THE
PEOPLE
CALLED

The Growth of
Community in the Bible

PAUL D. HANSON

1817

Harper & Row, Publishers, San Francisco

Cambridge, Hagerstown, New York, Philadelphia, Washington
London, Mexico City, São Paulo, Singapore, Sydney

Other books by Paul D. Hanson

The Dawn of Apocalyptic
The Diversity of Scripture
Dynamic Transcendence
Visionaries and Their Apocalypses

Acknowledgment is made for excerpts from "Choruses from 'The Rock' " in *Collected Poems 1909–1962* by T. S. Eliot copyright 1936 by Harcourt Brace Jovanovich, Inc.; copyright © 1963, 1964 by T. S. Eliot. Reprinted by permission of the publisher and by permission of Faber and Faber Ltd.

Unless otherwise noted, Scripture quotations contained herein are from the Revised Standard Version of the Bible, copyrighted 1946, 1952, 1971 by the Division of Christian Education of the National Council of the Churches of Christ in the U.S.A., and are used by permission. All rights reserved.

FIRST EDITION

Library of Congress Cataloging in Publication Data

Hanson, Paul D.
  The people called.

  Bibliography: p.
  Includes index.
  1. Bible—History of Biblical events. 2. Community—History. I. Title.
BS635.2.H36   1986   220.6   84–47725
ISBN 0-06-063700-5

86 87 88 89 90 HC 10 9 8 7 6 5 4 3 2 1

To
Amy Elizabeth
Mark Christopher
Nathaniel Ross

Contents

Preface   x

Abbreviations   xii

I.   The Nature of This Study   1

II.   The Birth of the Yahwistic Notion of Community
(Genesis 12–39, Exodus 1–15)   10

     A.   The Biblical Sources and the Historical
Question   10

     B.   Ancestral (Patriarchal) Background   13

     C.   Out of the House of Bondage: The Exodus   20

     D.   Encounter with the Deliverer God Yahweh
as Catalyst of the Yahwistic Notion of
Community   21

         1.   Worship as Response to God's
Antecedent Grace   24

         2.   Yahweh Majestic in Holiness   26

         3.   Yahweh's Steadfast Love   27

III.   The Growth of a Triadic Notion of Community
(Exodus 19–23, Joshua, and Judges)   30

     A.   Conquest Traditions in Joshua   31

     B.   Israel's Judges   34

     C.   Evidence for the Forms of Worship and
Tôrâ in the Early Yahwistic Community   38

         1.   Forms of Worship: Exodus 19:3–8
and 24:3–8   39

         2.   *Tôrâ*: Faith Coming to Expression in
Communal Forms and Structures   41

             a.   The Book of the Covenant:
Exodus 20:21–23:19   42

             b.   The Decalogue   53

             c.   The Distribution of Land
According to the *Naḥalâ*   63

         3.   A Celebration of Israel's Early Notion
of Community: The Song of Hannah   65

     D.   Summary of the Characteristics of the Early
Yahwistic Notion of Community   69

1. Community as Response to God's
Initiating Saving Activity 69
2. Devotion to the One True God as the
Unifying Heart of Community 69
3. The Community Defined by the Triad
of Righteousness, Compassion, and
Worship 70
   a. Righteousness 71
   b. Compassion 72
   c. Worship 73
   d. The Dynamic Interrelationships
   Among Righteousness,
   Compassion, and Worship 75
4. Implications of the Yahwistic Notion
of Community for Contemporary
Communities of Faith 78

IV. The Yahwistic Notion of Community Tested and
Refined: The Age of Kings and Prophets (1 and 2
Samuel, 1 Kings, and the Psalms) 87
  A. From Early Yahwism to Prophetic Yahwism 87
  B. Saul and Samuel 89
  C. David and Nathan 100
  D. Solomon 104
    1. Forms of Worship 107
    2. Structures of Society 112
  E. The Theme of Creation: A Community
  Describes Its Home in Nature 127
  F. The Divided Kingdom 132

V. Growth Through Adversity: Prophecy and Kingship
in the Northern Kingdom (Deuteronomy, 1 Kings,
Amos, and Hosea) 136
  A. The Prophetic Response to Jeroboam's Cult 137
  B. Ahab and His Prophetic Adversary Elijah 140
  C. The Prophetic Reform Movement
  Exploited by the Cynical King Jehu 147
  D. Amos Attacks a Perverted Cult on Behalf
  of the God Seeking True Worship
  Expressed in Compassion and Justice 148
  E. Hosea: "Israel Has Forgotten His Maker" 158
  F. Deuteronomy: A New Formulation of the
  Community of Faith 167

VI. A Variegated Portrait: The Contribution of Southern
     Kings, Prophets, and Sages to the Yahwistic Notion
     of Community (Kings, Chronicles, Isaiah, Micah,
     Jeremiah, Proverbs, Job, and Ecclesiastes)   177
     A. An Overview of the Seventh and Sixth
         Centuries in Judah   178
     B. Isaiah   181
     C. Micah   194
     D. The Reform Efforts of Faithful Kings   197
     E. The Prophet Jeremiah and Josiah's Cultic
         Reform   198
     F. Community of Faith in Israelite Wisdom
         Tradition   208

VII. The Exile: Crisis and Reformulation (Ezekiel,
      the Priestly Writing, Isaiah 40–55)   215
      A. The Traditional Notion of Covenant
          Community Called into Question   215
      B. Ezekiel: A Program for the Restoration
          of Purity   216
      C. The Priestly Writing ("P")   224
      D. Second Isaiah   233

VIII. Return from Exile and Attempts to Reconstitute
       Community (Chronicles, Haggai, Zechariah, Malachi,
       Isaiah 24–27, 56–66, and Ezekiel 38–39, 44)   253
       A. Second Isaiah's Visionary Followers   253
       B. The Restoration Program of the Zadokites   259
       C. The Growth of an Apocalyptic Response
           to Adversity   269
       D. Malachi   277

IX. The Consolidation of the Community Around the
     Torah (Chronicles, Ezra, and Nehemiah)   291
     A. The Reform under Ezra and Nehemiah   291
     B. The Chronicler's History   300

X. Witnesses to an Alternative Vision (Joel, Ruth,
    and Jonah)   312
    A. Joel   313
    B. Ruth   314
    C. Jonah   316
    D. The Theological Importance of the
        Alternative Vision   321

XI. The People of the Torah: From Ezra to the
     Maccabean Revolt (Judith and Ecclesiasticus)   325

	A.	The Encounter with Hellenism	326
	B.	The Samaritans	327
	C.	Pro-Hellenistic Positions	328
	D.	Temple and Torah, Priests and Scribes	330
	E.	Judith	332
	F.	Ecclesiasticus (The Wisdom of Jesus the Son of Sirach)	333
XII.		Diverse Notions of Community in the Last Two Centuries B.C.E. (Daniel, 1 Maccabees)	340
	A.	The Traditional Faith under Siege	340
	B.	The Maccabean Revolt and the Position of the Ḥasîdîm	343
	C.	The Emergence of the Threefold Division: Sadducees, Pharisees, and Essenes	347
	D.	The Pharisees	349
	E.	The Essenes	358
	F.	The Apocalyptic Community of the Dead Sea Scrolls	364
	G.	Implications of Second and First Century B.C.E. Developments for Later Communities of Faith	372
XIII.		Community in the Teaching of Jesus (Matthew, Mark, and Luke)	382
	A.	Continuity and Change	383
	B.	Jesus' Announcement of the Kingdom and Call to Discipleship as the Primal Events in the Birth of the Church	395
		1. Jesus Teaches the Way of the Kingdom	398
		2. Jesus' Life: The Manifestation of the Kingdom	413
		3. Jesus Dies for the Kingdom	421
		4. The Renewal of the Triadic Notion of Community	423
XIV.		The Birth of the Church as Response to God's New Initiative (Matthew, John, James, 1 and 2 Timothy, and Luke–Acts)	427
	A.	The First Generation	430
	B.	The Pauline Church: A Community Without Distinctions	438
	C.	The Church after the First Jewish Revolt (The Third Generation)	451

XV. The Biblical Notion of Community: Contemporary
Implications   467

    A. A Summary of the Biblical Legacy   469

    B. Recapturing a Vision: Faith Communities
Today   487

        1. Community Structure   489

        2. Relation to Civil Authorities   493

        3. Jewish-Christian Relations   496

    C. The Abiding Validity of a Biblical Notion
of Community   499

        1. Life-Sustaining Fellowship   501

        2. Agent of Healing   503

Appendix: Underlying Presuppositions and Method   519

    A. World Crisis and the Responsibility of
Communities of Faith   519

    B. A Scriptural Basis That Includes the
Hebrew Bible   520

    C. The Method Used in This Study   522

        1. Presuppositions   523

        2. The Process of Interpretation and the
Importance of the Faith Community
as Context   525

        3. A Hermeneutic of Engagement   527

          a. The Nature of This Method
of Interpretation   527

          b. Two-Dimensional Exegesis:
Word and World   529

          c. Levels of Discernment: Paradigms
and a Vision of Divine Purpose   529

          d. A Hermeneutic of Engagement and
the Problem of Biblical Authority   535

    D. Why a Historical Study Is Essential to
Understanding the Nature of Contemporary
Communities of Faith   537

    E. The Historical Relationship Between the
Communities of the Two Testaments   540

    F. Scripture: The Foundational Chapters in
a Faith Community's Autobiography   544

A Select List of Related Books   547

General Index   553

Scripture Index   560

Index of Authors   563

Preface

Since the publication of the biblical theologies by Walther Eichrodt[1] and Gerhard von Rad,[2] no volume has appeared in this field that can be characterized as a new synthesis on the grand scale of their works. Nevertheless, fresh insights into the meaning of the biblical writings have appeared in many smaller publications, yielding a corpus of scholarship that has stimulated considerable recent interest. These insights have prepared a foundation for renewed attempts to address biblical theology in a unified way.

This book does not seek to present a new biblical theology on the scale of Eichrodt or von Rad. The objective is more limited, inasmuch as one theme has been chosen as the unifying thread guiding treatment of the writings of the Bible, that theme being "community." In two other respects, however, this book seeks to transcend certain limitations found in the theologies of Eichrodt and von Rad.

First, I have attempted to treat the wide diversity of theological traditions found in the Bible with an appreciation for the unique contribution each makes to the theology of the Bible as a whole, and specifically, in this study, to our understanding of community. Accordingly, priestly, sapiental, and apocalyptic traditions take their place alongside the traditionally more favored historical and prophetic traditions as fully legitimate contributors to biblical theology. For reasons intimately tied to the particular development of Western Christianity, certain segments of Scripture such as Jeremiah 30–31 and Isaiah 40–55 have deeply influenced the formation of Christian thought. But neglected writings such as Ezekiel 40–48 and the so-called priestly stratum of the Pentateuch also contain profound insight into the nature of religious community. Since any attempt simply to supplement existing studies with these neglected aspects of biblical theology would lead to patchwork, a new unified approach is called for—the beginnings of which I hope will be detected in this book.

A second way in which this work seeks to transcend earlier limitations is by going beyond the writings of the Hebrew Bible (Old Testament). When a historical approach is taken to biblical theology (the approach most adapted to biblical faith), it seems artificial to end study with Daniel. To do so has suggested a far greater gap between the two testaments than is

---

1. Walther Eichrodt, *Theology of the Old Testament*, 2 vols., trans. J. A. Baker (Philadelphia: Westminster Press, 1961, 1967).
2. Gerhard von Rad, *Old Testament Theology*, 2 vols., trans. D. M. G. Stalker (New York: Harper & Row, 1962, 1965).

historically or theologically justifiable. The emergence of Christian communities knows no such absolute gaps. This study, by including the New Testament, redresses the narrowness of most earlier scholarship. Often, too, the exclusion of writings lying outside of the (Protestant) Christian canon has impaired theological understanding. Here, historical methodology encourages treatment of extrabiblical writings where they shed light on community development.

The basic idea of this study unfolded in the course of preparing the Thomas White Currie Lectures, entitled "Community of Faith: The Christian Way of Being in the World," delivered at Austin Presbyterian Seminary, Austin, Texas, on February 2–5, 1981. Further development occurred in lectures at Miami University, Gettysburg Seminary, Universität München, Union Theological Seminary in Virginia, Concordia College (Moorhead), University of North Carolina at Wilmington, Dropsie College, and Drew University. I am grateful for the helpful criticism I received at each of these institutions. The time needed to consolidate ideas through a full-scale, systematic program of research was provided by the Alexander von Humboldt Foundation of the Bundesrepublik Deutschland, sponsors of my sabbatical leave in Tübingen during the academic year 1981–82.

I am especially grateful to Professor Michael D. Coogan, who read through the penultimate draft and contributed innumerable valuable suggestions. I owe a debt of gratitude also to Professors Michael Fishbane and W. Sibley Towner, who generously offered their time in reading Chapters XI and XII, much to my benefit.

For the careful typing of this manuscript, I offer sincere thanks to Margaret Studier, a person of remarkable energy, wisdom, and grace. I have also appreciated deeply the editorial direction of John B. Shopp of Harper & Row.

In claiming sole responsibility for the final form of this book, I am not only conforming to convention, but am also admitting that it marks merely a serious beginning.

Seeking as it does to understand the biblical roots of true, life-sustaining community, this book is largely a product of the community that has sustained me. I count no greater blessing than the circle of intimacy within which tenderness and growth have been fostered and permitted to flourish in my life. To the three younger members of that circle, from whom I have learned so profoundly of love and life together in praise of God, I dedicate this book.

Abbreviations

AB	Anchor Bible
ANET	J. B. Pritchard (ed.), *Ancient Near Eastern Texts*
ATANT	*Abhandlungen zur Theologie des Alten und Neuen Testaments*
ATD	Das Alte Testament Deutsch
BA	*Biblical Archaeologist*
BAR	*Biblical Archaeologist Reader*
BASOR	*Bulletin of the American Schools of Oriental Research*
BEvTh	Beitrage zur evangelischen Theologie
BK	Biblische Kommentar
BZAW	Beihefte zur *ZAW*
CBQ	*Catholic Biblical Quarterly*
CMHE	F. M. Cross, *Canaanite Myth and Hebrew Epic*
ConBOT	Coniectanea biblica, Old Testament
EvTh	*Evangelische Theologie*
Evv.	English verses
FOTL	The Forms of Old Testament Literature
FRLANT	Forschungen zur Religion und Literatur des Alten und Neuen Testaments
HAT	Handbuch zum Alten Testament
HSM	Harvard Semitic Monographs
HTR	*Harvard Theological Review*
ICC	International Critical Commentary
IDB	G. A. Buttrick, Ed., *Interpreter's Dictionary of the Bible*
IDBSuppl	Supplementary volume to IDB
Int	*Interpretation*
JAOS	*Journal of the American Oriental Society*
JBL	*Journal of Biblical Literature*
JCS	*Journal of Cuneiform Studies*
JNES	*Journal of Near Eastern Studies*
JPOS	*Journal of the Palestine Oriental Society*
JR	*Journal of Religion*
JSOTSuppl	Journal for the Study of the Old Testament, Supplements
JSS	*Journal of Semitic Studies*
JTS	*Journal of Theological Studies*
NEB	*New English Bible*
OBT	Overtures to Biblical Theology
OTL	Old Testament Library
RSV	Revised Standard Version of the Bible
SBLDS	Society of Biblical Literature Dissertation Series
SBS	Stuttgarter Bibelstudien
SBT	Studies in Biblical Theology
SNTSMS	Society for New Testament Studies Monograph Series
ThB	Theologische Bücherei
ThZ	*Theologische Zeitschrift*
VT	*Vetus Testamentum*
VTSuppl	Vetus Testamentum, Supplements
WMANT	Wissenschaftliche Monographien zum Alten und Neuen Testaments
ZAW	*Zeitschrift für die alttestamentliche Wissenschaft*

I

The Nature of This Study

What life have you if you have not life together?
There is no life that is not in community,
And no community not lived in praise of GOD.[1]

This study focuses on a very basic human theme, the tender art of living together in community. T. S. Eliot posed the question succinctly: "What life have you if you have not life together?" He thereby pointed to a truth verified both by social scientists and by our own practical experience: we receive life, we foster life, and we pass life on within the context of fellow humans. But how varied is the quality of life experienced by different humans, or even by the individual at different stages of life! Any thoughtful, sensitive person is deeply aware of the fragile treasure that life is, with remarkable potential for warmth, friendship, joy, creativity, and generosity, yet so frequently threatened or destroyed by anxiety, bitterness, greed, anger, and hostility.

The Bible presents a rich pageant of life in community. Its stories, hymns, and proverbs cover the whole range of human feelings and experiences. It gives the story of a people who puzzled through the riddle of life from the midst of life, and came to a conclusion strikingly similar to Eliot's: "There is no life that is not in community. And no community not lived in praise of God."

What enabled one people to peer so deeply into life as to become the tutor of future ages? For one thing, no people in world history has been more intimately acquainted with tragedy than the Jews. In biblical times, they experienced repeatedly the ravages of passions and deeds, both from foreign hostility and from intracommunal conflict. Out of a history combining tragedy and comedy and joy, nevertheless arose a profound understanding of the only source promising deliverance *from*

---

1. From T. S. Eliot, "Choruses from 'The Rock,'" in *The Complete Poems and Plays, 1909–1950* (New York: Harcourt, Brace, 1952), p. 101. These lines from T. S. Eliot are complemented nicely by this statement by R. Scroggs in *Paul for a New Day* (Philadelphia: Fortress Press, 1977): ". . . God has created persons *for* community, and only within this sustaining community is his creation of authentic humanity complete" (p. 39).

that which destroys life, *to* that which creates and fosters and upholds life—the advent of divine grace.

Many thoughtful people might ask today whether such a model of deliverance is applicable to our modern situation. Ancient peoples may have found comfort in the thought that a god or gods would intervene to pluck them out of dilemmas of their own making or crises caused by the hostility of others. But our problems will be solved, many people assume today, if humans take responsiblity for their errors and begin building a more peaceful world.

Although this response is very common, it oversimplifies both the ancient world and our own. Israel did not derive from its sense of a Deliverer God an attitude of moral complacency, but inferred from the experience of divine deliverance a remarkably dynamic moral universe. As for modern experience, most people are no longer optimistic about our ability to undo our own errors and build a better world. It may be the time to ask whether Israel's acknowledgment of a Reality transcending every penultimate reality, and relativizing every mortal claim on privilege and authority, may not offer a far more hopeful basis for world peace and justice than more reductionary alternatives. At any rate, for inquiring into the notion of community that unfolded in ancient Israel, all that is required of us is that we free ourselves of misleading stereotypes regarding both the so-called mythic otherworldliness of biblical communities and the purportedly self-sufficient this-worldliness of individuals and groups in our own time. We need to study antiquity and modernity alike with an unbiased vision.

An open-minded entry into the world of the Bible may hold some surprises. The first event recorded in the Bible that can be called "historical"—the exodus—presents a mixed company (ʿēreb) of people challenging the widespread mythopoeic orthodoxy of their time. They did so on the basis of real experiences that broke the credibility of the official religion of special privilege and that initiated a search for a radically different grounding for life. The resulting movement from hopeless slave bondage into freedom gave birth to a notion of community dedicated to the ordering of *all* life, for the good of *all* life, under the guidance and empowerment of a righteous, compassionate God.

This notion, unlike the one it challenged, did not offer a finished program; it inaugurated a process. It did not commend to its members static answers; it offered the perspective of those who had experienced deliverance to others who suffered under various kinds of oppression. The result was a fascinating history of fresh discoveries, in which the alternative vision and the dynamic notion of community it fostered underwent revision amid further threats, many defeats, some retreats, inner conflicts, new starts, and remarkable perseverance. This entire history was accompanied by the confession that the process was not a matter of accident or whimsy. Taken as a whole, it manifested a purpose dedicated to the redemption and restoration of the entire created order. Early Israel named the author of that purpose *Yahweh*.

The dynamic, forward-looking nature of biblical community eventually found an appropriate form of expression in eschatology, a perspective regarding history as directed purposefully toward a final goal by God. Although the presence of God was discerned in the experiences of this world, and life was patterned after the nature of the God thus encountered, no human form or institution was deemed capable of capturing the fullness of God's nature and purpose. The community of faith was thus a pilgrim community. It oriented its life toward God's future, as the people called to participate in the inbreaking of a divine order into the imperfect structures of this world—an order we shall refer to as "God's reign," or God's "order of *šālôm* (shalom)."[2] Since communal structures were drawn inferentially from the experience of God's ongoing activity, the biblical narrative thus remains open-ended also with regard to forms of community, right up to the last writings to be included in the canon.

Attempts to argue that certain specific community structures are definitive for all time on the basis of an appeal to Scripture may contribute to a superficial sense of clarity. However, they not only oversimplify, but fail to grasp the most profound biblical insight into authentic communal structures—namely, that they are in every age an aspect of the community of faith's response to the *living* God. The first point that must be extrapolated from this insight by any modern community seeking to pattern its life on a biblical model, therefore, is that ideas concerning communal structure must arise from engagement with the God who is creatively and redemptively active in its own world. The most fundamental characteristic of such a notion of community thus seems to be that it is based on the pattern of *divine initiative and human response*. That is, forms of community arise as a people, peering into the heart of life and seeking to align itself with God, who is ceaselessly active to create fellowship where there is alienation, to reconcile where there is enmity, to redeem where there is bondage, adopt those structures of community that best equip it to incarnate God's purpose in its own life.

From the confession that God remains active in our world, it naturally follows that our vision of divine purpose and the dynamic notion of community that it fosters will continue to grow in response to God's

---

2. The Hebrew word *šālôm* is commonly translated "peace," which captures only an approximate and partial meaning. *Šālôm* describes the cosmic harmony that exists where the world and all its inhabitants are reconciled with God. Israel described this state with its concept of covenant; that is, the bond of fellowship within which "I (Yahweh) shall be your God and you shall be my people." The qualities of the community living in harmony with God in covenant are variously described as prosperity, peace, and righteousness, which taken together begin to describe *šālôm* (cf. P. D. Hanson, "War and Peace in the Hebrew Bible," *Interp* 38 (1984): 341–362).

initiatives. Although some individuals, including members of ecclesiastical hierarchies, may find in this context the word *dynamic* to be a eu-
phemism for *chaotic*, this study of the growth of community in the Bible
shows that communal order and stability are founded on something far
more profound and spiritual than rigid conformity to the forms of an
earlier period. While the inferential process of deriving forms of community from the ongoing relationship with God implies continuous reform, the resulting development is not chaotic, but dependable, for it
rests on a vision of a divine purpose that extends over the entire span
of time and space. To be sure, each generation of the community of
faith receives new insight into that purpose, even as each historical period gives rise to changed circumstances to which that vision must be
applied. But it is a fundamental confession of biblical faith that,
through all times and changes, God remains steadfast to the creative,
redemptive purpose that has guided the world from the beginning.

This confession does not imply that the life of the community of faith
will in all ages be characterized by smooth transition. The Bible records periods of harsh, even violent change, resulting not from an
abrupt change in divine purpose, but from human decisions to be guided by strategies running contrary to that purpose. Even through such
periods, however, the community was served by prophets and teachers
who upheld the vision of God's order of righteousness and compassion
to which the people of God were called. And always such prophets and
teachers were guided by a clear understanding and deep appreciation
of their religious heritage. Indeed, in every biblical period the confessional heritage provided the unique perspective from which the new
generation was able to discern God's presence and find the faithful response, both in gathering into community and in moving back into the
world with a new sense of commitment. The dynamic, forward-moving
quality of the community building in the Bible thus does not exclude,
but fosters what on a deeper level can be recognized as a continuity of
purpose and a dependable vision of the future.

The vision of divine purpose from which communal structures were
derived, however, was not always grasped with unanimity or group consensus. In fact, many periods were characterized by division between
conflicting opinions. Such periods themselves offer a vital lesson in the
nature of a historical faith, within which ambiguity is an unavoidable
aspect of seeking God in this world and of living according to the encounter. Even the intracommunal conflicts that inevitably arise tutor
the faithful in the art of grasping the delicate truths that are often
found not by identifying exclusively with one side of a controversy.
Such truths are found by recognizing, in the partial visions of contending sides, important aspects of a universal order of justice and peace
that transcends all parties, programs, and ideologies.

The insistence that the essential truth about community found in the

Bible arises from an awareness of its dynamic relational character thus does not lead to a chaotic relativism. Granted, the Bible does not seek truth by taking the sum total of all natural, historical, and personal phenomena and extrapolating from them a metaphysical principle. Rather, the Bible records happenings from the concrete and the every-day, and seeks among such particularities to understand life and life's Author. The insights gained by biblical writers into the nature of com-munity did not come in the form of abstractions. Such insights were les-sons derived from everyday experiences concerning the style of living that leads to the discovery of a dependable basis for authentic humanity and true community within the ever-changing vicissitudes of life. Nev-ertheless, out of such particularities arises a vision of the order of life willed by God for all creatures, and a corresponding notion of the voca-tion to which this vision calls the faithful. Once again, we are viewing a moving object when we focus on that vision and that notion of commu-nity. But as long as the relational nature of biblical truth is recognized, we can identify certain cardinal characteristics that develop in biblical history. We shall see especially that a unique triadic notion of communi-ty persists from earliest Yahwistic times down through the early rab-binical and Christian period. The understanding of the righteousness, compassion, and worship that characterizes this triad and defines the realm of šālôm to which God invites the faithful to live undergoes con-stant change. Yet its persistence over centuries can be taken as testimo-ny to the trustworthiness of the Bible as a guide for those communities of faith that today seek to bring all humans to the fullness of life that seems to be in harmony with our deepest spiritual insights.

It is my personal conviction that this testimony cannot be divorced from its basis in the biblical confession that our life together in commu-nity arises solely as a gift of a loving God. This in turn leads to the be-lief that the dynamic and life-enhancing notion of community found in the Bible reflects more than one people's history; in fact, this notion of community opens up to people of all ages a dependable vision of the One who is active in all history to guide the human family to a common life of justice, compassion, and shared prosperity on a mended and peaceful earth. Although richly diverse and multifaceted in its unfold-ing, the entire history of the biblical notion of community points to the same transcendent referent—the God who creates out of nothing, de-livers the enslaved, defends the vulnerable, nurtures the weak, and en-lists in a universal purpose of šālôm all those responsive to the divine call. The biblical notion of community therefore finds its final unity and focus in worship of the one true God. From that center alone, it derives its understanding of what is true, just, and good, along with the courage and power to stand on the side of truth and justice, whatever the cost.

The notion of community thus arising from our biblical heritage has a potentially profound contribution to make to a threatened world groping for direction. To be sure, the petty, self-serving, and imperialistic assumptions so frequently brought by individuals and contemporary religious groups to the Bible will not be supported by this study, for they are motivated by a selfish, narrow vision of divine purpose that runs counter to the biblical vision. But however inadequate our previous visions, rigorous biblical study provides training for individual and community alike in a way of life dedicated to universal justice, compassion, and peace in response to the God who will not rest until the last slave is freed and last malnourished person fed.

I turn now to several matters regarding the design of this book. In keeping with the intention to trace the growth of the notion of community over the entire history of the Bible, this study is divided into chapters that cover the various periods in historical sequence. Since the order in which books appear in the Bible does not always coincide with the actual order of their historical origin, I introduce each of chapters II–XIV with a brief historical note specifying which biblical books will be treated and describing the historical period covered by the chapter. Within the main body of the chapter, I trace the development of the community of faith within the historical and social context of that time, as accurately as I can reconstruct it from the available biblical and extrabiblical evidence. Each chapter ends with a theological evaluation of the notion or notions of community found in the period covered, with suggestions of implications for future developments.

A special word might be added concerning Chapters XI and XII, which deal with the period from Ezra up to the time of Jesus. This period is woefully neglected in theological studies of the Bible, though without an adequate understanding of the developments within Judaism during this period, rabbinical Judaism, early Christianity, and the relation between the two cannot adequately be illuminated. While it is undeniable that further work must be devoted to this period before the serious effects of long neglect can be redressed, I offer these two chapters as a modest beginning.

A word is also called for regarding terminology, and specifically the problem of finding a fitting designation for the phenomenon I seek to identify and describe in its historical development. When we consider the phenomenon of people gathering into a common life in response to what is experienced as divine initiative, whether in ancient times or today, one of the most obvious characteristics encountered is diversity and multiplicity. In the Bible, we do not find *one* faithful, unified people of God extending from Adam to Hillel and Paul. Instead, we find a long chronicle of faithfulness mixed with perfidy and rebellion against God, leading to separate congregations, diverse cults, competing nations, and rival parties. In spite of this diversity, however, we believe we can discern an underlying divine initiative, albeit grasped imperfectly by humans and often leading to a bewilderingly fragmented history of response. What do we call those people whose life together grows out of that response?

The situation is the same when we turn our attention to the contemporary world. Some ot those communities understanding their roots as tracing back to the faith of Israel gather in synagogues, others in churches. What is more, Jews cannot refer to themselves corporately as "the Synagogue," for they are divided into separate groups due to differences in the way the heritage is appropriated and applied. Similarly, all Christians do not fall within one organization that can simply be designated "the Church." Churches are also multiple.

We are faced with the problem of finding a term, or set of terms, that will convey the conviction that it is God who calls people into community, while denying neither the multiplicity, diversity, nor imperfection of the actual communities we are studying.

A certain fluidity seems necessary. In most cases, the term "community of faith" or "faith community" designates a group defining its identity in relation to divine initiative and call. In cases where more than one such group are being discussed, I use the plural. In the later chapters, the focus is specifically on "churches" or "synagogues," or in certain cases, more generally on "the church" or "the synagogue." Finally I express my conviction that these various groups manifest in their diversity and multiplicity a human response to the call of God by seeking to trace, as an underlying stream, the biblical notion of the community of faith. That this conviction goes beyond historical description to theological construction is obvious, as is the fact that the results must remain tentative and open to revision.

Regarding the approach taken in this study, it is thus clearly theological in nature. My own understanding of biblical faith is rigorously historical, thereby leading to careful attention to a historical reconstruction of the community of faith in each period. Yet my underlying belief that the essential quality of biblical community can be grasped only if historical, sociological, and philological methods are placed in the service of theological analysis determines the form of this study. While drawing repeatedly on the insights of the social sciences, for example, a social scientific perspective alone is inadequate for grasping for theological meaning of community in the Bible. The word study approach taken by earlier scholars is inadequate for a related set of reasons. First, while studies focusing on such words as $q\bar{a}h\bar{a}l$, $\bar{e}d\hat{a}$, and $ekklesia$ have shed important light on aspects of biblical community consciousness, the wide range of meanings emerging from such studies has not been amenable to synthesis without forced results. More seriously, much of the information found in the Bible regarding community is not found in association with specific words for community (as illustrated, for example, by the infrequent appearance of the word $ekklesia$ in the gospels). Above all, to get at the essence of the Yahwistic community or the New Testament church, we must penetrate beyond individual word studies to a recognition of the community-forming power created through encounter of groups of believers with God's presence in their world.

After the theological character of this study has been explained, however, it is important to note that this character in no way excludes the importance of social, anthropological, and psychological dimensions of biblical history. Any rigid separation of the various dimensions of community is ultimately forced and artificial. In all cultures, religious and social dimensions of human life are intricately intertwined. Harvard sociologist Daniel Bell recently suggested that at the root of the modern crisis, calling into question the confident optimism of modernity, is a *spiritual* crisis. Our headstrong civilization believed it had come of age and could dispense with the authority of sacred tradition. Now it has begun to lose nerve as it stares into the void and finds that secularization and profanation fail to answer age-old existential questions dealing with death and tragedy, obligation and love. Bell suggests that this crisis is preparing the way for "the return of the sacred." Religion restores our sense of purpose by reminding us of our connections with the past. Through remembering our religious roots, we recapture those moments that taught our ancestors those lessons in humility and caring without which a humane society is impossible.[3]

In recounting our heritage and its lessons in the art of living together, we are reaching back to our essential humanity. Since this study is historical in orientation and limited to one segment of our past, it does not constitute a completed task. Yet I hope it will make a contribution to the ceaseless challenge of rediscovering who we are by remembering whence we have come. As suggested earlier, the concreteness with which the basic questions of life are raised in the Bible does not preclude the possibility of grasping overarching themes in its notion of community. Conceptually, the reader will be aided in grasping both that concreteness and the broader themes by distinguishing between two levels of inquiry. On the level of the concrete and the particular, the reader will recognize in different periods specific events that in their specificity give such clear insight into the nature of community as to be exemplary and particularly helpful to future generations in their ongoing efforts to define themselves in relation to God. These I designate "paradigmatic events." Since according to biblical faith the same God is the ultimate reality encountered within each of these specific examples or paradigms, and since that God is believed to be true to one

---

3. Daniel Bell, *The Winding Passage: Essays and Sociological Journeys, 1960–1980* (Cambridge, Mass.: Abt Books, 1980). Michael Waltzer's most recent book, *Exodus and Revolution* (New York: Basic Books, 1984), gives expression in an equally persuasive manner to the importance of our ancient religious traditions, both in significant events of past history and in contemporary liberation and revolutionary movements.

universal purpose, the paradigms taken together in turn plot a trajectory through the entire biblical period that I designate as the community of faith's "vision of divine purpose." A full discussion of how this understanding of paradigms and the vision of divine purpose function in the overall structure of this book is offered in the Appendix, together with a much more detailed description of the theological presuppositions underlying this work than just given. Many readers will therefore want to read the Appendix before proceeding to the actual study of the growth of community through the various periods of biblical history, which begins in the next chapter.

II

The Birth of the Yahwistic Notion of Community
(Genesis 12–39; Exodus 1–15)

Historical Note: It was probably during the reign of Ramesses II (ca. 1290–1224 B.C.E.) that a band of Hebrew slaves slipped from their bondage in Egypt and experienced a miraculous escape from the Pharaoh's army at the Sea, which they attributed to the saving grace of their God Yahweh. Although these Hebrews likely were aware of a prehistory in the form of ancestral legends, their birth as a people occurred within the chain of events beginning with their exodus from Egypt and culminating in their settlement in the land of the Canaanites. Of fundamental importance in that birth process was the enactment of a covenant in which the people acknowledged the sole sovereignty of the Deliverer God Yahweh, and bound themselves by solemn oath to obey Yahweh's will.

A. THE BIBLICAL SOURCES AND THE HISTORICAL QUESTION

Where does the history of the biblical notion of community begin? Every history has an antecedent history, so in a sense we are referred back to the dawn of human consciousness in search of the first episodes in the chronicle. But since the detail available for reconstruction vanishes from our ken as we move back through the ages, it seems best to begin with the historical tradition that Israel itself identified as descriptive of its birthplace as a people of God, the exodus tradition. In addition, one important group of antecedent traditions will be referred to, those centering around the theme of divine promise to Israel's ancestors. In a manner suggested by the history of the growth of biblical tradition itself, however, it seems best to treat the ancestral traditions in connection with the exodus narrative rather than separately.[1]

Since some scholars would argue that even the exodus narrative is too tenuously related to historically reliable traditions to allow us to sketch

---

1. Cf. M. Noth, *A History of Pentateuchal Traditions*, ed. and trans. B. W. Anderson (Englewood Cliffs, N.J.: Prentice-Hall, 1972), pp. 47–51.

a historical development, we must turn briefly to this specific historiographic problem. In this particular study, the form this problem takes can be expressed by the question "Does the biblical narrative dealing with the theme of the exodus contain sufficient evidence for the reconstruction of the event (construed in the broad sense defined in the Appendix) that gave birth to the biblical notion of community and set the direction of its subsequent development?" Anyone applying a narrowly positivistic methodology must answer this question negatively, for the sources do not allow us to reconstruct a newsreel-like account of the escape of slaves from Egypt and their encounter with the Deliverer God at the Sea. If we ask, however, whether the Bible gives us a reliable picture of this early period in a portrayal that interprets the theological significance of the happenings and conditions experienced and then preserved in the collective memory of the people, we can answer affirmatively. For the theme of Israel being called into being as a people through the God Yahweh's delivering them from slavery in Egypt is the most ubiquitous theme of Hebrew scripture, permeating hymns, historical narratives, and legal documents from the earliest to the latest point of oral and then written transmission. Already in hymns and legal corpora stemming from the premonarchical period, such as Exodus 15 and Exodus 20:21 to 23:19, Yahweh is remembered as the God who delivered the slaves out of Egypt. As the very cautious scholar Martin Noth observed, in the case of this theme we are dealing with a "primary confession (*Urbekenntnis*) of Israel," indeed, with "the Kernel of the whole subsequent Pentateuchal tradition."[2]

The centrality of the exodus confession can be illustrated by referring to the epitome of biblical *tôrâ*[3] in the Decalogue, which begins with the formula, "I am the Lord your God, who brought you out of the land of Egypt, out of the house of bondage" (Exod. 20:2). This is probably an archaic liturgical formula from the cult of the League,[4] still preserved in its original parallelistic form, and recalling at the heart of *tôrâ* Israel's primal confession that the covenant relationship with Yahweh has its origin in Yahweh's antecedent acts of grace. Although the

---

2. *Ibid.*, p. 49.

3. The Hebrew word *tôrâ* will be used in this book rather than its common English translation "law," since the latter contains connotations that are misleading and inaccurate. Beginning with the practice of translating *tôrâ* with *nomos* in Greek, a tendency is discernible in Christian interpretation to impute a type of legalism onto the concept of *tôrâ* that is not present within its original biblical context. The basic meaning of *tôrâ* is "teaching," "instruction," "guidance." In the Persian period, it came to designate the first five books of the Bible, the so-called Books of Moses, or Pentateuch. When referring specifically to the Pentateuch, we shall depart from a scientific transliteration of the Hebrew word and use the form Torah.

4. We use the term "League" interchangeably with "tribal confederacy" to refer to the confederacy of Israelite tribes prior to the introduction of kingship. Although the separate tribes had their own chiefs and insisted on a high degree of autonomy, two types of events brought them into a unified body, annual cultic festivals and the call to the military muster.

covenant was affirmed through a wholehearted human response, the initiative was seen to be solely God's. Apart from prevenient divine grace, obedience is impossible.

The very structure of Israel's collections of statutes and commandments affords the opportunity to look behind the present literary form to evidence of the community-building effect that this early confession and its underlying historical memory had in premonarchical Israel. For example, in the Book of the Covenant, in Exodus 20:21 to 23:19, those laws that are imbued with the liberating dynamic that is the hallmark of Israel's notion of community are drawn explicitly from the exodus tradition and its confession of faith in the compassionate divine Deliverer of oppressed slaves.[5]

The shape of the development of Israel's earliest oral and literary traditions was determined through and through by the confession of the God Yahweh who delivered Hebrews from Egyptian bondage. The laws and social structures of earliest Israel were imbued so thoroughly by this same confession as to set them apart—in spite of many formal and thematic similarities—from the laws and social structures of contemporaneous neighboring cultures. As we trace these traditions back through their many stages of development, we find ourselves coming to the twelfth century as their point of origin, which is to say, within a century of the time regarded by most scholars as the time of the exodus (that is, the reign of Ramesses II in the thirteenth century B.C.E.). It seems to me to be an instance of excessive skepticism to doubt that the exodus confession arose out of a very powerful experience of some of Israel's ancestors. Within the cult, they subsequently preserved a vivid memory of their extraordinary birth as a people during the period we would now designate as transitional from the Late Bronze Age to the Iron Age, a memory recalling the escape from Egypt of a group of slaves under the leadership of a leader named Moses, an escape in which the activity of the God Yahweh was recognized.[6]

---

5. Cf. P. D. Hanson, "The Theological Significance of Contradiction in the Book of the Covenant," in G. W. Coats and B. O. Long, eds., *Canon and Authority* (Philadelphia, Fortress Press, 1977), p. 110–131.

6. What is here argued about the historical reliability of the exodus traditions applies specifically to the broad question of the emergence of the early Yahwistic notion of community. The problem varies, however, when one moves to other questions. For example, the attempt to reconstruct the historical happenings of early Israel in the narrower sense is beset with difficulties, as seen in the methodological discussions of Martin Noth and John Bright, and most recently in a volume edited by John Hayes and J. Maxwell Miller (*Israelite and Judaean History* [Philadelphia: Westminster Press, 1977]). In the case of writing the political history of Israel, the historian must strive to isolate the brute facts of history from the interpretation of those facts that is so prominent in writings that originated in large part as confessional statements, and were subsequently transmitted as Scripture. In our case, however, where the objective is to trace the notion of community as it developed in Israel, the writings of the Bible are quite ideally suited for the task, because the interpretive-confessional dimension preserves important traces of that very development.

This particular event made such a profound impact on those involved as to forge earlier impressions of divine providence and folk traditions concerning theophanies and divine promises to ancient patriarchs and matriarchs into a thematic focus capable of generating a whole new understanding of the nature of God and the quality of the community drawn into fellowship with God. For this reason, we are on a historically solid foundation when we draw on critically interpreted biblical sources to describe the birth of a new notion of community in the exodus; that is, in the deliverance from Egyptian slavery in which the early Hebrews recognized the redemptive activity of Yahweh.[7]

B. ANCESTRAL (PATRIARCHAL) BACKGROUND

The new community born of the exodus must first be seen against the background of the old order from which it emerged. In Egypt the people who were to emerge as the Hebrews of the exodus narrative belonged to a larger class of Semitic slaves who, in the course of migrations occasioned by economic necessity, had been absorbed into a society notoriously conservative in its attitudes toward religion and culture. Tensions and even open conflicts did arise within the history of relationships between pharaohs and priests in Egypt, but both were united in commitment to a social system that buttressed their own personal power and wealth, and that was accordingly deaf to the concerns of those at the bottom of the social pyramid. Although we must be cautious in describing one ancient culture for purposes of comparing with another, it is clear that the nineteenth dynasty in Egypt was a kingdom that supported the ambitious building programs of its kings and the luxury of its upper echelons through the exploitation of its human resources in a workforce living close to the subsistence level. The latter had little hope of upward mobility, and lived with the constant danger of decline into slavery through indebtedness.

---

7. Other evidence has been adduced by various scholars to demonstrate the historical reliability of this basic confession; for example, Moses's Egyptian name, Egyptian border reports of movements of Semitic peoples into Egypt in the Late Bronze Age, the building activities recorded by Ramesses in the Delta (cf. Pithom and Ramesses in Exod. 1:11), etc. Care must be exercised, however, not to oversimplify the picture, for it is the character of the confessional style of Israel's historical narrative to grasp the heart of an historical event, and to leave out what the modern historian would regard as essential detail. It is furthermore the character of Israelite historical tradition to reinterpret and reapply the exodus narrative at every stage of transmission. When the traditions are interpreted as a whole in their richness and complexity, it becomes evident that the exodus confession, born in the experience of a relatively small group, was subsequently adopted by other groups. These groups were involved in the complex convergence of clans that led to a loose tribal confederation, a short-lived nationhood under one king, and finally to the separate existence of two states under separate kings. In this ongoing history of transmission, other themes born of new experiences were added to the exodus theme, sometimes by way of amplification, sometimes by way of contrast. Nevertheless, in most streams of tradition, the exodus theme continued to play a significant role down to the final stages of the history of tradition.

The burden of such a social system weighed heaviest, of course, on the corvées of foreign slaves. Without any human rights to which they could lay claim, they were at the mercy of their overlords. Although the description of slavery in Egypt found in the opening chapters of the Book of Exodus has been shaped by theological concerns, the depictions of foreign slaves found on the reliefs of the Ramesside period leave no doubt that the experiences of Moses's kinsfolk in Egypt would have been typical of slave experience throughout the ancient world. It would have been marked by an inhumane workload aimed at pressing every bit of work out of persons whose only purpose in life was deemed to be that of delivering services to their owners. The episode of the Egyptian beating the Hebrew slave in Exodus 2:11, coupled with the motif of the increased burden placed on the brickmakers, fits the usual pattern followed by masters, namely, that of maintaining a level of productivity just short of the breaking point as a means of keeping slaves in a servile state of mind, deprived of the will and physical strength necessary for resistance or rebellion.

The Egyptian system under which the Hebrews labored was a carefully structured one, the result of centuries of refinement. Perhaps its major strength was the stability it maintained in the land through the cultivation and central distribution of all available resources. Within this system, every individual was aware of his or her assigned role, and the expectations associated with that role, a fact true for slaves as well as for all other social castes. While we recognize in Moses's rebellious followers' demanding a return to the "fleshpots of Egypt" a narrative motif serving a particular theological point, it also depicts a basic social reality: even for slaves the rigidly stratified system of Egypt ordered life in a predictable manner. As the experience of some slaves in the period after the American Civil War indicates, freedom can come as a dreadful threat for those accustomed to such order, even to the point of making re-enslavement preferable to the agony of self-determination.

We still see, however, that the slaves escaping from Egypt, together with whatever other groups joined them on the basis of identifying with their experience, forged within the liminal period between bondage and self-determination a sense of personhood that viewed freedom and spiritual development as essential qualities distinguishing the human world from the realm of the beasts. They accordingly considered the static structures that had maintained their bondage as an intolerable price to pay for security. Our contrast is not intended to deny the often remarkable accomplishments of ancient Egyptian civilization, as a visit to Luxor, Gizeh, or the British Museum readily illustrates. It simply points to a difference in value systems. In the case of the Egyptian system, life was graded on a scale beginning with the "divine" Pharaoh and descending all the way down to the slave. It was only natural that from the vantage point of the upper Egyptian classes the slave was of no intrinsic value or interest, but like a beast of burden functioned as a cog in the smooth functioning of an eternal kingdom.

Against this background, we are able to interpret several complexes of tradition that in the present form of the biblical narrative derive their deepest theological significance from their relation to the exodus theme. It is this theme, in fact, that lies at the heart of the Yahwistic Document, a historical-theological work composed in the tenth century B.C.E., that has the dual distinction of being the oldest literary source in the Pentateuch and of giving the first five books of the Bible their overall thematic structure. The Yahwistic Document in turn drew on antecedent oral traditions, among them an epic that already contained the basic narrative structure of promise to the ancestors, migration to Egypt, enslavement of Hebrews under the Pharaoh, exodus, covenant, and settlement in Palestine.[8]

From the very beginning of the development of the exodus theme, connections seem to have been drawn with ancestral traditions. The antiquity of much of the material associated with Abraham and Sarah, Isaac and Rebekah, Jacob and Rachel remains well established, in spite of recent attempts to assign the bulk of Genesis 12–50 to the monarchical and exilic periods.[9] For one thing, the complex literary structure of the ancestral stories bears the marks of a long history of oral and written transmission, the early stages of which must antedate the period of kingship in Israel. Moreover, application of modern socioanthropological methods of study to the Genesis legends and related texts from the Mesopotamian area (especially the eighteenth-century tablets from Mari) has led to the plausible suggestion that the original setting of the ancestral stories is a dimorphic type of society that existed—as commonly in the history of the human race—in the Near East in the second millennium.[10] Accordingly, these stories can be taken as evidence for the emergence of social forms that stood in contrast to those prevailing especially in the large city-states of that time.[11] Within the Middle Bronze Age Ugaritic epics discovered at Ras Shamra, we find evidence of customs and practices closely parallel to those found in the Book of Genesis. Although literary texts are still lacking, it is tempting to look also to the early history of Moab, Edom, Ammon, Midian, and Qedar, where bits and pieces of evidence suggest a process of nations growing

---

8. Noth, *Tradition*, pp. 38–41 and Cross, *CMHE*, 84–86.

9. T. L. Thompson, *The Historicity of the Patriarchal Narratives*, BZAW 133 (Berlin: Walter de Gruyter, 1974); J. van Seters, *Abraham in History and Tradition* (New Haven, Conn.: Yale University Press, 1975).

10. For a summary of recent study on this problem, see W. G. Dever and W. M. Clark, "The Patriarchal Traditions," in J. H. Hayes and J. M. Miller, eds., *Israelite and Judean History* (Philadelphia: Westminster Press, 1977), pp. 70–148.

11. Cf. J. J. Finkelstein, "The Genealogy of the Hammurapi Dynasty," *JCS* 20 (1966), 95–118.

out of clan confederacies or leagues that runs parallel to the transition from the League to kingship in Israel.[12]

Intimately related to this sharp contrast between imperial and tribal sociopolitical structures was an equally sharp contrast between religious views. In the myth and ritual pattern associated with the cults of the major city-states and empires, we find a rigidly hierarchical conception of authority. The chief deity residing in the main temple was the absolute sovereign, whose rule was adminstered by the king. The authority of the king was in turn established by the ascription of divine attributes. This conception determined the sociopolitical structures of the state. Essential to social harmony was the obedient acceptance by each individual of his or her assigned station in life, be that as priest, free landowner, peasant, or slave.

The religious views growing out of the tribally organized village-pastoral society—of which the biblical patriarchs and matriarchs seem to have been a part—contrast sharply from those of the highly centralized city-states. Although the extrabiblical evidence is fragmentary, it supports impressions gained from the biblical narrative, and delineates a pattern of belief in which the clan related to its deity in an intimate way that created a close bond between the patron god and the members of the clan. Within this bond, the god was acknowledged as the source of health, prosperity, and offspring, a belief reflected in the personal names found both in the biblical ancestral stories and in the onomastica (name lists) of Mari and related societies. An example is the name Jacob (*ya'ăqōb* in the Hebrew Bible; *Iaḫqub-el* in the Mari tablets), which, though subject to folk-etymologizing in the Bible, probably carried the original meaning "May God protect." Growing out of this understanding of the close bond between deity and people are genealogies of the linear rather than the segmented type, for the deity is pictured not in primary relationship to one sacred place or to one perpetual dynasty, but to the experiences of the particular tribe—in effect to its "history," that is, its search for new pasturage, its victories over enemies under the leadership of its patron god, its migrations, and so on. Recent scholars have rightfully noted the importance of such genealogies in the development of the historiography of early Israel.[13] Moreover, the historical dimension of religious faith so essential to the exodus theme can be seen in direct relation to this important aspect of the religion of Israel's ancestors as found in the Book of Genesis.

Abraham, as portrayed in Genesis, fits the sociopolitical type just described, as well as the related religious view. According to Genesis 15, the deity (who identifies self as Abram's "Shield") promises Abram de-

---

12. Cross, *CMHE*, p. 105; W. J. Dumbrell, "The Midianites and Their Transjordanian Successors," unpublished doctoral dissertation, Harvard University 1970).

13. Especially important is the study of R. R. Wilson, *Genealogy and History in the Biblical World* (New Haven, Conn.: Yale University Press, 1977).

scendants. What is required of Abram is faith: "And he believed in the Lord; and he reckoned it to him as righteousness" (Gen. 15:6). Amid sacrifice and theophany, this god makes a covenant with Abram, on the basis of which the patriarch is able to face the future with courage.

An important quality of the ancestral faith as described in the Genesis narratives is the intimacy of fellowship existing between the patron god and the human follower. A divine theophany becomes the occasion of a feast in which Abraham and Sarah serve as hosts for the divine company (Gen. 18). Moreover, though the deity tests Abraham, he does not forsake him in the moment of the most dreadful crisis, but provides a substitute sacrifice for Isaac, and then renews the covenant, "because you have obeyed my voice" (Gen. 22:18). This same covenant pattern already illustrated in relation to Abraham and Sarah characterizes also the stories of Isaac and Rebekah (Gen. 26) and Jacob and Rachel (Gen. 28).

Biblical tradition seems to preserve an important historical connection in describing the Hebrew slaves in Egypt as descendants of the ancestors of Genesis. And indeed, those slaves likely stemmed from the same village-pastoral class of people encountered in the traditions in Genesis. Due no doubt to economic adversity (drought, famine), they first had been forced to take up the ways of the 'apiru (those falling outside the structures of the urban cultures), and subsequently had become slaves of the Pharaoh. In Exodus 1–3, the two earliest documentary sources (J and E) portray the plight of the enslaved Hebrews in terms of oppression under the Egyptians, a condition observed by their patron God (e.g., J 3:7–8 and E 3:9–12).[14] The same theme is concisely epitomized in the P stratum:

And the people of Israel groaned under their bondage, and cried out for help, and their cry under bondage came up to God. And God heard their groaning, and God remembered his covenant with Abraham, with Isaac, and with Jacob. And God saw the people of Israel, and God knew their condition. (Exod. 2:23b–25)

The early narrators of Israel's history felt that it was important to stress the contrast between the experiences of the Hebrew slaves in Egypt and the earlier experiences of their ancestors. Slavery was a contradiction of earlier promises given by the god(s) of Abraham, Isaac, and Jacob. Early tradition accordingly portrays Yahweh as instructing Moses to introduce himself thus: "The Lord [Yahweh], the God of your fathers, the God of Abraham, the God of Isaac, and the God of Jacob, has sent me to you" (Exod. 3:15). And P offers even more detail in describing the nature of the historical connection:

14. The Yahwistic Document (J) is a literary stratum recognized by most scholars in the first four books of the Bible and assigned to the tenth century B.C.E. The Elohist Document (E) in turn is viewed to be a parallel history (more fragmentary than J) from the ninth century B.C.E. The Priestly Writing (P) is considered by most scholars to be exilic in its final form. It gives the first five books of the Bible their present form.

And God said to Moses, "I am the Lord. I appeared to Abraham, to Isaac, and to Jacob, as God Almighty [El Shaddai], but by my name the Lord I did not make myself known to them. I also established my covenant with them, to give them the land of Canaan, the land in which they dwelt as sojourners. Moreover I have heard the groaning of the people of Israel whom the Egyptians hold in bondage and I have remembered my covenant. Say therefore to the people of Israel, 'I am the Lord, and I will bring you out from under the burdens of the Egyptians, and I will deliver you from their bondage, and I will redeem you with an outstretched arm and with great acts of judgment, and I will take you for my people, and I will be your God; and you shall know that I am the Lord your God, who has brought you out from under the burdens of the Egyptians. And I will bring you into the land which I swore to give to Abraham, to Isaac, and to Jacob; I will give it to you for a possession. I am the Lord. (Exod. 6:2–9).

Aided by this reconstruction of the sociopolitical background of the Genesis ancestors and their descendants, we can begin to understand the social matrix underlying the legends gathered by tradition to describe the birth and childhood of Moses. The following hints are important: The reference to the Hebrew midwives who would not collaborate with the Pharaoh because "they feared God, and did not do as the king of Egypt commanded them but let the male children live" (Exod. 1:17); the detail that Moses, while raised in the Pharaoh's palace, had his own Hebrew mother as a nurse (Exod. 2:10); the episode describing Moses's violent reaction to the situation in which "he saw an Egyptian beating a Hebrew, one of his people" (Exod. 2:11–15). These legends all bear witness to a common folk memory: these slaves were conscious of being distinct from the others by virtue of a religious tradition that had been kept alive among them, a tradition of a God who had related to their ancestors in the intimacy of a covenant of promise. This memory was the source of the conviction that their present slave status was not the inevitable result of divine decree, but an evil their God would one day redress. Interesting in this connection is the motif associated with Moses and his mother: only an upper echelon of the He-brew slave people—to which the Egyptian system had assigned a less oppressive role—could keep alive this faith in the God who had not forgotten them. This motif reflects a social phenomenon recognized by revolutionary theorists down to our time, namely, that the masses of an oppressed people often are too drained of energy and broken of spirit to effect their own means of escape. A human catalyst, somehow spared from the depths of oppression, is required. Thus Moses, having benefitted from a privileged upbringing, and yet having been nurtured within the ethnoreligious traditions of his kinsfolk by his nurse-mother, became the representative who stood firmly against both the grumbling skepticism of his broken people and the Pharaoh's hard heart.

From the perspective of Yahwistic faith, Moses accordingly was called by the same God who had earlier entered fellowship with the patriarchs, and thus became Yahweh's agent in the deliverance of a people not intended for slavery. We therefore see that while such legends do not provide us with the raw facts of history, they do preserve dimensions of the exodus event that are of great importance for understanding the prehistory of Israel, dimensions such as the antecedent religious tradition of the Hebrews, which distinguished them sharply from the Egyptians, and the sociopolitical context within which the exodus occurred.

The ancestral narratives of Genesis, therefore, are an important source for understanding the background of Yahwistic faith. While the deliverance from Egypt was the revelatory event through which early Israel grasped the most distinctive aspects of her faith, the ancestral narratives of Genesis, interpreted within the larger sociopolitical matrix of the village and pastoral tribalism of the second millennium, help us recognize the alternative view of reality that maintained in the Hebrew slaves in Egypt an openness to a divine act of deliverance. According to that view, the individual Hebrew clan was under the special care of the patron god of its founder. The religion of Egypt and the oppressive social system it sanctified, were not beyond question and challenge, because the patron deity was not a member of the Egyptian pantheon. Doubtless the experiences in Egypt, as later the experiences of Jews in Babylonian exile, raised questions regarding the efficacy of this patron god vis-à-vis the mighty gods of their captors. But the old faith maintained an openness, even a longing, for an event that would demonstrate their god's continued care and power, even in their threatening alien setting.

As will be seen through the unfolding of Yahwistic belief in the Bible, the acts of God were not encountered as knee-jerk reactions by a whimsical deity, but as episodes preceded by long, careful preparation, and as parts of a plan that faith could discern running through and guiding all history. It becomes apparent that "the exodus event" was a vastly more complicated phenomenon than may appear on the surface.[15] We recognize God's preparation for this birth of a people hundreds of years earlier, in the migratory movements of peoples from the northeast into the Mesopotamian and Syro-Palestinian areas, in the traditions maintained by Hebrew clans in Egypt amid their trying experiences, and in the life of one Hebrew whose advantaged position did not dull his sensitivity to the plight, and hopes, of his kinsfolk. Of course, the extant records leave many aspects of this event unclear. For example, while existing traditions explain plausibly how the social and religious structures of the ancestors of the Genesis narratives prepared for belief in a God who hears the cries of his people, we are left to speculate over the historical circumstances under which the Hebrews come

15. For a more detailed description of the "exodus event," understood broadly and in a manner comprehensible to the modern mind, see P. D. Hanson, *Dynamic Transcendence: The Correlation of Confessional Heritage and Contemporary Experience in a Biblical Model of Divine Activity* (Philadelphia: Fortress Press, 1978).

to name that god *Yahweh*. Earlier scholarship pointed to the early contact reported in Exodus between Moses and the Kenite (Midianite)
priest Jethro, and speculated that important aspects of Yahwism arose
through that contact (cf. Exod. 3–4 and 18). It now appears likely that a
close relationship did exist between proto-Israelite clans and an early
Midianite League, a relationship remembered and fostered especially
by the Mushite priesthood in Israel. Moreover, reference to Seir,
Mount Paran, and Teman in Yahwistic poems such as Deuteronomy 33,
Judges 5, and Habakkuk 3 suggest that the Midianite region was the
home of an important southern sanctuary, a place of pilgrimage for
Yahweh worshippers of the League period.[16] Thus bits and pieces of
evidence point to the general context within which early Yahwism took
shape. In it various structural, legal, and conceptual elements were
drawn into the new experience of deliverance, and by being interpreted against the background of earlier ancestral traditions, the basic con-
tours of early Yahwism began to emerge.

C. OUT OF THE HOUSE OF BONDAGE: THE EXODUS

While the exodus event broadly construed was multifaceted and complex, it did have a nucleus that brought into sharp focus the theological
meaning of the whole. We are brought close to that nucleus by the remarkable hymn found in Exodus 15, whose oral form was the product
of a vivid recollection of the event of deliverance. Once again, it does
not represent history reporting in the narrow sense, but should be interpreted as a response to an experience in which the encounter with
historical realities led to a discernment of a deeper underlying significance. The genre used was that of the hymn.[17] The community, newly
delivered from the oppressor and recipient of God's promise of blessing and land and progeny, responded in the manner it found most fitting—through an expression of praise and gratitude to a gracious and
mighty God. It seems clear that the historical episode underlying the
hymn involved the escape of a band of Hebrews from the armies of the
Pharaoh. In this episode, the exact details of which are beyond our ken,
the majesty and compassion of Yahweh were displayed in a manner so
vivid that it gave rise to an image that seemed to reveal the heart of
Israel's God. Through this glorious triumph, Yahweh became Israel's
"strength" and "victory" even as God had earlier been the protector of
Israel's ancestors. The hymn goes on to describe that triumph: Yahweh
defeated the armies of the Pharaoh, and thwarted their efforts to recapture the people of Israel. Yahweh was incomparable among the
gods! The redeemer God was experienced as Israel's sustainer as well,

---

16. See T. Hiebert, *God of My Victory: An Ancient Hymn of Triumph in Habakkuk 3*, HSM
(Chico, Calif.: Scholars Press, in press).
17. Cross, *CHME*, pp. 112–133.

leading the people in steadfast love, protecting them from hostile peoples, and establishing them in a place that was Yahweh's own sanctuary. Although the metaphor of God as warrior understandably creates serious problems for many modern interpreters, its importance for the system of belief of a people born of deliverance from slavery must not be overlooked.[18]

The exodus event was a broad one and a deep one, encompassing ancestral promises, Egyptian social and religious structures, tribal customs, and many other specific happenings and concrete details not preserved by tradition. Yet its nucleus was captured by the hymn in Exodus 15. In a unique way, after a rich gestation period, the moment of Israel's birth as a community occurred in the experience of Yahweh's majesty placed at the service of an oppressed and threatened people, the experience of deliverance from the hosts of the Pharaoh at the Sea. Israel's birth thus occurred in this miraculous passage from bondage to freedom. And in essence there was already revealed in this event both the nature of the God Yahweh, and the nature of the community of faith that Yahweh's nature implied. By becoming the metonomy of the whole exodus event, this theme of deliverance at the Sea became a symbol of Israel's birth as a people of God. Subsequently this symbol was handed down through the ages. The canonical shape of Exodus 1–15 shows how hymnic celebration of the deliverance at the sea became the nucleus around which developed an entire exodus pageant.[19] This celebration echoes through the Bible as its most persistent theme. And it continues today to find annual expression in the Jewish celebration of the Passover.[20]

D. ENCOUNTER WITH THE DELIVERER GOD YAHWEH AS CATALYST OF THE YAHWISTIC NOTION OF COMMUNITY

With the birth of this people, a new order of life and a new notion of community were also born. The implications for human life and life in community found within the exodus experience were profound, as can be seen by contrasting the old gods with the new God. In the deliverance from Egyptian slavery, Israel encountered a God whose nature

18. For a theological discussion of this problem, cf. P. D. Hanson, *Int* 38 (1984), "War and Peace in the Hebrew Bible," pp. 341–362.

19. The classic study of this pageant remains J. Pedersen's "The Crossing of the Reed Sea and the Paschal Legend," in *Israel*, Vols. 3–4 (London: Oxford University Press, 1940), pp. 728–737.

20. G. von Rad expresses the central importance of the exodus event thus: "In the deliverance from Egypt, Israel saw the guarantee for all the future, the absolute surety for Yahweh's will to save, something like a warrant to which faith could appeal in times of trial (Ps. 74:2)." *Old Testament Theology*, vol. 1, trans. D. M. G. Stalker (New York: Harper & Row, 1962), p. 176.

and whose corresponding plan for reality stood in diametric opposition to the gods of the Pharaoh. The latter were the divine sponsors of the ruling class, similar to the high gods of the Mesopotamian city-states, alongside of which arose belief in the "personal god," who took a parental interest in ordinary human beings.[21] In the exodus was revealed the heart of a God whose sovereignty spanned the heavens, but who at the same time embraced the cause of the most humble and oppressed members of society, a God neither impressed with nor influenced by the pedigrees, proud claims, or pompous displays of power, erudition, and wealth of kings and other earthly potentates.

What were the implications of the encounter with the God of the exodus for the development of social structures and patterns of community? First, it must be recognized that emergent Israel was a people living within a world in which slavery and the exploitation of aliens were unquestioned parts of the economic system. And as we shall see, the young community, recognizing the need for communal norms and social structures as a matter of survival within a threatening world, naturally borrowed from laws and practices existing among its neighbors. This reality, together with the obvious fact that the members of the early Yahwistic community were vulnerable to the same human passions that foster oppression and inequality in every society, serves sufficient warning against temptations to view early Israel in romantically idealistic terms. Once this grounded view is clear, however, we can go on to recognize the long-range significance of the exodus experience: for its life as a free people, this community was indebted to the God who chose to take the side of slaves against the "divine" Pharaoh. So long as this primal experience was preserved in memory, it would have a decisive impact on the development of communal values and social structures. The exodus experience cannot be understood if its social implications are not recognized clearly: in this act of deliverance, the God Yahweh annulled religious and social systems predicated on assumptions of special privilege, and abolished the caste system as a fundamental structure of human society. Again, we dare not overlook the sad fact that this understanding of the exodus experience was more often neglected than preserved in ancient Israel, because of forgetfulness and the seduction of alternate ideologies. But the simple fact of the exodus event and the God encountered in that event implanted into the consciousness of the people a reality that refused to be silenced. As godly leaders in all ages of Israelite history pointed out, that reality continued to be present with this people, true to the same saving purpose that underlay the exodus.

Thus a new notion of community was born with the exodus. In com-

---

21. T. Jacobsen, *Toward the Image of Tammuz and Other Essays on Mesopotamian History and Culture* (Cambridge, Mass.: Harvard University Press, 1970), pp. 45–46.

promising it or denying it, as Israel repeatedly would, Israel would compromise or deny its own essential being as a people called by God, a community of freed slaves within which the pyramid of social stratification consigning certain classes to lives of ease and others to relentless suffering and deprivation was to be banned forever. But the notion of the alternative community would be kept alive and deepened in the resulting fray. As this study indicates, an unbroken chain of witnesses drew from Israel's birth experience its essential lesson: within this community, every individual was equally precious to God, regardless of social standing, and thus to be protected from exploitation and oppression by the structures intrinsic to the covenant between God and people.

However much denied by actual practices, there was accordingly an organic connection between the exodus event and the communal structures that were true to Israel's origins in God's gracious act of deliverance. That connection could not be preserved solely by abstract formulations of belief, but demanded a quality of life relating inextricably to systems of justice, land distribution, use of capital, treatment of vulnerable classes within the society, and the like. These institutions are not formal accidents, but essential structures already implicit in the nature of the God revealed in the exodus. Because of their ultimate source in God's nature, Israel's understanding of these structures would be deepened and refined over the entire history of its relating to the living God of the Covenant.

Thus God's deliverance of a slave people inaugurated a new order of life for Israel and, concretely, a new notion of community. Israel began to draw out some of the cardinal qualities of that new order as the Israelites lived in the wake of this memorable foundational event. Beyond these early beginnings, the act of deliverance in the exodus set in motion a dynamic process among those people who owed their freedom to that event, a process of defining themselves as the people of God. That process moved powerfully and creatively through the entire unfolding of Scripture, in spite of diverse forms of opposition from outside and from within. Anticipating later parts of this study, I may add that this same dynamic process continues today wherever religious communities seek to understand themselves in relation to God's liberating activity on behalf of the oppressed. Over the long history of the Judeo-Christian traditions, the reference point give by the exodus event for self-definition and understanding has remained a cardinal feature of communities who base their identity on the God of the Bible.[22] It is in recognizing God's activity in the deliverance of the op-

---

22. The exodus theme, for example, is central to the black liberation theology of J. K. Cone, as seen in his *A Black Theology of Liberation* (Philadelphia: J. B. Lippincott, 1970). It also plays an important role in the theological writings of G. Gutierrez, as illustrated by his book, *A Theology of Liberation: History, Politics and Salvation* (Maryknoll, N.Y.: Orbis Books, 1973).

pressed of all ages that the community of faith grasps the meaning of being called to be a *people of God*.

It is difficult to conceptualize the magnitude of the challenge raised by the Hebrew clans as they went forth to tell of their deliverance experience to other clans, some of them related by blood, others related through the experience of oppression under Canaanite overlords whose pattern of rule and treatment of their subjects was essentialy the same as that of the Egyptian pharaohs. The alternative their experience presented called into question the fundamental presuppositions of the dominant mythopoeic world view of that time. Not Egypt alone, but all the major ancient empires of the Near East built their social systems on the assumption that by divine intention some human beings were created to enjoy far greater esteem, privilege, and material comfort than others. This view was a logical extrapolation from their view of heavenly realities, where diverse levels of gods accorded special benefits to human beings on the basis of whim or favor. When Moses intervened on behalf of a Hebrew slave being beaten by an Egyptian guard and then took flight into the wilderness, his sojourn proved to be a passage in the night, which opened up to him a radically new notion of community. Wilderness—that austere, severe, and quiet place—created the brokenness and openness necessary to prepare for God's revealing a new plan for the human family.

What essential qualities of community did the Hebrews derive from their experience of deliverance from slavery?

1. WORSHIP AS RESPONSE TO GOD'S ANTECEDENT GRACE

Israel became a people because of divine initiative. Its birth rested on no human merit. It was explainable solely in terms of God's grace. The particular nature of the initiating act revealed the unique nature of the God Yahweh, a God who embraced the cause of the most humble and oppressed, making them a people with dignity and freedom. The notion of community that unfolds in the Bible can be understood adequately only by clearly recognizing its origin in the initiative of a gracious God. Israel became God's people by responding to divine grace. All the terms for the community of faith in the Old and the New Testament have this response quality; for example, *qāhāl* (assembly), *ʿēdâ* (congregation), *sôd* (assembly), and *ekklesia* (assembly, congregation, church). In each case, God is understood as the One who has gathered the people. For this reason, only a thoroughly theological approach promises to uncover the essential nature and meaning of the biblical notion of community. Concentration on social qualities, or structural features, or specific patterns of organization uncovers only certain aspects of the response to God's call to community in particular times and settings. The generative dynamic of the notion, however, is grasped only by seeing the first Hebrew community, as well as all subsequent generations of the faithful, as those responding to God's creative and redemptive activity, a response that is the human side of the living covenantal relationship.

We recognize in the exodus story a particular characteristic of the Hebrew slaves that is of theological importance. It is the condition of openness to the divine initiative, the desire to be saved from the bonds of slavery. More specifically, this openness is characterized by a sense of brokenness as regards human resources and dependency before God. In contrast, a smugly proud community draws a circle around its self-understanding that is no longer permeable by divine initiative. Self-understanding becomes a static quality defined from within, and ceases to be construed as response to action coming from beyond self. Confession of need, however, opens as people to a definition that is self-transcending, and to a saving presence that is not ensconced in institutional structures but experienced as breaking in afresh. This prerequisite human condition underscores the theological significance of the fact that the Hebrews were prompted by their suffering to cry to God for help. Unlike their overlords, they were receptive to God's new plan because of the openness that arose out of their oppression. As suggested by the New Testament metaphor of the camel's difficulty passing through the needle's eye, it is very difficult for those accustomed only to wealth and privilege to embrace the new order of humanity that God initiates in acts of deliverance of the oppressed and redemption of those in bondage, for in that order all people are equal and status is not recognized. The pedagogy of brokenness seems to play an important role in preparing a people for that new vision.

From this early Yahwistic perspective, it follows that those not tutored in the pedagogy of brokenness can hope to embrace God's new order only be denouncing their own roles of privilege and oppression, and by identifying with the poor and the oppressed. This notion is expressed clearly by Marie Augusta Neal's appeal to the "First World" to respond to the liberation movements of the oppressed not by feeble attempts to adapt liberation theology to situations to which it does not fit, but by developing the only theology that corresponds authentically to liberation theology from the side of those not suffering from, but contributing to the oppression of others—namely, a theology of relinquishment.[23]

Returning to the specific situation of the oppressed Hebrews, we find that when the slaves in Egypt cried from their bondage and distress, it was not the potentates of this world who responded to their plight, but a gracious, divine Deliverer. The hope of these slaves was therefore based solidly on their faith in a divine power that relativized all earthly power, thus placing an absolute limit on the hardships they could inflict

---

23. Marie Augusta Neal, *A Socio-theology of Letting Go* (New York: Paulist Press, 1977).

on their subjects. Notions of God's majesty and glory thus did not increase the slaves' feeling of deprivation and helplessness, but gave them a sense of empowerment in dealing with their situation. As the prophet of the "second exodus" realized centuries later, the message that "all flesh is grass" and that God's word alone endures forever, while threatening to the tyrants of this world, is the quintessence of good news for those lacking all earthly recourse (Isa. 40:8)[24]

In the response of slaves to God's act of deliverance, the biblical notion of community was born. And we can be more specific in describing the primary quality of that response: it was a response in worship. This quality is apparent already in the oldest biblical description of their deliverance from the armies of the Pharaoh, found in the Song of Miriam (Exod. 15), because the form of that composition is hymnic. Only in worship and praise did the people find the fitting response to the gracious, saving God: "I will sing to the Lord!" (Exod. 15:1).

Because God's initiating, gracious activity was the foundation of the biblical notion of community, worship was its primal quality. Worship acknowledges the source and center of life and freedom, and places all other realities in their proper relation to that source and center. In fact, all other realities in the world are derivative; that is, they have meaning only in relation to the divine Reality.

We can go on, moreover, to define more closely the nature of the worship of Yahweh in Exodus 15. In that ancient hymn, the response in worship involved recital; that is, it described the saving act of God in vivid detail, locating it in the midst of history, within the specific and the concrete, "for he has triumphed gloriously; the horse and rider he has thrown into the sea." As this and the numerous other details in verses 4–10 indicate, this deliverance was not construed as a timeless episode in a mythic scenario, but as a manifestation of God's purpose in history. While employing mythological images to interpret the transcendent significance of the historical event, the celebrants left no doubt that Yahweh was encountered within the realities of this world.

2. YAHWEH MAJESTIC IN HOLINESS

On the basis of this description of Yahweh's act of deliverance, the hymn makes a daring move. In an interrogative style that continues the tenor of awe and praise, it describes this incomparable God: "majestic

---

24. It is significant to note that today as in antiquity liberation movements involving the socially and economically oppressed do not find the concept of God's sovereignty a contributor to their oppression, but a source, indeed often the only source of hope for deliverance from earthly oppressors. It is only among movements originating among the socially and economically privileged that the concept of divine sovereignty is sometimes attacked as an obstacle to human fulfillment. For the individual or group possessing no means to withstand earthly powers and having no recourse to those in control, the reduction of the divine to equal status with humans would be tantamount with removing the only source of hope for vindication.

in holiness, terrible in glorious deeds, doing wonders" (Exod. 15:11).
Israel's sole Lord was the absolutely unique and incomparable Yahweh.
At the center of Israelite worship, and at the heart of Hebrew community, was thus a norm that relativized all other authorities. We have
here a classic expression of the numinous quality that Rudolph Otto
identified as the central feature of worship, namely, encounter with the
mysterium tremendum et fascinans.[25] In the presence of this holy God,
wickedness perished: "Thou didst stretch out thy right hand, the earth
swallowed them" (15:12). In this act of judgment, the Hebrews came
into the presence of a strict, new standard of righteousness. The holy
God Yahweh did not look on injustice with indifference, but with incisive action. Neither the cries of the oppressed, nor the reveling of the
oppressor were unheeded. When we turn to the Book of the Covenant,
we will see how this holy Deliverer Yahweh functioned as the norm for
early Israel's formulation of laws and social structures. Yahweh, majestic in holiness, became the standard of righteousness within this nascent community.

3. YAHWEH'S STEADFAST LOVE

In verse 13, the hymn returns to the descriptive mode. And in so doing it extrapolates from historical experience a second aspect of God's
nature: "Thou hast led in thy steadfast love the people whom thou has
redeemed, thou hast guided them by thy strength to thy holy abode."
Yahweh first appeared to the Hebrew slaves as Redeemer. In a gracious
act of deliverance, he led them out of bondage. But after this dramatic
act he did not just leave them in the wilderness to fend for themselves.
God's redemptive act was followed by God's sustaining presence with
the people. Without this abiding care, the redemptive act could not
have brought a community to maturity. The birth would have culminated in infant mortality. Indeed, the wilderness stories, and the entire
subsequent history of Israel recorded by Scripture, suggest that this
second stage in the creation of a people dependent on God's sustaining
activity was more difficult than the original redemptive act in the deliverance from Egypt. The second quality of God's nature inferred from
this ongoing activity of leading, guiding, and sustaining was thus described with a very significant word, *ḥésed.* Translated variously as
"goodness," "kindness," "mercy," "compassion," and "steadfast love,"
ḥésed in reference to God describes the divine quality of fidelity to the
covenant, the kind of love that was utterly trustworthy, and thus served
as a norm for all relationships (e.g., Ps. 89:2–5; Isa. 54:10, 55:3). The
history of God's relation to the community he had created in the exodus was qualitatively described by this term, even as it drew attention to

---

25. Rudolph Otto, *The Idea of the Holy*, trans. J. W. Harvey (London: Oxford University Press, 1950).

the roots of this community in the promises made earlier by God to Israel's ancestors. According to this description, the entire process of communal growth from birth to fulfillment in the perfect fellowship intended by God was to be faithfully directed by God within the shelter of divine covenant. God's *ḥésed* assured that throughout the long difficult path of history, a dependable stream was directing the community in becoming God's people. The deliverance that had introduced the people to Yahweh and had brought forth the birth of their community was thus only the beginning of a creative activity that would stretch through many ages, and would be guided from start to finish by God's covenant fidelity.

In Exodus 15, this guidance is portrayed very concretely: God leads the people "to thy holy abode." In verse 17, this guidance is further elaborated with the phrases "thy own mountain," and "the sanctuary which thy hands have established." Here the land of promise, in which Israel would develop as a free people, is described as a sanctuary of Yahweh—indeed, as the cosmic mountain on which the divine king of ancient Semitic mythology typically lived. Thus ancient symbolism is applied to confess that Yahweh would continue to be with this people intimately and steadfastly. His presence would abide in their midst. In this way, God would show that the exodus was not a mere stroke of good fortune, not even just a passing favor from heaven. That this was truly a "people . . . whom thou has purchased" would be demonstrated to the world by God's abiding presence (cf. Exod. 33:17–23 and 34:5–9).

The nature of Yahweh's guidance and sustaining power is described in specific terms in verses 14–17, again demonstrating the roots of Yahwistic belief in historical experience. The hymn then concludes with an ascription of praise to this holy Redeemer and steadfast Sustainer, who as the only God deserving of devotion and worship is Israel's King forever: "The Lord will reign for ever and ever."

In Exodus 15, then, we find the essential qualities of the early Yahwistic notion of community. With its source in the initiating activity of Yahweh, community arose as a grateful response centered in worship. In this worship, Yahweh was praised as the one who acted in a specific event of history to deliver the oppressed from their oppressor, thereby revealing self as the incomparable God, majestic in holiness. Moreover, Yahweh was praised also as the Sustainer, who continued to guide and uphold his people in steadfast love and deep compassion. Yahweh, unrivaled in holy majesty and steadfast in love, as righteous Judge and as compassionate Deliverer, is also the Reality that unifies the drama running through Exodus 1–15 in its final canonical form. In this larger unit, the openness and brokenness of the people is portrayed, accompanied by the unfolding theme of Yahweh's hearing their cry and then responding in righteous judgment and compassionate redemption. Moses, before receiving divine instruction, acts blindly on the basis of a sense of kinship with the oppressed. While his impulsive act gives noble expression to the sense of communal solidarity vis-à-vis the developed city cultures that was characteristic of the village pastoralism encountered in the patriarchal stories of Genesis, Moses's individual initiation can lead only to an impasse, which necessitates flight into the liminality of Midian. The failure of human schemes, however, sets the stage for introduction of the Divine Purpose. Out of the burning bush, which evokes in Moses the sense of awe fostering openness to God's plan, Yahweh introduces self as "the God of Abraham, the God of Isaac, the God of Jacob." With this important connection with the earlier tribal cult established, Yahweh goes on to reveal his specific plan, commissioning Moses as his agent in the redemption of Israel. And in contrast to Moses's former powerlessness, Yahweh now entrusts Moses with the divine name, with which he is to commend himself to the people: "Say this to the people of Israel, The Lord, the God of Abraham, the God of Isaac, and the God of Jacob, has sent me to you: this is my name forever, and thus I am to be remembered throughout all generations" (Exod. 3:15). Yahweh, in revealing his name, commits self to this suffering people and their leader. The divine name is a sign of Yahweh's faithfulness and trustworthiness: "This is my name forever."

The entire scenario that follows is seen as the unfolding of the plan of the sole Lord Yahweh. Against the hard-hearted Pharaoh, God stands as the righteous Judge. On behalf of the suffering Hebrews, he acts as the compassionate Savior. As the drama began with the worship of Moses before the burning bush, so too it ends with worship and praise, in the Passover ritual and the Song of Miriam. In thus comparing Exodus 15 with the final canonical form of Exodus 1–15 we see that the pattern of antecedent acts of the righteous, compassionate God Yahweh, followed by the grateful response of the people in worhship and praise, shaped the exodus tradition from beginning to end.

III

The Growth of a Triadic Notion of Community
(Exodus 19–23, Joshua, and Judges)

" . . . the time of the desert is that when one has strictly no other support, no other assurance than the grace of God."[1]

Historical Note: The period between the exodus and the introduction of kingship into Israel (ca. 1250–1029 B.C.E.) was one in which a distinctive notion of community developed that would abide as a powerful influence on Israel's self-understanding throughout its subsequent history as a people. We are able to reconstruct important stages in the growth of that community notion during the so-called League or Tribal Confederacy period on the basis of ancient materials embedded in Exodus 19–23 and the books of Joshua and Judges, materials arising within the early Yahwistic cult at Gilgal. It was clearly a period of severe testing as converts to the God Yahweh encountered the animosity of hostile neighbors, the seduction of other cults, and intracommunity tensions and divisions. But testing proved to be the mother of a remarkably progressive and humane notion of community: through no merit of its own, Israel had been drawn into a covenant relationship with Yahweh. Yahweh alone was to be worshipped as sovereign. And it was in imitation of Yahweh's righteousness and compassion that Israel was to live as a holy nation. From this period, therefore, we see worship and *tôrâ* emerge as the twin human responses to God's antecedent gracious initiative.

We have seen on the basis of the Song of Miriam how the experience of God's gracious deliverance led to worship and praise. In this response Israel focused especially on God's holiness and steadfast love, two divine qualities that would guide the subsequent development of Israel's notion of the community of faith as a people of God seeking to embody divine righteousness and compassion in every facet of life.

Now we need to ask what materials might contribute to our understanding of that subsequent development. First let us examine the con-

1. Jacques Ellul, *Apocalypse*, trans. G. W. Schreiner (New York: Seabury Press, 1977), p. 90.

quest traditions contained in Joshua and the stories of tribal leaders in Judges, and then return to early materials contained in Exodus 19–23.

A. CONQUEST TRADITIONS IN JOSHUA

The complex tradition that underlies the Book of Joshua does not permit us to reconstruct the development of Israel's notion of community in the "conquest" period on a *prima facie* reading. Critical study, however, has led to the discovery of very old traditions embedded in this section of the Deuteronomistic History (Deuteronomy through 2 Kings), that cast important light on our problem.

First we turn our attention to Joshua 3:1 to 5:1, an ancient festival legend from the sanctuary located at Gilgal.[2] This legend, whose present form preserves the marks of a long history of revision and conflation of sources, focuses on the theme of Yahweh leading Israel into the land of promise. We are led to ask more precisely, "What was the history of the Gilgal cult, and what was the nature of its central tradition?" Two important clues are found in the cult legend itself.

The first clue is found in the obvious interconnectedness between the theme of the exodus and the theme of the Jordan crossing. In answer to the children's question of what the twelve stones at this cult site signify, the confession was made, "Israel passed over this Jordan on dry ground. For the Lord your God dried up the waters of the Jordan for you until you passed over, as the Lord your God did to the Red Sea, which he dried up for us until we passed over" (4:22b–23). The parallel drawn between these two episodes suggests that we are dealing with a cultic tradition that focused on the deliverance from Egypt and the entry into the promised land as one unified confessional strand. This impression is reinforced by signs of interaction between Exodus 14–15 and Joshua 3:1–5:1. Joshua 5:1, for example, summarizes the theme found in Exodus 15:15 of the dismay of the inhabitants of Canaan as the Israelites moved forward under God's mighty hand. Exodus 14:21–29, on the other hand, reflects the influence of the Jordan crossing (Josh. 3:14–17). This is all very understandable if the exodus and the Jordan narratives were both parts of one cult legend, the legend of the spring festival of Passover held at the Gilgal sanctuary (cf. Josh. 4:19 and 5:10 for indications of the calendar date). Indeed, Exodus 15 is best understood as an ancient hymn of the Gilgal cult, in its oral form having originated as early as the twelfth century B.C.E., and tracing in one dramatic movement the exodus, the approach to the Promised Land, and finally Yahweh's bringing the people into the land.[3]

---

2. H.-J. Kraus, "Gilgal. Ein Beitrag zur Kultgeschichte Israels," *VT* 1 (1951), 188–199; J. A. Soggin, "Gilgal, Passah und Landnahme," VTSuppl 15 (1966), 263–277; Cross, *CMHE*, 103–105.

3. Cross, *CHME*, 137–139.

The second clue to the Gilgal cult and the tradition handed down there is found in the description of Joshua, for it points to another parallelism between the exodus and Jordan narratives: Joshua is portrayed as a second Moses. In Exodus 14:31, the exodus experience was summarized thus: "And Israel saw the great work which the Lord did against the Egyptians, and the people feared the Lord: and they believed in the Lord and in his servant Moses." Similarly, at the point where the people have completed their passage over the Jordan, the Joshua narrative concludes, "on that day the Lord exalted Joshua in the sight of all Israel, and they stood in awe of him, as they had stood in awe of Moses, all the days of his life" (Josh. 4:14; also compare Exod. 3:5–12 with Josh. 5:15). The fact that other biblical traditions give a very different picture of Moses[4] lends support to the following conclusion: the positive, parallel portrayal of Moses and Joshua found in Exodus 14 and Joshua 3:1–5:1 reflects a common source in the ancient Yahwistic cult at Gilgal.

When the broad significance of the early Gilgal cult is understood, other problems find their most plausible solution. First, in relation to the Book of Joshua itself, it has been correctly observed that the conquest traditions have their focal point in Benjaminite territory.[5] But why then is Joshua—who according to the grave tradition in Joshua 24:30 was an Ephraimite—the central figure in the conquest legends? One explanation, of course, is that the figure of Joshua has secondarily entered the Benjaminite conquest material.[6] But since Joshua is so centrally a part of this material on all levels, early to late, another explanation seems more plausible.

Joshua, like Moses, was likely an original figure in the exodus and conquest tradition of the Gilgal cult (and indeed, there is no reason to doubt that the source of both figures in this material is historial). The close association between Gilgal and the Benjaminites in early tradition indicates that the tribe played an active part in the Gilgal sanctuary. We can go further, moreover, and suggest that the tribe of Joseph (i.e., Ephraim and Manasseh) was also among the participants in this cult, for the tie between the two Rachel tribes of Benjamin and Joseph is too ancient and persistent to be explained in any other way than that their association stems from the early League period.[7] It is altogether possible that the common history of both tribes traces back to the exodus itself. At any rate, this reconstruction best explains the role of Joshua

4. Note, for example, the following: the tradition of the people's bitter complaints against Moses (Exod. 15:22–26; 16:1–36; 17:1–8; etc.); the rebellion of the people in the golden calf incident (Exod. 32); and the insubordination of Miriam and Aaron (Num. 12).

5. M. Noth, *Das Buch Joshua*, HAT 7 2d ed. (Tübingen: Mohr [Siebeck], 1953).

6. *Ibid.*, 12. And earlier, A. Alt, "Josua," *Kleine Schriften I* (München: C. H. Beck, 1953), p. 176.

7. Cf. H.W. Herzberg, *Die Bücher Joshua, Richter, Ruth*, ATD 9 (Göttingen: Vandenhoeck & Ruprecht, 1959), pp. 11–12; and S. Herrmann, *A History of Israel in Old Testament Times*, trans. J. Bowden (Philadelphia: Fortress Press, 1981), pp. 96–97.

in both Josephite and Ephramite tradition, as it does the unity of exodus and conquest themes within the sacred legend of Gilgal.

Gilgal thus emerges, under the light of critical examination, as a very ancient carrier of the exodus confession and of the notion of community that grew out of that confession. Exodus 15, as the ancient hymn celebrating God's great saving act at the sea, may in fact even be a fairly well-preserved fragment of the epic that had taken shape within that cult.

Other questions that emerge can be answered with less certainty. For example, might other clans or tribes also have participated in the Gilgal cult? The tradition of the twelve-stone memorial in both of the versions combined in Joshua 3:1–5:1 suggests that over the course of this sanctuary's development other tribes came to identify themselves with the exodus confession, and entered into the covenant of those acknowledging their origins as a people in God's gracious initiative in saving the oppressed. Equally intriguing is the relation of Gilgal to other cult centers mentioned in biblical tradition describing the premonarchical period. What is the relation, for example, between Joshua 3:1–5:1 and the covenant ceremony of Shechem described in Joshua 24, where confession of the exodus and conquest plays a central role and Joshua officiates? While later traditionalists, especially from the Deuteronomistic group, have thoroughly reworked this narrative, it likely contains earlier layers, which however are extremely difficult to disentangle.

One is also led to inquire into the history of the ark's relation to Joshua 3:1–5:1, and thus to the Gilgal sanctuary. Since the ark is firmly rooted in archaic tradition concerning the exodus and conquest, we are convinced that it was a sacred relic of the Gilgal sanctuary from the beginning of its history. This ancient palladium symbolized the presence of Yahweh, both in confrontations with hostile armies and in cultic reenactments of Yahweh's guidance of the people, such as that ritually celebrated at Gilgal.[8] Similarly, the story of Joshua's circumcision of the people suggests that in the Gilgal cult that rite was practiced as a sign of the covenant. The parallel between the twelve stories of the Joshua story and the twelve pillars erected by Moses in the tradition of Exodus 24:3–8 opens up the question of the nature of the covenant theology in the Yahweh cult at Gilgal, and its relation to early formulations of *tôrâ* preserved in the Hebrew Bible, such as the Book of the Covenant in Exodus 21–23. Because of the importance and magnitude of these problems, they are reserved for special treatment later.

Here we need to note one final theme in the Book of Joshua, and indeed a very major one, the allotment of the land described in Chapters 13–19. As in the case of the conquest, the portrait we receive is a theological idealization growing out of and reflecting a more complex his-

---

8. Cross, *CMHE*, pp. 94–97, 100–105.

torical reality. That reality likely involved the practice of land apportionment carried out as a condition stipulated by the community's covenant with its deity.

Thus when we read of Joshua's alloting the land to the clans at Shiloh, we can recognize the structural implementation within an early gathering of Ephraimite and Benjaminite tribes of a cardinal Yahwistic belief that all the land belonged to one Sovereign alone, namely Yahweh. No earthly lord was therefore empowered to purchase or hold title to property. Use of the land was to be made available equally to all, as a condition laid down by the divine Sovereign. Since that Sovereign was a righteous God, the allotment was to be even-handed, determined by divine decision alone (the casting of lots being the customary technique for ascertaining divine will).

In the final form that we find in Joshua, this practice is portrayed as pertaining to all twelve tribes gathered together in one place. A more limited, local practice such as suggested earlier seems plausible as the historical reality out of which this idealized portrait grew, since it is consistent with the features of early Yahwism seen elsewhere, especially the sole sovereignty of Yahweh and the interpretation of all life within the context of the covenant. Within the context of such a concept of convenant community, with its dedication to the well-being of all members, it is understandable that the basic condition on which human well-being depended, namely, land sufficient to sustain each social unit, would be protected, especially when one considers the threat posed by the contradictory attitudes and practices of the Canaanites. Such protection is entirely in keeping with the attention to the protection of aliens, the poor, widows, and orphans that arises in the premonarchical period.

B. ISRAEL'S JUDGES

Careful scholarly analysis of the Book of Judges has made an important contribution to our understanding of the general situation within which the early Yahwistic community developed its confessions and forms of worship and society. As in the case of the Book of Joshua, one must carefully distinguish between earlier and later levels of tradition. Once again the stories have been fitted into the imposing theological framework of the Deuteronomistic History, according to which the period between Joshua and Samuel was a time of political chaos. The historiographic schema into which the stories of the judges were placed, and which is seen especially clearly in the Deuteronomistic commentaries in 2:1–5, 6:7–10 and 10:6–16, is that of the repetition of the following cycle: the apostasy of the people, subjugation to the enemy, their cry to Yahweh, Yahweh's sending a "judge" (šōpēṭ) to deliver them, a period of peace under the šōpēṭ.

It is what antedates the Deuteronomistic stratum, however, that is of greatest interest for us, for there we find local traditions of various tribal heroes that, while not being historical sources in the modern sense of the word, nevertheless preserve a broad picture of the premonarchical period that seems authentic and reliable. Since there seems to be no other period in biblical history that could have given rise to such stories, we can safely assume that we are dealing with narratives that arose out of the struggles of that time. Even a cursory reading of these stories indicates why they suited the Deuteronomists' purpose of using them as illustrations of the instability of that age, and of the necessity of a new form of rule. They portray a land torn and threatened by diverse problems: fragmentation on political, social, and religious levels; struggles within the tribes to define their Yahwistic confession as opposed to the Baal religion of their Canaanite neighbors; stress and strain between centrifugal and centripetal forces as the separate tribes sought to work out a common *modus operandi*; and disagreement over the question of alternative forms of government.

Since instability on all these levels accurately describes the time of the Judges, out of fairness to the Deuteronomistic tradents one must also observe the following: Comparison of the pre-Deuteronomistic stories and the Deuteronomistic interpretation of them illustrates the high degree of sensitivity and seriousness with which Israel's historians treated their material. They did not simply impose an alien framework, but rather allowed their theological interpretation to grow out of and accurately reflect the realities described by their historical sources.

Chapter 1, which is unique among the pre-Deuteronomistic traditions of the book, describes a process of Israelite occupation of the land that varies markedly from that presented in Joshua. Rather than a massive pan-Israelite military onslaught leading to total conquest, separate battles were fought by various tribes and coalitions with such varying success that the large Canaanite settlements, especially in the plains, retained their independence. This picture seems to reflect more accurately the realities of the League period than does the more sweeping theological picture of the Book of Joshua, which in effect telescopes the period between Joshua and David in order to give greater emphasis to the confession that Yahweh, in fulfillment of earlier promise, gave the land to Israel as an inheritance. Judges 1, in contrast, describes a political situation consistent with the setting found in the stories of the judges that follow. It was a time of political fragmentation, with Yahwists living alongside Baalists, with Israelite settlements, scattered among Canaanite populations, vulnerable to attack and repeatedly in need of defending themselves. At times their defense was mounted through the unified force of a coalition of tribes (e.g., Judg. 5); at other times, we find them adopting the tactics of guerrilla warfare to compensate for the military superiority of the enemy (e.g., Judg. 6:1–8:32).

Here we do not aspire to a full survey of the stories of the Judges, but rather intend to limit ourselves to details that reflect conditions within the premonarchical community. It is interesting to note, for example, the presence of Canaanite divine elements among the names of the judges, such as Shamgar son of Anat (Judg. 3:31) and Jerubbaal (alias Gideon, Judg. 6:32; 7:1, 8:29, 35; 9:1). In Jerubbaal's case, his name is understandable against the background of his father's Baal-Asherah shrine. Gideon's destroying the Baal altar, and his constructing, by Yahweh's order, a Yahweh altar in its place vividly illustrates the bitter conflict between religious confessions of that time, as does his fear of the reaction of "the men of the town" to his sacrilege. Of related interest in this connection are the ephod and teraphim of Micah, the Levite whom Micah installed as priest, and the latter's adoption by the tribe of Dan (Judg. 17–18).

These various episodes invite one to try to identify the Yahwistic tradition involved in this conflict with Canaanite religion. An important clue is given in Gideon's plea to the angelic messenger: "Pray, sir, if the Lord is with us, why then has all this befallen us? And where are all his wonderful deeds which our fathers recounted to us, saying, 'Did not the Lord bring us up from Egypt?'" (Judg. 6:13). This confession suggests a connection with the exodus tradition of the Gilgal cult, which is plausible in light of the story's Ephraimite setting. Of further interest in the Gideon story is the incident concerning the ephod made by Gideon (8:24–27), which, symbolizing a pretension to unauthorized power, illustrates the unclarity over forms of governance that characterized the period. This impression is reinforced when this incident is compared on the one hand with Gideon's refusal of kingship in the preceding episode (8:22–23), and on the other hand with the grisly story of Abimelech's ill-fated kingship in Shechem that follows. The latter, of course, is an extreme example of the centrifugal force that threatened to tear the nascent coalition of clans apart. A similar example of this is the ganging up of Israelite clans against the tribe of Benjamin in Judges 19–21. In these stories, we are dealing not with historical reports in any strict sense, but with hero stories that bear the imprint of the general conditions of the times within which they arose. They seem to reflect a patchwork of settlements unified by varying degrees of kinship feeling, making their way, together or alone, within a culture dominated by Canaanite religious and social customs. It is clear that the confession of the Deliverer God Yahweh was not simply embraced by all the clans of the Palestinian region, but rather was obliged to compete in a climate of political, moral, and religious pluralism. If Gilgal was the center of a Yahwistic confession that had adherents among some of the tribes, especially Benjamin and Joseph, it is apparent that not all clans hastened to adopt "Yahweh, who brought you out of the land of Egypt" as their own God. The Samson story, in fact, reflects a milieu very remote from the Yahwistic tradition of the Gilgal cult. Is it accurate, then, to attribute any special role at all during this time to the cult that had the Yahweh of the exodus at its center?

We can answer this question in the affirmative, and even give an indication of the role this form of Yahwism played, on the basis of an archaic composition we have thus far left out of the account, namely, the Song of Deborah in Judges 5. Here is a song imbued with the same fervent Yahwism that produced the Song of Miriam. Portrayed is the Divine Warrior, Yahweh, now marching forth from the southern mountains to lead his people to victory against its foes (5:4–5). In Seir and Edom, we can perhaps recognize references to the southern sanctuary in which worshippers from Gilgal made religious pilgrimages.[9] In his hymn, Yahweh was portrayed as coming from that holy place to fight for his people against its Canaanite oppressors. As in the Song of Miriam, the people's response to Yahweh's gracious act of deliverance was one of praise. Through this hymn we gain insight into the community-building force of early Yahwism. Its setting was an attack by "the kings of Canaan," a coalition arising out of the inevitable conflicts between the new settlers (strengthened by converts from the indigenous population) and the local Canaanite rulers. The rallying point of the clans responding to the muster was not merely a sense of kinship, but acknowledgment of a common allegiance to "Yahweh, the God of Israel."[10] Not all the groups that would later constitute the twelve tribes of Israel were in the muster (note for example the conspicuous absence of Judah),[11] but what is significant is the positive response of a significant number of clans to a common threat *in the name of Yahweh*. This response is particularly significant when seen against the background of the centrifugal and community-disrupting forces so conspicuous in the stories of the judges in general.

What prevented total assimilation of Yahweh belief into Canaanite culture? What constituted the community-building dynamic that enabled disparate clans to act in consort against a common enemy? These questions, if unanswered, leave unexplained the rise of (Judah and) Israel. Fortunately, both are addressed in the following lines of the Song of Deborah:[12]

> Lord, when thou didst go forth from Se'ir,
>   when thou didst march from the region of Edom,
>   the earth trembled, and the heavens dropped,

9. On the biblical evidence for a southern Yahwistic sanctuary and its relation to the cult of Gilgal, see T. Hiebert, *God of My Victory: An Ancient Hymn of Triumph in Habakkuk 3*, HSM (Chico, Calif.: Scholars Press, in press).

10. Judges 5:5 and 5:12–18. Contrast with this the abdication of covenant obligations by Meroz in Verse 23.

11. Cf. Herrmann, *History*, 118–119.

12. For a thorough textual study and fresh translation of Judges 5, see M. D. Coogan, "A Structural and Literary Analysis of the Song of Deborah," *CBQ* 40 (1978), 143–166.

> yea, the clouds dropped water,
> The mountains quaked before the Lord,
> yon Sinai before the Lord, the God of Israel.
> Then down marched the remnant of the noble;
> the people of the Lord marched down for him against
> the mighty. (Judg. 5:4–5 and 13)

By the time Merneptah made his march from Egypt into Palestine in 1230 B.C.E. and included Israel among the nations inscribed on his victory stele, we can assume that the group rallying around the name of Yahweh was already noticeable enough to elicit the attention of an Egyptian commander. And during the chaotic times of the premonarchic period, the factor that alone satisfactorily accounts for the growth of this common identity is the faith in Yahweh we have been able to associate with the Gilgal cult and its exodus-conquest confession. In episodes such as the battle of the Israelite clans agains the Canaanite kings, the community-building effect of Yahwism was demonstrated in a way that undoubtedly won converts to the God who delivered the oppressed out of their bondage under powerful rulers. Here, then, was the dynamic that was able to nurture the growth of the community notion born in the exodus even through the first chaotic centuries of Israel's life in Palestine.[13]

C. EVIDENCE FOR THE FORMS OF WORSHIP AND TÔRÂ IN THE EARLY YAHWISTIC COMMUNITY

The Book of Joshua gives evidence pointing to Gilgal as the home of a confession in Yahweh the Deliverer that had a powerful community-building effect on participating clans. The Book of Judges in turn permits a glimpse of the chaotic conditions in the period between the exodus and the monarchy within which that confession persisted and developed. Specifically, Judges 5 illustrates how faith in Yahweh fostered among the otherwise loosely associated clans a sense of common allegiance and purpose.

Against the general background of the period furnished by these books, two other kinds of material add important detail to this study of

---

13. The scholarly discussion relating to the early stages of Israelite community formation was greatly enriched by study of the Amarna letters and related finds. Added to this study has been new perspectives derived from the field of social anthropology. The literature is vast, though deserving of special mention are G. Mendenhall, "The Hebrew Conquest of Palestine," in E. F. Campbell and D. N. Freedman, eds., *The Biblical Archaeologist Reader*, Vol. 3 (New York: Doubleday Anchor Books, 1970), pp. 100–120; E. F. Campbell, "The Amarna Letters and the Amarna Period," pp. 54–75 in the same volume; N. K. Gottwald, *The Tribes of Yahweh: A Sociology of the Religion of Liberated Israel, 1250–1050* (Maryknoll, N.Y.: Orbis Books, 1979); and the essays collected by D. N. Freedman and D. F. Graf, eds., *Palestine in Transition: The Emergence of Ancient Israel* (Sheffield: Almond Press, 1983), of which the contribution by M. Chaney is especially worthy of close attention.

the early Yahwistic notion of community, namely, liturgical texts illustrating the form worship took in this period, and legal texts describing the emerging social structures. Since specific forms of worship and community structures deeply affect the lives of individuals, and in fact serve as a kind of index to the quality of life in a given society, these materials are especially important to this study.

1. FORMS OF WORSHIP: EXODUS 19:3–8 AND 24:3–8.

The festival narrative in Josh 3:1–5:1 makes reference to a twelve-stone memorial erected at Gilgal. I have already suggested an historical connection between this reference and the tradition referring to twelve pillars erected by Moses in Exodus 24:4. In the archaic liturgical composition preserved by the Elohist in Exodus 19:3–8 and 24:3–8 is described a covenant ceremony that likely developed within the exodus-conquest confession identified with the Gilgal sanctuary. It is therefore a promising place to turn for a more detailed understanding of the forms of worship developed within the Yahwistic community in this early period.

Early Israel was mindful of the fact that the vitality of its community life depended on constant renewal from its source, Yahweh. Cultic forms among the Israelites developed out of this consciousness. The primal quality of response to Yahweh's initiating activity found in early hymns such as Exodus 15 and Judges 5 was not lost in this development, but was expressed in a form that renewed Yahweh's blessing through rehearsal of the redemption drama of the exodus, through symbolical representation of Yahweh's presence in theophany, and through the people's response in sacrifice and in commitment to the stipulations of the covenant. This phenomenon of renewal and reenactment through worship is portrayed in two fragments of an archaic liturgy to which we now turn:

And Moses went up to God, and Yahweh called him out of the mountain, saying, "Thus you shall say to the house of Jacob, and tell the people of Israel: you have seen what I did to the Egyptians, and how I bore you on eagles' wings, and brought you to myself. Now therefore, if you will obey my voice and keep my covenant, you shall be my own possession among all peoples; for all the earth is mine, and you shall be to me a kingdom of priests and a holy nation. These are the words which you shall speak to the children of Israel." So Moses came and called the elders of the people, and set before them all these words which the Lord had commanded him. And all the people answered together and said, "All that the Lord has spoken we will do." And Moses reported the words of the people to the Lord. (Exod. 19:3–8)

Moses came and told the people all the words of the Lord and all the ordinances; and all the people answered with one voice, and said, "All the words which the Lord has spoken we will do." And Moses wrote all the words of the Lord. And he rose early in the morning, and built an altar at the foot of the mountain, and twelve pillars, according to the twelve tribes of Israel. And he sent young men of the people of Israel, who offered burnt offerings and sacrificed peace offerings of oxen to the Lord. And Moses took half of the blood and put it in basin, and half of the blood he threw against the altar. Then he took the book of the covenant, and read it in the hearing of the people; and they said, "All that the Lord has spoken we will do, and we will be obedient." And Moses took the blood and threw it upon the people, and said, "Behold the blood of the covenant which the Lord has made with you in accordance with all these words. (Exod. 24:3–8)

In this liturgy, we find the following three-part ritual pattern. First, Moses (i.e., the priestly representative of the congregation) encounters Yahweh in a theophany, and is instructed by Yahweh to remind the people of how their God had delivered them from the Egyptians. Against the background of this initiating act of God, there comes a condition and a promise. If the people are obedient to Yahweh, and keep his covenant, they will be "my own possession among all the peoples; for all the earth is mine, and you shall be to me a kingdom of priests and a holy nation." Second, Moses delivers Yahweh's word to the people, and they respond by affirming the covenant. Third, sacrifices and a blood ritual seal the promise.

Plainly, the primal pattern of initiating divine act and human response observed earlier in Exodus 15 underlies the structure of this ritual as well. The form of the response, moreover, is described in terms that would remain valid throughout Israel's history. It is understood as a response within a covenant established by Yahweh. If the people would remain faithful to his covenant, the blessings of Yahweh would be fulfilled. The terms describing the community of faith into which the obedient people were drawn by Yahweh are extremely rich and theologically significant: "my own possession," "kingdom of priests," "holy nation." No basis of security could rival that of being Yahweh's own possession, a theme expressed in another ancient text, Deuteronomy 32:8–9, with the terms "his people," and "his allotted heritage":

> When the Most High gave to the nations their inheritance,
> when he separated the sons of men,
> he fixed the bounds of the peoples
>   according to the number of the sons of God,
> For the Lord's portion is his people,
>   Jacob his allotted heritage.

In Exodus 19:6, the phrase "kingdom of priests" is notable for its inclusiveness. Rigid distinctions between laity and different orders of priests did not divide this people. This inclusiveness underscores the archaic nature of this ritual fragment. Moreover, to be a holy nation meant to participate in the quality of holiness that characterized Yahweh. The divine power present in this covenant renewal ceremony came to expression in the blood ritual: The blood, representing the vital substance of the sacrificial victim, was divided, half being offered to Yahweh (i.e., thrown against the altar), half being thrown on the people with the words: "Behold the blood of the covenant which the Lord has made with you in accordance with all these words." Through this ritual, the two parties to the covenant were united in intimate fellowship.

Another ancient ritual fragment, Exodus 24:1–2 and 9–11, preserved by J, portrays the theophany in a less terrifying manner, though its portrayal of divine majesty is remarkable. It emphasizes the intimacy enjoyed by the faithful with the God of Israel in a festive meal: "They saw the God of Israel . . . , and he did not lay his hand on the chief men of the people of Israel; they beheld God, and ate and drank."

Worship, as Israel's primal response to God's gracious act of deliverance, and as the creative center of its life as a community of faith, thus found early ritual form in the covenant renewal ceremony preserved in Exodus 19 and 24. It was a form, moreover, that enjoyed a long subsequent story, first in the spring festival of the Yahwistic tribes held at Gilgal, then at other cult centers during both the spring and autumnal festivals, then as a theological concept in the thought of prophets, priests, and historians of Judah and Israel, finally as the central feature in the reform movements of Hezekiah and Josiah.[14] Two monuments bearing witness to the history of this form are Joshua 24 and the Book of Deuteronomy, to which we shall turn at a later point.

2. *TÔRÂ*: FAITH COMING TO EXPRESSION IN COMMUNAL FORMS AND STRUCTURES

Social practices and legal codes may not appear to be the most exciting sources for studying the beliefs of a community. But the writer of the Letter of James is not alone in teaching a lesson that lies at the heart of the biblical heritage:

If a brother or a sister is ill-clad and in lack of daily food, and one of you says to them, "Go in peace, be warmed and filled," without giving them the things needed for the body, what does it profit? So faith by itself, if it has no works, is dead. (James 2:15–17)

At the beginning of our spiritual ancestors' history as a community of faith, the God Yahweh was moved to action by the suffering of the weak and impoverished of the earth. And concern with the concrete needs of the poor and oppressed, and with the translation of confessions of faith into acts of justice, flows deeply through Scripture. This concern, moreover, continues to address our world with prophetic poignancy, for many voices still advocate a gospel of comfort for the comfortable in merciless disregard of the consequent suffering of the poor. Biblical faith reacted against attempts to spiritualize religion out of the

---

14. Cf. K. Baltzer, *The Covenant Formulary in Old Testament, Jewish and Early Christian Writings*, trans. D. E. Green (Philadelphia: Fortress Press 1971).

everyday realm of social structures and individual behavior, for such spiritualization was deemed contradictory to faith in the God first encountered as the divine Deliverer of the oppressed. The Hebrew Bible's careful attention to laws and ordinances, therefore, is not a sign of its impoverishment, but of its persistent attention to the structures that affect everyday life. As the author of James insisted, a living faith in God will express itself in acts of compassion toward those in need. And a living community of faith will translate its experiences of divine grace into forms of community that safeguard the liberating dynamic that nurtures healing and reconciliation in all areas of life.

We turn, therefore, to structures of community such as the practices of law in the gates, regulation of land use, and manumission of slaves. We must be aware, as we do this, that in Israel an intimate connection existed between such communal structures and forms of worship. Both grew as twin expressions of one unified response to Yahweh's antecedent redemptive activity. Moreover, structures of community unfolded in Israel under the influence of and in close connection with the cult. This interrelationship was integral to the ancient ritual fragment from Exodus 24 cited earlier, in which Moses "took the Book of the Covenant, and read it in the hearing of the people; and they said, 'All that the Lord has spoken we will do, and we will be obedient'" (Exod. 24:7). A formulation of the basic principles structuring community in Israel thus played a central role in the cult, even as the confessions of the cult influenced that formulation. For a more detailed picture of the relation between workship and *tôrâ* as community-building aspects of one basic response to the antecedent gracious acts of Yahweh, we turn to the Book of the Covenant itself. It is preserved in Exodus 20:21–23:19 and, like the ancient ritual within which it was read, comes from the premonarchical period.

a. The Book of the Covenant: Exodus 20:21–23:19

Structural forms deemed acceptable by the majority of the free members of a society stand as a prerequisite for a viable social contract. But of course the nature of these structural forms varies greatly from one case to another. Indeed, they offer an important index to the values and beliefs of a society, especially when studied with an eye to their historical transformation and in relation to the social systems of neighboring peoples.

Although Israel's values and beliefs have roots that run far deeper than the time of the exodus, and can in part be glimpsed in the ancestral stories, we have observed that the birth of what we can identify as a distinctly Israelite notion of community occurs in intimate relation to one foundational event, the experience of escape from Egyptian bondage interpreted as deliverance by the God Yahweh. The metonymy of this event, as we have seen, took the form of a narrative of deliverance from the pursuing armies of Pharaoh at the Sea. Testimony to this foundational experience of the Yahwistic religious community was expressed in the form of praise; that is, as a hymnic response to the divine Deliverer. And we have seen that Israel's experience of her birth as a people in God's gracious deliverance was followed by the conviction that the possibility of a future for this people depended on God's presence abiding with the new community. This conviction gave rise to the development of forms of worship, such as recitation of Yahweh's saving acts, sacrifice, and vows of obedience, by means of which God's abiding presence was assured. By drawing on treaty forms current in her world, early Israel conceptualized the relationship between God and people in terms of covenant. God's presence at the point of the Hebrews' deepest need, as experienced in the exodus, was neither accident of nature or history, nor the effect of divine whimsy, but revelation of God's will to enter into an everlasting bond of fellowship with this people. The quality of this bond was expressed as fidelity (ḥesed) that could be depended on under all circumstances and forever. This conviction ultimately derived from the primal experience of totally unmerited divine grace, through which a people was created from the nothingness of abject bondage and made God's own possession.

As Rudolph Otto has indicated, the basic human response to encounter with the *mysterium tremendum* is awe and worship.[15] In Israel, the specific form that worship took was the outgrowth of the nature of the event in which the glory of God was encountered. A positive correlation between the nature of the revelatory event and the form of response is found also in the case of the communal forms and structures that arose within the people as its members asked how they could conduct their lives in a way befitting a people belonging to the holy God revealed as Deliverer of the oppressed. The dynamic moral quality characterizing the early Israelite notion of community derives from its origin in a response to the God of the exodus. Corresponding to the covenant fidelity of God was to be the people's fidelity to the new order of life revealed to it by God.

Although God's grace was prevenient and unmerited, a trifling or hard-hearted response was a repudiation of God's covenant and an insult to God's majesty and holiness. From those called to be God's people a response was required that was patterned after God's holiness. Holiness was the quality that characterized the God Yahweh, and the command for communal holiness is to be understood in relation to Israel's deeply felt dependence on God's abiding presence. The people could be confident of God's presence with them only if their life together was a reflection of God's nature and of God's concern for jus-

---

15. R. Otto, *The Idea of the Holy*, trans. J.W. Harvey (London: Oxford University Press, 1950).

tice. In Israel's earliest attempts to express this notion of community, the dominant pattern was that of *imitatio dei*: to assure Yahweh's continued presence with the people meant acting toward other humans even as Yahweh had first acted toward them.

Theologically, then, we can see Israel's communal structures develop out of the desire to preserve within the people a state of holiness befitting God's holy presence. Concretely, we can see these structures develop as inferences from God's acts on behalf of the people. The theological understanding of being holy before Yahweh comes to particularly clear expressed in the so-called Priestly Writing.[16] However, the development of communal laws and structures by means of inference from God's antecedent acts (especially the act of delivering the people from bondage) is seen already, and in fact most vividly, in the earliest code of law preserved in the Bible, the Book of the Covenant (Exod. 20:21–23:19).[17]

The Book of the Covenant is a fascinating source for the study of community in early Israel in part because of its rough-hewn nature. Unlike the Decalogue, it has not been worked and reworked over the centuries so as to emerge as a polished jewel. Its history of development is confined to the period before the monarchy, and its baroque, eclectic nature allows us to glimpse into the process of transmission that culminated in its present form and even to reconstruct the general nature of the community that produce it.

Especially significant is the clear distinction between two blocks within the Book of the Covenant, a block of *case laws* in 21:1–22:16 (Evv. 22:17) and a block of what I call *Yahwistic laws* in 20:22–26 and 22:17 (Evv. 22:18)—23:19.

The case laws are typical of the ordinances found in the great cultures of Mesopotamia from the late third millennium on down. They enumerate cases and describe punishments for different offenses that threaten the order of society. Reflected is a sharply stratified order, with, for example, more generous treatment being accorded males than females (21:1–11), and less severe punishment being prescribed for a person injuring a slave than for a person injuring a free citizen (21:12–14, 18–19). The presence of numerous parallels with other law codes of the ancient Near East combines with the lack of parenetic clauses and themes deriving specifically from Yahwism in arguing for

---

16. The Priestly Writing ("P") is the literary stratum that gave final shape to Genesis, Exodus, Leviticus, and Numbers (plus the very end of Deuteronomy). It probably dates in its final shape to the sixth century B.C.E., though in recent years scholars increasingly have drawn attention to considerable pre-exilic material in P.

17. For a more detailed study of the Book of the Covenant and the evidence it provides for our understanding of the Israelite league of the premonarchical period, see P. D. Hanson, "The Theological Significance of Contradiction Within the Book of the Covenant," in *Canon and Authority*, G. W. Coats and B. O. Long, eds., (Philadelphia: Fortress Press, 1977), pp. 110–131.

an origin of this block in the basic communal need to order life on the basis of conventions widely accepted within the prevailing culture. In adjudicating legal cases in an early period of the Israelite tribes, the elders apparently drew on forms known to them from their immediate cultural environment. These laws had nothing specifically to do with Yahwism. In fact, they betray a continuity with the status quo of the prevailing social order that at specific points runs contrary to the essential meaning of the exodus event. It is obvious that not all those affiliated with the early tribes of Israel were thoroughly and exclusively imbued with the unique quality of life implied by Yahweh's saving slaves from their bondage, a state of affairs totally in keeping with the portrait of the premonarchical period given by the pre-Deuteronomistic strata of Joshua. A pervasive ancient Near Eastern social system continued to exert its influence and to furnish forms for a young community in search of life-ordering structures.

In comparison with the conservative orientation of the case laws, the material in the second block found in the Book of the Covenant is remarkably dynamic in its thrust. And the source of that dynamism is immediately apparent: whereas the case laws betray no intrinsic relation to the cult, the "Yahwistic laws" betray an intimate connection with the specific confessions of early Yahwistic faith. Indeed, they can be understood as inferences drawn from the nature of the God rvealed in the deliverance of slaves from their bondage. This second block, therefore, allows us to see how the early community of Israel, living in the memory of deliverance from slavery and seeking to define itself in its new land as a people of the gracious and holy God Yahweh, inferred guidelines and structures for life from the confession that formed the heart of its cultic celebrations.

Unlike the first block, this block goes beyond the promulgation of laws dedicated to the maintenance of social order. It sets forth patterns of behavior that constitute a quality of life in keeping with the nature of the God revealed in their own deliverance from slavery, a life of compassionate justice. It seeks not to impose social order derived from an external authority, but to draw forth social harmony from within, from the heart of life—that is, from God's compassion—and then from the hearts of those responding to the divine compassion by acknowledging God's lordship. Even as Yahweh's initiating act sought out the vulnerable, the weak, and the oppressed, these laws guide the people in a life of looking after the vulnerable among them, the debtors, the widows, the orphans, and those without the rights of citizenship.[18] The source of laws and community structures in God's compassion and in God's antecedent gracious acts can be recognized even on the basic

---

18. For a discussion of the special attention paid to the widow and the orphan more generally in the ancient Near East, see F. C. Fensham, "Widow, Orphan, and the Poor in Ancient Near Eastern Legal and Wisdom Literature," *JNES* 21 (1962), 129–139.

level of the syntax of the Yahwistic laws, a point we shall now illustrate with concrete examples.

The first example relates to the gēr, that is, the stranger or sojourner in the land, the individual lacking the status of citizenship and the rights belonging to that status—what we would today call the *alien*. In antiquity, aliens represented a vulnerable class, as illustrated by the numerous cases of sojourning peoples becoming victims of indebtedness and falling into slavery in the host country. Without inheritance, without the protection of extended family and clan, they were easy prey for exploitation and extortion. This precarious situation drew the attention of the Yahwistic community to the plight of the stranger: "You shall not oppress a stranger; you know the heart of a stranger, for you were strangers in the land of Egypt" (Exod. 23:9).

The viability of most ancient societies was predicated in part on the cheap source of labor supplied by homeless sojourners. In Israel, exploiting this class of people was forbidden, and it is noteworthy that this prohibition was not based on rational principles, or even in the first instance on Mosaic authority or theophanic verification. The law draws its motivating force concretely from Israel's memory of its past bondage. Israel's insight into the plight of the vulnerable gēr is derived from the most personal of all sources; empathy, the kind of understanding born of identification with the fellow human's experience. "You know (yd') the nēpeš of the stranger." Nēpeš is translated as "heart" in the RSV, an acceptable translation if heart is understood as the "essential being" of the stranger, and if yd' is understood as the deeply personal knowledge derived from close involvement with the other person. Why Israel was capable of this compassionate justice vis-à-vis the gēr is further specified: Knowledge of the heart of the stranger had a personal source, "for you were strangers in the land of Egypt." The moral quality that was to be the hallmark of the Yahwistic community was derived from memory of a specific event in the past, the condition of homelessness in Egypt. Whenever an Israelite looked on an alien, that Israelite did so as one who had also been alienated in a foreign land—and still would be, were it not for God's gracious act of deliverance. The freedom within which Israel could now construct structures of communal life was derived from God's grace in delivering strangers from bondage and giving them a home. Memory of that event and its divine gift quality was to motivate the Israelite's merciful treatment of every stranger in the land.

In the second example, we find a law providing special protection for another vulnerable class, the widow and the orphan. In antiquity, the widow could easily be cast into a destitute state resembling that of the oppressed sojourner, for her security depended on the household of her husband and his heirs. If the household dissolved due to her husband's premature death, the widow was thrust into a precarious situation. Having left her own family to marry, she was admitted into the new family by viture of her status as wife. But the husband's death severed tht connection, and she was thrust into the ambivalent space between clans, without claim to inheritance. If she had no grown-up children, or if those children refused to receive her, she could easily find herself without a home. Obviously, the widow represented a vulnerable class, in need of special care and compassion on the part of her relatives through marriage, for if they did not offer her protection, both she and her young children could rapidly fall into impoverishment and slavery.

As always with vulnerable classes that can become victimized by falling through gaps in the legal structures of a society, appeal to case laws was insufficient. What is more, general reference to the responsibilities of the king to look after the interests of the widow and orphan, as found, for example, in the prologue of the Code of Hammurabi, proved to be a deficient safeguard. The Book of the Covenant, in contrast, provided members of this vulnerable class with protection that was both dynamic and concrete by making their well-being the concern of the whole worshipping community.

This responsibility was tied to the community's ultimate commitment, inasmuch as the cause of the widow and the orphan was identified in the first instance with the divine Deliverer of the oppressed. Yahweh responded to their plight with the same passion and compassion earlier shown to Israel in Egypt:

You shall not afflict any widow or orphan. If you do afflict them, and they cry out to me, I will surely hear their cry; and my wrath will burn and I will kill you with the sword, and your wives shall become widows and your children fatherless. (Exod. 22:21–23 [Evv. 22:22–24])

The command is apodictic in form: "You shall not afflict any widow or orphan." And it is clothed in a sense of urgency and seriousness by being related to the vow of the lawgiver Yahweh. Yahweh surely will not stand by idly if the widow or orphan cry out in affliction. Yahweh is the Champion of the weak and the vulnerable, and if any Israelite should mock God by responding to God's prevenient grace by using it as an occasion to exploit the weak, Yahweh's wrath will burn, and the tables will be turned: the wives of the oppressors will in turn become widows, their sons orphans.

Coming to expression here is the complementarity between mercy and justice. The mercy of the God of the exodus was not viewed as pampering, but as a severe mercy. Compassion entailed incisive repudiation of the evil of the oppressor. The complementary side of God's compassion for the oppressed was God's wrath toward those who victimized the weak. In the case of this second class of vulnerable people, therefore, we again find that protection was provided by appeal to the dynamic heart of Israel's confession, the God who acted on behalf of the weak and who correspondingly expected of his people a just and merciful response to the widow and the orphan.

Turning to a third example, we realize that the poor constitute in every age a particularly vulnerable class, for they by definition live on the razor's edge between bare subsistence and deprivation. Any disruption of this precarious balance, whether occurring within the economic system of the society in general or in the orbit of an individual poor person's own existence, threatens that person with indebtedness and then the attendant spiral of compounding interest, forfeiture of property, and the harsh bonds of enslavement. Especially in an ancient world in which vast portions of the population were held in some form of bondage to the rich and powerful through indebtedness, and in which merciless creditors with their cruel weapons of interest and threats of foreclosure posed such a terrifying threat, what protection could be offered the poor? Once again, the answer given by the Book of the Covenant is concrete, and radical:

If you lend money to any of my people with you who are poor, you shall not be to him as creditor, and you shall not exact interest from him. If ever you take your neighbor's garment in pledge, you shall restore it to him before the sun goes down; for that is his only covering, it is his mantle for his body; in what else shall he sleep? And if he cries to me, I shall hear, for I am compassionate. (Exod. 2:24–26 [Evv. 22:25–27])

The Yahwistic community's response to poverty was not limited to adjustments in existing legal structures. It began with the exposure of poverty as a phenomenon that by its very presence called the viability of the entire society into question. Poverty represented an assault on God's order. The laws that emerged can thus be viewed as efforts to restore a quality of life that would banish distincitions between superfluity and want. Against this background, we can understand the specific laws prohibiting lending on interest and retention of security. And lest such laws should fall inconspicuously into place alongside countless other rules and regulations, they were bound to the heart of Israel's existence as a people, the God who had been revealed in the deliverance of slaves from Egypt as a compassionate God. In relation to this God, poverty took on a radical new dimension. Indebtedness leading to bondage represented a reversal of the process that had given birth to this people. The exploitation of some Israelites by others contradicted the heart of the Yahwistic notion of community. God had called them into being as a people by delivering them from slavery. To permit the reentry into Israel of practices that abetted impoverishment and slavery would not simply represent the neglect of social justice, but would constitute a mockery of divine grace. For this reason, one of the most widespread and pernicious causes of impoverishment of poorer by healthier members of the community was prohibited, namely, lending on interest.

Similarly addressed was the related problem of possessions taken in pledge, a problem elucidated with the concreteness typical of early Israelite law. What if a person had to give up his or her garment as security? Although dealing with a specific legal problem, even this case was interpreted and resolved in relation to the well-being of the individuals involved. No human was to go through a night shivering because of a lending law, or any other kind of law. Why? Because all laws in Israel were to be related to a heart. And that was the heart of Yahweh. Yahweh had shown in Israel's history what sort of God had called the nation into existence. And the nature of the community was to be inferred from the divine nature revealed in the exodus: "And if he cries to me, I will hear, for I am compassionate."

Here we have the explicit naming of a concept central to the notion of community structure in early Israel, divine *compassion*. It is a quality that is dynamic in nature, because it describes the living God known in the redemptive acts of history. And by being at the center of the Yahwistic notion of community it insisted that the ordering achieved by social structure must never become a barrier to those excluded from the community by reason of poverty or enslavement. The quality of divine compassion as the model for the community implied openness to the excluded, a point of access for the disenfranchised. In fact, taken in its most fundamental and original meaning, the compassion of the Deliverer God Yahweh implied that this community was present in the world precisely as a home for the enslaved, the poor, the bereaved. We shall see later how this quality of compassion functioned as an aspect of a notion of community that was dynamic in its ability to develop and expand. We shall also observe how it functioned as a safeguard against the domination of more reactionary forces in the society. For though the temptation to forsake the example of divine compassion was to take many seductive forms throughout the history of Israel, tribal leaders, kings, priests, prophets, and common people alike would repeatedly be reminded of the compassionate One:

> Father of the fatherless and protector of widows
>   is God in his holy habitation.
> God gives the desolate a home to dwell in;
>   he leads out the prisoners to prosperity;
>   but the rebellious dwell in a parched land. (Ps. 68:5–6)

By drawing communal structures inferentially from the acts of the Deliverer God Yahweh, Israel acknowledged a norm that was both dynamic and transcendent, dynamic in that the acts of this God were not confined to one period but were ongoing, transcendent in that no individual or class could make special or exclusive claims on God's protection and blessing. Here was a norm, then, that resisted co-option, a norm that the prophet or the righteous remnant could appeal to when assailed by a tyrant king or ungodly masses. This quality comes to clear expression in Exodus 23:1–8: following this norm implied that the just person would often have to follow a solitary path, one along which the pressure to show partiality to poor or rich was resisted firmly: "You shall not follow a multitude to do evil; nor shall you bear witness in a suit, turning aside after a multitude, so as to pervert justice; nor shall you be partial to a poor man in his suit" (23:2–3). Likewise, "You shall not pervert the justice due to your poor in his suit" (23:6). It was a path that implied fair treatment even of one's enemy: "If you meet your enemy's ox or his ass going astray, you shall bring it back to him. If you see the ass of one who hates you lying under its burden, you shall refrain from leaving him with it, you shall help him to lift it up" (23:4–5). In these examples of a norm that is both as dynamic as the historical development of Israel and as transcendent as the one true God, we find the source of a notion of community capable of remarkable adaptation and growth.

As we move from these specific examples back to the question of the function of the Book of the Covenant as a whole within early Israel, we are struck with its inner tensions. On the one hand, we find the case laws, emphasizing an ordering of society largely in continuity with the other societies of the ancient world. On the other hand, we see laws articulating a community ideal dedicated to justice embracing all members and emphasizing compassion to those whose economic or social status make them vulnerable to abuse. Especially noteworthy is the source of the motivation for this latter community ideal, namely, the antecedent, gracious, saving activity of Yahweh. This source underscores the basic theological unity between forms of worship and forms of communal structures in early Israel: both arise as response to God's initiating act of deliverance.

This grounding of the ethos, or moral ideal of the people in their life or worship is expressed by the introduction and the conclusion of the Book of the Covenant that forms its framework. In Exodus 20:22–26, both the *quality* of worship and the *place* of worship are described. It is to be a worship free of distractions by penultimate realities: "You shall not make gods of silver to be with me, nor shall you make for yourself gods of gold." This is not to say that it is to be an unfocused, nebulous worship, however. Distractions are removed, enabling God and humans to relate intimately in specific places in this world. "An altar you shall make for me and sacrifice on it . . . ; in every place where I cause my name to be remembered I will come to you and bless you." The God who delivered them from their bondage has provided for the unbroken continuation of the historical relationship. God has made God's self accessible—yes, *present*—to the people, thereby extending to them a life of fulfillment and well-being: "I will come to you and bless you."

The other half of the framework in Exodus 23:14–19 specifies special times of worship. Three times yearly, at critical points in the life of a people living in intimate contact with nature and its seasons, they were to appear before the presence of the Lord, to communicate God's presence with the people God had redeemed not only within the specificity of a place, but within the specificity of time as well.[19] God's relation to the community of faith was thus an integral part of their historical existence. From that relation, celebrated in the worship occurring in the cult place and during the cult festivals, Israel's communal laws and structures arose.

The case laws, for their part, in betraying frequent points of similarity with legal practices found generally in Israel's larger cultural environment, draw attention to one need addressed by the process of structure building that gave rise to the Book of the Covenant, the need to order society on the basis of practices acceptable to the majority of the citizens. It is notable, however, that the case laws were not compiled in the form of a civil law code independently exercising authority within a strictly legal setting. Although giving rise to tensions and even contradictions, these laws were combined with admonitions and confessions that imbued the forms of community with more than a social-structuring function. At the heart of this community was a redemptive purpose it derived from and shared with its God. At the same time as they contributed stability to society, Israel's laws were to be instruments of the liberating, healing process initiated by the God who freed slaves from their bondage. While materials borrowed from other cultures could satisfy certain needs for order in this nascent community, the essential redemptive purpose of this people determined that the principal qualities constituting the communal notion born of the exodus could not be borrowed from existent sources, but would have to unfold within the ongoing relationship with the God who acted on behalf of the slave, the poor, the widow, and the orphan. In other words, here was a notion that would continue to develop as long as the community of the faithful related to the events of this world as episodes in an ongoing drama on salvation.

Israel's legal structures, therefore, like its forms of worship, can be understood properly only when seen as aspects of its ongoing effort to describe the nature of a people owing its existence to God's gracious act of deliverance. Whenever forms and structures were borrowed from neighboring cultures, they were subjected to the transforming power of this self-perception, for it was imprinted indelibly on Israel's

---

19. The history of the cult festivals is similar to that of the history of the social laws in Israel in that we can observe how celebrations drawn in large part from Canaanite roots were assimilated to the historical confessions of Israel. For a discussion of this process, see R. de Vaux, *Ancient Israel: Its Life and Institutions*, trans. J. McHugh (New York: McGraw-Hill, 1961), pp. 484–506.

consciousness. Memory of the exodus would never let the people of the exodus forget that before Yahweh's initiative they had been slaves, whereas after Yahweh's victory on their behalf they were free.

It is interesting to note that Israel preserved this primal fact of her existence as a people even on the semantic level. The term used in Hebrew Scripture to describe the free person in contrast to the slave is *ḥopši*. Cognates of this word in Assyrian texts and in the Amarna tablets have the sense of "serf" or "a person subject to a corvee" (*ṣab ḥubši, awîl ḥubši*). The verb underlying these cognates has the meaning "to bind." Thus even on the level of language development, we glimpse how this nation of former slaves retained their earlier designation, but defiantly clothed it with new meaning born of the passage from bondage to freedom.[20]

In a threatening world, a community seeking to establish itself in the small space between hostile rivals was keenly aware of the need for social order. But this social need was worked out in earliest Israel within the context of Israel's primal confession in the God who led it out of bondage, and hence it was tempered with the unique qualities of justice and compassion that constituted the nature of Israel's God. The Book of the Covenant regulates the life of this people as a life in the presence of God. They are to acknowledge one God alone (Exod. 20:23; 22:19 [Evv. 22:20]; 23:13); they are to be consecrated to Yahweh (22:30 [Evv. 22:31]); they are to be aware that obedience brings blessing (20:24b), disobedience the curse (22:22–23, 26b [Evv. 22:22–24, 27b]; 23:7b). These features indicate clearly that the Book of the Covenant grew within the context of Israel's worship life. Community life, like worship, was a response to the antecedent act of a gracious God. Community was Israel's concrete way of saying thank you to God.

Given this dynamic and transcendent heart of Israel's notion of community, it is not surprising that the earliest document describing the social forms of this community was not a polished memorial, but a rough-hewn signpost. Or, expressed with a slightly different metaphor, it was not a completed ediface dazzling the viewer with its monolithic columns and perfect cornices, but an emerging structure whose unfinished walls and unvaulted ceilings pointed beyond themselves toward a meetingplace between a gracious God and a responding people that promised to be a source of blessing for all the families of the earth.

---

20. Cf. W. F. Albright, "Canaanite *ḥapši* and Hebrew *ḥofši* Again," *JPOS* 6 (1926), 106–108. Albright comes to the following conclusions: "I would suggest that *ḥofši* meant primarily "serf or peon, attached to the land," then "peasant landholder" or "freeholder," as distinct from "serf" and "slave." The time at which this alteration of meaning took place is not easy to establish but it was very possibly at the Hebrew conquest, when the Hebrews may have adopted the word for "peasant" from the Canaanites, and given it a wholly new connotation, in keeping with the complete transformation in social conditions" (p. 107).

b. The Decalogue

The implications of Israel's dynamic notion of life as God's people for the future development of communal structures were profound. As expressions of the desire to respond faithfully to the living God, these structures could not be frozen into the form of immutable regulations. Inferences drawn from God's future acts would have to be taken as seriously as the inferences drawn from earlier divine acts. We have here a model combining continuity and change, a phenomenon paralleled by Israel's credal traditions. In the cult, the credo was not frozen. But neither was it replaced in every new age. Rather, it grew, as Israel's experiences with God continued.

Along with this growth in the credal traditions occurred a corresponding growth in communal structures and laws. For example, when the Deuteronomistic School sought to reformulate *tôrâ* at a later point in time, its discernment of God's presence in new events led to the conclusion that the distinction between male and female slaves found in the Book of the Covenant was inconsistent with God's nature. As a comparison of Exodus 21:2–11 with Deuteronomy 5:12–18 indicates, the view of *tôrâ* derived from Israel's dynamic and transcendent norm led to an elimination of the earlier discriminatory distinction. Later still, the practice of holding a fellow Israelite as a slave was prohibited categorically, though foreign slaves were permitted (Lev. 25:35–46). Similarly, the restriction of participation in the central cult to males found in the Book of the Covenant was broken open, with worship becoming a celebration embracing all (Deut. 16:14; cf. Neh. 8:2–3). With passion and power, Deuteronomy presented *tôrâ* as the substance of a blessed life in constant communion with God.

This same process of growth produced the most remarkable formulation of *tôrâ* in the Hebrew Bible, the Decalogue. Here the effects of centuries of reflection and revision based on covenant fellowship with the living God are clearly seen. The rough edges and inconsistencies so conspicuous in the Book of the Covenant were replaced by the symmetry of a sublime expression of divine will. We can easily understand the position of honor that Jewish and Christian tradition has accorded it over the ages. Alone in the Bible it carries the simple name, "the ten words." Here, in majesty and economy of words, God's will was summarized, and a space was created in which Israel could experience the blessed life (i.e., *šālôm*) intended by God for this people.[21] Commands and prohibitions were not presented to the community as harsh and onerous impositions, but as loving protections safeguarding this space for fellowship with God.

---

21. Cf. H. Gese, *Von Sinai zum Zion*, BEvTh 64 (München: Chr. Kaiser Verlag, 1974), pp. 66–67.

Appropriately, therefore, the introduction to the Decalogue in Deuteronomy stressed the completeness of this unique expression of divine will: "These words the Lord spoke to all your assembly at the mountain out of the midst of the fire, the cloud, the deep gloom, with a loud voice; and he added no more" (Deut. 5:22).

Even as modern scientific theories enrich rather than detract from our appreciation of the majestic confessions of Genesis 1–3, so too modern biblical criticism enriches our appreciation of the divine address that gave our ancestors in the faith this remarkable guide to life. That address, symbolized by the theophany of Sinai, occurred not in the timeless realm of mythology, but in the familiar realm of Israel's day-to-day life of worship and service. God's will was revealed to this people as it lived in the presence of the God encountered in the real events of personal and communal experience. There Israel grapsed the divine imperative with a clarity stemming from God's own reaching out in delivering this people from bondage and entering into covenant fellowship with them. The Decalogue is thus the culmination of a centuries-long process of a community's identifying itself in response to the creative, redemptive, sustaining, and sanctifying acts of God. In being blessed for obedience, in being judged for rebelliousness, in suffering both in faithfulness and in obduracy, Israel was tutored in the way of šālôm expressed in the Decalogue. By applying the tools of biblical criticism, we see the literary traces left by this long history, a history first of oral transmission, and subsequently continuing in written form, as the significant differences between the versions of the Decalogue in Deuteronomy 5 and Exodus 20 indicate.

Since the early Yahwistic community was the historic matrix within which the essential qualities coming to expression in the Decalogue took shape, it seems appropriate to examine this document in this chapter, even though the literary process producing the final versions found in Exodus and Deuteronomy extended well into the period of the monarchy.[22]

When we turn to the earlier stages of oral and written tradition lying behind the final versions of the Decalogue, we recognize roots that reach back into the time before kings ruled in Israel. In general, the following pattern can be detected: The earlier formulations had tended to address a specific concrete legal case. The later formulations, which were taken up into the Decalogue, broadened the application of the law to a much wider area of life. For example, the second (third)[23]

22. For a fuller discussion of the Decalogue, cf. P. D. Hanson, "The Decalogue within the Covenant Community," *Lutheran Theological Seminary Bulletin* 61 (1981), 14–36; and W. Harrelson, *The Ten Commandments and Human Rights* (Philadelphia: Fortress Press, 1980).

23. Two different numbering systems exist for the Decalogue, depending on whether Exodus 20:3 and 4–6 are treated together as the first commandment (Luther) or treated separately as the first and second commandments (Calvin).

commandment originally put an interdiction against the false witness, under oath, of one person against another in a trial. In the Decalogue, a stage was reached at which the commandment forbade the misuse of the divine name in *all* settings. The fourth (fifth) commendment had originated in a specific law against cursing parents (cf. Exod. 21:17), which was broadened until reaching the present formulation to honor father and mother, accompanied with the promise of ensuing blessing. The fifth (sixth) and sixth (seventh) commandments were broadened by dropping the objects that in an earlier formulation had prohibited the killing of free Israelites and the stealing of a human being (cf. Exod. 21:12 and 16). For the simple commands, "Thou shalt not steal" and "Thou shalt not kill," without designating the object, are shorter formulations with a much broader range of application.[24]

The other finding of scholarly research is that the Decalogue's long list of ten commandments is itself a sign of this code being the culmination of a long antecedent history of formation. For where the specific commandments in their earlier forms are found elsewhere, they are found either singularly or in clusters of two or three at the most.

Together, these two findings suggest that the Decalogue represented a very special document in Israel by the time it had reached literary form in the early period of the monarchy. It represented the gathering together of the most important commandments relating to the quality of life that Israel's spiritual leaders believed God intended for the community. Nowhere else in the Bible do we find a collection of commandments that is so life encompassing and universal in scope, in spite of its remarkable brevity. Its individual formulations are no longer tied to any particular stage of Israelite history, or to any specific institution, or to any single social class. In this respect, the Decalogue is unlike the Covenant Code in Exodus 21–23, the Cultic Decalogue in Exodus 34, or the Holiness Code in Leviticus. It is a carefully reflected theological formulation of the parameters that define God's people. The preponderance of negative commands indicates that those who broke one of these commandments had set themselves outside of the covenant community.

The awesome importance of the Decalogue is reflected by two other characteristics: First, although we know from parallels of these commandments elsewhere in the Bible that they were punishable by death—that is, that they touched on areas of extreme importance to the community—in the Decalogue no sanctions are mentioned. The holiness of the document in itself makes mention of punishments unnecessary. Second, tradition has placed the Decalogue as the crown on the head of the entire Sinai corpus, which extends from Exodus 20

24. Cf. W. H. Schmidt, "Überlieferungsgeschichtliche Erwägungen zur Komposition des Dekalogs," VTSuppl 22 (1971), 201–220.

through Leviticus, Numbers, and Deuteronomy. And until this centrality was obscured in medieval times by efforts to systematize the law, resulting in the assimilation of the Decalogue into hundreds of others percepts, "the ten words" continued to enjoy the distinction of being the *epitome* of God's will for God's people.

These considerations lead us to designate the Decalogue as the "charter" of the covenant community. Although it probably was not handed down in its present form by Moses, it embodies and immortalizes for all ages the essence of the covenant community ideal that originated in the band of freed slaves led by Moses. It is a powerful testimony to the resilience of early Yahwistic faith that it could produce such an eloquent formulation of the divine imperative stemming from its primal encounter with Yahweh without losing the awesome power inherent in the original experience.

The awesome power of Israel's primal encounter was relived in the hearing of the divine name. Thus the Decalogue opens majestically with the self-prediction: "I am Yahweh." From the unique nature of Yahweh emanated all the richness and rightness of life. Attention was thus directed from the outset toward the one Reality worthy of undivided allegiance: "I am Yahweh."

But how had this unique God chosen to reveal self to humans? It is the hallmark of biblical faith that this revelation occurred within the concrete events of history through which Yahweh interacted with the people. This hallmark is observable to us already at the earliest discernible stage of Yahwistic faith. When the tribes gathered to give expression to the common faith, they recalled the God who delivered them from Egypt. The starting point of the Yahwistic community, therefore, was neither a cosmic vision, nor a timeless code of law. It was an experience of God entering the concreteness and particularity of human life to save humans from their bondage. The first word of Yahwistic faith was thus divine grace, unmerited, unexpected, coming to the people on the basis of one fact alone, "I am Yahweh."

Israel's birth as a covenant people took place in a specific event, the memory of which was a constant source of renewal and reorientation. For this reason, the divine name was amplified in the prologue with the relative clause, "who brought you out of the land of Egypt, out of the house of bondage." To preserve the posture that was pleasing to God, Israel needed to remember its origin as a slave people, once destitute, now delivered from bondage to freedom by a gracious God. This memory was secured by the assimilation of the relative clause describing the primal act of deliverance to the name Yahweh, even as it was engraved in the consciousness of the Jewish community by the Passover, the annual reliving of the birth of this community in divine grace.

The prologue of the Decalogue therefore established the context for the proper understanding and application of the ensuing commands.

The primal fact of Israel's existence was God's initiating activity, in which God had called a people into being. The first word of Israel's sacred story was the good news of deliverance from slavery. The commandments grew out of this message of grace as a response in gratitude for all Yahweh had done. Recognition of this relationship does nothing to diminish the importance *tôrâ*, but rather safeguards its dynamic character from being obscured by legalistic interpetations.

We must take issue, therefore, with the position of Gerhard von Rad, according to which the connection between the exodus and law-giving themes in the Pentateuch is to be regarded as secondary.[25] From the point of view of structure, such a separation is impossible in the case of the Decalogue, where the "gospel" theme of deliverance and the "law" theme of the commandments are inextricably bound into one covenant formulary. The same is true of the great covenant text in Joshua 24. Corroborating this structural connection are Hittite inscriptions from the fourteenth century that document the political treaty form that early Isreal borrowed to express its covenant theology. They begin with a historical prologue describing what the suzerain had done for the vassal, and then go on to specify the treaty conditions incumbent on that vassal.[26]

From the theological point of view, such division between "law" and "gospel" endangers the dynamic heart of early Yahwistic faith, for from the beginning it knew of no such division. Deliverance originating in divine grace and obedience based on the human response of gratitude were indivisible aspects of Israel's primal experience as a people.

The profound theological sensitivity reflected in the overall structure of the Decalogue also came to expression in the ordering of the individual commandments. This is seen already in the position of the first commandment. Even as the Decalogue was the crown on the entire corpus of *tôrâ* in the Pentateuch, the first commandment was the jewel in that crown: "You shall have no other gods before me." With those words early Israel described life's center, for the individual, for the community and for the cosmos. Where other gods came to rival the sole lordship of Yahweh, life lost focus, was scattered, moving in many directions at once, with the result that order lapsed into meaninglessness, bringing tragic results. False gods moved in to capture the allegiance of the community, the bond of trust that sustained corporate life was broken, and the community disintegrated into life-destructive greed and exploitation of others. And as the Deuteronomic curses for covenant violation indicate, the collapse of the moral universe inevit-

25. G. von Rad, "The Form-Critical Problem of the Hexateuch," in *The Problem of the Hexateuch and Other Essays*, trans. E. W. Trueman Dicken (New York: McGraw-Hill, 1966), pp. 1–78.

26. G. E. Mendenhall, "Law and Covenant in Israel and the Ancient Near East," *BA* 17 (1954), 26–46, 49–76.

ably sent shock waves through the entire realm of nature, threatening the delicate cosmos inhabited by humans (Deut. 27–28).

Life could be whole and blessed only where the consciousness of the individual and the community was filled with one reality alone, the holy God. The first commandment went on to give classic expression to a fundamental truth already expressed in the archaic texts we examined from the Gilgal cult, namely, that worship was absolutely central to the life of faith. In fact, the Bible viewed life's most basic struggle as that between true and false worship. Where Israel's devotion was singular and focused, Yahweh's promise pertained: "You shall be my people, and I shall be your God." This constituted šālôm in its fullest sense. But where Israel was disobedient to the first commandment, prophets such as Hosea were instructed to deliver a devastating message: "Call [your son's] name Not my people, for you are not my people, and I am not your God" (Hos. 1:9).

The Decalogue, by opening with its numinous "I am Yahweh . . . you shall have no other God besides me," contributed the fundamental axiom of all theology worthy of calling itself biblical. This cornerstone of faith has found many expressions in the history of our confessional heritage, from the "Hear O Israel, the Lord your God is one Lord" of Deuteronomy 6, to Augustine's "You have made us for yourself, and our heart is restless until it rests in you,"[27] and down to Paul Tillich's definition of God in terms of Ultimate Concern. Martin Luther, in his sermons on the Decalogue, delivered in 1528 C.E., also gave eloquent expression to the centrality of the first commandment, referring to it as "the sum and the light of all the others."[28] In this Large Catechism, he wrote, "Thus the first commandment is to shine and impart its splendor to all the others. Therefore you must also allow [it] to run through all of the commandments like the clasp or loop in a garland, which joins the end and the beginning and holds them all together."[29] Modern form-critical study can add little to this image in explicating the theological unity imparted to the Decalogue by the first commandment.

Not all traditions have placed the divisions between the first and second commandments at the same point in the text. Already the versions found in Exodus an Deuteronomy reflect the tendency toward differentiation. And this tendency continued. In the well-known catechism of Martin Luther, the prohibition of images was included in the first commandment. Originally images of Yahweh may have been the object of concern, though in its present form this object has been broadened to include every representation, thereby making it an amplification of the first. Calvin subscribed to a different division. The disparity results

---

27. *Confessions* I.1.

28. Luther, *Luther's Works*, ed. J. W. Doberstein, vol. 51 (Philadelphia: Muhlenberg Press, 1959), p. 144.

29. Weimar Aufgabe 30; pp. 180–181.

from Calvin accentuating the prohibition of images of Yahweh, thereby establishing it as a second commandment separate from the first, and Luther accentuating the prohibition of all representations, thereby making it an amplification of the first.

However one divides the commandments, the aniconic theme, which was such an important one in early Yahwism, is powerfully expressed. Yahweh was categorically distinct from all other beings, and simply could not be represented by any image. This commandment repudiates the presumptiousness of any human claiming to be able to capture the essence of God in an earthly form. The God who related self to this world in the freedom of holy majesty and mystery simply could not be encompassed in any manner by human effort. Walter Zimmerli has commented thus: "God has chosen to make himself known, not in a 'static' image, but in the ambiguity of dynamic history. The command-ment protects God's entry into the sphere of human life by guarding against an abuse which seeks to exploit his revelation for one's own use."[30] We find here the introduction into our confessional heritage of an aniconic theme that should be applied not only to images, but to written theological statements as well. Although the Bible displays a high degree of imagination in describing God's nature (e.g., God as shepherd, warrior, parent, and spouse), the first commandment stands as a reminder that all these metaphors constitute nothing more than human efforts to describe an ineffable mystery, the reality before whom stammering efforts at description properly end in silent worship. What Kiekegaard described as "the infinite qualitative distinction" sep-arates God from humanity,[31] which places an awesome qualification on every theological endeavor, and thus stands guard against the most an-cient of sins, hubris.

Around the center of devotion to the one true God was added a fur-ther prohibition in the second commandment, namely, against "taking the Lord's name in vain." This originally had related to false oaths in court, but in its final form prohibited any attempt to use God's name to unrighteous purpose. It is customary today to trivialize the divine name, applying it so often and so vainly as to desacralize it. This stands in marked contrast to the holy fear with which Israel approached "the Name." Israel related stories of priests who, approaching God's pres-ence with unholy purpose, were struck dead. This sense of reverence before God is still to be observed in the awe that prohibits the ortho-dox Jew from pronouncing the divine name directly, and in the fear that inspires the pious Jew reverently to cover the head before God. If a community's focus is on the one true God, in worship and in all of

30. W. Zimmerli, *Gottes Offenbarung* (München: Chr. Kaiser Verlag, 1963), pp. 245–246.

31. Søren Kierkegaard, *Training in Christianity*, trans. W. Lowrie (Princeton, N.J.: Princeton University Press, 1944), p. 139.

life, its use of God's name is purged of every vain use, and resounds to God's glory alone.

In the community centered in worship around the one true God, there was also observed a rhythm that embraced all life. Israel, like the cultures around it, sought within the cult to give expression to the solidarity of the human family with the world of which it was a part. This solidarity was symbolized in the third commandment of sabbath observance, when all work-a-day activities ceased, and the heart was opened wide to be refreshed by the creator God. This commandment was amplified in two directions in the canon as we have received it, testifying to the fluidity of the tradition down to a relatively late period. In both cases, the pattern observed earlier of Israel's inferring divine will from antecedent divine actions was followed. The Deuteronomic version rooted motivation in Yahweh's delivering the people from Egypt. The Priestly version in Exodus referred back further to the creation, commanding that because God rested from labor on the seventh day the people were to do likewise.

The third commandment serves as a good illustration of the need to interpret the Decalogue from its dynamic center in the first commandment. According to gospel narrative Jesus disputed with those who removed this commandment from that center and applied it legalistically. By insisting that "the sabbath is made for humans and not humans for the sabbath," he affirmed the heart of this commandment by directing attention to its historical-relational context in the covenant (Mark 2:27).[32] The sabbath observance derives its meaning directly from the context of Israel's covenant with Yahweh. Throughout Israel's history as a people, this special day served to sanctify the relationship between humans and their God by being "a sabbath day to your Lord," and to enhance the quality of life in the human family by including all members of society and even the beasts of the field in a day of renewal.

The first three commandments, therefore, secured the heart of Israelite faith and worship. And from this heart the fear and love of God were able to flow into all aspects of life to secure the kind of community that was consistent with God's compassionate nature. The God described in the prologue of the Decalogue was a God who had delivered and sustained the outcasts of society, thereby establishing a new, humane order of life. In harmony with that inaugural act, the remaining commandments were dedicated to the protection of all members in that new order. *All* humans were the object of God's loving concern, a

---

32. Luther commented, "You have the first commandment in the second and third, fear and love God . . . . Thus it was not intended as a command to idleness, or mindless obedience of a law." He sought, through interpreting the third commandment in light of the first, to draw out its positive meaning: "I should live holily on this day; for this day is given to us in order that we may use it for the exercise of holiness" (*Luther's Works*, vol. 51, p. 154). When interpreted within the context of the covenant with the God who relates unceasingly to the faithful community, the third commandment finds its intended setting.

theme in complete harmony with the deep moral concerns of the Book of the Covenant. Through the commandments a space was secured, an orbit of šālôm, within which God's people could flourish, safe from harm or fear of harm. Within that space they could thus devote themselves to life's consummate purpose, worship, and praise.

Attention turned first to a group that was critically important in a family-centered society such as that of the early Hebrews: "Honor your father and your mother." Of concern here was the vulnerability accompanying old age, when the ability to contribute productively had waned, and the prospect of neglect and abuse increased. In Israel, the elderly were to live free from fears of ending their years in misery, for Yahweh, the compassionate God, looked on them not as economic resources, but as beings whose worth was intrinsic, who were deserving of protection and loving care. The promise attached to this commandment draws attention to the organic connection between God's will and the šālôm of the entire created order. Obedience leads to the kind of blessing visionaries of every age have described as God's intention for the human family: "that your days may be long in the land which the Lord your God gives you."

Next to be addressed was the violence that engulfs a society when people are permitted to take the law into their own hands: "You shall not kill." Originally this law related specifically to premeditated murder of a fellow Israelite leading to blood vengeance. In its final form without the object, it declared that all forms of violence against another person contradicted the quality of community intended by God. This was to be a community in which all, young and old, weak and strong, were able to live without fear, sharing the love and protection of their God with one another.

Also of importance to the community of righteousness was the sanctity of marriage. Early Israelite society, growing up in full exposure to the fertility cults of the Canaanites, was as aware as we are of the degrading of life that occurs when faithfulness in marriage is disdained. As illustrated most graphically in Hosea, the Jews perceptively recognized in the intimate relationship of marriage a pertinent analogy for the relationship between God and humans. Within their relationship with the loving God, they discerned the qualities that were to characterize marriage, a tender union that was to be assured the opportunity to flourish by being free from the blight of adultery. And within the steadfast bond of marriage fidelity, a secure home was maintained for one of God's most marvelous gifts to humanity, happy children. Although the covenant community provided all its people with the blessings of life-sustaining relationships, those entering into the intimate relationship of marriage were to realize that the bond was secure when rooted in the love and fear of the righteous and compassionate God.

Once again in the seventh commandment, the dropping of the object lent to the command its widest possible field of application. In the circle of protection around the community of faith provided by the Decalogue, a form of harm against the neighbor was banned that has always had ravaging effects on the fabric of human life, namely thievery. At stake was not just the taking of something that rightfully belonged to another, but, especially in relation to the poorest and most vulnerable members of the society, a flagrant act of oppression. And from the point of view of Yahwistic faith, such oppression is present whenever any members of a society are denied their share of the commonwealth, whether as a result of outright theft or unjust laws and social structures. Luther's insight into the profound social significance of this commandment is as true to its meaning within the early Israelite community as it is relevant today:

It is stealing whenever I get my neighbor's goods into my possession by any means whatsoever. That's why there is no more common trade or larger craft on earth than thievery. And usually we hang the petty thieves; the big ones, however, go walking around in the highest esteem.[33]

To the rich you do no wrong; but here is the great mass of poor people; these are the ones you cheat and afflict. These are the ones who go out of the butcher's with weeping eyes and cry out to heaven. These are the ones to fear, the multitude of the poor does it, and God regards their tears.[34]

Perhaps Luther had in mind here the motive clauses we discussed earlier in the Book of the Covenant: "If you do afflict them, and they cry out to me, I will surely hear their cry" (Exod. 22:23). At any rate, he recognized clearly that the biblical basis of personal and social morality was theological, for in all of life's dealings the one to whom one is relating is the God who cares for every member of the human family, however humble, poor or obscure:

But when you steal something from me or do me the slightest injury, you are not attacking me, but rather God. Therefore every artisan, butcher, and the like should write this commandment on his scales, the miller on his sacks, the baker on his bread, the shoemaker on his last.[35]

The terrible wrong suffered by the one addressed by the eighth commandment, the one falsely accused, is illustrated most vividly in the Bible by the Naboth story in 1 Kings 21, where Jezebel, operating outside of the Israelite covenant ideal, had accomplices bring false charges against the innocent vintner. Again, we are dealing with an abuse of human rights that early Isreal insisted could not be tolerated within a god-fearing society.

Finally, the last two commandments move beneath external acts of

---

33. Luther, *Luther's Works*, vol. 51, p. 155.
34. Ibid., p. 156.
35. Ibid., p. 156.

harm to the neighbor to their affective source. Acts of harm were to be eliminated where they originated, in the covetous heart. We see clearly here, as we shall see below in relation to the story of Tamar, that the law codes of the Hebrew Bible emphatically were not based on a legalistic understanding of righteousness. Although every community must struggle against the temptation to reduce the function of law to a system of external rewards and punishments, it was of the essence of biblical morality to locate the source of right and wrong in the human heart, and to define obedience within the context of the covenant with the righteous and compassionate God. Reform efforts, from the Deuteronomistic era to the time of Jesus, were thus appeals to the original meaning of the *tôrâ* rather than introductions of new concepts of morality. This is why it is so essential that the study of biblical *tôrâ* be carried out as an aspect of the larger study of the biblical covenantal community.

This brief exposition of the Decalogue indicates how it embodied the unique notion of covenant community that had been born in the exodus experience, and that had developed in the early years of the tribal league. It sought to create, as it were, a protective wall around this community of freed slaves, and to secure a space within which they could live in peace and justice. This it was able to do by maintaining an unbroken connection with the deliverer God whose prevenient grace had called Israel forth as a people from nothing. From this starting point, it sought to keep Israel's focus on the only possible source of continued freedom and well-being: Israel could avoid falling back into bondage and chaos, could remain a free people, only by holding securely to its source in faith and obedience. From fidelity to the one true God stemmed the motivation and strength to embody the righteousness and compassion that constituted this people as a blessed people.

The Decalogue thus gave classic expression to the pattern that lay at the heart of early Israel's sense of being a community of faith, the pattern of divine initiative and human response. Obedience to the commandments was not regarded as an onerous work, but rather as the fitting response of those recognizing their life together as derivative—originally and continually—of divine grace.

c. The Distribution of Land According to the Naḥălâ

From the classical formulation of community in the Decalogue, we turn to a legal structure that arose in relation to a specific problem, namely, that of equitable distribution of the land. In the Ugaritic texts of the fourteenth century B.C.E., we get a glimpse of the religiosocial structures of the dominant culture Israel encountered in Palestine and surrounding environs. As in Egypt, the society was strictly stratified, and laws and social structures strengthened the hands of the rich as opposed to the poor and impoverished. This disparity is seen in the case of entitlement to land, for land was bought and sold as any commodity on purely commercial terms. Like any personal property, it could be bought by those with sufficient purchasing power, in any quantity whatsoever. The result was the amassing of real estate by the wealthy, and the concomitant impoverishment of the poor.[36]

As a safeguard against the misuse of land ownership, there arose in early Israel the concept of the *naḥălâ*, the sacred patrimony, according to which the land was to be divided equitably among the people.[37] As in the case of the laws studied earlier from the Book of the Covenant, this concept arose out of a central confession of Yahwistic faith: the land Yahweh first promised and then conferred on Israel was Yahweh's own possession. No tribe or individual could claim private ownership. Nor were Israelites free to buy additional land or sell the portion allotted to them. A portion of land was granted, in accordance with the size of each tribe, as a sacred trust from Yahweh, to be used and enjoyed in perpetuity (cf. Num. 26:52–56). Here we witness the radical faith of freed slaves expressing itself in concrete social terms. If the re-enslavement of parts of the community was to be prevented, each family had to be guaranteed a portion of land sufficient for its physical sustenance. This was a right based not merely upon a social ideal, but on the Yahwistic confession that every Israelite was a child of the same parent, a heavenly Parent to whom belonged the whole earth, who had chosen Israel as an inheritance out of all the families of the earth (Deut. 32:8–9); 9:26, 29; Ps. 28:9; 79:1; Jer. 10:16), and who now distributed, with even-handed fairness, the land among the people. Of course, in a cultural milieu dominated by a strictly secular attitude toward ownership of land, this radically egalitarian concept was constantly under attack. Micah 2:1–2 expresses this threat vividly:

> Woe to those who devise wickedness and work
> evil upon their beds!
> When the morning dawns, they perform it,
> because it is in the power of their hand.
> They covet fields, and seize them; and houses,
> and take them away;
> They oppress a man and his house, a man and
> his inheritance (*naḥălâ*).

Scattered through the Bible, we find laws and prophetic proclamations that seek to safeguard the concept of the *naḥălâ*. In Numbers 27, the case of the daughters of Zelophehad is presented as precedent for a

---

36. It is revealing to note the parties with whom early Israelites entered into real estate transactions. For example, David purchased land from the *Jebusite* (i.e., Canaanite) Araunah (2 Sam. 24:25), even as Omri bought the estate of the *Canaanite* noble, Shemen (1 Kings 16:24).

37. In this connection, comparison with the terms *niḥlatum* found in eighteenth-century texts from Mari is interesting, since customs at Mari reflect the influx of the Amorite elements to which the biblical patriarchs were likely related. Cf. A. Malamat, "Mari and the Bible: Some Patterns of Tribal Organization and Institution" *JAOS* 82 (1961), 143–150.

"statute and ordinance" in Israel that if a father has no sons, the inheritance shall be kept within the family by being conferred on the daughters. The ruling in fact goes further, to assure that even if the deceased has no daughters, it shall go to his brothers; if no brothers, to his father's brothers; and so on. In Numbers 36:6, marriage outside the tribe is prohibited, so as to prevent a tribe's forfeiture of land. In the reallotment of the land envisioned for the restoration, it is notable that the early Israelite sensitivity to the alien is preserved: "They shall be to you as native-born sons of Israel; with you they shall be allotted an inheritance among the tribes of Israel" (Ezek. 47:2b). The substance of the concept of the *naḥălâ* comes to classic expression in the conflict between King Ahab, who as king had been convinced by his Phoenician wife to treat property in his kingdom in the style of a Canaanite, and the determined vintner Naboth, who adhered faithfully to the ancient Yahwistic view of property: "the Lord forbid that I should give you the inheritance (*naḥălâ*) of my fathers" (1 Kings 21:3). We return to the Ahab-Naboth story in the next chapter, discussing the threat to the early Israelite notion of community posed by kingship.

Because of the incomplete nature of the evidence, it is not possible to sketch a complete history of the *naḥălâ* in ancient Israel. In discussing evidence pertaining to the early Yahwistic community found in the Book of Joshua, we concluded that the tribes of Benjamin and Joseph likely subscribed to the idea of an even-handed distribution of land as a part of their understanding of covenant. This conclusion holds even though the picture of all twelve tribes gathered together at one time to divide the land is a later idealization of a more modest historical phenomenon.

Although abused and neglected in practice, the testimony of the prophets assures us that the concept of the *naḥălâ* did not disappear as a force in the religious and social life of the Israelite community. When Amos, Micah, and Isaiah inveighed against those who bought and sold property and amassed real estate at the expense of the impoverished, they were appealing to the early Yahwistic notion of equal distribution to which the right of the *naḥălâ* gave social form. This concept was an inseparable part of the deep sense of justice and equality that grew out of Israel's primal experience of the Deliverer God Yahweh. Since the source of the idea of the *naḥălâ* was located in the nature and acts of Israel's God, it was one that would continue to resurface among those who sought to give concrete form to their confession in the God who delivered slaves from bondage and gave them a land in which to live in freedom.

3. A CELEBRATION OF ISRAEL'S EARLY NOTION OF COMMUNITY: THE SONG OF HANNAH

Within Israel's formative period, a notion of community grew as a bold alternative to the oppressive societal structures of the surrounding kingdoms. I have paid particular attention to early legal and institutional materials in the Bible to demonstrate that this notion was not merely given symbolic expression, but was translated into the concrete realities of life. The dangers of institutionalized oppression and the legitimization of positions of special privilege for the powerful and rich were dealt with systematically through the outlawing of lending on interest, through laws placing limits on the then universal practice of slavery, through special legal protections for widows and orphans, and through the entitlement of each family to a portion of land protected against forfeiture by the right of the nahălâ.

A pattern of social construction thus arose in Israel that resisted the dominant one in antiquity: here was a society constructed not by the privileged and the elite, but by ordinary folk, by former slaves drawing their guidelines from the example of a God who embraced the cause of the weak against the powerful oppressor. The contrast is equally striking with regard to purpose: in place of a social system designed by the powerful as a means of protecting their privileges against the underprivileged, we see here a community ideal by which former slaves sought to safeguard their God-given freedom. This unusual process of constructing community from the bottom up is documented in hymnic form by the beautiful Song of Hannah, which is to be dated (with the exception of the royal addition on the end of verse 10) to the premonarchical period:

> Hannah also prayed and said:
> "My heart exalts in the Lord;
>   my strength is exalted in the Lord.
> My mouth derides my enemies,
>   because I rejoice in thy salvation.
> There is none holy like the Lord,
>   there is none besides thee;
>   there is no rock like our God.
> Talk no more so very proudly,
>   let not arrogance come from your mouth;
> for the Lord is a God of knowlege,
>   and by him actions are weighed.
> The bows of the mighty are broken,
>   but the feeble gird on strength.
> Those who were full have hired
>   themselves our for bread,
>   but those who were hungry have
>   ceased to hunger.
> The barren has borne seven,
>   but she who has many children is forlorn.
> The Lord kills and brings to life;
>   he brings down to Sheol and raises up.
> The Lord makes poor and makes rich;
>   he brings low, he also exalts.

> He raises up the poor from the dust;
>   he lifts the needy from the ash heap,
> to make them sit with princes
>   and inherit a seat of honor.
> For the pillars of the earth are the Lord's,
>   and on them he has set the world.
> He will guard the feet of his faithful ones;
>   but the wicked shall be cut off in the darkness;
>   for not by might shall a man prevail.
> The adversaries of the Lord shall
>   be broken to pieces;
>   against them he will thunder in heaven. (1 Sam. 2:1–10a)

This hymn articulates the response of a powerless one to the saving act of a compassionate and powerful champion of the weak (v. 1). It thus reflects the primal pattern underlying Israel's early forms of worship and community: antecedent divine act leads to human response.

Praise first focuses on the incomparable holiness and majesty of the savior God. All other heavenly powers are depotentized (v.2), all earthly powers are relativized (v. 3). The only Lord deserving of devotion is Yahweh, the universal Savior and the all-knowing Judge.

The hymn then goes on to give exquisite poetic expression to the social vision of the released Hebrew slaves. Under Yahweh's exclusive lordship, the world is no longer the playground of the tyrant, where those with much accumulate more and the weak are driven deeper and deeper into impoverishment. In the new order instituted by Yahweh, the tables have been turned. And indeed, it is the destruction of the power of the mighty ("the bows of the mighty are broken") which enables the empowerment of the weak ("the feeble gird on strength"). The ideals of equality and the democratization of power, which alone explain the new laws and institutions we have seen emerging in Israel's early period, are described vividly in the imagery of exquisite poetry:

> [The Lord] raises up the poor from the dust;
>   he lifts the needy from the ash heap,
> to make them sit with the princes
>   and inherit a seat of honor. (v. 8a)

This new communal order, moreover, is not a fragile innovation whose existence is threatened by the presumptuous cosmologies sanctioning the social systems of pharoahs and tyrant kings. For this order is in harmony with the Author of cosmic order: Yahweh is the sovereign over all structures, social and cosmic (v. 8b).

Verses 9 and 10, in hymnic style, identify the source of Israel's strength once again, in the God who guards the feet of his faithful ones, and destroys the wicked. From this, a poignant lesson is derived, a lesson that Israel would forget only at the loss of all she had received: "for not by might shall a [hu]man prevail" (v. 9b).

Here then is a vision of a community that derived its basic structure from a God who acted to save the weak and the impoverished from the powerful wicked oppressor, a vision of a people that depended for its well-being solely on the holy and compassionate God Yahweh, a people that accordingly found its fitting response in a life of worship and praise.

This confessional foundation of the early Israelite notion of community was expressed vividly in another early hymn, Psalm 82. It acknowledged a period when other gods had exercised rule over their respective peoples (cf. Deut. 32:8–9). Their mandate had been identical to that which Israel had extrapolated from its encounter with the God who takes up the cause of the weak and the oppressed:

> Give justice to the weak and the fatherless;
>   maintain the right of the afflicted and the destitute.
> Rescue the weak and the needy;
>   deliver them from the hand of the wicked. (Ps. 82:3–4)

But those gods had ruled in disregard of that mandate. The result was that the harmony between the social and the cosmic order had been threatened: "All the foundations of the earth are shaken." This imbalance led to an incisive turn of events: the one true God reestablished justice and harmony in the world by condemning the false gods to the death of mortals (vv. 6–7). A new era thus began, in which the one true God's sovereignty came to embrace all the earth (v. 8).

Although we have seen that early Isreal borrowed freely from her neighbors,[38] it is clear that the heart of Israel's notion of community was unique in the ancient world. And that notion became the foundation for a novel development within the religions of antiquity. When one seeks to explain that uniqueness, it is not enough to make references to differences in social background (e.g., nomadic versus agrarian) or in temperament, for early Yahwism encompassed truly a "mixed company" in these and other respects. If one wishes to offer an adequate explanation of that uniqueness, one cannot avoid a theological answer. Involved was encounter with the God Yahweh during the nativity period of Israel's life, for among the gods of antiquity, Yahweh was unique. We can show the direct correlation between confessions and communal structures by citing an ancient liturgical fragment found in Exodus 34:6–8. In answer to the question, "What accounts for the unusual qualities of early Israel's notion of community?" this liturgical fragment offers a concise answer:

The Lord passed before him, and proclaimed, "The Lord, the Lord, a God merciful and gracious, slow to anger, and abounding in steadfast love and faith-

---

38. A stimulating exploration of some of the important connections between Israelite categories of thought and those of other ancient Near Eastern cultures is found in B. Albrektson, *History and the Gods* (Lund: Gleerup, 1967).

fulness, keeping steadfast love for thousands, forgiving iniquity and transgression and sin, but who will by no means clear the guilty, visiting the iniquity of the fathers upon the children, to the third and the fourth generation. (Exod. 34:6–7)

And true to the response pattern we have found at the basis of the community notion in this early period was Moses's reaction in this narrative tradition: "And Moses made haste to bow his head toward the earth, worshipped" (Exod. 34:8).

D. SUMMARY OF THE CHARACTERISTICS OF THE EARLY YAHWISTIC NOTION OF COMMUNITY

Having examined the earliest traditions in the Bible dealing with Israel's community structures and underlying beliefs, I shall now describe in a more systematic manner the main characteristics of the Yahwistic community in the pre-monarchical period.

1. COMMUNITY AS RESPONSE TO GOD'S INITIATING SAVING ACTIVITY

Psychological or sociological methods alone are inadequate to uncover the essential key to the early Israelite notion of community. Even a philosophical approach seeking to discover the principal human ideal that gave rise to community in Israel will miss the most basic point. It was not the deliberations of Hebrew philosophers over the *summum bonum* of all life that issued forth in the founding principles of Hebrew community, but encounter with the God who delivered slaves from bondage. Israel understood community essentially as a response to God's gracious act of salvation. Israel was called into existence as a people when it was called forth from bondage to be a nation of priests consecrated to God's redemptive purposes.

2. DEVOTION TO THE ONE TRUE GOD AS THE UNIFYING HEART OF COMMUNITY

In being delivered from slavery by Yahweh, the Hebrews encountered the only reality in the world that was holy, and that could claim their absolute allegiance. In this encounter with the "wholly other," all else was relativized, all other gods, all earthly powers, all material goods. Stripped and exposed, driven to deepest need and helpless, and then experiencing all needs satisfied by the one true God, Israel discovered the true object of worship, and at the same time, the only dependable basis for human community. The šĕmāʿ of Deuteronomy 6:4–5 stands alongside the first commandment of the Decalogue as the classic formulation of this central devotion: "Hear, O Israel: The Lord our God is one Lord; and you shall love the Love your God with all your heart, and with all our soul, and with all your might."

In ancient Israel, as today, these words no doubt tended to become mere formulas for people forgetting their origins. But then as now, betrayal of this central devotion led to the flirtation with rival gods, or to the search for grounding in human devices, with the inevitable result of the disintegration of true community. Israel thus was educated by its own experiences to become the teacher of countless communities to come: with the betrayal of the heart of faith, unity is lost and community is torn into segments as factions form on the basis of conflicting allegiances. Without an object of devotion that transcends human self-interests, human efforts fail to reconcile differences. No common court of appeal remains where disputes may be brought for open debate and resolution. What in a healthy community of faith are acknowledged as penultimate convictions take on the status of ultimacy, and a pantheon arises. Personal ambition, material gain, group privilege, royal status, and other human goals are exempted from relativization before the Holy, and assume divine status themselves. As soon as God is neither acknowledged as sole author of life and as Lord, nor loved and obeyed with the whole heart, soul and might, myriad idols enter the lives of the people, claim their devotion, and destroy the only trustworthy foundation for genuine community.

Ancient Israel contributed to future generations the first commandment and the šĕmāᶜ as timeless monuments to its notion of community, for Israel understood that worship as a response to God's prevenient grace was central to the life of those gathered into covenant fellowship. "I will be their God, and they shall be my people." This was the relationship on which all other meaningful relationships could be built. This was the covenant on which life and community could be constructed.

3. THE COMMUNITY DEFINED BY THE TRIAD OF RIGHTEOUSNESS, COMPASSION, AND WORSHIP

We have observed that from the outset Israel's notion of community was a developing one. Arising out of a confessional response to a God perceived as active in the drama of history, and from the beginning offering itself as an alternative to the more static systems of neighboring kingdoms, there was an intrinsically dynamic quality in Hebrew communal structure. In Yahweh, Israel found a source of community life that was dynamic and transcendent; that is, ever creatively and redemptively involved with the world, and yet ever holy in majesty.

How can we summarize the qualities of this dynamic notion of community as they emerge in this early period as inferences from God's acts and from the divine nature revealed in these acts? Implied in every such effort at summarizing is the danger of replacing living qualities with static categories. This rigidity can be avoided, however, by keeping clearly in mind the pattern of interrelationships that safeguards their dynamic quality.

a. Righteousness

Yahweh was a God who created order out of chaos and established structure where there was anomie. The wilderness legends describe the state of anomie, in which clans, removed from a system to which they had grown accustomed, were disquieted by the prevailing social vacuum to the point of wanting to return to the security of their former slavery, which to them appeared preferable to the vicissitudes of the new life of freedom.

The impressions given by these legends perhaps are not far off the mark in describing the earliest stage of community-building in Isreal. Involved was a search for a means of ordering disparate groups within a new setting. No doubt much effort was expended in the mixed company of freed slaves to find structures conducive of social harmony. The Book of the Covenant contains one block of laws, the mišpāṭîm, or case laws, which were apparently borrowed from Israel's neighbors for purposes of ordering this endangered nascent community. This process went hand in hand with the amalgamation of various tribal groups into a community consciousness on the basis of their identification with the exodus confession. In this ordering process, such typical problems were addressed as personal injury, homicide, repayment of debts, and redress of property damage. Noticeable in the mišpāṭîm is the distinctly conservative tendency characteristic of civil law in general, as illustrated by the lex talionis (Exod. 21:23–24) and the acceptance of social stratification as a social assumption (Exod. 21:28–32). But beginning already in the composition history of the Book of the Covenant, and continuing on throughout the history of Israelite law, such laws were subjected to the dynamism inherent in the confession of the God Yahweh who delivered the Hebrew slaves from their bondage. This confession, and the covenantal concept that grew out of it, drew the various legal materials and social customs found among the early Hebrews into a particular notion of justice that is best described as "righteousness" (ṣêdeq or ṣĕdāqâ). We can take a law from the Holiness Code, which regulated the measures used in commerce, to illustrate the quality of righteousness that permeated Israelite law from the earliest to the latest stages of biblical tradition:

You shall do no wrong in judgment, in measures of length or weight or quantity. You shall have just balances, just weights, a just ephah, and a just hin: I am the Lord your God, who brought you out of the land of Egypt. (Lev. 19:35–36)

In the Hebrew text the individual measurements are specified with the genitive construction; "an ephah of ṣêdeq," "a hin of ṣêdeq," and so on. This formula may seem like a rather belabored way to regulate a straightforward practice. When one takes into account, however, that just measures are of basic importance to order and harmony in a society, and that those most often harmed by dishonest measures are the weak and the poor, it becomes apparent why the full eight of the concept "righteousness" is applied to the ephah and the hin. Righteousness was too essential a quality of life to exclude any domain from its influence if harmony was to prevail. And in this law the source of that quality was identified specifically by the motive clause with which it concludes: "I am the Lord your God, who brought you out of the land of Egypt." Even at the relatively late stage of tradition represented by the Holiness Code, the exodus confession continued to safeguard the specifically Yahwistic quality of justice, which was its relational quality as defined by the covenant between God and people.

b. Compassion

Reference to the Deliverer God Yahweh—which if not explicitly mentioned was nevertheless assumed in all the laws regulating Israelite society—bound the standard of righteousness to the second quality central to the early Hebrew notion of community, divine compassion. This was a quality underlying the J narrative in Exodus 3:7–8, the E narrative in Exodus 3:9–12, the P narrative in Exodus 2:23–25, and formulated explicitly by the Deuteronomist in Deuteronomy 7:8: ". . . it is because the Lord loves you, and is keeping the oath which he swore to your fathers, that the Lord has brought you out with a mightly hand, and redemmed you from the house of bondage, from the hand of Pharaoh king of Egypt."

We have observed earlier the tension created in the Book of the Covenant by the juxtaposition of the rather conservative "case laws" and the more dynamic "Yahwistic laws" with their motive clauses referring to the compassionate Deliverer God Yahweh. The order established by the former was of the type deemed necessary by all societies for social stability. But order can assume vastly different forms. And not all such forms foster the development of a humane society. For example, the Egypt of the Pharoahs was a strictly ordered society that remained essentially unchanged for over a millennium. From the vantage point of the Hebrew slaves, what was lacking in this stable environment was an opening for those excluded from its benefits, especially the weak, the poor, the enslaved, the alien. This openness was a quality that, however, eluded codification. It could be infused into a community's consciousness only by personal example, and indeed, a personal example of such unique stature as to be acknowledged by, and to exert its influence over, all members of that community.

In Israel, that example was supplied by memory of the Deliverer God Yahweh, who out of compassion redeemed slaves and brought them to a land of freedom. Without denying the need for order, the compassion of Yahweh awakened consciousness of the fact that in and of itself order can be oppressive. For a community to have a heart, justice had to be infused with compassion. For those redeemed from the oppression of a heartless social order, justice was not to be allowed to become an abstraction, codified in immutable formulations. Justice in the new community was to be understood specifically and concretely as the righteousness of the God Yahweh. As such, it maintained its inseparable bond with the compassion of the God who delivered the oppressed from their bondage. A righteous standard capable of ordering the new society was thus to be accompanied with a heart reaching out to embrace all—especially the weak and the poor and the alien—within the protective habitation of God's šālôm.

c. Worship

The harmonious wedding of righteousness with compassion is unfortunately not a characteristic of most societies, either in antiquity or in modern times. More commonly the need for order hardens into a rigid administration of justice, or the reassertion of human passion leads to the dismissal of the stringent standard of righteousness in favor of a sentimental permissiveness conducive of social chaos. How can these two qualities be held together? In Israel, this link was possible because both were unified in the reality of the God who entered history for the sake of a slave people and thus came to be known as "Yahweh, who delivered you from bondage." The ultimate reference point for Israel was this God, and the eternal touchstone for faith was the personal commitment conveyed by revelation of the divine name, "I am Yahweh." To Yahweh alone Israel owed existence, and to Yahweh alone Israel was to pledge its undivided devotion. When faithful in this commitment, Israel was capable of facing every new decision and crisis with courage. Yahweh was the righteous and compassionate God who was active in the events of history consistent with a creative and redemptive purpose embracing all. Tensions and crises were not therefore eschewed in favor of flight into the timeless realm of myth, but were interpreted as signs of Yahweh's ongoing struggle against evil on behalf of the oppressed and of those suffering from physical or spiritual bondage. Judgment and redemption were both parts of this struggle. Reality, seen from the perspective of Yahwism, was thus not simple, static, and timeless, but complex and forward moving, and presented itself to the responsive as a summons to participation.

Once we have recognized the source of Israel's dynamic view of reality in this ultimate point of reference or external touchstone, the righteous and compassionate God Yahweh, we can appreciate the importance of the third cardinal quality of the early Israelite notion of community: acknowledgment of the sole lordship of this one true God in worship. In worship, Israel confessed the holy name of Yahweh, recited Yahweh's glorious acts, and thus kept alive the divine example of the bond of righteousness and compassion in its life. In worship, therefore, the potentially disruptive tension between these first two qualities was transformed into a generative force capable of molding a people into an agent of God's purpose in the world.

Within the earliest hymnic literature of Israel, we are able to glimpse how in worship the dramatic interplay of Yahweh's righteousness and compassion infused the faithful with the qualities empowering them to become a community dedicated to God's justice and peace. In the Song of Miriam, for example, the congregation confessed, "Yahweh is a warrior, Yahweh is his name," and then went on to recall how by shattering the enemy Yahweh delivered the people. In the Song of Hannah, descriptive praise relived how Yahweh broke the bows of the mighty, enabling the feeble to gird on strength, indeed, how Yahweh "kills and brings to life," "brings down to Sheol and raises up," "makes poor and makes rich," "brings low" and "also exalts." Here Yahweh, the God steadfast and true to covenant through all generations, was acknowledged on the basis of concrete historical memory as the source of unbounded redemptive vitality. Righteousness and compassion, judgment and redemption, destruction and restoration, killing and bringing to life, were awesome polarities that normally threaten to engulf life and to undermine a community's foundations to the advantage of the ruthless oppressor. But by being related to the redemptive activity of the God of covenant fidelity, these polarities were drawn into the creative, redemptive current that Israel discerned at the heart of life and believed to be constitutive of all reality. Only in worship of this unique God, Israel believed, could righteousness and compassion intertwine as strands of one life-enhancing pattern. Because Yahweh was one, the full life-transforming force of righteousness and compassion was not only a possibility, but in worship became the holy fascination enabling a people to engage in life as agents of a divinely ordained process of transformation. The steadfastness and at the same time the dynamism of this process can be seen in the development of the divine epithet; that is, in the elaboration of that primal expression of Israel's ultimate reference point, "I am Yahweh." For example, in the ancient liturgical fragment in Exodus 34:6–7, belief in the eternal oneness and stedfastness of Yahweh generated a remarkably dynamic epithet embodying righteousness and compassion: "The Lord, the Lord, a God merciful and gracious, slow to anger, and abounding in steadfast love and faithfulness, keeping steadfast love for thousands, forgiving iniquity."

Worship of such a God of course did not only generate such epithets, but had an equally dynamic effect on the community. Complacency was not an option open to a community called to a way of lie befitting a people claimed as a holy possession by this God. Excluded were recourse both to a safe legalism and a normless sentimentalism for a community worshipping "the faithful God who keeps covenant and steadfast love with those who love him and keep his commandments, to a thousand generations, and requites to their face those who hate him, by destroying them" (Deut. 7:9–10). Fellowship in worship with a God of righteous compassion and compassionate righteousness commended to the community of faith a distinct style of relating to life: declaring oneself for the God who in righteousness and compassion had delivered slaves from the house of bondage was simultaneously a decision for a life of commitment to all who were in bondage. Wherever the faithful pronounced the name of "Yahweh, who led you out of the house of bondage," they not only reaffirmed the divine basis of their own deliverance, but simultaneously became recipients of a commission: "Because in my saving acts I revealed myself to be a righteous and compassionate God, you accordingly shall be righteous and compassionate toward others." Israel's forms of worship and structures of community, which arose in response to this God, therefore embodied both righteousness and compassion, and in spite of the tension implied in this union, they resisted reduction to pure legalism or pure emotionalism. Instead, sustained by ongoing communion with the living God, they became strands in a communal fabric that ordered life without excluding, that created harmony without stultifying, that sustained the community without extinguishing the challenge to develop and grow.

d. The Dynamic Interrelationships Among Righteousness, Compassion, and Worship

According to this analysis, then, a triad of qualities underlies the early Yahwistic notion of community. In their interrelationship, they clarify the dynamism discernible in Israelite community in the premonarchical period. The righteousness of God represented a universal standard of justice that ordered life, defined the realm in which Yahweh's šālôm could be received, and gave rise to ordinances and institutions that formed a protective wall around the people that sheltered it from life-threatening dangers. Compassion allowed righteousness in Israel to maintain its stringency as a clear and dependable standard by giving it a heart, and by wedding its just requirements with openness and concern for the salvation of all members of God's family. Finally the two were able to work together as a life-enhancing polarity in maintaining an ordered but open society by finding their unity in worship of the one holy God, the Judge of the wicked and the Redeemer of the repentant and the innocent oppressed. At the beginning of its life as a people, Israel encountered a God revealed as "I am Yahweh, who brought you out of the land of Egypt, out of the house of bondage."

Israel's understanding of this God would undergo profound change, for as Yahweh was first encountered in the context of history, even so those encounters could continue throughout Israel's life as a people. Yet the name Yahweh and Yahweh's commitment to a covenant with Israel would abide, signifying God's fidelity throughout all historical change and all changes in human understanding. Because the utter trustworthiness of God was already assured in the self-commitment conveyed in the revelation of the name and in the covenant, Israel was enabled to deepen its understanding of Yahweh on the basis of further experiences within the covenant relationship.

The development of Israel's laws and the elaboration of the divine epithet that historical-critical study allows us to trace thus document this deepening of understanding accompanying the ongoing encounter of new generations of the faithful community with its God. The result was both continuity and change, a dialectic characteristic of the entire history of tradition in the Bible. Continuity was assured by the commitment made by God at the beginning in the revelation of the name Yahweh and through the covenant promise, "I shall be your God, and you shall be my people." And indeed, continuity is discernible throughout the transmission history of Scripture, as seen, for example, in the organic relationship between the various law codes. Clearly Israel did not adopt a new view of righteousness with each generation, but deepened and refined its understanding over its whole history. Israel confessed the steadfastness of God, which meant that the truth and justice revealed in Yahweh's earliest encounters with this people remained a trustworthy guide to future encounters. The vitality of Yahwism is seen in the fact, however, that this conviction did not exclude the belief that every new generation was afforded the opportunity of gaining a deeper insight into God's righteousness on the basis of new chapters in God's involvement with this world. This continuousness lends the progressive quality that is so characteristic of Israel's forms of worship and community in the early period, and explains the ability of this community to adopt to profound changes without forsaking the distinctive quality of righteousness already revealed in the exodus. Reform and revision, therefore, did not contradict Israel's faith in God's trustworthiness, but kept the community alert to the implications of being related to a living God who was encountered in the real stuff of life. The early Yahwistic community expected from experience new lessons in righteousness and compassion as an essential part of life understood within the context of fellowship with the living God.

There is no question that this openness to change entailed a precariousness that would have been intolerable to other ancient cults. Indeed, the flux represented by historical existence was precisely the awful threat that ancient cults sought to oppose by appeal to the changeless verities rooted in the timeless, mythic realm of the gods. How could Israel tolerate, even embody at the center of her understanding of reality, the tension implied by this dynamic view of righteousness and compassion? We have come to recognize that this courageous posture was grounded in the encounter with a God revealed to them as a personal agent committed to the battle against injustice and oppression in the world. In terms of Israel's ongoing life, this confessional grounding alone made possible the wedding of a stringent sense of righteousness with a generous openness to those beyond the protective shelter of the community. In a word, the source of Israel's vitality was found in worship. When God, in creed and theophanic presence, was encountered as personal Reality, individuals were empowered to live into the future both with confidence and expectation. Change, which for other cultures raised the specter of deadly chaos, actually summoned the community of faith to action on behalf of those threatened by wickedness, for the movement discernible in change was interpreted as evidence of God's relentless struggle against evil for the sake of the oppressed, the sick, and the homelss. In Israel's worship, therefore, tattered nerves, waning courage, and faltering faith were renewed in the presence of the righteous and compassionate One, who first delivered, and then drew the delivered into a partnership of overcoming wickedness and heartlessness with divine righteousness and mercy. In the presence of such a God, Israel experienced the forgiveness of sin and the healing that freed it for commitment to the order of life intended by God for all.

Although the dynamism created by the interrelationship between righteousness, compassion, and worship implied ongoing development within Israel's notion of community, these three qualities themselves continued to function throughout the biblical period to define the creative, redeptive space within which Israel lived as the people of God. This fact we can illustrate by reference to two passages from later periods that embody the same dynamic triad. One is found in the eighth-century prophetic book of Micah; the other is from a Matthean saying of Jesus. First, the Micah passage:

> He has showed you, O [hu]man, what is good;
> and what does the Lord require of you
> but to do justice, and to love mankind,
> and to walk humbly with your God? (Mic. 6:8)

In this word, the prophet addresses the question of true worship: With what shall I come before the Lord, and bow myself before God on high?" (v. 6). The answer describes worship as the place where the two cardinal qualities of righteousness and compassion are unified in a manner constitutive of both life and worship.

In Matthew, Jesus is presented attacking the scribes and Pharisees for their narrow view of cult, "for you tithe mint and dill and cummin, and have neglected the weightier matters of the law, justice and mercy and faith; these you ought to have done, without neglecting the others" (Matt. 23:23). Here controversy becomes this occasion of Jesus' reviving the classical biblical notion of community discernible already at the earliest stages of Israelite history. The life that embodies God's order—that is, the life true to the weightier matters of the *tôrâ*—is discribable in terms of a triad: justice, mercy, and faith. Justice is guardian over the norms without which life disintegrates into chaos. Mercy contributes the special quality of a heart within the ordered community that reaches out to all, particularly those in need. And finally, there is the quality of life within which justice and mercy find their source and unity, faith in the living God expressed in true worship.

This passage from Matthew, and others especially in the Sermon on the Mount, need to receive far greater attention if the contribution of the early Yahwistic notion of community to a renewal of contemporary Christian communities of faith is to be reclaimed. Failure to see this organic connection has contributed to a distored view of *tôrâ* and a disintegration of the profound and dynamic view of community that emerges from an adequate biblical theology.

4. IMPLICATIONS OF THE YAHWISTIC NOTION OF COMMUNITY FOR CONTEMPORARY COMMUNITIES OF FAITH

"The weightier matters of the law, justice, mercy, and faith"; that this Matthean characterization of the *tôrâ* coincides with the three cardinal qualities discernible at the heart of early Israel's notion of community already suggests how important a source of understanding is neglected when the Hebrew Bible is left outside of the discussion of the nature of contemporary communities of faith. Why is it that so many people seem prepared, at best, to append insights from late prophecy, especially Second Isaiah and Jeremiah, to their New Testament understanding while neglecting large portions of the Hebrew Bible, including the *Torah* (Genesis, Exodus, Leviticus, Numbers, and Deuteronomy)? In the Jesus logion in Matthew, it is not just the prophets that are mentioned: "Think not that I have come to abolish the law and the prophets; I have come not to abolish them but to fulfill them. For truly, I say to you, till heaven and earth pass away, not an iota, not a dot, will pass from the law until all is accomplished" (Matt. 5:17–18). Unless these words are simply to be excluded from the discussion by *a priori* claims that they represent an invasion into the gospel by Judaism, modern Christians must pose with much more seriousness the qustion of the *tôrâ*'s role in maintaining the health of communities of faith today. We have obviously raised a major problem within Christian theology today, one moreover that has vexed theologians since the early history of the church. This problem arises largely from an unbiblical understanding of *tôrâ*. *Tôrâ*, translated "law" on the basis of the Greek *nomos*, has all too often been summarily dismissed from serious discussion within Christian circles with something like the following reasoning: Paul states the Christian view of the law in Romans 10:14: "Christ is the end of the law." This position is supported by Martin Luther: "Moses is dead." Therefore the problem of the law is resolved for Christians. We live in the freedom of the gospel as sinners justified by grace apart from the law; any reference to the law in discussion of the nature of the church is a reversion to Judaism.

That the matter is not so simple can be suggested in a preliminary way by applying the same method of proof texting in support of the opposite conclusion. In Romans 3:31, Paul writes, "Do we then overthrow the law by this faith? By no means! On the contrary, we uphold the law." Luther, in turn, made the Decalogue the starting point of his small and large catechisms, preached several sermon series on those same Ten Commandments of Moses, and even appealed directly to Moses's authority in admonishing his flock. For example, in a sermon from 1528 C.E. he proclaimed:

Fear God and give to the needy whatever he is lacking, as Moses says: "If there is among you a poor man, one of your brethren, in any of your towns within your land which the Lord your God gives you, you shall not harden your heart or shut your hand against your poor brother, but you shall open your hand to him, and lend him sufficient for his need, whatever it may be" (Deut. 15:7–8). Don't say, I don't have it. Here Moses himself is taking the fear of God from the first commandment and applying it to all ten of them.[39]

Once a selective reading of the Gospel writers, Paul, or Luther is replaced by a full contextual reading, it becomes apparent that a carefully nuanced interpretation of tôrâ is found that in no way justifies one-sided interpretations. Even when this problem is acknowledged, however, firm interpretive procedure is not assured, for the longing for systematic clarity often issues forth in the simple statement produced in the effort to find the middle ground between the declaration that the law is dead and the belief that the law remains a faithful guide to those seeking to live in obedience to God. Too often the resulting compromise position reduces theology both to shallow faith and to superficial ethics. How, then, can the problem of the relation between law and gospel be approached in order to redress mistakes of the past?

In approaching this question anew, several points are germane. First, a weakness of much current theology in addressing the areas of personal morality and social ethics is traceable to an inadequate understanding of the role of the Hebrew Bible. On the other hand, in communities of faith where biblical tôrâ is studied seriously as a guide to faith and ethics, one often finds the cardinal teaching of the reformers blunted or lost. This teaching is that justification is by faith alone, that mortals can contribute nothing to their salvation, no matter how zealously they work to obey the law, that in fact all efforts to be justified before the law ultimately condemn sinners by proving them helpless to contribute anything to the redemptive precess.

In light of these two points, it is clear that our question will not be

---

39. Luther, *Luther's Works*, vol. 51, p. 153.

answered by efforts to reduce the polarity of *tôrâ* and gospel to one simple proposition. At the heart of the problem is a dialectic. And this dialectic will neither be resolved nor will its theological importance be explicated by synchronic analysis alone. Rather, explanation can come only through careful historical study; that is, by tracing the problem through the progressive stages of biblical tradition.

This study of the earliest stage of development in the notion of community in Israel revealed a significant result precisely in relation to this question. The dialectic found in New Testament and subsequent Christian theology was already at the heart of Israel's definition of community. And in the earliest history of this dialectic, *tôrâ* was not a realm opposed to gospel! *Tôrâ* originated as a response to gospel; that is, to God's saving activity on behalf of Hebrew slaves, who, within the context of their new freedom, sought to create patterns of community that were consistent with the righteousness and compassion of Yahweh revealed in the exodus. Nowhere in the literature of this period do we find righteousness to be a prideful posture on the basis of which the mortal sought to prove worthiness before God. Righteousness and compassion were rather qualities of a lifestyle that found their unity in humility before God; that is, in worship. This *imitatio dei* was not motivated by anxious efforts to save self, but as a response of gratitude for a deliverance already accomplished by divine grace, a response taking the form of praise in worship and a building up of communal structures that were befitting a covenant people. Growing out of a response to God's antecedent acts of mercy, righteousness was not directed inward in the manner of the "introspective consciousness of the West,"[40] but was directed outward in dedication to the construction of a healthy community, that is, a community in which a compassionate openness to those falling outside of its orbit of protection would be preserved. Moreover, righteousness oriented outward toward the *šālôm* of the whole community was not construed in terms of human achievement—which inevitably leads to the pride and exclusivism of work righteousness—but in terms of the ongoing manifestations of God's creative, redemptive activity. By deriving its existence and self-understanding from belief in the antecedent and the ongoing gracious acts of God, this was a community that felt drawn into the universal purposes of God, thereby fulfilling the Abrahamic promise of being a blessing to all nations.

Since early Yahwism's laws and communal structures arose as responses to God's acts of grace, acts that were understood to be ongoing in the course of history, neither the notion of righteousness and com-

---

40. This phrase is taken from the insightful article of K. Stendahl, an article very germane to the question of the relation of Hebrew Scripture to Christian theology, "The Apostle Paul and the Introspective Conscience of the West," *HTR* 56 (1963), 199–125; reprinted in *Paul Among Jews and Gentiles* (Philadelphia: Fortress Press, 1976), pp. 78–96.

passion nor the forms of worship and *tôrâ* were static. They too were part of the ongoing redemptive process to which Israel owed its birth, and as such were subject to constant revision and reformulation in harmony with the God who addressed each age anew. Although contributing a dynamic, progressive quality to Israel's faith, the result was not spiritual chaos, for the foundation of that faith was firmly established on the reality of the God who committed self in the revelation of the name, "I am Yahweh, who brought you out of the land of Egypt, out of the house of bondage," and in the invitation to covenant fellowship, "I shall be your God, and you will be my people." All else—laws, forms of worship, communal structures—were subservient to the one ultimate Reality revealed in that holy name. As instruments of that Reality, they were to be dedicated solely to the purposes of the one true God. If they were made subservient to any other end, such as securing the special privileges of certain classes or exploiting vulnerable members of the society, they contradicted their essential warrants, and had to be changed.

Within Israel's earliest collections of *tôrâ*, we have examined examples of this radical dedication to one object of devotion, and have observed the dynamic, progressive quality of life that it fostered. This quality is found not only in the legal traditions, however, but is an essential part of Israel's historical and legendary traditions as well. Earlier we examined some of these traditions. One final example will illustrate the point with special clarity and simplicity. It is the story of Tamar and Judah in Genesis 38.[41] Like Hannah, whose majestic hymn in praise of Yahweh, the righteous and compassionate God, served as a key to Luke's version of the gospel (Luke 1:46–55), Tamar was remembered with special favor by New Testament tradition, as indicated by her place of honor in Matthew's genealogy of Jesus (Matt. 1:3). And for good reason. Tamar's story is a gospel narrative, a story of good news to the oppressed.

To understand the Tamar story, we must dispel the usual stereotyped view of *tôrâ*, something especially difficult for many Christians to do. In this story we see one of Israel's ancient patriarchal figures confronting a young woman of his tribe who has been accused of committing adultery, and whose condition of pregnancy and widowed state seem to corroborate the accusation: "Bring her out, and let her be burned." This picture quite irresistibly calls to mind the popular misconception of the function of the law within Jewish society and of the consequences incurred by someone breaking a commandment of the Decalogue. How

41. Although it is difficult to place the development of a story like that of Tamar and Judah into a chronological framework, within the overall framework of the development of Israelite religion, it corresponds closely in spirit to early Yahwistic documents. Apparently it stems either from the formative period or from a tradition that preserved the ideals of early Yahwism.

natural it seems that punishment should take the form of death by
burning or stoning! This presupposition we bring to the text probably
derives in part from the Johannine story about the woman caught in
adultery:[42]

The scribes and Pharisees brought a woman who had been caught in adultery,
and placing her in the midst, they said to him, "Teacher, this woman has been
caught in the act of adultery. Now in the law Moses commanded us to stone
such. What do you say about her?" This they said to test him, that they might
have some charge to bring against him. (John 8:3–6a)

In this passage we find a sharp contrast between certain Jewish leaders and the teacher seeking to uphold the unity of divine righteousness
and compassion. Commonly Christians extrapolate from such texts that
the interpretation of the law attributed by certain late New Testament
traditions to the Pharisees is an accurate picture of all Pharisees, or
even of the function of law at all stages of Israelite religion.

But let us look carefully at the story of Judah and Tamar itself. The
action at first proceeds according to the popular stereotype. Judah is
informed, "Tamar your daughter-in-law has played the harlot, and
moreover she is with child by harlotry." And Judah said, "Bring her
out, and let her be burned." Now all that is in keeping with the commandments found in the Decalogue. The specific connotation is perhaps that Tamar has been consorting with other gods through cult
prostitution, and has disgraced the careful protection of sexual purity
in which her host clan prided itself. In the company of all women
through the ages who have worn the "scarlet letter," she must suffer
the terrible consequences of her sin. But from this point the story skill-
fully develops into an attack on this sentence as a superficial and heartless legalism, and indeed, it does this in a manner Christians associate
with Jesus, or Paul, or Augustine, or Luther. We are told by the narra-
tor that there is more to Tamar's story than appears on the surface,
and that to judge fairly we need to know about the total life context of
Tamar's crisis. In fact, *she* is the wronged party, having been grievously
wronged by Judah's sons Er and Onan, with the result that she has
been denied offspring. As we have seen in discussing the Book of the
Covenant, this entailed the harshest of fates in ancient society, where a
widow's only security in old age was her children. Moreover, Judah
himself had added to the hurt by deceiving her with an unkept promise
of giving to her his next son when he came of age.

Tamar is thus presented as a woman whose rights had been denied
her, and who, confident nevertheless of the rightness of action when
measured against the ultimate norms of her society, dares to press on to

---

42. The story of the woman caught in adultery is a late addition into the Gospel of
John, as indicated by the evidence of the Greek manuscripts (cf. C. H. Dodd, *The Gospel of
St. John* [London: SPCK, 1962], pp. 490–493).

a public hearing. By disguising herself as a harlot, she becomes pregnant by Judah. Thus, unknown to him, the woman on whom he proceeds to pronounce the death sentence is bearing his own child!

The closing scene is powerful, and bears witness against misconceptions concerning a rigid legalism in the early Hebrew society that could expose the heart of *tôrâ* in the form of such a remarkable story. Tamar produces the personal belongings of Judah, which she wisely had kept from the time of their fleeting union, and then states simply, "By the man to whom these belong, I am with child . . . Mark I pray you, whose these are, the signet and the cord and the staff" (Gen. 38:25). Judah's reply is just as direct, and incorporates the courage he has encountered in this brave woman: "She is more righteous than I, inasmuch as I did not give her to my son Shelah" (Gen. 38:26).

What sort of relation between grace and law do we find here? Is it not of the same quality as that embodied by Jesus when he said, "Let him who is without sin among you be the first to throw a stone at her"? Is it not of the sort articulated by Paul, the Apostle to the Gentiles, who searched for the heart of the commandments and concluded,

The commandments, "You shall not commit adultery, You shall not kill, You shall not steal, You shall not covet," and any other commandment, are summed up in this sentence, "You shall love your neighbor as yourself." Love does no wrong to a neighbor; therefore love is the fulfilling of the law. (Rm. 13:9–10)

Is it not similar to that rediscovered by the Bishop of Hipp, who taught that God's law is ultimately love?

It would be too much to say that all God's teaching on the relation between law and grace was completed within the Hebrew Bible. But it would be an act of insensitivity and ingratitude to our Jewish heritage to miss the deep roots of that teaching in Hebrew Scripture. This becomes even clearer if we examine more closely Judah's confession: "She is more righteous than I."

The norm appealed to here is that of righteousness (*ṣĕdāqâ*). Once Judah has been shocked to his senses, his attention shifts from simply applying a law to grappling with the essential quality of "being right" before God. Why was he forced to conclude that this woman Tamar possessed this quality in a measure that he did not? To answer this question necessitates consideration of what we have learned about the early Israelite notion of covenant community as righteous community, for the Tamar story on its deepest level functions as a reflection on the true nature of righteousness within its communal context.

We have seen that the early Yahwistic community extended special protection and care to those who were helpless or vulnerable. Three classes accordingly protected by special laws in the Book of the Covenant were the alien, the widow, and the poor. Tamar belongs to all three classes! But his membership not only implied triple vulnerability, but in Israelite society triple protection as well. In this story, attention focuses primarily on the protection accorded by the levirate marriage law: if a woman's husband died, it was the responsibility of the relatives of the deceased to provide a new marriage partner and thus a means of procuring offspring. This law was treated with utter seriousness because it derived from Israel's ultimate standard of righteousness, the God who personally takes the side of the widow and orphan, and commands the people gathered in God's name to do the same. In a society modeling its life on the acts of the righteous and compassionate God Yahweh, the rights of every individual were to be honored, in this case, the rights of a woman to pass on the name of her husband to future generations and to enjoy security in old age. Relating as it did to the compassion of Israel's God, this ideal could not be regulated by external rules alone, not even by strict enforcement of the Decalogue. It called for attitudes and actions between indivudals that embodied God's compassion and that thus enhanced the wholeness of the entire community. Judah's original actions, although correct to the letter of the law, violated the spirit of the covenant. Tamar's actions, while breaking the letter of law, grew out of a profound understanding of the meaning of the community of faith in which the widow is protected and allowed to contribute to the health of the whole body. This then is the meaning of Judah's honest confession: "She is more righteous than I."

The Tamar story thus gives flesh and blood to the essential qualities of early Israelite community we described above by a more formal analysis. It was a society ordered by law, as every stable society must be. In fact, its standard of righteousness was very stringent in comparison with neighboring societies, in keeping with a lofty concept of divine holiness and fidelity. It was, moreover, a society according special protection to vulnerable members such as the widow. But due to the penetrating view of human relationships derived from the encounter with the compassionate Deliverer God Yahweh, Israel was aware of an abiding truth: all good intentions of wise lawmakers notwithstanding, the quality of compassion—that alone can safeguard an ordered society against a harsh legalism that oppressed the weak—cannot be codified. While important in its function of influencing the form that laws assume, ultimately its only reliable habitation is in the hearts of those who make decisions and hold leadership positions in the community. And that habitation can be established only relationally; that is, on the basis of personal example that is compelling by its steadfastness and truthfulness.

Israel's hope of maintaining a compassionate heart within the ordering structures of *tôrâ* derived from faith in the righteous, compassionate Deliverer God Yahweh, a faith nutured by memory of Yahweh's saving acts. Within the drama of this story, the convert Tamar knew of the stringency of the laws protecting this society from decay. But for a Canaanite widow, on the fringe of the protective structures of this community, the more important knowledge was of the nature of the Author of those laws, the righteous and compassionate God who was moved to action by the cry of the oppressed widow.

This story allows us to glimpse how the early Israelite community used its patriarchal traditions to show how the exodus faith and its radical social ramifications had deep roots reaching back to Israel's most ancient ancestors. In hory antiquity, God had already promised to bless Abraham with a land and abundant offspring and to make him a blessing to the nations. Even in the life of the Canaanite widow Tamar, the staedfastness and fidelity of God to those promises were visible in God's assuring her a place in the family of Judah. Naturally, those giving form to this story were mindful of the long history that lay ahead in God's relating to this family, but that history of change would not detract from, but only substantiate, the faithfulness of God to those original promises. To Tamar, as to Hannah, God was the righteous and compassionate God who called people into a community where ordering structures provided a home for a loving heart. The commonality between the story of Tamar and the Book of the Covenant is thus unmistakable:

You shall not wrong a stranger or oppress him, for you were strangers in the land of Egypt. You shall not afflict any widow or orphan. If you do afflict them, and they cry out to me, I will surely hear their cry; and my wrath will burn, and I will kill you with the sword, and your wives shall become widows and your children fatherless. (Exod. 22:21–24)

Not only is the story of Tamar compatible with the attitude toward tôrâ which we have seen in Matthew and Paul, but it exemplifies the remarkable notion of community that is the tap root out of which would grow God's new people in Christ, a people living from the promises of the God who saves the weak and the oppressed. The meaning of the church will be grasped, therefore, not by denying that root, but by carefully tracing its history of growth. It is a long way from the radical experimentation of freed slaves with new forms of social structure like those embodied in the notion of the Jubilee year to Jesus' announcement that he was commissioned "to proclaim the acceptable year of the Lord." But it is a path that repays patience with a deeper understanding of the God whose faithfulness extends from Abrahamic promise to the vision of a universal kingdom of righteousness and peace. Only such historical study of our confessional ancestry, for example, can provide a basis for an understanding of important theological polarities such as law and gospel, an understanding capable of avoiding both one-sided solutions and shallow compromises.

As shown in subsequent chapters, this approach to the question of the biblical basis for understanding contemporary communities of faith does not result in a denial of the central importance of the New Testament for a proper understanding of Christianity. The study of roots does not result in an equating of periods of persons. Moses and Jesus are not identical. What a historical approach to this theological problem does exemplify, however, is that the righteous and compassionate God who was present so fully in Christ most surely was active in the Mosaic era to redeem the human family. The history of Western Christianity verifies the importance of this thesis, for where the roots of the new covenant in the first covenant have been neglected, a host of demons have followed: privatistic piety, abdication of social responsibility, a narrow sectarianism, neglect of caring for the realm of nature, anti-Semitism, and shallow theology. An adequate appreciation of the community of faith in the Hebrew Bible alone is able to outline the parameters within which the act of God in Christ can be understood in its amazing fulness, which is an important preliminary step both in the effort to understand and renew the Christian communities of faith and to enrich and deepen understanding between Judaism and Christianity.

IV

The Yahwistic Notion
of Community Tested
and Refined: The Age of Kings
and Prophets
(1 and 2 Samuel, 1 Kings, and the Psalms)

> *Historical Note:* The early Yahwistic notion of community,
> which was born of the experience of divine deliverance from
> the oppressive structures of an absolute monarchy, was sub-
> jected to a severe testing with the introducion of monarchy
> into Israel. This chapter draws on 1 and 2 Samuel, 1 Kings,
> and the Psalter to describe the impact that this new political
> development had on community structures and ideals in the
> period of the united monarchy under Saul, David, and Solo-
> mon (1029–932 B.C.E.).

A. FROM EARLY YAHWISM TO PROPHETIC YAHWISM

Chapter III described the birth of a dynamic notion of community
among a people seeking to discern the meaning of its recent passage
from bondage to freedom, finding that meaning in a confession of divine deliverance, and then giving expression to that confession in forms
of worship and communal structures aimed at preserving a quality of life
drawn from the example of a righteous and compassionate God. There
is, of course, always the danger of idealizing the origins of such a notion,
a tendency often encountered in the epic literature of a people and expressing itself in a "golden age" mentality. As the stories found in the
Pentateuch and the Deuteronomistic History (Deuteronomy through 2
Kings) indicate, however, early Israel resisted such a romantic picture of
its origins. Rather, this notion of community, with its profound sense of
worship and moral responsibility, emerged not within an idyllic setting,
but amid the same type of historical ambiguity and human frailty that
characterizes human experiences in general. The dominant mood in early Israel was not one of deep gratitude seeking expression in worship and

acts of moral commitment. More often than not the hymns of the faithful were drowned out by the grumbling complaints of the masses and by cowardly requests to be returned to the security of the earlier bondage. One is impressed by the verisimilitude of the biblical portrait of the majority rebelling against its spiritual leaders and adopting the wanton practices of its neighbors. Far from the conglomeration of peoples subsequently drawn into its tribal organization being infused with Yahweh's righteous compassion, they instead slipped into a manner of life that, as portrayed by the Book of Judges, amounted to a rather indistinguishable mixture of Yahwism and Canaanite Baalism.

What is remarkable about early Yahwism, then, is not the people as such, but rather the fact that such a unique notion of community could survive, and even develop, under such inhospitable, and often downright hostile, circumstances. How is it that in the period of the judges Yahwism did not simply succumb to the powerful lure of Baalism? The latter was the religious system that most immediately addressed the agrarian life the Hebrews came to adopt. As they adopted many of the festivals, symbols, and customs of their Canaanite neighbors, how was it that they did not blend back into the ancient Near Eastern mythopoeic environment from which they had emerged?

The answer must be that some Hebrews had been captivated on a sufficiently profound level by the memory of the Deliverer God of the exodus to keep alive the dynamic process of becoming that allowed the Yahwistic notion of community to grow with new experiences, even adverse ones, rather than to cling blindly to earlier confessions until they no longer addressed new experiences or to regress into the static repose of the chthonian and fertility cults of Canaan. We are able to understand neither the transmission history of biblical narrative nor the actual history of the community of faith in Israel without a clear recognition of this essential fact. This memory of deliverance, representing for the faithful "the absolute surety of Yahweh's will be save,"[1] constituted the basis of a historical faith that was both durable and dynamic. In fact, it was because of this "absolute surety" that early Yahwism could be flexible in adapting to new circumstances without losing its distinctive identity. Since Yahweh was faithful to the covenant and was the trustworthy sovereign of the world, Israel could expect of events evidence of the further unfolding of divine purpose. This posture was not conducive to a religion of ethereal tranquility, for the events of Israel's history were often ambiguous and thus troubling for those seeking to interpret them from the perspective of a faithful God. But this posture allowed Yahwism to be an extremely durable faith while yet remaining capable of remarkable adaptability and growth.

Chapter III described this characteristic of early Yahwism in relation

---

1. G. von Rad, *Old Testament Theology*, Vol. 1, trans. D. M. G. Stalker (New York: Harper & Row, 1962), p. 176.

to the self-disclosure of the divine name. In revealing God's self as Yahweh, Israel's God made a commitment to eternal trustworthiness and fidelity. But as the God who not only acted to create and save in the past, but who would continue to do so in the future, the relative clauses amplifyng the divine name, and revealing new aspects of the divine mystery, were not frozen, but were capable of dynamic growth. This chapter discusses a testing of this dialectic of durability and adaptability that proved to be more severe than any previous one. In this case the amplificaiton of the divine name took the form, "who gives victory to kings, who rescuest David his servant" (Ps. 144:10). How this new confession could be related to the earlier Yahwistic confession in "Yahweh, who brought you out of the house of bondage," involves a truly intriguing story. Could the old belief in Yahweh as the sole king of Israel be combined with a royal ideology according to which God binds self by oath to the king by promising to establish the king's reign forever (2 Sam. 7 and Ps. 89)? And could this accommodation be accomplished without sacrificing those essential qualities that give rise to the early Yahwistic notion of community? Tracing how these questions were answered demonstrates a transformation in the biblical notion of community as it passed from early Yahwism to prophetic Yahwism.

B. SAUL AND SAMUEL

In tracing the development of Israel's notion of community during the early years of the monarchy, one is confronted with the rich but complicated evidence in 1 Samuel. As in the Book of Judges, the final form of the book has been shaped from the perspective of the theological program of the Deuteronomistic school. The essential lines of the book were already present, however, in the antecedent tradition used by the Deuteronomists, which interpreted the careers of Israel's early kings from a prophetic perspective. This tradition in turn incorporated older sources, some of which are remarkable for their historiographic quality, especially the Succession Narrative (2 Sam. 9–20 and 1 Kings 1–2). Other old sources used were the History of Saul's Rise (1 Sam. 9–10:16; 11; and 14), and the Ark Narrative (1 Sam. 4–6 and 2 Sam. 6).

Of the Saul material, the narrative in 1 Samuel 10:27b–11:15 seems to give the most accurate account of the circumstances that led to his being anointed king. In important respects, the narrative follows the pattern found in the stories of the early judges. In this case, the threat is described as arising out of an Ammonite attack on Jabesh-Gilead. The cry of the people was answered by Yahweh's spirit coming mightily on Saul, who mustered the tribes in the characteristic manner of the charismatic leader, and then led them to victory. The final stage in the League pattern would have followed naturally, according to which the šôpēṭ, after having performed his or her duty, would have returned to his or her position within the local clan. But the departure from the pattern we now note points to the introduction of a change, subtle in its starting point, but pregnant with future implications for Israel's understanding of community. The departure was this: Saul does not return to his field in Gibeah: "So all the people went to Gilgal, and there they made Saul king before the Lord Gilgal. There they sacrificed peace offerings before the Lord, and there Saul and the men of Israel rejoiced greatly" (1 Sam. 11:15).

We see in this narrative both continuity and change in relation, for example, to the Song of Deborah. In the later, under Yahweh's guidance, a number of tribes went out to defeat the common enemy. Yahwism was the unifying factor that gave the diverse clans their sense of solidarity in war. Similarly, in 1 Samuel Saul's own tribe of Benjamin was joined by others (perhaps Ephraim and the Galilean tribes) under the same God. In this case, however, a further step toward solidarity was taken, in the naming of the deliverer to a *permanent* office. In all likelihood, this measure was taken to increase the capability of the tribes to defend themselves against the increasing threats coming from all sides. The new unstable condition, caused especially by the aggressiveness of the Philistines, seemed to demand a new, centralized form of leadership.

What was the nature of this new form of leadership? Its essential features were twofold: (1) designation by Yahweh, and (2) acclamation by the people.[2] In continuity with the early Yahwistic notion of the Judges period, there was to be no leader over God's people except by God's own choosing. The thoroughly spiritual nature of the people as Yahweh's chosen nation was thereby acknowledged in the form of divine designation of the anointed ruler. This feature combined with the second, moreover, to thwart the efforts of ambitious opportunists (in the style of Abimelech, son of Jerrubbabel, in Judges 9) to build up a base of power from which to impose their personal claims on the people. The role of the people in the acclamation of the king preserved the democratic dimension in the Yahwistic community, which derived from its birth in the exodus.[3]

These two essential features allow us to designate the kingship bestowed on Saul by the people as a "limited kingship." Moreover, the source of these features, which placed strict limits on the power of kings, is unmistakable—namely, the early Yahwistic notion of community. After all, the group gathered in this acclamation of Saul's leadership was not an amorphous or *ad hoc* entity. It was the Yahwistic com-

2. Cf. A. Alt, "The Formation of the Israelite State in Palestine," *Essays in Old Testament History and Religion*, trans. R. A. Wilson (New York: Doubleday, 1968), pp. 225–309.
3. Cf. S. Herrmann, *A History of Israel in Old Testament Times*, trans. J. Bowden (Philadelphia: Fortress Press, 1981), pp. 131–137.

munity gathered once again at its oldest cult center of Gilgal.[4] Here followers of Yahweh introduced a new form of rule at the holy shrine that more than any other reminded them of their primal confession of Yahweh's deliverance from oppression. Clearly, that confession would influence the conception of kingship they were willing to adopt. Negatively stated, any form of kingship contradicting Yahweh's sole lordship over the people would have been repudiated by those adhering to the cherished beliefs of early Yahwism. On that central confession was based (1) the standard of righteousness that safeguarded them against re-enslavement and (2) the quality of compassion that disallowed their becoming oppressors of others.

On the other hand, why did the people move as far as they did in the direction of a different form of leadership? Did not even the move of making the charismatic office permanent contradict the radical anti-monarchical bias of Yahwism, which had come to expression, for example, in the Gideon story? There the narrative sources had spoken of the flat repudiation of kingship based on the sole claim reserved for Yahweh:

Then the men of Israel said to Gideon, "Rule over us, you and your son and your grandson also; for you have delivered us out of the hand of Midian." Gideon said to them, "I will not rule over you, and my son will not rule over you; the Lord will rule over you." (Judg. 8:22–23)

What were the actual historical circumstances accompanying the introduction of kingship under Saul? Although the traditions preserved in Judges and 1 Samuel reflect a complex history of transmission, they do seem to indicate that a persistent groundswell of opposition, even to limited notions of kingship, existed from earliest times in Israel, an attitude consonant with tribalism. Supporting this judgment are the stories treating Saul's career: he is portrayed as a tragic figure destroyed by his internalizing the tension between early Yahwism and the innovations his office represented. The running conflict between him and Samuel perhaps rests on reliable historical memory, and surely preserves the strains within Yahwism during the early monarchy. Moreover, the evidence supports the majority view in biblical scholarship today, which rejects the earlier tendency to regard the strand of tradition in Samuel that is critical of kingship as late and historically unreliable. It seems more accurate to ascribe an early origin to both of the traditions now fused in 1 Samuel, the one kindly disposed to kingship, the other bitterly opposed.[5]

---

4. Alt emphasizes the decisive role of earlier covenant tradition in this ceremony at Gilgal, for here we see the tribes "paying homage, not on the battlefield, but far away from it in a holy place, so that the whole procedure was under the guarantee and control of Yahweh, which was necessary to any 'covenant' in the Israelite sense of the word." Alt, *Essays*, pp. 254–254.

5. Cf. A. Weiser, *Samuel. Seine geschichtliche Aufgabe und religiose Bedeutung*, FRLANT 8 (Göttingen: Vandenhoeck and Ruprecht, 1962); P. K. McCarter, *I Samuel*, AB 8 (Garden City, N.Y.: Doubleday, 1980), pp. 12–30.

In other words, the tension inherent in the sources should not be attributed to the late introduction of a prophetic perspective. One expects rather that early Yahwism, by its very nature, would have been constrained to be critical of Saul's new office. That Yahwistic community gathered at its ancient shrine initially could see Yahweh's designation behind Saul's success and thereby add its acclamation is perhaps understandable under the circumstances. Its survival was at stake. Yahweh did not will its destruction under the enemy. Yahweh, through the more steady leadership of the "permanent judge," would protect them. This anointing could have been interpreted as further manifestation of divine protection and compassion. But that re-evaluation would resurface as soon as circumstances permitted reflection and the expression of dissenting opinion is equally plausible. It is clear that later tradition, especially under the inspiration of the prophets who came to regard themselves as the guardians of the early Yahwistic faith, elaborated on the theme of resistance to kingship. However, there is no reason to doubt that the roots of this criticism are as old as the office of kingship itself.

The time of Saul, therefore, introduced a *novum*, but a carefully limited one. Yahweh alone could designate the king, and if the king was unfaithful to his commission, he could readily be dismissed by Yahweh—as Saul in fact was. F. M. Cross correctly observes, "Certainly Saul's exaltation to the office of *nāgîd* or *mêlek*, 'king,' was conceived by the tribesmen as a conditional appointment or covenant, so long as the 'Spirit of God' was upon him, and so long as he did not violate the legal traditions or constitution of the league."[6] This limited concept of kingship excluded by definition the dynastic principle subsequently introduced by David and Solomon. In fact, implicit in the concept was a standard for evaluating kingship that would later be refined and then vigorously applied by the prophets, a standard resting squarely on the early Yahwistic notion of community examined in Chapter III. In a community tracing its origins to the antecedent gracious acts of Yahweh and understanding its existence as a response to the sole lordship of that God, a form of leadership that preserved the Yahwistic triad of righteousness, compassion, and worship from inner and outer threat was compatible with its cherished values. But any form of leadership that drew the attention of the people away from that righteousness, compassion, and sole worship of Yahweh by fostering *self*-glorification of the earthly king and of the elite of the nation contradicted the very heart of Yahwistic faith. It would invoke powerful resistance, for the early followers of Yahweh were unaccustomed to the language of high royal ideology, such as the following:

---

6. F. M. Cross, *CMHE*, 221

Therefore God, your God, has anointed you
  with the oil of gladness above your fellows;
  your robes are all fragrant with
    myrrh and aloes and cassia.
From ivory palaces stringed
  instruments make you glad;
  daughters of kings are among
    your ladies of honor;
  at your right hand stands the
    queen in gold of Ophir. (Ps. 45:7–9)

That kingship could become a spiritual snare was likely feared already during Saul's reign. The social background of the members of this community, including their inherited clan values and their memory of suffering under foreign kings, in itself makes such suspicion comprehensible. Powerfully reinforcing this suspicion was the central confession of Yahwism, that Israel's God made self known precisely in opposing the power of the king of Egypt. Yahweh's kingship of righteousness and compassion was diametrically opposed to the unjust and unmerciful reign of earthly kings.

In the attempt to understand the problematic posed by kingship for early Yahwism, it is instructive to notice how the communal qualities of righteousness, compassion, and worship, as defined in Chapter III, were at the basis of the tradition of criticism of kingship that developed during the course of the tradition history of 1 Samuel. For example, already in the pre-Deuteronomistic stratum found in 1 Samuel 8 (excluding the Deuteronomistic addition in v. 9), the practices of Israel's future king are described by Samuel. The repetitive pattern is striking: "He will take your X to be his Y." All that was most dear to the people would be taken by the king to add to his luxury and military might. The list concludes with this terse summary statement: "and *you* shall be *his* slaves." In other words, the social system the kings would introduce would violate the very heart of the early Yahwistic notion of community; that is, the quality of righteousness that protected the rights of each individual, including the weak and the vulnerable. Instead, the king would establish his own self-serving standards in the place of Yahweh's holy ones; for example, he would tax the people and give the proceeds to his own retainers; he would take their sons and daughters and force them into military and police service.

By locking the people into structures that defined some members as lords and others as slaves, the openness of the community—which was the fitting reflection of divine compassion for the alien and the outcast—was also repudiated. And with exact perceptiveness, the source of this twofold perversion of early Yahwistic values is located in the third and fundamental quality of the early Yahwistic community, sole worship of Yahweh: "They have rejected me from being king over them." In a profound theological sense, then, the type of leadership the people chose was a reflection of, and thus a judgment on, their own perverted values. Hegel maintained that the king of any nation embodied the values of his people. That opinion is already expressed by the tradition of criticisms found in 1 Samuel. Why was Israel's king characterized by greed, hubris, and lust for personal power and glory:

But the people refused to listen to the voice of Samuel; and they said, "No! but we will have a king over us, that we also may be like all the nations, and that our king may govern us and go out before us and fight our battles." (1 Sam. 8:19–20).

Thus at the beginning of Israel's experience with kingship, we find the basis of a tradition of criticism that would extend throughout the history of prophecy. Kings and nation would be evaluated on the basis of the qualities discerned in Yahweh's own acts, namely, righteousness and compassion. And ultimately these qualities could be incorporated by the people and their leaders only to the extent that they were integrated within the context of worship of the one true God.

But if kingship represented such an ambivalent phenomenon in Israel, being necessary for national defense and yet being a threat to the fundamental qualities of the Yahwistic faith, how could Yahwism respond? Granted, threats were not new to Yahwism. From the early moments of communal life under Yahweh, and certainly throughout the period of the judges, Yahwism was assailed by various threats, such as the impatience of the people, the lure of Baalism, and the aggression of hostile neighbors. And in each instance courageous leaders responded in a succession that seemed from the perspective of faith to be attributable to the providential grace of Yahweh, a belief some supported by reference to the charisma that seemed to characterize the savior judges. Within the circles of faithful Yahwists who resisted the syncretizing tendencies of the period of the judges, the alternative vision of early Yahwism managed to maintain itself.

As severe as was the testing of the judges period for the young faith, a more difficult time was to follow. No previous threat to Yahwistic faith could equal that posed by the introduction of kingship into Israel. A community had visualized itself as a social protest community offering to the persecuted and the disenfranchised an alternative to the oppression of the normative societies of antiquity by relating all life to the standards and purposes of the one true God. This people stood in danger of being transformed by national greed and royal hubris into a society construing itself as normative in its own right and for its own sake, and capable of inflicting oppression and inequality matching that of any other kingdom. Saul thus came at the beginning of a period in Israelite history that raised fundamental questions regarding the future of the Yahwistic community. For the sake of survival, would it have to make concessions that would obliterate its essential character? Or stubbornly clinging to its primitive values and beliefs, would it sacrifice itself in a futile struggle against inevitable change? Would its early successes under the royal scepter lead it to emulate the prideful ways of other kingdoms, and thus to sacrifice its distinctiveness? Or, in nostalgically clinging to the archaic customs of its tribal militia, would it be ground into the earth by a mighty movement of warring peoples extending from the crumbling Mycenaean Empire to the waters of the Nile, the Tigris, and the Euphrates?

These are not simple questions. At no point in either the united or the divided monarchy could they be answered with a clear yes or no. They point to a tension woven into the very fabric of Yahwism in the age of monarchy. Kingship, messiah, royal dynasty, Davidic covenant, unconditional divine promise—these and similar phenomena were the stuff of a bitter struggle for self-definition and survival. Like Saul or David or Solomon, they were not *ipso facto* either pro- or anti-Yahwistic. They were rather forms, concepts, and structures capable of being applied either on the side of or against Yahwistic faith and the humane ideals to which it was dedicated.[7]

It is not even possible to give an unequivocal answer to the question, "Did the early Yahwistic notion of community end or continue with the dawn of kingship?" With Israel's desire to become "like the other nations," there was no doubt an ending, an ending within certain circles united around the Gilgal cult, of an idealistic vitality, sacrificed—perhaps inevitably from the perspective of normal processes of social change—as an aspect of passage from communal infancy to civil maturity. But the Bible is in a real sense a story of many endings and beginnings, which can be explained theologically in light of the biblical concept of God's covenant fidelity (*ḥēsed*). The Genesis story did not end with the expulsion of Adam and Eve from the garden, though the expulsion was in a sense an important ending. For even the passage from what Tillich called "dreaming innocence" into the harsher "existence" of their descendants outside of Eden can be seen as a beginning, a beginning of the drama of God's struggle with the human race as we humans experience it.[8]

Similarly in the transformation from Samuel to Saul, an ending would carry with it promise of a new beginning. While it proved to be a very precarious beginning, its very ambiguity and complexity relates authentically to our own difficult world. If some Israelites had retained romantic notions of being a perfect people under God, their "dream-

---

7. P. D. Hanson, *The Diversity of Scripture* (Philadelphia: Fortress Press, 1982), pp. 14–36.

8. P. Tillich, *Systematic Theology*, Vol. 2 (Chicago: University of Chicago Press, 1957), pp. 28–44.

ing innocence" was rudely replaced by a harsher realism: judged on the basis of political or social structures, this was a nation like any other. But this harsher realism did bear with it the possibility of a new beginning, characterized by a deepending of the Yahwistic community's understanding of what it meant to be God's people. Since the meaning of Israel's being a people of God could not be understood along nationalistic lines, those wishing to define their spiritual identity would have to search more deeply. They would have to look to less tangible, more essential qualities, such as righteousness, compassion, and faith, taking Yahweh's covenant fidelity as a starting point. And they would have to be prepared to struggle to preserve these qualities in the face of political structures and social practices that often contradicted the principles of Yahwism.

But in such an ambivalent situation, could this people keep the earlier Yahwistic vision alive, and thereby continue to function as bearer of hope to the oppressed within Israel and beyond? The answer that arose during the period of the monarchy was totally in keeping with the compassionate righteousness manifested in Yahweh's deliverance of slaves from bondage. The Yahwistic notion of community could be preserved only by a renewed struggle on the part of the righteous God Yahweh and Yahweh's followers against the ungodly oppressors of this world. And since the latter now included many of Israel's own leaders, the struggle entered a new phase: God was now perceived as having to enter into controversy with God's own people, in order to prevent the slave-vision from being reduced to the worldly pragmatics of kings. God turned to an oppressed minority within Israel in search of a faithful community, dedicated to preserving the Yahwistic principles of righteousness, compassion, and undivided worship. But whom could this persevering God find to serve as mediators in this struggle? The age of the savior judges, when God's spirit seemed to designate and fill the people's leaders, seemed to be past. Unlike the judges before them, who had returned to their farms after battles had been fought, Israel's kings, knowing that their term of rule extended over a lifetime, frequently turned to plans motivated by personal ambition. The remnant that remained dedicated to the righteous rule of Yahweh accordingly felt the call to rise up in opposition to those worldly plans.

In the new situation, one thing was very clear. The introduction of kingship had represented a fundamental *institutional* change. And if Yahwism was to survive, and if its notion of community was to remain a creative and redemptive force in the nation, its response had to be institutionally commensurate. The institutionally commensurate response of Yahwism to kingship was *prophetism*. Prophetism was the new Yahwistic office that arose to cope with the new civil office of kingship. In large part, then, the struggle between Yahwism and forces seeking to distract from its essential nature was carried on between kings and prophets. It is no accident that prophecy comes on the scene with the introduction of kingship, and ceases with the demise of kingship. It is accurate to observe, moreover, that the offices of king and prophet can be understood as a splitting of the office of the charismatic *šôpēṭ* ("judge") into its two component parts. The civil duties of the *šôpēṭ*, involving rule, civil judgment, and war, fell to the king. The spiritual duties of being spokesperson for Yahweh, of calling the people to holy war on behalf of the oppressed against the oppressor, of holding up to the people God's standards of righteousness and compassion, of calling them to sole worship of the one true God, and of threatening judgment for sin, fell to the prophet. And in keeping with the egalitarianism of the early Yahwistic notion of community, according to which no member of the community was excluded from either the promises or the curses of the covenant, kings were measured by the prophets against the same standards as all other classes of the population. Indeed, their heightened visibility and responsibility attracted the particularly close scrutiny of the prophets. When they deviated from the standards of the Yahwistic covenant, the prophets threatened them with judgment. In the case where kings grew resolute in their opposition to divine will, prophets did not hestitate to declare that Yahweh had nullified the kings' mandate to rule. The prophets could even announce that Yahweh had declared war against the king and nation. Thus the institution of prophecy developed as a sort of counterbalance to kingship. In the office of the prophet was preserved the immediacy of God's presence that earlier had been manifested by the charisma of the *šôpēṭ*. For example, designation of the king by the prophet indicated that it was God who appointed kings, to which the people could only add their acclamation. And in the office of the prophet, the participation of all the people in the community of faith was kept alive, for the prophets acted to "muster the clans" in opposition to every foe, domestic or foreign, who threatened the fundamental qualities of the Yahwistic covenant.

In 1 Samuel, Samuel, the last judge, is also portrayed as the first prophet, as he carries out the responsibilities just described. Samuel is thus a figure of pivotal significance. This is the portrait given by the Deuteronomistic redactors, but it also characterized the underlying prophetic stratum drawn on by the eighth-century Deuteronomists. And there is no reason to doubt that this role originated in historical realities. Through Samuel, Yahweh spoke to the people. Samuel spoke on behalf of the early Yahwistic values in the process of selecting a king. Samuel sought to guide Saul along the strictly defined path of limited kingship, and finally Samuel pronounced Yahweh's hard word of rejection when Saul failed. The various levels of tradition in 1 Samuel document the development of prophetic thought regarding kingship, and the responsibilities of Yahwistic prophecy vis-á-vis kingship. The tradition history underlying 1 Samuel is a particularly complex one.[9] Nevertheless, a pre-Deuteronomistic prophetic tradition, which is faithful to the fundamental principles of Yahwism in its critique of kingship, is discernible running throughout the materials used by the later editors. This tradition of prophetic tradition is comprehensible only as the outgrowth of a premonarchical form of Yahwism that was organized along the decentralized lines of a tribal confederacy. Ancient societies organized from the beginning as monarchies simply did not generate the persistent antimonarchical critique that persisted throughout Israel's history.

Within the history of that prophetic critique, 1 Samuel 12 stands as a stately monument. In Samuel's farewell address, a clear profile is drawn, that of the prophet who throughout his career has stood on the side of righteousness and compassion: "You have not defrauded us or oppressed us or taken anything from any man's hand" (v. 40), truly a picture of even-handed justice. Implicit in this profile was, of course, a contrast with that of the king given in chapter 8, one consisting of injustice and mercilessness! Moreover, the prophet was the one empowered by Yahweh's Spirit, as the thunderstorm described in verses 16–18 emphatically demonstrated. The passage concludes with one of the most intriguing insights into the relationship between kings and prophets found in the Old Testament:

And all the people said to Samuel, "Pray for your servants to the Lord your God, that we may not die; for we have added to all our sins this evil, to ask for ourselves a king." And Samuel said to the people, "Fear not; you have done all this evil, yet do not turn aside from following the Lord, but serve the Lord with all your heart; and do not turn aside after vain things which cannot profit or save, for they are vain. For the Lord will not cast away his people, for his great name's sake, because it has pleased the Lord to make you a people for himself. Moreover as for me, far be it from me that I should sin against the Lord by ceasing to pray for you; and I will instruct you in the good and the right way. Only fear the Lord and serve him faithfully with all your heart; for consider what great things he has done for you. But if you still do wickedly, you shall be swept away, both you and your king." (1 Sam. 12:19–25)

Here we see how Yahwism, now under the guidance of Yahweh's "gadflies" the prophets, would be enabled to live forth courageously into the new era. Neither co-option nor resignation would characterize its response. Rather, the fundamental qualities of righteousness, compassion, and true worship would enlighten the path for the faithful,

---

9. For an analysis of the various traditions brought together in 1 Samuel, see T. N. D. Mettinger, *King and Messiah: The Civil and Sacramental Legitimation of Israelite Kings* (Lund: Gleerup, 1976), pp. 80–98; P. K. McCarter, *I Samuel*, pp. 12–30. B. C. Birch, *The Rise of the Israelite Monarchy: The Growth and Development of I Samuel 7–15*, SBLDS 27 (Missoula, Montana: Scholars Press, 1976); and B. Halpern, *The Constitution of the Monarchy*, HSM 25 (Chico, Calif.: Scholars Press, 1981), pp. 340–381.

even under harshly altered circumstances. Against that standard all institutions and human actions would be judged, and from that standard life would be infused with transforming power.

The religious realism of the passage is truly remarkable. In the election of the king, Yahwism had suffered a serious setback. What could be done? In a mythopoeic faith, return to the timeless *Urzeit*, the pristine original state, could be resorted to. From within the historical realism of Yahwism, the situation was different. In contrast to the world of the Olympian or Mesopotamian gods, Yahweh was not a heavenly actor who deigned not to become sullied by mundane affairs. Yahweh chose to encounter humans within the flux of history. Accordingly, new developments in the realm of history could not be ignored, but needed to be interpreted. Thus the prophets did not preserve the early Yahwistic ideal of the covenant community by elevating it to a supermundane level where it could not be challenged by historical changes. The temptation to spiritualize the sacral realm into a strictly heavenly concept was resisted. Instead the prophets took up the battle of interpreting the principles of their faith in relation to the new political developments. They deemed it their duty to bring the newly introduced structures into conformity with the fundamental qualities of their faith. In this process, the new was not romanticized or idealized. The sinister potential of the new kingship was recognized, and was traced to its source in the sinfulness and lack of trust of the people: "for we have added to all our sins this evil, to ask for ourselves a king." On the other hand, neither was the new kingship ignored. It was, rather, taken into full account in the attempt to chart a trustworthy path into the future: "Fear not; you have done all this evil, yet do not turn aside from following the Lord." This phrase paints the vast backdrop of the religious struggle of the monarchy period. Within this tension of "done evil . . . yet . . . ," prophecy would carry on the struggle for righteousness and compassion. There no longer being any doubt about the nation being *peccator*, the prophets would turn to the struggle of keeping alive the possibility that could arise only from divine grace and forgiveness: *simul justus*. There being no question of the worthiness of a people who would reject Yahweh's kingship in favor of a human reign, the prophets would call attention to the only remaining hope: "The Lord will not cast away his people, for his great name's sake."

The passage goes on, moreover, to outline the role of prophecy in this new situation: "Moreover, as for me," Samuel says, "far be it from me that I should sin against the Lord by ceasing to pray for you; and I will instruct you in the good and the right way." There might yet be a future beyond their great sin. Yahweh would not abandon the people. He would still accompany them on the precarious journey ahead through his mediators, the prophets. True, kings would rule over them, and as a reflection of their own lust for glory, these kings would abide as a potential snare for them. But alongside their civil ruler would be the spiritual one, as a reminder that the fundamental qualities of Yahwism could never be reduced to or regulated by a civil structure. Prophecy would keep alive the battle of transforming rule in Israel to Yahweh's sole rule. And that meant that the prophets would seek to draw even the structures of kingship into conformity with the righteousness, compassion, and worship that formed the heart of the Yahwistic community from the beginning. That some of the structures of kingship, however, drew heavily on an ideology resistant to the reform efforts of the prophets, became painfully clear already in the reigns of the two kings who followed David. Israel did not wait long for her bitter instruction in "the ways of the king who shall reign over them" (1 Sam. 8:9). Eventually, therefore, the prophets would find the bittersweet diet of faith in Yahweh and disappointment with the reigning kings directing their attention to plans Yahweh had for this people in an era beyond the age of earthly kings. Over the course of the monarchy, the prophets became increasingly aware that most of Israel's kings were not fostering Yahweh's order of šālôm but were leading the people into a disorder so complete that it could be overcome only by the creative power of the God who in hoary antiquity had created a universe out of murky chaos. This awareness eventually led to the transmutation of prophecy into apocalyptic.

C. DAVID AND NATHAN

The form of kingship that arose when the people accepted Saul as their permanent military commander was shaped by the abiding dynamism of early Yahwism. In accord with its theological and communal principles, Saul was obliged to act within the carefully defined restraints of a "limited monarchy." And it is the unified testimony of the various traditions in the Bible that he was tormented and torn by the tensions this limited role raised. The final result of these tensions was the ignominious fall of Israel's first king and his house. F.M. Cross identifies the source of this fall in the old Yahwistic tradition of the League period: "All our sources, whatever their attitude towards the nascent monarchy, are in accord in reporting that Saul forfeited the kingship, for himself and his house, by his breach of old law, namely by attempts (in one way or another) to manipulate the fixed forms of holy war in his own interests."[10] Tenaciously the faithful Yahwists maintained their commitment to the integration of life in devotion to one Lord, Yahweh. The king who drew attention away from God toward himself placed himself under the curse of the covenant. Saul's fall is thus testimony to the abiding vitality of early Yahwism during the reign of Israel's first, tragic king.

---

10. F. M. Cross, *CMHE*, p. 221.

David's rise to power occurred under circumstances that continued to bode ill for the Israelites. Saul's ignominious defeat at Gilboa left the young kingdom on the brink of collapse. The cause of antimonarchical Yahwists was strengthened by Saul's failure. But nevertheless, the awesome threat posed by the Philistines called for greater centralization, not a reversion to the loose, archaic structures of the League. Unlike Saul, however, David was equal to the challenge, and his keen strategy and remarkable success left a deep imprint on future generations, especially in the Southern Kingdom of Judah, but also in post exilic apocalyptic circles.

The History of David's Rise (1 Sam. 16:14 to 2 Sam. 5) gives a vivid description of David's path to power. As Saul, David began his career as a charismatic leader, but he added astonishing cunning and political prowess. Having fled from the jealous wrath of his father-in-law the king, he established as his base in the South a condottiere. He went on to win the trust of the Judean people through his courage and generosity. In the description of the band that gathered around David in 1 Samuel 22:2, one senses a line of continuity with the liberation movement to which early Yahwism traced its birth: "And every one who was in distress, and every one who was in debt, and every one who was discontented, gathered to him; and he became captain over them." One can readily understand how David was embraced by Yahwists as one who would both protect them for the enemy (cf. 1 Sam. 23:1–13 and 1 Sam. 24–26) and support their cherished traditions. And it seems that David strove to honor that trust, as the following description indicates.

The essential duality of what is commonly designated with the one name "Israel" is clearly seen in the double anointing of David. First he was anointed king in Hebron by the elders of Judah (2 Sam. 2:4). Only after Abner (Saul's general) and Ishbaal (Saul's son) were ruined by intrigue and blood—through which David, again with consummate skill, managed to maintain an image of innocence—a delegation representing the tribe of Israel came to Hebron, "and King David made a covenant with them at Hebron before the Lord, and they anointed David king over Israel" (2 Sam. 5:3). It is significant that these proceedings were carried out in conformity with the terms of "limited kingship" discussed earlier: (1) David's rule rested on Yahweh's designation; and (2) in both anointings, the people were represented—that is, to Yahweh's designation they added their acclamation. The terminology used to describe his second coronation is significant: David "made a covenant" with the northern tribes "before Yahweh." This phrasing implies that from his side David made commitments to the people, even as their anointing him was a sign of their commitment. A deeper dimension of this covenant is also very important: It also involved Yahweh's commitment to his anointed, as seen in 2 Samuel 23:5 and Psalm 132:11. This dimension placed the kingship of David on a firmer basis than Saul's. While the latter rested on the old model of the temporary charismatic designation of the šōpēṭ, Yahweh's covenant with David was understood as one of lifelong duration.

David's cautious, balanced policy continued on into his reign. Rather than show favor to either the north or the south, he captured Jerusalem, a city belonging to neither and lying between both, and made it his capital. And then, as if to counteract any suspicions that this, and the private army he had assembled, represented a threat to the cherished beliefs of the League, he demonstrated his commitment to early Yahwistic tradition by taking personal oversight in bringing the ark of the covenant to Jerusalem. Jerusalem thus took its place in the succession of Yahwistic sanctuaries: Gilgal, Shiloh, and Jerusalem. And the ark reassured traditionalists that Yahweh, who delivered his people from the land of Egypt, and accompanied them in their wanderings and battles leading to occupation of their new land, was still at the center of David's Jerusalem cult. For the ark, on which Yahweh was invisibly enthroned, was a powerful symbol of the continuity between the old and the new. This continuity was further demonstrated by David's choice of Abiathar, priest of the Mushite line associated with Shiloh, to serve as priest alongside Zadok.

An excellent expression of David's balanced approach to his office is preserved in Psalm 132. First his zeal on behalf of Yahweh is described in connection with his "finding a place for Yahweh;" that is, for the old sacred League symbol of the ark. Then the covenant between Yahweh and his anointed is described:

> The Lord swore to David a sure oath
>   from which he will not turn back:
> "One of the sons of your body
>   I will set on your throne.
> If your sons keep my covenant
>   and my testimonies which I shall teach them,
> their sons also for ever
>   shall sit upon your throne." (Ps. 132:11–12)

It is very significant that Yahweh's promise to David concerning succession is accompanied by a condition, for this serves as another indication of the restraints imposed on royal ideology by Yahwistic tradition. The innovations inaugurated by David are undeniable, and the heightened importance of king and royal city are visible throughout the psalm. But the abiding influence of early Yahwism for the time being has retarded the development of royal ideology in the direction of absolute monarchy and unconditional covenant. This tension between the old and the new is also evident in the last words of David in 2 Samuel 23:1–7, which refer to Yahweh's eternal covenant with David, but add a condition relating to the king's responsibility to uphold justice and to place God first in his life:

> The God of Israel has spoken,
>   the Rock of Israel has said to me:
> When one rules justly over men
>   ruling in the fear of God,
> he dawns on them like the morning light,
>   like the sun shining forth upon a cloudless morning,
>   like rain that makes grass to sprout from the earth. (2 Sam. 23. 3–4)

The tension between innovations fostered by royal ideology and the restraining influence of old Yahwistic tradition is seen nowhere more clearly than in the accounts describing interactions between kings and prophets. 2 Samuel 7 is the result of a very complex tradition history, at the basis of which seems to stand a dialogue between king and prophet in which Nathan is spokesman of an old antitemple tradition with deep roots in the early Yahwism of the League:

> But that same night the word of the Lord came to Nathan, "Go and tell my servant David, 'Thus says the Lord: Would you build me a house to dwell in? I have not dwelt in a house since the day I brought up the people of Israel from Egypt to this day, but I have been moving about in a tent for my dwelling. In all places where I have moved with all the people of Israel, did I speak a word with any of the judges of Israel, whom I commanded to shepherd my people Israel, saying, 'Why have you not built me a house of cedar?' " (2 Sam. 7:4–7)

David, according to this account, respected the old Yahwistic sanctuary tradition. He put aside plans to build the type of holy place appropriate to a Near Eastern royal dynasty, and retained the rustic tent shrine at home in the cult of the League. Later we shall see how the growth of royal ideology in Israel that broke out of the restraints imposed by early Yahwism is reflected in the subsequent layers of interpretive tradition added to 2 Samuel 7.

The role of the prophet in keeping the king mindful of the special conditions that applied to kingship in Israel is seen in Nathan's reproof of David in the matter of Uriah the Hittite and his wife Bathsheba (2 Samuel 11–12). In Nathan's exquisite parable of the poor man's lamb, the qualities of righteousness and compassion find powerful expression, and are related to their source in Yahwistic worship by Nathan's blunt question: "Why have you despised the word of the Lord, to do what is evil in his sight?" (2 Sam. 12:9). According to the early Yahwistic notion of community, though a foreigner, the Hittite was not excluded from Yahweh's compassion, nor was the king exempted from the standard of Yahweh's righteousness. David had violated both qualities of the covenant, and on the deepest level, had thus despised Yahweh's word. The curses of the covenant accordingly came to rest on his house, as the entire remaining chapters of the Succession Narrative (2 Sam. 9–12 and 1 Kings 1–2) illustrate. During David's lifetime, the old Yahwistic covenant notion retained much of its force, giving rise to tensions that only the unusual genius and piety of David could convert into stability and growth, at least in the earliest years of his reign.

Increasingly, however, the tremendous tensions introduced into Yahwism by kingship came to the surface, as one can discern in the traditions dealing with David's reign. In the actions of faithful Yahwists, in the courageous opposition of the prophets, and to some extent, in the restraint exhibited by David himself, the resiliency of early Yahwism can be glimpsed. But like an ineluctable force the aggressive self-assertiveness of ancient Near Eastern royal ideology can be recognized as a counterpoint in the narrative. David, true to the manner of a king seeking to organize his human resources, ordered a military census. But this move precipitated a direct clash with the sacred traditions of the League and specifically with its unique attitude toward personal property (the naḥălâ). David fell under the curses of the covenant, as announced by the prophet Gad (2 Sam. 24). Most especially in the bloodshed and court intrigue that accompanied Solomon's rise to the throne, one sees the alien climate that had begun to enshroud the land. At the end of David's reign, we are only one step away from the silencing of the old Yahwistic voice and the self-assertion of the royal ideology as it was about to break out of the restraints thus far maintaining the fragile structure of a "limited monarchy." All that was needed for that final step to be taken was a king who no longer felt committed to the early Yahwistic notions at the base of a "limited kingship," and who instead desired to shift the tender balance implied in the Davidic interpretation of royal office, covenant, and cult in the direction of absolute monarchy.

D. SOLOMON

The question of the impact that kingship had on the notion of religious community in Israel is a difficult and complex one. It would be a gross oversimplification to claim that kingship was to blame for all that went awry in Israel in the centuries after David and Solomon. But it would also be false to claim that kingship had nothing to do with Israel's woes, as if institutions were neutral in matters of faith and morality. The introduction of kingship placed tremendous power in the hands of one person and one family. Involved was an important structural change accompanied in the ancient Near East by an attitude of veneration of the king. Thus Israel's kings were sorely tempted to use their power for personal ambition and dynastic pretension. Kingship also provided an opening for the importation of foreign religious and social ideas. There is some truth to the claim, then, that an institutional innovation, once introduced, develops with a momentum of its own.

The other half of the truth, however, is suggested by the view that the type of king ruling over a people actually is a reflection of that people's own beliefs and values. This is verified by the history of Israel, for there are notable cases where the people, through prophetic advocates or by group action, disrupted the dynastic succession to bring kingship more in line with the values of the governed. When both sides of the issue are held in mind, it becomes apparent that kingship in Israel was a complex phenomenon. Accordingly, its effects on the quality of community life must be evaluated with careful attention to the textual evidence.

The sources at our disposal for the reign of Solomon are of a different character from those focused on David. While the latter gave a picture of David that was remarkably true to life, the stories about Solomon have a distinct legendary quality (with the exception of short excerpts from royal annals). But the difference in the nature of the sources is itself revealing: David was accessible to the people, and open to scrutiny and critique. Solomon, in the style of the oriental monarch, was visible only through the splendor of his office, and consequently the Nathans and Gads, with their critiques of the king, are replaced by foreign kings and queens extolling the virtures, wisdom, and riches of an ideal monarch.

When read critically, what picture emerges of Solomon's reign? It begins with a consolidation of power predicated on a policy of harsh suppression of all criticism and opposition. Adonijah, the rival to the throne, was liquidated on a pretext. In a program of intrigue sponsored by Bathsheba on behalf of her son, and flimsily attributed to the death-bed instructions of David, Adonijah's supporters Joab and Shimei were summarily executed. Abiathar, David's Mushite priest, was banished to Anathoth. This move betrays the departure of the cult sponsored by Solomon away from the older traditions his father still sought to honor. With the removal of Abiathar from the priestly office, Solomon broke an important link with the early Yahwistic traditions handed down at the League shrines of Gilgal and Shiloh, shrines served by the Mushite priesthood of which Abiathar was a member. A further sign of Solomon's suppression of League traditions is the conspicuous absence of any prophetic voice in the traditions dealing with Solomon.[11] The "checks and balances" built into the limited kingship by the presence of the prophet at the side of the king were removed. Solomon obviously chose to interpret the word of Yahweh without the "help" of those "gadflies" who so often differed with kings. As for the priestly office, Solomon was careful to select the priest whose allegiance to the king was demonstrated and sure. Not surprisingly, the account of the harsh, repressive measures of Solomon in 1 Kings 1–2 concludes with the sentence "So the kingdom was established in the hand of Solomon."

11. The only reference to prophets having any relation to Solomon is found in the historiographic note of the Chronicler in 2 Chron. 9:29.

This consolidation accomplished, Solomon was able to introduce changes into the cult which his father, influenced by the Yahwism of the prophets Nathan and Gad, had eschewed. The first order of business was to construct a magnificent acropolis, as symbol of his royal glory. Standing side by side were palace and temple, the one serving as home of the king, the other as home of a cult placed under the aegis of the monarchy. The royal ideology on which Solomon drew can be recognized both in relation to the source of his workmen and materials (the Phoenician city-state of Tyre) and to the pattern and symbolism of his temple. The Solomonic temple was constructed completely in the style of Canaanite models. An authentic imperial shrine had come to replace David's rustic tent as the new home of Yahweh.

In keeping with the architecture of his temple and palace was his reorganization of the royal administration. Drawing on Egyptian and Phoenician models, it introduced an elaborate bureaucracy (1 Kings 4:2–6), a large professional army replete with chariotry, and a "levy of forced labor out of all Israel" (1 Kings 5:12). This bureaucratiztion led to the superimposition of an elite adminstration and military class on the society, to which repayment for services took the form of royal land grants. The effect was not only the enrichment of a privileged class, but the creation of an aristocracy whose allegiance was bound to the crown. Finally, to cover the enormous costs of this elaborate structure, Solomon obliterated the old tribal boundaries in favor of the more rational system of twelve tax districts administered by court appointees. In all this, those cherishing the structures and traditions of early Yahwism must have looked on in dismay at what their king had wrought to make them a nation "like all the nations."

All of Solomon's domestic changes were matched by a similarly innovative foreign policy: with Egypt, Tyre, Moab, Ammon, Edom and Sidon, Solomon entered into military and economic treaties, symbolized cultically by the introduction of shrines to the gods of those nations into his acropolis. This of course constituted a frontal attack on the cherished belief of early Yahwism that Yahweh was the sole guarantor of the people's security. It as, moreover, vivid proof of the conviction that such treaty engagements led to entanglements with foreign gods. For all these reasons, after the ark of the covenant had been brought in royal procession amid the sacrificing of so many sheep and oxen "that they could not be counted or numbered" and had been placed into the deep darkness of the inner sanctuary, the question must have arisen in the minds of many faithful Yahwists: "Was this a day of conquest for Yahweh, or of captivity?"

The question of whether Yahweh was the conqueror or the conquered in the Solomonic cult presents itself as a serious one in our study of the Yahwistic community as well. What effect would the newly asserted sacral autonomy of the king have on a community founded on belief in the sole sovereignty of Yahweh, and dedicated to a unique understanding of righteousness and compassion that stemmed from the experience of deliverance from the bondage of kings? To gain some insight into this important question, we return to the two areas of life that in Chapters II and III furnish the primary evidence for describing the early Yahwistic notion of community—namely, forms of worship and structures of society.

1. FORMS OF WORSHIP

King Solomon built a temple as "a place for [Yahweh] to dwell in for ever" (1 Kings 8:13) adjacent to his palace on his new Jerusalem acropolis. To this temple he assigned the priestly personnel. He paid for temple expenses from the royal treasury. He personally offered sacrifices there (1 Kings 9:25; cf. 1 Sam. 13:7b–15a). From Solomon stems the ideal of the priest-king, which deduces legitimization from the divine oath expressed in Psalm 110: "The Lord has sworn and will not change his mind, 'You are a priest forever after the order of Melchizedek.' " We encounter then in Solomon themes that move far beyond anything thus far introduced into Yahwistic worship, themes such as a royal chapel proclaimed as the permanent dwelling of Yahweh, and the sacral autonomy of the king resting on an eternal divine decree. It was inevitable that such themes would alter the forms of worship in Israel. As we observe some of these innovations, however, it is important to remember that the older forms (mentioned earlier) that focused on the themes of Yahweh's deliverance of slaves from bondage and the conquest, while eclipsed by the new Jerusalem cult, were not eradicated. In shrines scattered throughout the countryside, these archaic themes lived on, exerting their influence especially on Israel's prophets, but also on the Deuteronomistic School.

First, as far as cult sites and dates are concerned, it is significant that the central celebration of the League period, namely, the spring New Year festival that had been held at Gilgal and Shiloh and that had commemorated the old covenant tradition of the exodus and conquest, receded into the background and virtually disappeared during the floruit of the Davidic dynasty in Jerusalem. Not until the time of Josiah was it reintroduced. In its place there arose, first in Jerusalem and then in the rival northern cult of Bethel, the autumn festival corresponding to the Canaanite and the Egyptian New Year (i.e., Ethanim, the seventh month, cf. 1 Kings 8:2).

Far more important than shifts in calendar and location, however, was the change in the central theme of the cult. Replacing the old covenantal theme of Yahweh's deliverance of the Hebrews from bondage in Egypt and his guiding them into a new land was a royal theme: the choice of David and Zion by the heavenly King Yahweh. Underlying this shift was a fundamental change in orientation. We have observed how the early Yahwistic credal traditon arose out of what was perceived as Yahweh's activity in historical events. The epic form of that tradition

is discernible from its earliest stages. It unfolded with the unfolding of
the historical experiences of the community gathered around the common confession in Yahweh the Deliverer. Following the alternative pattern of ancient Near Eastern royal ideology, the new theme of Yahweh's choice of an earthly king and dwelling place drew in the first
instance on a heavenly drama, that is, on the realm of myth.[12] This
source is clearly discernible in Psalm 2:

> Why do the nations conspire,
>   and the peoples plot in vain?
> The kings of the earth set themselves,
>   and the rulers take counsel together,
>   against the Lord and his anointed, saying,
> "Let us burst their bonds asunder, and cast
>   their cords from us."
> He who sits in the heavens laughs;
>   the Lord has them in derision.
> Then he will speak to them in his wrath,
>   and terrify them in his fury, saying,
> "I have set my king
>   on Zion, my holy hill."
> I will tell of the decree of the Lord:
> He said to me, "You are my son,
>   today I have begotten you.
> Ask of me,
>   and I will make the nations your heritage,
>   and the ends of the earth your possession.
> You shall break them with a rod of iron,
>   and dash them in pieces like a potter's vessel." (Ps. 2:1–9)

The psalm begins with an ominous scene. With a sweep and universality reflecting the theme familiar in ancient Near Eastern myth of the
revolt of the inimical gods and their hosts in heaven, we hear of plans
for a massive attack against "Yahweh and his anointed." Yahweh's terrifying reply tersely expresses the twin themes of royal ideology: "I
have set my king on Zion, my holy hill." It is this establishment of king
and royal city that secures the cosmic order by making provision for
the sure defeat of the unruly forces that threaten life. Yahweh is pictured as seated in heaven, or more precisely in the imagery of the underlying myth, in his temple on the cosmic mountain. Corresponding
to his stance is the anointed king whom Yahweh has set "on Zion, my
holy hill," the earthly counterpart of the heavenly mountain and temple of God. The anointed king's lofty position is contingent neither on
proof of his ability to defend his people in battle nor on the accla-

---

12. For a survey of the royal psalms and the mythical background of their main
themes, see P. D. Hanson, *The Dawn of Apocalyptic*, 2d ed. (Philadelphia: Fortress Press,
1979), pp. 299–315.

mation and continued support of the congregation. It rests on a divine decree: "You are my son, today I have begotten you." While not implying the full divinity of the king, but rather suggesting an adoption occurring on the day of coronation, it is nevertheless clear that a mythic pattern is the source of this view of election of king and temple mountain.

One effect of this re-orientation was that the conditional nature of the Mosaic covenant between Yahweh and people in the exodus-conquest tradition was supplanted with an unconditional covenant between Yahweh and his anointed:

> Once and for all I have sworn by my holiness:
>   I will not lie to David.
> His line shall endure for ever,
>   his throne as long as the sun before me. (Ps. 89:35–36)

Here, as elsewhere in the royal psalms (cf. 78:67–72; 132:13–14), the election of the royal Davidic dynasty is traced to an eternal decree made by the heavenly suzerain Yahweh. The setting of this election in the cosmogonic battle that imposed order on the murky chaos represented by the unruly enemies of mythology, Sea and River, is revealed by verse 25 of Psalm 89:

> I will set his hand on the sea
> and his right hand on the river.

Coming to expression in this and related psalms is a concern that lies at the heart of all the cosmogonic myths of the great ancient Near Eastern kingdoms. It is the concern for order, the order (in the first instance) of the cosmos, which was established by the warrior god's defeat of the forces of chaos—the order (in the second instance) of the earth, which was secured derivatively by the warrior god's human representative, the king, through his battles and through proper administration of his kingdom.

The order over which kingship presided was thus conceived of as one grounded in the essential nature of reality. Its central institution, the temple, was patterned after its heavenly prototype in celebration of the defeat of chaos in the creation event, and its head, the king, derived his appointment from a decree belonging to the original "orders of creation."

The unfolding of this high royal ideology is visible in many variations. In Psalm 48, the heavenly king Yahweh is praised "in the city of our God,' which city is then designated with an ascription belonging to the divine mountain of Northwest Semitic mythology as attested in Ugaritic, an ascription that ill fits the geographical and topographical particularities of Jerusalem, but that perfectly suits the spiritual significance of this replica of heavenly realities:

> His holy mountain, beautiful in elevation
>   is the joy of all the earth,
> Mount Zion, in the far north,
>   the city of the great King. (Ps. 48:1b–2)

In this psalm as well, the drama of cosmogonic myth accompanies the description of Zion. The kings gather to attack, but the divine warrior god scatters them in a panic, thus securing the safety of the holy city, "the city of our God, which God establishes for ever" (v. 8b).

Psalm 68 serves as another illustration of the appropriation of mythic motifs related to kingship and temple. The divine warrior king rides out against his enemies. Like the storm god Baal of Ugaritic mythology, he "rides upon the clouds," accompanied by thunder, lightning, and the copious rains that refructify the land (vv. 1–10). The enemies flee, Yahweh delivers the prisoners, and mighty Mount Bashan looks with envy "at the mount which God desired for his abode, yea, where the Lord will dwell for ever" (v. 16). Next, the victorious procession moves festively to the temple on Mount Zion (vv. 17–18, 24–27).

> Thy solemn processions are seen, O God,
>   the processions of my God, my King, into the sanctuary—
> the singers in front, the minstrels last,
>   between them maidens playing timbrels:
> 'Bless God in the great congregation,
>   the Lord, O you who are of Israel's fountain.' (vv. 24–26)

Here we glimpse the ritual of the royal temple itself, celebrating Yahweh's victory over chaos, his establishing order and fertility, and closely related to this, his taking up habitation in his temple amid the festivities of his people. The remainder of the psalm describes the universal compass of Yahweh's reign, and the beneficent effect this has on his people:

> Terrible is God in his sanctuary, the God of Israel,
>   he gives power and strength to his people. (v. 35)

In the storm god language of Psalm 68, we recognize the original matrix of the underlying cosmogonic myth in a temple ritual that tied the victory of Baal to the renewed fertility of the land. This deep concern of agrarian cultures, which was scarcely visible in early Yahwism, permeates the royal psalms, suggesting that the temple taught the people to enjoy the benefits of a God whose reign assured the fertility of their crops. Psalm 104 develops this motif most extensively. First the cosmogonic conflict of the storm god "who makes the clouds thy chariot" is described, with careful attention to the resultant ordering of the heavens, the earth and the waters under the earth (vv. 1–9). Yahweh "stretched out the heavens like a tent," "laid the beams of thy chambers on the waters," "set the earth in its foundations so that it should never be shaken," drove back the chaotic waters, and "set a bound which they should not pass so that they might not again cover the earth." Having rebuked and bound all that is inimical to life, Yahweh then releases the fertility of the earth: "Thou makest springs gush forth in the valleys . . . " This line issues forth in a virtual rite of spring, in which all is beautiful, bountiful, and teeming with life (vv. 10–30).

These examples vividly illustrate two facets of the royal theme of the choice of David and Zion by the heavenly King Yahweh; Yahweh's majesty (cf. also Ps. 29, 93, and 97) and the beneficence of his reign for his people (cf. also Ps. 72). It is not difficult to imagine the sense of fascination and awe that could encompass a congregation that, amid the smoke of frankincense and sacrifices, would sing:

> Let us come into his presence with thanksgiving:
>   let us make a joyful noise to him with songs of praise!
> For the Lord is a great God
>   and a great King above all gods.
> In his hand are the depths of the earth;
>   the heights of the mountains are his also.
> The sea is his, for he made it
>   for his hands formed the dry land. (Ps. 95:2–5)

At the same time, of course, it is clear that the close association drawn by the royal psalms between the glorious heavenly King and his anointed Davidic king also accorded to the latter a very lofty position in the royal temple:

> The Lord sends forth from Zion your mighty scepter.
>   Rule in the midst of your foes.
> Your people will offer themselves freely
>   on the day you lead your host upon the holy mountains. (Ps. 110:2–3)

Although this look at the form of worship of the temple cult introduced by Solomon has been brief and sketchy, it suffices to give an impression of the new mood that prevailed, when contrasted to the rites of the early Yahwistic cults of Gilgal and Shiloh.[13] What Solomon achieved in architecture was matched in liturgy, namely, a cosmopolitan elan befitting a once rustic nation now aspiring to compete with the great kingdoms of the world. David's legitimization of his reign was too homespun, having been based on sacral anointing by an old seer and acclamation by the people. Equally intolerable within the strident new royal climate was David's earlier consent to rule without a proper temple, out of deference to the views of an old prophet. Far more appropriate was the language familiar to the Phoenicians and the Egyptians, the language of a divine decree according to which the king was adopt-

---

13. The problem of dating the Psalms is notoriously difficult. The royal psalms I have drawn on are likely traceable to the temple and priesthood established by Solomon. Although there is room for debate in details, the general picture of the Solomonic temple that such psalms give is sufficiently reliable for our purposes.

ed to sonship, and the celebration of the resulting dignity and power of the king in a glorious temple reflecting the splendor of the heavenly temple of the king's divine patron.

Another sign of the liberal, cosmopolitan spirit of Solomon's reign is the pursuit of wisdom mentioned in 1 Kings 4:29–34 and 10:1–10. Reference to his 3,000 proverbs and 1,005 songs is followed by a list of subjects he covered. It resembles the encyclopedic science known from the Egyptian Onomasticon of Amenophis from roughly a hundred years earlier. When these notices are combined with the observation that the literary masterpiece called the Yahwistic Document (which forms the narrative structure of Genesis, Exodus, and Numbers) likely comes from the Solomonic period, it seems safe to describe the Solomonic court as the center of a remarkable floruit of culture.

2. STRUCTURES OF SOCIETY

Having observed some of the effects of Solomon's innovations on forms of worship, we move on to ask, "What effect did Solomon's orientation away from the traditions of the League in the direction of a royal ideology drawing on customs and myths of the great kingdoms of that time have on social structure?" Certainly it would not be accurate simply to state that he disregarded matters pertaining to justice in the land. The royal ideal on which he drew emphasized the responsibility of the king for his subjects. For example, in the prologue to the Code of Hammurabi, coeval with the designation of the god Marduk's responsibilities vis-à-vis human beings, and the naming of the royal city Babylon, Anum and Enlil named Hammurabi

> to promote the welfare of the people,
> me, Hammurabi, the devout, god-fearing prince,
> to cause justice to prevail in the land,
> to destroy the wicked and the evil,
> that the strong might not oppress the weak,
> to rise like the sun
> over the black-headed (people),
> and to light up the land.
> Hammurabi, the shepherd, called by Enlil, am I;
> the one who makes affluence and plenty abound. (1:22–51)[14]

As the representative and son of Marduk, Hammurabi was responsible to maintain the order and welfare of the land. Solomon, as representative and son of Yahweh, was similarly charged:

> Give the king thy justice, O God,
>   and thy righteousness to the royal son!
> May he judge thy people with righteousness,
>   and thy poor with justice!

---

14. T. J. Meek, *ANET*, 3d ed., p. 164.

> Let the mountains bear prosperity for the people,
>> and the hills, in righteousness!
> May he defend the cause of the poor of the people,
>> give deliverance to the needy,
>> and crush the oppressor! (Ps. 72:1–4)

Even as the temple symbolized the divine power that ordered the heavens and fructified the land, so too it symbolized divine justice that established order and averted social chaos. It is apparent that Solomon and his followers sought to integrate the judicial functions formerly associated with "the gates" of the villages and with the local sanctuaries into the temple order:

> I was glad when they said to me,
>> "Let us go to the house of the Lord!"
> Our feet have been standing
>> within your gates, O Jerusalem!
> Jerusalem, built as a city
>> which is bound firmly together,
> to which the tribes go up,
>> the tribes of the Lord,
> as was decreed for Israel,
>> to give thanks to the name of the Lord.
> There thrones for judgment were set,
>> the thrones of the house of David. (Ps. 122:1–5)

Temple worship was by no means ethically neutral. Like the appointment of the king, it derived the structures of the society from the "eternal orders of creation." Therefore, the pilgrims who wished to enter the gates of the temple were subjected to careful examination:

> O Lord, who shall sojourn in thy tent?
>> Who shall dwell on thy holy hill?
> He who walks blamelessly, and does what it right,
>> and speaks truth from his heart;
> who does not slander with his tongue,
>> and does no evil to his friend,
>> nor takes up a reproach against his neighbor;
> in whose eyes a reprobate is despised,
>> but who honors those who fear the Lord;
> who swears to his own hurt and does not change;
> who does not put out his money at interest,
>> and does not take a bribe against the innocent.
> He who does these things shall never be moved. (Ps. 15:1–5)

A similar "entrance *tôrâ*" is found in Psalm 24, which includes these words in its examination section:

> Who shall ascend the hill of the Lord?
>> And who shall stand in his holy place?
> He who has clean hands and a pure heart,

> who does not lift up his soul to what is false,
>   and does not swear deceitfully.
> He will receive blessing from the Lord,
>   and vindication from the God of his salvation. (Ps. 24:3–5)

This passage is followed by the majestic announcement of Yahweh's entry, echoing a festive shout from the Ugaritic Baal cycle:

> Lift up your heads, O gates!
>   that the King of glory may come in.
> Who is the King of glory?
>   The Lord, strong and mighty,
>   the Lord, mighty in battle! (Ps. 24:7–8)

Also the legendary portrait of Solomon given by the traditions in 1 Kings supports the view that Solomon in all his splendor was conscious of his responsibility for justice in the land, for the story of the two harlots in 1 Kings 3:16–27 describes a wise and discerning judge. The verse concluding that story makes explicit the connection between the king's wisdom and its divine source: "And all Israel heard of the judgment which the king had rendered; and they stood in awe of the king, because they perceived that wisdom of God was in him, to render justice" (1 Kings 3:28).

What basis is there then for criticism of Solomon's innovations? Did he not place the security and prosperity of the land on a firm basis, and assure the maintenance of order through his own administration of justice? In principle the picture looks very attractive, as it does in the prologue to Hammurabi's Code. But as we know from alternate sources of the plight of the impoverished and enslaved in Babylonian society, so too we know from other biblical texts of the harsher realities arising during Solomon's reign and during the reigns of subsequent Davidic kings as the result of the innovations of Solomon and his successors. First we shall mention some of these realities, and then return to observe more closely the forms of worship and structures of society he introduced, in order to evaluate their effect on the community of faith in Israel.

Solomon created social and political structures aimed at consolidating and securing a large, complex nation under the firm, centralized control of the royal house. The process observable in the development of the early Yahwistic community was thus reversed. In that case the former slaves and those coming to share their confession in Yahweh the Deliverer built a society from the bottom up, with the corresponding determination not to allow their simple egalitarianism to be threatened by the hierarchical structures under which they had suffered in Egypt. Solomon, the first leader of Israel born in a royal house and assuming office by right of birth, looked from his lofty perspective down upon an inefficiently organized nation, located midway between a rustic clan confederacy and a modern nation. When one recognizes Solomon's background, one is in a position to understand how, from the top down, he imposed on his nation a rational structure patterned on Egyptian and Phoenician models. The first stratum below the king was his personal cabinet (ʿabdê hammêlek), including his finance minister, minister of trade, and minister of forced labor. The next elite class consisted of the military nobility. Then came the land-owning aristocracy, whose wealth increased greatly through the benefits bestowed by the increased trade opened up by Solomon's far-reaching treaty relationships. And, of course, the strata of his national social pyramid continued downward through the classes whose well-being decreased in proportion to the enrichment of the elite classes. At the bottom was a growing class of impoverished whose increasing indebtedness was swelling the pool of indentured Hebrew slaves in Israel. It must have been a bitter irony for Yahwists, whose principles forbade their accepting elite positions of leadership because they required unquestioning loyalty to the king, to find *themselves* slipping into impoverishment in their own land. Israelites were being brought back into "the house of bondage" without stepping outside of their own boundaries. It is not difficult to understand the passion and resolve that motivated the revolt of the northern tribes immediately on the death of Solomon. Indeed, it strikes the historian as an inevitability. The resistance to royal innovations that had begun already during David's reign (2 Sam. 20:1) reached the breaking point in Solomon's last year.

> What portion have we in David?
> We have no inheritance in the son of Jesse.
> To your tents, O Israel!
> Look now to your own house, David. (1 Kings 12:16)

What is more, the bitter fruits of the reintroduction of a stratified society continued to be harvested throughout the period of the divided monarchy, as we shall see in studying the prophetic books.

What was wrong with the social structures introduced by Solomon? Perhaps we can discern a source of the problem in the vast increase of wealth and power that resulted from the expansion of the empire under David and its clever exploitation by Solomon, for this increase was not accompanied by the development of equitable distribution. Instead, Solomon's reorganization moved increasingly along the hierarchical lines familiar in Egypt and Phoenicia. As a result, within the society a powerful structural discrimination arose against the lower classes, which stood in principled contradiction to the early Yahwistic notion of community. The creation of an elite class increased the power of some Israelites over others. And this imbalance created bondage both at the top and on the bottom of the social pyramid: the elite were bound to the king by their oaths of allegiance, and of course the lower classes were bound to their creditors.

Quite naturally the concentration of wealth in the hands of the aristocracy led to the demand for protections, both from internal threats and from foreign adversaries. Internally, the laws protecting the vulnerable members of society (for example, the *naḥălâ*) were neglected, and the growing cases of social injustice were overlooked by those whose self-interests were bound up with their court-appointed offices, thereby inhibiting the even-handed administration of justice. Perhaps the acts of discrimintion and injustice described in the prophetic books can be seen as an inevitable result of the clamoring after wealth, security, and order by the privileged within a stratified society.

As far as national security is concerned, the professional army was modernized and expanded under Solomon. The accelerated militarization of the land can also be viewed as an inevitable outgrowth of the social transformation already described, for the vast accumulation of wealth among the landed aristocracy and the royal court attracted the attention of foreign powers. The result of this accumulation, and the vast building projects that accompanied it, was loss of freedom for vast numbers of citizens through conscription. In addition, there was the even more ominous threat of an increasingly heavy burden of taxation, not infrequently leading to impoverishment, loss of family inheritance, and slavery.

Against the background of this description of the social conditions characterizing Solomon's kingdom, we return to the question of the notion of the community of faith. In the light of these social realities (one could be led to ask), can one even speak of the contribution of kingship to the Yahwistic notion of community? Is not the united testimony of the historiographic and prophetic sources sufficient to conclude that kingship was simply antithetical to Yahwism? Could one not simply argue that the notion of community was carried from early Yahwism down to later periods in circles that circumvented the temple, circles such as the Rechabites, who continued to live from the ancient confessions of the League without being influenced by the royal theology?

There are two reasons why this alternative must be excluded. First, the introduction of kingship resulted from the inability of the old League structures to cope with the new complicated international situation represented by the Philistine threat. For the Yahwistic community of faith simply to have insisted on its virginal purity by repudiating the new forms of political and social structure imposed on Israel by historical developments, would perhaps have pronounced its own untimely death. By stepping from the League into kingship, Israel stepped from a youthful state into civil maturity, an inevitable step fraught with dangers. The question, therefore, was not *whether* the Yahwistic community had to accompany the nation in this move, but *how* it would do so. This is the perspective from which critique must be exercised, which implies a complex process of theological inquiry.

A second reason why the question of the contribution of kingship cannot be dismissed out of hand is the contribution to Yahwistic worship made by the temple cult. This point can be made in the form of a question: "Is it conceivable to give a complete picture of the community of faith in the Hebrew Bible without due attention to the psalms arising out of worship in the Jerusalem temple?" And, of course, the impact of temple worship goes far beyond the Psalter, permeating the historical books, the prophets, and contributing major motifs to biblical tradition, including Messianism, without which later developments in Judaism and Christianity would remain incomprehensible. The temple cult was thus not something antithetical to Yahwism *per se*. It and its rituals were fully capable of serving true worship, if their proper function in relation to God was not lost. The theological basis of that proper function is described well by A. C. Welch in a comment on the Psalms: "The significance of the cult, according to these hymns, rested, not on the rite *per se*, but on the character of Him who had commanded it, and on the attitude of those who fulfilled it."[15]

How then do we get a handle on this complex question of the relation of the Solomonic monarchy to the Yahwistic community of faith? We propose that a reliable guide is the triad of qualities discerned at the heart of the early Yahwistic community—namely, worship, compassion, and righteousness. How did the Solomonic innovations affect these three qualities and their integration in the community of faith?

Chapter III recognized the source of early Israel's notion of righteousness in the activity of Yahweh, by which Yahweh called a people into being. This notion of righteousness provided the early Israelites with a standard of justice on which they could construct social structures, laws and institutions that would safeguard their new life as free people. We also noted how the stringent demands entailed by these laws and institutions were taken very seriously by God. They were seen as an integral part of the covenant God had established between God and people. Flagrant disobedience in fact jeopardized the covenant, which was in this sense conditional.

Certainly God's righteousness as the standard of the divinely ordered society continued as a theme in the royal cult in Jerusalem: "The heavens declare his righteousness, for God himself is judge," the hymnist exclaims in Psalm 50. And we have seen how the king, in continuity with ancient Near Eastern royal ideology understood as the shepherd of his people, represented the divine king in administering justice in the land:

> Give the king thy justice, O God
> and thy righteousness to the royal son
> May he judge thy people with righteousness,
> and thy poor with justice? (Ps. 72:1–2)

---

15. A. C. Welch, *Prophet and Priest in Old Israel* (New York: Macmillan, 1953), p. 133.

Moreover, the importance of Yahweh's righteous standard in ordering the universe and setting a limit beyond which chaos was not permitted to pass received greater emphasis than in early Yahwism:

> Bless the Lord, O my soul!
>> O Lord my God, thou art very great!
> Thou art clothed with honor and majesty,
>> who coverest thyself with light as with a garment,
> who has stretched out the heavens like a tent,
>> who has laid the beams of thy chambers on the waters,
> who makest the clouds thy chariot,
>> who ridest on the wings of the wind,
> who makest the winds thy messengers,
>> fire and flame thy ministers.
> Thoud didst set the earth on its foundations,
>> so that it should never be shaken.
> Thou didst cover it with the deep as with a garment;
>> the waters stood above the mountains . . . .
> Thou didst set a bound which they should not pass,
>> so that they might not again cover the earth. (Ps. 104:1–6, 9)

Emphasis on Yahweh's cosmogonic activity led to an enrichment of images pertaining to God's ordering of the realm of nature for the benefit of God's people:

> Thou visitest the earth and waterest it,
>> thou greatly enrichest it;
> the river of God is full of water;
>> thou providest their grain,
>> for so thou has prepared it.
> Thou waterest its furrows abundantly,
>> settling its ridges,
> softening it with showers,
>> and blessing its growth.
> Thou crownest the year with thy bounty;
>> the tracks of thy chariot drip with fatness.
> The pastures of the wilderness drip,
>> the hills gird themselves with joy,
> the meadows clothe themselves with flocks,
>> the valleys deck themselves with grain,
>> they shout and sing together for joy. (Ps. 65:9–13)

All this evidence shows what I have referred to in another study as the important contributions of kingship to the cosmic vector within biblical faith. That is, it shows contributions to the exploration of God's presence in those structures and dimensions of reality that support life by virtue of their dependability and resistance to change.[16]

But as can be seen in early Yahwism, God's standard of righteousness

---

16. P. D. Hanson, *Dynamic Transcendance* (Philadelphia: Fortress Press, 1978).

implies as well a teleological dimension that does not allow order to rigidify into structures that oppress and exclude. We observed how the Egypt of the Pharaohs was a meticulously ordered society, but its order was an oppressive monolith that Yahweh opposed on behalf of those victimized by its eternal bonds. It is the liberating aspect of Yahweh's righteousness that Solomon failed to keep alive; indeed, he placed serious impediments in the way of its development. Order and security were not held in harmony with the liberation of the oppressed. To the contrary, bondage was the price many of Solomon's subjects paid for his system of order and security, whereas its benefits were largely restricted to the elite. Therefore, the standard of righteousness in Solomon's reign ceased to be primarily "Yahweh, who brought you out of the house of bondage," and became bound up with a concept of the "orders of creation" at home in the imposing cosmogonies of the ancient Near Eastern kingdoms. Solomon abandoned the archaic practice of defining righteousness by stepping into the sandals of the sojourning Hebrew in Egypt through recitation of the old Yahwistic credo. Instead, he located himself at the right hand of God, whose earthly representative he regarded himself in the administration of an eternal law. The covenant on which his election rested was no longer construed in conditional, but in absolute terms. The result was an abstraction of the concept of righteousness, which could find expression in lofty hymnic forms that rarely made contact with life.

In early Yahwism, derivation of the standard of righteousness from Yahweh the Deliverer of the oppressed tied this standard inextricably to the corresponding quality of the triad—compassion. This tie prevented laws and structures from becoming abstract formulations applied mechanically to judicial proceedings, for their heavenly Author was the Deliverer and the Judge who heard the cry of the widow, the orphan, the debtor. The administration of justice could not be divorced from the quality of life implied by the presence of a compassionate God. This quality, however, threatened to disappear in the Solomonic court with the disappearance of the old Yahwistic confessions and their guardians, the Mushite priests and especially the prophets. Solomon's administration was a bureaucratically rational one, ordered from the top to achieve maximum efficiency and durability. In early Yahwism, compassion tempered the righteous orders and structures of the community to offer special protection for the vulnerable and a means of access for those otherwise rejected or excluded. In place of this compassion for the weak and openness to the disenfranchised, in Solomon's kingdom are found structures dedicated to enhancing the life of the privileged at the expense and to the exclusion of the vulnerable. In the construction of a large military force to protect the sprawling empire and trade routes, in the proscription of citizens into forced labor to build temple, palace, and many other imperial projects, in the maintenance of the elaborate court and bureaucracy, the effect was the same: A rational ordering of society which rigidified barriers between the classes and led to exclusion of increasing numbers from the benefits of God's land. In such a climate, laws and customs such as the *naḥălâ* and laws against usury, derived from the example of Yahweh's compassion, could not compete with the fascination and lure of wealth emanating from the example of the king's military successes and his magnificent reign.

In Solomon's kingdom, then, the unity between righteousness and compassion dissolved, as an abstract, rational concept of righteousness excluded the personal, emotional qualities of compassion. Why did this happen? Chapter III noted that the union of righteousness and compassion was possible in early Yahwism only because of the powerful example of their embodiment in Yahweh the Deliverer, which example was experienced in worship. What effect did Solomon's innovations have on the quality forming the heart and center of early Yahwism, the sole worship of Yahweh?

There can be no doubt that the beauty and solemnity of the Solomonic temple inspired a deep sense of awe and praise in the hearts of pilgrims gathering there for sacrifice and worship (cf. 1 Kings 8:10–13; Isa. 6:1–8):

> How lovely is thy dwelling place, O Lord of hosts!
> My soul longs, yea, faints for the courts of the Lord;
> my heart and flesh sing for joy to the living God. (Ps. 84:1–2)

Nevertheless, it is obvious that when the Jerusalem sanctuary is compared, for example, with the sanctuary at Gilgal, a vast difference becomes apparent. In the place of the earlier simple structure, there stood a magnificent edifice. And whom did it immortalize? Yahweh, of course, but in contrast to the earlier tent sanctuary where the divine presence had been unrivaled by human majesty, the earthly king in his function of temple patron now moved into the center of attention as well. This was a *royal* chapel, and its services celebrated not only the reign of Yahweh, but also the reign of Yahweh's counterpart on earth, the Davidic king. The redactional layers of 2 Samuel 7 illustrate the transformation that occurred in the short time between David's and Solomon's reigns.[17] David, Yahweh's servant, had requested permission to build a temple for Yahweh to dwell in, but Yahweh's prophet Nathan delivered Yahweh's word denying the request. Conversely, in the Solomonic redaction, Solomon was granted the permission that had been denied David, and added to the permission was a divine promise of an eternal dynasty, and a father-son relationship between king and deity: "He shall build a house for my name, and I will establish the throne of his kingdom forever. I will be his father, and he shall be my son'" (2 Sam. 7:13–14).

The redactional history of 2 Samuel 7 thus records the tendency

17. Cf. F. M. Cross, *CMHE*, pp. 241–258.

within the Jerusalem temple to move the person of the king ever closer to the divine presence, and to move the congregation correspondingly into the background, a tendency seen already in Solomon's investiture as king, which (unlike David's) seems to have been a closed ceremony of the court, directed by the king and excluding the assembly of the people.[18]

What evidence do we see in the Psalms of the effects of this growing distance between king and people and simultaneous narrowing of the gap between king and deity? Most obvious is the exalted position ascribed to the king in the Psalms, and correspondingly, in the temple worship. Psalm 2 is a striking example. First, it is noteworthy how closely king and deity are identified in the description of the plotting of the kings of the earth against Zion, "against the Lord and his anointed." Secondly, Yahweh's words spoken in this situation exalt the king, and promise him an imposing dominion over the earth:

> You are my son, today I have begotten you.
> Ask of me, and I will make the nations your heritage,
>   and the ends of the earth your possession.
> You shall break them with a rod of iron,
>   and dash them in pieces like a potter's vessel. (Ps. 2:7–9)

Equally imposing is the dignity and power ascribed to the king by Yahweh in Psalm 110: "Sit at my right hand, till I make your enemies your footstool," "The Lord sends forth from Zion your mighty scepter," "Your people will offer themselves freely . . . ," "You are a priest for ever after the order of Melchezedek," "The Lord is at your right hand."

Other examples could be added from Psalms 21, 72, 89, and 132. Here we shall discuss only one further example, however, Psalm 45, where the veneration of Yahweh takes second position behind that of the king:

> My heart overflows with a goodly theme
>   I address my verses to the king . . . .
> You are the fairest of the sons of men;
>   grace is poured upon your lips;
>   therefore God has blessed you for ever.
> Gird your sword upon your thigh, O mighty one,
>   in your glory and majesty! (Ps. 45:1–3)

The psalm goes on to celebrate the king's power, his zeal for righteousness, the luxury and splendor that surrounds him on all sides, the beauty of the king's female attendants, and especially of his bride to be. In these lines of praise, the following are especially noteworthy: Verse 6a is particularly controversial, since its literal meaning is "Your throne,

---

18. Cf. 1 Kings 1:32–40, and T. N. D. Mettinger, *King and Messiah* (Lund: Gleerup, 1976), pp. 119–124.

O God, endures for ever and ever"—the one addressed being the (human) king! Verse 7b accentuates Yahweh's elevation of the king over the rest of the people: "Therefore God, your God, has anointed you with the oil of gladness above your fellows." Finally, the concluding verse is noteworthy, since its lavish promise of immortal fame would seem to be appropriate for God alone: "I will cause your name to be celebrated in all generations; therefore the people will praise you for ever and ever."

Thus we discern a pattern that permeated all levels of Israelite society under Solomon, involving centralizaton of political power, which rescinded important rights earlier enjoyed by the people, consolidation of all social structures to the benefit of the royal court and its favored elite at the cost of the majority of the poeple, concentration of military power in the hands of the king through a professional army that replaced the tribal militia, and absolute control over a captive labor force through a corvee that suspended the civil liberties of the citizenry. Finally, it is not surprising to discover that this pattern permeated temple worship as well, where the king was exalted to a level that threatened to divert the attention of the worshippers away from the central quality of early Yahwism, sole worship of Yahweh.

This last facet of Solomon's program provides the key for understanding the serious problems attending Solomon's reign also in regard to the other qualities of the Yahwistic community, righteousness and compassion. As observed earlier, Yahwism was able to hold these qualities together in a dynamic unity only because of its sense of the living presence of the God whose acts demonstrated the indivisibility of righteousness and compassion. In worship of this one true God, all other norms, powers, and points of reference were relativized. Undistracted by earthly norms or powers, Israel could focus on the holy and merciful God, who out of righteousness and compassion created, redeemed, and judged people and world, and who in the covenant called Israel to participate as a kingdom of priests. But what happens if one earthly norm becomes excluded from the relativization of all that is mundane, thereby obliterating one of the marks of true worship? The solidarity of a people constituted as equal and responsible under God is weakened as one of them is elevated to a categorically higher status.

Naturally, in the League there were also leaders, but their ultimate solidarity with the people was safeguarded by the limits set on their offices, offices determined only by God's Spirit and dissolved with the resolution of the crisis the individual leader was called to address. Moreover, in the League leaders were subjected to the same conditions of the covenant as were all other members of the community.

Under Solomon, these limits were removed, for he became king by dynastic succession and held his office according to eternal divine decree for life. Moreover, this throne, and its extension to his sons in perpetuity, was guaranteed by an unconditional covenant. Of such a one it could be said, "Your throne, O God, endures for ever and ever" (even the weakened translation, "Your divine throne endures for ever and ever," conveys the lofty pretensions introduced by the royal court). In Solomon's temple, the exalted presence of the king threatened to draw the worshipful attention of the people to itself, which within the theology of early Yahwism constituted idolatry. Once this human norm was introduced alongside Yahweh, thereby compromising the primal quality of Yahwistic community—namely, worship—its other two qualities of righteousness and compassion were simultaneously vitiated. Alone in the example of Yahweh did Israel experience the integrating force capable of holding these two qualities together in one life-enhancing unity. No king could imitate this divine example, not even Solomon in all his glory. This is seen in the fact that all the hyperbolic praise of the Solomon legends in 1 Kings 3–10 could not prevent the traditionalists from allowing the real Solomon to appear in chapter 11 (the assignment of all his evil to his old age was transparently the device used by the Deuteronomists to harmonize the discrepancy between the idealistic picture of the legends and historical records describing his pagan shrines and many foreign wives). Here we read that Solomon's heart "was not wholly true to the Lord his God." Solomon's heart went after Solomon's women, Solomon's idols, Solomon's wealth. His heart, amid all this royal praise and splendor, became preoccupied with Solomon, not God. Israel's king clearly was a faithful example neither of true worship nor of godly righteousness nor of divine compassion.[19]

Thus the legacy of Solomonic kingship is a very mixed one. We have observed that kingship resulted from political necessity. In the victories of the king, the nation experienced God's care for God's people, God's

---

19. We can depict the development in kingship during the reigns of Saul, David, and Solomon as follows, with each section within the rectangle representing the relative influence of each group:

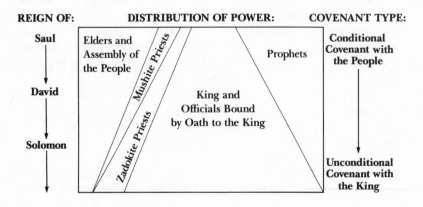

REIGN OF:	DISTRIBUTION OF POWER:	COVENANT TYPE:
Saul	Elders and Assembly of the People — Mushite Priests — Zadokite Priests — King and Officials Bound by Oath to the King — Prophets	Conditional Covenant with the People
David		
Solomon		Unconditional Covenant with the King

ordering of a fickle universe, God's defense of Zion against hostile kings, God's blessing of the land with fertility and abundance. In the Psalms, we are inspired by the deep longing for the fullness and immediacy of God's presence. And it is undeniable that through the borrowing of mythic images and patterns, Israel's theological vocabulary, and thus Israel's capacity for understanding the depths of the universality of God's majesty were enriched. Where then lay the flaw in this high form of kingship?

We can perhaps take our clue from the prophetic critique in 1 Samuel 8, which cites the people as insisting, "No, but we will have a king over us, that we also may be like all the nations . . . " In the royal psalms, we sense that Israel was reaching out with a deep longing for God's kingdom of righteousness and peace, but in allowing its attention to be diverted away from the only King who can bring such a kingdom and instead turning toward an earthly king, Israel was slipping into a dangerous diversion away from God's intention for God's people. God's kingdom, intended by God for the human family from the beginning, could not come through the desire to be like the other nations, or through a king elected to conquer new territory. To identify God's purpose with such a program was to confuse God's universal kingdom with a petty human imitation and to seek to institutionalize God's kingdom within human structures. It was to bind God to an unconditional commitment and to define God's will in human terms. According to early Yahwism, the only god that would allow itself to be a party to such a national program of self-glorification was an idol. The danger of idolatry lurking in the Solomonic royal ideal, therefore, must not be ignored: "For they have not rejected you (Samuel), but they have rejected me (Yahweh) from being king over them" (1 Sam. 8:7).

Thus Israel faced the temptation that has plagued the community of believers in every age. In the desire to defend itself against adversity, it was tempted to pledge allegiance to penultimate powers, and the inevitable result was a confusion of God's kingdom with their own petty state. Life needs order, societies need structures, communities need leaders, but there is only one reliable safeguard against any of these penultimate entities being mistaken for the ultimate, and that is acknowledgment and sole worship of the true ultimate Being by the members of the community of faith.

We can point, therefore, to much that was politically inevitable, much that was socially deplorable, and much that was morally neutral in Solomon's kingdom. Furthermore, taken within the context of the longer history of Israel as a covenant people, we, like the Deuteronomistic historians, can detect a dangerous drift in the life of the nation. We fail to grasp the only key that can explain all these conflicting data, however, if we do not see the underlying truth the perspective of early Yahwism opens up for us. Despite all human longing for the kingdom combining righteousness with compassion, despite all human effort to achieve it, despite the reign of kings as clever as David or as wise as Solomon—the end result will be futile if the fundamental truth of Yahwism is forgotten. Yahweh alone can assure the reign of righteousness and compassion in the community, and indeed, for that to be possible Yahweh must be present at the center of that community's life together. Moreover, because of God's nature, that presence cannot be imitated by an abstract concept or a mythological prototype, nor can it be represented by an earthly image or a human mediator. The living God can be present only where all idols are renounced, and the community recalls in praise and relives in recital the salvation history in which God was personally present on behalf of the people: "I am Yahweh, who brought you out of the house of bondage . . . " For it is within that salvation history that God's people continues to live in the presence of the one true God, a history that did not end with an event of the past, but that continues in the lives of the community of faith as a testimony to God's faithfulness to a covenant of righteousness and compassion.

There was a future for the Yahwistic community of faith, therefore, not because of the magnificent achievements of kings, but because of God's faithfulness. But how are the innovations of kingship to be evaluated from this Yahwistic perspective, innovations that included the concept of Yahweh's anointed king and the eternal covenant of Yahweh with David? The importance of these contributions can be grasped only if Israel's fascination with a penultimate referent is replaced with their only proper ultimate referent. God's promise to establish a universal kingdom of righteousness and compassion and šālôm was an eternal promise, and as the message of Second Isaiah indicated, even in adversity and exile God would continue to draw the servant people into that task. Moreover, as the central theme of the kerygma of the early Church announced, God's promise of an anointed son also was a faithful promise. To be sure, under their Davidic kings, the united kingdom and then Judah sought to grasp this kingdom on their own terms, which was modeled largely after what they had observed of earthly kingdoms such as Phoenicia and Egypt. But by building on a concept of kingdom that adulterated God's plan with human substitutes, the Solomonic era, instead of inaugurating God's kingdom, initiated a long period of testing and learning. For until this people could be purged of their earthly ideas of God's reign, they would continue to confuse their penultimate kingdom with God's ultimate Kingdom.

If the League period can be viewed as a time when the Yahwistic notion of community was born and in which its fundamental qualities emerged in response to Yahweh, the period of kingship can then be seen as a time of testing and refining. In this period the prophets sought to keep alive the perspective of early Yahwism as they interpreted the events of their time to their people. Consistent with their belief that God was the absolute standard of righteousness and compassion who relativized all earthly norms and powers, the prophets subjected all institutions and leaders to the critique of their Yahwistic perspective. They detected the reintroduction of an order of earthly values in the royal ideology and the royal cult, and condemned it as idolatry. They condemned the people's running after earthly rulers as apostasy away from Yahweh, and foreign alliances as a breach of Israel's only legitimate covenant. If it were not for this critique, if Israelite religion had been embodied from this time forth exclusively within the forms of the royal temple of Solomon, it could well have blended into the other imperial cults of that age. It is because the perspective of early Yahwism was kept alive by the prophets and others upholding the earlier confessions that a faith and a notion of community continued to develop in Israel that resisted assimilation to the ways of "all the nations."

The prophets, however, did not flee from involvement in the social and political issues of their time as a means of preserving their confessions. True to the historical realism of Yahwism, they sought rather, for centuries, to convert kings to the Yahwistic ideal of worship, righteousness, and compassion, and to mold monarchy in Israel along lines compatible with faith in Yahweh. For example, Isaiah's royal pronouncements (cf. especially in chapters 7–11) portray the prophet as intensely engaged in drawing kings toward a Yahwistic ideal of kingship.

It is probably accurate to say that the prophets, especially in the north, held to a model of a strictly "limited kingship," such as we saw Samuel advocating vis-à-vis Saul and David. But gradually their struggle with kings and people as Yahweh's messengers taught the prophets a harsh lesson. By being consistent with their early Yahwistic perspective of a community formed around worship, righteousness and compassion, the prophets courageously held up before king and nation a standard that was repeatedly broken. Kings continued to act on behalf of their own glory rather than Yahweh's, and the people continued to seek earthly splendor rather than righteousness and compassion. The history of kingship was thus a history of increasing disappointment. Was Yahweh's promise unreliable after all? Either it was, or the people were looking for its fulfillment in the wrong place. The prophets became firmly convinced that the latter was true. And this led to three very important developments in the Yahwhistic notion of community: God's people came to be understood as a remnant, God's kingdom as an eschatological reign, and God's king as an eschatological messiah. All three of these developments were actually expressions of a return to the early Yahwistic belief in God's sole sovereignty and the accompanying relativization of all earthly norms and powers. The remnant concept was a reaction against the temptation to define God's reign in terms of earthly nations or institutions. The concept of God's eschatological reign represented a return to the belief that only God could establish the kingdom of righteousness and compassion. Messianism reestablished the clear distinction between the human and the divine: The anointed one, whom the people could trust as leading them to the true worship, righteousness, and compassion that constituted God's kingdom, could not be expected to appear in the triumphal splendor of earthly kings. The true Messiah's way of leading the people remained a mystery that only God could reveal, but that would probably involve suffering.

Although here anticipating the discussion of the final chapter of this book, I may observe that the reassessment of the theological significance of kingship just described could lead one to view in a new light what may otherwise seem to be a peculiar exegetical feature of a bygone era—namely, Luther's christological exegesis of the Psalms. In the Psalms, the pious were reaching for a personal and intimate communion with the one true God. When they sought to satisfy that longing by focusing on their earthly king, they were left empty and confused. What they were reaching for in these beautiful expressions of longing and hope was God's own presence, a longing and hope that would be satisfied when God sent the long-awaited messiah. According to Luther, this truth was clear to the prophets, due to their grounding in the perspective of true faith. And he felt that it was clear to the faithful of Israel who let the splendor of no earthly ruler distract them from the splendor of God's anointed one, even when his appearance came in the humblest of human conditions.[20]

E. THE THEME OF CREATION: A COMMUNITY DESCRIBES ITS HOME IN NATURE

The theme of creation, like the theme of wisdom, permeates much of the Old Testament. There were certain times and settings, however, in which such themes enjoyed a special floruit. In the case of creation, one such time was the early monarchy. Indeed, it would appear that it was in the era inaugurated by David and Solomon that focused attention was first turned to the realm of nature in the effort to explain the relation of the God revealed in historical experiences to the mysterious and wondrous qualities of nature.

---

20. For an example of Luther's christological interpretation of the royal psalms, see his commentary on Psalm 2, *Luther's Works*, Vol.12, edited by J. Pelikan (St. Louis: Concordia, 1955), 4–93. In discussing verse 6, Luther writes, "The world also has its kings, who rule by divine authority, as St. Paul says: 'All authority is from God' (Rom. 13:1). And yet they are, as St. Peter calls them, a 'human institution' (1 Pet. 2:13), that is, established by a human arrangement, with only the care of external and corporeal things entrusted to them. But this King, our Lord Jesus Christ, is appointed directly by the eternal Father Himself to be King and to be called the Father's King, or the King established by the Father. 'I,' He says, 'have set My King.' Therefore He sets Him apart from all the kings of the world" (pp. 36–37).

Why the monarchy would provide a setting within which interest in nature would flourish is evident. As indicated earlier in this chapter, a central concern of Israel's kings, in keeping with their counterparts in other nations, was to maintain the kind of order in their realm that assured both the security of their subjects and the perpetuity of their own dynasty. Within the cultural setting within which they lived, it was inevitable that this concern led to an interest in the larger natural order tha surrounded them, for throughout the ancient Near East it was assumed that social and political order was directly related to the maintenance of cosmic harmony. In that ancient world, cosmic harmony was of course the responsiblity of the gods. As the kings of Mesopotamia, Canaan, and Egypt devoted much energy and vast resources to cultivating the proper ritual enactment of the myths of creation, so too Israel's kings fostered the development of creation themes within the temple cult. Earlier in this chapter I noted numerous examples of this, and here recall one typical couplet from Psalm 89:25: "I will set his hand on sea/and his right hand on the rivers." In this promise of Yahweh to the king of Jerusalem, we see reflected the direct connection between the theme of cosmic order and the concern for social and political stability. Social and political stability was possible only in a world secured by Yahweh from the chaos represented by the sea and the rivers—a state of affairs manifested on earth by Yahweh's election of the Davidic king and the temple on Zion.

Thus far we have referred to the theme of creation as a concern of the king. It must be added that it was a concern shared by many others, especially those who had a direct investment in the monarchical structures such as priests and courtiers. But the royal psalms afford a glimpse of a culture within which the influence of the royal ideology reached out to influence wide circles within the populace as well, as the ritual of temple worship fostered an appreciation for the beauty and fruitfulness of the world around them and an awareness of its origin in God's creative activity. It is obvious that the priests of the temple, as well as the teachers and storytellers among the people, would have turned their attention to this theme of creation. In the first instance, their intent would have been confessional: The God whose might and grace is manifested in the world of nature and in the vast reaches of the cosmos is none other than Yahweh. In searching for the specific literary vehicles for this confession, however, Israel's priests, bards, and poets naturally looked to their larger cultural environment; that is, they used the creation language familiar to them. In contrast to our own tendency to raise the question of whether this involved syncretism, the Israelites would have found the idioms of creation that we find in Genesis and the Psalter to be the familiar parlance appropriate for such a subject, though, as is widely recognized, these idioms were taken from the common stock of mythical themes current in the ancient Near-ern kingdoms of that time. Alongside beautiful hymns such as Psalm

104, we thus find in the stories of Genesis 1–11 evidence of Israel's discovery of its relation to the natural environment.

This discovery led to a profound enrichment of the Yahwistic notion of community. It was a community living in a beautiful and fragile world, beautiful because it was the product of God's creative activity, fragile because its intricate harmony could be disrupted by human thoughtlessness and rebellion. Already in the tenth century, perhaps within the context of the Jerusalem court, the writer we call the Yahwist drew together older stories of creation and wedded them to the epic of Israel's birth in God's gracious deliverance of slaves from Egypt. This wedding had a remarkable effect on the epic. Israel was not a people detached from its natural environment, or forever wandering like a bedouin without a home to call its own. God had created for all humans, and thus Israel as well, a good home, one supportive of life and capable of benefitting its human inhabitants with great blessing. The effect of this introduction of the theme of creation was that the Yahwistic community would not only direct attention to its passing through history toward a goal promised by Yahweh, but it would also focus attention on the world of nature as a home—yes, even a garden—for which it was to care tenderly in partnership with the creator God.

To be sure, the Canaanites long before had described with force and beauty the intimate connection between the human and nature. But in contrast to the fertility cult of the Canaanites, which we can best glimpse from the Baal myths found in the literature of ancient Ugarit,[21] we find that within the Israelite cult the historical dimension of Israel's experience had an important effect on the theme of the community's relation to nature. In the cult of Baal, that relation was characterized by a mythological and naturalistic determinism. The fate of humans was determined by the gods manifested in the forces of nature. Humans were thus caught up in the ever recurring cycles of nature and bound by the social structures inferentially drawn from those cycles within the royal ideology. The dialectical relation between nature and history effected by the wedding of historical and creation traditions within the Yahwistic community led to a view of the human race as a part of a potentially harmonious natural order, but also raised to a consciousness of not being bound to its cycles and forces, but being led according to the plan of a God who freely directed cosmos and history and who called the community of faith to participate in that plan. As Gerhard von Rad has noted, this transformation in the attitude toward nature was achieved by the Yahwist's placing the creation traditions as a prelude to the historical traditions of the epic.[22]

It would be going too far, however, to say that the creation traditions were thereby simply subsumed under the historical aspects of Yahwis-

---

21. An excellent translation of and introduction to these myths is found in M. Coogan, *Stories from Ancient Canaan* (Philadelphia: Westminster Press, 1978).

22. Von Rad, *Theology*, Vol. 1, 138–139.

tic faith, depriving them of a unique contribution to biblical thought. As Psalms 29, 89, and 104 indicate, creation as a theme was present in Yahwistic thought as a source of theological reflection on aspects of experience inadequately addressed by a perspective strictly historical in orientation. And as Isaiah 34–35, Proverbs 8:22–31, and Job 38–42 indicate, at times in Israel's historical pilgrimage the historicist perspective proved ill equipped to explain the riddles of life. At those times, creation traditions offered a fresh perspective and even a basis for new hope.

The stories of Genesis 1–11 themselves indicate how profoundly the Yahwistic community was enriched by being located explicitly within its larger natural and world environment. At a later time the Priestly Writing, in turn drawing on older liturgical material from the Jerusalem temple, described the order of which Israel was a part in its widest reaches (Gen. 1:1–2:4a). But from its more anthropocentric perspective, the Yahwist already gave rich description of the relation of the human race to its world, pointing in symbols both bright and dark to the heights and depths of that relationship.

At the very beginning of the Yahwist's account of the earliest history of the human race, we read of Yahweh's creating the first human. Formed from the dust of the ground, this being is distinguished from the divine much more clearly and emphatically than, for example, in the Babylonian *Enūma eliš*, where the human race is fashioned from the blood of the slain god Kingu. The connection the creator God established with this creature is spiritual rather than material, for Yahweh "breathed into his nostrils the breath of life; and ['ādām] became a living being" (Gen. 2:7b). No sooner has the goodness and beauty of the natural home Yahweh provided 'ādām been described, however, than the ambiguity of the human's relation to nature begins to appear. In the garden is a tree 'ādām is forbidden to eat, under threat of death (Gen. 2:17). This establishes the rightful home of the human on this earth, for while one finds in ancient Near Eastern mythology the search for the food of immortality as an expression of the human's longing for escape from the mundane realm to the realm of the gods,[23] the biblical story makes the emphatic point that the attempt to deny one's mortality by eating the food of immortality can only lead to a degrading of the good life given by God to humans within their earthly habitation.

It next becomes evident that Yahweh has not established this home in order that 'ādām might live in stark isolation, but that 'ādām might enjoy a full life as a social and relational being. After the animal world has

---

23. Of the ancient Near Eastern stories dealing with the search for immortality, pride of place goes to the adventures of Gilgamesh, which tell of his ill-fated meeting with the one to whom the gods had awarded immmortality, Utnapishtim (E. A. Speiser, "The Epic of Gilgamesh," *ANET*, 3d ed., pp. 72–99).

been formed around '*ādām*, the climax of the creativity of God is reached when the human partnership between man and woman is established. With simple beauty, the essentially communal nature of the human and the profound interconnectedness between man and woman is expressed by the creation of the partner from the rib of '*ādām*.

The ambiguity already hinted at by the description of the tree of the knowledge of good and evil deepens into a dark shadow in the form of the serpent in Genesis 3:1–7. Although humans have an intimation of the harmony that should characterize their relation to nature, to one another, and to God, the harsh realities of life have taught them of labor and pain and strife. This dark side is taken up not only in the curses of serpent, woman, and man in 3:14–19, but is developed over the course of the remaining stories in Genesis 1–11. The brothers Cain and Abel contend, and the earth is stained by the blood of homicide (Gen. 4:1–16). The discoveries of early inventors turn into implements of further violence (4:17–24). The sin and rebellion escalates even to heaven (6:1–4), and becomes so grave as to prompt God to regret having created the human race and to send the flood. Although Yahweh is gracious, and promises not to repeat the flood, even then the survivor plays the part of the fool by becoming hopelessly drunk on the fruits of the good earth (9:20–27). Noah's cursing Canaan and blessing Shem points to a startling manner of distinguishing between the nations, although this and the genealogical tables that follow, with their division of the human family along the lines of Shem, Ham, and Jephtah give us an intriguing glimpse at Israel's early efforts to locate herself not only within the natural world but also within the world of the nations.

The Yahwistic primeval narrative ends on a very ominous note. The last united effort of the human race was to build a tower to heaven, quite clearly another attempt to transcend the mortal state and to attain to the realm of the divine. The division of the world into its vast array of nations and tongues arose of the necessity felt by God to thwart this act of rebellion. The Yahwistic account of the earliest history of humanity thus poses a serious question: What is to come of a race both given such a beautiful and fruitful natural home and yet apparently determined to degrade it? The Yahwist was aware, of course, that the national epic to which he attached the primordial history would address that question, beginning already in Genesis 12 with the promise of blessing given by Yahweh to Abraham. From our perspective, we can see that the answer was even broader, extending over the entire Bible, and on through the long confessional heritage beyond.

The extent of the contribution of the creation theme to Israel's reflection on its identity as a people of God thus does not only become clear in writings like Job or Second Isaiah, but is evident in Genesis 1–11 as well. The world around was not simply a matter of indifference, to be exploited mindlessly and callously. It was a part of a harmonious divinely created order to which humans were closely related. Within that order, antedating Israel's own history as a people and reaching far beyond its own borders, members of the community of faith were to live in faithfulness to God and in uprightness toward one another. The bright and dark symbols of these stories together emphasize how delicate was the created order within which God had placed humans. To be a faithful people thus implied not only being faithful witnesses to God's saving events in history, but also being responsible caretakers of their natural habitat and trustworthy neighbors of the many peoples with whom they shared this good earth.

The importance of the creation theme for contemporary communities of faith by and large has not received the attention it deserves in the history of the West. Focus has often been almost exclusively directed toward the historical traditions. Nature has been treated with cold indifference as an object to be used pretty much according to human caprice. What must be regarded as a narrow and misleading interpretation of Genesis 1:26 has even been used in defense of the exploitation of nature.[24] Especially at a time when the beauty and fragility of our natural home is being rediscovered, partly out of alarm over the devastating centuries of arrogant and insensitive human plundering of the natural world's riches, much more attention needs to be paid to the broad context within which the community of faith is placed in the Bible according to the creation traditions. This context in turn influences the way in which other traditions are read and understood. As with other neglected traditions such as wisdom and apocalyptic, the creation traditions of Genesis, Job, Proverbs, the Psalms, and Second Isaiah beckon sensitive people of faith to broaden their perspectives by an openness to the manifestation of God not only in historical events, but in other broad spheres Western thought has often failed to comprehend.

F. THE DIVIDED KINGDOM

It may be that biblical historians are too hasty in assuming that the division of the Davidic-Solomonic kingdom into north and south was a political inevitability. After all, the hitherto separate tribes had united under David, for they had recognized in him a leader who was sensitive to the values and traditions they cherished the most. And in the important area of the cult, this involved David's respect for and accommodation to their understanding of worship, righteousness, and compassion. Conversely, Solomon's insensitivity to this places a great strain on the union. The north and south parted company for some very clear reasons. Those reasons were deeply related to Solomon's high-handed administration of nation and cult.

---

24. Cf. Lynn White, Jr., "The Historical Roots of Our Ecologic Crisis," *Science* 155 (1967), pp. 1203–1207.

The despotic court style of Solomon was brought to a high degree of refinement by his son Rehoboam. It seems that his succession to the throne occurred in Judah without protest. In the north a very different situation prevailed. The biblical narrative in 1 Kings 12 pictures the northern clans gathered at Shechem. In their negotiations with Rehoboam, their point of reference was the concept of a "limited monarchy" that could foster a fair synthesis between early Yahwism and the monarchical form of rule. Their standard was the one with which we have grown familiar, involving righteousness and compassion; that is, order blended with sensitivity to human need that was inclusive of all the people. On the basis of that standard, they made the reasonable request that the severe policies of Solomon be modified: "Your father made our yoke heavy. Now therefore lighten the hard service of your father and his heavy yoke upon us, and we will serve you" (1 Kings 12:4). After repudiating the sage advice of older court counselors in favor of the impudence of his young companions, Rehoboam brought back to these fair-minded citizens a stinging insult to their cherished notion of community: "My father made your yoke heavy, but I will add to your yoke; my father chastized you with whips, but I will chastize you with scorpions" (1 Kings 12:14).

Immediately the call for secession went out: "To your tents, O Israel!" In a further sign of his insensitivity to Israel's sense of righteousness and compassion, Rehoboam sent the one who symbolized like none other the odiousness of absolute monarchy, "Adoram, who was taskmaster over the forced laber," obviously to bring the rebels to submission! The narrative concludes by describing the grim consequences of Rehoboam's tactless action. The terse style is masterfully suited to the content: "And all Israel stoned him to death with stones. And King Rehoboam made haste to mount his chariot, to flee to Jerusalem" (1 Kings 12:18).

The tradition behind this break of the northern tribes with the absolute kingship of Solomon is the early Yahwism associated with the sanctuaries of Gilgal, Shiloh, and Shechem. This is suggested by the use of the word 'ēdâ to designate the group gathered to negotiate with Rehoboam, for this is the archaic term used for the "sacral assembly" of the League. Moreover, it is significant that they met at Shechem; that is, at one of their sanctuaries.

The nature of the conflict that culminated in secession is also revealed by the story of Jeroboam and Ahijah in 1 Kings 11. In Jeroboam, we meet a person whose role and destiny resemble Moses's in several important respects. Due to his strong personal qualities, he was drawn from the ranks of his fellow countrymen and placed in a privileged position: Solomon made him captain "over all the forced labor of the house of Joseph" (1 Kings 11:28). That is, he was drawn from the ranks of his kinsmen to become their slavemaster! Rather than enjoy personal benefits at the expense of the oppression of his fellow Ephraimites, however, he "lifted up his hand against the king" (v. 26b). With these new facts, this story informs us that Jeroboam was unwilling to tolerate Solomon's flagrant disregard of the old Yahwistic standard of righteousness.

Ahijah's appearance in the story is particularly important. We have seen how Solomon's reign began with the removal of all opposition and the silencing of all criticism, and how it ran its course with no interference from the prophets. But finally, after the restiveness of the common people had erupted in a powerful distrust of Solomon, a prophet appeared. His home, significantly, was Shiloh, for also at home there were the Mushite priests, who like Jeroboam, had been banished from the court of Solomon. Following the archaic Yahwistic pattern reminiscent of Samuel, Ahijah designated the fugitive Jeroboam as future king of Israel, using a vivid sign act in which he tore a garment into twelve pieces. Clearly early Yahwism was reasserting its concept of governance by insisting on the limitation of kingship and the freedom of Yahweh to appoint leaders out of the ranks of the people through the prophetic oracle. Indeed, the rending of the garment into twelve pieces evokes memory of Yahweh's holy war against his enemies in the period of the League (cf. Judg. 19:29–30, 1 Sm. 11:7). Against this background, the full significance of the call to revolt in 1 Kings 12:16 becomes recognizable. By reaffirming their archaic values, the northern tribes were able to declare that their "portion," their "inheritance," was not to be found in the Davidic monarchy, but in the old traditions of their monarchical past: 'To your tents, O Israel! Look now to your own house, David" (1 Kings 12:16).

Thus the phenomenon of Israelite monarchy developed another complicated facet: In Judah, the Davidic dynasty continued. In the north, the older "limited kingship" ideal of Samuel was reintroduced as more compatible with the early Yahwistic beliefs cherished by the clans north of Judah. And so the reconstituted assembly ('ēdâ) summoned Jeroboam, the Ephraimite who had had the courage to oppose his patron Solomon. The archaic pattern of the League was restored as the assembly of the people added their acclamation to the divine designation mediated by the Shilonite prophet Ahijah.

The story of the division of the Solomonic kingdom is interesting in a study of the Yahwistic notion of community especially for the following reason. It indicates that the early Yahwism of Gilgal, Shiloh, and Shechem, which played such a decisive role in defining the qualities of community in terms of worship, righteousness, and compassion, persisted as a living force. Its effects were more visible at this time in the north than in the south (where the royal ideology was successful in minimizing its role). The group that emerged as the courageous defender of the old Yahwistic ideal was the prophets.

Our task would be greatly simplified if after the tense period of the division of the kingdom all significant developments in the Yahwistic notion of community were henceforth confined to the north. Then, in a manner quite contrary to that of the Chronicler, we could trace the history of Israel and ignore Judah. But a disturbing fact disallows this approach: Although the Northern Kingdom evolved a form of kingship that in important respects was more compatible with early Yahwism than were the institutions of the Jerusalem court, it sadly proved to be less than the ideal foster parent of Yahwistic faith. Not only were its kings in general hostile to the qualities at the heart of the Yahwistic community of faith, but also the pattern of kingship that developed in the north seemed to abet a far higher degree of instability than was found in the south. Out of this complex set of circumstances, one truth stands out all the more clearly: the true Yahwistic notion of community was no longer identifiable with a political entity. Its nature and qualities would develop in the less tangible (though certainly not less real) spiritual community of those worshipping the one true God, and seeking to embody God's righteousness and compassion. This community would grow and develop in the south under Davidic rule, and in the north under a somewhat different type of kingship. It would draw on Jerusalem temple theology, the wisdom of the seers, and the language and praxis of priests; and as often it would grow through opposition to these institutions and traditions. But throughout its history it would never forsake the root from which it had grown and that still gave it is most dependable sustenance, the early Yahwistic confessions about "Yahweh, who brought you out of the house of bondage." Moreover, this memory would be kept alive especially because of the tireless efforts of the prophets, the group that more than any other proved itself to be Yahweh's chosen instrument for preserving a faithful people of God through the troubling times of the monarchy.

V

Growth Through Adversity: Prophecy and Kingship in the Northern Kingdom
(Deuteronomy, 1 Kings, Amos, and Hosea)

> *Historical Note:* Imposed on Israel as an historical inevitability
> and presenting both an opportunity for significant growth
> and a temptation to turn from the central ideals of Yahwism,
> kingship was met by a worthy challenger—prophecy. The
> traditions clustered around the figure of Elijah in 1 Kings,
> the oracles of Amos and Hosea, and the Book of Deuteron-
> omy provide a sound basis for studying the growth of the
> Yahwistic notion of community in the Northern Kingdom in
> the period 932–722 B.C.E. It was a period in which the outside
> world pressed mightily on the people of Yahweh, in the form
> of the Egyptian and Assyrian empires, necessitating a rethink-
> ing of the earlier confessions within a much larger and more
> threatening universe.

Prophecy did not introduce a new form of religion in Israel. Rather,
the prophets, having experienced a call to proclaim God's word and to
preserve a people of God amid a maelstrom of competing commitments, spoke from a confessional heritage already having centuries of
history behind it. While never giving a systematic description of the notion of the community of faith, it is clear from their messages that they
spoke on behalf of a tradition committed to the sole worship of the
God Yahweh, whose righteousness and compassion as revealed in their
own history of redemption they felt called to embody as a testimony to
God's presence in the world. In the unsettled centuries of the monarchies of Israel and Judah, it was not primarily in the royal sanctuaries,
but among the circles of the prophets and their disciples that the Yahwistic notion of community developed. The prophets stood apart from
their compatriots by virtue of their radical commitment to God's will.
Their openness to transcendence placed them in their ecstatic experiences in the presence of God, which in the idiom of that time meant

that they were privy to the deliberations of the divine assembly; that is, Yahweh and the council of divine beings gathered around Yahweh. Thus they construed their vocations in terms of placing themselves at the disposal of God. Consequently, even at times when the vast majority of these two nations and their rulers were dedicated to other primary devotions than Yahweh, the Yahwistic notion of community did not die, but grew through testing and refinement.

Since Solomon's policy of repressing prophetic criticism was continued with a vengeance by his son Rehoboam, we need to turn at first to the Northern Kingdom, where the earlier idea of a "limited kingship" assured the prophets a voice in the life of the people.

A. THE PROPHETIC RESPONSE TO JEROBOAM'S CULT

Jeroboam became king of Israel with the aid of the prophet Ahijah of Shiloh, who recognized him to be an opponent of the oppressive policies of Solomon, a defender of the older Yahwistic notion of righteousness, and thus an appropriate civil leader of the people. But Jeroboam, after having accepted Ahijah's prophetic designation as king, soon broke off the relationship between king and prophet that was essential to the concept of "limited monarchy." Indeed, he took cultic matters into his own hands with a zeal unequaled by Solomon. According to 1 Kings 12:25–33, he recognized the threat that the Jerusalem cult posed to the independence of his own reign, and took radical measures to provide a religious cult that would tie the religious allegiance of the people to his own territory. Accordingly, he created two cult objects, set one up in Dan and one in Bethel, identified the God represented by the cult objects with the god "who brought you up out of the land of Egypt" (v. 28), appointed priests of his own choosing and a festival date "which he had devised of his own heart" (v. 33). It is apparent that the Deuteronomistic editors have heightened the offensiveness of Jeroboam's action in keeping with the role they assigned to him as the paradigm of sinfulness in the entire subsequent history of the Northern Kingdom. The bulls are portrayed as idols of "your *gods*, O Israel," and the point is made that the priests were illegitimate ("not of the Levites"). As has frequently been argued, it is unimaginable that Jeroboam could have attempted to introduce the worship of a duality of gods into Israel. Rather likely here was his attempt to provide the people with an iconography with an even older history than the ark. And evidence suggests that the priests placed in Bethel and Dan were of priestly families claiming descent from Aaron and Moses, respectively.[1] Jeroboam tried mightily to consolidate his kingdom around cult centers

---

1. For a full development of this line of interpretation, cf. F. M. Cross, *Canaanite Myth and Hebrew Epic* (Cambridge, Mass.: Harvard University Press, 1973), pp. 73–75.

that could be acceptable to his subjects, thereby keeping their hearts from longing for Jerusalem.

But precisely here we have the point at which the prophet Ahijah—and the northern prophetic tradition after him all the way down to the Deuteronomistic School—took offense. Ahijah's designation of Jeroboam as king indicates that he was able to recognize the legitimacy of a political division in Israel; after all, he viewed Solomon's reign from the old Yahwistic perspective of a conditional covenant, a covenant that Solomon had broken, leading to a disruption in the Davidic reign (1 Kings 11:33). By the same token, while serving as Yahweh's prophetic agent in Jeroboam's designation as king over the northern tribes, Ahijah, as he was remembered and portrayed by the Deuteronomistic School, viewed Jeroboam's royal mandate in the same strictly conditional terms: "And if you will hearken to all that I command you, and will walk in my ways, and do what is right in my eyes by keeping my statutes and my commandments, as David my servant did, I will be with you, and will build you a sure house, as I built for David, and I will give Israel to you" (1 Kings 11:38). Now, at a point well into Jeroboam's reign, Ahijah evaluates the king he had designated and over against whom he still sees himself as Yahweh's prophetic spokesman, and against the standard of early Yahwistic faith he finds that Jeroboam has broken covenant ("done evil above all that was before you"). The exact formulation of the condemnation in 1 Kings 14:7–11 again is colored with the unitary themes of the Deuteronomistic History. But there is no reason to doubt that at the basis of the chapter lies an old report of Ahijah's judgment on Jeroboam for this king's betrayal of his divine charge. Jeroboam has removed the sole worship of Yahweh from the center of his cult, and overlaid the ancient Yahwistic centers of Bethel and Dan with a royal ideology designed to serve the monarchy. And all this he has done in the effort to control the lives of his subjects, including their spiritual devotion. In a profound theological sense, then, the Deuteronomic coloring of the story in 1 Kings makes the essential point: Jeroboam's construction of the Bethel and Dan sanctuaries with their symbols did constitute idolatry, for they were intended to bind the allegiance of the people to a kingship other than Yahweh's.

The theological significance of this cultic innovation of Jeroboam is indicated also by the prophetic legend in 1 Kings 13, with its scathing condemnation of the altar of Bethel. There was thus introduced at this point a theme, taken from early Yahwism, which would run throughout prophecy: As soon as the religious community had allowed penultimate concerns to encroach on the sole worship of Yahweh, it had broken the covenant on which its life was based, and faced death. By clearly recognizing its point of reference within the premonarchical conception of the Yahwistic community with the triadic notion of worship, righteousness, and compassion, we are able to understand that the prophetic position rests on more than a rash vindictiveness. Without the heart of the people sustained by sole worship of its God, the triad falls into decay, and the people of God come to naught. Kings, like judges before them, were called to safeguard and enhance righteousness and compassion, but this they could do only by allowing their people to turn in worship to the one true God. Where they placed their own interests between their subjects and God, they became enemies of God, and thus enemies of the prophets. In such a case, the prophets, if they remained true to their mandate as messengers of Yahweh, had no choice other than to deliver an oracle of judgment.

In the biblical description of the early years of David, we are able to catch a glimpse of the kind of kingship with which the prophets were able to cooperate. It was one in which the king submitted, along with his subjects, to the stringent demands of righteousness and where the religious leaders taught the old Yahwistic confessions and thus preserved the motivational force for Israel's obedience in the example of the compassionate Deliverer God. Within such a kingdom, the hearts of all the people, including the kings, united in worship of the one true God. In the early years of the Northern Kingdom, however, we observe how King Jeroboam jeopardized the essential Yahwistic triad of worship, righteousness, and compassion by placing personal ambitions at the center of his program. Clearly, Jeroboam was not solely to blame. His fears of losing the hearts of his subjects, and the control of his kingdom, were not imagined, as the frequent border skirmishes between the northern and southern armies attest. Moreover, a legacy of unfaithfulness had already accumulated, including both Rehoboam's repudiation of the reasonable terms of his Yahwistic subjects and Solomon's self-glorification, which left no room for the prophets. Naturally, we could go on tracing this sordid legacy beyond Solomon to the aging David, to the unstable Saul, to the derelict priests of Shiloh, and so on. The leitmotif we can trace through this long, tragic history is the broken covenant relationship.

The only possible remedy would have been thoroughgoing repentance and reform, based on the old Yahwistic ideals. But with the kings of this period little disposed to reform, we witness an ungodly succession of sin and blood from Jeroboam and Nadab to Baasha, and from Baasha and Elah to Zimri. These were years of border disputes between Israel and Judah, the loss of territory with the subsequent reduction of the kingdoms to petty states, and in general little worth remembering aside from details such as the humiliation suffered by the land in Pharoah Shishak's invasion, King Elah's drinking bout that ended in this assassination, and Zimri's ill-fated seven-day reign.

B. AHAB AND HIS PROPHETIC ADVERSARY ELIJAH

The Northern Kingdom had experienced two ill-fated attempts to establish a royal dynasty, with Nadab succeeding his father Jeroboam and Elah his father Baasha. Zimri was an outright usurper with a thin support base, hence his week-long reign. It seemed that this chaotic succession history was to continue as the people then divided in following two different aspirants, Tibni and Omri. But the supporters of the latter prevailed, with Omri going on to establish the first significant dynasty in the north, and building up a kingdom whose strength was acknowledged as far away as Assyria.

Little is recorded about Omri in the Bible, aside from his founding of Samaria as the new capital of Israel and a summary note from the Deuteronomists that he "did more evil than all who were before him" (1 Kings 16:25). Between these two notes, however, we are able to glimpse a political and socioreligious situation that would be of critical importance for the destiny of Yahwism in the following century and a half.

The note about Omri's purchase reads, "He bought the hill of Samaria from Shemer for two talents of silver; and he fortified the hill, and called the name of the city which he built, Samaria, after the name of Shemer, the owner of the hill" (1 Kings 16:24). In moving from Tirzah to a new capital, Omri's intentions seem clear. No longer would his royal city be bound to the customs and traditions of the Israelite settlements. Like David's Jerusalem, Samaria would be private property of the crown, to be constructed as the king desires. Moreover, this independent city, again in a manner reminiscent of David's Jerusalem, was situated between two distinct elements of the population, both which could best be appeased from an independent royal city between them. But here the similarity ends, for while David's two populations were both Yahwistic, Omri was seeking to unify the Yahwistic elements of the old tribal holdings with the Baal-worshipping Canaanite population in the plains to the west and the north of Samaria. It is therefore significant that the orientation of Samaria, in contrast to Tirzah, is toward Canaanite Phoenicia. Omri's close relationship to the royal house of Tyre was ratified by the marriage of his son Ahab to Jezebel, daughter of King Ethbaal (named "king of the Sidonians" in 1 Kings 16:3, which is a general term for the Phoenicians at this period).

Ahab continued the policy of his father, encouraged now, of course, by his Phoenician wife. Solomon had accommodated to the religious practices of his foreign wives by building shrines dedicated to their gods on Mount Carmel. But Ahab went a significant step further. Although the report in 1 Kings is written from the point of view of the Deuteronomists, and is thus both southern and Yahwistic in orienta-

tion, the general situation seems clear: Ahab built a Baal temple in Samaria, which was intended to be the official sanctuary of his kingdom.
This was indeed a very daring way to effect a rapprochment with the
Canaanite elements within his kingdom. But in fact it drove a sharp
wedge into the society, as illustrated by the clash between the two
strong individuals named Jezebel and Obadiah. The former was the
daughter of a Canaanite king now seeking to purge her newly adopted
home of Yahweh-worshippers out of her zeal for Baal. And Obadiah
was devoted to Yahweh, and doing his best to give refuge to the hunted
prophets: "Now Obadiah revered the Lord greatly; and when Jezebel
cut off the prophets of the Lord, Obadiah took a hundred prophets
and hid them by fifties in a cave, and fed them with bread and water"
(1 Kings 18:3b–4).

The nucleus of Yahwistic opposition to Ahab's syncretistic policies
was propheticism, in the form of wandering bands gathered around
their charismatic leaders. Of the latter, the one most highly revered by
tradition for his courageous defense of Yahwistic faith and the early
Yahwistic notion of community was Elijah the Tisbite, whom, on their
first recorded encounter, king Ahab named "troubler of Israel." Elijah's reply to the king introduces the conflict between king and prophet with terse accuracy: "I have not troubled Israel; but you have, and
your father's house, because you have forsaken the commandments of
the Lord and followed the Baals." The roots of the trouble that
plagued the community are clear from the perspective of Elijah's Yahwistic faith: Betrayal of the one true God, and the inevitable subsequent violation of the commandments; that is, of those guidelines describing the embodiment of God's righteousness and compassion in the
community.

The contest to which Elijah challenged Ahab focuses directly on this
betrayal of Israel's covenant with Yahweh. And Mount Carmel was an
appropriate place, since it was a traditional holy mountain between
Phoenician (Baalistic) and Israelite (Yahwistic) territory. Elijah's opening questions to the people attacked Ahab's policy of a middle road between Baalism and Yahwism head on: "How long will you go limping
with two different opinions? If the Lord is God, follow him; but if Baal,
follow him" (1 Kings 18:2). After the Baal priests had failed to awaken
their god ("there was no voice; no one answered, no one heeded"), Elijah made preparation for his appeal to Yahweh. The description of his
actions and his speech reveal the roots of his perspective in the early
Yahwistic exodus-conquest tradition: The altar he erected consists of
twelve stones, and he addresses his God as "Yahweh, God of Abraham,
Isaac and Israel." After Yahweh's dramatic reply in consuming fire, the
people respond according to the ancient pattern we observed in early
Yahwistic tradition, namely, in worship: "And when the people saw it,
they fell on their faces." And their confession gives emphatic and

memorable expression to the heart of Yahwistic community: "The Lord, he is God; the Lord he is God" (1 Kings 18:39). Acknowledgment of the sovereignty of Yahweh and undivided devotion to the one true God: here we see vividly the austere Yahwistic alternative to Ahab's syncretistic flirtation with Canaanite deities and foreign alliances! And the great rain that follows establishes Yahweh as supreme precisely in the realm Baal supposedly controlled—fertility (v. 45)!

Elijah's harsh treatment of Jezebel's Baal priests placed him under her curse, and a hunt ensued. The story of the prophet's flight to Horeb, and of the theophany that took place there, depict Elijah as a second Moses, another way of underlining the roots of prophecy in early Yahwism (cf. also 2 Kings 1:8). But the newness of the prophetic era is also described: Yahweh speaks not in the conventional wind, earthquake, and fire of theophany, but in a whisper; that is to say, in a word perceptible only to Yahweh's attentive hearers, the prophets. For in this mode Yahweh would henceforth speak to the community of faithful followers.

The role of the prophet as Yahweh's representative in both the political and sacral realms finds powerful expression in the following threefold commission of Elijah: to anoint Hazael to be king of Syria, Jehu to be king over Israel, and Elisha to be his successor as prophet (1 Kings 19:15–18). In this emphatic formulation, prophetic Yahwism declared its commitment to the concept of "limited kingship," according to which the prophets would be charged with the weighty responsibilities of designating and dismissing kings, and of keeping king and people mindful of their true sovereign, Yahweh.

Another responsibility falling to the prophets in this tradition was the declaration of holy war against Yahweh's enemies, a theme coming to expression in 1 Kings 20 and 22. Of special note in this connection is the first appearance of a class of prophets whose primary allegiance was to the king rather than to Yahweh. 1 Kings 22 portrays four hundred of them giving the war oracle King Ahab desires. The phenomenon of court prophecy can be interpreted as evidence for an attempt made by Israel's kings to gain control of the prophetic office, and thus to eliminate the criticism coming from the perspective of early Yahwism. But the appearance of the king's troupe of professional soothsayers prophesying victory (a scene familiar from the Assyrian annals) is not convincing to Ahab's ally, King Jehoshaphat of Judah, a king remembered by tradition as a faithful Yahwist. The latter's request for another opinion leads Ahab to admit, "There is yet one man by whom we may inquire of the Lord, Micaiah the son of Imlah; but I hate him for he never prophesies good concerning me, but evil" (v. 18).

Micaiah is summoned, and after mocking the king by parroting the word of the court prophets (or just playing it safe?), he comes forth and proclaims his true prophetic word, a stinging message of judgment (v.

7). Then follows a vivid description of the transcendent source of his true word and of the false word of his rivals: "I saw the Lord sitting on his throne, and all the host of heaven standing beside him on his right hand and on his left" (v. 19). This Micaiah tradition obviously stems from Yahwistic circles closely related to the Elijah tradition with its claim that there was in Israel a means by which Yahweh's continued presence in the lives of people could be experienced. This means was not associated with the king's pretensions to godlike power, but with the God-fearing obedience of the prophets, which prepared in them an openness to the disclosure of divine will.

Also coming from the prophetic circles active during the Omride dynasty is the majestic narrative in 1 Kings 21, Naboth's Vineyard. Whether Elijah was the original prophetic figure in this story has been questioned, since the reference to the Naboth incident found in 2 Kings 9:25–26 quotes the prophetic word of 1 Kings 21 without attributing it to Elijah.[2] What is clear is that it describes an attack on the heart of the Yahwistic notion of community that offered such a poignant illustration of the conflict between the two ideals then dividing the people that it came to enjoy a prominent place within the traditions of those resisting the excesses of kingship in the name of Yahwistic faith.

The Naboth story describes what occurred in Israel whenever the sole worship of the one true God was repudiated in favor of idols: righteousness and compassion, the other essential qualities of the healthy society, collapsed and were replaced by the whims of ungodly rulers. In many important details, the account describes the conflict between two diametrically opposed notions of community, one based on the unlimited claims of absolute kingship, the other on the early Yahwistic covenant tradition associated with Gilgal, Shiloh, and Shechem. This becomes apparent already in the opening scene. Guided by the predisposition of Israel's wealthy to "join house to house" and "add field to field until there is no more room" (Isa. 5:5), which incensed the prophets of both kingdoms, Ahab's covetous eyes turned to the vineyard of Naboth, which bordered his Jezreel palace. Ahab said, "Give me your vineyard . . . and I will give you a better vineyard for it; or, if it seems good to you, I will give you its value in money" (1 Kings 21:2). Ahab's attitude toward his subject's property was consistent with that of the Canaanites, as indicated by the Ugaritic texts of ancient Ras Shamra, and by Egyptian attitudes toward real estate, including the Pharoah's unlimited claims over property.[3] But Naboth responds from a completely different perspective: "The Lord forbid that I should give

2. Cf. O. H. Steck, *Überlieferung und Zeitgeschichte in den Elia-Erzählungen*, WMANT 26 (Neukirchen-Vluyn: Neukirchener Verlag, 1968), and P. Welten, "Naboths Weinberg" (I König 21), *EvTh* 33 (1973), 18–32.

3. Cf. K. Baltzer, "Nabothsweinberg," *Wort und Dienst* NF 8 (1965), 81–84.

you the inheritance (*naḥălâ*) of my fathers" (v. 3). He thereby appeals to the early Yahwistic institution of the *naḥălâ*, described in Chapter III as a means in early Israel of protecting the rights of each family against the self-aggrandizement of the powerful. The proposition of the king is something that from the perspective of Naboth's understanding of God is simply unthinkable and impossible. In contrast to the king's thinking, he does not have free disposition over the land. In Israel, the land is Yahweh's, held by the individual in trust in perpetuity. This understanding comes to vivid expression in a subtle shift in vocabulary. In his offer, the king used the ordinary word "vineyard" (*kérem*) to describe Naboth's property (v. 2). Naboth, in his reply, substitutes for the objective language of one dealing in real estate, a term loaded with theological meaning: "inheritance" (*naḥălâ*) (v. 3 and 4). The two do not speak the same language; they represent two different worlds![4]

In the second scene, we discover why Ahab, an Israelite, represents an anti-Yahwistic, Canaanite view. Behind the king stands a powerful queen. So after Jezebel finds her husband sulking on his bed and refusing to eat, and has asked him to explain his problem (again he uses the word "vineyard" and not "inheritance" in referring to Naboth's property [v. 6]), she replies incisively, "Do you now govern Israel? Arise, and eat bread, and let your heart be cheerful; I will give you the vineyard (*kérem*) of Naboth the Jezreelite" (v. 7). Here now is the true exponent of royal majesty, certainly not willing to allow the archaic beliefs of a common vintner to stand in the way of the crown!

It is interesting, though, that this clever and ruthless Canaanite queen nevertheless has to reckon with the customs of her adopted land. Here the royal court cannot merely seize the property. Such matters go through the assembly of the people. Therefore, using Ahab's royal seal, she writes letters to the elders and nobles of Jezreel, ordering a fast, and arranging to have false witnesses accuse Naboth of cursing God and king, heinous acts threatening the order of the community and thereby calling for purgation of the offender by stoning. Her scheme carried out, she is able to revert back to the customs associated with absolute monarchy, according to which the property of one thus executed would fall to the royal house. And thus we see Ahab entering Naboth's vineyard to take possession.

There the king meets the third person of the narrative, Elijah the prophet, whom he "greets" with the words, "Have you found me, O my enemy?" (v. 20). Elijah enters the scene as a representative of another king, Yahweh, the protector of those oppressed by the ungodly powerful. In early Israel the *naḥălâ* had been understood as a gift from Yahweh designed to spare people from the impoverishment that Hebrew slaves had experienced under the Pharaohs. But the *naḥălâ* of Na-

---

4. This point is brought out by P. Welten in the article mentioned in n. 2 above.

both had been violated, he had been unjustly sentenced to death as a blasphemer, and the specter of destitution and slavery had fallen on his descendents, who were henceforth deprived of their share in the land and in Yahweh's order of *šālôm*.

As we have seen, however, absolute kingship had been unable to silence those bearing witness to an earlier ideal of community in Israel, the ideal cherished by people covenanted with the God who had revealed the essential features of a righteous and compassionate society long before kingship had been introduced in Israel. As one of those witnesses to the earlier Yahwistic ideal, Elijah speaks in the name of the only king who was entitled to unlimited authority in Israel. And on that authority he announces that it is not Naboth who has blasphemed and thus incurred the sentence of death, but the king. For in arrogating to himself godly prerogatives, in killing and taking possession, he has incurred the guilt for which Naboth was unjustly punished. As defender of that early Yahwistic notion of community, Elijah takes the side of the innocently slain Naboth, and as spokesman of the God of that covenant community he pronounces judgment on the actual offender. The Naboth story thus stands in Hebrew Scripture as a stately monument to an ideal that the royal house itself was unable to destroy: There was but one authority in Israel, and that was Yahweh, God of righteousness and compassion. Accordingly every individual, king and commoner alike, enjoyed the same protections and bore the same responsibilities under the just commandments of that divine authority.

This remarkable narrative thus testifies to the fact that even in the face of formidable competition from other ideals, the early Yahwistic notion of community continued to develop, albeit in the refining fires of recurrent persecution. The triad forming the center of that notion—worship, righteousness, and compassion—could not be portrayed more clearly than in this story, which moreover explicates their dynamic interrelationship. Chapter III of this book observed how righteous as the standard of the just, ordered society could be wedded with compassion, the generous quality of tender openness to those excluded from family and community protection, only where the one true God was worshipped in single-hearted devotion by the people. This interrelationship formed the heart of the Book of the Covenant, and found classical expression in the Decalogue. In the story of Naboth, it comes to expression within the concreteness and specificity of real-life experience by describing a king whose heart strayed from Yahweh, to be ensnared in the deadly clutches of false gods. In this betrayal of sole devotion to the one true God, the very viability of the kingdom was threatened. For Ahab had repudiated the principle on which Israelite society was based: "I am the Lord your God who brought you out of the land of Egypt, out of the house of bondage. You shall have no other gods before me."

The result of this primal sin was the collapse of the other two essential qualities of community. First, righteousness, the basis of a just society, disintegrated as attention turned away from the only trustworthy standard of justice and equality, the one true God. Ahab, no longer acknowledging the God in whose sight all Israelites were judged against the same standard of righteousness revealed in the covenant commandments, proceeded to create his own standards, and in the process trampled on the precious laws that safeguarded a realm of God-given šālôm for the Yahwistic community. One by one they fell: "You shall not take the name of the Lord your God in vain," "You shall not kill," "You shall not steal," "You shall not bear false witness against your neighbor," "You shall not covet your neighbor's house."

Ahab thus introduced an alien ideal of kingship that contradicted the very essence of the Yahwistic notion of community that had offered an alternative to the social structures of ancient Near Eastern societies. Discarding all efforts at limiting the claims of kingship out of respect for the principles of Yahwistic faith, dedicated instead to a program of appeasement of the Canaanites in his land, he strove diligently to make Israel "like all the other nations," with all the frightening consequences enumerated in 1 Samuel 8:10–18 (a passage reflecting the same northern prophetic tradition to which the Naboth story belongs). There is no question that by continuing in the tradition of his father Omri, Ahab provided order in his kingdom, which fostered far more political stability than had characterized the era immediately preceding. But according to prophetic Yahwism, order in Israel was to be defined and judged against the specific criterion of Yahweh's acts. And all of Ahab's diplomatic and political achievements could not hide the fact that against that standard the forms he had constructed had no substance. That is, they lacked the righteousness that can arise only among those patterning their lives on the example of the God who treats all according to one norm of justice.

Second, in Ahab's betrayal of true worship, the third essential quality of early Yahwistic community was egregiously violated, namely, compassion. One can scarcely think of an example that could be more remote from the compassion of the Deliverer God who harkened to the cry of slaves, widows, orphans, and the impoverished than this king— surrounded by gold and ivory, and yet coveting one more vineyard, and not stopping short of murder to get it from one of his own subjects! Rather than compassionately hearing the cries of the widows and orphans of his kingdom, he increased their number and added to their plight.

Little wonder that the Deuteronomistic tradition, in its effort to continue in the south the earlier efforts of the northern prophetic tradition to defend Yahwistic faith against the threat of a paganized royal ideology, adopted and elaborated on the story of Naboth, Ahab, and

Elijah! Later we shall see how the Deuteronomists, as a part of their own theological reform, gave modern expression to the old Yahwistic notion of the covenant community. But we turn first to the excessive zeal of the cynical king Jehu, and then to the eighth-century prophetic defenders of Yahwism against the apostasy of northern kings and their subjects.

C. THE PROPHETIC REFORM MOVEMENT EXPLOITED BY THE CYNICAL KING JEHU

Jehu came to the throne in the pattern of the limited kingship ideal of the Northern Kingdom, being anointed by a prophet from Elisha's circle and acclaimed by the army, which represented the people (2 Kings 9:1–13). One could suspect our judgment on Jehu's cynicism and excessive violence to be the product of modern sensibilities alien to prophetic Yahwism were it not for the fact that prophetic Yahwism itself rendered a similar judgment (Hos. 1:4–5). Prophetic Yahwism, similar to the early Yahwism from which it derived its essential theological themes, was not a simple-minded phenomenon, as the triadic notion of community itself indicates. It addressed all facets of life with subtlety and balance, and insisted that a community built on the qualities of righteousness and compassion integrated in worship was to be committed not to needless bloodshed and excessive violence, but to order and harmony conducive to šālôm . We shall readily see how Jehu's reform, while taking its start in the reform movement of prophetic Yahwism, posed a threat to the Yahwistic notion of community, though to be sure, a very different kind of threat than that represented by the Omrides.

Jehu's rise to power can be interpreted against a twofold background: the growing resistance to the Baalism of the Omride dynasty, and the aggressive encroachment on Israelite territory by Syria. That prophetic circles, with their tradition of holy war, could come to recognize in a commander of the army a vehicle of God's Spirit is not surprising. After all, the twin threats from the outside and the inside were very formidable. But what strikes one in the Jehu story in 1 Kings 9–10 is how this king transferred the authority divinely conferred on him within the carefully formulated conditions of the covenant into a personal authority, and how he exploited both the reform zeal of Yahwism and the power of his office to his own benefit. Moreover, he accomplished all this with an unflinching vehemence and cynicism. What after all remained of the delicate Yahwistic balance between righteousness and compassion in Jehu's writing to the rulers and elders of Samaria and the guardians of the royal family? Jehu ordered them to deliver the heads of the seventy kings' sons to him at Jezreel, and had them laid in two heaps at the gate. Then he inquired of the people who had committed such an act, and used this as instigation for a bloodbath on the house of Ahab (2 Kings 10–11). This, together with the incident of the extermination of the visiting royal family of Judah (vv. 12–14) and his great "sacrifice" of the Baal priests (vv. 15–27), points beyond Jehu's disdain for righteousness and compassion to the ultimate source of his violence and cynicism, a hubris that placed the mortal Jehu in the place of the immortal God as the ultimate point of reference in his program of reform. Jehu was not a true advocate of prophetic Yahwism, and although he opposed Baalism, he was not an ally of those who had courageously sought to keep alive the testimony to the true God of Israel. Jehu was an opportunist who exploited his supporters for his own personal ambition, and therefore it is with justification that the prophet Hosea emphatically disassociated Yahweh's cause from the cause of Jehu: "I will punish the house of Jehu for the blood of Jezreel, and I will put an end to the kingdom of the house of Israel" (Hos. 1:4). This oracle does not represent a compromise of the stringent prophetic understanding of righteousness, but arises from the vision of God's order of šālôm wherein righteousness and compassion would be harmoniously one.

D. AMOS ATTACKS A PERVERTED CULT ON BEHALF OF THE GOD SEEKING TRUE WORSHIP EXPRESSED IN COMPASSION AND JUSTICE

The period between Jehu's reform and Hosea's condemnation of it spans nearly one hundred years. It is a period during which we know more about events in neighboring countries than within Israel and Judah (the whole period is covered by 2 Kings 12–15, whereas we have considerable information about Syria and Assyria from extrabiblical sources covering this time). At first the Syrians pressed mightily from the north, and Israel was weakened by a loss of territory. And then a far more formidable foe raised its head, the neo-Assyrian empire under Ashurnasirpal II and Shalmanesar III. In the middle of the eighth century, this threat was felt more acutely by Syria than by Israel, with the result that the fourth king of the Jehu dynasty, Jeroboam II (786–746), was able to restore much of the territory previously lost to Syria and to establish a considerable degree of internal stability in the land. The result was an improvement in Israel's economic situation. But due to the change in the economic and social structure of the land that had been introduced by earlier kings, the increased prosperity was limited to the royal house, the bureaucratic class which it had created, the landed nobility, and the wealthy merchants.

Basically, the land was sharply divided by the time of Jeroboam II into two systems. On the one side was the egalitarian-agrarian system stemming from the premonarchical period, which sought to protect the rights of each person through the institution of the *naḥălâ* and the laws of the Mosaic covenant. On the other was the system introduced by kingship on the basis of Canaanite models, in which land was treated like any other commodity, allowing certain individuals to amass vast holdings, and thereby to increase their power over other citizens. The leader of this latter system was the king. We read earlier that David had purchased a parcel of real estate from Araunah the Jebusite (2 Sam. 24:18–25) and that Omri had bought the hill of Samaria from another Canaanite, Shemer (1 Kings 16:23). These are examples of a process that likely became increasingly common in the era of the kings, namely, the purchase of land from a people uninfluenced by the early Yahwistic view of the land as property of Yahweh, which was to be used gratefully but not sold by its human caretakers. The result of this disregard of the institution of the *naḥălâ* was plain: Alongside, and even encroaching on the tribal tracts, there grew the royal holdings. And with this growth there arose the need for an increasingly complex system of overlords and serfs to manage and work it. To the overlords came personal holdings of their own as payment for their services to the royal house. To the serfs fell the precarious existence of those dependent on the whims of a feudal lord, as well as on the vicissitudes of personal, natural, and historical events. A huge gap between the wealthy and the poor had opened by the time of Jeroboam II's reign, with all the evils and injustices attending social stratification. Those in the privileged position either to uphold Israel's traditions of law or to neglect them found it increasingly in their self-interest to neglect them. On the other hand, the victims of this neglect were driven into the powerlessness of abject dependence on their oppressors and the constant threat of falling from a subsistence level of existence to indebtedness, impoverishment, and finally bonded slavery. Moreover, the one who according to this royal system alone had the authority to protect the vulnerable—the king— was the one benefiting most from the existing exploitative structures, making him an unlikely source for the badly needed reform. Thus we witness the emergence into full form of the system called the "ways of the king" in 1 Samuel 8:10–18. It is the classic condition for the type of cruel exploitation of the poor alluded to in 2 Kings 4:1, which like the Naboth story contributes less to the reconstruction of the details of history than to our understanding of the social conditions of ninth- and eighth-century Israel in general: "Now the wife of one of the sons of the prophets cried to Elisha, 'Your servant my husband is dead; and you know that your servant feared the Lord, but the creditor has come to take my two children to be his slaves.' "

In the older Yahwistic system, there was obviously no lack of sin and injustice. But there the recourse open to every individual was clear, namely, "judgment in the gates," which was the open court in which the elders as representatives of the people tried cases guided by the laws of the Mosaic covenant. In this old system, all were regarded as equally liable to the judgment of the only ultimate authority, Yahweh. And as the Book of the Covenant indicated, the presence of Yahweh, the righteous and compassionate God, was felt in the legal proceedings, a presence assuring a fair hearing for all, including the poor and the weak (e.g., Exod. 23:6).

But in the new system, with final authority no longer entrusted to an impartial judge, but retained by the one who was often the chief protagonist of the privileged classes, namely, the king, who was to protect the rights of the afflicted and oppressed poor against the greed and exploitation of the wealthy powerful? We have seen in the Naboth story (1 Kings 21) how grievous the plight of the common person had become in the Omride dynasty. Had the situation improved during the new dynasty of Jehu?

True, Jehu himself came to power as a reformer, seeking to purge Yahwism of Tyrian Baalism; and indeed he did remove the temple of Baal from Samaria. But I have already referred to a dangerous tendency that accompanied his rise to power: the tendency to use the Yahweh cult for his own political and personal ends. And as already noted, from the time of Solomon and Rehoboam, the sanctuary that placed the king in a place rivaling Yahweh's kingship ceased to be a source of righteousness and compassion within the nation, for it became bound to a system of privilege for the powerful and oppression for the poor and vulnerable. Such was the case with the sanctuary sponsored by Jeroboam II, the great-grandson of Jehu, a sanctuary subservient to the whims of the king, served by a co-opted priesthood, hostile to the true prophets of Yahweh, and overlaid with a resurgent Baalism (note that already Jehu's son Jehoahaz reverted to Baalism, according to 2 Kings 13:7, which is not surprising in a cult subservient to the wishes of a king who no doubt still faced the problem of keeping the large Canaanite population of the land content).

The clash between the two systems could not be displayed more clearly than in the encounter between Amos and Amaziah, the priest of Bethel (Amos 7:10–17). The background to the story was a previous word of judgment spoken by Amos against King Jeroboam. That word had not been accepted as a warning from a spokesperson of God, but was given the most sinister of all possible political interpretations: "Amos has conspired against you in the midst of Israel; the land is not able to bear all his words," the priest reports to his king. The antithesis is thus absolute. The two offices intended to work together in the Yahwistic concept of "limited kingship" had been torn asunder. There was room for only one authority in Israel, which meant that the authoritative word of Yahweh had to be removed, and that the cult had to be regarded strictly as the king's domain. Amaziah drew out the implications of this system for the prophet: "O seer, go, flee away to the land of Judah, and eat bread there, and prophesy there; but never again prophesy at Bethel, for it is the king's sanctuary, and it is a temple of the kingdom" (Amos 7:12–13). Bethel, set up originally by Jeroboam I to bind the allegiance of the populace to the king, was now under Jeroboam II to tolerate no authority save the king's, for it was to be perceived as a *royal* sanctuary. Amos was accordingly instructed to go back home to Judah, and to stop obstructing the cult by citing an authority other than the king.

Amos, in his reply to the priest, explained that unlike the official prophets, who were assigned and dismissed like any royal official by command of the king, he belonged to no earthly order, but stood exclusively under the authority of Yahweh's word: "I am no prophet, nor a prophet's son" (better, "nor one of the sons of the prophets"; i.e., a professional), "but a dresser of sycamore trees, and the Lord took me from following the flock, and the Lord said to me, 'Go, prophesy to my people Israel' " (Amos 7:14–15). According to the old system represented by Amos, the authority of the king and the co-opted royal cult was a mockery of the only true authority. That true authority, moreover, was no longer known to an apostate priesthood or kingship, but only to God's "servants the prophets"; that is, to those called to an office regulated by no earthly institution or authority, but by God alone:

> Surely the Lord God does nothing
>   without revealing his secret to his servants the prophets.
> The lion has roared; who will not fear?
> The Lord God has spoken; who can but prophesy? (Amos 3:7–8)

The prophetic office, moreover, experienced a significant twofold development in Amos and his slightly later contemporary Hosea: its address went beyond the king and the royal family to encompass the nation as a whole, and it went beyond the borders of Israel and Judah to embrace Israeh's neighbors as well.

Yahweh's suzerainty over the other nations is seen especially in Amos 1 and 2. These chapters add impetus to a developing universalism in Yahwism that would be carried further by later prophets. Because Yahweh was understood to be the suzerain of all nations (cf. Amos 9:7), one standard applied to all, that being the standard of righteousness and compassion that had been revealed to Israel through Yahweh's presence in her history. This is seen clearly in the specific indictments raised against the various nations: "they have threshed Gilead with threshing sledges of iron," "they carried into exile a whole people," "they did not remember the covenant of brotherhood," "he pursued his brother with the sword and cast off all pity," "they have riped up women with child in Gilead, that they might enlarge their border." The other side of this message of judgment must not be overlooked, for its significance for biblical faith is vast: if the nations would order their lives in accord with the standards of righteousness and compassion, there would emerge a real basis for peace throughout the world. The idea of a universal covenant of peace was to become a very important amplification of the Abrahamic covenant's blessing to the nations. Although it was not developed further by Amos, it was planted by him as a seed within the fruitful soil of prophetic faith, and would later burst forth into a new form of expression in the message of Second Isaiah.

We now move to a closer look at Amos's message to Israel in relation to our specific interest in the Yahwistic notion of community. One is first struck by the harshness of that message. Although Israel continued to apply the important concepts of early Yahwism, such as covenant, election, and promise, and to exercise the familiar forms of worship, Amos observed this was being done in a manner directly opposed to their intended purpose. They were being used to keep the one true God, the standard of compassion and righteousness, at a distance. They were being applied as a means of deception so as to cause the prostitution of true worship to give the appearance of an obedience deserving the divine blessing.

This development in the prophetic office was extremely important for the consequent development of the Yahwistic notion of community. It signified that the institutional structures of the land, such as kingship and cult, could not be relied on to define the people of God. Instead a redefinition would arise in large part in a running controversy with those institutional structures. And through that process of redefinition God's people would become a righteous remnant characterized by repentance and faithfulness in persecution.

The new setting and mission of prophecy in the eighth century explains the form of discourse so commonly applied by the classical prophets, the disputation (rîb). Presupposed by this prophetic form of discourse was Yahweh's covenant with Israel, and Israel's commitment to the laws of the Mosaic covenant. Since covenant and stipulations had been flagrantly broken, the prophet spoke for God in bringing charges against the people, and in announcing the judgment incurred by disobedience: "You only have I known of all families of the earth; therefore I will punish you for all your iniquities" (Amos 3:2).

In this controversy, the prophets were not operating with a vague, personalistic or novel notion of covenant and community. As can be demonstrated by the example of Amos, they were speaking on behalf of the early Yahwistic notion growing out of the exodus-conquest tradition of Gilgal, Shiloh, and Shechem. Due to the prostitution of the old sanctuaries by the royal cult, the prophets were forced to make their debut as outsiders, but their point of reference was clear to them: It was the classic Yahwistic faith dedicated to God's righteousness and compassion grounded in worship of the one true God. Belonging to this faith was a notion of community in which all were precious to Yahweh and protected by the laws of the covenant. The prophetic controversy (rîb) expressed the same understanding, and more specifically relflected the entitlement of every Israelite to trial in the gates in the event that personal rights had been violated. For the rîb, in which Yahweh was judge, demonstrated that when the poor or oppressed cried out from their affliction, even though earthly leaders and judges turned a deaf ear, the compassionate Judge of all heard their cry and acted to defend and to deliver.

But what were the guardians of that notion of community to do with a nation that had violated the laws of the covenant, indeed, had turned the fundamental intention of the early Yahwistic community on its head by suspending the righteous laws, falsifying the just standards, and blocking the due process of tôrâ in order to enhance the opportunities of the wealthy and powerful to oppress, extort, and impoverish the week and the poor? Or as Amos characterized their intention, "that we may make the ephah small and the shekel great, and deal deceitfully with false balances" (Amos 8:5b). What was to be done in a land in which the one responsible for justice, the king and his officials, lived in luxury oblivious of the plight of the poor, and were themselves party of the oppression of the righteous?

> Woe to those who are at ease in Zion,
> and to those who feel secure on
>   the mountain of Samaria, . . .
> Woe to those who lie upon beds of ivory,
>   and stretch themselves upon their couches,
> and eat lambs from the flock,
>   and calves from the midst of the stall;
> who sing idle songs to the sound of the harp,
>   and like David invent for themselves instruments of music;
> who drink wine in bowls,
>   and anoint themselves with the finest oils,
>   but are not grieved over the ruin of Joseph! (Amos 6:1a, 4–6)

> "I will smite the winter house with the summer house;
>   and the houses of ivory shall perish,
> and the great houses shall come to an end,"
>
> says the Lord. (Amos 3:15)

What was to be done in a situation in which a divine standard of justice and compassion had been replaced by a mockery of justice subservient to the desires of oppressors? "Oh you who turn justice to wormwood, and cast down righteousness to the earth!" (Amos 5:7).

The Naboth story already adumbrated the prophetic answer to these questions. Where the institutions of the land had been corrupted, and no longer stood for the compassion and righteousness of Yahweh, the prophets came to the side of the oppressed poor. They set up, as it

were, a court of law in place of the one corrupted by Israel's officials.
They entered into controversy with the oppressors as Yahweh's agents
on behalf of the innocent, the poor, and the afflicted. It was an unpop-
ular and dangerous advocacy position, but Amos for one did not flinch:

> They hate him who reproves in the gate,
>   and they abhor him who speaks the truth.
> Therefore because you trample upon the poor
>   and take from him exactions of wheat,
> you have built houses of hewn stone,
>   but you shall not dwell in them;
> you have planted pleasant vineyards,
>   but you shall not drink their wine.
> For I know how many are your transgressions,
>   and how great are your sins—
> you who afflict the righteous, who take a bribe,
>   and turn aside the needy in the gate.
> Therefore he who is prudent will keep silent in such a time;
>   for it is an evil time. (Amos 5:10–13)

Amos 2:6–12 clearly identifies this prophet's roots in the early Yahwistic notion of community by its many allusions to the Book of the
Covenant. In verse 6, he attacks those who "sell the righteous for silver," and thus comes to the side of the innocent and righteous party,
whom (according to Exod. 23:7) it is the court's responsibility to defend. Verse 7 indicts those "that trample the head of the poor into the
dust of the earth, and turn aside the way of the afflicted," and thus applies Exodus 23:6, "You shall not pervert the justice due to the poor in
his suit." Verse 7b recalls Exodus 21:8 in condemning "the violation of
the rights of a female bondservant by making her into a concubine for
father and son."[5] And in verse 8 we read of "the garments taken in
pledge" from the poor and obviously not returned before sundown,
thus violating Exodus 22:26–27.

All these applications of the laws from the Book of the Covenant
unite around a common theme. In Israel, the structures that had been
established to protect the poor and the vulnerable as an expression of
divine righteousness and compassion had been corrupted into means of
further oppression of the innocent and the righteous.

As an astute attorney and advocate, Amos, in a continuation of the
court scene in chapter 2, searched deeply for the root cause of the corruption of justice in the gates, and the cause he found was the profanation of Yahweh's holy name (v. 7b). False worship, and a turning away
from the holy God of Israel, lay at the heart of the matter. Amos therefore went on to paint a shocking picture of the cult life of his day,
where the same ones who made a mockery of the sacred laws of the tôrâ

---

5. J. L. Mays, *Amos, A Commentary* (London: SCM, 1969), p. 46.

sprawl "beside every altar upon garments taken in pledge," "and in the house of their God they drink the wine of those who have been fined" (v. 8). The sanctuary had become a place where the wealthy could indulge in the profits they had pressed from the poor. Worship had been hopelessly corrupted, and where the true God was no longer the object of worship, the foundation was taken from under righteousness and compassion in the land.

Against the background of this indictment, verses 9–12 take on a poignant meaning. They describe the history of God's saving acts, on which the covenant had been based, and to which the faithful had earlier responded in worship and in obedience to the covenant stipulations. In Israel's earlier history, the recounting of God's antecedent gracious acts functioned as prologue for the *tôrâ* (e.g., Exod. 20:2), for this gave expression to Israel's belief that it was God's deliverance that made obedience to the commandments a blessed possibility. In this passage, however, the order is reversed, for the entire moral universe had been turned on its head by Israel. In verses 6–8, the commandments, and their violation by Israel, are listed. In verses 9–11, Yahweh's acts in Israel's history are recitated. And because of Israel's apostasy, that recitation no longer celebrates salvation but announces judgment (vv. 13–16).

It is interesting to note that in addition to the usual series of divine acts (exodus, wilderness, conquest), Amos added another, namely, "I raised up some of your sons for prophets" (v. 11). Yahweh's saving acts were not to be construed as a thing of the past, to be recited mindlessly in the cult as a basis for smug assurance of Yahweh's blessing. Yahweh's acts were rather to be regarded as ongoing, meaning that a fresh response to each new situation was required of the community. Yahweh's latest act had been the raising up of prophets to witness to the covenant broken by king and people. In commanding the prophets, "you shall not prophesy," king, priest, and people had repudiated Yahweh's gracious initiative, a perversion that would bring with it the covenant curses and judgment. And all the clever human scheming in such proud display in Jeroboam's kingdom would have no effect in delaying Yahweh's terrible day of judgment (v. 13–16).

The root of Israel's pride and self-confidence was its perverted sense of worship. This was the reason for Amos's scathing attack on the cult places. What had a sanctuary, in which the sole acknowledged authority was the king, any longer to do with Yahweh? Thus, with stinging irony, Amos intoned,

> Come to Bethel, and transgress;
> to Gilgal, and multiply transgression;
> bring your sacrifices every morning,
> your tithes every three days
> offer a sacrifice of thanksgiving of that which is leavened,

and proclaim freewill offerings, publish them;
for so you love to do, O people of Israel!
    says the Lord God.   (Amos 4:4–5)

What Israel so sorely needed was fellowship with God, but Yahweh was not to be found in the royal sanctuaries: "Seek me and live; but do not seek Bethel, and do not enter into Gilgal, or cross over to Beersheba (Amos 5:4b–5a). Where was Yahweh then to be found? Amos's dominant word is clear: Because of Israel's repudiation of the true God in its acts of worship and its espousal of false gods and hypocritical worship, because of its refusal to repent and return in spite of Yahweh's repeated overtures (Amos 4:6–11), she faced a dreadful day of meeting: "Prepare to meet your God, O Israel." All of her deceptions would not disguise the holiness of God on that day, a holiness that consumed all unrighteousness:

Woe to you who desire the day of the Lord!
   Why would you have the day of the Lord?
   It is darkness and not light.   (Amos 5:18)

Alongside this dominant message of judgment, however, another message is found in Amos. It held up to the people an alternative to judgment and death. The alternative was a remote one perhaps, given Israel's stubbornness, but one nevertheless consonant with the quality of compassion in the Yahwistic notion of community that patiently kept open the door to those excluded. This alternative was not a compromise of the divine righteousness that was expressed in the judgment pronouncements, but revealed that God's righteousness itself was an expression of divine compassion. The wedding of these two qualities is found in Amos 5:21–24:

I hate, I despise your feasts,
   and I take no delight in your solemn assemblies,
Even though you offer me your burnt offerings and cereal
    offering,
   I will not accept them,
and the peace offerings of your fatted beasts
   I will not look upon.
Take away from me the noise of your songs;
   to the melody of your harps I will not listen.
But let justice roll down like water,
   and righteousness like an everflowing stream.

According to this eighth-century prophet, there was but one hope for Israel, and that was the hope that "Yahweh, the God of hosts, will be with you." But this could occur only if Israel realized that under its kings, and its new system of justice, the nation was in effect back in the slavery of Egypt. Only by repentance begetting the acknowledgment of brokenness, and the need for Yahweh's new saving act (through the prophets? or through deliverance following judgment by a foreign enemy?), could there be hope: "it may be that the Lord, the God of hosts, will be gracious to the remnant of Joseph" (5:15b). On the basis of this hope, a later writer was able to append the glorious prophecy of restoration found in 9:11–15.

How then did the notion of community develop in the prophetic word of Amos? First, on the basis of his Yahwistic perspective Amos was able to locate the root of the decadent social conditions of his time in a collapse of the primal quality of early Yahwistic community, worship of the one true God. The prostitution of the cult into a sanctuary of the king pushed Yahweh from the center, and placed an idol at the heart of the nation's worship. No longer did a people look alone to God in praise and thanksgiving, but congratulated itself for its achievements. This hubris left no room for the true God in the cult, who could therefore only speak from the outside through a prophet:

> The Lord has sworn by himself
> (says the Lord, the God of hosts):
> "I abhor the pride of Jacob,
>   and hate his strongholds;
>   and I will deliver up the city and
>   all that is in it."   (Amos 6:8)

Second, where Yahweh was removed from the center of Israel's worship there was no longer a standard for righteousness and compassion in the land. The king provided standards fitting his desires, and in the feudal system that was rapidly supplanting the more egalitarian tribal system of early Yahwism, each feudal lord in turn tailored standards for his own domain that enhanced his personal aspirations and designs. In the place of justice in the gates, protection of the rights of the poor, and compassion for the widow and the debtor and the sojourner, the new system introduced extortion, oppression, deprivation of the rights of the weak, corruption, impoverishment, and a social decay that made the land increasingly vulnerable to foreign aggressors: "Fallen, no more to rise, is the virgin Israel; forsaken on her land, with none to raise her up" (5:2). But as clear as his judgment was Amos's word of hope. In returning to Yahweh, in undivided worship of the one true God, and in the grateful embodiment of God's compassion and righteousness, in "loving good" and "establishing justice in the gate," God's presence could return to the land, bringing šālôm to the remnant of Joseph. Although Amos's message was severe, a lighter message in this setting would not have been more compassionate, but would merely have contributed further to Israel's act of self-deception. Amos's message of severe mercy was able to wed God's righteousness with

God's compassion, because it found both united within the nature of the one true God, a God whose majesty was clearly seen to encompass all nations, and whose compassion relentlessly pursued the lost, even when the only word they were capable of hearing was the harsh word of judgment.

E. HOSEA: "ISRAEL HAS FORGOTTEN HIS MAKER"

Hosea represents the covenant theology of early Yahwism in a very clear form. For him, the heart of this community of faith was the relationship in which Yahweh was the God of Israel and Israel was the people of Yahweh. The terms of this covenant relationship and the nature of this God were known according to Hosea within the context of Israel's particular history of exodus, wilderness, and conquest. It was in this history that Yahweh had called Israel to be his people, and had taught it the way of blessing: "I am the Lord your God from the land of Egypt; you know no God but me, and beside me there is no savior. It was I who knew you in the wilderness, in the land of drought" (13:4–5; cf. 11:1).

But this long history, according to Hosea, was a tragic history: "when they had fed to the full, they were filled, and their heart was lifted up; therefore they forgot me" (13:6). "The more I called them, the more they went from me; they kept sacrificing to the Baals, and burning incense to idols" (11:2). Hosea, with daring and imagination, focused directly on the heart of Israel's problem, giving expression to it in diverse metaphors. That problem was Israel's forsaking Yahweh, which led to the collapse of the primal quality of the early Yahwistic notion of community, worship of the one true God. Hosea stood in the tradition of Elijah in attacking the Baal worship that was drawing the heart of the people away from the true God of Israel. Taking into account the dominant fertility theme of the Baal cult, he used harlotry as the master metaphor for describing Israel's idolatrous behavior, a device picked up later by the Deuteronomists and Jeremiah:

> My people inquire of a thing of wood,
>   and their staff gives them oracles.
> For a spirit of harlotry has led them astray,
>   and they have left their God to play the harlot.
> They sacrifice on the tops of the mountains,
>   and make offerings upon the hills,
> under oak, poplar, and terebinth,
>   because their shade is good. (Hos 4:12–13a)

Although this indictment was very broad, Hosea was also careful to specify those particularly responsible for Israel's apostasy: the priests, prophets, and royal family. Hosea would have agreed emphatically with Chaucer:

> And this figure he added eek thereto,
> That if gold ruste, what shal yren do?
> For if a preest be foul, on whom we truste,
> No wonder is a lewed man to ruste.[6]

According to Hosea's view, the community's leaders were entrusted with the holy tradition, including the stories of exodus and wilderness and conquest, and the commandments given by God to the people as a part of their covenant relationship. That holy tradition in fact constituted the heart of Israel's identity as a community. Without "knowledge" and "the law of your God," the people had no guide to preserve them from the enticements of Baal.[7] Therefore the priests and prophets were the particular objects of Hosea's *rib*:

> . . . for with you is my contention, O priest.
> You shall stumble by day,
>> the prophet also shall stumble with you by night;
>> and I will destroy your mother.
> My people are destroyed for lack of knowledge;
>> because you have rejected knowledge,
>> I reject you from being a priest to me.
> And since you have forgotten the law of your God,
>> I also will forget your children.   (Hosea 4:4b–6)

The whole affair is reminiscent of the corruption of the priests at Shiloh, and indeed Hosea foresaw the same ignominious end: "They feed on the sin of my people; they are greedy for their iniquity . . . I will punish them for their ways" (Hos. 4:7–10, cf. 10:5–6; 13:1–3).

The chief protagonist of this decadent system was the very one under whose authority the priests and professional prophets served, namely, the king. Hosea was very bleak in his assessment of the current state of kingship in Israel, and we see reflected in some of the oracles from the latter half of his career the chaotic conditions in the years after Jeroboam II, years in which a rash of assassinations accompanied the rapid succession of four kings in fifteen years. In his critique of kingship, he proves to be a staunch defender of the prophetic tradition that gave its pessimistic description of kingship in 1 Samuel 8. Hosea charged, "They made kings, but not through me. They set up princes, but without my knowledge" (8:4a). The very existence of kingship in Israel thereby testified to the godlessness of the people! Also the harsh prophetic critique of Jeroboam I's royal cult was reiterated by Hosea (cf.

---

6. The Prologue to *The Canterbury Tales*, lines 499–502, in *English Literature and Its Background*, vol. 1, edited by B. D. Grebanier et al. (New York: Dryden Press, 1956), p. 141.

7. H. W. Wolff sees in the expression "knowledge of God" reference to the early Yahwistic tradition of the exodus and conquest and the covenant with its laws, " 'Wissen um Gott' bei Hosea als Urform von Theologie," *Gesammelte Studien zum Alten Testament*, ThB 22 (München: Ch. Kaiser, 1973), pp. 182–105.

1 Kings 12:25–14:20): "With their silver and gold they made idols for their own destruction. I have spurned your calf, O Samaria. My anger burns against them" (8:4b–5). The king, as sponsor of an idolatrous cult, was guilty of diverting the attention of the people from their true God, and of hastening the day of calamity.

The frantic godlessness of the kingdom was described by Hosea with the metaphor of a hot oven: "By their wickedness they make the king glad, and the princes by their treachery. They are all adulterers; they are like a heated oven" (7:3–4a). In a land lacking the "knowledge" and "law" of God, the rejoicing on the king's enthronement day was not of an uplifting quality, but of the drunken sort reeking of disorder and death: "on the day of our king the princes became sick with the heat of wine; he stretched out his hand with mockers" (7:5). Indeed, in a land where God's "knowledge" and "law" were lacking, no trustworthy standard remained for guiding the land. In the resulting vacuum, chaos rushed in, and like a consuming fire, the drunken intrigue of the princes destroyed the land and its leaders:

> For like an oven their hearts burn with intrigue;
>   all night their anger smolders;
>   in the morning it blazes like a flaming fire.
> All of them are hot as an oven,
>   and they devour their rulers.
> All their kings have fallen;
>   and none of them calls upon me.   (Hos. 7:6–7)

At the same time that the land was rotting from within, Hosea was keenly aware of the rising strength of Assyria. But in the absence of a center of devotion to Yahweh, he observed a foreign policy as frantic and scattered as the chaotic conditions within the land (7:11; 8:7–10; 12:1). In the prophetic role of the herald of the holy warrior Yahweh, Hosea raised the battle alarm. But the graveness of the situation could not have been more emphatically described, for the object of attack was not a foreign host, but Israel! Yahweh, the One who had created the people Israel by delivering slaves from bondage, was about to turn against his own people:

> Set the trumpet to your lips,
>   for a vulture is over the house of the Lord,
> because they have broken my covenant,
>   and transgressed my law.   (Hos. 8:1)

The Assyrians did in fact engulf Israel as a part of their westward expansion and specifically as a reply to Israel's participation in an anti-Assyrian coalition. The land was thereby reduced in 733 B.C.E. to a rump state consisting merely of the environs around Samaria. And following King Hosea's rebellion against Assyria and Shalmaneser's devastating campaign in the years 724–722, the Northern Kingdom was erased from the annals of history.

Might Israel's fate have been different had her leaders followed an alternative foreign policy? The Book of Hosea does not give us a direct answer to this political question. This prophet did not enter into speculative policymaking. He rather focused on the heart of Israel's life as a community of faith, and described the only possible source of life, health and security, namely, trust and obedience in the relationship with the one true God. On that basis, Hosea did say with confidence that trust and obedience would issue forth in God's fulfillment of the covenant promises. But in place of trust, Hosea saw that "Ephraim has multiplied altars for sinning." And what of obedience? "Were I to write for him my laws by ten thousands, they would be regarded as a strange thing" (8:11–12). Israel's worship was blatant mockery of God, for "they love to sacrifice; they sacrifice flesh and eat it; but the Lord has no delight in them" (8:13a). Israel had become blind to the heart that constituted it as a people. By removing Yahweh as the sole object of its devotion, Israel had placed its trust in itself and its fortifications: "For Israel has forgotten his Maker, and built palaces; and Judah has multiplied fortified cities; but I will send a fire upon his cities, and it shall devour his strongholds" (8:14).

Such were the effects of a perverted cult. With the loss of the heart of the community collapsed its standard of righteousness. The resulting moral decay left the nation vulnerable and helpless in the face of enemy attack. But the ravages of Israel's unfaithfulness went far beyond its political borders. Repudiation of God's grace and disregard for God's *tôrâ* set in motion a cataclysm that would leave no aspect of creation unaffected. Therefore, in Hosea 4:1 the prophet announced that Yahweh was taking the inhabitants of the land to trial. The indictment that follows in effect gave a summary of the contents of the Decalogue, again an indication of Hosea's roots in early Yahwistic tradition. As the Decalogue had begun with the heart of Israelite faith, so too in Yahweh's trial speech delivered by Hosea, the first question addressed was the question of devotion to God. In being tested against that norm, Israel was found wanting, desperately wanting: "There is no faithfulness or kindness, and no knowledge of God in the land." Once the heart of the community, its grounding in true worship, had failed, the land was left without defense against the onslaught of moral chaos. Thus the remaining commandments of the Decalogue were called to witness against the people: "There is swearing, lying, killing, stealing, and committing adultery: they break all bounds and murder follows murder." Like shock waves, the effects of Israel's guilt moved out in ever widening circles to engulf the entire created order: "Therefore the land mourns, and all who dwell in it languish, and also the beasts of the field, and the birds of the air, and even the fish of the sea are taken away." So perfect was the covenant order established by Yahweh that faithfulness at the center expressed in true worship had the effect of releasing the šālôm God intended for the whole world and of channeling it into all areas of life and creation. As intimated already within early Yahwistic tradition, and as would be brought out explicitly by Second Isaiah, Israel's vocation as a people could most clearly be understood as the vocation of servants of Yahweh's šālôm in the world. But unfaithfulness at the center had an equally assured result: the chaos that engulfed the people who had broken Yahweh's covenant would spread forth like a curse to consume all life and creation. Herein lies the reason for the urgency and severity of Yahweh's controversy with Israel reported by Hosea. This world was a beautiful, delicate organism. The community gathered by Yahweh formed its nucleus. The quality of life and the health of that nucleus had a profound effect on the quality and health of the whole organism.

But in the mind of Hosea, was there any remaining hope for that organism? Given the history of a sin that ran so deeply, and the threat of a judgment so devastating, was not Hosea proclaiming and end of Yahweh's dealing with this wayward and wanton nation, thereby implying an end as well to the whole concept of an order of šālôm? Some commentators interpret Hosea, as well as Amos, as a preacher of unmitigated doom, and assign all words of hope and salvation to later editors who supposedly found the harshness of the original prophecy too disturbing to leave unaltered. But this interpretation misses a dimension of Hosea's message implicit even in the judgment oracles. The reason for the judgment was clear: Israel's repudiation of the true God in favor of idols, its blatant disregard of the laws of God, its choice of rulers without consulting Yahweh (i.e., without prophetic oracle), its pursuit of foreign policy mindless of God's will (again without prophetic oracle), and corruption of its priests and professional prophets. But this message of judgment implied a corresponding message of salvation, for the same divine standard that was a source of dread for the ungodly was a source of hope for the faithful. Hosea's look beyond judgment is thus an essential part of his theology. Indeed, his message is remarkable in the way it spans the entire gamut of divine passion from righteousness to compassion, judgment to salvation, uncompromising realism to brilliant hope. Hosea was unusual in his penetration into the depths of severe mercy; that is, God's righteousness and compassion known most intimately in true worship.

Given the stubborn sinfulness of the people, and the impending judgment visible on the horizon, where did Hosea find a basis for hope? This he found in his unshakeable conviction that Yahweh was faithful to the same purpose that had guided God's saving acts from the beginning of Israel's history. This conviction allowed Hosea to recognize Yahweh even in the judgment descending on the people. The ultimate purposer was not the king of Assyria, but Yahweh: "I, even I, will rend and go away, I will carry off, and none shall rescue" (5:14b). And even this severe act was in the service of Yahweh's salvific plan:

> Come, let us return to the Lord;
> for he has torn, that he may heal us;
>   he has stricken, and he will bind us up,
> After two days he will revive us;
>   on the third day he will raise us up,
>   that we may live before him.
> Let us know, let us press on to know the Lord;
>   his going forth is sure as the dawn;
> he will come to us as the showers,
>   as the spring rains that water the earth.   (Hos. 6:1–3)

In this remarkable confession, the prophet gave clear expression to the inseparability of God's tearing and healing. To have upheld a people in their apostasy and wantonness would have been the most cruel of acts, tantamount to sealing their covenant with death. But to rend and tear until in their brokenness their mesmerization with their idols would be ended and their attention would be redirected to the true God was an act of profound mercy. In it, the opportunity was renewed of "living before him"—that is, of forswearing death and of entering into the covenant of life and šālôm based on knowledge of God.

Hosea was specific in describing how the opportunity to renew the covenant could unfold beyond judgment. And, indeed, his description was not an invention, but a legacy of the theological heritage that nourished him, that is, the early Yahwistic exodus, wilderness, conquest tradition. This tradition allowed Hosea to realize that even in this bleak time there was a community of faith in Israel. It was the community of those remaining faithful to that ancient confession. And in an era of opportunistic kings and corrupt priests, its leaders were the prophets, the spokespersons of God who stood in the succession of the faithful from Moses to the present time: "By a prophet the Lord brought Israel up from Egypt, and by a prophet he was preserved" (12:13). "The prophet is the watchman of Ephraim, the people of my God, yet a fowler's snare is on all his ways, and hatred in the house of his God" (9:8). The message of that long chain of prophetic witnesses to the community of the faithful had been clear and consistent:

> Therefore I have hewn them by the prophets,
>   I have slain them by the words of my mouth,
>   and my judgment goes forth as the light.
> For I desire steadfast love and not sacrifice,
>   the knowledge of God, rather than burnt offerings.   (Hos. 6:5–6)

The prophets, then, were the carriers of the message of hope in Israel, a message of repentance and covenant renewal, a message of centering true worship in love and knowledge of God rather than in a shallow cult piety degenerating into a disguise of self-centered godlessness.

The salvation history to which the prophets bore witness went beyond recitation of past events to an announcement of the only way back to wholeness, the way of repentance and renewal! Since Israel's state of bondage to sin was tantamount to slave bondage, the first step announced by Hosea was the harsh one involving subjugation under the yoke of the enemy:

> They shall return to the land of Egypt,
> and Assyria shall be their king,
> because they have refused to return to me.
> The sword shall rage against their cities,
> consume the bars of their gates,
> and devour them in their fortresses.
> My people are bent on turning away from me;
> so they are appointed to the yoke,
> and none shall remove it.   (Hos. 11:5–7)

This return to the zero point of existence, however, was not the end of Israel's history with God. In the passionate divine speech in chapter 11, we find the exodus-wilderness tradition used to point to the second step in Yahweh's redemptive activity. In that earlier history, though they had turned away from Yahweh to idols, Yahweh's deep compassion had persisted: "I led them with cords of compassion, with bands of love, and I became to them as one who eases the yoke on their jaws, and I bent down to them and fed them" (11:4). In his own dark time, Hosea peered into the heart of the same God, and we see a remarkable spanning of the gap between judgment and compassion:

> How can I give you up, O Ephraim!
> How can I hand you over, O Israel!
> How can I make you like Admah!
> How can I treat you like Zeboiim!
> My heart recoils within me,
> my compasssion grows warm and tender.
> I will not execute my fierce anger,
> I will not again destroy Ephraim;
> for I am God and not man,
> the Holy One in your midst,
> and I will not come to destroy.   (Hos. 11:8–9)

Yahweh's dealings with Israel had not ended. There was a basis for hope, and it resided in Yahweh's compassion, which even in judgment was actively engaged in rescuing a lost people.

It seems probable that Hosea's profound insight into the heights of divine righteousness and the depts of divine compassion was intimately tied to his own personal life, especially his marriage to a prostitute. Through the adulterous conduct of Gomer, Hosea was instructed in the profound sorrow and angry judgment experienced by the divine Lover forced to look on Israel's wanton pursuit of Baal (2:1–13).[8] The very children born to Gomer bore the prophetic message in their names, "Jezreel" as a reminder of the blood guilt on the dynasty of Jehu, "Not pitied" as an ominous prophecy of impending judgment, and "Not my people" as a sign of the broken covenant. But beyond punishment Hosea saw the ultimate designs of divine compassion, a return to the beginning, a new start that would wash away the stain of sin: "Therefore, behold, I will allure her, and bring her into the wilderness, and speak tenderly to her . . . there she will answer me as in the days of her youth" (2:14–15). The names of the Baals would be removed from Israel, and the covenant would be renewed that would clothe all creation with šālôm.

And I will betroth you to me for ever; I will betroth you to me in righteousness and in justice, in steadfast love, and in mercy. I will betroth you to me in faithfulness and you shall know the Lord.   (Hos. 2:19–20)

Here we see portrayed the healing of the lethal sickness of the people Israel, the healing of a heart that had turned against its Maker. With the restoration of Israel's primal devotion, the principal qualities of righteousness and justice, love and mercy, returned to the life of the community. Israel's covenant with Yahweh, which from the beginning had constituted it as a community of faith, was restored: "And I will have pity on Not pitied, and I will say to Not my people, 'You are my people'; and he shall say, 'Thou art my God' " (2:23).

When we consider Hosea's message as a whole, it is obvious that the early Yahwistic notion of community was deeply enriched by his prophetic word. His observation concerning the role of the prophet was emphatically confirmed in his own ministry: "The prophet is the watchman of Ephraim, the people of my God" (9:8). At a point when the community of faith in Israel was endangered more sorely than at any previous time, he bore witness to Yahweh's righteousness and compassion with a courage and skill that compromised neither, but deepened understanding of both by grounding them in the heart of God. What did he commend to this endangered people? Trust in Yahweh's covenant fidelity, repentance, and a return to true faith! To this lesson he added the example of Jacob, who persevered in his struggle with the

8. It must be acknowledged that the androcentric bias of ancient Israelite culture led to the unfortunate result that when the realm of human relations was drawn on as a metaphor for the breakdown of the divine-human relationship, the fault was assigned primarily to the female partner in the relationship (Jer. 2:20–25; 3:1–5; Ezek. 22). It is one of the challenges of biblical theology to capture the central point conveyed by such metaphors without perpetuating the negative effects of such culturally conditioned gender bias. Beyond this, it behooves all communities seeking to be true to the profoundly positive legacy of biblical faith to dedicate themselves to a way of life in which women and men enjoy equal opportunity to envision, symbolize and embody a life-sustaining and life-giving way of life.

angel and "met God at Bethel" (12:4). In the new threatening era, Hosea pointed to an old faith, now more profoundly understood through his own suffering: "So you, by the help of your God, return, hold fast to love and justice, and wait continually for your God" (12:6). Repeatedly we see Hosea summoning the people back to the only true basis of community, the early Yahwistic triad of worship, righteousness, and compassion!

We can finally summarize Hosea's contribution to a deepened understanding of the early Yahwistic notion of community in relation to that triad. First, nowhere before had the meaning and significance of the primal quality of Yahwistic community been so profoundly explicated. Nowhere before had the hues and qualities of the false gods been so clearly described, nor the chaos and death that lay behind their seductive veil, than in this "final battle [of Yahweh] against Baal for the soul of Israel."[9] Nowhere before had the heart of the one true God been exposed so daringly to the worshipper, or the true blessedness of covenant fidelity expressed in such moving terms and metaphors.

Second, the dynamic nature of faith in Yahweh was portrayed with uncommon power in the interplay in Hosea's message between the judgment born of Yahweh's righteous standard and the compassion that perseveres in spite of sin. Here the uncompromising, sterling quality of God's righteousness was held up before a people enamored with its own identification with death. The tenaciousness of habitual sin, and the futility of superficial treatment, were exposed with stunning clarity precisely because Hosea bore witness so faithfully to this standard of righteousness. And this faithful portrayal in turn exposed the mysterious quality of divine compassion, whose transcendent quality was revealed, according to Hosea, precisely in its perfect union with righteousness. And Hosea's final verdict was clear: Only this divine union could provide the basis for the true order of šālôm that was the hope of all creation.

Finally we are amazed at how comprehensive Hosea's covenant theology was in describing reality. The triad of worship, righteousness, and compassion moved in ever expanding concentric circles from cult to social institutions and structures to the vast order of nature. Where God was worshipped and God's laws were obeyed, šālôm radiated from that holy center through the community of faith to the "beasts of the field, the birds of the air, and the fish of the sea." Where idols stole the heart of the people, the collapse was correspondingly total. This remarkable comprehensiveness was possible because Hosea, rather than being threatened by Baal worship, moved confidently from his Yahwistic confession to claim nature for its rightful "husband" (2:16). This made possible the enrichment of the historical images of early Yahwism with

---

9. J. L. Mays, *Hosea, A Commentary* (London: SCM, 1969), p. 1.

the nature images of Canaanite religion. Thus Hosea could remain true to the triadic confession of his heritage, even as he combined it with the freshness of a natural order revivified by the one true God, who was the Sovereign One not only of history but of nature as well:

> Sow for yourselves righteousness,
>   reap the fruit of steadfast love;
>   break up your fallow ground,
> for it is the time to seek the Lord,
>   that he may come and rain salvation upon you.   (Hos. 10:12)

F. DEUTERONOMY: A NEW FORMULATION OF THE COMMUNITY OF FAITH

Early Yahwism formulated its vision of what it meant to be the people covenanted with God in the Book of the Covenant and the Decalogue. This formulation served as a light guiding the faithful through many troubled times, times in which the covenant notion was challenged by rival Baal cults and even by a rival conception of covenant coming from within the nation itself in the form of the royal ideology of Jerusalem. In the prophets, we have come to recognize the chief defenders of the early Yahwistic notion of community against both of these threats. Especially in northern prophecy, the qualities of community embodied in the Book of the Covenant and the Decalogue, as well as in the narrative traditions reporting the saving deeds of Yahweh, were interpreted and refined in the light of God's new activity in the prophetic word. During this entire span of time down to the mid-seventh century, however, no new formulation of the community of faith was attempted.

Amos and Hosea, however, prepared the way for such an attempt by maintaining the independence of the Yahwistic notion of God's people from entanglements with Baal worship or the native forms of royal ideology. According to them Yahweh was neither the patron of a royal temple nor the instrument of a nationalistic policy. Yahweh was the righteous and compassionate God who desired "steadfast love and not sacrifice, the knowledge of God, rather than burnt offerings" (Hos. 6:6). By thus resisting co-option by political or religious institutions, prophetic Yahwism survived the collapse of both Northern Kingdom and cult during the Assyrian invasion of 724–722. In fact, the resulting destruction itself called attention to the truthfulness of the severe mercy proclaimed by these prophets. If there was to be a future for God's people, surely it was to be found among a people confessing, "Assyria shall not save us, we will not ride upon horses; and we will say no more, 'Our God,' to the word of our hands" (Hos. 14:3). The deep darkness of the times allowed the light the prophets had refused to extinguish through compromise or assimilation to shine forth as Israel's only hope: "Hate evil, and love good, and establish justice in the gate; it may be that the Lord, the God of hosts, will be gracious to the remnant of Joseph" (Amos 5:15).

The task formally undertaken by the authors of Deuteronomy was thus already anticipated in the activity of Amos and Hosea. They acknowledged one norm alone for the life of the community, the one true God, whose will was revealed in the Mosaic covenant and its law. And in anticipation of the Book of Deuteronomy, they sought to apply that norm to the new situations facing the people. Although their engagement with concrete situations as they arose did not give rise to as comprehensive and systematic a reformulation of the covenant understanding of community as that found in Deuteronomy, their address was not haphazard, but was always consistent with a clear vision of what it meant to be God's people, that being the vision of early Yahwism. One God, one covenant, one *tôrâ* interpreting that covenant to the community united under the sovereignty of God—this was the background of their prophecy. If they had sat down to formulate it in comprehensive terms, it would have resembled the Book of Deuteronomy, with one exception: the emphasis on the centrality of worship in one sanctuary would have been lacking. That likely entered this northern tradition after its migration to the south.

Often the positive vision of the righteous covenant community is not noticed by readers of the eighth-century prophets, since the unrighteousness of the people forced them repeatedly to carry on God's controversy and to intone the corresponding indictments and sentences. But it was precisely their vision of God's intended order that led them fearlessly to take up the cause of the poor and the oppressed, and to oppose any person or group that by commission or neglect contributed to the impoverishment of the land and the people. For them the greed and abuse of power by kings, priests, nobles, and false prophets were not a mere matter of personal misconduct, but an attack on the righteous community intended by God, and thus a repudiation of God's sovereignty. These prophets were thus the unflinching defenders of the early Yahwistic notion of community formulated in the Book of the Covenant and the Decalogue. In a spiritual succession reaching them from Gilgal, Shechem, and Shiloh, they stood in unbroken continuity with the redeemed slaves who first were gathered by Yahweh into the covenant community. Thus even to the rampant apostasy of that time, for example, Hosea responded with a unique formulation of Yahweh's judgment: It would be a return to the wilderness, where God could speak to them undistracted by the Baals and other seductions of the fertile land. The wilderness, as a return to the beginning, as a place for a new start, as an opportunity for covenant renewal, was the most promising place for the reformulation of the Yahwistic notion of the covenant community.

"These are the words that Moses spoke to all Israel beyond the Jordan in the wilderness" (Deut. 1:1a). Deuteronomy picks up on Hosea's suggestion that the wilderness was the location where the covenant could be re-presented to the people of Israel. In the austerity of the desert could be found the intimacy of undistracted communion with their Deliverer.

But where might the carriers of this northern prophetic tradition recreate this wilderness setting? Their original home in the Northern Kingdom was no longer the place of new beginnings. There God had spoken a definitive word of judgment on the nation, its king, and its cult. Amos's vision of a remnant was accurate. Only a small circle of witnesses survived the dispersion of a nation. But beyond judgment Amos and Hosea had glimpsed a new beginning. Where could the remnant proclaim their message of repentance and covenant renewal?

Since the time of Ahijah of Shiloh, the prophets, while conceding a political division of Israel, never recognized a religious division. Their hope remained fixed on the restoration of Yahweh's whole people. It was quite natural, therefore, that when Samaria fell in 722 B.C.E., the heirs to the prophetic tradition moved to Judah to carry on their work. And specifically, the traditions preserved by northern prophecy seemed to be borne by a circle of levitical teacher-priests, no doubt in company with followers of such prophets as Hosea. Their teaching and exhortation is recorded in the Book of Deuteronomy.

These Levites asked a life-and-death question: What could prevent the catastrophe of the north from repeating itself in Judah? Only a return to the true covenant of God, was their reply, that is, to the covenant that early Yahwistic tradition traced to Sinai (Horeb), in which the one true God elected Israel to be a holy people living in obedience to the will of God expressed in the *tôrâ*. Deuteronomy is nothing less than a new formulation of this notion of the community of faith, embodying the traditions of early Yahwism as they had been handed down especially in the north, now applied to the new setting in seventh-century Judah. Here the testimony of freed slaves to a new notion of community would live on in that portion of Israel that had escaped the destruction of the Assyrians. Here was the wilderness where God could again speak to the hearts of his people:

Hear, O Israel, the statutes and the ordinances which I speak in your hearing this day, and you shall learn them and be careful to do them. The Lord our God made a covenant with us in Horeb. Not with our fathers did the Lord make this covenant, but with us, who are all of us here alive this day. (Deut. 5:1–3)

Deuteronomy was thus an invitation to Israel to renew the covenant with Yahweh "that you may live" (5:33). It also reformulated the *tôrâ* in which Yahweh described for the people the conditions and the qualities of the covenant of life. It is thus no accident that close connections exist between the Book of the Covenant and this "second *tôrâ*."[10] Nor is it a coincidence that the major themes of the northern prophetic tradition that succeeded early Yahwism find their systematic formulation here: "Their concern for the observance of covenant law, their adherence to the ideology of Holy War, their strong attachment to the principles of charismatic leadership and their critical attitudes toward the monarchy."[11] For Hosea, prophetic Yahwism (as the authentic carrier of early Yahwism) began with Moses and the exodus (Hos. 12:13). And in Deuteronomy, Moses again takes up the discourse in formulating God's word for the people. In the words of the introduction to the original edition of book: "This is the law which Moses set before the children of Israel; these are the testimonies, the statutes, and the ordinances, which Moses spoke to the children of Israel when they came out of Egypt" (4:44–45).

The reformulation of what it meant to be God's covenanted community found in Deuteronomy is an impressive witness to the vitality of this tradition. It moved from the ashes of the Northern Kingdom into the south as a daring effort to return what remained of Israel to the God of the exodus and Horeb. As is necessary in any viable hermeneutical effort, it made necessary adjustments to the new environment. It acknowledged implicitly (without mentioning Jerusalem, which in the mouth of Moses may have been deemed unacceptable anachronism) the central sanctuary of the Southern Kingdom as the place where "the Lord your God will choose out of all your tribes to put his name and make his habitation there" (12:5). It likewise acknowledged the office of kingship (17:14–20). But remarkably, it made these adjustments without compromising the principal themes of prophetic Yahwism. Thus at no point is the legitimacy of the Davidic Covenant (with its unconditional commitments to the House of David and to Zion) granted, which could have been accomplished without disrupting the literary fiction of the wilderness address by making reference to it in the law of the king in chapter 17. Rather, the sole authority of the conditional covenant permeates the entire book. Even the king is to follow carefully "the words of this law and these statutes, . . . doing them, that his heart may not be lifted up above his brethren, and that he may not turn aside from the commandment . . . , so that he may continue long in his kingdom, he and his children in Israel" (17:19b–20).

The boldness of this effort is also seen in its consistent reference to the nation as a whole. The message of Deuteronomy was not limited to a remnant, but appealed to all Israel. As R. E. Clements has written, "Deuteronomy therefore stands out as a last great attempt to call Is-

---

10. O. Eissfeldt, *The Old Testament: An Introduction* (New York: Harper & Row, 1915), pp. 220–221.

11. E. W. Nicholson, *Deuteronomy and Tradition* (Oxford, England: Blackwell, 1967), p. 69. Cf. A. Alt, "Die Heimat des Deuteronomiums," *Kleine Schriften zur Geschichte des Volkes Israel*, vol. 2 (München: C. H. Beck, 1953), pp. 271–272.

rael to national reform, including everyone in its appeal to repentance and renewal."[12] In it the attempt was made to show how every aspect of life, personal and public, could be conformed to the righteous standards of the holy God. Deuteronomy reformulated Israel's covenant as a total program for the whole people. The liturgical format used to structure the book would have awakened in its audience memory of the covenant renewal ceremony celebrated by Joshua at the beginning of Israel's history as God's people.[13] What were the essential features of the Deuteronomic program for renewal?

As is the case of the unbroken continuity that can be recognized running through the Book of the Covenant, the Decalogue and the early prophets, in Deuteronomy the people of Judah were not presented with a new theology, but rather with a fresh formulation of God's original revelation. Thus they found the Decalogue at the head of the Torah section (5:6–21). And its definitive nature was emphasized: "These words the Lord spoke to all your assembly at the mountain . . . and he added no more" (5:22). What follows, therefore, would have been understood as an elaboration, one that—we can add on the basis of modern study—beautifully dignified the original "charter document" of the Yahwistic community.

Fully in the spirit of the Decalogue, the *tôrâ* of Deuteronomy focused first on the heart of Yahwism; that is, on worship of the one true God:

Hear, O Israel: The Lord our God is one Lord; and you shall love the Lord your God with all your heart, and with all your soul, and with all your might. And these words which I command you this day shall be upon your heart: and you shall teach them diligently to your children, and shall talk of them when you sit in your house, and when you walk by the way, and when you lie down, and when you rise. And you shall bind them as a sign upon your hand, and they shall be as frontlets between your eyes. And you shall write them on the doorposts of your house and on your gates.   (Deut. 6:4–9)

As subsequent generations of Jews have realized down to our own day, acknowledgment of the sole sovereignty of God, and a response to this Sovereign in a love that is undivided and total, constitutes the center of faith. It was from this center that the entire Book of Deuteronomy emanated. From this center arose the covenant and the *tôrâ* that described it (Deut. 7–26). Through the worship of this one Sovereign and through obedience to God's holy will, God's *šālôm* was allowed to permeate the entire community and its habitation in the world of nature (Deut. 27–28).

Not only was Yahweh acknowledged as the center of faith. Yahweh was also confessed to be the source of the specific qualities that entered the life of the community so as to establish it in peace and righteousness:

12. R. E. Clements, *God's Chosen People: A Theological Interpretation of the Book of Deuteronomy* (London: SCM, 1968), p. 37.

13. Cf. Joshua 24, and commentaries that draw attention to the covenantal structure of the Book of Deuteronomy, such as G. von Rad, *Deuteronomy*, trans. D. Barton (Philadelphia: Westminster Press, 1956).

When your son asks you in time to come, "What is the meaning of the testimonies and the statutes and the ordinances which the Lord our God has commanded you?" then you shall say to your son, "We were Pharaoh's slaves in Egypt; and the Lord brought us out of Egypt with a mighty hand; . . . and he brought us out from there, that he might bring us in and give us the land which he swore to give to our fathers. And the Lord commanded us to do all these statutes, to fear the Lord our God, for our good always, that he might preserve us alive, as at this day. And it will be righteousness for us, if we are careful to do all this commandment before the Lord our God, as he has commanded us." (Deut. 6:20–21; 23–25)

The qualities Israel was to embody in its community were justice and love. Israel was to be a holy people because God was holy. Israel was to be a righteous and compassionate people, because God was righteous and compassionate. For this reason, the remembering of the exodus tradition was so important to the Deuteronomists, "that you may live" (8:1–10), even as forgetting Yahweh's gracious saving acts elicited the most dreadful of threats, "you shall surely perish" (8:11–20). Therefore, occasions for remembering were instituted as a regular part of Israel's life as a community, such as the Passover, with its pageant of the exodus (Deut. 16), and the festival of first fruits with its recitation of the *magnalia dei* (26:1–11). God's grace had thus been manifested in God's delivering Israel from its bondage, and drawing it into a covenant of love, even as God's grace continued to be shown in the gift of the *tôrâ*. For in remembering and in obedience Israel was to find the abundant life. But not only in forgetting could Israel go astray. The very consciousness of the covenant relationship, of being "a people holy to the Lord your God," of being chosen "to be a people for his own possession, out of all the peoples that are on the face of the earth" (7:6) could become the occasion for a terrible sin, hubris. We have seen how Amos and Hosea struggled with this distortion of God's election, and with its repercussions in a perverted cult. In their moving homiletic style, the Deuteronomists also struggled to guard the hearts of the people from sinful pride:

It was not because you were more in number than any other people that the Lord set his love upon you and chose you, for you were the fewest of all peoples; but it is because the Lord loves you, and is keeping the oath which he swore to your fathers, that the Lord had brought you out with a mighty hand, and redeemed you from the house of bondage, from the hand of Pharaoh king of Egypt. (Deut. 7:7–8)

Life in community for Israel was life in an intimate and life-sustaining relationship. Israel was called into existence solely by the gracious initiating act of God. To this Israel contributed nothing, neither unique beauty nor numerical advantage that could draw Yahweh's attention, nor special power to assist in its deliverance—nor, as 9:4–5 adds, was it "your righteousness or the uprightness of your hearts." To the contrary, these people were present in the world as the fewest of all peoples. One source of motivation alone explained Israel's deliverance from bondage to freedom: God's love and God's faithfulness to the promises made to Israel's ancestors.

For the community of faith, the divine gifts of deliverance and freedom had created the context for the authentic life; that is, life of service and joyful obedience to God's will. But the God who was true to promises made centuries earlier to Israel's patriarchs could scarcely tolerate on the part of the people a response of unfaithfulness and contempt of the covenant relationship. They were called to a holy purpose, they were drawn into a distinct mission, and if they cast aside the life of righteousness for a life of greed and shamefulness, they became a hindrance to God's will rather than a blessing on the earth. The Deuteronomic theology made perfectly clear, therefore, that the response demanded by God's gracious acts of deliverance and creation of a people was unequivocal:

Know therefore that the Lord your God is God, the faithful God who keeps covenant and steadfast love with those who love him and keep his commandments, to a thousand generations, and requites to their face those who hate him, by destroying them; he will not be slack with him who hates him, he will requite him to his face. You shall therefore be careful to do the commandment, and the statutes, and the ordinances, which I command you this day. (Deut. 7:9–11)

When tempted to take their freedom for granted and to insult God's grace, the people of Israel had the commandments of the covenant to remind them that even as deliverance of the enslaved was a matter of great urgency for God, obedience and zeal for justice were to be matters of urgency and greatest seriousness for them as well. They were God's possession not for a life of sinful self-indulgence, but righteous service. For it was in sharing God's love with others that they remained open to God's life-sustaining love.

Deuteronomy thus reformulated the notion of the community of faith of early Yahwism. And in so doing, its authors remained true to the original vision of a people called into being solely by the antecedent grace of God, and called to "be to me a kingdom of priests and a holy nation" (Exod. 19:6a). It also demonstrated that the Yahwistic notion of community was a dynamic one, based on faith in a God active in every new generation. Thus Deuteronomy placed a new generation, faced with serious threats to faith and nationhood, before the God whose will had been revealed at Horeb. The result was a deepening of the essential qualities of the Yahwistic notion of community.

In this formulation, the Yahwistic understanding of righteousness was broadened to demonstrate how God's holiness applied to every aspect of life, cultic, social and political. With a remarkable comprehensiveness, *tôrâ* was explicated so as to leave no area uncovered, no social class unaddressed. At the same time, comprehensiveness did not lead to an abstract legalism, for Deuteronomy was infused with an urgent and passionate appeal to the heart of every Israelite. Here was not a vocation reserved exclusively for kings and priests. Every individual was responsible for upholding the covenant in everyday life.

In a depth hitherto not reached, righteousness was clothed in compassion, creating a dynamic interaction between these two qualities that had a profound effect on the Yahwistic notion of community. Using an idiom earlier favored by Hosea, the Deuteronomists traced the quality of compassion to Yahweh's *love* for Israel; there was no explanation for Israel's election aside from the fact "that the Lord set his love upon you and chose you." Moreover, "the Lord your God is God, the faithful God who keeps covenant and steadfast love with those who love him and keep his commandments" (7:7b and 9a). Love between God and humans was thus characterized by a reciprocity that tied cult and morality together in an indivisible relationship.

Here we can note only a few examples of the effects of this deepening of understanding of righteousness and compassion and of their interrelationship. In the section regarding the release of slaves, the discrimination against female slaves found in the Book of the Covenant was eliminated:[14]

If your brother, a Hebrew man, or a Hebrew woman, is sold to you, he shall serve you six years, and in the seventh year you shall let him go free from you. And when you let him go free from you, you shall not let him go empty-handed; you shall furnish him liberally out of your flock, out of your threshing floor, and out of your wine press; as the Lord your God has blessed you, you shall give to him. (Deut. 15:12–14).

Moreover, the motivational basis for this new sense of equality was located explicitly in the antecedent gracious acts of God: "You shall remember that you were a slave in the land of Egypt, and the Lord your God redeemed you, therefore I command you this day" (15:15). Similarly, in the cultic festivals, the discrimination found in the Book of the Covenant was eliminated: All were to attend, "you and your son and your daughter, your manservant and your maidservant, the Levite who is within your towns, the sojourner, the fatherless, and the widow who are among you" (7:11), and again motivation was grounded in Yahweh's initiating act of grace: "You shall remember that you were a slave in Egypt; and you shall be careful to observe these statutes" (17:12).

Other vivid examples of the wedding of righteousness and compassion in laws derived from the gracious acts of Yahweh related to "the justice due to the sojourner" and "the fatherless" and "the widow"

14. Cf. P. D. Hanson, "The Theological Significance of Contradiction Within the Book of the Covenant," in G. Coats and B. Long, eds., *Canon and Authority* (Philadelphia: Fortress Press, 1977), p. 116.

(Deut. 24:17-18), and to the provision of gleanings for these same vulnerable classes (24:19-22). A deepened sensitivity is also found in the Book of Deuteronomy to the ramifications of the Yahwistic belief that the land was a gift from Yahweh, a gift for all the people to enjoy. Since some could find this right denied them due to misfortune, the specific provision of the third-year tithe was made for the Levite (who had no possession), the sojourner, the fatherless, and the widow (14:28-29). Such observance of the *tôrâ* was not merely a legal observance, but was an integral part of the order of *šālôm* established by Yahweh: That these vulnerable classes may "come and eat and be filled" was inextricably related to the blessing "of all of the work of your hands that you do" (14:29b).

The organic relation between God's antecedent grace toward Israel and their response in compassionate righteousness is beautifully expressed in the transition from the description of Yahweh to the commandment to Israel in Deuteronomy 10:17-19: "For the Lord your God is God of gods and Lord of lords, the great, the mighty and the terrible God, who is not partial and takes no bribe. He executes justice for the fatherless and the widow, and loves the sojourner, giving him food and clothing. Love the sojourner therefore; for you were sojourners in the land of Egypt."

This passage leads us to the third quality of the Yahwistic notion of community, for in it we can discern how righteousness and compassion could be maintained in such a dynamic relationship in Israel: they were already wedded in the heart of God. When Israel responded to the love of God in worship, it found the motivation from which righteousness and compassion alone could enter the life of community and individual. In Deuteronomy, the center of life—the one true God, celebrated in worship—was described more vividly than in any previous Yahwistic document, from its most sublime formulation in the *šĕmā* (Deut. 6:4-9) to the persistent application of this belief to every area of life in its specific expositions of *tôrâ*. The effects of this central confession can be seen throughout the book. As one example we note that, although the Deuteronomists accepted the existence of kingship, at no point was the privileged status of the king normally associated with the Davidic covenant allowed to encroach on Yahweh's sole sovereignty. The king, like every Israelite, stood under the sole authority of the Horeb covenant, with its unconditional stipulations and absolute commandments. Similarly, while the centrality of the cult was accepted, the royal traditions according Zion unconditional promises are nowhere to be found. Even in the implication that the ark might represent a special material link between God and people was removed. No longer was it described as the throne on which the invisible deity was seated, but rather as the container for the tablets of the law. As for Yahweh's presence, it was expressed through a carefully formulated theologumenon; that is, by reference to the divine name, which Yahweh would put in the place of his choosing (e.g., 12:5), a concept again congruous with early Yahwism (cf. Exod. 20:24) and resistant to the royal theology's concept of the election of David and Zion. Against the background of this strict observance of the central theme of early Yahwism, one can understand why the Deuteronomic law itself included both a very careful formulation of "limited kingship" (17:14–20) and provision for the charismatic presence of the prophet such as Moses (18:15–22); both were intended as guardians of the central confession of Yahwism.

We thus see how the Deuteronomistic notion of community was essentially faithful to the early Yahwistic notion, and dynamic in the way it broadened and deepened the concept. With beauty and power, it pictured a people whose holiness derived solely from its center in worship of the one true God. From this center there emanated outward into the community a powerful divine example of acts of righteous compassion, interpreted by *tôrâ* and inviting embodiment in the life of the people. The obedient response of the people in turn facilitated the flow of Yahweh's *šālôm* into all nature, restoring a covenant of universal blessing. Passionately, therefore, the book appealed to the people to remember and to live. For in remembering what Yahweh had done, Israel would respond in grateful obedience to the *tôrâ*, which is to say, in a life of worship, righteousness, and compassion. And in that dynamic triad alone was the life of blessing and peace to be found.

VI

A Variegated Portrait: The Contribution of Southern Kings, Prophets, and Sages to the Yahwistic Notion of Community

(Kings, Chronicles, Isaiah, Micah, Jeremiah, Proverbs, Job, and Ecclesiastes)

The Word of the LORD came unto me, saying:
O miserable cities of designing men,
O wretched generation of enlightened men,
Betrayed in the mazes of your ingenuities,
Sold by the proceeds of your proper inventions:
I have given you hands which you turn from worship,
I have given you speech, for endless palaver,
I have given you my Law, and you set up commissions,
I have given you lips, to express friendly sentiments,
I have given you hearts, for reciprocal distrust.
I have given you power of choice, and you only alternate
Between futile speculation and unconsidered action . . .
Much is your reading, but not the Word of GOD,
Much is your building, but not the House of GOD.[1]

Historical Note: The development of community forms and ideals took a somewhat different direction in the Southern Kingdom than in the Northern, in part because of the major impact that the Davidic house had on the religious thinking of the south. Evidence of the growth of the Yahwistic notion of community in Judah up to the Babylonian destruction of Jerusalem in 587 comes from the books of Kings and Chronicles, and from the prophecies of Isaiah, Micah, and Jeremiah.

---

1. From T. S. Eliot, "Choruses from 'The Rock,' " *The Complete Poems and Plays, 1909–1950* (New York: Harcourt, Brace, 1952), p. 102.

International events, including the powerful rise of the neo-Babylonian empire at the expense of Assyria, continued to induce the prophets to formulate their vision of the future of God's people in broadly universal terms.

A. AN OVERVIEW OF THE SEVENTH AND SIXTH CENTURIES IN JUDAH

In the kingdom of Judah, the problems faced by those seeking to incorporate the qualities of worship, righteousness, and compassion in response to the saving acts of Yahweh were different in certain respects from those with which the northern prophets struggled and were similar in others. In Judah, the influence of Baalism on the cult, though by no means absent, was less pronounced than in the Northern Kingdom. In the Jerusalem temple, Yahweh reigned, although a serious theological problem continued to be posed by the special covenant with the deity claimed by the royal house. The resulting influence of the king over the temple and its priesthood was accompanied not only by the danger of a veneration of the king, which encroached on Yahweh's sole sovereignty, but also by the tendency of kings to introduce ingredients of non-Yahwistic cults into the religious life of the nation when such moves served the aims of foreign policy. The similarities, however, far outweighed the differences in the struggles faced by faithful Yahwists in the north and south, and for a fundamental reason. Whether caused by attraction to Baal worship, or by inordinate veneration of the king, the impingement on the sole sovereignty of Yahweh over the people had similar results: The disintegration of the dynamic triad of worship, righteousness, and compassion with the attendant perversion of cult and degeneration of social justice. This accounts for the considerable thematic overlap between, for example, Hosea and Isaiah, even though one comes from a rural Yahwism of the north with deep roots in tribal customs of the League period, the other from the urban Yahwism that had developed in Jerusalem in close association with the Davidic monarchy.

At the same time an important fact should be observed: Not all southern kings sought to exploit the Davidic covenant and the temple cult at the cost of the centrality of Yahweh worship in the temple. As many of the psalms originating in the Jerusalem sanctuary attest, the temple was a place where worship was offered to God by sincere and penitent hearts, and among those hearts were the hearts of several of Judah's kings. When the Deuteronomists reconstructed the history of kingship on the basis of sources available to them, they acknowledged the efforts of Asa, Jehoshaphat, Joash, Hezekiah, and Josiah to reform the cult along Yahwistic lines. And although the inspiration for the Josianic reform was at least in part tied to the discovery of the Book of Deuteronomy (that is, a vehicle primarily of northern prophetic tradition), the other reforms were apparently indigenous southern phenomena.

This is not surprising when one recalls the early history of the Davidic dynasty. In the ideology of the south, the Davidic covenant did not of necessity replace the earlier traditions associated with Sinai, Gilgal, Shechem, and Shiloh. As the narrative tradition in 2 Samuel 6 relates and Psalm 132 recalls, David took great pains to draw the symbol of early Yahwism, the ark, into his sanctuary. And he paid heed to the words of his prophetic advisors Nathan and Gad, men speaking for the Yahwistic traditions of the League. Thus a choice faced each of the kings of Judah either to follow the model of David in integrating Davidic and Sinaitic covenants (that is, God's covenant with the king and God's covenant with the people) through acknowledgment of Yahweh's sovereignty over all Israel, or to emancipate self from the conditions of the Sinaitic covenant, and with exclusive emphasis on the unconditional promises of the Davidic covenant, to claim absolute authority over people and cult, thereby compromising the sovereignty of Yahweh. In the cases of kings choosing the former option, we read of the cooperation of king with Yahwistic prophets and other people faithful to the traditions of early Yahwism. In the cases of those choosing the latter, we hear of no such cooperation. Either the prophets are not mentioned, or they are mentioned as the victims of persecution.

It is particularly instructive in this connection to note that when the Deuteronomists recounted the reform efforts of the several godly kings, the starting point and main emphasis of each reform was the cleansing of the cult of idols and practices that encroached upon the sole worship of Yahweh. The first such reform was carried out by Asa:

And Asa did what was right in the eyes of the Lord, as David his father had done. He put away the male cult prostitutes out of the land, and removed all the idols that his fathers had made. He also removed Maacah his mother from being queen mother because she had an abominable image made for Asherah; and Asa cut down her image and burned it at the brook Kidron. (1 Kings 15:11–13)

We can recognize here the influence of early Yahwism with its primal commandment to worship no god but Yahweh. And the Chronicler seems to be drawing on reliable, old tradition in reporting that this restoration of sole worship of Yahweh was construed as a covenant renewal ceremony in the archaic style of the League cult:

And they entered into a covenant to seek the Lord, the God of their fathers, with all their heart and with all their soul; and that whoever would not seek the Lord, the God of Israel, should be put to death, whether young or old, man or woman. They took oath to the Lord with a loud voice, and with shouting, and with trumpets, and with horns. And all Judah rejoiced over the oath; for they had sworn with all their heart, and had sought him with their whole desire, and he was found by them, and the Lord gave them rest round about. (2 Chron. 15:12–15)

As expressed both in early Yahwistic law (e.g., Exod. 10:3–6; 20:23, and 23:20) and early Yahwistic cultic ritual (Josh. 24:14–28), the undivided devotion of the people to God was the heart of the Yahwistic community. Asa, after the model of David, proved himself true to the covenant beliefs and practices of early Yahwism. For him, the Davidic covenant did not annul the early covenant of God with the people, but fit into it. And thus in spite of Asa's not removing the high places, the Deuteronomists could conclude: "Nevertheless the heart of Asa was wholly true to the Lord all his days" (1 Kings 15:14b).

Asa's son Jehoshaphat continued the Yahwistic practices of his father (1 Kings 22:41–46). It is interesting that the Chronicler, again in all probability drawing on an old tradition, gives an account of a reform of the land's judicial system that played a part in Jehoshaphat's leading the people "back to the Lord, the God of their fathers." Again, the pattern of early Yahwistic community, with the rooting of righteousness and compassion in sole worship of God, is visible, as is beautifully expressed in the king's admonition of his judges:

Consider what you do, for you judge not for man but for the Lord; he is with you in giving judgment. Now then, let the fear of the Lord be upon you; take heed what you do, for there is no perversion of justice with the Lord our God, or partiality, or taking bribes. (2 Chron. 19:6–7)

The next king cited as a reformer by tradition is Joash, son of Ahaziah, whose life was spared from the assassin Queen Athaliah by his sister, and whose rightful claim to the throne was advanced by the priest Jehoiada. After his coronation, the young king, under the tutorship of the priest Jehoiada, set to work on reform, and again his program was connected with covenant renewal: "And Jehoiada made [the] covenant between the Lord and the king and people, that they should be the Lord's people; and also between the king and the poeple" (2 Kings 11:17). Although this is overlooked in the RSV translation, the Hebrew refers to *"the* covenant" (in contrast, for example, to 11:4), obviously to emphasize the fact that this was the covenant *par excellence*, which, since League times, constituted the people as Yahweh's people. It is also important to note that in this covenant, the king stood in solidarity with his people in the relationship with Yahweh, "that they should be the Lord's people." We observe, moreover, how this covenant led immediately to the urgent task of removing idolatrous worship from the land (vv. 18–20), highlighting the cardinal Yahwistic theme that without acknowledgment in the cult of the sole sovereignty of Yahweh, covenant was impossible. Finally, it is significant that when the opportunity presented itself (in this case due to the king's youthfulness), the leading priest of the Jerusalem temple, supported by "the people of the land" (v. 14), reintroduced the covenant theology of early Yahwism, evidence that that tradition maintained itself tenaciously in certain circles, against the absolute claims of some of Judah's kings. In the thought of those circles, there was still one people of Israel, and that community was reconstituted whenever false gods were renounced, the saving acts of Yahweh were recalled, the covenant was renewed, and the *tôrâ* was obediently followed.

B. ISAIAH

Nowhere are both the similarities and the differences that characterize the relationship between northern and southern prophecy as clearly seen as in the prophet Isaiah. Living in close personal contact with the royal house and the temple of Jerusalem and steeped in the traditions of Yahweh's election of Zion and the anointed ruler, he nevertheless remained true to the qualities of the early Yahwistic community, defending the sole sovereignty of Yahweh and the the stringent standard of divine righteousness with a dedication equal to that of Amos and Hosea. In the case of Solomon and Rehoboam, we noticed the seriousness of the threat to Yahwism that resided in royal ideology, though the genuine longing for God's presence found in many of the psalms stemming from the Jerusalem cult gives an indication of the spiritual depth and beauty of Jerusalem temple worship. Isaiah masterfully synthesized the diverse traditions of early Yahwism and Jerusalem royal theology in a way that broadened and deepened the Yahwistic notion of community without threatening its dynamic core. This he was able to do because of an understanding of the essential qualities of the Yahwistic notion of community so profound as to enable him to draw freely on a wide range of themes and images with the effect that they enriched rather than detracted from these essential qualities.

This remarkable transformation is visible in the master symbol of his formulation of the religious community: the righteous, faithful city (e.g., 1:26). This symbol referred, of course, to Zion, the royal habitation chosen by Yahweh according to the royal theology. And indeed, Isaiah incorporated into his picture of this community many of the themes belonging to that royal theology. In royal psalms such as 46, 48, and 76, we recognized the motif of the attack of the enemy hordes on the Holy City and their defeat by Yahweh, a motif stemming from the conflict myth with its picture of the assault on the Divine Mountain. In tirelessly relating his vision of the righteous, faithful city to the events and crises of his day, Isaiah applied this motif as a part of his admonition to king and people to trust Yahweh (cf. 10:27b–34; 14:24–27; 14:28–32; 30:27–33; 31:4–9). An especially vivid example arose in response to Sennacherib's invasion of Judah in 701:

> Ah, the thunder of many peoples,
>> they thunder like the thundering of the sea!
> Ah, the roar of nations,
>> they roar like the roaring of mighty waters!
> The nations roar like the roaring of many waters,
>> but he will rebuke them, and they will flee far away,
> chased like chaff on the mountains before the wind
>> and whirling dust before the storm.
> At evening time, behold, terror!
>> Before morning, they are no more!
> This is the portion of those who despoil us,
>> and the lot of those who plunder us. (Isa. 17:1–4)

The attack of the nations on Israel is likened to the waters of chaos breaking in to destroy the created order, but between the setting and the rising of the sun Yahweh has blasted them away like dust. This mythological motif, lifted far above the details of historical happenings, resembles later apocalypticism. But this is insufficient reason to assign this passage to a post-Isaianic author, for it is rather illustrative of Isaiah's use of motifs from the royal cult of Jerusalem.

Similarly, Isaiah drew deeply on the theme of Yahweh's anointed one of the house of David. Isaiah had in mind not the temporary, charismatic ruler of the League, but rather the king at home in the Jerusalem royal theology on whom Yahweh's spirit and the corresponding charismata had come to rest as a lifelong endowment (11:1–2), the king whose rule was to assure the end-time *šālôm* familiar from the royal psalms and ultimately traceable to ancient Near Eastern royal mythology.

How Isaiah transformed these themes from the royal theology is, however, far more significant than the recognition of their source. Zion became the citadel of righteousness and the beacon of justice in the land, even as the anointed one was portrayed as the bearer of the qualities of the righteous, compassionate, deliverer God Yahweh. As David had previously drawn into the heart of the new royal sanctuary the essential qualities of early Yahwism (symbolized by his bringing the ark to Jerusalem), Isaiah at this later time incorporated into his vision of Zion the righteous laws and structures of early Yahwism:

> And I will restore your judges as at the first,
>> and your counselors as at the beginning.
> Afterward you shall be called the city of righteousness,
>> the faithful city. (Isa. 1:26)

In the righteous, faithful city, the anointed representative of God, the Davidic king, would exemplify the primal confession of Yahwism, drawing veneration not to himself, but to God. In the manner of early Yahwism, from this grounding in worship of the one true God he would foster righteousness and compassion in the land:

> And his delight shall be in the fear of the Lord.
> He shall not judge by what his eyes see,
>   or decide by what his ears hear;
> but with righteousness he shall judge the poor,
>   and decide with equity for the meek of the earth;
> and he shall smite the earth with the rod of his mouth,
>   and with the breath of his lips he shall slay the wicked.
> Righteousness shall be the girdle of his waist,
>   and faithfulness the girdle of his loins. (Isa. 11:3–5)

While using royal and even mythological motifs, Isaiah placed them in the service of early prophetic Yahwism, due to his unflinching dedication to the Yahwistic qualities of worship, righteousness, and compassion. It is significant, therefore, that between the charismatic anointing of the Davidic king in 11:1–2 and the description of the *šālôm* characterizing his reign in 11:6–9, verses 3–5 describe the king's devotion to Yahweh, and his commitment to God's righteousness and compassion. As we have seen, Yahwistic faith acknowledged no way to peace save through this divinely given triad, and for Isaiah the "shoot from the stump of Jesse" was to be the perfect embodiment of this ancient Yahwistic conviction.

Isaiah matched the earlier prophets' hard-hitting attack on every violation of the early Yahwistic standard of righteous compassion, therefore, because he had fully integrated that ideal into his notion of the righteous, faithful city. Zion and God's anointed on Zion were not symbols of national pride and human glory, but of covenant responsibility and godly devotion. And *šālôm* could be expected only where God was worshiped in faithfulness and his *tôrâ* was obeyed in grateful devotion. It is this notion of the righteous, faithful city that Isaiah held up as a standard before the nation and the resulting assessment was devastating:

> How the faithful city has become a harlot,
>   she that was full of justice!
> Righteousness lodged in her,
>   but now murderers.
> Your silver has become dross,
>   your wine mixed with water,
> Your princes are rebels
>   and companions of thieves.
> Everyone loves a bribe
>   and runs after gifts.
> They do not defend the fatherless,
>   and the widow's cause does not come to them. (Isa. 1:21–23)

In the spirit of the defenders of the Yahwistic ideal before him, Isaiah viewed this moral turpitude in radically theological terms. What he recognized was not merely the violation of a code of human conduct, but a

frontal attack on the one holy God. Therefore, even as God was acknowledged to be the ultimate source of this standard of righteousness,
so too he was confessed to be Israel's judge:

> The Lord has taken his place to contend,
>   he stands to judge his people.
> The Lord enters into judgment
>   with the elders and princes of his people;
> "It is you who have devoured the vineyard,
>   the spoil of the poor is in your houses.
> What do you mean by crushing my people,
>   by grinding the face of the poor?"
> says the Lord God of hosts.   (Isa. 3:13—15)

The motif of the vineyard found here Isaiah applied and exquisitely
elaborated in 5:1–7. As the singer guided his audience through the levels of his song of unrequited love, he prepared them for a message recalling the passion of Hosea:

> For the vineyard of the Lord of hosts
>   is the house of Israel,
> and the men of Judah
>   are his pleasant planting;
> and he looked for justice,
>   but behold, bloodshed:
> for righteousness,
>   but behold, a cry!   (Isa. 5:7)

Isaiah was very mindful of the long history of Yahweh's covenant with
Israel, a history beginning with gracious, saving deeds and developing
under Yahweh's constant attention and care. Through this long history, God had sought to create a righteous and compassionate people, a
city offering the refuge of the Lord to its afflicted: "The Lord has
founded Zion, and in her the afflicted of his people find refuge"
(14:32). But where had that long history led? Not to justice and righteousness, but to bloodshed and the cry of the oppressed, for godless
greed ruled instead of the righteousness of the covenant community
(5:8–12; 10:1–4). Indeed, from the perspective of this prophet, the perversion seemed egregious, with standards completely reversed: "Woe
to those who call evil good and good evil, who put darkness for light
and light for darkness who put bitter for sweet and sweet for bitter"
(5:20). With this perversion of righteousness, there arose correspondingly suitable leaders: "I will make boys their princes, and babes shall
rule over them" (3:4). From this broad historical perspective, Isaiah
was only able to assume that this was a people committed to sin from
the beginning. This he expressed in a divine word that was placed as an
introduction to the Book of Isaiah: "Sons I have reared and brought
up, but they have rebelled against me. The ox knows its owner, and the

ass its master's crib; but Israel does not know, my people does not understand" (1:2b–3). This elicited for Isaiah the deepest, darkest riddle of his prophetic career, which was even incorporated into his commissioning. This was a people with a hardened heart (6:9–13), which seem determined to refuse the invitation of God to be saved. They were indeed a covenanted people, but their covenant was with death (28:15a)! They were a people confident of a refuge, but their refuge was not Yahweh: "for we have made lies our refuge, and in falsehood we have taken shelter" (28:15b).

Isaiah's use of themes taken from his Jerusalem temple environment, therefore, was not at all an uncritical one. Šālôm did not reside in Zion on the basis of a natural law. Nor did the reigning Davidic king provide a guarantee of security by virtue of his royal blood. For Israel, Zion, its cult, and its king all were solely responsible to Yahweh, and they could become true agents of peace only in relationship to that great King. Isaiah's harsh attack on the cult, therefore, did not contradict, but grew out of his concept of Zion and the anointed king, tied as they were in his theology to the covenantal thought of early Yahwism. This is seen vividly in 1:10–20, where Yahweh rejects with loathing the people's sacrifices, assemblies, and prayers (vv. 10–15). And the reason is stated clearly: "Your hands are full of blood" (v. 15b). Not in splendid temple structures and liturgies, nor in beautiful hymns and abundant sacrifices, but in their daily relationship to God's righteousness and compassion was the heart of the people revealed. Isaiah's admonition was accordingly a straightforward lesson out of the early Yahwistic notion of the community of faith:

> Wash yourselves; make yourselves clean;
>> remove the evil of your doings
>> from before my eyes;
> cease to do evil,
>> learn to do good;
> seek justice,
>> correct oppression;
> defend the fatherless,
>> plead for the widow.   (Isa. 1:16–17)

Forgiveness, even at this late hour, was offered to the people. If only they could be brought to their senses (1:18)! And šālôm was offered too, but not as a gift to be taken for granted, but as an inxtricable part of a relationship to the God of righteousness and compassion:

> If you are willing and obedient,
>> you shall eat the good of the land;
> But if you refuse and rebel,
>> you shall be devoured by the sword;
>> for the mouth of the Lord has spoken.   (Isa. 1:19–20)

Against the background of these rich traditions, and within the context of the crises of the late eighth century, Isaiah pondered over the riddle of this people, blessed with such opportunity and yet choosing the covenant with death. Wherein lay the roots of this madness? Isaiah's answer was "pride." This he portrayed powerfully in the image of the haughty daughters of Zion, who "walk with outstretched necks, glancing wantonly with their eyes, mincing along as they go, tinkling with their feet" (3:16–26). Such vain, self-destructive human hubris was a terrible offense to "the Lord of host [who] has a day against all that is proud and lofty" (2:6–22). There was no place for human pride before the God of Isaiah, whose holy majesty was experienced so powerfully by the prophet in his call vision (6:1–3). Not even kings were excluded from this judgment:

> Man is bowed down, and men are brought low,
>   and the eyes of the haughty are humbled.
> But the Lord of hosts is exalted in justice,
>   and the Holy God shows himself holy in
>   righteousness. (Isa. 5:15–16)

Isaiah was able to condemn human pride so consistently because of his overwhelming sense of God's holy majesty, and from this the rightful posture of the human before God was also manifested, the posture of absolute trust in the one true God: "Behold, I am laying in Zion for a foundation of stone, a tested stone, a precious cornerstone, of a sure foundation: 'He who believes will not be in haste' " (28:16). With beauty and clarity, Isaiah reaffirmed the primal quality of early Yahwism, namely undivided devotion to the one true God. No other foundation existed for the righteous, faithful city of Isaiah's vision. The destruction of all other foundations was assured: "I will make justice the line, and righteousness the plummet; and hail will sweep away the refuge of lies, and waters will overwhelm the shelter" (28:17). Here we begin to see the inner connection between Isaiah's harsh words of judgment against the land and his hope for Zion. The righteous, faithful city could arise after the city of lies had been removed. The threatening clouds gathering around the land were not evidence of Yahweh's absence, but of Yahweh's nearness "to do his deed—strange is his deed! and to work his work—alien is his work!" (28:21b). Thus the tragic flaw in the proud attitude of the people that their own strength was sufficient to defend themselves was that it blinded them to the true Purposer. In 22:8b–11, Isaiah enumerated all the measures taken by the leaders of Jerusalem to guard themselves against the seige of Sennacherib, and then lamented, "but you did not look to him who did it, or have regard for him who planned it long ago."

The "precious cornerstone" and the "sure foundation," that is, Yahweh's majesty, called for trust and righteous compassion. With fresh, new images, Isaiah thus described the central quality of true community, and then proceeded to apply it to every circumstance and event, both in the everyday society and in the historic events taking shape in Assyria and Egypt. Having already drawn attention to Isaiah's attack on those bending justice to their advantage at the cost of widows, orphans, and the poor, those luxuriating as the land decayed, and those perverting all sense of right and wrong, we now turn to illustrate his application of this same standard to international events.

In each of the crises of his time, Isaiah made the same appeal: Trust in Yahweh alone; rely on no league or treaty with a foreign land, for they are not from Yahweh, but represent the sinful, prideful attempts of mortals to produce their own security (30:1–5; 31:1–3). In the international arena, too, hubris manifested itself as the refusal of humans to acknowledge their ultimate dependence: "Woe to those who go down to Egypt for help and rely on horses, who trust in chariots because they are many and in horsemen because they are very strong, but do not look to the Holy One of Israel or consult the Lord!" (31:1). The basic problem that Isaiah had with human alliances was that they overlooked the fact that one plan alone guided all history: "As I have planned, so shall it be, and as I have proposed, so shall it stand" (14:24). This plan encompassed not only Israel, but all nations. Thus Yahweh could use Assyria as the rod of punishment against his people, but when the Assyrian king vaunted himself in his haughty pride, and claimed "by the strength of my hand have I done it," he too stumbled against the Holy One of Israel and was brought low (10:5–15).

Nowhere else did Isaiah's emphasis on absolute trust in Yahweh, and the relation of that emphasis to the themes of Zion and Yahweh's anointed, come to clearer expression than in the material coming from the Syro-Ephramite war crisis found in 7:1–9:6. To a frightened king facing the attack of Israel and Syria and contemplating an appeal to Assyria for help, Isaiah was sent with his son Shearjashub ("a remnant shall return"). This was an hour of dreadful decision for the king. The name of Isaiah's son bore witness to this fact. At hand was one of those fateful moments demanding declaration of one's ultimate allegiance.

Isaiah pointed to the Lord as the One under whose sovereignty the entire affair rested: "Take heed, be quiet, do not fear, and do not let your heart be faint because of these two smoldering stumps of firebrands" (7:4). The posture described by Isaiah was identical to the one previously required of the people in the exodus and in the subsequent holy wars of Yahweh against Israel's enemies. Isaiah admonished Ahaz to give up his clever plans to save himself and instead to make his plans in relation to God. It is not possible to determine exactly what this would have meant in political terms. But it would be injudicious to extrapolate from this word a pacifism binding on all times. What is clear is that the king, in consultation with Yahweh's messenger the prophet, was to work out his policy quietly and confidently on the basis of absolute trust in Yahweh's sovereignty. Moreover, the opposite side of the coin was dreadfully clear to the prophet: "If you will not believe, surely you shall not be established" (7:9b). The outcome of this encounter between prophet and king was that Ahaz refused to believe, and even refused a sign from Yahweh. He chose to pursue his own program of self-help, the fateful terms of which corroborate Isaiah's warning.

So Ahaz sent messengers to Tiglath-pileser king of Assyria, saying, "I am your servant and your son. Come up and rescue me from the hand of the king of Syria and from the hand of the king of Israel, who are attacking me." Ahaz also took the silver and gold that was in the treasures of the house of the Lord and in the treasures in the king's house, and sent a present to the king of Assyria.
(2 Kings 16:7-8)

One of the consequences of Ahaz's acknowledgement of Tiglath-pileser's sovereignty was the erection of an Assyrian-type altar in the Jerusalem temple (2 Kings 16:10–18), which was the beginning of an entanglement with Assyrian religion that would culminate in the apostasy of Manasseh. Thus it becomes clear that what Isaiah was defending was the heart of the community gathered in the name of Yahweh, namely, acknowledgement of the sovereignty of one King alone, and undivided worship of and trust in that divine King—in other words, the primal quality of Yahwism formulated by the first commandment and the šĕmāᶜ of Deuteronomy 6. Once this primal quality was abandoned, Israel ceased to be a people covenanted with Yahweh, and like the other nations sought security through strength of armaments and military treaties (31:1). This for Isaiah was a covenant with death (28:14–22). The alternatives thus facing Ahaz were clearly described by Isaiah within the context of a later crisis:

> For thus said the Lord God, the Holy One of Israel,
>   "In returning and rest you shall be saved;
>   in quietness and in trust shall be your strength."
> And you would not, but you said,
> "No! We will speed upon horses,"
>   therefore you shall speed away;
> and, "We will ride upon swift steeds,"
>   therefore your pursuers shall be swift.
> A thousand shall flee at the threat of one,
>   at the threat of five you shall flee,
> till you are left
>   like a flagstaff on top of a mountain,
>   like a signal on a hill.   (Isa. 30:15–17)

In Isaiah's prophecy, Yahweh was extending to the king yet another opportunity to return to Israel's true source of life and security. But the king's answer was emphatic: "No."

This scene of the encounter between prophet and king vividly portrays an important aspect of the Yahwistic community's relation to the realm of society and politics. Undivided allegiance to Yahweh was not only a matter of the cult. It was to serve as the central perspective for every political and social question facing the nation. Isaiah saw it as his responsibility to declare to king and people alike the terms of this faith, and the consequences of its denial. This was seen already in Isaiah's call vision in the temple, where any temptation to spiritualize his vocation within the congenial setting of the temple precincts was countered with the command: "Go, and say to this people" (6:9a). The somber message given to Isaiah to declare to the people in his call (6:6b–13) accords with the description of Ahaz's response to Isaiah. Both express what we might call "prophetic realism:" Those extending the prophetic invitation to undivided allegiance to Yahweh as that which alone could constitute a viable community would have to be prepared to face rejection by the nation and its leaders! The pessimism of this message is striking, and raises the question of how it might be assessed. In the case of the Book of Deuteronomy's appeal to the whole people to acknowledge the sole sovereignty of Yahweh and to build its life on the *tôrâ*, one can detect the potential of Yahwism as a program for reform, a potentiality that surfaced powerfully during the reign of Josiah. But what future was there for a message that seemed convinced of its own rejection by an unbelieving king and people? Isaiah developed his answer to this question in 7:10–9:6. It is an answer that represents a significant new contribution of prophecy to the Yahwistic notion of community.

Ahaz's pious refusal of a sign gave proof of his unwillingness to submit to Yahweh and cast himself on Yahweh's plan for the future. His mind was set on his own course of action. But to Isaiah the stubborn unfaithfulness of the king did not alter the fact that Yahweh had a plan for Israel, and that plan would prevail against all obstacles. The nature of the divine plan was revealed under the sign of Immanuel: "Therefore the Lord himself shall give you a sign: A young woman is with child, and she will bear a son, and will call him Immanuel" (NEB, Isa 7:14). To this prophet, whose mind was so attentively focused on the holy Lord God of Hosts and whose life was so drawn into the will and activity of that God, there was no question that "God is with us" (Hebrew: *ʿimmānû'ēl*). But how was God to be with a people that bore a promise of blessing and nevertheless persisted in rejecting its Lord? In interpreting the sign of Immanuel, Isaiah sought to take fully into account both the riddle of Israel's incorrigibility, and the faithfulness of God to the promises regarding Zion and the Anointed One.

In 7:16 Isaiah addressed the question of the Syro-Ephraimite threat, and, in keeping with the message of 7:5–9, announced that before the child would be able to discern between evil and good, those two lands would be deserted, a theme further elaborated on in 8:1–4. But with that the "strange" and "alien" deed of Yahweh was not completed.

Judgment would come to Judah as well when Immanuel had grown to the age of discerning between evil and good, symbolized by his eating curds and honey, foods not of a high urban civilization, but of a land reduced to nomadism (7:15, 17, 21, and 22). In 8:5–10 Isaiah elaborated on this theme of judgment with another image: "this people have refused the waters of Shiloh that flow gently." Here we recognize a symbol of the quiet trust in Yahweh that was central to Isaiah's message. When the people of Judah betrayed their trust in God by taking history into their own hands and appealing to Tiglath-pileser, they had not removed the future from Yahweh's hands, but had set in motion Yahweh's judgment on their faithlessness: the king of Assyria would be to them like the waters of primeval chaos engulfing the land of Immanuel, the land that due to its unrepentance was about to experience God's presence as judgment. In other words, in his worldly plan to avert chaos by appealing to Assyria for help, Ahaz had cast his lot with a far more ominous chaos!

In Isaiah 8:11–15 we find the central theme of Yahwism expressed yet another time in the form of a warning to the prophet (no doubt intended for his disciples as well; cf. v. 16) not to follow the frantic path of those who based their plans on fear of Syria and Israel. For they were looking at reality from a false perspective that interpreted earthly potentates as free agents who were to be dreaded. In verse 13, the attention of the people is called back to the only trustworthy vantage point, sole acknowledgement of Yahweh's sovereignty: "But the Lord of Hosts, him you shall regard as holy; let him be your fear, and let him be your dread." Immanuel was to be a sign that Yahweh was present, but present not as a tool at the disposal of the people, but as the one who directed all reality according to a holy plan. That holy presence was accordingly "a sanctuary" for the faithful, but "a stone of offense, and a rock of stumbling to both houses of Israel, and a trap and a snare to the inhabitants of Jerusalem," because in their pride they had pursued their own course and had repudiated God.

The implications of the sign of Immanuel for impending judgment is thus clear. But what of "the sanctuary"? What of the promise? That aspect of the message of Immanuel was first to involve a period of waiting, for it was not possible for a message of repentance and trust to be heard by a people instructing its prophets to "consult the mediums and the wizards who chirp and mutter," but refusing to "consult their God." In a purely pagan manner, "they consult the dead on behalf of the living" (8:19). This covenant of death would have to be broken before the covenant of life could be renewed. And hence the prophet was instructed to wait for Yahweh's "strange deed" to run its course by having his teaching sealed among his disciples and leaving his children with their sign names as testimony to God's plan. By this withdrawal, the prophet symbolized the people's rejection of God in favor of its own schemes, which augured very darkly for the immediate future: "Surely for this word which they speak there is no dawn" (v. 21), a time of "distress and darkness, the gloom of anguish; and they will be thrust into thick darkness" (v. 22).

Remarkably, the prophet was not himself disspirited by this bleak outlook: "I will wait for the Lord, who is hiding his face from the house of Jacob, and I will hope in him" (v.1 7). Nothing could demonstrate more clearly that the prophet viewed the future solely from the perspective of faith in the one true Sovereign, the Lord of Hosts. Clearer than any of his contemporaries, he was aware of the political disaster assured by Israel's courtship with the Assyrians and later the Egyptians. Nevertheless, he looked beyond disaster wth hope. Indeed, the present darkness seemed to accentuate all the more the future brilliance. Yahweh's alien deed itself was an integral part of the plan of the righteous, compassionate God. With Hosea he believed that Israel's haughty pride and its fascination with false gods first had to be broken for her again to experience the grace of Immanuel.

Whereas Hosea, with his background in League traditions, viewed return to the zero point as a new wilderness experience, Isaiah drew on the Jerusalem theology with its promises concerning Zion and the Anointed of Yahweh who would reign over a righteous city filled with Yahweh's šālôm. But his synthesis of the early Yahwistic themes of sole worship of Yahweh, righteousness, and compassion with the themes of royal theology led to a profound transformatin of the Zion and Davidic promises. The present Zion was not the glorious habitation of Yahweh. The reigning Davidide was not the blessed and obedient anointed son of God. The promises of the royal theology were thoroughly eschatologized. They would be fulfilled after the great judgment when Yahweh's alien deed would be complete, and a people open to God's new deed of salvation would inhabit Zion to receive Yahweh's reign of righteousness. This transformation of the royal theology was given powerful expression in the Ariel prophecy of 29:1–8, where the city of David is depicted first as being reduced to the dust by Yahweh, from which low estate it would be raised miraculously and delivered from the assaulting hordes. Trust in Yahweh was according to Isaiah not a blind trust in the invincibility of a holy city. It was a firm trust in the future of a righteous, compassionate God who would surely bring a plan to fulfillment. It was a severe trust, that spoke not in terms of national pride and glory, but of God's righteous judgment on all that was proud (2:12–22), and of God's compassionate deliverance of the remnant that would "lean upon the Lord, the Holy One of Israel, in truth" (10:20–23; cf. 7:3).

From the perspective of his absolute trust in the faithfulness of the righteous, compassionate God to his promises, Isaiah could speak as clearly of the salvation beyond the judgment as he did of the judgment itself. Thus after the "distress and darkness," "the gloom of anguish" and the "thick darkness" of 8:22 we read of a remarkable transformation: "But there will be no gloom for her that was in anguish . . . the people who walked in darkness have seen a great light" (9:1–2). Addressed by this passage was not just Judah, but all Israel, as indicated by the fact that verse 1 describes the sections of the Northern Kingdom that had been assimilated into the Assyrian provincial system of Tiglath-pileser in 734 and 732. Once judgment had broken the deceptive sense of self-confidence of the land, and had ended the succession of kings whose personal pride and refusal to submit to Yahweh made them unsuitable as leaders of God's people, a remnant would survive that would look to Yahweh with hope and trust. And the faithful survivors would not be disappointed, for Yahweh would act as in the days of Israel's birth as a people. Darkness would be turned to light, and in response to Yahweh's deliverance the grateful people would respond with great rejoicing. The life of fear and oppression under foreign rulers would be broken as emphatically as "on the day of Midian" (cf. Judg. 6–7), that is, not by the strength and plans of humans, but by Yahweh's own act, which would end war and the implements of war forever.

As in the exodus, Yahweh would not leave those delivered from slavery to wander aimlessly, so as to fall back into new forms of bondage, but would give them structures and laws supportive of a life of blessing. Indeed, as Yahweh's victory over the oppressor was to be definitive, so too Yahweh's sustaining activity would outstrip that of former times. In contrast to the long line of kings who betrayed Yahweh and the people through their own selfish inclinations, Yahweh would provide the people with a leader who would end this history of disappointment, a leader given utterly to God's kingdom of justice and righteousness. In his coronation, names would be given to him which, in keeping with West Semitic custom,[2] would describe the nature of the God with whom he was covenanted as faithful son and servant: "Wonderful Counselor, mighty God, Everlasting Father, Prince of Peace" (9:6b). Through this faithful anointed one, God's counsel, power and šālôm would be mediated to the people. It is noteworthy that in naming this new occupant of the Davidic throne Isaiah used not the title "king" (mêlek), but "prince" (śar in v. 5[EV v. 6]; similarly, Micah in 5:2 uses "ruler," môšēl). Their anointed one was not simply to be identified with the former line of Davidic kings. His relation to God was to be categorically new, his reign qualitatively distinct form any earlier reigns: "Of the increase of his government and of peace there will be no end, upon the throne of David, and over his kingdom, to establish it, and to uphold it with justice and righteousness from this time forth and for evermore" (v.7). In this formulation we see how Isaiah used the imagery of the royal theology

2. Cf. 2 Samuel 12:25; Jeremiah 23:5–6 and M. Coogan, *West Semitic Personal Names in the Muraṣû Documents*, HSM 1 (Missoula, Mont.; Scholars, 1976), p. 70.

of Jerusalem, but at the same time radically transformed it into an eschatological vision of Yahweh's reign of eternal rightousness administered by a faithful ruler. The importance of God's earlier history with the nation was thus acknowledged, but with limitations: That former history had been a *praeparatio* for God's definitive reign. The compassionate deliverance of Hebrew slaves from Egypt, the Sinai covenant and its righteous laws, the promises to Zion and the House of David, were all signs of God's faithfulness to his plan of salvation. But they would all be gathered up into a definitive demonstration that the God who long ago began a work with Israel would bring it to completion, for through the mediation of this righteous ruler God would reign over the people forever: "The zeal of the Lord of hosts will do this" (9:7b). This blessed era would begin within the nation where all citizens acknowledged the sovereignty of God, and looked to God alone as their source of strength and well-being. Where the one true God was worshipped, righteousness and justice would be established, and *šālôm* would reign forever.

Isaiah was a remarkably creative spokesperson of the Yahwistic faith, and his prophecy stimulated growth in the biblical notion of the community of faith for centuries to come. His ability to draw together materials as divergent as the exodus-conquest and the Zion-Davidic traditions in a manner true to the spirit of early Yahwism, and at the same time both relevant to contemporary realities and pregnant with meaning for the future, is a parade example of the dialectic between continuity and change that characterizes the history of the biblical notion of community. One is first of all struck by Isaiah's profound sense of the holy majesty of the one true God, a sense enriched by the symbolism of the Jerusalem temple. Life in the community of believers was sustained solely within a relationship of undivided worship of the Lord of Hosts. This relationship expressed itself in absolute trust, excluding reliance on human schemes and worldly lords. Trust in Yahweh was thus dramatically opposed to every form of human pride.

Secondly it is clear that Isaiah maintained an unbroken connection with earlier Yahwism in his insisting that proper worship express itself in righteousness and compassion. Although deeply influenced by the Jerusalem theology, he refused to accommodate the demanding standards of the *tôrâ* to the claims of kings and nobles. Instead he attacked all who violated the rights of the weak, who perverted justice, and who amassed wealth and power at the expense of the poor. Such acts represented not only misconduct, but apostasy. For Isaiah, a right relationship with God was expressed in the first instance in the even-handed administration of justice. We have seen that Isaiah's refusal to compromise his vision of the righteous, faithful city led him to a bleak outlook on the immediate future. But his perspective, derived from the faithful promises of Yahweh, enabled him to peer beyond judgment to the inbreaking of a new era of righteousness. In a land freed forever from violence by the Deliverer God, and under a prince living in closest communion with the divine King, a people of God would dwell in peace, justice, and righteousness that would be unending.

This vision, classically formulated in Isaiah 9, would capture the imagination of the faithful of subsequent generations who, though continuing to experience the world less as the "great light" of the blessed era than as "the contempt of the land of Zebulon," nevertheless refused to abandon their longing for the *faithful* city. In the next chapter, we shall see that it was a vision capable of being misused in two directions, either as a model to be scaled down and identified with an existing form of community, or as an invitation to escape existing realities in anticipation of exaltation to a *heavenly* city. Within the careful balance maintained by Isaiah, however, both the reductionary accommodation of pragmatism and the visionary escapism of apocalypticism were eschewed. With what we might call a visionary realism, the righteous, faithful city was embraced as the norm from which all contemporary realities were evaluated and criticized, including the conduct of national leaders, the relation of the wealthy to the poor, the quality of religious institutions, and even the relations between the nations.

Although actively engaged in holding vision and reality together, Isaiah at no point interpreted human reform programs as that which could inaugurate the era of šālôm, but merely as the community of faith's ongoing response to the God at work bringing to fulfillment a plan of salvation. Righteousness and compassion thus were held together and related to their intended vocation by being focused on the one "who planned it long ago" (22:11). As for the kingdom of righteousness and šālôm, "the zeal of the Lord of hosts will do this" (9:7). For Isaiah, absolute trust in what God was doing alone supplied the perspective from which humans could recognize the nature of their daily task: "cease to do evil, learn to do good; seek justice, correct oppression; defend the fatherless, plead for the widow" (1:16b–17). Isaiah's message was not an uncomplicated one, but in its fine nuances and its rich assortment of symbols and images there nevertheless came to expression a hitherto unequaled depiction of the faithful community characterized by worship, righteousness, and compassion.

C. MICAH

Micah spoke to the same situation as that addressed by his contemporary Isaiah. He also shared with Isaiah a starting point in the covenant theology of early Yahwism. In one respect he proceeded even further than Isaiah in his judgment on the land: There remains in his prophecy no trace of the divine promise to Zion upon which to base a hope for reform. As Samaria "is the transgression of Jacob," Jerusalem 'is the sin of the house of Judah" (1:5b). And as Samaria would be made by Yahweh "a heap in the open country" (1:6), "Zion shall be plowed as a field, Jerusalem shall become a heap of ruins, and the mountain of the house a wooded height" (3:12). A sharper attack on the tradition of Yahweh's election of Zion can scarcely be imagined. Micah's list of indictments was devastating and complete, focusing especially on the land's leadership: its rulers "abhor justice and pervert all equity . . . its heads give judgment for a bribe, its priests teach for hire, its prophets divine for money; yet they lean upon the Lord and say, 'Is not the Lord in the midst of us? No evil will come upon us' " (3:9–11). Those whose responsibility it was to oversee the administration of justice "hate the good and love the evil" and devour the people (3:1–3). Those whose commission it was to warn the people of divine judgment on their sin instead "lead my people astray," and "cry 'Peace' when they have something to eat, but declare war against him who puts nothing into their mouths" (3:5). With such decadent leadership, the powerful rich had "open season" on the people: "They covet fields, and seize them; and houses, and take them away; they oppress a man and his house, a man and his inheritance" (2:2).

The fundamental structures of the Yahwistic notion of community were thus under attack, for with the loss of house (bēt) and inheritance (naḥălâ) by the common people to wealthy landowners, the egalitarian ideal protected by the tôrâ was forced to yield to the feudalism of Israel's neighbors. Micah very perceptively traced the source of such practices to a system diametrically opposed to the Yahwistic covenant: "for you have kept the statutes of Omri, and all the works of the house of Ahab; and you have walked in their counsels" (6:16a). Here Micah made explicit reference to the Canaanite system introduced earlier by the Omride dynasty. It was identified as the source of the profanation of the naḥălâ and the use of "wicked scales" and "deceitful weights" (6:11). Through such devices, the people were removed from the protection of the tôrâ. The community no longer was ordered on the basis of the righteous standard. The result was social chaos:

> Put no trust in a neighbor,
>   have no confidence in a friend;
> guard the doors of your mouth
>   from her who lies in your bosom;
> for the son treats the father with contempt,
>   the daughter rises up against her mother,
> the daughter-in-law against her mother-in-law;
>   a man's enemies are the men of his own house.   (Mic. 7:5–6)

With such total perversion of all that was righteous and good, the land fell under the curses of the covenant (6:13–16). But Micah, very similarly to Hosea and Isaiah, interpreted even the impending doom as part of God's plan to save this people. For unlike most of his contemporaries, he focused on God alone, and was confident that God would not remain silent: "But as for me, I will look to the Lord, I will wait for the God of my salvation; my God will hear me" (7:7).

In looking to the Lord, rather than to the false leaders of the land, what did Micah see? The answer to this question is complicated by uncertainty concerning the extent of later additions to the Book of Micah. It seems clear, however, that Micah looked in the first instance to the early Yahwistic traditions of exodus and conquest for a perspective from which to view Yahweh's future activity (6:3–5). It was in spurning the gracious deliverer Yahweh, and in disregarding God's holy laws, that Israel incurred divine wrath and judgment. Hope seemed tied, therefore, to remembering again what Yahweh had done, and what Yahweh had commanded (6:5).

When later disciples of Micah looked on the terrible judgment that actually fell on the land at the hands of the Babylonians, they looked beyond judgment to Yahweh's reassembling a people from the lame, the outcast, and the afflicted. Over this remnant Yahweh would reign in Mount Zion forever (4:6–7). Another prophecy, which calls to mind Isaiah 9:1–7, envisions a ruler from Bethlehem (obviously a second David) who would "feed his flock in the strength of the Lord," thereby inaugurating an era of peace (5:1–4). The beautiful concluding verses of the book identify the source of Israel's future hope in the incomparable love of God and in God's faithfulness to ancient promises:

> Who is a God like thee, pardoning iniquity
>   and passing over transgression
>   for the remnant of his inheritance?
> He does not retain his anger for ever
>   because he delights in steadfast love.
> He will again have compassion upon us,
>   he will tread out iniquities under foot.
> Thou wilt cast all our sins
>   into the depths of the sea.
> Thou wilt show faithfulness to Jacob
>   and steadfast love to Abraham,
> as thou has sworn to our fathers
>   from the days of old.   (Mic. 7:18–20)

In the light of the earlier words of their prophetic leader, followers of Micah, like followers of Isaiah (cf. Isa. 2:1–4; 4:3; 11:11, 16; 10:20; 28:5), were able at a later day to offer comfort to those who had experienced Yahweh's judgment. And as the remnant of God's people reflected on what was required of them if they were to experience Immanuel in the future as the bringer of šālôm rather than further judgment, they were guided by one of the most beautiful summaries of prophetic Yahwism in the Bible, woven out of the classical triad of true worship, righteousness, and compassion.

With what should I come before the Lord,
   and bow myself before God on high? . . .
He has showed you, O [hu]man, what is good;
   and what does the Lord require of you
but to do justice, and to love kindness,
   and to walk humbly with your God?   (Mic. 6:6a and 8)

D. THE REFORM EFFORTS OF FAITHFUL KINGS

Earlier we recognized in Isaiah an imposing example of one conforming his entire life to the urgent sense of having been called to return the king and the people to the only source of deliverance from the calamity that seemed to loom on every horizon. Isaiah 36–39 and 2 Kings 18–20 show the influential role played by Isaiah in the life of King Hezekiah. And 2 Kings 18:4 describes Hezekiah's cleansing of the cult from Canaanite objects and practices. That narrative ties this activity explicitly to Hezekiah's acknowlegement of the sole sovereignty of Yahweh, thereby establishing a link with the message of the prophet Isaiah, and more generally, with the primal Yahwistic commandment to worship no God but Yahweh: "He trusted in the Lord the God of Israel . . . he held fast to the Lord; he did not depart from following him, but kept the commandments which the Lord commanded Moses" (2 Kings 18:5–6). Hezekiah was a king who followed his prophetic advisor in integrating the covenant theology of early Yahwism into the central Jerusalem cult.

In a report whose overall credibility has been corroborated by recent research,[3] the Chronicler (in 2 Chron. 29–31) gives a rather complete picture of Hezekiah's thoroughgoing reform of the cult, interpreting it as a renewal of the covenant reminiscent of those carried out by Asa (cf. 2 Chron. 15:12–15) and Joash (2 Kings 11:17–20). Involved was confession of past neglect of true worship that had invoked God's wrath, the cleansing of the temple, and then celebration of the Passover, to which invitations were sent also to the Israelites who had survived the Assyrian conquest of the Northern Kingdom. Although in the Deuteronomist's account in 2 Kings little was reported of Hezekiah's reform (apparently because the focus of interest is so concentrated on Josiah), the Chronicler was likely relying on old, authentic tradition in recalling a reform of the temple cult that reintroduced early Yahwistic beliefs and practices in a manner unprecedented since the time of David.

On the basis of these accounts, we see that kings were potential supporters of the Yahwistic notion of community centered on worship,

---

3. J. Rosenbaum, "Hezekiah's Reform and the Deuteronomistic Tradition," *HTR* 72 (1979), 214–43.

righteousness, and compassion—that is, the notion of community based on renewal of the covenant with Yahweh and obedience to the Mosaic *tôrâ*. But within a land whose kings were generally so inclined to put their own will above Yahweh's, and to exploit the Davidic covenant to the neglect of the earlier covenant between Yahweh and the whole people, it was primarily the prophets and faithful Yahwists from the priesthood (e.g., Jehoida) and from the people in general (e.g., the "people of the land" in 2 Kings 11:14) who kept alive the early Yahwistic notion of community as the only true way for Israel to live in response to a righteous, compassionate God. It is thus apparent that in the monarchical period, the Yahwistic community of faith cannot be identified with any cultic or political institution. It was rather a reality fostered by a vision of the righteous, compassionate, God-centered community kept alive in the witness of the prophets and their followers, a vision deepened and refined in their ongoing effort to draw king and nation into the orbit of God's healing power. As the reforms of Asa, Jehoshaphat, Joash, and Hezekiah show, it was not a vision confined to an otherworldly realm. It was always present as a God-given invitation to renew the covenant, to live as the people of God, to choose life over death.

E. THE PROPHET JEREMIAH AND JOSIAH'S CULTIC REFORM

Jeremiah stands as a monumental example of the tenacity of the early Yahwistic tradition based on the Mosaic covenant (e.g., 11:1–14) and incorporating the themes of exodus, wilderness, and conquest (e.g., 2:4–7 and 32:16–23). This is not surprising when one recalls that Jeremiah originated from a priestly family of Anathoth, a village in Benjamin; that is, in the territory of one of the tribes of the Rachel group within which the archaic Yahwistic traditions originated and flourished. In contrast to Isaiah, there is in Jeremiah's message no trace of the Zion tradition, and Davidic tradition is applied only in a very carefully defined way in his eschatological vision. This spiritual lineage is also corroborated by the numerous points of contact between Jeremiah and Hosea, both in theme and style (e.g., 2:2–3; 3:20).

Jeremiah's roots in the covenant theology of early Yahwism also are manifested by what he says, and by what he refrains from saying, in relation to the Josianic reform. Before turning to this, we must consider Jeremiah's message in the period before the reform of Josiah.

From 627 to 622, Jeremiah proclaimed a message of judgment reminiscent, both in metaphor and in substance, of the message of Hosea. Israel, in a way defying understanding, had betrayed God (2:9–13), and had gone in feverish pursuit of the abominations of the Baal cult (2:23–25 and 3:1–5). The consequence of this apostasy was the one documented repeatedly by the prophets of Yahweh, namely a blatant disregard for the *tôrâ*: No one "does justice," "they swear falsely," "they refused to take correction," "refused to repent," "have sworn by those who are no gods," "committed adultery," "they judge not with justice the cause of the fatherless, to make it prosper, and they do not defend the rights of the needy" (5:1–3, 7, 28). This interlocked process of betrayal of the one true God and the substitution of God's life-giving *tôrâ* with a self-destructive form of life Jeremiah described in a poignant metaphor: "For my people have committed two evils: they have forsaken me, the fountain of the living waters, and hewed out cisterns for themselves, broken cisterns, that can hold no water" (2:13). The result was that the land had fallen under the curses of the broken covenant. Indeed, the collapsing moral order had brought the entire created order to the brink of chaos (4:23–6; cf. Hosea 4:1–3). To this deplorable condition of inner decay, Jeremiah related the assault of the invaders from the north, interpreting them as the instrument of Yahweh's righteous wrath (1:14; 4:5–8 and 6:1–26). Yet, even at this late hour, Jeremiah discerned a glimmer of hope. For Yahweh did not will the destruction of this people, but their repentance. This conviction prompted Jeremiah to admonish (3:21–23), to plead (3:12–14), to struggle passionately with the people to bring them back to their senses:

> A voice on the bare heights is heard,
> the weeping and pleading of Israel's sons,
> because they have perverted their way,
> they have forgotten the Lord their God.
> "Return, O faithless sons,
> I will heal your faithfulness."
> "Behold, we come to thee;
> for thou art the Lord our God.
> Truly the hills are a delusion,
> the orgies on the mountains.
> Truly in the Lord our God
> is the salvation of Israel.   (Jer. 3:21–23)

After several years of proclaiming this message of judgment (interspersed with admonitions to the people to return to Yahweh), Jeremiah witnessed what was apparently an extensive reform carried out by King Josiah. Attempts to reconstruct the history of that reform must proceed with caution, to be sure, given the fact that our major source of information is the Deuteronomistic History, which—it has been convincingly argued—is itself a partisan work of the Josianic reform movement.[4] The existence of an account of the same period in the Chronicler's History, which is in important respects independent of the Deuteronomist's History, is of course welcomed evidence. Indeed, the

---

4. Cross, *CMHE*, 274–289.

Chronicler's version, according to which Josiah's reform was conducted in several stages culminating in renewal of the covenant, is probably more accurate than the account in 2 Kings, which portrays the entire reform as concentrated in one year. At any rate, it seems that the reform reached its apex in the year 622 as the result of the discovery of "the book of the law in the house of the Lord," a discovery made during repair of the temple. The reading of this "book of the law," generally assumed to be the original edition of the Book of Deuteronomy, is described as having had a profound effect on King Josiah. He recognized in it a sharp indictment on the sin of the land (2 Kings 22:11–13), a response corroborated by consultation with Huldah the prophet (22:14–20).

In its main lines the description of what follows makes a strong claim to historical fact, for it draws together several details into a very plausible pattern. We see a king acknowledging his responsibility to uphold the tôrâ of the land. Indeed, he seems guided by the model of kingship described in the "law of the king" in Deuteronomy 17:14–20, according to which the king is to read in the tôrâ "all the days of his life, that he may learn to fear the Lord his God, by keeping all the words of this law and these statutes, and doing them; that his heart may not be lifted up above his brethren, and that he may not turn aside from the commandment, either to the right hand or to the left; so that he may continue long in his kingdom, he and his children, in Israel" (Deut. 17:19–20). In what was probably the deliberate attempt to obey the long-neglected law regarding the periodic reading of "this law before all Israel in their hearing" (Deuteronomy 31:9–13), Josiah, before "all the men of Judah and all the inhabitants of Jerusalem, and the priests and the prophets, all the people, both small and great . . . read in their hearing all the words of the book of the covenant which had been found in the house of the Lord" (2 Kings 23:2).

Josiah is thus portrayed as one of the kings of Judah who remained committed to the early Yahwistic ideals of covenant and faithfulness to the tôrâ. True to the pattern seen in the reforms of Asa, Joash, and Hezekiah, a pattern stemming ultimately from the early, premonarchical Yahwistic cult of Gilgal, Shechem, and Shiloh, "the king stood by the pillar and made a covenant before the Lord, to walk after the Lord and to keep his commandments and testimonies and his statutes, with all his heart and all his soul, to perform the words of this covenant that were written in this book; and all the people joined in the covenant" (2 Kings 23:3). This, again true to the pattern observed in the other reforms, was followed by the cleansing of the temple and the land of all objects, practices, and personnel that distracted from the sole worship of Yahweh. Indeed, as described in 2 Kings 23:4–20, this cleansing of the land was more extensive than any previous one. Finally, the entire process culminated in the celebration of Passover.

Even after the likely blending of programmatic with historical elements in the Deuteronomistic report of Josiah's reform is taken into account, one can still recognize the significance of this reform. Josiah, like Hezekiah before him, sought to shape kingship in a way faithful to early Yahwistic tradition. The celebration of Passover was a sign of this commitment. Josiah and Hezekiah (cf. 2 Chron. 30) apparently stood alone among Judah's kings in seeking to retrieve Passover from the shadow cast over it by the popular fall New Year's festival. Passover, as the central re-enactment of the foundational event of the early Yahwistic community, was reinstated to a place of honor and returned to the center of Israel's cultic calendar. Apparently in Josiah the Deuteronomists found a willing pupil, one who added the authority of the throne to their effort to restore respect for the archaic traditions and practices of premonarchical Israel.

We thus find in the reform of Josiah as described in 2 Kings the culmination of the synthesis between Jerusalem temple tradition and the traditions of early Yahwism that had been advanced by the Book of Deuteronomy and by the prophet Isaiah. Here the early Yahwistic covenant theology with its basis in the Mosaic *tôrâ*, a theology that had been preserved and handed down by northern prophetic circles and had been brought to Judah and adapted to the central cult in Jerusalem by the Levitical-prophetic Deuteronomists, was acknowledged by a Davidic king as the only authentic basis for the nation. King joined with subjects in humbling himself before the Lord and accepting the commandments of Moses as the basis of covenant renewal.

At the same time it remains clear that the royal theology of Jerusalem was not abandoned, for the role of covenant mediator was played by the Davidic king. From the perspective of the supporters of Josiah (which is also, of course, the perspective of the Deuteronomistic source), a high point had been reached in God's history with this people, as indicated by the lavish praise of the Deuteronomists:

No such passover had been kept since the days of the judges who judged Israel, or during all the days of the kings of Israel or of the kings of Judah. Before him there was no king like him, who turned to the Lord with all his heart and with all his soul and with all his might, according to all the laws of Moses; nor did any like him arise after him. (2 Kings 23:22, 25)

The partisan nature of the Deuteronomistic History is detected when one contrasts this high praise with the similar theme related to Hezekiah in 2 Kings 18:5. It is not unlikely, in fact, that at one stage the Deuteronomistic History culminated with the reign of Hezekiah, with the later Josianic edition patterning itself after that earlier version. In the case of both kings, however, the praise was likely not without historical basis. Josiah, like Hezekiah, sought to reverse the course of a long history of sin (2 Kings 23:13), which, according to Deuteronomistic thought, was tied to neglect of the early Yahwistic covenant in the temple cult and within the royal family. There was little room in the policy of the Judean kings (with the four exceptions noted previously) for many of the stipulations of the Mosaic *tôrâ*. The unconditional promise of the Davidic covenant suited their purposes much better. At the same time it should not be forgotten that Josiah, like Hezekiah before him, was in an important sense restoring the faltering balance first struck by David, when he wedded the old customs of early Yahwism with the innovations of the new monarchy. It is apparent why Josiah's supporters saw fit to herald him as a *David redivivus*.

What, in the meantime, was Jeremiah's response to this reform movement, that seemed to draw together such diverse traditions and offices, this reform precipitated by a priest's discovery of a book of the law, supported by a prophetess's confirming word, guided no doubt by protagonists of the Deuteronomistic "school,' and carried through by the zeal of a god-fearing king? Since it embraced the Mosaic covenant, which was also central to Jeremiah's message, one might expect to read of the prophet's support of the king. On the other hand, the tying of early Yahwistic tradition to kingship and the Jerusalem temple cult, a process already begun in the original Deuteronomic Law and carried a significant step further by the first edition of the Deuteronomistic History,[5] was less compatible with the theological tradition from which Jeremiah stemmed. It is against the background of this ambiguity that one must seek to understand the fact that no Jeremianic word appears to have been preserved from the period of Josiah's reform. It seems he kept his silence, torn perhaps between hope that his call to repentance had been heeded and that Josiah actually would lead the people back to acknowledgement of Yahweh's sole sovereignty, and a nagging fear that the tie to the throne and to the Jerusalem temple would direct the hearts of the people, as it had repeatedly in the past, to false gods and to a sense of trust in king and cult.

Subsequent events rapidly dashed Jeremiah's hopes, even as they confirmed his fears. The god-fearing reform king, whom the Deuteronomists expected to lead the people into the kind of blessed era of righteousness and peace described in the royal psalms and in Isaiah 9 and 11, came to an ignominious end that baffled his devout followers. The report of Josiah's death was entered into the Deuteronomistic History—just four verses after the lavish praise quoted above—with a terseness as cold as the bronze of Pharaoh Neco's deadly sword: "Pharaoh Neco King of Egypt went up to the king of Assyria to the river Euphrates. King Josiah went to meet him; and Pharaoh Neco slew him at Megiddo, when he saw him" (2 Kings 23:29). In the succeeding reigns of Josiah's two sons and grandson, the land was thrust right back

---

5. Cf. Cross, *CMHE*, pp. 278–285.

into the ungodliness Josiah had sought to remove, and its perfidious and unrighteous leaders were ill suited to cope with the threatening international deelopments that quickly engulfed the small country, hastening it to its bitter end.

When Jeremiah broke his silence, and resumed his prophetic discourse, he spoke with a deeper pessimism and harshness than before. After Jehoahaz's brief reign of three months, Jehoiakim occupied the throne, and with every aspect of his reign made a mockery of God and God's righteousness and compassion. In a passage from the biographical narrative of Jeremiah's secretary Baruch, a passage that likely derives from an authentic Jeremianic oracle addressed to Jehoiakim, we find Jeremiah's version of "the law of the king," and it is based solidly on the central qualities of early Yahwism:

Thus says the Lord: Do justice and righteousness, and deliver from the hand of the oppressor him who has been robbed. And do no wrong or violence to the alien, the fatherless, and the widow, nor shed innocent blood in this place. For if you will indeed obey this word, then there shall enter the gates of this house kings who sit on the throne of David, riding in chariots and on horses, and their servants, and their people. But if you will not heed these words, I swear by myself, says the Lord, that this house shall become a desolation. (Jer. 22:3–5)

The theme of this passage is the familiar one from classic Yahwism: the security of the nation derived not from the might and authority of the kings, but from observance of the divine order given by Yahweh, an order based on righteousness and compassion. It was by obedience to this order that the Davidic kings were to be established, and not by virtue of an unconditional promise. We recognize an unbroken line of continuity running from the Book of the Covenant, through Samuel's concept of limited kingship, into the defense of the early Yahwistic laws based on righteousness and compassion in the prophets, on to the reformulation of Mosaic covenant and *tôrâ* in Deuteronomy, and finally coming to expression once again in the prophet from Anathoth. Measured against this classic standard of Yahwism, how did Johoiakim appear to Jeremiah? We find his verdict in Jeremiah 22:13–17. Jehoiakim represented for him the direct antithesis of the godly king: "Woe to him who builds his house by unrighteousness, and his upper rooms by injustice; who makes his neighbors serve him for nothing, and does not give him his wages" (v. 13). Described was a king who disdained the twin qualities of Yahwistic community, righteousness and compassion. The source of this disdain was clear to Jeremiah: Jehoiakim did not fear Yahweh, but instead placed himself at the pinnacle of his kingdom, declaring, "I will build myself a great house," to which Jeremiah caustically replied, "Do you think you are a king because you compete in cedar?" (v. 14a and 15a). The prophet went on to cite Josiah as an example of the godly king: "Did not your father eat and drink and do justice and righteousness? Then it was well with him. He judged the cause of the poor and needy; then it was well. Is not this to know me? says the Lord? (vv. 15b–16). Against this example of the proper wedding between true worship and a life of compassionate righteousness, Jeremiah resumed his portrait of Jehoiakim: "but you have eyes and heart only for dishonest gain, for shedding innocent blood, and for practicing oppression and violence" (v. 17). On such a perverted foundation a kingdom could not stand, Jeremiah declared, and accordingly be handed down Yahweh's devastating sentence on the king (vv. 18–19).

For Jeremiah, the symbol of the land's perverted religious understanding was the temple. Therefore, at the beginning of Jehoiakim's reign (cf. Jer. 26:1) he stood in the temple gate and delivered a harsh speech (Jer. 7:1–15). He first drew attention to the deadly temptation that lurked in the royal theology of Jerusalem since its inception, that of ensnaring the people in a false sense of security. In this respect Jeremiah was more perceptive than were either Isaiah or the southern compilers of the Deuteronomic Law. It is entirely possible that included among those against whom this polemic was directed were individuals claiming Isaianic support for their temple theology. Moreover, his distance from the Deuteronomistic theology became very clear in this period, for he associated himself with a familiar aniconic tradition reaching back to the original Nathan oracle in 2 Samuel 7:5–7, running through the northern prophets, and resurfacing here and in Isaiah 66. In his temple speech, Jeremiah stated with searing clarity that the identity of God's community was defined neither by the temple, nor by any other institution or structure, but strictly by the life of righteousness and compassion that was the sign of true worship. When divorced from this manner of life, temple worship was a mockery of God and a self-delusion, a trusting in "deceptive" words: "This is the temple of the Lord, the temple of the Lord, the temple of the Lord."

In stating the conditions of true security, Jeremiah drew on the classic formulations of early Yahwism: "For if you truly amend your ways and your doings, if you truly execute justice one with another, if you do not oppress the alien, the fatherless or the widow, or shed innocent blood in this place, and if you do not go after other gods to your own hurt, then I will let you dwell in this place, in the land that I gave of old to your fathers for ever" (7:5–7). But he witnessed instead a people persisting in their self-deception, breaking the Decalogue ("you steal, murder, commit adultery, swear falsely, burn incense to Baal, and go after other gods that you have not known" [v. 9]), and then taking flight into the "security" of the temple, claiming "we are delivered" (v. 10).

As proof against those claiming the invincibility of the temple, Jeremiah pointed to Shiloh, and delivered an oracle announcing that Yahweh likewise would destory the Jerusalem temple (vv. 12–15)! In other words, institutions and structures, even Solomonic temple and Davidic kingship, would offer no security from the wrath of God if the covenant had been broken. There was only one basis for security in Israel, namely, "the words of this covenant which I commanded your fathers when I brought them out of the land of Egypt, from the iron furnace, saying, Listen to my voice, and do all that I command you. So shall you be my people, and I will be your God, that I may perform the oath which I swore to your fathers, to give them a land flowing with milk and honey, as at this day" (11:3–5). Since, however, both kingdoms "have broken my covenant which I made with their fathers" (11:10b), no temple or dynasty could avert the curses of the broken covenant. The divine word Jeremiah delivered was therefore extremely harsh: "Behold, I am bringing evil upon them which they cannot escape; though they cry to me I will not listen to them" (11:11). The prophet was even forbidden to intercede for the people (7:16; 11:14).

For a prophet who felt solidarity with his kinsfolk, this message tore deeply into his own heart (e.g., 23:9–11). The covenant had been broken. Judgment must follow. The Babylonian invaders were not a sign of Yahweh's weakness. They stood under the command of the sovereign of the whole earth (27:5–6). Israel had placed human glory where God's glory alone belonged, with the resulting disintegration of righteousness and compassion in the land. In the midst of this collapse, Jeremiah reaffirmed the dynamic triad at the heart of the Yahwistic community:

Thus says the Lord: "Let not the wise man glory in his wisdom, let not the mighty man glory in his might, let not the rich man glory in his riches; but let him who glories glory in this, that he understands and knows me, that I am the Lord who practice kindness, justice and righteousness in the earth; for in these things I delight, says the Lord." (Jer. 9:23–24)

In the midst of the social and political chaos, with the vain, the rich and the mighty offering their plans for a cure, Jeremiah pointed to the center of life, which alone was capable of healing and security. Without knowledge of this center, all human efforts were futile, and all human self-glorification an absurdity. For the qualities that constituted life and community were not products of human ingenuity or effort. They derived solely from "I am the Lord who practice steadfast love, justice, and righteousness in the earth." Life and community were to be found in knowing and being drawn to this center, becoming agents of his love, justice and righteousness.

The passage just quoted (9:23–24), spoken during the godless reign of Jehoiakim, suggests that in the mind of Jeremiah, the possibility of covenant renewal had not ceased. For Yahweh was a God whose steadfastness led to repeated attempts to win back the people (cf. 24:4–7). But what could open their hearts to acknowledgement of the one object worthy or worship, Yahweh, the source of righteousness and compassion?

In reflecting on this puzzling theological question, Jeremiah delved more deeply into the basis of true faith than perhaps anyone before him. And in so doing, he located the source of the problem in the human heart: "The heart is deceitful above all things, and desperately corrupt; who can understand it?" (17:9). Of course Jeremiah did not come to this conclusion strictly on the basis of private research. Rather, there culminated in him a process of discernment that had run throughout the history of prophecy. Called to bring the people back to life in fellowship with Yahweh, the prophets had witnessed repeatedly the stubborn resistance of kings and people alike. They had grown dismayed at Israel's persistence in worshipping the gods of wealth and military power and in devoting themselves to merciless exploitation of the weak and the poor. They had been appalled to see their warnings against foreign entanglements go unheeded, as kings and princes courted the great empires within the vortex of rapidly changing international conditions. And these collective experiences culminated in Jeremiah's deepened consciousness of the gravity of the sinful condition of humanity. This represented a real crisis in Yahwism. If Jeremiah was right, there was no easy transition possible out of this bleak dilemma; no king's reform could change such a corrupt heart. A harshly realistic anthropology emerged that dismissed every plan of human reform as grossly inadequate. If prophetic thought was to raise itself above a hardened nihilism, it would have to discover a basis for hope that could prove capable of dealing with a nation resembling a camel in heat, racing madly after lovers with nothing seemingly capable of restraining its lust (2:23–24).

Jeremiah did venture to suggest a basis for hope. The divine word he delivered was daring and hopeful precisely because it was mediated by a prophet who had drunk fully from the bitter cup of divine wrath, suffering grievously for the sin of his people, and confessing a deep, personal sense of brokenness and despair. The wilderness described by Hosea, within which Yahweh could again address the people, had been transformed in Jeremiah's experience into a wilderness of the heart. Perhaps there God could address the people, within the brokenness of human pride and rebelliousness caused by calamity:

Behold, the days are coming, says the Lord, when I will make a new covenant with the house of Israel and the House of Judah, not like the covenant which I made with their fathers when I took them by the hand to bring them out of the land of Egypt, my covenant which they broke, though I was their husband, says the Lord. But this is the covenant which I will make with the house of Israel after those days, says the Lord: I will put my law within them, and I will write it upon their hearts; and I will be their God, and they shall be my people. And no longer shall each man teach his neighbor and teach his brother, saying, "Know the Lord," for they shall all know me, from the least of them to the greatest, says the Lord; for I will forgive their iniquity, and I will remember their sin no more. (Jer. 31:31–34).

It is important to specify exactly what was new in this formulation, for it must not be construed as a promise of a new *tôrâ*. Repeatedly we have observed that for Jeremiah the conditions for a renewal of the covenant between God and people were already stated in the classic formulations of the Book of the Covenant and the Decalogue. The novum was rather this: in the new covenant God would employ a new manner of conveying *tôrâ* to the people. No longer would it be presented from the outside, only to be rejected by stubborn hearts. Rather, the source of the problem would be addressed: The heart of humans would be changed; Yahweh would put his law "within them," would "write it upon their hearts." In this transformation of the heart from an instrument that was "deceitful" and "corrupt" and resistant to God into an agent of inner testimony to God's will, the sole impediment between God and humans would be removed, and the covenant would be renewed. Jeremiah's vision of inner transformation emphatically rejected a legalistic concept of obedience. Envisioned was a new divine act, based on forgiveness, that could create knowledge of God in the hearts of all the people. In other words, Jeremiah described the restoration of the center of life, namely, acknowledgement of the sole Sovereign of all, in which acknowledgement was to be found the only true source of the righteousness and compassion expressed in the *tôrâ*. This centering on life's source came to expression also in another passage (32:36–41), concerned with the restoration of the people to the land after the exile: "I will give them one heart and one way, that they may fear me for ever . . . I will put the fear of me in their hearts, that they may not turn from me" (vv. 39a and 40b). In this passage again, the source of hope lies solely in the gracious and faithful heart of Yahweh: "I will rejoice in doing them good, and I will plant them in this land in faithfulness, with all my heart and all my soul" (v. 41).[6]

With this all-important keystone in place, the whole beautiful structure of life planned by God for God's people could arise from the dust and flourish. The Northern and Southern kingdoms would be reunited (3:18), the scattered would be gathered (23:3), the fruitfulness of the land would be restored (33:10–13), and Yahweh would set shepherds over them who would care for them (23:4). All this would occur not because of the might of Israel's kings, but solely because of Yahweh's power and grace. Within this carefully constructed framework, Jeremiah was able to integrate three themes that would be of abiding importance in the centuries ahead, as devout Yahwists continued to forge a way of life that was both true to their confessional heritage and viable within the social and political realities of a changing world.

6. That Jeremiah 31:31–34 and 32:36–41 are both prophetic words of Jeremiah, each with its own emphasis, has been most recently supported by H. Weippert, *Schöpfer des Himmels und der Erde: Ein Beitrag zur Theologie des Jeremiabuches* (Stuttgart: Katholisches Bibelwerk, 1981), pp. 57 and 95–102.

First is the theme of continuity and change. Jeremiah drew deeply on the classic conception of Yahwistic community in his stress on acknowledgment of the sole sovereignty of Yahweh, on the high standards set by Yahweh's righteousness, and on the passionate care for other humans motivated by compassion. At the same time, he was able to recognize the impasse created by a tragic history of rebelliousness and sin, and hence to proclaim boldly God's new initiative as the only hope for a lost people.

Secondly, he was able to combine a harsh critique of the reigning Judaean kings with a clear sense of trust that Yahweh would ultimately fulfill the promise of a righteous Anointed One of the House of David who would lead the people back to obedience and righteousness: "Behold, the days are coming, says the Lord, when I will raise up for David a righteous Branch, and he shall reign as king and deal wisely, and shall execute justice and righteousness in the land" (23:5). The emphasis on his role in safeguarding the fundamental qualities of the Yahwistic covenant is striking. And to make this point even clearer, as well as to engrave into the office of the Anointed One its source of righteousness in the only true Lord, the righteous Branch of the house of David was accorded another name: "The Lord is our righteousness" (23:6b).[7]

Thirdly, Jeremiah gave expression to the inseparability of the faith of the individual and the health of the community as a whole. Negatively he traced the tragic decline of the nation to the deceitful and desperately corrupt human heart, and did not hesitate to single out sinful individuals like Hananiah and Jehoiakim in pointing to specific causes for the impending judgment. Positively he looked to the restoration of Israel as a time when a wise and righteous king would rule over a godly populace, each member of which would obey Yahweh from the heart. Ezekiel would develop further the theme of the significance of the individual within the faithful community (chapter 18), thereby contributing to a clarificaiton of the biblical notion of community as one in which the individual finds full personhood not through self-indulgent personalism, but by becoming an unstinting contributor to the vitality of the whole people.

F. COMMUNITY OF FAITH IN ISRAELITE WISDOM TRADITION

Jeremiah was not alone in exploring the relations between the individual and the community. This relationship was a major theme also within a stream of tradition that was tutored for this task by centuries of observation of and reflection on the conduct of human beings within their various life settings, that tradition being the rather amorphous

---

7. As in Isaiah 9:6, the faithful king of the future will bear names describing his divine Sovereign, thereby emphasizing both his subservience to God and his faithful representation of God's righteousness, compassion, and šālôm on earth.

one we designate "sapiental" or "wisdom." Within Israel and beyond the questions of the wise had remained essentially the same for centuries: What are the characteristics of the righteous person and the evil person? What constitutes a healthy community? What maintains the harmony of the realm of nature, including its many classes of living beings and the heavenly bodies? How is the presence of evil to be explained, or the suffering of the righteous and the prosperity of the wicked?

The actual settings within which reflection on these universal questions was conducted are elusive, since the aim of abstracting general truths from specific instances did not necessitate a description of the settings within which the sages were active.[8] Some of the proverbs treat the affairs of the household, and may have originated in the instructions of parents to their children (e.g., 4:1–27; 15:20; 17:21, 25; 19:13–14, 18, 26–27; 20:20; 22:6, 15; 22:13–14; 29:15, 17).

We know from Mesopotamian and Egyptian sources that the royal courts sponsored schools for the purpose of training scribes. Although direct evidence is lacking, it is likely that such schools also existed in Israel from the time of Solomon on, as a means of supplying the bureaucrats required by the elaborate structures of the monarchy. Perhaps the traditional attribution of wisdom sayings to Solomon reflects this phenomenon, as might also the mention of the "men of Hezekiah" in Proverbs 25:1. The king is often the focal point of sayings in the Book of Proverbs (e.g., 14:28, 35; 16:12–15; 19:12; 20:2, 8, 28; 21:1; 22:11, 29; 24:21–22; 25:1–15; 31:1–9;), and the conventional etiquette that pervades this book probably is influenced in part by the protocol of the royal court. This social conventionalism was reinforced also by the influence of the wisdom traditions of other cultures, a fact corroborated by the dependence of Proverbs 22:17 through 24:22 on the Egyptian "Instruction of Amenemopet."[9]

It is a tribute to the vitality of Yahwistic faith that what is in general terms a collection of wisdom sayings and instructions in the style of the conventions of the ancient world has nevertheless been permeated by the qualities identified at the heart of the Yahwistic notion of community. This orientation was stated explicitly in the introduction to the book by its final editors: The purpose of the work is that people might come to "know wisdom, . . . receive instruction in wise dealing, righteousness, justice, and equity," with the understanding that "the fear of the Lord is the beginning of knowledge" (Prov. 1:1–7). That the fear of Yahweh is the source of wisdom is a theme carried through the entire book (3:5–8; 14:27–28; 15:16–17, 33; 19:23; 23:17; 28:14; 29:25).

---

8. On the question of the setting of the sapiental writings, see R. E. Murphy, O. Carm., *Wisdom Literature: Job, Proverbs, Ruth, Canticles, Ecclesiastes, and Esther*, FOT XIII (Grand Rapids, Mich.: Eerdmans, 1981), pp. 6–9.

9. J. A. Wilson, *ANET*, 3d ed., pp. 421–424.

The instructions contained in chapters 1–9 in particular are character-ized by a Yahwistic orientation. Yahweh stands solidly on the side of the righteous, guarding their paths from those who would distract their at-tention from the ways of integrity and righteousness (2:6–22). Notable is the personification of Wisdom, who is both the source of instruction in righteousness and prosperity and the agent of Yahweh in the cre-ation of the heavens and the earth (chapter 8). This vast embrace of all reality within the realm of discourse of wisdom, and the resulting uni-fied view of reality under the sovereignty of Israel's God was one of the most noble achievements of Israel's sages, and would be a legacy wor-thily developed further by Jesus ben Sirach and the great rabbis.

In addition to this general Yahwistic focus, the specific qualities of true worship, righteousness, and compassion are also commended by the sages of the Book of Proverbs. To be sure, there is much which is quite conventional, like the retribution doctrine with its confident assurances that the righteous are blessed with prosperity, whereas the wicked are punished (10:3, 24, 32; 11:9, 21; 22:24). And in many cases, observation of human traits is recorded without further evaluation (18:23; 19:4, 6–7; 22:7). But amidst such conventions one discovers deep insights into some of the basic issues of life, where the centuries of accumulated wisdom is combined with the distinctive qualities of Yahwistic faith. Thus a por-trait of life takes shape in which the chief building blocks are righteous-ness, integrity, truth telling, dependability, prudence, caring, and love (10:9–12; 11:28; 13:6, 14), and in which the ultimate basis is Yahweh's order of righteousness (15:3, 25; 16:1–11; 19:21; 21:30–31).

Many of the specific themes that developed within the Yahwistic *tôrâ* to describe righteousness recur in the Book of Proverbs. The righteous are to use just weights and measures (11:1; 16:11; 20:10, 23). They are to show impartiality in court (24:23–26). They are to speak the truth, and eschew false witness (12:17–22; 24:28; 25:18). They are to be good neighbors (11:12–13; 14:21). When compared with similar themes in the Book of the Covenant, Deuteronomy, or the Priestly Writing, it is clear that the grounding of motivation in historical memory is absent here. This can be attributed primarily to the aphoristic style of Prov-erbs. Occasionally, however, the parenesis is tied directly to the believ-er's relationship with Yahweh, lending a sense of freshness and power reminiscent of the Book of the Covenant: "[The one] who oppresses [one who is poor] insults his Maker, but [the one] who is kind to the needy honors him" (14:31; cf. 17:5; 15; 19:17). Even the deference to the king that permeates Proverbs is not unaffected by the Yahwistic no-tion of righteousness:

> Open your mouth for the dumb,
>   for the rights of all who are left desolate.
> Open your mouth, judge righteously,
>   maintain the rights of the poor and needy.   (Prov. 31:9)

The second cardinal quality of the Yahwistic notion of community, namely compassion, also permeates the Book of Proverbs. As is proper, it is so inextricably tied to the concept of righteousness as to lend a particular quality to the various descriptions of the righteous person (10:10–12). But the most distinctive insight into compassion is that it is to be measured especially by one's attitude toward the poor (14:21; 19:17; 22:9; 28:27; 29:7). And as in the case of righteousness, the quality of righteous compassion toward the poor and the oppressed is rooted on the most profound level in divine compassion:

> Do not rob the poor, because [they] are poor,
> or crush the afflicted at the gate;
> for the Lord will plead their cause
> and despoil the life of those who despoil them.   (Prov. 22:22–32)

Once again, the divine passion stirred up by the plight of the vulnerable in the society has not been forgotten (cf. Prov. 21:13 with Exod. 22:22–24). And indeed, the expansive quality of divine compassion, that is, its reaching out to draw toward the šālôm of the community those excluded for whatever reasons, is expressed in the following: "If your enemy is hungry, give him bread to eat; and if he is thirsty, give him water to drink" (25:21; cf. 12:10, where even one's beast is to be treated with consideration!).

Although the gnomic style of the proverbs tends to focus on the qualities of righteousness and compassion in the life of the individual, it is clear both implicitly and explicitly that these qualities are deemed the only reliable basis for a healthy life *in community*: "By the blessing of the upright a city is exalted, but it is overthrown by the mouth of the wicked" (11:11; cf. 14:34). Moreover, only if the king and others in authority live true to the standards of righteousness and compassion can a nation hope to be secure and blessed (29:2, 4, 14, 16, 18).

We thus see that the legacy of centuries of observation and reflection of sages both in Israel and beyond combines in the Book of Proverbs with distinctly Yahwistic themes to offer guidelines for a good life for both the individual and the community as a whole. Although the most distinctive Yahwistic theme of all in the biblical notion of community is developed more fully in other streams of tradition, we have already seen in the theme of "the fear of Yahweh" that the aura of worship is not lacking in the book. And there are even a couple of descriptions of true worship that are reminiscent of the prophets:

> The sacrifice of the wicked is an abomination to the Lord,
> but the prayer of the upright is his delight. (Prov. 15:8)

> To do righteousness and justice
> is more acceptable to the Lord than sacrifice. (Prov. 21:3)

Finally, in chapter 30, Agur son of Jakeh strikes a new theme relating to worship, namely, the divine mystery before which humans are finally reduced to silence and awe. But this is a theme developed more richly by Job, a book less confident than Proverbs of the accessibility of wisdom, and perhaps for that reason more profound in its description of the queen of the Yahwistic triad, namely, worship.

The question of what led to the profound level of inquiry found in the Book of Job is as intriguing as it is difficult. Does it reflect the catastrophic experiences of the early sixth century B.C.E.? What compelled the sages to probe more deeply than ever before the basic questions of life that were their professional agenda? When one compares the persistent retributive doctrine of Proverbs with the agonized searching of Job in the dialogues, it seems clear that something of the magnitude of the destruction of the Holy City had led to a heightening of the contradiction already felt by ancient Egyptians, Sumerians, Babylonians, and Canaanites between the individual's moral character and the "rewards" of this life.[10]

At any rate, the Book of Job displays an uncommon courage and passion in subjecting the received traditions to the acid tests of life on the basis of a faith that is open, questioning, and honest. In the dialogues of the book, we find Job's "friends" trying strenuously to defend the traditional notion of community based on the doctrine of retribution and belief in a rational, moral universe. With a freshness and poetic quality equal to that of Second Isaiah, the author of the dialogues in chapters 3–31 and 38–42:6 rises up in opposition to a facile orthodoxy that would reduce life in human community to a set of rigid doctrines and rules, to be forced on all life situations regardless of the cost in human pain and anguish (8:3–7; 22:29–30). By pleading that faith ultimately comes down to trust in one Reality alone, and acknowledging that the road to such trust often entails doubt, anger, and agony that cannot be dismissed with facile doctrines, Job spoke out clearly on behalf of a more honest, sensitive, humane, and at the same time, godly community (12:3–6; 23:1–17). Within such a community, there could be both the freedom to cry out in despair to God (7:11–21; 9:21–24), and the freedom to acknowledge that comfort sometimes may best be given to the suffering one by a love incapable of finding words, but precious nonetheless in its compassionate, understanding silence (19:21–

---

10. For fragments of a Sumerian account of the righteous sufferer, see S. N. Kramer, "Man and His God: A Sumerian Variation on the 'Job' Motif," 170–182 in M. Noth and D. W. Thomas, eds., *Wisdom in Israel and in the Ancient Near East*, VTSuppl 3 (Leiden: Brill, 1955), pp. 170–182. For a Babylonian version, see R. S. Pfeiffer's translation of "I Will Praise the Lord of Wisdom," *ANET*, 3d ed., pp. 424–437. (See also 437–438). Compare the Egyptian "A Dialogue of the Man Weary of Life with His Soul," trans. J. A. Wilson, *ANET*, 3d ed., pp. 405–407; and "The Epic of King Kirta," trans. M. D. Coogan, in *Stories from Ancient Canaan* (Philadelphia: Westminster Press, 1978), pp. 58–74. Excellent recent commentaries on the Book of Job are: M. Pope, *Job*, AB 15 (Garden City, N.Y.: Doubleday and Co., 1973); J. G. Janzen, *Job*, Interpretation (Atlanta: John Knox Press, 1985).

22). This honest doubt and courageous faith significantly deepened the primal quality of the Yahwistic notion of community, the quality of worship of the one true God. For worship is distinguished in Job from an activity reserved for life's winners. God is portrayed not as an abstract principle of retribution, but as the mysterious power at the center of life. Empirical categories and rational systems of proof simply falter within the context of true worship. In a later era, another faithful sufferer would similarly rediscover the mysterious nature of true faith. In prison, Dietrich Bonhoeffer wrote, "The transcendence of theory based on perception has nothing to do with the transcendence of God. God is the 'beyond' in the midst of our life.' "[11] In Job, suffering and reversal moved the mortal back to the nadir point from which the earliest Yahwistic community had been born, and this return resulted in the rediscovery that true worship arises when one is stripped of all penultimate realities, and God alone is acknowledged as true Reality:

> For I know that my Redeemer lives,
>   and at last he will stand upon the earth;
> and after my skin has been thus destroyed,
>   then from my flesh I shall see God . . . (Job 19:24–26)

Job did not answer all the questions of the sages. But he pointed the wisdom tradition, and the Yahwistic community as a whole, to something more important than answers to riddles—namely, the mysterious, holy center of life, in relation to whom alone the mortal could find a meaning transcending all doubt, suffering, and even death:

> I had heard of thee by the hearing of the ear,
>   but now my eye sees thee;
> therefore I despise myself,
>   and repent in dust and ashes. (Job 42:5–6)

This holy mystery is expressed beautifully also by the Psalmist (73:26):

> My flesh and my heart may fail,
>   but God is the strength of my heart and my portion forever.

At a somewhat later period (probably the fourth century B.C.E.) another sage continued the tradition of honest questioning, namely, the Preacher (Ecclesiastes or Qoheleth). The Preacher pays homage to the profession: "Who is like the [sage] (ḥākām)? And who knows the interpretation of a thing: A [person's] wisdom makes his face shine, and the hardness of his countenance is changed" (Eccles. 8:1). But relentlessly, in the style of Job, the Preacher probes beneath conventional wisdom and its facile ordering of life according to rational principles to the more elusive wisdom best described and safeguarded by honest ques-

---

11. D. Bonhoeffer, *Letters and Papers from Prison: The Enlarged Edition*, (ed. E. Bethge [London: SCM Press, 1971], p. 282).

tioning and reflection. Embracing such openness to the lessons of life and the testimony of faith gives one the freedom to affirm (2:24–26) and to doubt (3:16–22), to construct (8:13–16) and to contradict (cf. 3:16 with 3:17 and 8:11–12a with 8:12b–13). And this in turn breaks one out of a paralysis in the face of inability to establish a definitive philosophy of life and frees one to go about the human vocation of living in full acceptance of life's limitations and possibilities. Without claiming more for the Preacher than is his due in the context of biblical thought, it seems important to accept his lessons in human modesty, honesty, and openness to life, as well as his "insistence upon God's transcendance and sovereignty, and upon the task of men to meet the present as it is, as it comes from the hand of God, with joy."[12]

The contribution of the so-called wisdom writings of the Bible to the biblical notion of community is thus undeniable. Their deep probings into the experiences of the individual, into the life of the community, and into the realm of nature, especially as these probings were related to God's sovereignty, enrich our understanding of communal life in important respects. We have also seen how the melding of earlier formulations of wisdom with a distinctively Yahwistic notion of tôrâ was leading to the transformation of rather conventional practitioners of wisdom into a refined class of theologians. As we shall see in Chapter XI and XII, this transformation would culminate in a highly refined scribe class capable of producing the Wisdom of Jesus the Son of Sirach and of becoming a powerful influence within the Jewish community during the Hellenistic and Roman periods.

---

12. R. Murphy, *Wisdom Literature*, p. 131.

VII

The Exile:
Crisis and Reformulation
(Ezekiel, the Priestly Writing, Isaiah 40–55)

> But their light was ever surrounded and shot
>   with darkness
> As the air of temperate seas is pierced by the
>   still dead breath of the Arctic Current;
> And they came to an end, a dead end stirred
>   with a flicker of life,
> And they came to the withered ancient look of
>   a child that has died of starvation.[1]

Historical Note: The destruction of Jerusalem, the burning of the temple, the loss of nationhood and exile into a foreign land shook the faith of Israel to its foundations. The year 587 B.C.E. thus thrust the religious leaders of Israel into a period of deep searching, as people questioned both Yahweh's compassion and Yahweh's power vis-à-vis other nations and cults. The result was a series of penetrating reformulations of what it meant to be a people of God, found in the prophet Ezekiel, the Priestly Writing (i.e., the final edition of the Pentateuch) and the author of Isaiah 40–55 (the so-called Second Isaiah). Once again, international events set the stage to which Yahweh's plan had to be related. Of special significance was the meteoric rise of Cyrus the Persian, whom Second Isaiah identified as the one anointed by Yahweh to restore the people of Israel to their homeland. In these three writings, we find not only the spiritual resources for renewal of a threatened faith, but the well-spring of important new directions of growth for the Yahwistic notion of community.

A. THE TRADITIONAL NOTION OF COVENANT COMMUNITY CALLED INTO QUESTION

In the Book of Jeremiah, we have already arrived at an important crossroads in the development of biblical thought on community. In

---

1. From T. S. Eliot, "Choruses from 'The Rock,'" in *The Complete Poems and Plays, 1909–1950* (New York: Harcourt Brace, 1952), p. 197.

Jeremiah's first period, prior to Josiah's reform, we found oracles of judgment interspersed with admonitions to repent and return to Yahweh, much in the style of earlier prophecy. After Josiah's death, however, and in the succeeding years marked by apostasy and the threat of Babylonian conquest, a very deep pessimism came to dominate Jeremiah's message. All of God's appeals through the prophets had come to nought. This people seemed utterly given to their idols. Destruction seemed inevitable, so deeply rooted was the evil: "The heart is deceitful above all things, and desperately corrupt" (17:9). Accompanying this deepened sense of evil, however, was a commensurately more radical formulation of salvation: Only a new covenant and a new act of salvation could restore a community related in obedience to God.

Jeremiah was not the only one who responded to the crises of the late seventh and early sixth centuries with a radical new analysis of the condition of Israel. Three events posed the question of whether God had forsaken this people forever. The first event was the seemingly senseless death of Josiah and the shocking end of the high hopes associated with his reform. Second was the advance of the Babylonians, which, unlike Sennacherib's invasion during the time of Hezekiah and Isaiah, did not end with the miraculous deliverance of Zion, but with the destruction of the holy city and the temple of Yahweh. And third was the deportation of the most prestigious and influential of the population to a pagan land. "The Lord will not do good, nor will he do ill" (Zeph. 1:12b), some Jerusalemites concluded. Jeremiah had to contend with apostates who compared the good fortune they had enjoyed when they worshipped the Queen of Heaven (during Manasseh's reign) with the calamity suffered since the Yahwistic reform of the cult (Jer. 44:15–19). The exilic period was a time in which people were questioning the very roots of Yahwism—the righteousness, compassion, and power of their God. If their questions could not be answered, the heart of the Yahwistic notion of community had been destroyed. Jeremiah looked at the bleak situation from the perspective of a prophet steeped in the traditions of early Yahwism, and concluded that Yahweh would have to act anew to implant the *tôrâ* within the hearts of the people if there was to be a future for his people. Three other attempts were made to reconcile natural and cultic calamity with faith in Yahweh, the God of Israel, and from each there emerged a new formulation of the notion of a faith community in covenant with God.

B. EZEKIEL: A PROGRAM FOR THE RESTORATION OF PURITY

From the perspective of one trained as a priest, Ezekiel witnessed the death of Josiah, and the ensuing spiritual and political decline of Judah culminating in the calamity of a temple reduced to rubble and a people exiled to a pagan land. This perspective he brought into the service of a prophetic career in the wake of a series of powerful visionary experiences. The result was a program for the restoration of the Yahwistic community combining priestly with prophetic elements in a daring composition that in subsequent centuries exerted considerable influence on temple priests and apocalyptic seers alike.

In Ezekiel, the majesty of Yahweh stands out more grandly than perhaps in any other biblical writing. The formula "and (or then) you shall know that I am the Lord" occurs eighty-six times in Ezekiel.[2] Yahweh spared Isreal for the sake of his name (e.g., 20:9, 14, 22); Yahweh was profaned through Israel in the sight of the nations (22:16); and finally, Yahweh would act in a radically new way, again, for his name's sake:

Therefore say to the house of Israel, Thus says the Lord God: It is not for your sake, O house of Israel, that I am about to act, but for the sake of my holy name, which you have profaned among the nations to which you came. And I will vindicate the holiness of my great name, which has been profaned among the nations, and which you have profaned among them; and the nations will know that I am the Lord, says the Lord God, when through you I vindicate my holiness before their eyes. (Ezek. 36:22–23)

As seen in the detailed figurative historical résumé found in chapter 20, he revised the exodus-conquest tradition to emphasize the primal command at the heart of Yahwism. Not first in the wilderness, but already in the land of Egypt, Yahweh had said to the people, "Cast away the detestable things your eyes feast on, every one of you, and do not defile yourselves with the idols of Egypt; I am the Lord your God" (20:7). In relation to this primal command issuing forth from Yahweh's majesty, the sin of Israel was to be understood. Stubbornly, "they rebelled against me and would not listen to me" (20:8). Yahweh spared them for the sake of his name, led them out of Egypt and into the wilderness, giving them his statutes, ordinances and "sabbaths, as a sign between me and them, that they may know that I the Lord sanctify them" (20:12). But again they rebelled, and thus the story continued until Yahweh, in his wrath, "gave them statutes that were not good and ordinances by which they could not have life" (20:25). With that ominous entry, Ezekiel brought the history of Israel up to the present. The resulting open-ended and threatening character of the future was reinforced structurally by Ezekiel through the deletion at this point of the refrain, which concluded the other chapters of Israel's history with a word of divine restraint (20:9, 14, 22).

Ezekiel taught that Israel was constituted as a people to give glory to God through its purity. Its sole purpose in life was that of glorifying God by a life of holiness. The key to that holiness was observance of

2. W. Zimmerli, *Erkenntnis Gottes nach dem Buche Ezekiel.* ATANT 27 (Zurich: Zwingli, 1984).

the first commandment. The statutes and ordinances in turn were the guidelines by which Israel could live in purity. The community living in obedience to God was not only a righteous, but also a blessed people, for in its midst—that is to say, in the temple—dwelt Yahweh's *kābôd* (glorious presence). But as Ezekiel sought to portray in chapters 16, 20, and 23, through its entire history Israel had lived in blatant disregard for God's commandments, thus preparing for the present time of wrath.

When Ezekiel turned to establish Yahweh's case against his rebellious people, he did not overlook the ethical concerns of the earlier prophets. The rights of parents, sojourners, widows, and orphans, and the laws forbidding adultery, shedding blood, interest, and extortion were reiterated (e.g., 22:6–12). Moreover, the tradition of harsh indictments against merciless rulers, unfaithful priests and false prophets found in the eighth-century prophets was renewed by Ezekiel (22:23–31). A difference, however, is apparent: these, and all other instances of injustice, were given a sacral interpretation. Together with Israel's harlotrous idol worship, they were all interpreted as examples of a massive ritual impurity that stained the land and had transformed it into an abomination in the eyes of the holy God: "You are a land that is not cleansed, or rained upon in the day of indignation" (22:23). Such a defilement was totally unsuitable as a context for the indwelling of the glory of the holy God. A purging was mandatory: "I will disperse you through the countries, and I will consume your filthiness out of you" (22:15).

The entire book of Ezekiel is structured around a series of visions that portray Yahweh's response to the sacral impurity of the land. In the opening vision (chapter 1), Ezekiel peers at the indescribable, "the appearance of the likeness of the glory of the Lord" (1:28b). Thus at the beginning of the book one is introduced to the holy center of Israel's existence as a people. It was from this holy center that Ezekiel received his commission. That commission already emphasized the total incompatibility of God and the people to whom the prophet was sent; they are "a nation of rebels," "impudent" and "stubborn." Therefore, the words he received to digest and utter were "of lamentation and mourning and woe" (2:3, 4, 10). The same terrible message was repeated in Ezekiel's second visionary encounter with the Glory of the Lord in the plain (3:22–27).

Next we find Ezekiel transported in visions to Jerusalem, where he is shown the abominations being committed by the priests and people in the temple precincts: worship of the image of jealousy, of zoomorphic gods, of the Mesopotamian vegetation god Tammuz and of the sun (chapter 8). The rationale of the people is simple: "The Lord does not see us, the Lord has forsaken the land" (8:10). Already in this chapter Yahweh explains the end result of their acts, "to drive me far from my sanctuary" (8:6). Chapters 10 and 11 describe the consequence, as Ezekiel watches the Glory of God lifted up by its cherubim chariot and carried away from temple and city. The glorious presence of Yahweh in the temple, on which Israel depended for its existence, had been forced to leave, due to the total ritual depravity of the land. The result was inevitable: The decayed city would fall victim to the enemy invaders, as portrayed by Ezekiel in words and picture, and then announced as historical fact (33:21). The rattling bones of the fourth vision sound an uncanny death knell: Israel was dead! Without the glory of Yahweh, the land was without the vital spirit upon which its life was utterly dependent.

The brokenness that prophets like Hosea and Jeremiah had described as the necessary precondition for Yahweh's turning again to the people in compassion was thus brought to its climax by Ezekiel. Among the dead, the hubris and defiance of haughty mortals had ended. In the valley of dry bones ("they were very dry"), and in the land of ashes it symbolized, nothing remained of human potential for the restoration of the people. In the face of the question "Can these bones live?" one could only look to the One who had "formed man of dust from the ground, and breathed (*wayyippah*) into his nostrils the breath of life (*nišmat hayyîm*), with the result that the human "became a living being" (Gen. 2:7). That is to say, only a new divine creative act, recapitulating the original creation of humanity, could bring this dead people back to life. This was the daring hope extended to the prophet in his vision:

Prophesy to the breath, prophesy, son of man, and say to the breath, Thus says the Lord God: Come from the four winds, O breath, and breathe (*ûpĕhî*) upon these slain, that they may live (*wĕyihyû*). So I prophesied as he commanded me, and the breath came into them, and they lived, and stood upon their feet, an exceedingly great host. (Ezek. 37:9–10)

Ezekiel, who had delivered Yahweh's harsh words of judgment with such seeming dispassion, thus was commanded to speak of a very different divine act. The judgment had fallen, and its culminating phase in 587 had left the people dumbfounded and broken: "Our bones are dried up, and our hope is lost; we are clean cut off" (37:11b). God's "alien" act had achieved its objective, and to a broken people opened finally to God's word, his ultimate saving purpose could be revealed:

And you, son of man, say to the house of Israel, Thus have you said: "Our transgressions and our sins are upon us, and we waste away because of them; how then can we live?" Say to them, As I live, says the Lord God, I have no pleasure in the death of the wicked, but that the wicked turn from his way and live; turn back, turn back from your evil ways; for why will you die, O house of Israel? (Ezek. 33:10–11)

Given the utter depravity of the people, and the testimony to their unrelenting stubbornness given by past history, those surviving the calamity would acknowledge the rightness of God's severe act of judgment (6:8–10 and 14:22–23), would repent and give up their idolatry, and thus open themselves to the miraculous act that only God could achieve, a new creation!

Therefore prophesy, and say to them, Thus says the Lord God: "Behold, I will open your graves, and raise you from your graves, O my people; and I will bring you home into the land of Israel. And you shall know that I am the Lord when I open your graves, and raise you from your graves, O my people. And I will put my Spirit within you, and I will place you in your own land; then you shall know that I, the Lord, have spoken and I have done it, says the Lord." (Ezek. 37:12–14)

Like Jeremiah, Ezekiel portrayed the outward manifestation of this new creative act, like return to the land, reunification of Judah and Israel, rebuilding of its cities and restoration of its fruitfulness (36:8–11; 37:15–23), without losing sight of its primary location, in the inner parts of the human. As the historical résumés in Ezekiel indicated, Israel's root sin was disobedience. Therefore, the most essential aspect of God's recreation of Israel was to be the cleansing of the people from all uncleanness, and the creation of a new heart and spirit:

A new heart I will give you, and a new spirit I will put within you; and I will take out of your flesh the heart of stone and give you a heart of flesh. And I will put my spirit within you, and cause you to walk in my statutes and be careful to observe my ordinances. (Ezek. 36:26–27)

With this wedding of divine will and human will, the covenant would be reconstituted: "You shall dwell in the land which I gave to your fathers; and you shall be my people, and I will be your God" (36:28). The promised result was the šālôm of the healthy covenant (36:29–32). And as Yahweh's first saving act had been followed by his sustaining care, after this new act Yahweh would protect them through his prince, "my servant David" (34:20–24). As 37:24–26 indicates, the Davidic tradition was bound by Ezekiel to the carefully defined conditions of the early Yahwistic Sinaiatic covenant. King and people, in the new blessed era, would be characterized by their careful observance of Yahweh's ordinances and statutes.

This entire saving act of Yahweh—return to the land, cleansing, creation of a new heart and spirit, compassionate rule by the Davidic prince—was to culminate in the event on which Israel's existence as a community was utterly dependent, the dwelling of Yahweh in the midst of the people:

My dwelling place shall be with them; and I will be their God, and they shall be my people. Then the nations will know that I the Lord will sanctify Israel, when my sanctuary is in the midst of them for evermore. (Ezek. 37:27–28)

It is fully in harmony with the central theme of Ezekiel's prophecy that the book's central concern with Yahweh's indwelling should culminate in an elaborate description of the "sanctuary in the midst of them." Although including considerable later detail from followers of Ezekiel, there is no question that the basic program for restoration in Ezekiel 40–48 stems from the prophet himself. National calamity had finally created the conditions for Yahweh's purification and new creation of a people living in obedience, a people which in Ezekiel's view would be drawn forth by Yahweh from among the exiles (11:14–21). With the restoration of purity, the *kābôd* of Yahweh, which had been forced to leave by the people's defilement of the land, could return once again. Thus the vision in 43:1–5 of the return of Yahweh's Glory to the temple parallels the vision of its departure in 11:22–25. In the carefully detailed portrait of chapters 40–48, the exilic community, once it had returned to the land, would have the blueprint for rebuilding Yahweh's dwelling place. Here Ezekiel's background in the Jerusalem temple priesthood came to clear expression. Through the careful observance of the sacral ordinances, the purity of the temple precinct and the whole land was to be maintained, that Yahweh's Glory would never again be forced to leave the temple. In keeping with Ezekiel's affiliation with the Zadokite priesthood, the exclusive claim of the Zadokites to full priestly status is acknowledged (40:44–47; 43:18–19), with the Levites receiving the assignment of assisting the Zadokites in duties other than "approaching the Lord" (45:4–5). This division into major and minor clergy was also projected onto the "blueprint" of the rebuilt city (45:1–5). Although there is no sign of a polemical thrust to this division in Ezekiel himself, it was to become a point of bitter contention in subsequent years, as indicated even in the Book of Ezekiel by the scathing attack on the Levites, and the corresponding praise of the Zadokites, in the later additions found in chapter 44 and 48:11. We shall see later that Zadokite superiority was a feature of the Ezekielian restoration program, which gave offense to a significant number of people.

Special safeguards were also to be observed to prevent defilement through the encroachment of Israel's kings on the sanctuary (43:6–9), which in the past had been the source of many unholy entanglements. In relation to the rights of the people, strict laws were imposed on the king or prince to prevent the abuse of royal power resulting in loss of property and impoverishment (45:7–8). Although sacral law certainly predominated in this priestly vision of a land strictly ordered in accordance with ritual purity, laws reminiscent of early Israel's deep concern with divine righteousness were not forgotten:

Enough, O princes of Israel! Put away violence and oppression, and execute justice and righteousness; cease your evictions of my people, says the Lord God. You shall have just balances, a just ephah, and a just bath. (Ezek. 45:9–10)

In the new era of salvation, the land would be allotted according to a pattern symbolizing the centrality of temple and temple personnel (Ezek. 45:1–8), and granting the twelve tribes equal portions (47:13–

48:29). With the land ordered in all ways according to these holy ordinances, Yahweh's šālôm would transform the Judean wilderness into a rich paradise, a theme employing the ancient mythic motif of the sacred river flowing from the temple (47:1–12). In all this one is reminded of Ezekiel's central message that everything depended on Yahweh's dwelling in the midst of the people, a message expressed in its tersest possible form in the new name given to the city in the last verse of the Book of Ezekiel: "The Lord is there."

When it comes to the evaluation of Ezekiel's contribution to the biblical notion of community, it is easy to be distracted both by the esoteric images of this prophet's vision and by the priestly language in which his ideas were expressed. Commonly Ezekiel's vision of community is dismissed as cold priestly ritualism and legalism. But one must not overlook the dynamism underlying the priestly language and esoteric images.

The expression Ezekiel gave to the primal quality of the biblical notion of community, sole worship of the one true God, was not only majestic, but dynamic as well. The austere image of the Glory (kābôd) of Yahweh mounted on its chariot throne must not obscure the fact that the God thus portrayed was an active, seeking God. Although his rightful habitation was in Jerusalem, when defilement forced his leavetaking, he did not disappear into the heavens, but reappeared in Babylon, to be with his people and to prepare them for a return to Zion. His judgment and his salvation were both parts of a universal plan of bringing the knowledge of Yahweh to all the world, and bringing šālôm to a people living in obedience, righteousness, and purity in a city named "Yahweh is there."

Although expressed in a unique idiom, it is thus clear that Ezekiel's message rested firmly on sole worship of Yahweh. What of the qualities of righteousness and compassion that form the other two essential points of the early Yahwistic notion of community? There is no denying the fact that the attention of the priest-prophet was focused in the first instance on the ordinances regulating the cult. Defilement of this sacral center of Israelite community had led to the departure of Yahweh's Glory. And without God's Glory at its center Israel was dead. Life could return to Israel only by the return of Yahweh's Glory, an event possible only if sanctity were restored in Israel, a sanctity beginning at the sacral center and radiating outward into all other spheres of life. In a couple of cases, however, we see Ezekiel addressing the issue of individual righteousness. The context was the complaint of the exiles that the punishment they were suffering was the result of their *fathers'* sins. The divine word Ezekiel delivered was a strong declaration of the responsibility of each individual for his or her *own* conduct. And the examples offered by the prophet to describe what constituted the life of righteousness give a good summary of early Yahwistic *tôrâ*, beginning with the first commandment, and then blending the stringent demands of the standard of righteousness with the tenderness of divine compassion:

If a man is righteous and does what is lawful and right—if he does not eat upon the mountains or lift up his eyes to the idols of the house of Israel, does not defile his neighbor's wife or approach a woman in her time of impurity, does not oppress anyone, but restores to the debtor his pledge, commits no robbery, gives his bread to the hungry and covers the naked with a garment, does not lend at interest or take any increase, withholds his land from iniquity, executes true justice between man and man, walks in my statutes, and is careful to observe my ordinances—he is righteous, he shall surely live, says the Lord God. (Ezek. 18:5-9)

Growing out of the trials of the early sixth century, we see in this description of righteousness the explication of a hitherto undeveloped facet. Members of the community were not to blame their own unrighteousness on their ancestors. Each of them stood before God with a personal answerability for his or her own life. Moreover, the fatalism of the one resigned to a life of iniquity due to the weight of past sin, or the smugness of the one who drew comfort from past righteousness, were both nullified by the principle of personal responsibility (18:19–28). In the role of "watchman" that Yahweh assigned to Ezekiel (3:16–21 and 33:1–20), we therefore see that this prophet's concept of righteousness was not limited to cultic ordinances, but described a way of life of the individual before God that was dynamic, personal, and in harmony with the spirit of early Yahwism.

The quality of compassion, while similarly less conspicuous than themes relating to Ezekiel's cultic concerns, nevertheless also came to expression. In the historical résumé in chapter 16, the source of Israel's notion of compassion was located in Yahweh's acts of pitying, saving, and nurturing Jerusalem, from infancy to adulthood (16:1–14). That same compassion was extended to the individual Israelite in exile by the God who swore, "I have no pleasure in the death of the wicked, but that the wicked turn from his way and live" (33:11a). Yahweh's compassion also came to expression with special clarity in the pastoral pleading carried on by Ezekiel on Yahweh's behalf:

Cast away from you all the transgressions which you have committed against me, and get yourselves a new heart and a new spirit! Why will you die, O house of Israel? For I have no pleasure in the death of anyone, says the Lord God; so turn, and live. (Ezek. 18:31–32)

From this divine source, compassion was to permeate the lives of the members of the community gathered in worship of Yahweh (18:6–9). Righteousness and compassion therefore were not qualities assigned by Ezekiel solely to an eschatological vision of the ideal Jerusalem. Righteousness and compassion, wedded in the lives of those devoted to the one true God, were to be the essential ingredients of the lifestyle of even those who found themselves in the imperfect setting of the exile. Through sole worship of Yahweh and the embodiment of righteousness and compassion in their relations with their fellow exiles, the faithful prepared the way for the return of Yahweh, and for their own return to the city named "The Lord is there."

At most, one might be critical of the degree to which Ezekiel couched the dynamic triadic notion of Yahwistic community in technical cultic-liturgical language. But this criticism is mollified when one remembers that Ezekiel's conceptual world was that of a Jerusalem priest in exile. His longing was for a return to the familiar setting of the temple, where God's presence radiated forth and enveloped the community with blessing. When this background is kept in mind, one may rightly be astonished at how far beyond purely cultic concerns the vision of Ezekiel reached.

C. THE PRIESTLY WRITING ("P")

The Priestly Writing[3] addressed itself to the same crisis situation to which Ezekiel had spoken. The community that had defined itself in terms of possession of a land given by God and in relation to the presence of that God in the temple now found itself without land and temple. Did this signify the end of Yahweh's relationship with Israel? Was the election that traced all the way back to Abraham now ended?

In responding to these questions, the prophets referred back to the faithfulness of Yahweh to his promises. There was a future, indeed a future that would far outstrip the past in glory and splendor. Isaiah, Jeremiah, Ezekiel, Second Isaiah, and their followers looked beyond judgment to an eschatological act of God that would establish an order of righteousness and peace hitherto unknown to humans. They awaited a new creation.

The Priestly Writing, while addressing the same crisis, approached the matter somewhat differently. Although it too appealed to the promises of Yahweh, it emphasized less the radical newness of Yahweh's fulfillment of those promises and more the dependableness and perfection of the order established by God long ago, to which the people in exile could hope to return. To present this message, the writer we call P applied the literary form of the historical narrative. And he used this form in a manner that betrayed an interest less in recording the course of past events than in accentuating the paradigmatic meaning of events of the past for the present generation in Babylon. Thus it is that the events narrated by P were those dealing with the establish-

---

3. The Priestly Writing (signified "P") was written during the exile within a priestly circle that drew on older traditions in describing the sacral ordinances they believed to be central to the life of Israel. Its basic form was subsequently supplemented with extensive new materials treating cultic regulations.

ment of the major cultic institutions and practices upon which depended the renewal of the Israelite religious community in the era after the
destruction of the temple by the Babylonians. Accordingly, the story of
creation was interpreted as an etiology of the sabbath, the celebration
of which could remind the exiles of the dependability of the good order
God had created and reassure them of the trustworthiness of the divine
promise: "Be fruitful and multiply, and fill the earth and subdue it"
(Gen. 1:28). The Noachic covenant, with its sign of the rainbow, assured Yahwists, confronted in Babylon by pagan cosmologies, of the
stability of the natural order established by the God of Israel (Gen. 9:8–
17). And the covenant with Abraham gave the homeless, decimated exilic community a solid basis of hope for the renewal of their offspring,
repossession of their land, and the return of God to their midst, promises etched into their memory by the sign of circumcision (Gen. 17:1–
27).

For P, the heart of God's promises to Israel was that he would be
their God, present among them to bless them. Accordingly, the central
point developed by the P narrative was the marvelous appearance of
the Glory (kābôd) of Yahweh on Mount Sinai, for in this form Yahweh
had chosen to be present to his community. It is noteworthy that P, in
contrast to J, E, and D, did not even mention a covenant ceremony or a
revelation of divine commandments on Sinai. The Glory of Yahweh
had descended on Sinai for one purpose, to reveal to Moses the plan of
the sanctuary in which Yahweh would be present to the people through
the mediators Moses, Aaron, and the sons of Aaron. Exodus 29:42b–
46, which gives a concise description of this purpose, has rightfully
been considered the heart of P.[4]

... the tent of meeting before the Lord, where I will meet with you, to speak
there to you. There I will meet with the people of Israel, and it shall be sanctified by my glory; I will consecrate the tent of meeting and the altar; Aaron also
and his son I will consecrate, to serve me as priests. And I will dwell among the
people of Israel, and will be their God. And they shall know that I am the Lord
their God, who brought them forth out of the land of Egypt that I might dwell
among them; I am the Lord their God.   (Exod. 29:42b–46)

The community of faith was constituted according to P solely by this
divine presence. In the form of the Glory, Yahweh was graciously reaching down to the people to enter into relationship with them. The exilic
community addressed by P was to regard itself, like its forefathers, as a
people in the wilderness, a place filled with threats and dangers, yet
dominated by hope based on the Glory of Yahweh in their midst. For the
Glory of Yahweh had not remained on Sinai, but had moved to the tent
of meeting Moses constructed according to divine instruction (Exod.

---

4. This point is persuasively argued by Bernd Janowski, *Sühne als Heilsgeschehen*,
WMANT 55 (Neukirchen-Vluyn: Neukirchener Verlag, 1982), pp. 317–328.

40:34–38). Yahweh's presence thus had revealed itself to be a presence also to those in the wilderness, a presence that would accompany them until they reached the land of promise, when they could worship Yahweh in his proper sanctuary (i.e., the Jerusalem temple).

In this highly imaginative way, then, P sought to assure the exiles that they had been forsaken by Yahweh no more than had their ancestors in the wilderness. Accompanying this promise, however, was an urgent word of admonition. This promise of Yahweh's presence was not an occasion for complacency. God was faithful to his promises: his sacred order was dependable; an obedient generation would always find Yahweh in its midst. But as the generation dying in the wilderness (and the exiles forced from their home to live in Babylon!) proved, the generation that was unfaithful to God would be severely punished. It is obvious that the stunning events of the early sixth century had led priestly circles to address the problem of sin with a new urgency. The doctrine of sin in itself was not new. Yahwism from earliest times looked on sin as a violation of God's order, which inevitably brought in its wake dreadful consequences.[5] It was for this reason offenders were dealt with so harshly, in the Book of the Covenant as well as in all subsequent law codes. If the source of the disruption of divine order were not removed by expulsion or stoning, or if atonement were not made, the inevitable result was the destruction of the entire community. The destruction of land and temple was obviously taken by the priests of Israel as a sign that God's order had been heinously violated. How could harmony within that order be restored?

The answer of P to that question is intimately related to another Yahwistic belief: namely, that in God's view the world was divided between two realms, the pure and the impure. For P—and in this respect similarities to Ezekiel are readily apparent—the nucleus of purity was the sanctuary, where the holy God was present. Among humans, the priests who are designated to enter into God's presence in the sanctuary had to exercise the most stringent laws regarding cleanness (in the nomenclature of P, they are the sons of Aaron, but designate the same group which Ezekiel and the Chronicler call the sons of Zadok). Next in order were those charged with serving the priests in the precincts of the temple, namely, the Levites. Then as one moved outward from the temple, one moved further from the nucleus of purity into the profane. For the individual layperson, life was lived in the gray area between purity and impurity, that is, in the tension between what upheld life and what threatened it. If the community were to be prevented from being engulfed by the chaos accompanying impurity, the sacral orders that maintained the state of purity in Israel were of paramount importance.

---

5. Regarding the connection between the deed and its consequences, see K. Koch, *Um das Princip der Vergeltung in Religion und Recht des Alten Testaments* (Darmstadt: Wissenschaftliche Buchgesellschaft, 1972).

For these orders were instituted by God, and out of them came forth the divine powers of healing and peace that alone could ward off the powers of death.[6]

From the period of early Yahwism on, this concern with purity had been related in a special way to cult, sacrifice, and the priesthood. In P, a further development of certain facets of this concern occurred. Increased emphasis was placed on the atoning aspect of sacrifice, and the exclusive claims of the Aaronide priests in regard to supervision over the sacral orders of the sanctuary led to the demotion of the Levitical priests to the status of assistants, or what one can call "minor clergy." This development within the relationships among the priestly families, which traces back in large part to Josiah's program of cult centralization and was reflected also in the restoration program of Ezekiel, heightened significantly the importance of the role of the Aaronide priests in mediating between Yahweh and Israel. Other Yahwistic offices disappeared, as focus came to bear exclusively on the sons of Aaron as the agents through which Yahweh dealt with the people.

Against this background we can reformulate our earlier question, relating it now specifically to the Priestly Writing: in the thought of these Aaronide priests, and in relation to their perception of themselves as mediators of God's presence, what response could be made to the exilic crisis? What they produced was a reply that was both comprehensive and theologically penetrating. It arose on the one hand out of a deep awareness of the impurity that had led to the destruction of temple and nation, and on the other, out of an abiding belief in Yahweh's commitment to being present in his sanctuary. In the life and death struggle between the sacred and the profane, they regarded the Aaronide priests to be Yahweh's agents in breaking the chain of sin and punishment that bound the people. The means of accomplishing this release had been given by God to Moses, and involved the sacral orders, at whose center stood the acts of atonement. Since the atonement sacrifices have frequently been misinterpreted as acts initiated and performed by humans to gain divine favor, it is essential to look more closely at this phenomenon.

According to P, the possibility of being reconciled with God rather than being destroyed for its sin existed for Israel solely because God had provided a means of atonement. Within the structure of early Yahwistic *tôrâ*, one who had incurred blood guilt could avoid the death incurred by his or her sin only by providing an appropriate substitute or ransom (e.g., Exod. 21:28–30; 2. Sam. 21:1–14). Deuteronomy 21:1–9 described how the land, profaned by the shedding of innocent blood, was to be atoned for by the blood of an unworked heifer that Yahweh

---

6. Cf. G. von Rad, *Old Testament Theology*, vol. 1, trans. D. M. G. Stalker (New York: Harper & Row, 1962), pp. 272–279.

would accept as a substitute for the blood of the inhabitants of the region. It was this atonement concept that P, following Ezekiel (43:18–28 and 45:13–17), drew into the cult and made the central ingredient of all sacrificial ritual (Lev. 9:7). Hartmut Gese has argued persuasively that one misses the central point of P's understanding of atonement if the laying on of hands is understood merely as the transfer of sin from the one sacrificing to the sacrificed victim. Something more profound was involved: by laying his hands on the head of the sacrificed animal, the one bringing the sacrifice identified himself with that animal.[7]

The sacrifice of the animal to God thereby stood for the dedication to God of the one bringing the sacrifice.[8] This identity was conveyed also by the other major sign of the atoning sacrifice, the pouring (or sprinkling) of the blood. The source of this sign was in rituals of dedication, whether of individuals such as the Aaronide priests (Lev. 8:5–22 and Exod. 29:19–21) or of objects such as the altar of burnt offerings (Exod. 29:10–18 and Ezek. 43:18–27). Blood thus symbolized the total dedication of the individual to God. This dedication involved nothing less than the sinner's giving him- or herself up to death through identification with the sacrificial animal, for only so could he or she hope to live in the presence of the holy God and not be destroyed. In thus dedicating self to God, the individual was drawn to and reconciled to God. The result was the fulfillment of what we earlier recognized as the deepest longing of the exilic community represented by P: to live in the presence of God, where alone the threat of sin's wages, death, could be nullified. Through atonement, P hoped for the destruction of the chain of sin and death that held the community in bondage. Through atonement, a life-giving relationship with God could be renewed. Through atonement, Israel could be drawn away from the realm of the profane, and placed in the realm of the pure and the holy: "Say to all the congregation of the people of Israel, You shall be holy; for I the Lord your God am holy" (Lev. 19:1). Secure in this realm of holiness, Israel would once again be empowered to keep the commandments, which, unlike those of the period of wrath "by which they could not have life" (Ezek. 20:23–26), would bring the fullness of life intended by God for his people: "Every one of you shall revere his mother and his father, and you shall keep my sabbaths: I am the Lord your God. Do not turn to idols or make yourselves molten gods: I am the Lord your God" (Lev. 19:3–4).

In P, rites of atonement were ranked, starting with those in which the individual brought an offering and culminating with the act of atone-

7. H. Gese, *Zur biblischen Theologie: Alttestamentliche Vorträge*, BzET 78 (München: Ch. Kaiser, 1977), p. 89.

8. Cf. H. W. Robinson, "Hebrew Sacrifice and Prophetic Symbolism," *JTS* 43 (1942), 130; and H. H. Rowley, *Worship in Ancient Israel: Its Forms and Meanings* (London: SPCK, 1967), p. 133.

ment celebrated once a year, the only time in which the high priest entered the holy of holies into the very presence of God. As the Glory of Yahweh had appeared to Moses on Sinai in the middle of a cloud, so Yahweh promised to be present with the community of the Aaronide priests: "I will appear in the cloud upon the mercy seat" (Lev. 16:2b). The "mercy seat" kappōret was the holiest of all places in Israel, for there God was enthroned, and there Yahweh of hosts (the hosts represented by the cherubim)—that is, the transcendant God of heaven—reached down to humans and offered them the life-giving opportunity to live in the presence of the source of all life and purity. Here the chief sign of the atonement ritual reached its climactic point: the Aaronide high priest, as representative of the people, took of the blood of the sacrificial bull and sprinkled "it with his finger on the front of the mercy seat" (Lev. 16:14). Israel thereby rededicated itself to God, restoring the one relationship on which all of life depended and making her deepest desire a reality, life in the presence of God.

Although regulated in minute detail, and presented in a factual manner without theological explanation, P's description of the sacral order binding on Israel was thus based on a profound sense of the centrality of God's presence to Israel's life as a community, and on a deep conviction that life in God's presence was possible only on the basis of divine grace. The relationship of these points to the blood of the sacrificial ritual came to clear expression in Leviticus 17:11: "For the life of the flesh is in the blood; and I have given it for you upon the altar to make atonement for your souls; for it is the blood that makes atonement, by reason of the life." God personally provided the blood as the life substance by which atonement could occur. And through this life-giving ritual, Israel, though in exile, was promised the blessing first experienced by its ancestors in the wilderness, the blessing of a God choosing to "dwell among the people of Israel," to "be their God" (Exod.29:45). In this blessing, P preserved a link with the oldest covenant ritual preserved from early Yahwism, in which Moses, after the sacrifice of burnt and peace offerings, threw half the blood against the altar and half on the people, symbolizing the at-one-ness of God and community (Exod. 24:3–8). For P, the intended result of the atonement ritual was the reestablishment of communion between God and the community. Also in this respect we can recognize an unbroken line of continuity from Israel's earliest cult down to P, for in another archaic liturgical fragment embedded in P we see that the culmination of worship was reached at the point of such communion:

Then Moses, and Aaron, Nadab, and Abihu, and seventy of the elders of Israel went up, and they saw the God of Israel; and there was under his feet as it were a pavement of sapphire stone, like the very heaven for clearness. And he did not lay his hand on the chief men of the people of Israel; they beheld God, and ate and drank. (Exod. 24:9–11)

This comparison points to the tenacity of the line of tradition running all the way from early Yahwism down to the reformulation of the sacral community in the Priestly Writing.

Throughout this study, however, we have seen that continuity was accompanied by development and change due to the dynamism of Yahwistic faith. The Deuteronomist, Ezekiel, and P all applied the traditions they had received from their confessional heritage to new settings. Before concluding this discussion of P, therefore, it is necessary to note the most significant changes that resulted, and to try to evaluate their significance.

Recent study has demonstrated the inadequacy of the view—often connected with the name of Julius Wellhausen—that regarded P as a descent from the heights of an earlier fresh and dynamic religion into a sterile legalism. We now see that in a setting within which nothing less than the very existence of the Israelite community of faith was at stake, the circle of exilic priests represented by P drew the hallowed traditions of the past into a powerful demonstration of the basis of Israel's hope for a future as God's people. In the events of Israel's past, Yahweh had established all the institutions necessary for life in the presence of God. At the heart of these institutions was the ritual of atonement, which was God's provision for removing the sin that had cut the people off from their Source.

Sensitivity to the vitality of the priestly theology in P must not lead, however, to an uncritical evaluation of the role of P in the total context of exilic faith. The theology of P represents a very energetic effort to restore order where chaos threatened, and it was carried out with a consistency and determination that left little room for disagreement. This is visible in two areas especially.

The first area is the interpretation of history in relation to the unfolding of God's will. For the prophets, history was the arena of God's ongoing activity. Even when Israel's apostasy had prepared the way for divine judgment, the promises made by Yahweh to Israel in the past allowed the prophets to see a brilliant new era beyond judgment. In relation to the realities of the present, whether social, political, or cultic, the future was expected to usher in realities that outstripped all forms of the past and present in significance. This was expressed with language such as "new covenant," "new creation," "new heart."

P's view of history was oriented somewhat differently. Promises, such as those to Adam and Eve in Genesis 1:28, though repeatedly threatened in the past (e.g., Exod. 1) and again under assault in P's own time, were proleptically fulfilled in the institutional structures revealed on Sinai and in the wilderness. From the future P did not await daring new disclosures of divine will, or new acts surpassing the old in glory and fullness, but rather a return to structures established in a bygone era. Naturally, ascription of the plan of the sanctuary, the rituals of sacrifice, and the priestly orders to the Mosaic period involved use of a literary device. And we have observed innovative elements in all these facets of the P theology. Nevertheless, all the structures and institutions described by P developed in continuity with the cultic realities that were present in the Jerusalem temple immediately prior to the destruction of the temple. Indeed, large blocks of P material probably originated in the pre-exilic period within the temple cult. P this was primarily a comprehensive plan of restoration, and while it is not accurate to claim that P was completely lacking in an eschatological dimension, its eschatology involved the anticipation of the fulfillment of the sacral orders already revealed to all Israel in the past.[9] In contrasting P with prophets such as Jeremiah or Second Isaiah, one may perhaps refer to P's eschatology as implicit in contrast to the explicit eschatology of the prophets. And as such it was amenable to further development in either of two directions.

The one direction drew P's implicit eschatology toward a fuller expression, and can be illustrated by the last chapter of Zechariah. In the following passage, which comes from one of the supplementary sections of the Book of Zechariah, we find a picture of Jerusalem and Judah according to which the division between the realms of purity and impurity would be superseded:

And on that day there shall be inscribed on the bells of the horses, "Holy to the Lord." And the pots in the house of the Lord shall be as the bowls before the altar; and every pot in Jerusalem and Judah shall be sacred to the Lord of hosts, so that all who sacrifice may come and take of them and boil the flesh of the sacrifice in them. And there shall no longer be a trader in the house of the Lord of hosts on that day. (Zech. 14:20–21)

Here is a vision that accords well with a theme of early Yahwism (e.g., Exod. 19:5–6). And in Numbers 14:21 we can recognize even a further extension of the eschatological vision in the phrase "as the earth shall be filled with the glory of the Lord."

The circles that guided the further development of the Priestly writing, however, did not foster the eschatological dimension of priestly traditon, but rather placed the emphasis elsewhere, namely, on the definitive nature of the *tôrâ* and the order of salvation ordained by God on Sinai. The facet of priestly tradition accentuated in this further development was its regulation of the priestly offices of the cult. With consistency and solemn divine authority, P ordained the strict division between priests (e.g., the Aaronides) and Levites. This division was basic to its entire sacral structure.[10] In the background of this move, of

---

9. Cf. N. Lohfink, "Die Priesterschrift und Geschichte," VTSupl 29 (1978), 224–225. Contrast R. W. Klein, "The Message of P," in *Die Botschaft und die Boten: Festschrift für Hans Walter Wolff* (Neukirchen-Vluyn: Neukirchener Verlag, 1981), pp. 57–66.

10. E.g., Leviticus 8–9.

course, lay a long and embattled history, tracing back to Solomon's exclusion of the Mushites in favor of the Zadokites, and culminating in Josiah's centralization of the cult in Jerusalem, which had the consequences of leaving the majority of Levites without a professional position. Traces of the bitter struggles that occurred between the priestly families are found in many parts of the Bible.[11] They are very visible in the priestly tradition of which P itself is a product. For example, the earliest literary stratum of Leviticus 1:1–17 referred to the person conducting the atoning sacrifice with the broad title "the priest" (hakkōhēn) (vv. 9, 12, 13). The second discernible stratum narrowed the description to the specific title, "the sons of Aaron" (benê 'ahārōn), which in turn led to the pluralization of "priest" to "priests" (vv. 5, 8, 11). Karl Elliger has correctly observed behind these alternations specific priestly interests. That is, we can discern here the effort of the Aaronides to reserve for themselves, to the exclusion of the broader circle of the descendants of Levi, the right of performing the sacrifice.[12]

The excluded Levites, for their part, responded with a vehemence expected on an excluded and threatened party by calling into question the entire priestly program.[13] Ezekiel 44, which is a supplement to the Ezekiel program of restoration, includes a scathing attack on the Levites, and serves as an indication of the bitterness of the controversy that issued forth from the theological program of P, primarily because of its position on the division of the priesthood into major and minor clergy.[14] Quite naturally, the priestly party excluded by the Aaronide and Zadokite priestly program moved increasingly toward an eschatological vision of the future, which in turn influenced those inheriting the program of P to neglect the implicit eschatological dimension in favor of an interpretation of God's revelatory activity as already completely fulfilled in the sacral structures over which they presided. Since this tendency, while not absent in the original P, was carried to the extremes just mentioned only in the period of the return from exile, I shall return to it at a later time.

Here I conclude by simply observing that the theology of P itself was a dynamic and penetrating response to the crisis of exile. It addressed the previous problem of sin and guilt honestly, drew together resources from previous cult tradition, and brought them together into a powerful new synthesis of theological understanding and practical application. A detailed sacrificial system was worked out that neglected no

11. Cf. F. M. Cross, *Canaanite Myth and Hebrew Epic* (CMHE) (Cambridge, Mass.: Harvard University Press, 1973), pp. 198–205.

12. K. Elliger, *Leviticus*, HAT 4 (Tübingen: J.C.B. Mohr [Paul Siebeck], 1966).

13. P. D. Hanson, *The Dawn of Apocalyptic*, 2d ed., (Philadelphia: Fortress Press, 1979), pp. 95–96, 220–240.

14. See W. Zimmerli, *Ezekiel 2*, trans. J. D. Martin (Philadelphia: Fortress Press, 1983), pp. 452–464; and P. D. Hanson, ibid., pp. 264–267.

area of life in assuring that the state of communal sanctity that assured Yahweh's blessing was maintained. And in spite of the emphasis on ritual and sacrifice, the Priestly theology did not overlook the deeper dimensions of human experience, dimensions without which the forms of worship could only remain ineffectual, especially the dimension of repentance and confession that must underlie every authentic cultic act (e.g., Lev. 5:5–6, Num. 5:6–7, 15:30–31). P was, moreover, a worthy heir to the high ethical ideals of early Yahwism and prophecy, capable of summarizing the laws of the *tôrâ* relating to fellow humans with the classic formulation "you shall love your neighbor as yourself" (Lev. 19:18). As we shall later observe, however, this profound theological response was soon adapted to serve in a bitter polemic, with the result that its strong points were blunted, and its weaknesses accentuated. Chief among such weaknesses were the Priestly Writing's emphasis on the definiteness of its program and the accompanying strict division of priestly orders into *clerus major* and *clerus minor*, a division exploited by later Zadokites in their strife with the broader circle of the Levites.

D. SECOND ISAIAH

Perhaps the most remarkable response to arise out of the desolation of exile was the one we designate "Second Isaiah" (Isaiah 40–55). It was inspired by a vision of events transpiring in heaven that were soon to bring about a remarkable transformation on the earth (40:1–11). From this starting point, it proceeded to draw important links between heavenly deliberations and mundane realities. For example, it identified the great conqueror of empires, Cyrus "the Mede," as God's anointed agent in carrying out the divine plan (44:24 through 45:7). And it went on to portray "the Servant of Yahweh"—a figure who, though defying precise identification, was surely an historical entity—as another agent charged with bringing God's justice to the nations and atoning for the sins of God's people (42:1–4; 49:1–6; 50:4–9; 52:13–53:12).

The historical presupposition of Second Isaiah was the same as that of Jeremiah, Ezekiel, and the Priestly Writer. Israel, punished for rebellion against God and for persistence in sin, had been reduced to the nadir point of its existence. Yet this deplorable state of affairs did not prove God's impotence vis-á-vis the gods of the Babylonian conquerors, but derived from God's righteousness. For this God applied one standard to all nations, according partiality to none:

> The Lord was pleased, for his righteousness' sake,
>   to magnify his law and make it glorious.
> but this is a people robbed and plundered,
>   they are all of them trapped in holes and hidden in prisons;
> they have become a prey with none to rescue,

> a spoil with none to say, "Restore!"
> Who among you will give ear to this,
>   will attend and listen for the time to come?
> Who gave up Jacob to the spoiler, and Israel to the Robbers?
> Was it not the Lord, against whom we have sinned,
>   in whose ways they would not walk,
>   and whose law they would not obey?
> So he poured upon him the heat of his anger
>   and the might of battle;
> it set him on fire round about, but he did not understand;
>   it burned him, but he did not take it to heart.   (Isa. 42:21–25)

Israel had been reduced to ashes. There was thus no longer a human basis for constructing hopes of restoration:

> Rouse yourself, rouse yourself,
>   stand up, O Jerusalem,
> you who have drunk at the hand of the Lord
>   the cup of his wrath,
> who have drunk to the dregs
>   the bowl of staggering.
> There is none to guide her
>   among all the sons she has born;
> there is none to take her by the hand
>   among the sons she has brought up.
> These two things have befallen you—
>   who will condole with you—
> devastation and destruction, famine and sword;
>   who will comfort you?
> Your sons have fainted,
>   they lie at the head of every street
>   like an antelope in a net;
> they are full of the wrath of the Lord,
>   the rebuke of your God. (Isa. 51:17–20)

Holy War, once fought by Yahweh to deliver an oppressed clan of Hebrews, had been turned against a people grown fat in its wantonness and neglectful of divine *tôrâ*. The Babylonians had been appointed agents of Yahweh's wrath: "I was angry with my people, I profaned my heritage; I gave them into your hand" (47:6a). As in the confessions comprising the Book of Lamentations, we find here the acknowledgement of the righteousness of God, which had come to expression in a national calamity.

Precisely at the point where all human pride had been broken, a remnant emerged that turned away from idols to the only true source of hope. Devastation and destruction, famine and sword, were accounted by the heavenly judge as having effected their intended purpose. The prophet was called to listen in on the divine assembly at the important moment when Yahweh charged the heavenly heralds with a new message:

> Comfort, comfort my people,
>   says your God.
> Speak tenderly to Jerusalem,
>   and cry to her
> that her warfare is ended,
>   that her iniquity is pardoned,
> that she has received from the Lord's hand
>   double for all her sins. (Isa. 40:1–2)

Israel's history had reached a decisive turning point. The era of punishment for sin was ended. A new era of salvation was about to begin. This was to be solely Yahweh's doing. For Yahweh was about to return to his people to deliver them from their bondage, to lead them back to Zion, and to rebuild Jerusalem. This happening was announced in dramatic form to the prophet in the divine council: "A voice cries: 'In the wilderness prepare the way of the Lord, make straight in the desert a highway for our God' " (40:3). And that same voice declared that the ultimate goal underlying this miraculous event was the manifestation of the Lord's sovereignty to all the earth: "And the glory of the Lord shall be revealed, and all flesh shall see it together, for the mouth of the Lord has spoken" (40:5).

The prophet's confidence in the truthfulness of his message rested on a profound understanding of the majesty, righteousness, and compassion of Yahweh, which since the time of early Yahwism had formed the substantive basis of the community of faith. In considering how the understanding of these three qualities continued to grow in Second Isaiah's message, we observe first how the sovereign majesty of Yahweh was described through the use of daring metaphors highlighting the unequaled glory of this unique God (cf. 40:12–31; 42:8; 48:11):

> Have you not known? Have you not heard?
>   Has it not been told you from the beginning?
> Have you not understood from the
>   foundations of the earth?
> It is he who sits above the circle of the earth,
>   and its inhabitants are like grasshoppers;
> who stretches out the heavens like a curtain,
>   and spreads them like a tent to dwell in;
> who brings princes to nought,
>   and makes the rulers of the earth as nothing. (Isa. 40:21–23)

Within the context of this universal vision of Yahweh's plan for history Second Isaiah explained the significance of the most imposing historical figure of that day, Cyrus. After a long history of Davidic "messiahs" (that is "anointed kings") who had neglected their duty and misused their power, Yahweh in his freedom had elected a pagan as his messiah (māšiaḥ, "anointed"): "He is my shepherd, and he shall fulfill all my purpose" (44:28a). The appointment of this Persian as Yahweh's instrument in the deliverance of the faithful nullified all narrow concepts of a nationalistic proprietorship over divine presence and activity. Yahweh was not bound to any human family, not even the house of David, in bringing about his purpose: "For the sake of my servant Jacob, and Israel my chosen, I call you by your name, I surname you, though you do not know me" (45:3). In the broad panorama of world history, Second Isaiah observed Cyrus's overthrow of the ruthless power of the Babylonians, his release of captive peoples, and his rebuilding of destroyed cities and sanctuaries, and from the perspective of his daring faith in the one true God Yahweh, he confidently announced: "This is all according to divine plan":

> "I have aroused him in righteousness,
>   and I will make straight all his ways;
> he shall build my city
>   and set my exiles free,
> not for price of reward,"
>   says the Lord of hosts. (Isa. 45:13)

The good news Second Isaiah was commissioned to bring to the exilic community reached out to a people that had exhausted all human resources. Indeed, its human brokenness proved to be an essential preparation for its hearing the prophetic word. For only a people acquainted with defeat and broken of pride could respond to the invitation: "Ho, every one who thirsts, come to the waters; and he who has no money, come, buy and eat! Come buy wine and milk without money and without price" (55:1). Only those prepared to denounce human devices and to open themselves up to divine grace were able to receive the advent of the God who came to save the poor and needy:

> When the poor and needy seek water,
>   and there is none,
>   and their tongue is parched with thirst,
> I the Lord will answer them,
>   I the God of Israel will not forsake them. (Isa. 41:17)

Only the breaking of human pride could enable a people to give up the clever theological systems of the past and admit their need for a radically new answer, one that the one true God alone could bring:

> I will open rivers on the bare heights,
>   and fountains in the midst of the valleys;
> I will make the wilderness a pool of water,
>   and the dry land springs of water.
> I will put in the wilderness the cedar,
>   the acacia, the myrtle, and the olive;
> I will set in the desert the cypress,
>   the plane and the pine together. (Isa. 41:18–19)

The pedagogy of brokenness earlier taught by Hosea thus found a new application in the mission of Second Isaiah. Patching up old structures was no longer possible. The decay had penetrated too deeply. Only a return to the wilderness, and a yearning for a new beginning with God offered hope to a broken nation. Second Isaiah was thus Yahweh's herald of a second exodus, a second chance, a new beginning (42:13–16; cf. 43:1–7):

> The Lord goes forth like a mighty man,
>   like a man of war he stirs up his fury;
> he cries out, he shouts aloud,
>   he shows himself mighty against his foes.
> For a long time I have held my peace,
>   I have kept still and restrained myself;
> now I will cry out like a woman in travail,
>   I will gasp and pant.
> I will lay waste mountains and hills,
>   and dry up all their herbage;
> I will turn the rivers into islands,
>   and dry up the pools.
> And I will lead the blind
>   in a way that they know not,
> in paths that they have not known
>   I will guide them.
> I will turn the darkness before them into light,
>   the rough places into level ground.
> These are the things I will do,
>   and I will not forsake them.

Out of the darkness of the exile there thus arose a brilliant message of deliverance, and of the recreation of a community owing its existence solely to divine grace. At the pinnacle of Second Isaiah's notion of community stood therefore a clear conception of the sole sovereignty of Yahweh, the incomparable God (40:25; 44:6–8) before whom all other gods were confounded (41:21–29; 45:20–25; 46:1–7). This of course was the identical starting point as used by earliest Yahwism. And as the hymnic style of Isaiah 40–55 indicates, the response of the exilic community was also identical to that of the community of the exodus, a response of worship and praise (51:9–11). It was by responding to Yahweh's saving acts in worship and by acknowledging its source solely in divine grace that this people became God's people. Its primal quality was therefore worship of the one true God, a quality that, due to Second Isaiah's universal vision, extended to the entire created order:

> Sing to the Lord a new song,
>   his praise from the end of the earth!
> Let the sea roar and all that fill it
>   the coastlands and their inhabitants.
> Let the desert and its cities lift up their voice,
>   the villages that Kedar inhabits;
> let the inhabitants of Sela sing for joy,

> let them shout from the top of the mountains.
> Let them give glory to the Lord,
>   and declare his praise in the coastlands.
> The Lord goes forth like a mighty man,
>   like a man of war he stirs up his fury,
> he cries out, he shouts aloud,
>   he shows himself mighty against his foes. (Isa. 42:10–13)

> Sing, O heavens, for the Lord has done it;
>   shout, O depths of the earth;
> break forth into singing, O mountains,
>   O forest, and every tree in it!
> For the Lord has redeemed Jacob,
>   and will be glorified in Israel. (Isa. 44:23)

> Sing for joy, O heavens, and exult, O earth;
>   break forth, O mountains, into singing!
> For the Lord has comforted his people,
>   and will have compassion on his afflicted. (Isa. 49:13)

In comparing the community of faithful of the exilic period to the community of the "first exodus" we thus discern a similarity of theme, style, and function between Exodus 15 and Isaiah 40–55. For a more complete picture of Second Isaiah's notion of community, we would also like to find materials corresponding to Exodus 19:3–8, 24:3–8, and 20:21 through 23:19—that is, materials preserving the forms of worship and structures of community of the exilic community after its reentry into the land. Unfortunately, materials corresponding to these were not preserved by the community of the "second exodus." The closest we come to such are found in Isaiah 60–62. But the ethereal quality of these chapters suggests that the followers of Second Isaiah were not successful in inferring from their experience of divine deliverance appropriate forms of worship and community. The concrete aspects of community building were taken up instead by another group, namely, those dedicated to the Zadokite program of restoration based on Ezekiel 40–48. The experience of deliverance in Second Isaiah and the community of faith implied by the nature of the divine Deliverer thus remain inchoate. Forms of worship and communal structures do not emerge as they had in the wake of the exodus from Egypt. We must be satisfied with indications of underlying theological principles and with hints concerning the communal forms they implied.

Nevertheless, it is clear that on a fundamental level the primal confession of Yahweh's sole sovereignty and the people's response in worship were wedded in Second Isaiah's proclamation to the other two essential qualities of Yahwistic community, namely, righteousness and compassion. Both in his punishment of his own people for their sin (Isa. 42:18–25; 43:22–28) and in his mighty intervention on the side of the afflicted against their Babylonian oppressors (47:1–15; 51:4–8, and

17–23), Yahweh had acted according to the standard of divine righteousness. From this we can be confident that, had their situation provided the opportunity, the community of the second exodus would have inferred from its experience of Yahweh's deliverance communal structures in harmony with the standard of righteousness found at the center of the Book of the Covenant, the Decalogue, and Deuteronomy. Indeed, as discussed later, the Servant Songs reflect a deepened insight into divine righteousness that no doubt had come to prophet and community through their growth in understanding the nature of the God who had heard their cry in a far-off land.

It is equally clear that the quality of divine righteousness was wedded in Second Isaiah to a profound insight into divine compassion. A people, having experienced the most devastating of human experiences, was able to face the future with hope and confidence because they were lifted from their brokenness by a God whose boundless compassion expressed itself in complete forgiveness and unconditional acceptance. We are reminded of Hosea's intimate acquaintance with the heart of God when we hear Yahweh's words to his people in Second Isaiah: "you are precious in my eyes, and honored, and I love you" (43:4a); "Can a woman forget her suckling child, that she should have no compassion on the son of her womb? Even these may forget, yet I will not forget you" (49:15). And even as this latter passage is reminiscent of Hosea 11, the following recalls the marriage metaphor of Hosea 1–3:

> For your Maker is your husband,
>   the Lord of hosts is his name;
> and the Holy One of Israel is your Redeemer,
>   the God of the whole earth he is called.
> For the Lord has called you
>   like a wife forsaken and grieved in spirit,
> like a wife of youth when she is cast off,
>   says your God.
> For a brief moment I forsook you,
>   but with great compassion I will gather you.
> In overflowing wrath for a moment
>   I hid my face from you,
> but with everlasting love I will have compassion on you,
>   says the Lord, your Redeemer.   (Isa. 54:5–8)

Moreover, 40:10–11 illustrates clearly how Yahweh's majesty, righteousness, and compassion are inextricably interwoven in his saving activity:

> Behold, the Lord God comes with might,
>   and his arm rules for him;
> behold, his reward is with him,
>   and his recompense before him.
> He will feed his flock like a shepherd,

> he will gather the lambs in his arms,
> he will carry them in his bosom,
> and gently lead those that are with young. (Isa. 40:10–11)

With roots in the classic Yahwistic vision of the righteous and compassionate God of all peoples, a dynamic and universal notion of community came to expression in Second Isaiah that was both a culminating point of Yahwistic faith and an adumbration of the vision of the eschatological kingdom in the kerygma of Jesus. Thus an ancient pattern of redemption received a profound reformulation, according to which human sin and brokenness were answered by divine righteousness and compassion, issuing forth in forgiveness and deliverance and evoking a response of praise in human hearts filled to overflowing with God's love.

The inextricable bond between Yahweh's antecedent grace and the compassionate response of the people is seen in 49:7–12 (a prophetic word of Second Isaiah addressed to Israel and later attached to the Second Servant Song).[15] To a despised and broken nation, Yahweh, in "a time of favor," in "a day of salvation," came to deliver and to sustain. But deliverance was not an end in itself. The redeemed themselves were to be drawn into the salvation drama, given by God as "a covenant to the people," that is, as an agency of mediation between God and the people. The two prepositional phrases that follow and the longer clause in verse 9a describe important tasks in that mediation. What was involved was the restoration of the righteous community established by Yahweh after the exodus. The family inheritances (nĕḥālôt), which had been decimated by the unjust practices of the powerful, were to be reapportioned. The imprisoned were to be released. Clearly, the expressions "time of favor" and the "day of salvation" were intended to call to mind the Jubilee Year, the time of God's restoring the conditions of righteousness that constituted the šālôm intended by God for all people (cf. 42:6–7). After the exilic community had been given this lesson regarding their role in Yahweh's drama, their attention was directed toward a description of God's ongoing sustenance of his people in language reminiscent of the exodus from Egypt (49:9b–12). Like the original community of redeemed slaves, the exilic community was to realize that it was embraced by divine grace. Preceding and following its own participation in God's drama was the ever present, all-sufficient grace of the righteous, compassionate Deliverer. It is most fitting that this confession issued forth in joyous praise (v. 13).

The role of mediation described in Isaiah 49:7–12, to which the redeemed of Israel were called, is a central theme also in the so-called Servant Songs (42:1–4; 49:1–6; 50:4–9; and 52:13–53:12). Indeed the

---

15. Cf. C. Westermann, *Isaiah 40–66*, trans. D. M. G. Stalker (London: SCM Press, 1969), pp. 212–216.

path toward the kingdom in which righteousness and compassion would be united in worship of the one true God was blazed in Second Isaiah, especially by the mysterious, intriguing figure of the Servant of Yahweh.

The much debated question regarding the identity of the Servant in Second Isaiah will not be taken up here.[16] Already in the Isaianic text itself one finds the polyvalence that is a natural part of every profound symbol. The Servant, though named Israel, nevertheless had a mission to Israel, and, though suffering vicariously for Israel, at the same was given by Yahweh as a light to the nations. In the subsequent history of interpretation, which cannot be overlooked in considering the reality portrayed by the Servant image, the symbol was enriched further: The Servant was interpreted as the righteous remnant in Third Isaiah (56–66), the martyr of a persecuted community in Second Zechariah (12:10), and Jesus of Nazareth in the Gospels. This polyvalence was fully in keeping with Yahwistic faith, according to which God was involved and present in the events of history in the form of human agents; that is, servants responding to the divine summons to become a part of the divine struggle for the hearts of humans. The Servant Songs give powerful expression to Second Isaiah's understanding of how God was present in history. This becomes clear when his message is contrasted with the earlier royal theology of Jerusalem, according to which God was represented on earth by glorious and powerful Davidic kings. According to Second Isaiah, God's entry into history occurred not through the agency of a dazzling king, but through that of a despised and suffering Servant. The new faithful community was to be constituted not through force, but through the depths of divine compassion encountered in obedience unto death. True, in overthrowing the bonds of Babylonian oppression, Yahweh had engaged the warrior Cyrus. Subsequently, however, with the stage set for Yahweh's salvation to reach outward, the agent was to be the patient, faithful Servant, who would neither break the "bruised reed" nor extinguish the "dimly burning wick" in bringing justice to the nations.

The Servant Songs contribute a dimension of meaning that profoundly affects the whole message of Second Isaiah. They stand guard against every attempt to interpret the message of salvation proclaimed by this prophet of the exile along narrow triumphalistic, nationalistic lines. Here was a message of salvation, to be sure, but it was salvation affected at a profound cost, the cost of innocent suffering. And it was a salvation not intended to culminate in personal or national pride, but in obedient service of the only One deserving of praise (48:11).

The motifs, allusions, and traditions applied by Second Isaiah in his

16. Cf. C. R. North, *The Suffering Servant in Deutero-Isaiah* (Oxford: Oxford University Press, 1948), and T. N. D. Mettinger, *A Farewell to the Servant Songs: A Critical Examination of an Exegetical Axiom* (Lund: Gleerup, 1982), pp. 43–46.

portrait of the Servant were not chosen haphazardly, but through careful reflection. Elements were drawn from the offices of charismatic judge (*šôpēṭ*), king and prophet, as well as from the language of the sacrificial cult, and were combined into a portrait of a new eschatological office through which Yahweh would call forth a faithful people and inaugurate a new era of *šālôm* for the entire human family. As Yahweh had commissioned and used other human instruments in former epochs, in the new age the Servant was being called as the instrument in a wonderful new plan of the heavenly Sovereign.

Lines of connection with Israel's earlier offices were carefully drawn in the description of the Servant. In the terms "servant" and "chosen," royal connotations were evoked. Like the judges, prophets, and kings, the Servant was clothed by Yahweh's "spirit." Like Jeremiah, he was called while yet in his mother's womb. We sense that, according to the eternal plan of Yahweh glimpsed by Second Isaiah, all those earlier offices had served to prepare the way for this one.[17] This sense of culmination is strengthened by the description of the Servant's mission. Like his predecessors, he was charged with caring for and restoring Jacob and Israel (49:5), but in keeping with the radical newness of Yahweh's immanent saving act, the horizon of the Servant's mission was vastly extended: "I will give you as a light to the nations, that my salvation may reach to the end of the earth" (49:6). Attempts to deny a universal vision in the message of Second Isaiah simply cannot do justice to the second Servant Song found in 49:1–6, for the entire composition, beginning with an address to the "coastlands" and "peoples from afar," and culminating with the verses quoted earlier, announced the extension of Yahweh's saving activity to all peoples through the office of the Servant.[18] Moreover, the first Servant Song in 42:1–4 contributed significantly to this theme of universal mission. In its background stood Yahweh's claim to sole sovereignty over all the earth, a theme coming to expression especially in the disputations with foreign gods (cf. 41:1–16; 21–24; 43:11–14; 44:6–8; 45:20–25; 46:8–11): "turn to me and be saved, all the ends of the earth! For I am God, and there is no other" (46:22). Through the mission of the Servant, Yahweh's sovereignty was to be extended over the nations. How this would take place was described in terms of his bringing forth justice to the nations, establishing

---

17. Cf. G. von Rad, *Old Testament Theology*, vol. 2, trans. D. M. G. Stalker (New York: Harper & Row, 1965), pp. 258–262.

18. Cf. N. H. Smith and H. M. Orlinsky, *Studies on the Second Part of the Book of Isaiah.* VTSupl 14 (Leiden: Brill, 1967), and H. M. Orlinsky, *The So-Called "Suffering Servant" in Isaiah 53* (Cincinnati: Hebrew Union College Press, 1964). The denial of a universal dimension in Second Isaiah's proclamation is commonly based on a failure to recognize the roots of aspects of that proclamation in royal Jerusalemite traditions, traditions that in turn draw on ancient royal-mythic themes (cf. Andrew Wilson, "The Nations in Deutero-Isaiah: A Study on Composition and Structure," doctoral thesis, Department of Near Eastern Languages and Civilization, Harvard University).

justice in the earth, as the coastlands waited for his law, a theme found also in 51:4:

> Listen to me, my people,
>   and give ear to me my nation:
> for a law will go forth from me,
>   and my justice for a light to the peoples.

Justice (*mišpāṭ*) and law (*tôrâ*) in this passage recalled the righteous order of life which Yahweh had revealed to the covenant community in the Book of the Covenant, the Decalogue, Deuteronomy, and the message of the prophets. In Israel Yahweh had disclosed an order wedding righteousness and compassion, which was now to become the basis for *šālôm* not only in Israel, but among all the nations of the earth. As Israel formerly had been given faith to recognize in its deliverance from slavery the divine basis for a righteous communal order, in the even more glorious act of salvation that Yahweh was about to inaugurate, this order was to be extended to the ends of the earth. This would take place through the office of the Servant—which is to say, not in the manner of mighty conquerors who forcefully impose their laws on subjugated peoples, but meekly and quietly, and with gentle regard for the fragile and the weak (42:2-3). This mission would succeed, moreover, because the nations, like the Hebrews in Egypt, "wait for his law;" that is, would themselves be aware of their need for deliverance and divine assistance. The addition to the first Servant Song found in 42:5-9 therefore appropriately interpreted this mission of the Servant as an extension of the Jubilee to the nations, as Yahweh's covenant extended itself along universal lines that already had been anticipated in the Abrahamic covenant:

> I am the Lord, I have called you in righteousness,
>   I have taken you by the hand and kept you;
> I have given you as a covenant to the people,
>   a light to the nations,
>   to open the eyes that are blind,
> to bring out the prisoners from the dungeon,
>   from the prison those who sit in darkness.   (Isa. 42:6-7)

It is difficult to grasp the magnitude of the change in Israel's vocation implied in the transition from being "my servant to raise up the tribes of Jacob and to restore the preserved of Israel" to becoming "a light to the nations, that my salvation may reach to the end of the earth" (49:6). Such a move was made possible only as the historical consequence of a vastly enlarged vision of Yahweh's majesty, such as we have already noted in 40:22-23.

As remarkable as was this extension of the vision of the Yahwistic community to encompass a plan of peace for the whole earth, it does not yet exhaust the contents of the Servant Songs. For this breadth is matched by a probing of some of the depth dimensions of community life. This probing can be seen in the latter two Servant Songs, 50:4–9 and especially 52:13 to 53:12. The breadth of the Servant's mission having been charted, the discourse has returned to the subject of Israel itself. The brilliant announcement of the return of Yahweh and the resulting restoration of the people seemed to require a further interpretation, one invoking a far more somber, even tragic tone. How this occurred within the career of Second Isaiah is enshrouded in as much mystery as the figure of the Servant itself. After the first exuberant phase of Second Isaiah's ministry, conducted in the light of Cyrus's dazzling conquests, the prophet probably was led by personal suffering and disappointment to see that much of Israel itself continued to resist Yahweh's invitation, and that the path to redemption would involve rejection, abuse, even death for the faithful Servant. But the result was a deeper understanding of community, as rejection and tragedy led to a far more penetrating insight into the enigma of sin, begetting in turn a shockingly new understanding of the way of redemption as the way of vicarious suffering.

It seems as though Second Isaiah himself had not realized the utter novelty of God's "new thing" he had been called to announce until he saw the mysterious lure of divine grace in the Suffering Servant. More conventional forms of address and modes of leadership had been incapable of bringing back a stubborn and wayward people, had been unable to reconcile Israel—not to mention the nations—with the one true God.

The theme of innocent, obedient suffering is presented in the personal testimony of the Servant in 50:4–8: "I gave my back to the smiters, and my cheeks to those who pulled out the bread; I hid not my face from shame and spitting" (50:6). Here it is combined with the confidence that even in suffering "the Lord God helps me; therefore I have not been confounded" (50:7a). It is in the fourth Servant Song, however, that the theological meaning of that suffering comes to most vivid expression.

The fourth Song is introduced by a word of Yahweh preparing the audience for a divine act of such novelty as to evoke disbelief: "As many were astonished at him—his appearance was so marred, beyond human semblance, and his form beyond that of the sons of man" (Isa. 52:14). Those expecting the advent of Yahweh in a manner inoffensive, undisturbing, and fully in keeping with existing conventions were thus warned of a shocking surprise. The light of Israelite faith and God's justice and *tôrâ* would not be carried to the nations by the fair sons of David, but by this disfigured one: "So shall he startle many nations; kings shall shut their mouths because of him" (52:15a). Accordingly Yahweh served notice that the world was to prepare itself for a chapter in human history for which prior experience was inadequate preparation: "for that which has not been told them they shall see, and that which they have not heard they shall understand" (52:15b).

To this introductory word of God, which has the effect of placing this Servant Song in an international setting, we find the community giving its response. This new act of God, this Servant who had come to them, evokes a sense of astonishment and wonder: "Who has believed what we have heard? And to whom has the arm of the Lord been revealed?" (Isa. 53:1).

The reason for this profound surprise is described vividly:

> For he grew up before him like a young plant,
>   and like a root out of dry ground;
> he had no form or comeliness that we should look at him,
>   and no beauty that we should desire him.
> He was despised and rejected by men;
>   a man of sorrows and acquainted with grief;
> and as one from whom men hide their faces
>   he was despised, and we esteemed him not. (Isa. 53:2–3)

What sort of person was being described with these shocking images? Within popular Hebrew thought, it could only have been one cursed by God, for the righteous were believed to enjoy divine favor in the form of health and prosperity. As observed by Job's friends, one suffering so grievously had to be living under God's curse. Otherwise how could he be removed so utterly from the orbit of divine šālôm?

But the startling news penetrates even more deeply, coming in a staccato series embodying a haunting he/we contrast that strikes at popular religious conventions until they lie like the frangments of Dagon's image scattered on the temple threshold:

> Surely he has borne our griefs
>   and carried our sorrows;
> yet we esteemed him stricken,
>   smitten by God and afflicted.
> But he was wounded for our transgressions,
>   he was bruised for our iniquities;
> upon him was the chastisement that made us whole,
>   and with his stripes we are healed. (Isa. 53:4–5)

Here was not a normal sinner, bearing in his flesh the just desserts of sin. "*He* was wounded for *our* transgressions!" That is, the community found itself gazing on one who suffered for others, for *them*. In fact, through his grievous punishment came their healing! And most startling of all was the recognition that this was the Lord's doing: "All we like sheep have gone astray; we have turned every one to his own way; and the Lord has laid on him the iniquity of us all" (Isa. 53:6).

Faced with a nation hopelessly lost in its own stubborn rejection of God, God had chosen the unprecedented course of bringing back the lost through the innocent suffering of God's Servant. The vicarious nature of that suffering was explicated through the image of the sacrificial lamb (v. 7), and by explicit reference to his being "stricken for the transgression of my people . . . although he had done no violence, and there was no deceit in this mouth" (vv. 8–10).

Verse 10a combines the language of cult sacrifice with theological interpretation.[19] A minor emendation restores what seems to be the intended meaning (compare RSV): "But the Lord was pleased with his bruised one, he has *restored the one* giving himself as a sin offering."

The Servant, living from the knowledge of God's new struggle for the hearts of his people, had devoted himself completely to the purpose of God. In the suffering that followed on this surrender, human dedication and divine will were united, and the fellowship between God and human that had been the divine intention from the very beginning found fulfillment. The resulting death of the Servant did not signal the end of that fellowship, but only a new beginning, for occurring within the context of oneness between human and divine will, death itself was drawn into the fulfillment of divine purpose. A verb used to designate divine acceptance of cultic sacrifice (*ḥpṣ*) was used to express God's approval of the Servant's self-sacrifice, an approval manifested in his restoring the Servant, and, as verses 10b–12 indicate, blessing him with *šālôm*. The profound significance of this theological interpretation can be explained by referring at this point to the prophetic and priestly thought on sacrifice that developed during the periods of the divided monarchy and the exile.

In Hosea 6:6 and Isaiah 1:11 (cf. Mal. 1:10), the same verb found in Isaiah 53:10 (*ḥpṣ*) was used with the negative participle to express Yahweh's rejection of the sacrifices of the Israelite cult. This entailed not a rejection of sacrificial practice as such, but rather of the delusion that sacrifice could be used by a corrupt people, against whom Yahweh through his prophets had proclaimed holy war, to avert divine wrath. But to Second Isaiah a totally different situation had been revealed by God: God's warfare against this people had ended. God was turning to Israel with favor. But even now reconciliation was not a trifling matter. Here the profound reflection on the nature of sacrifice and atonement found in the Priestly Writing should be called to mind.

The exilic period was one deeply conscious of the magnitude of human sin. And according to P, Yahweh alone could provide a means of atonement. This occurred when the one bringing the sacrificial animal, by laying his hands on the head of the animal, identified himself with the sacrifice and thereby confessed dedication to God unto death. We have seen that the blood, furnished by God, and sprinkled before the

---

19. Cf. E. Haag, "Das Opfer des Gottesknechts (Jes. 53:10)," *Trierer Theologische Zeitschrift* 86 (1977), 81–98.

altar, conveyed this same dedication. To this sacrificial act, God responded by accepting the animal in place of the sinner, thereby breaking the chain of sin and death, and renewing a life-giving relationship between God and human. It is also important to recall that once a year, on the great Day of Atonement, the high priest in like manner made atonement for the whole people.

In this sacrificial theology, we find the background of the notion developed in Isaiah 53:10. In "the time of favor," the "day of salvation,"—that is, the day marking the cessation of Yahweh's warfare against this people—genuine sacrifice was again possible, sacrifice through which God provided the means of renewed fellowship with humans. In contemplating the meaning of the tragic suffering of the Servant, Second Isaiah deepened the notion of atonement sacrifice found in the Priestly theology.[20] In his obedience unto death, the Servant was recognized as having given himself as a sin offering ('āšām). But on an even deeper level, this was grasped as an act of divine compassion, for Yahweh accepted with favor (ḥpṣ) this sacrifice, and regarded it as atoning for the sins of the people. A more profound basis for understanding community was thus established. The righteousness enabling a people to live in fellowship with God had eluded humans bound to sin. But now God had taken the initiative of making a reality of the righteousness that was basic to the covenant community. A sacrifice had been provided by God, "and with his stripes we are healed." Stated in another idiom, "by his knowledge (that is, by the understanding revealed to him by God of God's new saving initiative) shall the righteous one, my servant, make many to be accounted righteous" (v. 11b). As observed by F. Crusemann, we have here the first clear insistence of the theological concept of justification in the Old Testament.[21] In the mystery of the Suffering Servant, Second Isaiah discerned Yahweh at work in a manner true to this new initiative both to save Israel, and through their redemption to bring the order of righteousness of which Israel was Yahweh's historical vehicle to all the nations of the earth.

In the message of Second Isaiah, we thus see evidence of a significant

---

20. R. T. Thompson correctly recognized the profound effect of the synthesis of priestly and prophetic perspectives in Second Isaiah's portrayal of the Servant: "While not accepting the view, on the one hand, that the efficacy of sacrifice was limited to inadvertent sins, which were no real sins at all, or, on the other, that the prophets and pious psalmists saw no value in sacrifice whatsoever, it remains true that the cult was liable to abuse, when the inward tie between worshipper and means of worship was loosed, and prophetic religion became necessary to emphasize the priority of a personal relation to God. It is no accident, however, that when priestly and prophetic religion meet in the figure of the Servant of the Lord in Isaiah 53, the highest point of Old Testament religion is reached, as all that is valuable in cult is taken up into a person, who makes a sacrificial atonement and calls for the love and personal allegiance of the human heart." *The New Bible Dictionary*, ed. J. D. Douglas (Grand Rapids, Mich.: Eerdmans, 1962), p. 1122a.

21. F. Crusemann, "Jahwes Gerechtigkeit im Alten Testament," *EvTh* 36 (1976), 427–450.

broadening and deepening of the Yahwistic notion of community. The horizon of Israel's mission as Yahweh's servant people was widened to embrace all the families of the earth. And out of trial and suffering had grown a more radical awareness of the depths of sin and of the incorrigibility of the human heart, which resisted every facile notion of fellowship with God and impelled the faithful to search for a deeper grounding for its understanding of the covenant community. People did not just grow by natural process into this community. Nor did it occur as an inevitable aspect of being children of Abraham. Simple formulas based on systems of merit were likewise inadequate. Rather, membership in the people of God was seen to involve the deep mystery of God's acting for the healing of Israel and the world in one who was suffering the fate of the accursed, one who was taking on himself this suffering by assuming the iniquities of his people. This one was approved in his self-surrender by a righteous and compassionate God who graciously extended the healing of the Servant to those confessing their bondage to sin and accepting purely as a gift of divine compassion the righteousness without which fellowship with God was impossible. Living out of the knowledge of this new entry of God into the community of humans, and devoting himself totally to God's purpose, the Servant, in his life, death and exaltation became God's instrument of atonement for the people. Thus a new side of the majesty of the one true sovereign God entered into the consciousness of the faithful of Israel: here the mighty Creator, capable of stretching out the heavens and establishing the earth, or causing them to vanish in an instant, entered into intimate fellowship with humans to win back their hearts not in a dazzling display of power, but in quiet, patient suffering. In the Servant of Yahweh, the community of faith came face to face with the righteousness and compassion of the one true God in a mystery so profound that centuries would be required to grasp the implications of this new act of God for the life of a people seeking to pattern its existence on the example of the God manifested in human experience as the God active to save the lost and to heal the broken.

The community of faith capable of integrating this profound new insight mediated by Second Isaiah into its self-image would be one recognizing at the center of its life the tragic reality of sin, the abyss that sin created between God and humans, and the costly path of grace necessary for atonement and reconciliation. After the exile, such a community of faith consisted of those continuing to experience the shock of recognizing the astonishing manner of God's advent to restore and redeem the lost and discovering in their own redemption the call to share God's grace with all peoples. We do well not to seek to dissolve the mystery left by Second Isaiah himself in forced attempts to identify precisely who the historical Servant was. Yet it is clear that he was God's human agent given as an alternative to alienation, desolation, and death;

that is, as a means of return from exile not only for the nation, but for the individual. Through the suffering of the Servant, God was calling forth life from death, and thereby was gathering a community together as those forgiven, atoned for by the sacrifice of an innocent victim, and given a new future solely as a gift of divine grace.

Thus the Servant is the pre-eminent manifestation in Second Isaiah of the new thing God was doing, which was nevertheless prepared for by God from the beginning of time. The novelty was thus not in God's plan, for in calling forth judges, priests, kings, and prophets God was preparing for the mission of the Servant. The newness rather was in the historical moment, the "time of favor" when God's new initiative and a particular human response united to bring God's plan for the world to the threshold of fulfillment.

But fulfillment remained a reality only in the hearts of a faithful remnant, for those within the community who identified with the mystery of the Servant's suffering were a minority. Nevertheless, the reality of God's Servant suffering for the atonement of those separated from God was not lost, for it was kept alive in future generations by other faithful Yahwists who, like the Servant, were acquainted with much suffering. There is thus a line of continuity connecting the community in exile and the apostle who could quote Second Isaiah in interpreting the meaning of Christ's passion, "At the acceptable time I have listened to you, and helped you on the day of salvation," and then bring the two together in announcing the good news, "Behold, now is the acceptable time, behold, now is the day of salvation" (2 Cor. 6:2).

In the wake of the crucifixion, the disciples of Jesus found in the Servant Songs a key to understanding the meaning of their master's life. For in his being bruised, oppressed, taken away in judgment, cut off from the land of the living, and then exalted by God, they recognized God's eternal plan for reconciling the human family manifesting itself anew. In Jesus, they witnessed one who had submitted completely to the will of God. The result was that he became a victim of human wrath. But in light of the Servant Songs, his death and resurrection were seen as God's act of identifying with a fallen humanity. Here was the supreme "sin offering" ('āšām), whereby atonement was accomplished for all acknowledging that God was in Christ, reconciling the world to God, and believing in the one by whose sacrifice many were "accounted righteous."

On the basis of the powerful eschatological thrust in Second Isaiah's portrayal of the Servant of Yahweh, the Christian Church has come to see itself as heir to the promise of God's atoning for the sins of humans through the obedient suffering of his Servant. But even the *praeparatio* seen in the Old Testament and the fulfillment discerned in Jesus are not consigned to past history, for God continued to draw the community responding to God's initiation into the ongoing mission of reconciliation. Old and new is therefore not a mere matter of chronology, but of distinguishing between the community based on a strictly human definition of fellowship and the community called together by the message of reconciliation. And in the latter the Suffering Servant continued to be found at the center of the communal life as the one shocking the faithful into an awareness of the radical depths of sin and into acknowledgment of the cost of divine grace manifested by the atoning sacrifice of the Innocent One.

As important as is the image of the Suffering Servant for the Church's self-understanding, the common practice of skipping over the entire period between Second Isaiah and the birth of the Christian Church in tracing the history of the biblical notion of the community of faith is a serious mistake. This study of the roots of the Church in the Hebrew Bible, therefore, does not end with Second Isaiah. The intervening period, though ill understood and in many ways downright confusing, was a period in which the diverse ingredients of that biblical notion were tested, reinterpreted, and further developed. Emphasized in this entire process were elements of the community notion that are commonly neglected by the Church, with harmful theological, social, and political results. It seems very easy therefore for the Church to sketch its life of descendency directly from Second Isaiah, while neglecting traditions which during the Second Temple period focused on the theological themes stemming from Ezekiel and the Priestly Writing. But the flaw in such one-sided interpretation can be illustrated already in relation to these three exilic works themselves. Second Isaiah unfolds a vision of divine purpose that would prompt the community of faith in succeeding centuries to reflect on the fundamental qualities of the life in fellowship with God. Nevertheless, it is not a complete program addressing all aspects of the covenant community.

Ezekiel and the Priestly Writing serve as important reminders that the vision of God's saving action must be translated into the forms of worship and the structures of community that shape the life of faith in this world. Although these forms and structures themselves are a part of God's dynamic saving activity and undergo change in keeping with the living reality they symbolize and embody, the stage represented by Ezekiel and P are of a significance often overlooked in the history of the Christian Church. The reality of the Divine Warrior in Isaiah 51:9–11 and of the Servant of Isaiah 52:13 to 53:12 must come to expression in the concrete forms of life and worship lest they be allowed to escape into a realm of religiosity remote from the world God seeks to bring to peace and wholeness.

It is perhaps theologically accurate to observe that the announcement of the Suffering Servant in Second Isaiah, and the gathering of a community of faith around the Nazarene it came to recognize as fulfilling that message, were separated by such a long period of time precisely because of the parting of ways between the vision of God's universal plan and its translation into the concrete forms of life during the period of the Second Temple. And perhaps it is possible to argue that that parting was often more at the expense of the visionary side than the pragmatic. For example, the programs of Ezra and Nehemiah seem to represent a narrowing of the more universal vision of Second Isaiah. But to abet the parting of the ways between the vision of God's universal plan and its translation into the structures of day-to-day life and praxis by neglect of the Second Temple period traditions, and by the one-sided emphasis on the visionary side of the biblical notion of community that inevitably follows this neglect, is equally unjustifiable. If Christians expect religious Jews to take seriously their interpretation of Second Isaiah's vision, they dare not neglect the carefully developed exposition of how God's righteousness and compassion can find embodiment in the everyday life of the faithful community that was developed within the stream of tradition reaching from Ezra and Nehemiah to Hillel and Judah the Patriarch.

STREAMS OF TRADITION IN THE SECOND TEMPLE PERIOD

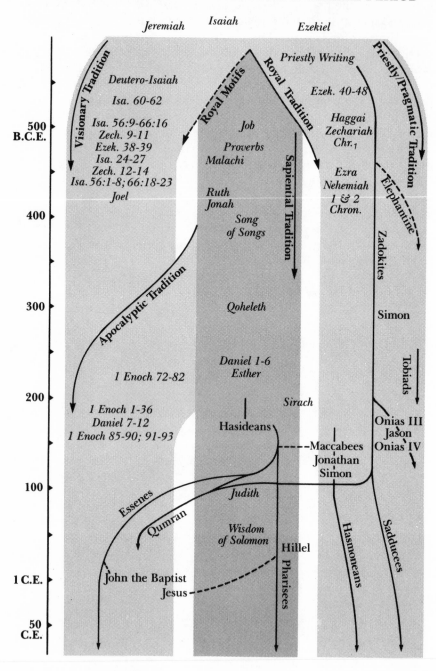

VIII

Return from Exile and Attempts to Reconstitute Community
(Chronicles, Haggai, Zechariah, Malachi, Isaiah 24–27, 56–66, and Ezekiel 38–39, 44)

Much to cast down, much to build, much to restore;
Let the work not delay, time and the arm not waste;
Let the clay be dug from the pit, let the saw cut the stone,
Let the fire not be quenched in the forge.[1]

Historical Note: Many Yahwists greeted the rise of Cyrus to a position of hegemony with enthusiasm and hope for the future, especially when it became clear that he would support the return of Jewish exiles to Jerusalem and the restoration of the cult (the Edict of Cyrus, 538 B.C.E.). As high hopes collided with the harsh realities of rebuilding a devastated land, however, frustration and despair began to descend like a shroud over the returnees. The problem was compounded by tension between rival groups as they struggled for control over the rebuilding of temple and community. The Zadokite priestly party was able to repress the dissident group coming to expression in Isaiah 56–66, and with the support of the prophets Haggai and Zechariah was able to rebuild the temple between 520 and 515 B.C.E. But a deep wound had torn into the tissue of the community, setting the stage for continued struggle between Zadokites and Levites, and between those with pragmatic and those with visionary predilections throughout the Second Temple period (cf. the diagram on p. 252). Our literary corpus for this period will be the books of Chronicles, Haggai, Zechariah, and Malachi, Ezra 1–6, Isaiah 24–27 and 56–66, and Ezekiel 38–39 and 44.

A. SECOND ISAIAH'S VISIONARY FOLLOWERS

Second Isaiah left to his followers a noble vision of God's plan for Israel and the world. It was a vision straining the limits of human lan-

---

1. T. S. Eliot, "Choruses from 'The Rock,' " in *The Complete Poems and Plays, 1909–1950* (New York: Harcourt, Brace, 1952), p. 102.

guage in the effort to identify the heart of the community of faith. Thus we find Second Isaiah drawing on myth to portray the basis of Israel's historical struggles in a cosmic conflict between order and chaos. But he was ever mindful that Israel's historical experiences offered the most vivid manifestation of Yahweh's creative, redemptive effort to establish the realm of *šālôm* against the threat of chaos in its many forms. To show how that was to be accomplished in Israel's life, Second Isaiah also drew on the priestly language of atonement ritual, and he crowned this entire bold synthesis with the image of the Suffering Servant, God's patient instrument in reconciling an estranged people with its God.

In this vision, we have seen that the early Yahwistic notion of community was both restored, and deepened and broadened. In the first instance, this was made possible by Second Isaiah's refocusing the attention of his audience on Israel's only true source of life and community, the one true God. In Israel's response to the gracious initiative of God in this second creation and second exodus, the qualities of righteousness and compassion derived from divine example by the people of the first exodus were again grasped as the marks of genuine community. Once again the triadic relationship of classical Yahwism was restored: righteousness and compassion grounded in worship of the one true God. That classical formulation, moreover, was broadened by the cosmic breadth of Second Isaiah's vision. An idea only hinted at in earlier formulations found explicit exposition: the God-given state of *šālôm* experienced by the people living within the community defined by worship, righteousness, and compassion was not to be limited to the inner life of this community, but was to be carried by the Servant people to all nations, for it was a salvation intended for the whole earth (49:6). The God active since the beginning to drive back chaos and to established an order of *šālôm* had thus drawn the faithful as partners into this universal salvation drama.

What would the disciples of Second Isaiah, and beyond them the future generations of the people of Israel do with this vision and its vocational mandate? Its symbolic language and poetic vision were powerful carriers of a program and a challenge. But it would fall to those actually moving from exile back to their own land to translate this vision and its rich symbolism into reality, a reality moreover usually very resistant and often even hostile to such translation. What would the effects of their efforts be on the future development of Israel's notion of community?

The answer to this question is found in part in the history of a group that viewed itself as the heir to Second Isaiah's vision.[2] In continuity

---

2. For a detailed reconstruction of the socioreligious setting of Isaiah 56–66, see P. D. Hanson, *The Dawn of Apocalyptic*, 2d ed. (Philadelphia: Fortress Press, 1979), pp. 32–208.

with Second Isaiah's message, they viewed the return of Yahweh to re-store his people as imminent, and saw thereby inaugurated an era of šālôm that would encompass the whole world from its center in Zion (Isa. 60). Again in the manner of Second Isaiah, the restoration of šālôm was expressed in terms of the Jubilee, "the year of the Lord's fa-vor," in which all creation would be restored (Isa. 61:1–4, cf. Isa. 35).

Initially the followers of Second Isaiah preserved the breadth of the vision as formulated by Second Isaiah. They issued a call to the whole people to a righteousness by which God was glorified: "Your people shall all be righteous, they shall possess the land forever, the shoot of my planting, the work of my hands, that I might be glorified" (Isa. 60:21). Israel's unity was to be grounded in common acknowledgment of Yahweh as the only true God. Moreover, the whole people was to be drawn into a sacral vocation, a priesthood and a ministry dedicated to God's righteous and compassionate purpose in the world: "You shall be called the priests of the Lord, [people] shall speak of you as the minis-ters of our God" (61:6).

In actual fact, however, in the early years after the return from exile, this group of disciples of Second Isaiah did not find the nation uniting in acknowledgment of Yahweh's sovereignty as a community of righ-teous priests. The Edict of Cyrus, which in 538 B.C.E. granted permis-sion to the Jews in exile to return to Israel and to restore their cultic community, had set in motion a rival program of restoration far better equipped to achieve its goals. Headed by the Zadokite priestly party (that is, the priesthood to which Josiah's reform in 622 B.C.E. had given exclusive charge of the temple cult and which had maintained its lead-ership status over the Jews during the exile) and officially sponsored by the Persian royal court, this party set forth the terms of restoration with a pragmatism and rationalism that called for a narrowing of Sec-ond Isaiah's vision in several important respects: (1) Rather than being guided by the early Yahwistic, egalitarian notion of a nation of priests (expressed in Exod. 19:6 and reaffirmed in Isa. 60:21 and 61:6), leader-ship was held firmly in the hands of the Zadokites; (2) the universal vi-sion of Israel's mission to the nations was replaced by a pragmatic pro-gram of domestic consolidation; (3) the cosmic vision of Yahweh's sovereignty was compromised by recognition of the sovereignty of the Persian emperor, even within the context of the official cult (cf. Ezra 6:10).

Although the coexistence of rival programs of restoration raises seri-ous problems for interpretation, it would be a theological oversimplifi-cation simply to declare one of the just mentioned programs as true to the early Yahwistic notion of community, the other as its betrayal. We have seen from the beginning and repeatedly that the Yahwistic com-munal notion was dynamic and developed within the context of the ac-tual circumstances of the world Israel lived in. For example, it is not possible to evaluate the theological validity of the Zadokite policy of accommodation to the Persian court against an abstract ideal. As before, we must seek to evaluate all responses within the context of the dynamic notion of community defined by sole acknowledgment of Yahweh and embodiment of the divine attributes of righteousness and compassion. In the struggle that ensued toward the end of the sixth century between visionaries and pragmatists, a people called to be one community under God's reign was divided into separate groups struggling for proprietorship over the vision of God's purpose and the role of Israel in that purpose.[3] On both sides of the struggle, a sharp distinction between winners and losers arose in terms of those deemed worthy of inclusion in the restoration of "true" Israel, and those who were to be excluded. This divisive element created a disharmony within the community, which then extended on into its attitude toward the other nations. The need to understand the theological causes of this breakdown can be answered only with the aid of careful analysis of both parties in the struggle, whereas uncritical identification with one side over against the other inevitably inhibits such understanding.

Although the followers of Second Isaiah based their hopes on a cosmic vision of Yahweh's reconstituting the people as a community of priests gathered around a restored sanctuary on Zion, the Zadokite party embarked on a much more pragmatic plan. The cultic structures they supported had already been described in detail in the program formulated in Ezekiel 40–48. That program in turn stood in continuity with the structures of the Jerusalem cult over which Zadokites had presided in the period immediately before the exile. It accorded central authority to the Zadokite high priest, alongside of whom the Davidic prince was to rule over civil affairs. The population was carefully divided into zones of relative holiness, beginning with the Zadokite priests who alone were allowed to perform temple sacrifice, and then on through a descending order of Levites, Davidides, and so on. The stratified structure of the monarchical period was thus not removed, but sacralized. It was moreover a system that could be implemented only by a policy of exclusion. This policy affected most directly the Levites by consigning them to the role of minor clergy, a policy culminating a long history of discrimination initiated by Solomon and abetted by Josiah's removal of the outlying local sanctuaries where many Le-

---

3. J. Levenson's plea for methodological fairness in the scholarly comparison of "temple" and "prophetic" traditions is entirely justified, and his own assessment of the rich theological meaning associated with the Jerusalem temple in the Bible provides a badly needed corrective to earlier overemphasis on prophetic elements of biblical tradition. At the same time, however, I do not feel that a descriptive term such as "hierocratic" need convey a more negative connotation than the term "visionary" if used accurately and properly (J. Levenson, "The Temple and the World," *JR* 64 [1984], 275–298; see also Levenson's *Sinai and Zion: An Entry into the Jewish Bible* [Minneapolis: Winston Press, 1985]).

vites had practiced their profession. When one calls to mind the magnitude of the class called Levitical priests—a class whose genealogy served as a constant reminder of what they deemed their rightful place at the center of the nation's cult life, but who were now denied priestly status by the Zadokites—one can easily comprehend why a significant coalition of priests and visionaries embraced the broadly egalitarian restoration vision of Second Isaiah and made it the basis of their future hope. Even in the earliest stage of their formulating this hope programmatically, as we find it in Isaiah 60–62, one can detect an inchoate polemical element. In the description of a community in which "your people shall all be righteous" (60:20), we can hear voices dissenting from the tight circle being drawn around the temple cult by the Zadokites, with its corresponding stratified order of holiness (cf. Ezek. 48).

Although the Zadokite group did not pursue its restoration program without difficulties—one difficulty being opposition from dissenters—the future was clearly on its side. To its members belonged both a realistic plan and the organizational ability to bring it into effect. Their pragmatic orientation gave them another huge advantage: a carefully balanced policy of accommodation earned for them the support of the Persian royal court. Finally, in Haggai and Zechariah they found two enthusiastic prophetic supporters, right at the critical time when a final effort was being made to complete the rebuilding of the temple.

All this the visionaries found completely objectionable, and one can trace the translation of their mounting anger and frustration into an increasingly vindictive polemic. They felt shunned by their own leaders (Isa. 63:16) and removed from their own sanctuary (63:18–19). Their helplessness to change the course of a restoration program that assured their exclusion vented itself in harsh condemnation pronounced in the name of Yahweh. Although their opponents were an abomination to Yahweh, they displayed to others a mock-righteous conceit (65:1–7). Through their iniquity, they had turned the day of salvation announced by Second Isaiah into a day of darkness (59:9). The whole order of righteousness ordained by God had been perverted: "Justice is turned back, and righteousness stands far off; for truth has fallen in the public squares, and uprightness cannot enter" (59:14). The visionaries identified their present suffering with that of the Suffering Servant, whose title and role they democratized and applied to themselves (65:9, 13–16). Therefore they anticipated as well the exaltation of the Servant, as the result of which they would regain possession of Zion: "But he who takes refuge in me shall possess the land, and shall inherit my holy mountain" (57:13b). Looking about themselves, however, they saw little sign of this vindication in the earthly sphere. To the contrary, they saw the Zadokite temple rising in Zion as a palpable sign of their adversaries' victory. This temple and its ritual they denounced as an abomination to Yahweh (66:1–4), which denunciation further exacerbated the division by leading to their excommunication from the Zado-kite-sponsored cultic community (66:5).

With this disintegration of the intracommunity situation came a transformation in the vision of Yahweh's advent. Gone was Second Isa-iah's brilliant picture of salvation and light, and of a nation, whose war-fare was ended, being returned in joyous procession to Zion. In a world perceived as completely fallen, in which "there was no justice" and "no one to intervene," Yahweh as portrayed as the Divine Warrior entering to inflict stinging punishment on his adversaries; that is, in the first in-stance, on the leadership group that had excluded and oppressed those who called themselves "the Servants." According to their deeds, so God would repay, "wrath to his adversaries, requital to his enemies; to the coastlands he will render requital" (59:18). Second Isaiah's empha-sis on universal salvation was replaced with a picture of universal slaughter:

> For behold, the Lord will come in fire,
>   and his chariots like the stormwind,
> to render his anger in fury,
>   and his rebuke with flames of fire.
> For by fire will the Lord execute judgment,
>   and by his sword, upon all flesh;
>   and those slain by the Lord shall be many. (Isa. 66:15–16)

This oracle is a grim reminder of the path eschatological thought was taking in this period. It led to the harshest condemnation of the nations of the world found in Scripture, beginning with Isaiah 63:1–6 and con-tinuing through the many oracles against the nations that were added to prophetic books such as Isaiah, Jeremiah, and Ezekiel. The disinte-gration of God's order of šālôm *within* the community seemed to poison the attitude of the visionaries toward their neighbors, making them in-capable of carrying out their divinely ordained vocation as light to the nations. As Yahweh would intervene to destroy their adversaries among their own people, so too Yahweh would destroy all the nations of the earth so as to secure their prosperity.

Why this reversion to inner and outer chaos? We recall that in early Israel Yahweh's answer to the chaos that according to ancient Near Eastern cosmology was ever poised to engulf the ordered life of the community was the institution of šālôm. The order of šālôm prevailed against chaos where God was acknowledged as sole sovereign, and where God's righteousness and compassion were embodied in the life of the community. We can best explain the chaotic communal situation portrayed in the literature of this time by evaluating it against the tri-adic notion of community traced to early Yahwism.

Such evaluation leads to this fundamental observation: Acknowledg-ment of the sole sovereignty of Yahweh in the form of a vivid commu-nal response to Yahweh's saving acts fell victim to the practice of viewing Yahweh primarily as a partisan on one side or the other in the bitter conflicts that tore into the fabric of the community. Yahweh's activity was no longer seen as that which drew the community into one worship-centered unity, but as that which divided the people along strict party lines. This change represented nothing less than an attack on the principal tenet of early Yahwism. God was no longer revered as the universal creator and redeemer, the transcendent norm above all human norms and ultimate point of reference, but became a projection of one or the other party's self-interest. The actual nexus of authority shifted from the nature of the God revealed in the saving events of history to the nature of the leadership claims of the individual parties. This shift in authority brought with it a corresponding shift in the means of defining the qualities undergirding the community. Righteousness ceased to be the impartial norm derived from the nature of the God who treats all people, regardless of class, with even-handed justice. Instead, it became an instrument by which those in power distinguished their positions and the position of others—and that meant, all too often, an instrument of exclusion of the vulnerable. Compassion ceased to be the open invitation extended by the community to those denied the protection of its structures and laws, and became a courtesy limited to members of one's own party.

Despite this distinction between sources of authority, the fact remains that all communities are tempted to clothe their image of God in their own images, early Israel being no exception. Nevertheless, it seems legitimate to be sensitive to the differing degrees to which this actually does or does not occur. The cultic group that earlier had expressed itself in the Book of the Covenant was one whose experience of the unmerited grace of the Deliverer God Yahweh had left an unmistakable imprint on all its beliefs and values. It had established at its heart a norm and a point of reference that safeguarded the rights of all its members with a remarkable equality. In contrast, the experiences that proved to be most influential in the groups contending in the early postexilic period grew out of their struggles for control of the cult. Not surprisingly, penultimate loci of authority threatened the sole authority that classic Yahwism had attributed to Yahweh, thereby undermining the only source of communal unity acknowledged by biblical faith. The result was a divided community. Having looked at the early stage of the visionary side of that struggle, we now turn to a closer look at its more pragmatic counterpart.

B. THE RESTORATION PROGRAM OF THE ZADOKITES

The exilic period, as we have seen, was a period of deep religious questioning. In many sectors of the community, people were asking whether Yahweh had the power or desire to reestablish the Jewish community as a free people in their own land. The continued vitality of the Yahwistic faith came to expression in the responses to this crisis that we have seen in the prophecy of Ezekiel, the programmatic history of the Priestly Writing, and in the daring vision of restoration in terms of a new creative act of God found in Second Isaiah.

The last chapter traced the history of those who clung to the visions of Second Isaiah as the basis for their hope for the future. That history was one of increasing disappointment and resentment toward leaders who seemed little disposed to make room in their restoration efforts for the visionary notion of a "nation of priests" in which sanctity and righteousness were to be shared by all of the people.

But who were the leaders against whom they responded with the intense vitriol witnessed in Isaiah 56–66? Or to formulate the question even more concretely, against whom was the oracle of Yahweh found in Isaiah 66:1–2 directed, "Heaven is my throne and earth is my footstool; what is the house which you would build for me, and what is the place of my rest?" The answer seems clear: the attack was directed against a group that interpreted Yahweh's will in a very different way. The extent of the gulf separating the two groups can be glimpsed by comparing the oracle of the visionaries just quoted with the divine word that epitomized the position of their rivals: "Go up to the hills and bring wood and build the house, that I may take pleasure in it and that I may appear in my glory, says the Lord" (Hag. 1:8).

The Jewish community of the early post exilic period was very fragile. Not only were its members still haunted by the remembered devastation of homeland and of exile, but in addition internal divisions had begun to threaten the viability of the new vassal state even before it had become established. Although we are unable to recognize all the factors that were abetting such division, it seems clear that strife between rival priestly groups played a significant role.[4] In particular, Ezekiel 44 indicates that the Zadokite priests were determined to establish themselves as undisputed heads over the cult, in continuity with the pre-eminence they had come to enjoy in Babylon. The effect of their efforts was to complete the process begun during the reign of Josiah, namely, demoting the Levites to a rank explicitly subservient to the Zadokites. Within the setting of increasing altercations, it was perhaps inevitable that the predisposition of the visionaries to view the restoration in highly idealistic terms and the inclination of the Zadokite leaders to pursue a path of pragmatism and accommodation grew in intensity, thus further exacerbating the polarization. Since we have already examined this polarization from the side of the visionaries, we must now follow the other side of the growing controversy.

---

4. Regarding the rivalry between opposing parties in the period 538–520 B.C.E., see P. D. Hanson, *Dawn of Apocalyptic*, pp. 209–279; P. D. Hanson, "Israelite Religion in the Early Post-Exilic Period," *Ancient Israelite Religion: Essays in Honor of Frank Moore Cross*, P. D. Miller, Jr., P. D. Hanson, S. D. McBride, Jr., eds. (Philadelphia: Fortress Press, in press).

First, it is necessary to reiterate that the conflict cannot be explained by identifying one side as the villain and the other as the victim. The visionaries were convinced (1) that they stood for the classic principles of Yahwism, (2) that the Zadokites had profaned those principles through a combination of accommodation to worldly powers and dedication to personal ambition, and (3) that Yahweh would intervene in a display of power to vindicate the innocently oppressed. The Zadokites, on the other hand, no doubt looked on the restoration visions of their opponents as fanciful and out of touch with the real world. They were dedicated to reestablishing structures they could trust on the basis of their proven utility, and that meant the sacral structures of their own cult, adjusted now to the new political setting of Persian domination.

The pragmatism of the Zadokites must not obscure the carefully defined theological basis of their program. It had been refined in detail by Ezekiel and the authors of the Priestly Writing. Its aim was nothing less than the restoration of a communal sanctity that would re-establish a suitable habitation for Yahweh's "Glory" (kābôd), that is, for the indwelling of the divine Presence that alone could preserve šalôm in the land. They believed that only through the restoration of communal sanctity as defined by their program could recurrence of the devastating events of the Babylonian destruction be averted.

Within this theological system, the temple assumed a vital, central position. Within the properly constituted temple, the ordering of the community took place that established safeguards against the various forms of profanation that could force the holy God to leave the temple and land as Ezekiel earlier had witnessed in his vision of Jerusalem (Ezek. 9–11). Such ordering and the resulting preservation of communal sanctity was tied to a sacerdotal structure that tolerated no flexibility. The high priestly service within the sacrificial system of the temple was the essential key to the vitality of the community. Through that service, a state of holiness was preserved, which alone could guarantee the abiding presence of the Glory of God. Moreover, that service was reserved exclusively for the Zadokites. As both the restoration program of Ezekiel (Ezek. 40–48) and the Priestly Writing legislated, the Levites were to be relegated to the Zadokites as the latter's assistants.

Amid the physical hardships that confronted the returnees in the early years after the exile, and perhaps due in part to the enervating effects of partisan divisions, the Zadokite leaders initially made little progress, finding it impossible, literally, to get their temple-building program off of the ground. In the years 520–518, however, the Zadokite cause found a powerful source of support in the prophets Haggai and Zechariah. The original leader of the community, Sheshbazzar, had disappeared from the scene, replaced by a more able leader named Zerubbabel. By his side stood a priest named Joshua. The two seemed to their supporters to be portents of a bright new era, for as a Davidide,

Zerubbabel seemed to fulfill Ezekiel's promise of a Davidic prince (Ezek. 34:23–24), and of course as a Zadokite, Joshua represented the priestly line believed by them to be divinely ordained to represent the people before God in the temple.

There was no ambiguity in Haggai's message. The hardships suffered by the people since their return from exile were nothing less than manifestation of a divine curse. And the cause of this curse was specific and clear: "Why?" says the Lord of hosts. Because of my house that lies in ruins" (Hag. 1:9). The solution was equally specific and clear: "build the house, that I may take pleasure in it and that I may appear in my glory, says the Lord" (Hag. 1:8). For those who devoted themselves to the Zadokite temple program, Haggai was the bearer of lavish promises: "Before a stone was placed upon a stone in the temple of the Lord" they had experienced drought, futility, devastating storms, and diseases that destroyed their crops, and economic chaos. "Since the day that the foundation of the Lord's temple was laid," they were to witness fertility and abundance. For with the temple rebuilt, Yahweh would once again have had a habitation in the midst of the people. And the results would be dramatic:

My Spirit abides among you; fear not. For thus says the Lord of hosts: Once again, in a little while, I will shake the heavens and the earth and the sea and the dry land; and I will shake all nations, so that the treasures of all nations shall come in, and I will fill this house with splendor, says the Lord of hosts. The latter splendor of this house shall be greater than the former, says the Lord of hosts; and in this place I will give prosperity, says the Lord of hosts. (Hag. 2:5b–9)

It is not difficult to recognize in Haggai's appeal a call to a specific program and an absolute authority. One either lined up on the side of the temple program and the leadership of Zerubbabel and Jeshua, or was marginalized. A movement was underway that did not tolerate dissent.

The form of support that Zechariah brought to the temple program of the Zadokites was theologically more subtle than that of Haggai. For at the same time as he agreed with Haggai that the rebuilding of the temple held the key to renewed prosperity (Zech. 8:9–13), he did not lose sight of the ethical dimensions of Yahwism (Zech. 8:16–17). Basically, however, both prophets can be recognized as protagonists of the same program, that of the Zadokites. Like Haggai, Zechariah therefore supported the rebuilding of the temple within which Yahweh's Glory (kābôd) could again dwell in the midst of the people (Zech. 1:16–17; 2:8–16 [EVV. 2:4–12]; 4:6–10a). The leadership that was to preside over temple and community was also stated unequivocally: Zerubbabel (whom Zechariah designates with the royal title "Branch" [ṣemaḥ] was to be joined in harmonious rule with the High Priest Joshua. The loftiness of the authority accorded these two figures by Zechariah is illustrated by the vision in chapter 4, for after describing the lampstand of the temple as the symbol of Yahweh's life-giving, community-sustaining presence in the temple, the vision goes on to describe as inseparably bound to the lampstand two olive trees symbolizing "the two anointed who stand by the Lord of the whole earth"—that is to say, Zerubbabel and Joshua (Zech. 4:14). This was of course a daring claim, that the restoration of the community was tied, by God's own choosing, to the leadership of the Zadokite party. All in all, it is clear both from the individual promises made in the oracles of Zechariah and in the overall movement of the vision cycle in chapters 1–6 that Zechariah awaited the dawn of a messianic era, under the tutelage of the Davidide Zerubbabel and the Zadokite Joshua.[5]

The fact that the goal the earlier returnees had been unable to accomplish under Sheshbazzar was in fact reached by this second wave of reform reflects skillful organization and an effective mobilization of the resources of the community. The effect of the prophetic activities of Haggai and Zechariah must have been considerable. In their oracles, many must have felt that they were hearing God's word, and its message was urgent: "Rally behind your Prince Zerubbabel, and your High Priest Joshua, for they have been chosen by God to lead you in rebuilding the temple." Obedience to this command would be rewarded by renewal of the covenant, security, and prosperity.

Recently some scholars have detected evidence for another major source of support for the temple-rebuilding program led by Zerubbabel and Joshua, namely, an early edition of the books of 1 and 2 Chronicles.[6] The support of Haggai and Zechariah came in the form of the prophetic word; that is, a new word from God calling for action. The support of Chr[1] (the abbreviation we shall use for the first edition and/ or author of the Chronicler's History, covering 1 Chron. 10 through Ezra 3:15;) came in the form of the less direct, but no less powerful lesson from history. By using the Deuteronomistic History (Deuteronomy, Joshua, Judges, 1 and 2 Samuel, and 1 and 2 Kings) as well as other traditions, and then shaping them in a distinct new form, Chr[1] sketched a national history that began with David and culminated in the restoration community living under its new Davidic prince and its Zadokite high priest. At the heart of the Jewish community was the temple and

5. Cf. P. D. Hanson, "In Defiance of Death: Zechariah's Symbolic Universe," in J. H. Marks, ed., *Love and Death*, Martin H. Pope Festschrift (New Haven, Conn.: Four Quarters Publishing, in press).

6. To my knowledge, this hypothesis was first suggested by D. N. Freedman, "The Chronicler's Purpose," *CBQ* 23 (1961), 436–442. The question of the date of composition of the Chronicler's History remains a much debated issue. Compare, for example, F. M. Cross, "A Reconsideration of the Judean Restoration," *Int* 29 (1975), 187–202, with T. Willi, *Die Chronik als Auslegung* (Göttingen: Vandenhoeck and Ruprecht, 1972), pp. 190–244, and P. Welten, *Geschichte und Geschichtsdarstellung in den Chronikbüchern* (Neukirchen-Vluyn: Neukirchener Verlag, 1973), pp. 199–200.

the cult that found its home there, overseen by the Zadokites. According to this interpretation of Israel's history, it was no less than the great David who, under God's command, had arranged in finest detail this entire sacral structure. When one compares the elaborate detail given to David's arrangement of temple and priesthood in the Chr[1] account with the corresponding section in the Deuteronomistic History, it becomes obvious that one is focusing on a matter of central concern for Chr[1]. And the message seems clear. As the building of the first temple was arranged by David under the command of God mediated by the prophetic word, so too would the rebuilding of the temple be carried out by a Davidide under the command of God mediated by the prophetic word. Other themes followed from this one: as security and prosperity were dependent throughout Israel's history on the fidelity of king and people to the temple cult, so too would security and prosperity be reestablished by a people returning to the true faith. And even as David had placed the temple cult in the charge of the Zadokites, with the Levites as minor clergy assisting them, so too the proper cult of the present would be so ordered (1 Chron. 23–28). Thus, while the entire tone of Chr[1] is positive and free from the vitriol found for example in Ezekiel 44, nevertheless the structure of the restoration community is set forth in no uncertain terms. It is the structure of the Zadokite program, emphasizing the importance of the rebuilding of the temple and the careful ordering of that temple under Zadokite leadership.

The alignment of Chr[1] with the Zadokite restoration program can be illustrated with a specific textual example. In 1 Chronicles 28, David declares to his subjects, "I had it in my heart to build (*bnwt*) a house (*byt*) of rest (*mnwḥh*) for the ark of the covenant of the Lord, and for the footstool (*hdm*) of our God" (v. 2). In Isaiah 66, we found the protest of those opposing the Zadokite temple-building program, a protest using the same technical terms, but to the opposite effect: "Thus says the Lord: 'Heaven is my throne and the earth is my footstool (*hdm*); what is the house (*byt*) which you would build (*tbnw*) for me, and what is the place of my rest (*mnwḥty*)?' " This contrast gives clear indication of the stream to which Chr[1] belongs. In effect, Chr[1] adds a historical dimension to the prophetic word expressed thus by Haggai: "Built (*bnw*) the house (*byt*)" (Hag. 1:8).[7]

The emphasis on the key role of David in the construction of temple and in the ordering of its personnel as presented by Chr[1] argues for its provenance in the early stages of the temple rebuilding. This was the last time in the post exilic period in which a prince of the Davidic house exercised some of the traditional royal duties. Indeed, before the temple reached completion, Zerubbabel, the last Davidic prince, seems to

---

7. See the preceding pp. 260–262 and Hanson, *Dawn of Apocalyptic*, pp. 174–177.

have disappeared, and this prompted changes in the Zadokite program. By the time the final edition of the Chronicler's History was completed (toward the end of the fifth century B.C.E.), the entire program has been adjusted to fit the new realities of a community, deprived of its Davidic prince and living under the sole leadership of the remaining member of the diarchy, the Zadokite high priest.[8] The final edition of the Chronicler's History is discussed in Chapter IX, section B, of this book.

Those later developments leading to a hierocratic form of community governance were already anticiapted in the earliest stages of the Zadokite restoration program. Already in the original words of Zechariah, the Zadokite member of the diarchy was accorded a special position of honor. A vision that seems to have been directed against dissidents who were calling into question the ritual purity of Joshua concludes with this lofty divine promise to the high priest: "If you will walk in my ways and keep my charge, then you shall rule my house and have charge of my courts, and I will give you the right of access among those who are standing here (i.e., the heavenly beings attending upon Yahweh)" (Zech. 3:7). We find here an unprecedented claim to authority on the part of the Zadokite high priest, claiming nothing less than access to the divine council. In addition to the claim that only a Zadokite could represent the people before God in the inner temple has been added a privilege that hitherto had been reserved for those called to be prophets of Yahweh, the right of access to the divine council (cf. 1 Kings 22, Isa. 6 and 40, Jer. 14:13–14 and 23:28).

In the text of Zechariah, traces have been left of a further enhancement of the power of the Zadokite high priest. In 6:9–14, we find a divine directive concerning the preparation of crowns, which in light of the focus of verses 12–14 on the diarchy consisting of Zerubbabel and Joshua must have been intended for the heads of these two leaders. But in verse 11, in spite of the plural form of the noun "crowns," a crown is placed only on the head of Joshua. Zerubbabel obviously has been deleted from the text! It seems clear that at a point soon after this word had been delivered by the prophet, Zerubbabel disappeared from the scene. Was he removed by the Persians as a threat to the vassal status of the Jewish community? If read by the Persians, the prophecies of Haggai and Zechariah could have aroused serious suspicions, suspicions that hostile neighbors to the north and east, eager to discredit their Jewish rival, would have readily abetted. If the hypothesis is correct concerning an early edition of the Chronicler's History written in support of a reconstituted Davidic house, we have evidence for another document that the Persians might have interpreted as a threat to their political and military interests in the region. At any rate, from royal

8. J. Myers, *I Chronicles*, AB 12 (Garden City, N.Y.: Doubleday, 1965), p. LXIX.

seals published in 1976 by Nahman Avigad,[9] it has become clear that after Zerubbabel, the governors of Judah ceased to be Davidides, in spite of the continuance of the Davidic line at least on into the fifth century (cf. 1 Chron. 3). Taken together, the evidence from the postexilic seals and the text of Zechariah 6 establish a significant fact: shortly after the rebuilding of the temple, which commenced in 520, the governance of Judah passed out of the possession of the Davidic house, henceforth to be determined by direct Persian appointment, leaving the Zadokite high priest as the only remaining indigenous authority in the Jewish community. That this led to a categorically very significant enhancement of Zadokite power is obvious.

The accomplishments of the Zadokite leadership group cannot be denied. Within a badly divided and languishing community, they were able to assert a degree of authority that repressed dissent and mobilized the resources of the nation around the rebuilding of the cult center. After what was apparently a crisis with the Persians leading to intervention and removal of the Davidic governor, the Zadokite priests under the leadership of their high priest seemed to emerge with their authority firmly established over against rival groups within the community, an authority backed by the Persian crown. With this enhancement of authority, the Zadokite priests began to asert an ever greater role in all aspects of the community's life. And an effect since repeated in history over and over was the result: secular interests began to interfere with the discharge of their spiritual responsibilities, until the demoralized state described by the Book of Malachi was reached in the first half of the fifth century.

The effects on the larger community of this consolidation of power is clear. True, the community once again had a temple. But the lavish promises proclaimed by Haggai did not accompany completion of the temple. Dissidents who had been forced to the side by the powerful Zadokite movement were quick to associate the continued hardships suffered by the community with the alleged impurity of the incumbent priests. And thus we witness the descendants of a people who once understood itself to be called by God to be a blessing to the nations, hurling back and forth against one another words of accusation and judgment, all in the name of the same God of Israel.

It is clear that the bitter oracles of Isaiah 66 and Ezekiel 44 are unlikely sources for a deepened understanding of the biblical notion of commuity. But in these materials we at least find an answer to the question of how it was that in the generation following Second Isaiah a broad vision of redemption was followed not by courageous new steps in the direction of becoming God's servant people, but by a rather

---

9. N. Avigad, *Bullae and Seals from a Post-Exilic Judean Archive*, Qedem 4 (Jerusalem: Hebrew University, 1976).

shocking collapse of intracommunity harmony leading to a harsh spirit of vindictiveness. That answer in the first instance emerges from a clear recognition of what had become the primary allegiance of large segments of the postexilic community. Whereas Second Isaiah, in the tradition of the classical prophets of Yahwism and true to the example of the Hebrews of the exodus, had focused on Yahweh's acts on behalf of all who were afflicted, contending groups within the early postexilic community focused primarily on their own partisan interests. That is to say, Second Isaiah's daring vision of what Yahweh was doing to restore the whole creation to divinely ordered šālôm was obscured by party strife. Each group increasingly derived its sense of direction and purpose from the mandates of its leaders, leaders intent on establishing their authority over all opposition, and not hesitating to call the judgment of God on the heads of their rivals. In the heat of polemic, human authorities thus became confused with the ultimate authority, and Yahweh was clothed in the ideologies of the striving parties. Since this was a reversal of the inferential process constitutive of early Yahwism's dynamic notion of community, the primal quality of sole acknowledgment of the sovereignty of the one true God by the central community was encroached on in a way reminiscent of what had happened earlier within the royal cult of Jerusalem.

The social effect of this focus on penultimate authorities was the exacerbation of intracommunity divisions, for as stated earlier, it was an established principle of Yahwism that the fundamental qualities of righteousness and compassion could be held together in their life-enhancing unity only by being grounded in the worship of the one true God.

The collapse of the triad of worship, righteousness, and compassion allowed the order of šālôm to be invaded by chaos in its various manifestations of strife, greed, oppression, and abuse of power, with no common court of appeal remaining for the oppressed except for the court of the heavenly judge. That intracommunity chaos can be seen as the social basis for the harsh vindictiveness expressed in the salvation-judgment oracles of this period in which Yahweh is depicted as intervening from heaven to save one group by destroying all others.

The contrast this creates in comparison with the earlier visions of the šālôm that was expected to emanate from Zion in ever widening circles is severe. In the place of a vision of universal peace, we see in the oracles the Zadokites addressed against Levites, and the Levites addressed against Zadokites, a surge of chaos welling forth within a strife-ridden community. And this inner chaos quickly became the cauldron from which arose not visions of universal šālôm but of divine wrath reaching out to engulf all nations. One result of the collapse of inner harmony was that the disquietude experienced by the early postexilic Jewish community was projected onto the wider world. Yahweh the warrior was enlisted not only to annihilate adversaries within the community, but to execute judgment against *all* flesh. The envisioned realm of šālôm was narrowed down further and further until the vast lot of humanity was excluded, and holiness was restriced to the tiny circle of those exempting themselves from God's wrath by virtue of their assertion of superior righteousness and special favor.

We have already documented this narrowing process among the visionary circles of the latter half of the sixth century. An example of the simultaneous narrowing of vision among the Zadokites is found in the section secondarily added to the Book of Ezekiel (likely in the last quarter of the sixth century) in chapter 44. It functions as a codicil added to Ezekiel's program of restoration, in which the Zadokite priestly party fabricates charges of idolatry against the Levites, using those charges to bar that wider circle of priests from the officiating priesthood:

> But the Levites who went far from me, going astray from me after their idols when Israel went astray, shall bear their punishment. . . . Because they ministered to them before their idols and became a stumbling block of iniquity to the house of Israel, therefore I have sworn concerning them, says the Lord God, that they shall bear their punishment. They shall not come near to me, to serve me as priest, nor come near any of my sacred things and the things that are most sacred; but they shall bear their shame, because of the abominations which they have committed. . . . But the Levitical priests, the sons of Zadok, who kept the charge of my sanctuary when the people of Israel went astray from me, shall come near to me to minister to me. (Ezek. 44:10, 12–13, 15)

Quite expectedly, the non-Zadokite priests responded in kind, heaping scorn upon those whom they alleged offered defiled sacrifices and yet spurned others with mock holiness: "Keep to yourself, do not come near to me, for I am set apart from you." But in the perception of these critics, the sacrifices of such priests, far from being well-pleasing to God, were "a smoke in [Yahweh's] nostrils, a fire that burns all the day" (Isa. 65:5).

Clearly, the early postexilic period was a very troubled time, and it is not surprising that the literature it produced is shocking. It was indeed the kind of situation that in later centuries would produce fully developed apocalyptic literature. In the late sixth and early fifth centuries, it hastened the transition from prophetic eschatology to apocalyptic eschatology within circles that felt disappointed with and excluded from the Zadokite program of restoration. Although this period and its literary monuments represent anything but a high point in biblical history, we shall turn now to look at a few more examples of the writings produced by dissidents who failed to be convinced that the rebuilding of the temple accomplished by the Zadokites had inaugurated the commonwealth intended by God for God's people. After that we shall seek to clarify the nature of the legacy of the early postexilic period for our understanding of the biblical notion of community.

C. THE GROWTH OF AN APOCALYPTIC RESPONSE
TO ADVERSITY

Recent intensified study of the way in which traditions within the Bible grew into their canonical shape, and an accompanying awareness of the rich diversity that characterizes those traditions, have led Bible students to appreciate the dynamic manner in which traditions were handed down, reapplied to new situations, and qualified by deletions, explanatory additions, and reordering. Thus the challenges represented by received traditions that were not corroborated by new experiences, challenges that within a more static religious system would have destroyed the credibility of the received confessions, were met by engaging the past in earnest dialogue. In the examples to which we now turn, we hear the voices of those questioning the claims of their hierocratic leaders that the new society centered around the temple fulfilled God's plan for God's people.

The very location of Ezekiel 38–39 says a great deal about its intended message. Chapters 34 through 48 of Ezekiel (after secondary sections such as chapter 44 have been set aside) move progressively toward an effective climax. In chapter 34, Yahweh promises that he, and his servant David (i.e., the Davidic prince of the restored community), would care for Israel as a loving shepherd cares for his flock. This is followed with images of a cleansing of the people, the granting of a new heart and spirit, and a description of unprecedented prosperity and security in the land. Chapter 37 then portrays a miraculous rebirth of the people in the vision of the dry bones, and adds a promise of the reunification of the divided kingdoms, with David ruling over a nation bound to Yahweh in an everlasting covenant of peace. All this is preparatory to the vision in chapters 40–48 of the rebuilding of the temple and the return of Yahweh's Glory to take up habitation in the midst of the sanctified people. The miraculous šālôm that would result is described with the image of the life-giving stream flowing from the temple and fructifying the desolations of the Dead Sea and the Arabah. After outlining the wide borders of the restored nation, the book reaches a fitting climax with the majestic words, "And the name of the city henceforth shall be, The Lord is there" (Ezek. 48:35).

How rudely this triumphant movement is interrupted by chapters 38–39! They scream out that the glorious age would not unfold as originally pictured by the prophet. Affliction and devastation lay ahead that would outstrip in magnitude and horror anything previously experienced by the people. Return from exile had not marked the end of trial; evil had retained a death grip on the world, and its most frightful moment was still in the future. In fact, only after a final climax of devastation, an expression of negation so absolute that only mythical images like the chaos monster (38:4) and the drinking of blood and eating of flesh in the frenzied excitement of the victory banquet (39{17–20), could salvation be awaited. That frightful moment is described as follows: Judah, "restored from war" and "gathered from many nations"—that is to say, returned from exile—is described in idyllic terms drawn from the optimistic prophecy of Zechariah as "the land of unwalled villages" and "the quiet people who dwell securely, all of them dwelling without walls, and having no bars or gates" (Ezek. 38:11; cf. Zech. 2:8–9 [Evv. 2:4–5]). How unprepared this land is for the next turn of history, one being called forth by none less than Yahweh, who, contrary to all the expectations of the people and the reassurances of their leaders, was once again declaring war on this people by summoning enemy hosts from the far reaches of the north (also an expression bearing mythological overtones!). Only after this final trial would Yahweh, through a display of natural cataclysm in keeping with the methods of the Divine Warrior, miraculously deliver the survivors. Only then would the land be cleansed, and would Yahweh pour out his spirit on the house of Israel.

This shocking portrait leaves many questions unanswered. Whose perspective does it represent? To what specific issues and conditions does it react? At least this much is clear: it inserts into the Book of Ezekiel a powerful qualification. But does this qualification represent a criticism of the theology of the original message of the prophet Ezekial, or of the way in which that message was being applied within the Zadokite program of restoration? In asking such a question, we must keep in mind that in biblical times as much as today proper application of a sacred text necessitated careful attention not only to that text, but also to the setting to which it was being applied. It is distinctly possible that Ezekiel himself would have concurred with this qualification—that is to say, would have agreed that the spiritual conditions that continued in the land did not equal the sanctity he had described as a necessary condition for the return of Yahweh's Glory, and that only further judgment could purge the land, and prepare for its proper sanctification. At any rate, the horrors of the destruction portrayed in Ezekiel 38–39 vividly show how wide was the gulf the visionaries who added these chapters perceived between the conditions within their community and the holy habitation within which Yahweh would be able to dwell. Only an emphatic new act by Yahweh could restore that habitation; only Yahweh could sanctify a land within which his holy name would be profaned no more (Ezek. 39:7). Unmistakably, we are able to recognize the perspective of apocalyptic eschatology exercising its critique of the specific application and implementation being made by the Zadokite party of the Ezekielian tradition, a tradition that would continue to be treasured and studied by visionary and hierocratic streams alike throughout the Second Temple period.

Isaiah 24–27, the so-called Isaiah Apocalypse, likely stems from the same general period as Ezekiel 38–39—that is, the decades following Cyrus's Edict of 538.[10] Its assessment of existing conditions was equally bleak, evoking the same vision of a Divine Warrior who would intervene to destroy a fallen order and through destruction inaugurate a new era of unprecedented glory for the righteous. Isaiah 24:1 through 25:9 is the first literary unit in these chapters, and can be used here as our second example of the apocalyptic response that was being spawned by opposition to the Zadokite restoration movement. From the perspective of this composition, reality is seen in sharply dualistic terms: curse-blessing, earth-heaven, past-future, chaos-new creation. Isaiah 24:1–20 gives a portrait of total devastation, with Yahweh engaged in undoing creation. The result of this cosmic war is not only a leveling of the earth and the heavens, but a leveling of all the class distinctions that charactreized the type of stratified society found in Judah during this period. In light of the hierocratic structures advanced by the Zadokite party, it is notable that the first pair is, "and it shall be, as with the people, so with the priest" (24:2). The reason given for this dreadful cataclysm is stated clearly:

> The earth lies polluted
> under its inhabitants;
> for they have transgressed the laws,
> violated the statutes,
> broken the everlasting covenant.
> Therefore a curse devours the earth,
> and its inhabitants suffer for their guilt;
> therefore the inhabitants of the earth are scorched,
> and few men are left. (Isa. 24:5–6)

The scathing judgment on the contemporary society proclaimed by this "apocalypse" is rooted in the tenet that comprised the heart of Yahwism from its earliest period, that life for this people was possible only within the context of a sound covenant relationship with the one true God, as manifested by obedience to the Torah. With singleness of focus, this criterion alone functions to establish the guilt of the people. And with a cosmic scope recalling Hosea 4:1–3, the moral nature of the entire creation and the caretaker responsibility of the covenant community within that creation are stressed: When that community is derelict in its covenant responsibility, the nucleus of the entire cosmos decays, and the devastation is total.[11]

The passage goes on to indicate, however, that this grim assessment is not shared by all. Indeed, the seer looks about and sees a world filled

---

10. Cf. W. R. Millar, *Isaiah 24–27 and the Origin of Apocalyptic*, HSM 11 (Missoula, Mont.: Scholars Press 1976).

11. See P. D. Hanson, "War and Peace in the Hebrew Bible," *Int* 38 (1984), 341–362

with exuberant optimism over the Glory of God (24:14–16a). The situation resembles the false optimism, with which the prophet Amos had to deal, of the nation eagerly awaiting the Day of Yahweh. And the response evoked in both cases is the same. Amos lashed back with a string of stinging images:

> Woe to you who desire the day of the Lord!
>> Why would you have the day of the Lord?
> It is darkness, and not light;
>> as if a man fled from a lion,
> and a bear met him;
>> or went into the house and leaned
> with his hand against the wall,
>> and a serpent bit him. (Amos 5:18–19)

And the seer here does likewise:

> But I say, "I pine away,
>> I pine away. Woe is me!
> For the treacherous deal treacherously,
>> the treacherous deal very treacherously."
> Terror, and the pit, and the snare
>> are upon you, O inhabitant of the earth!
> He who flees at the sound of the terror
>> shall fall into the pit;
> and he who climbs out of the pit
>> shall be caught in the snare. (Isa. 24:16b–18a)

Although every attempt to reconstruct the sociohistorical setting of an undated passage like this must remain tentative, this scathing attack on the optimism of those rejoicing over Yahweh's majesty would fit extremely well into the polemic of visionary dissidents against the Zadokite temple-rebuilding program.

The passage then moves to a climax with a picture based on ancient Near Eastern cosmology. As in the primordial flood, now in the end-time, the "windows of heaven are opened, and the foundations of the earth tremble" (Isa. 24:18b). This creates the mythological backdrop for the next episode, in which the Divine Warrior moves into battle against the forces of chaos: "On that day the Lord will punish the host of heaven, in heaven, and the kings of the earth, on the earth" (24:21). Here we see one of the major contributions of ancient mythology to the development of apocalyptic eschatology: the events of earth are but a mere reflection of the real drama, the drama of heaven. And of course, this perspective offers the basis for hope for the visionaries. Developments on earth may seem to give the lie to all the hopes of the afflicted group. But these woes are to be endured in view of the seer's vision of heavenly events. The victory of the Divine Warrior against the host of heaven will soon be reflected in the defeat of this earth's adversaries.

This verse thus marks the turning point of the composition: the victorious reign of the Divine warrior, Yahweh of hosts, will be celebrated on Mount Zion, where his Glory will be manifested before "his elders" (an archaic image with polemical intent, i.e., the Glory does not appear to the Zadokite priests in the temple, but to the elders). This leads to a hymn of praise in 25:1–5, celebrating the vindication of "the poor" and "the needy in his distress" and their deliverance from "the ruthless." Finally, the composition ends with a depiction of the victory banquet prepared by Yahweh, which will inaugurate the blessed era that banishes forever the darkness and gloom of the past (25:6–8).

The eschatological pattern and the apocalyptic judgment it proclaims is strikingly similar to that expressed in Ezekiel 38–39. The pattern that structures the composition is borrowed intact from the Conflict Myth, a pattern stemming ultimately from the great cultures of the ancient Near East and preserved during the monarchy within the royal cult in Jerusalem. Basic to this pattern is the dualism distinguishing between chaos and order, and the drama depicting that interrelationship. Here the description of chaos, or the collapse of the cosmos (Isa. 24:1–20), sets the stage for Yahweh's battle against the inimical hosts, a battle ending in a great victory and the restoration of this King's reign on his mountain (24:21–23). The worshippers, grateful for their deliverance, sing hymns of praise (25:1–5), all of which climaxes in the victory banquet prepared by the Divine Warrior (25:6–9). It is a pattern familiar to us from proto-apocalyptic and apocalyptic compositions covering the entire Second Temple period, compositions in which visionaries proclaim judgment on the leaders of their world and salvation for their own following.

Since the polemical application of this same pattern in the compositions found in Zechariah 10–14 has been discussed elsewhere, it need not be discussed anew here.[12] Suffice it to say that in those compositions, stemming from the same general period with which we are dealing here, dissident visionaries attack leaders and institutions they judge to be hostile to divine will, and then go on to depict the battles of the Divine Warrior who will come to deliver them and establish them in a kingdom of perfect peace and prosperity, where sacred status will not be restricted to a priestly elite, for "every pot in Jerusalem and Judah shall be sacred to the Lord of hosts, so that all who sacrifice may come and take of them and boil the flesh of the sacrifice in them" (Zech. 14:21). In other words, a community setting is reflected in which groups feeling frustrated in their attempts to influence the direction of the restoration find their only recourse to be a vision of violent divine intervention.

When taken together with the oracles of Third Isaiah, the visionary

12. Hanson, *Dawn of Apocalyptic*, pp. 280–401.

material sampled in this section raises the question of the contribution made by these earliest expressions of apocalyptic eschatology in Israel to the biblical notion of community. I have already pointed in the direction of a negative consideration, namely, that the type of polarization experienced between different groups within the early years after the return of Babylonian exiles to the land was inimical to the growth of a profound communal experience. Since Israel's understanding of religion was dynamic, and inextricably related to historical experiences, the conditions of life in any period had an effect on theological understanding. The quality of that life could not be divorced from the question of the quality of Israel's relationship with God.

In the earliest period of that relationship, self-understanding as a people grew out of the experience of God as Deliverer. From that experience arose the norms and values of the community. A very natural extension of that self-understanding was Second Isaiah's description of true Israel in terms of Yahweh's Servant. Israel was delivered and preserved in preparation for participating in God's plan of salvation as that plan unfolded to embrace all peoples. This was of course an awesome challenge, and it placed on true Israel a tremendous responsibility, for to be the agent of the God who redeemed by being present with humans meant embodying that God's nature, especially God's righteousness and compassion, which eschewed self-assertion in favor of patient, steadfast care for those lost in sin. Needless to say, this outer-directedness could arise only within the community gaining its orientation and self-understanding from a plan transcending human designs.

It is in the very nature of an historical faith that a specific generation either builds on the deepest insights of the generation preceding it, or fails to grow. At worst, it loses the orientation given by the best of its tradition, and degenerates into a more petty or even harmful self-concept. As we examine both (or all) sides of the controversies of the early postexilic period, we look in vain for a further development of the notion of the community as Servant of Yahweh. At first glance, the Third Isaiah group's transformation of the term "servant" into the plural might be interpreted as a commendable "democratization." Although I once interpreted it in this sense, I no longer believe this accounts for the whole phenomenon. Pluralization of the notion of servant may have helped some to understand their relationship to God in more personal terms. On the other hand, the final effect was not to broaden its application, but to cut it down in size so as to make it applicable only to the individuals belonging to one side of an increasingly divided community. By thus restricting and circumscribing its meaning, all that was awry within the community could be blamed on "the other side." This partitioning of course led to the ascription to one's own side of the divine promises of unlimited blessing, and to the other side of all of the curses of the covenant:

Therefore thus says the Lord God;
"Behold, my servants shall eat,
　but you shall be hungry;
behold, my servants shall drink,
　but you shall be thirsty;
behold, my servants shall rejoice,
　but you shall be put to shame;
behold, my servants shall sing for gladness of heart,
　but you shall cry out for pain of heart,
　and wail for anguish of spirit.
You shall leave your name to my chosen for a curse,
　and the Lord God will slay you
　but his servants he will call by a different name. (Isa. 65:13–15)

How different is the spirit behind this word spoken in the name of Yahweh from the divine word of Isaiah 49:6: "It is too light a thing that you should be my servant to raise up the tribes of Jacob and to restore the preserved of Israel; I will give you as a light to the nations, that my salvation may reach to the end of the earth." In these words, we find the image of the Servant being used to develop a concept of election for the sake of the salvation of "the other." In Isaiah 65, that image and the underlying concept of election become the basis for the condemnation, in the name of God, of "the other."

The first lesson the harsh literature of this period teaches us is thus a negative one: a fractured religious community is illsuited for the task of participating in God's redemptive plan for humanity. Energy intended for extending the orbit of šālôm to others becomes directed back in upon the agent community. In the form of interparty strife, it wreaks havoc with the ideals of that community. Partisan interests become confused with divine will, and religious practices become a mockery of the community's confessional heritage and even an offense to basic principles of human integrity. To be capable of serving as an agent of God's šālôm in the world, a religious community must restrain and relativize all party allegiances through acknowledgment of the sole sovereignty of God. This acknowledgment enables the community to imitate God's righteousness and compassion, to experience the harmony of the order God intends for the human family, and to serve faithfully in extending that harmony to others. Accordingly, the religious community experiencing painful divisions should eschew the temptation of adapting its vision of divine will to its partisan interests by condemning all opposition in the name of God, and instead should be prompted to ask what those divisions are saying about the quality of its own relationship to God.

A second lesson drawn from this tension-filled time in the history of Israel is this: although emerging badly scarred from this period, as a result both of the wounds inflicted by foreign adversaries and of those occurring through internal strife, those who remained faithful to traditional Yahwism had been tutored in a kind of realism that would equip them for the trials that awaited them in the coming centuries. As much as we are drawn to the sublime promises of Second Isaiah, and as much as the contemporaries of Haggai were no doubt drawn to his portrait of the heavens showering their treasures on the rebuilders of the temple, the authors of Ezekiel 38–39, Isaiah 24–27, and Zechariah 10–14 introduce what was probably a necessary corrective if the Yahwistic faith was to survive in the troubled times ahead. For they portrayed evil as a persistent and continuing threat to the community of faith. Unlike many of the Zadokite leaders of their time, they refused to regard any existing institution as elevated above this sinful state. The main theological insight emerging from this was the helplessness of humans, be they priests, prophets, or laity, to inaugurate the blessed era. For this they looked in yearning to God alone.

Finally, we recognize in the protest literature of this time the tendency to view the problem of evil and the need for divine deliverance on a universal, even cosmic scale. Human society had fallen to such a low point that minor change held out no basis for hope. Only a radical transformation affecting all creation could save the world from destruction. This insight would not be forgotten in future centuries, and can be credited with adding both greater depth and greater breadth to late biblical, "intertestamental," and New Testament theology.

Drawing attention to the lasting contribution of certain early apocalyptic writings is not intended to detract from the earlier observation that an important insight of early Yahwism was also threatened by these writings—namely, that the vision of God's deliverance was not to be left in the head of the seer, but was to become a norm for political and social reform. Even at this point, however, we must not overlook the persistence of an essential prophetic theme in these writings, namely, the moral responsibility born by the community of faith. This we have seen, for example, in one of the most shocking of all apocalyptic pictures, that found in Isaiah 24–25. There Yahweh is seen reducing the earth and the heavens to chaos. But the reason is neither divine caprice nor blind vengeance. The universe is still interpreted as a strictly moral universe. The lesson being taught is that preservation of the fragile beauty of life both in society and in nature is inextricably tied to the response of the human community to God's gracious initiatives and to its observance of the righteous order established by God in the Mosaic covenant. The threat of a world returned to primeval chaos is the threat of a covenant community's abdication of its primary responsibility of acknowledging the sole sovereignty of the Deliverer God Yahweh through acts of compassion and righteousness. In the realm of human communities as in nature, when the nucleus of a living cell disintegrates, the viability of the entire cell is destroyed, and ultimately the whole organism is threatened. Even the late offspring of the prophets, the apocalyptic seers, did not lose sight of the central theme of Yahwism regarding the relation of the community called into being by God to other peoples. Indeed, they pointed in the direction of a new and wider application still: That community, as agent of God's *šālôm*, was vital to the wholeness of the entire universe. Its dereliction in relation to the covenant and its *tôrâ* threatened to bring with it the most dire of consequences: "The earth lies polluted under its inhabitants; for they have transgressed the laws, violated the statutes, broken the everlasting covenant" (Isa. 24:5).

From this assessment of the contributions of some of Israel's earliest apocalyptic writings—especially when those contributions are viewed in relation to the writings of the Zadokite leadership group examined in the previous section—it becomes clear that we inherit from this period a very mixed legacy. But given the fractured nature of the community in the early postexilic period, we are saddened but hardly surprised to find a response to life filled with violent images and visions of frightful retribution. We are dealing here as before with a community of faith seeking to live faithfully to its heritage within hitherto unexperienced circumstances. But the quality of its intracommunity life was such as to ill prepare it to blaze courageous new paths. One leaves this period with the feeling that much searching and testing lay ahead before new forms of community could evolve that would be capable of sustaining the people of God in a world vastly different from that of their ancestors.

D. MALACHI

The inner community struggle for leadership in the restoration of the society and cult in the years 538–515, while producing a very mixed theological legacy, issued forth in a very clear political result: the Zadokite priestly party emerged as the head of the reconstituted community, both in cultic and civil matters. Although leadership was at first shared between Davidic prince and Zadokite high priest—that is, between Zerubbabel and Joshua—the former disappeared from the scene by the time of the temple's dedication in 515, leaving the Zadokite high priest as the sole head over the people in all domestic matters. The qualification "domestic" is important, inasmuch as all matters whose significance extended beyond the borders of Judah were governed by the ultimate sovereign of the land, the Persian king. The reconstituted Judah was the product of Persian international policy, and its continued existence would depend on its accommodating to this larger reality.

The victory of the Zadokites no doubt reduced open conflicts in the land, at least momentarily. And this was precisely the motivation behind the Persian court's support of the Zadokite leadership, for it achieved the strategic goal of creating a dependable buffer on the southwestern flank of its empire bordering on the territory of one of the enemies of the Persians, the Egyptians. But it is equally evident that this political victory was not without its social, cultural, and religious costs within Jewish society. As a bonded vassal of the Persians, the state of Judah was obliged to honor military, economic, and cultic commitments that in some cases created direct conflicts with important principles of Yahwistic faith. Moreover, dissident voices that since 538 had been seeking to establish their alternative visions of the restoration, were silenced, leaving wounds that would continue to fester. And from a theological perspective, we have already suggested that the intensification of the pragmatic facets of the Zadokite program led to the repression of important aspects of Yahwistic faith that the disenfranchised visionaries held dear, but which they were no longer in a position to represent within the life of the community. The people of Judah accordingly entered the fifth century as a hierocratic community dominated by a priestly class dedicated to the pragmatic concerns of consolidating and maintaining control over the land and its cult, and not hesitating to use the political power at its disposal to accomplish its purposes.

From the viewpoint of many traditional Yahwists, Judah's leaders had turned away from Israel's ultimate allegiance, and had turned instead to penultimate concerns. This constituted within their traditional theological understanding a breach of covenant, and brought with it both the threat of further social decay and finally divine judgment, unless the people repented and returned to Yahweh as their sole sovereign.

When we next come on sources reflecting the conditions in the land, we find that the decades immediately following the dedication of the Second Temple were marked by social stagnation and religious decline. The first half of the fifth century B.C.E. was apparently lacking in outstanding leaders. As for the opposition, it had been left in disarray by the Zadokite domination of cult and land. A solitary voice crying out against the ominous new trends and appealing to the traditional values of ancient Yahwism was an anonymous figure who came to be designated Malachi (as the result of a misreading of the title "my messenger," mal'ākî, in Mal. 1:1 as a proper name). The question of the identity of the opposition group for which Malachi served as spokesperson is of great interest, and is addressed shortly. But first it is important to sketch the major themes of the book itself.

The degeneration of the community as portrayed in the Book of Malachi engulfed a broad cross section of the people. The situation was marked by violence, disregard of fidelity in marriage, and consorting with devotees of foreign gods. And as if that were not enough, the members of this community are portrayed as going further to assert insolently that "everyone who does evil is good in the sight of the Lord, and he delights in them." And then, apparently feeling immune from divine punishment, they quip, "Where is the God of justice?" (Mal. 1:17). Although such polemical rhetoric must be interpreted as a reflection of a particular perspective, it is significant to observe that in the minds of the opposition the land is diabolically locked into a situation of total perversion of justice:

You have said, "it is vain to serve God." What is the good of our keeping his charge or of walking as in mourning before the Lord of hosts? Henceforth we deem the arrogant blessed; evildoers not only prosper but when they put God to the test they escape." (Mal. 3:14–15)

This perception bears striking resemblance to that of the group opposed to the Zadokite leadership two generations earlier as reflected in the oracles of Third Isaiah:

> Justice is turned back,
>   and righteousness stands afar off;
> for truth has fallen in the public squares
>   and uprightness cannot enter.
> Truth is lacking,
>   and he who departs from evil makes himself a prey. (Isa. 59:14–15)

In both cases, the judgment on the moral and religious state of the community is total. And in both cases hope resides in the minority group's confidence that Yahweh would not allow such a situation to continue for long. For what had occurred in the land was nothing less than a rejection of Yahweh's rule and a profanation of "the covenant of our fathers" (Mal. 2:10).

Although the indictment found in Malachi is against the people quite generally, it does single out one group as uniquely responsible for the sad state of affairs. And that group is the priesthood, and more specifically in this period this means the Zadokite priests. They are condemned for neither honoring nor fearing Yahweh, thereby giving a pathetic example for the people to follow. One recalls a similar attack on the nation's leaders in anonymous words attached to the Book of Zechariah that likely stem from roughly the same period and setting:

> For the teraphim utter nonsense,
>   and the diviners see lies;
> the dreamers tell false dreams,
>   and give empty consolation.
> Therefore the people wander like sheep;
>   they are afflicted for want of a shepherd.
> My anger is hot against the shepherds,
>   and I will punish the leaders;
> for the Lord of hosts cares for his flocks. (Zech. 10:2–3a)

As regards the specific accusations, the priests are charged with offering animals they have gotten by violence (Mal. 1:13), or that are blind, lame, or sick. Thus they affront the honor of Yahweh in a way they would not even consider in relation to their governor (Mal. 1:6–8). Yahweh's response is commensurate with the quality of their service: "Oh, that there were one among you who would shut the doors, that you might not kindle fire upon my altar in vain! I have no pleasure in you, says the Lord of hosts, and I will not accept an offering from your hand" (Mal. 1:10). But from the side of the priests there is no sign of repentance, but only brazen defiance and smug arrogance: " 'What a weariness this is,' you say, and you sniff at me, says the Lord of hosts" (Mal. 1:13a). Here too we hear an echo of the bitter complaint in Isaiah 65:5 against priests who say, "Keep to yourself, do not come near me, for I am set apart from you." In that context Yahweh replied,

> These are a smoke in my nostrils,
>   a fire that burns all the day.
> Behold it is written before me:
>   I will not keep silent, but I will repay,
> yea, I will repay into their bosom
>   their iniquities and their fathers' iniquities together
>   says the Lord.   (Isa. 65:5b–7)

In Malachi, the judgment on the priests is correspondingly harsh: "Behold, I will rebuke your offspring, and spread dung upon your faces, the dung of your offerings, and I will put you out of my presence" (Mal. 2:3). A stronger word of repudiation could scarcely have been pronounced against the presiding priests![13]

The indictment developed in the oracles of Malachi is stinging. But it is not an example of blind vindictiveness. It is apparent that its critique of people and priests is based on an alternative notion of community to the one embodied by the Zadokites. And indeed its close ties to earlier prophetic oracles and the archaic Yahwistic notion of community make

13. In this connection, it is interesting to take note of a suggestion recently made by Michael Fishbane that Malachi 1:16–2:9 is an exegetical oration on the priestly blessing of Numbers 6:23–27, composed to press the accusation that "the priests have despised the divine name and service," leading "to a threatened suspension of the divine blessing." According to this opposition position, the result of such dereliction on the part of the officiating priests was that the šālôm which through their agency was to permeate the community, had been supplanted by a curse. In a reversal of the traditional Yahwistic pattern of true worship followed by an even-handed and impartial imitation of Yahweh's righteousness and compassion, the accusation states that the priests "raise the countenance" in overt partiality and misuse of tôrâ. Fishbane concludes: "A more violent condemnation of the priests can hardly be imagined. . . . By unfolding the negative semantic range of most of the key terms used positively in the [Priestly Blessing of Numbers 6], the rotten core and consequences of the language and behaviors of the priests echoes throughout the diatribe. . . . The prophetic speech of Malachi, itself spoken as a divine word, is thus revealed to be no less than a divine exegesis and mockery of the priests who presume to bless in His Name." M. Fishbane, "Form and Reformulation of the Biblical Priestly Blessing," *JAOS* 103 (1983), 119.

it clear that in Malachi the appeal was being made for a return to an earlier ideal. In the plea to return to acknowledgment of Yahweh as sole sovereign and to the imitation of Yahweh's righteousness and compassion, one discerns unmistakeably the triadic notion of community characteristic of earlier Israel. Indeed it is that notion that underlies every one of the pronouncements in Malachi. Priests and people are on this basis charged with betraying true worship, and thereby hastening the unraveling of the moral fabric of the nation. But even in a setting where the people dare to taunt Yahweh with the words, "Where is the God of Justice?" this group holds fast to its belief in a God who stands at the side of the poor, the widow, the orphan, and the sojourner against all who oppress them (Mal. 3:5). The roots of Malachi in the notion of community expressed by the Book of the Covenant, Deuteronomy, and the classical prophets are deep and clear.

Now to return specifically to the question of the identity of the opposition group represented by Malachi, the numerous parallels in theme and underlying setting between Isaiah 56–66 and Malachi are suggestive. Although the sources are not complete enough to enable us to describe precisely the opposition groups coming to expression in the anonymous materials found in Isaiah 56–66, Malachi, and Zechariah 10–11, it is at least clear that they are all united in a harsh, and often vitriolic critique of the Zadokite leadership. For common in all these materials is the appeal to earlier norms as the basis for opposition to the policies and practices of the Zadokites. To be sure, one would have to go beyond conclusions warranted by the evidence to conclude that we are dealing in all these protest materials with one well-organized party with a carefully formulated opposition program and a consistent political policy. Instead, one must be sensitive to the specificity of each group represented. In the case of Malachi, we are probably witnessing the protest of a group very close to the temple cult itself, for the book is permeated by "priestly" interests. In the case of the material in Isaiah 56–66, disenfranchised Levitical elements making common cause with disciples of Second Isaiah were likely behind the attack on the Zadokite leadership. It is not impossible that the combination of cultic concerns and apocalyptic themes in Malachi hints at a similar coalition of prophetic and priestly elements active some fifty years later. Support for this suggestion might be found in the salvation-judgment oracular form that appears in fully developed form for the first time in Isaiah 56–66 and recurs in the Book of Malachi.[14] It is equally possible, however, that the harsh critique coming to expression in Malachi arises out of a new split within the priesthood. That is to say, it may be that the degeneration in praxis and in general morality inveighed against by this book, while characteristic of the majority of the Zadokite priest-

14. Hanson, *Dawn of Apocalyptic*, pp. 106–107, 143–145.

hood, was resisted by some of the Zadokites, with the result that their protests and reform efforts led to their disenfranchisement and marginalization. In this case, the resulting alliance would have been similar to that which produced the writings of Isaiah 56–66, for such dissident Zadokite priests would have found a new home within circles that continued to criticize the existing institutions and leaders from a prophetic point of view, circles that were responding to repression by inclining toward an apocalyptic form of eschatological hope.

As in the case of the opposition group to which Isaiah 56–66 bears witness, the group coming to expression in the oracles of Malachi based its protest on an appeal to an ideal of Yahwism more archaic than that of its opponents. In Malachi, that archaic ideal is in fact named expressly as Yahweh's "covenant with Levi." The passage that describes this ideal is an important piece of evidence for anyone attempting to identify the group raising its voice in protest against what it judges to be a corrupt temple priesthood. It follows directly on Yahweh's pronouncement of a curse against the unfaithful Zadokite priests, which curse is resumed again at the conclusion of the description of the "covenant with Levi." The result of this structural "envelope" is that the fallenness of the Zadokites is placed in sharpest possible contrast with the Levitical ideal:

. . . and I will put you out of my presence. So shall you know that I have sent this command to you, that my covenant with Levi may hold, says the Lord of hosts. My covenant with him was a covenant of life and peace, and I gave them to him, that he might fear; and he feared me, he stood in awe of my name. True instruction [tôrâ] was in his mouth, and no wrong was found on his lips. He walked with me in peace and uprightness, and he turned many away from iniquity. For the lips of a priest should guard knowledge, and men should seek instruction [tôrâ] from his mouth, for he is the messenger of the Lord of hosts. But you have turned aside from the way; you have caused many to stumble by your instruction [tôrâ]; you have corrupted the covenant of Levi, says the Lord of hosts, and so I make you despised and abased before all the people, inasmuch as you have not kept my ways but have shown partiality in your instruction [tôrâ]. (Mal. 2:3b–9)

In searching for a model to hold up before a corrupt priesthood, the opposition group coming to expression in the Book of Malachi thus goes behind the Zadokite victory to an earlier stage of Israel's history, when the Levites served Yahweh as priests. In this move we see unmistakably the ideal of priesthood espoused by this opposition group, as it seeks to re-establish itself in the priesthood as a means of restoring health to the community: "Then the offering of Judah and Jerusalem will be pleasing to the Lord as in the days of old and as in former years" (Mal. 3:4). In sharp contrast to the division between priests and Levites that had developed under the leadership of the Zadokites, that is reflected in the Priestly Writing and Ezekiel 44, Malachi's "covenant with

Levi" recognizes no such distinction. It reflects instead the earlier ideal expressed in Deuteronomy 18:1–8.

As in the case of the visionary followers of Second Isaiah, however, in the case of the "Malachi" group the vision of a righteous community of priests has been frustrated by the bitter experience of opposition from the very priestly party leading the people deeper into social decay and its dreadful consequences. This bleak social setting seems to explain the other major characteristic of the oracles of Malachi, namely, their eschatological overtone, which moves powerfully in the direction of later apocalyptic eschatology. In circles convinced that the wickedness of the community and its leaders had once again banished Yahweh from the land, hope was maintained in the form of a vision of Yahweh's return as Divine Warrior to banish evil and to refine a remnant capable of reconstituting a holy cult in Jerusalem (Mal. 3:1–4 and 3:19–21 [Evv. 4:1–3]). Yahweh would personally attend to restoring a pure priesthood out of the sons of Levi. The community would be reconstituted in faithfulness and holiness, enabling Yahweh to abide in its midst. Although Yahweh's sudden return as Divine Warrior to purge and refine anticipates the mode of divine intervention found in later apocalyptic writings, the oracles of Malachi do not abdicate responsibility for the present order in the manner characteristic of later apocalyptic writings. The opposition group seems to cling to the hope that through its agency God would be able to call the community back to its senses. A curse rests on the land, and especially on the apostate Zadokite priests, but even the latter were not placed beyond the realm of possible repentance: "Return to me, and I will return to you, says the Lord of hosts" (Mal. 3:7).

But what would be the mark of the faithful people, once Yahweh had refined and restored land and temple? Clearly, as noted earlier, it would be a people acknowledging the sole lordship of Yahweh, and a people embodying Yahweh's righteousness and compassion. Equally clearly, it would not be a people defined by the facile criterion of Zadokite party affiliation. That approach, which had gained such influence in the late sixth and early fifth centuries, was emphatically repudiated by Malachi. If the Zadokites were not God's chosen agents in the restoration, then who were? The Book of Malachi offers a surprising answer, the significance of which for the subsequent history of Judaism (and Christianity) can scarcely be overestimated:

Then those who feared the Lord [yir'ê yhwh] spoke with one another; the Lord heeded and heard them, and a book of remembrance was written before him of those who feared the Lord and thought on his name. "They shall be mine, says the Lord of hosts, my special possession on the day when I act, and I will spare them as a man spares his son who serves him. Then once more you shall distinguish between the righteous and the wicked, between one who serves God and one who does not serve him." (Mal. 3:16–18)

In reference to the awesome day of Yahweh's advent to restore a righteous poeple, Yahweh's "special possession" is specified. Surprisingly it was not to be the high priest, or the Zadokites, or the Davidic king, but "those who feared the Lord (yir'ê yhwh)." What is the significance of this term, and to whom does it apply?

An important clue relating to this question is found in several Psalms that likely stem from roughly the same period as the Book of Malachi. They seem to reflect a ritual setting, since they list in a formal manner groups involved in a liturgical proceeding:

> O Israel, trust in the Lord!
>   He is their help and their shield.
> O house of Aaron, put your trust in the Lord!
>   He is their help and their shield.
> You who fear the Lord, trust in the Lord!
>   He is their help and their shield.
> The Lord has been mindful of us; he will bless us;
>   he will bless the house of Israel;
>   he will bless the house of Aaron;
> he will bless those who fear the Lord,
>   both small and great. (Ps. 115:9–13)

> O give thanks to the Lord, for he is good;
>   his steadfast love endures for ever!
> Let Israel say,
>   "His steadfast love endures for ever."
> Let those who fear the Lord say,
>   "His steadfast love endures for ever." (Ps. 118:1–4)

> O house of Israel, bless the Lord!
>   O house of Aaron, bless the Lord!
>   O house of Levi, bless the Lord!
>   You who fear the Lord, bless the Lord. (Ps. 135:19–20)

"Those who fear the Lord" in these psalms seems to designate a group entitled to a place of honor in the worship life of the people equivalent to that of the priestly house, and quite apart from any special status or quality other than their fear of Yahweh. It seems that the protest group expressing its views in Malachi, in its effort to call the people to a communal and cultic ideal that is both more archaic and more open than that of the Zadokites, found the designation "those who fear the Lord" an appropriate one for describing Yahweh's "special possession"; that is, the eschatological community remaining faithful to the Lord, and standing in readiness to serve as Yahweh's agent in restoring true worship, righteousness, and compassion in the land. No doubt Psalm 147:10–11, by contrasting "those who fear the Lord" with that which is powerful in the world, would also have enhanced their sense of identification with this term (cf. also Ps. 119:74):

> [The Lord's] delight is not in the strengh of the horse,
> nor his pleasure in the legs of a man,
> but the Lord takes pleasure in those who fear him,
> in those who hope in his steadfast love. (Ps. 147:10–11)

A close parallel to this term and its usage in Malachi is found in the kindred passage Isaiah 66:1–2, where Yahweh, after repudiating the group that under Zadokite leadership was rebuilding the Jerusalem temple, gives this description of the favored one:

> But this is the man to whom I will look,
> He that is humble and contrite in spirit,
> and trembles at my word. (Isa. 66:2b)

While the two terms are not identical, both seem to describe the same notion, thereby lending support to the view that the "Malachi" group was related historically in some way to the dissidents of Isaiah 56–66.

All in all, it seems clear that the protagonists of Malachi found in the epithet "those who fear Yahweh" (which occurs also in Ps. 14:4; 119:79; and in Eccles. 7:18) the designation of faithful followers of God who, often in contrast and even in opposition to those of power and authority, placed God and God's will over all else through pure worship and through godly conduct of their lives. With this epithet, they were able to identify wholeheartedly. While this survey of the use of the term "those who fear Yahweh" in other biblical texts supplies important background information, its application in the Book of Malachi represents a fresh formulation of the term that makes a significant contribution to postexilic thought. Here is a bold claim that in the "day of Yahweh" all criteria would dissolve before the one based on distinguishing between those who did and did not fear Yahweh. Those who feared Yahweh would be Yahweh's chosen, more specifically, Yahweh's "special possession" (segullâ). In the case of all others, even priestly status would not save them from the wrath to come.

The term "special possession" was doubtlessly used to amplify the meaning of "those who fear Yahweh" because of its rich associations. It is the term used in the ancient liturgical text in Exodus 19:1–8 as Yahweh's designation of the people called into covenant relationship on Sinai, along with the terms "kingdom of priests" and "holy nation." Malachi 3:16–18 seems to be proposing a radical redefinition of what constituted the true people of God. When God had reestablished those who "feared Yahweh" as God's special possession, then the order of righteousness and compassion that was the divine order intended by God would supplant the existing fallen order and its corrupt priestly leaders. True Israel would be reconstituted in holiness, and Yahweh would again be present in its midst. The confusion and moral chaos perpetrated by Israel's unfaithful leaders would finally yield to a true sense of justice: "Then once more you shall distinguish between the righteous and the wicked, between one who serves God and one who does not serve him" (3:18).

In the verses immediately following, the participation of "those who fear my name" in Yahweh's act of judgment and restoration is described. While in that dread day "all the arrogant and all evildoers" would be burned like stubble, a wonderful promise was given to the faithful: "But for you who fear my name the sun of righteousness shall rise, with healing in its wings. You shall go forth leaping like calves from the stall. And you shall tread down the wicked" (Mal. 3:20–21 [Evv. 4:23]). The broken and embattled community of faithful was thus encouraged to persevere, confident in the promise that soon it would be drawn to the only true source of healing, the God of righteousness whose "rising" was near. Although social and political realities seemed to contradict that hope, they could rest confidently in the knowledge that their words to one another did not go unheeded by God, and that their names were written in "a book of remembrance . . . before him" (Mal. 3:16).

One characteristic of the circles described as "visionary" was a tendency to construe Yahweh's final act of judgment and salvation with a breadth that went beyond tribal or national boundaries. This was apparent in Isaiah 49, as well as in oracles coming from Second Isaiah's followers (Isa. 59 and 66). This "universalistic" tendency is also apparent in Malachi, both in Yahweh's judgment against "all evildoers" and in the vision of Yahweh's reign that was to embrace all nations: "For from the rising of the sun to its setting my name is great among the nations, and in every place incense is offered to my name, and a pure offering; for my name is great among the nations, says the Lord of hosts" (Mal. 1:11). Even within the bleak circumstances of the first half of the fifth century the narrowing of the restoration vision, and the accompanying accommodation to the political realities of the Persian empire that characterized the official policy of the Zadokites, were being resisted in certain circles on the basis of the vision of a divine purpose that was to embrace all of the families of the earth. Although that vision at times hardened into a pronouncement of divine judgment on all except the "elect," what is more remarkable is the degree to which God's saving activity was seen to extend to all the families of the earth.

Since many Protestant scholars seem to identify indications of a universal vision in the Hebrew Bible with a purported de-emphasis on the role of the *tôrâ*, it is important to note that in Malachi, as indeed in the classic formulation of Israel's universal mission in Isaiah 42 and 49, *tôrâ* continues to enjoy its position at the center of the vision of the restored community: "Remember the law of my servant Moses, the statutes and ordinances that I commanded him at Horeb for all Israel" (Mal. 3:22 [Evv. 4:4]). What we witness in Malachi, as in Third Isaiah and Zechariah 9–14, is not an antinominian, anticlerical, or antitemple movement, but rather opposition to specific policies and practices of the Zadokites, especially (1) their realized eschatology, which seemed to equate God's plan with their own institutional structures; (2) their accommodating attitude toward the Persian empire, and (3) their exclusion of priestly groups outside of their own. Specifically as regards temple praxis, they advocated a far more stringent observance of *tôrâ* than they observed in the officiating priests. Although the intracommunity conflicts of the early postexilic period were often bitter, and involved sharp differences both in theology and praxis, there is no indication during this period that any of the contending groups denied the centrality of *tôrâ* in the life of the community.

Once this is clear, the significance of the actual points of contention can be evaluated, especially in light of the bearing they would have on future developments. In this connection, another piece of evidence for the oppostiion movement of the early fifth century is of interest. It is found in the editorial framework around the oracles of Isaiah 56–66, which likely derives from the same group that produced the Book of Malachi. We have already made frequent reference to similarities between the oracles of Third Isaiah and the themes of Malachi. It is not surprising, therefore, that the group out of which Malachi arose also saw fit to edit the oracles of Third Isaiah, and to add a framework that served to highlight the themes at the center of its concerns, like the restoration of justice in the land, the reestablishment of a faithful priesthood, and the opening up of the cult to elements excluded by the Zadokites:

> Thus says the Lord:
> "Keep justice, and do righteousness,
> for soon my salvation will come,
>   and my deliverance be revealed.
> Blessed is the man who does this,
>   and the son of man who holds it fast,
> who keeps the sabbath, not profaning it,
>   and keeps his hand from doing any evil." (Isa. 56:1–2)

As in the case of the Book of Malachi, emphasis on fidelity to *tôrâ*, and specifically to sabbath observance, is wedded with an attitude of cultic toleration that stands in starkest contrast to the exclusivism of the Zadokite priesthood. In opposition to their elitism, Yahweh is depicted as a God seeking to embrace most especially those who had suffered exclusion due to physical defect or accident of birth. The polemical nature of the entire oracle in Isaiah 56:1–8 is unmistakable, for it stands as a frontal attack on the priestly ordinance that the Zadokite priests used to sanction their exclusion of all rivals, an ordinance preserved in Deuteronomy 23:1–6:

He whose testicles are crushed or whose male member is cut off shall not enter the assembly of the Lord. No bastard shall enter the assembly of the Lord; even to the tenth generation none of his descendants shall enter the assembly of the Lord; even to the tenth generation none belonging to them shall enter the assembly of the Lord for ever. . . .

On what basis could this trend toward exclusion, and the accompanying narrowing of leadership status to one priestly group be resisted by the visionary-Levitical opposition? The answer is given by the concluding verse of the oracle in Isaiah 56:1–8, which identifies the divine speaker as the one whose action was directed toward ever greater inclusion rather than toward exclusion:

> Thus says the Lord God,
>   who gathers the outcasts of Israel,
> I will gather yet others to him
>   besides those already gathered. (Isa. 56:8)

It seems likely that their own bitter experience of exclusion had created among the dissident visionaries and Levites an awareness of the presence in the wider world of others suffering as outcasts. In this way they came to grasp anew the central confession of early Yahwism that Israel's God was a merciful Deliverer. It would seem that this central confession and the communal qualities of righteousness and compassion that derived from it and that had constituted the heart of the early Yahwistic notion of community were better understood by those losing the struggle for pre-eminence in the restoration era than by the Zadokite victors. It was within such circles that the archaic notion of "a kingdom of priests" (Exod. 19:6) and the exilic vision of a nation in which "your people shall all be righteous," and be "called the priests of the Lord" (Isa. 60:21 and 61:6) were reaffirmed during the bleak years prior to the arrival of Ezra and Nehemiah. For those struggling to retain their membership in a cult whose leaders sought to exclude them, the confession in the God who vindicated those unjustly oppressed took on a new poignancy. And their own suffering no doubt helped foster an awareness of God's concern for all others who suffered the ignominy of exclusion:

> Let not the foreigner who has joined
>   himself to the Lord say,
>   "The Lord will surely separate
>   me from his people;"
> and let not the eunuch say,
>   "Behold, I am a dry tree."
> For thus says the Lord:
> "To the eunuchs who keep my sabbaths,
>   who choose the things that please me,
>   and hold fast my covenant,
> I will give in my house and within my walls
>   a monument and a name
>   better than sons and daughters;

> I will give them an everlasting name
>> which shall not be cut off.
> And the foreigners who join themselves to the Lord,
>> to minister to him, to love the name of the Lord,
>> and to be his servants,
> every one who keeps the sabbath, and does not profane it,
>> and holds fast my covenant—
> these I will bring to my holy mountain,
>> and make them joyful in my house of prayer;
> their burnt offerings and their sacrifices
>> will be accepted on my altar
> for my house shall be called a house of prayer
>> for all peoples. (Isa. 56:3–7)

The remarkable inclusiveness of this oracle extends even beyond that found in Malachi 1:11, for while the latter passage acknowledges Yahweh's universal sovereignty, this oracle announces that outcasts and foreigners would even participate within the cult! While noting this difference, however, we must be equally aware of the common quality underlying both, an outer-directedness that comes to expression in the concluding formulas of both of the passages: ". . . in every place incense is offered to my name, and a pure offering; for my name is great among the nations, says the Lord of hosts" (Mal. 1:11); ". . . their burnt offerings and their sacrifices will be accepted on my altar; for my house shall be called a house of prayer for all peoples" (Isa. 56:7).

In the latter half of the editorial framework of Isaiah 56–66, we once again encounter the visionary perspective, with Yahweh being depicted as One coming "to gather all nations and tongues" (Isa. 66:18). Within the context of this universal restoration, in which the narrow exclusivism of the Zadokite leaders would be forced to yield to God's cosmic plan, ample space of course would be created for the reinstatement of Levites who since Josiah's reform had been forced to live outside the priesthood. For those suffering at the hands of their powerful leaders, hope resided in the vison of a new order in which Yahweh alone would designate leaders. The breadth of vision and generosity toward other outcasts characteristic of the dissidents of the fifth century is thus intimately related to their own yearning for inclusion:

And from them I will send survivors to the nations, . . . And they shall bring all your brethren from all the nations as an offering to the Lord. . . . And some of them also I will take for priests and for Levites, says the Lord. (Isa 66:19–21)

While the officiating priests were devoting their energies to the pragmatic concerns of cult and nation, those who fell outside the benefits of the present social structures dreamed of a radically new order in which their rights would be restored:

> For as the new heavens and the new earth
>> which I will make
> shall remain before me, says the Lord,
>> so shall your descendants and your name remain.
> From new moon to new moon,
>> and from sabbath to sabbath,
> all flesh shall come to worship before me,
>> says the Lord. (Isa. 66:22–23)

Within the broad context of the history of the development of the notion of community in the Hebrew Bible, we thus come to recognize that the dissident stream consisting of protesting visionaries and disenfranchsed Levites (and possibly including even some disaffected Zadokite priests) made a notable contribution. In their own time, their message was unable to stem the tide of Zadokite consolidation and priestly monopoly. As we shall see later, the exclusivism of Judah's leaders actually increased in the latter half of the fifth century. But beyond that century, the effect of this minority's witness was not inconsiderable. It contributed within important segments of the Jewish community to a renewal of commitment to bringing the Torah to the nations. It also encouraged ongoing critique of the pragmatic equation that was abetting the parochialism of the time and encouraging a policy of political expediency and religious accommodation. Partly as a result of the perseverance of the circles that produced Malachi, Zechariah 9–14, and the editorial framework of Third Isaiah, Israel did not lose the early Yahwistic vision of a kingdom living in righteousness and compassion under the sole sovereignty of Yahweh and dedicated to an extension of the kingdom of šālôm to all peoples. Indeed, the central confession in Yahweh the Deliverer and key terms like "those who fear Yahweh" recurs among believers of later generations who took their clues from the visionaries of the late sixth and early fifth centuries. But first we turn to trace further the history of the hierocratic majority.

IX

The Consolidation of the Community Around the Torah
(Chronicles, Ezra, and Nehemiah)

You have seen the house built, you have seen it adorned
By one who came in the night, it is now dedicated to GOD.[1]

Historical Note: From 583 until 332 B.C.E., Judah was a vassal
state within the Persian Empire. From roughly 510 on, it was
organized as a hierocracy under the leadership of the Zadokite
high priest. Although struggling for survival and threatened
by a low morale and internal dissension in the first half of the
fifth century, a thoroughgoing reform occurred beginning in
the middle and latter half of that century, which consolidated
the community around the temple and established the social
and cultic structures that prevailed through the next three
centuries, and ultimately provided the foundation on which
rabbinical Judaism was constructed. The central figures in the
reform were Ezra and Nehemiah. The central authority on
which they based the specific aspects of their reform was the
Torah of Moses. The principal documents on which we can
draw for this period are Chronicles, Ezra, and Nehemiah.

A. THE REFORM UNDER EZRA AND NEHEMIAH

By the mid-fifth century, the religious community gathered around
the Jerusalem temple was in a very vulnerable position. Priests neglected their duties, the nobility's high rates of interest were impoverishing
the populace, governors were living lives of luxury at the expense of
their destitute subjects. In a broader political context, where the leaders of the province to the north centered in Samaria greeted every adversity in Judah as an enhancement of their own chances of being able
to annex their southern neighbors, a process was thus set in motion
that was virtually certain to lead to disaster if powerful measures were
not taken to reverse the trend. We have already called attention to one

1. T. S. Eliot, "Choruses from 'The Rock,' " in *The Complete Poems and Plays, 1909–
1950* (New York: Harcourt, Brace, 1952), p. 112.

stream of tradition, fostered down to this period by elements excluded from positions of leadership in temple and community, which interpreted every setback as further evidence of God's impending judgment. According to this view, only after the land had been purged of its present leaders could God inaugurate a new era of blessing and prosperity, an era in which those disenfranchised by the Zadokites would be elevated to positions of honor and in which all the nations would bring tribute to the glorified Zion.

This visionary position in turn had been discredited by so many unfulfilled prophecies that the stage was set for a pragmatic program of reform coming from within the existing cultic and communal structures and offices. All that was necessary was a catalyst. That role was filled powerfully and impressively by Ezra and Nehemiah, who came to Jerusalem from Persia with royal permission to reform the languishing community. In a propitious manner, the interests of the religious leaders of Judah and the established foreign policy of the Persian empire converged: Judah was to be strengthened as a buffer state bordering Persia's chief enemy Egypt by the renewal of the cult on the basis of the Torah. This state of affairs was ideally suited for a Zadokite leadership class willing to collaborate with the Persian authorities as a means of safeguarding its own position of pre-eminence and of strengthening the cause of its own program of community reform.

The question of whether Ezra preceded Nehemiah, or vice versa, is still debated, and cannot be taken up anew here. Each contributed specific elements to the overall reform associated with these two figures, and therefore the historical question does not affect the analysis of the reform in general. More important in this context is the relation of the Ezra and Nehemiah literary sources to the interpretative work of the Chronicler, who drew those sources into his larger history, which extends from 1 and 2 Chronicles through Ezra and Nehemiah. Most valuable as an historical source are the Nehemiah Memoirs in Nehemiah 1:1–7:5, 11–13, and 9:38–10:39 (with mention of Ezra added secondarily in 12:26 and 36), for they give us a reliable account of Nehemiah's work between 445 and 433. The Ezra source in Ezra 7–10 and Nehemiah 8:1–9:37 (with mention of Nehemiah added secondarily in 8:9) combines historically reliable sources (like the Artaxerxes Edict in Ezra 7:12–16) and oral traditions about Ezra with the Chronicler's own commentary. The latter is also the dominant element in Ezra 1–6 and Nehemiah 7:6–73a (Heb. 72a).

On all levels of tradition, Ezra is identified with the mission of reading the Torah of Moses to the assembly of Jews gathered in Jerusalem and of renewing the covenant between God and community on the basis of this Torah. There is no doubt that this accurately describes Ezra's chief contribution to reform.[2] It is a picture that can be filled in with a fair degree of probability. As indicated by the genealogy in Ezra 7:1–5,

2. Cf. K. Koch, "Ezra and the Origins of Judaism," *JSS* 19 (1974), 173–197.

Ezra himself was a Zadokite priest (Ezra 7:1–5). "The law of Moses" [*tôrat mōšeh*] in which he was skilled as a scribe (7:6) may have been some form of the Pentateuch, that is to say the Torah as it had been developed toward its authoritative form by Zadokite priests in Babylon. At any rate, in Chronicles, Ezra, Nehemiah, and writings coming from later in the Persian and Hellenistic periods, *tôrâ* frequently refers specifically to the "Books of Moses"; that is, the Pentateuch. Whereas we have used the transliterated form of "*tôrâ*" in this study whenever that word was applied in its broad sense, we shall render the narrower sense of the "Five Books of Moses" with the form "Torah."

The Aramaic "Letter of Artaxerxes" in Ezra 7:12–26, though reworked somewhat from the Chronicle's perspective, likely gives an accurate account of the commission granted Ezra by the Persian court: "For you are sent by the king and his seven counselors to make inquiries about Judah and Jerusalem according to the law [Aramaic *dāt*] of your God, which is in your hand (Ezra 7:14). In this task Ezra was granted both financial and legal support by the Persians, and exemption from taxes for himself and his priestly colleagues.

Ezra's assignment is described in more detail in the concluding paragraph of the royal letter:

And you, Ezra, according to the wisdom of your God which is in your hand, appoint magistrates and judges who may judge all the people in the province Beyond the River, all such as know the laws of your God; and those who do not know them, you shall teach. Whoever will not obey the law of your God and the law of the king, let judgment be strictly executed upon him, whether for death or for banishment or for confiscation of his goods or for imprisonment. (Ezra 7:25–26)

The Torah (*dāt*) in Ezra's hand is here defined as the constitutional document of the Jewish community.[3] By acceptance or rejection of the Torah, individuals define themselves as either inside of or outside of that community. Ezra is empowered both to set up structures of administration and granted the supreme powers of enforcement. The significance of this development can scarcely be overstressed, for it meant that in the official judgment of the world power of that day, the priestly version of Yahwistic faith contained in the Torah of Moses was the *religio licita* in the land. For the Persians, this meant that a basis had been established for the restoration of order in a land that, hitherto torn by rival factions, had proven to be a buffer of dubious dependability between the Persian empire and its rival to the south, Egypt. For Jewish religion itself, it means that tremendous legal clout had been added to the Zadokite cause: the Persian empire stood unequivocally on the side of its claim that acceptance of the Torah of Moses, as interpreted and enforced by the Zadokite priestly leadership, constituted citizenship in the true community of Israel. An accommodation with the powers and

3. Cf. S. Talmon, "The Sectarian *yḥd*—A Biblical Noun," *VT* 3 (195), 133–140.

structures of this world had been worked out that, in accordance with divine will as explicated by Zadokite interpretation (e.g., Ezra 7:27–28), implied that the lofty eschatalogical visions of the visionaries had been superseded. This line of interpretation was carried further by the Chronicler in his monumental effort to demonstrate that the postexilic Jewish community living under the leadership of the high priest was the culmination of the community structures instituted by God through David. But first we consider Nehemiah's contribution to the reform of the Jewish community in Jerusalem and Judah.

Nehemiah, a royal official of Artaxerxes I (464–424 B.C.E.) who became governor of Judah, had a range of interests that complemented those of Ezra the Scribe. No sooner had he arrived in Jerusalem in 445 B.C.E. than he turned to the problem of rebuilding the city's broken fortifications, a project complicated by the harassment of enemies like Sanballat, the governor of Samaria, Tobiah, and Geshem, of the Arab state of Qedar. Through prayer and perseverance, the task was completed, thus creating a bulwark against external threats to the struggling community's existence. Nehemiah quickly recognized that external defenses were not enough, for the country was weakened from within by economic abuses perpetrated by the ruling classes, which were driving the common people to mortgage their property, borrow money to pay taxes, sell their children into slavery, and even to lose their fields and vineyards to creditors. On the basis of Mosaic law, Nehemiah ordered the nobles and officials to stop charging their fellow Jews interest, and to return to them "their fields, their vineyards, their olive orchards, and their houses, and the hundredth of money, grain, wine, and oil which you have been exacting of them" (Neh. 5:11). By this act Nehemiah restored fundamental aspects of the egalitarian community ideal tracing back all the way to the early Yahwism of the pre-monarchical period, involving the rights of each family to its *naḥălâ*, as well as laws forbidding lending on interest. To these reform measures, Nehemiah added his personal example of a godly life, free of the luxuries customarily belonging to the governor, and given to prayer.

After a brief return to the court of Artaxerxes, Nehemiah took up his second term as governor in Judah (beginning at some point between 433 and 424 B.C.E.), and extended his reform to temple regulations, sabbath observance, and the enforcement of laws against mixed marriages.[4] In the separation from Israel of "all those of foreign descent," we find the intracommunal counterpart to the rebuilding of the walls around the city completed earlier by Nehemiah. To a community battered by internal strife and beleagured by foreign adversaries, self-preservation seemed to necessitate both the stringent ordering of the struc-

---

4. On the theological significance of the issue of mixed marriages in the reform of Nehemiah, see H. G. M. Williamson, *Israel in the Books of Chronicles* (Cambridge, England: Cambridge University Press, 1977), pp. 60–61.

tures regulating the internal life of the people and a strict separation from non-Jews. In one incisive reform, both Zechariah's vision of Jerusalem "inhabited as villages without walls" (Zech. 2:4 [Heb. 2:9]) and Second Isaiah's vision of Israel given by God as "a light to the nations" (Isa. 49:6) seemed to vanish. Nehemiah introduced an era whose energies were dedicated to establishing a community intent on defining its identify as opposed to "all those of foreign descent" (Neh. 13:3). We recognize the powerful historical determinants that led to this protectionist and segregationist position, and even suggest that without thorough reform and consolidation such as that inaugurated by Ezra and Nehemiah the Jewish community may have been assimilated to its reli-giocultural environment, much like the Jewish community of Elephantine on the Nile. Nevertheless, we cannot neglect the task of assessing this period from the overall point of view of the biblical notion of community. And in doing so, we recognize both important gains and some implicit dangers.

Guided by the triadic model of Yahwistic community, we first observe how central worship was in the life of Nehemiah. His trust in God's guidance and protection was unswerving, and this expressed itself in worship and praise that grew naturally out of the matters of everyday life. This is seen for example in the festival of dedication of the wall in Nehemiah 12:27–43, celebrated "with gladness, with thanksgivings and with singing, with cymbals, harps, and lyres." "And they offered great sacrifices that day and rejoiced, for God had made them rejoice with great joy; the women and children also rejoiced. And the joy of Jerusalem was heard afar off" (Neh. 12:27 and 12:43).

Second, on the basis of the Mosaic Torah the dependable standard of God's righteousness was again established at the center of Jewish life. The reform of Ezra and Nehemiah, seen against the background of the deplorable conditions reflected by the Book of Malachi, serves as a powerful reminder that without concrete communal structures capable of regulating a society and maintaining a just order, the high ideals of the Yahwistic community of faith could not be maintained. Their practical response to the concrete problems facing the land also offers a legitimate corrective to the tendency in certain apocalyptic circles to withdraw from communal involvement in anticipation of Yahweh's final, decisive act of vindication. The covenant renewal ceremony described in Nehemiah 9:38–10:39 in particular illustrates that the dynamic quality characteristic of the earlier *tôrâ* tradition had not been lost. For here we are told that as part of the ceremony of covenant renewal the congregation bound itself to a series of new obligations hitherto not covered by existing codices. As in the early Yahwistic and prophetic periods, *tôrâ* retained a living quality requiring extension to new areas of life as they unfolded within the community.

In relation to the third quality of compassion, the question arises whether this aspect of the Yahwistic notion of community was not actually thwarted by the reform program of Ezra and Nehemiah. One is struck by the absence of the central characteristic of the early Yahwistic concept of compassion, namely, its reaching out to draw excluded elements into the healing orbit of its communal life. Their reform efforts emphasized instead structures that encouraged separatism by inhibiting inclusion of anyone of foreign origin, by defining legitimacy in terms of birth within the house of Judah, and by narrowing the priesthood to members of the Zadokite family. Since earlier confessions had portrayed Yahweh as the God who created Israel from nothing by having compassion on sojourners and by drawing a mixed company into covenant community, how is one to account for and evaluate the tendency in the fifth century to compromise a broad, dynamic understanding of compassion through such intradirectedness?

It is possible to avoid an overly simplistic, and even distorted answer to this question only by recognizing at the heart of the situation a very fragile polarity. On the one hand, the fifth-century Jewish community, like any community, was able to maintain its viability only to the extent that it clarified for its members that which made it distinct from other social groups. Should a sense of uniqueness have been lost, assimilation and ultimately extinction as a distinct community would have been inevitable. The other side of the polarity, however, was represented by the wedding within early and prophetic Yahwism of Israel's unique sense of righteousness with the capacity to reach out to and assimilate foreign elements, a capacity best designated as compassion. It was this latter quality that fostered within Yahwism the universalistic tendency that found classic expression in the message of Second Isaiah, a quality that defined Israel's existence as a community in terms of the extension of Yahweh's šālôm to all the peoples of the earth.

An adequate evaluation of the contribution of Ezra and Nehemiah to the Yahwistic notion of community therefore must keep in mind both sides of this essential polarity. First, it must not minimize the significance of the reform measures of these two figures. Many of the abuses that had threatened to destroy the Jewish community, abuses that had also troubled critics of the Zadokite priesthood such as Malachi, were effectively dealt with by Ezra and Nehemiah. To a significant degree, the Yahwistic quality of righteousness was re-established in Judah. But the effects of their ultrastrict divorce policy and their regulation of community membership on the basis of a narrowly parochial definition of "Israel" on the Yahwistic concept of compassion must also be considered.[5]

In some respects, the period of early kingship already anticipated the

5. That the rather open attitude toward larger Israel found in what I have designated Chr[1] is considerably narrowed in Nehemiah has been arqued by H. G. M. Williamson on pp. 61–68 of the monograph cited in note 4.

fifth-century situation. This is true with respect to the role of compassion in the self-image of the community. During the monarchy, we noted periods when the definition of righteousness based on royal authority and the accompanying eclipse of compassion as a significant quality in the policy of the state were symptoms of a deeper problem—namely, the dislocation of the "keystone" of Yahwistic community, acknowledgment of the sole sovereignty of Yahweh, by the penultimate reality of the king. The earlier process of extrapolating the qualities of the community from the example of the God experienced as deliverer of the oppressed was forced to yield to the more rational process of determining the laws of the land on the basis of the needs for order and security as perceived by the king. The dynamism and openness that characterized the early period began to diminish as structures became more rigid and closed.

The Jewish community of the fifth century faced threats to its existence similar in important respects to threats faced by Israel in the early years of kingship: the menace of hostile neighbors, the inability of the people to muster sufficient strength to defend themselves, and centrifugal tendencies that were threatening to tear the society apart. In the eleventh century, the answer had been found in the centralization of the authority in the king. In the fifth century, it was found in the centralization of leadership in two figures authorized by the Persians, Ezra the Scribe, and Nehemiah the Governor. In both cases the imputation of order on an unstable situation brought with it a ridigifying of social norms that tended to close the community to the dynamic outreach characteristic of more expansive periods. And a distinct rationalization was developed in support of this rigidification in each period. In the case of early kingship, appeal was made to the eternal order of myth; in the case of the fifth-century hierocracy, to the Torah, understood increasingly as an eternal order handed down to Moses from heaven—which is of course also a mythological notion.[6] A corresponding change occurred in the understanding of social and cultic continuity. In more creative periods, continuity was located in the trustworthiness of God, who, though understood as ever acting in new ways, was seen as acting in fidelity to one purpose. This flexibility permitted a high degree of change in the customs and institutions of the Yahwistic community, and a capacity to assimilate foreign elements. Continuity was safeguarded in a noticeably different way in the period of early kingship and in the fifth century. In the former, attention turned away from Yahweh's ongoing action into history, with continuity being located increasingly in the notion of the "royal seed"; that is, in the dynastic succession of the Davidic house. In the fifth century, it was defined on

---

6. In important respects, the development of the concept of the eternal, heavenly Torah anticipates the exalted position of the Torah in the Hellenistic and Roman periods.

the basis of the "holy seed"; that is, the race stemming from the exiles of the house of Judah. It is clear that Ezra's and Nehemiah's severe opposition to mixed marriages was in response to an acute problem. Given the threatened position of the Judean community, a clear definition had to be made of what constituted membership in the people of Israel. Ezra 9:1–2 gives the most precise formulation of the threat as perceived by the community's leaders:

The people of Israel and the priests and the Levites have not separated themselves from the people of the lands with their abominations, from the Canaanites, the Hittites, the Perizzites, the Jebusites, the Ammonites, and Moabites, the Egyptians, and the Amorites. For they have taken some of their daughters to be wives for themselves and for their sons; so that the holy race has mixed itself [wĕhitʿārĕbû zéraʿ haqqōdeš] with the peoples of the lands.

In response to this threat, Ezra and Nehemiah produced a definition of membership based on a very specific criterion, that of "the holy seed" (zéraʿ haqqōdeš), which was to be preserved by avoiding contamination with other ethnic groups. The clarity of this definition is evident, involving a criterion all members could understand, even those who might lack the courage to believe that in a world dominated by the Persians, Israel's Yahweh was the only Power determining and guiding all nations and events. For such individuals, the earlier process of defining peoplehood strictly on the basis of the nature of the God encountered in history represented too much ambiguity. As the people of an earlier era had asked Samuel for a king to provide their identity for them, in the fifth century many were prepared to have the principle of heredity supply their self-definition.

Ezra and Nehemiah were not the first to concern themselves with the threat of loss of identity through assimilation to other peoples. Both the Yahwistic Writing (Exod. 34:16) and the Deuteronomic Law (Deut. 7:3; 23:3–5) sought to safeguard the community from this danger. But in adopting this approach as the sole means of defining membership, another tradition that runs throughout the Bible was displaced. Both in early tradition (e.g., Joseph in Gen. 41:45, Moses in Num. 12:1; cf. Gen. 38) and in later tradition (Mahlon and Chilion in Ruth 1), marriages with foreign wives were accepted.

The verb used in Ezra 9:2 to describe contamination through mixed marriages is telling, since it is probably a denominative form of the noun used in early tradition to describe those accompanying the early Israelites in their escape from Egypt (Exod. 12:38), a group not rejected by early Yahwism, but incorporated into the life of the people and offered the special protection of the law guaranteed by Yahweh's compassion (cf. Exod. 22:22–28 [Evv. 21–27] and 23:3). Under Ezra and Nehemiah, this openness of the community to outsiders was reversed, for on the basis of their interpretation of the Torah, they took strong measures against the group that, in disregard of its being the "holy seed," had mixed itself (*hit ʿārĕbû*) with "the peoples of the land," and accordingly "they separated from Israel all the mixed company" (*ʿēreb*). This inversion of the application of the root *ʿrb* points to a radical change in attitude toward those falling outside of the community of faith. For in the exodus story, the "mixed company" (*ʿēreb*), far from being excluded, helped constitute the young covenant community.

We are led to the conclusion that in elevating the criterion of heredity to an important position in defining the people of Israel, the dimension of other-directedness that was essential to early Yahwism's understanding of compassion was endangered. The reasons for this change are historically very comprehensible, even as were the circumstances leading to Israel's earlier attempt to find a source of definition and security in its earthly king. But in the one case as in the other, it seems that a criterion entered the picture that encroached on the primal confession of Yahwism, the sole sovereignty of Yahweh, from whose example alone the qualities of life in community were to be derived. This change in turn had an impact on another aspect of Yahwism that developed especially in the prophetic period, namely, the positive role Israel was seen to play in relation to the other nations. How was this chosen people to be a source of blessing to the families of the earth and a servant nation in bringing Yahweh's Torah and *šālôm* to the nations if its chosenness was no longer construed in terms of agency on behalf of the nations but in terms of the avoidance of all contact with "the peoples of the lands"?

In the previous chapter, we noted that the polarization between pragmatic and visionary tendencies in the early postexilic period led to the tearing asunder of polarities that lay at the heart of Yahwistic faith. Perhaps it is accurate to acknowledge that in the period of Ezra and Nehemiah one of the victims of this struggle was the polarity constituted by a clear understanding of the community's uniqueness among the families of the world on the one hand and a healthy sense of mission in the name of the God of all nations on the other. As in the case of all of the important polarities of faith, this one could be preserved only if rooted in a keen sense of being a distinct people solely as a response to the saving activity of God in history, activity acknowledging no limitations and thereby drawing the responsive community into a mission that ultimately was to encompass all peoples. This observation serves as a reminder once again that the study of the unfolding of the notion of community in the Bible must be aware of divergent streams within Scripture, especially during periods of division and controversy. Such awareness will allow us to grasp the importance of the contribution of Ezra and Nehemiah to the survival of the community during a very threatening period without failing to detect its deficiencies. Without their courageous efforts, and their skill in working out a *modus vivendi* with the ruling power of the day, the disintegration of the quality of righteousness that defined Israel's position among the nations may well have continued unabated, leading to the destruction of the Yahwistic community. At the same time, the tendency to identify righteousness too closely with a narrow partisan view of community muted the earlier prophetic understanding of compassion as God's all-inclusive outreach. If unqualified by the witness of dissenting voices within the community, the result of this tendency could be the substitution for a salvific understanding of community by an ethnic one. Similarly, the unqualified extension of this parochialization would lead to the loss of a lively eschatological dimension such as one encounters in prophetic Yahwism, for if election to the community is defined by a criterion set in pre-existing hereditary structures and definitively revealed in immutable regulations, future acts of God dedicated to a universal plan of salvation would be precluded. It is fortunate indeed that alongside the reports of the activities of Ezra and Nehemiah the Bible has included the stories of Ruth and Jonah. We turn to such dissenting voices later; first we trace the culmination of the Zadokite reformation in the Chronicler's History.

B. THE CHRONICLER'S HISTORY

In the historical work referred to as the Chronicler's History and consiting of 1 and 2 Chronicles, Ezra, and Nehemiah, more than one editorial level can be recognized. Chapter VIII, section B, described the earliest discernible level (designated Chr[1]) as a historical narrative written in support of the restoration program, and especially of the temple-rebuilding aspect of that program, under the leadership of the Davidic prince Zerubbabel and the high priest Joshua. Also, before the sixth century had come to a close significant adjustments had to be made in the restoration program sponsored by the Zadokite priesthood as a result of the sudden exit from the postexilic scene of the Davidic member of the priest-prince hierarchy.

This section shows how the Zadokite party drew on all the traditions in its rich legacy, including its historical source Chr[1], the prophetic traditions of Ezekiel, Haggai, and Zechariah, and from more recent times, the memoirs and traditions of Ezra and Nehemiah, and forged them into what became the final edition of the Chronicler's History. This document deserves careful attention, for it offers a detailed plan of the hierocratic community that represents the culmination of the theological reflection of the Zadokite tradition. It both reflects the principles and structures that had emerged by the time of its composition at about 400 B.C.E., and went on to occupy a position of considerable influence in enforcing those principles and structures in subsequent years.

When we read the Chronicler's History in its final form, we are confronted with a message that goes beyond the recording of events of past history. Here we find theological minds seeking to address the question that also underlies the Priestly Writing: After the calamity of the Babylonian destruction of temple and nation, how can life as a people of God be structured and preserved against recurrent disaster?

The answer given by the final editor(s) of the Chronicler's History was a bold one. Judah, a vassal state under the Persians whose essential social structures were determined by a temple cult with a high priest at its head, was nothing less than the extension of the holy community established by God through King David. In presenting this history, therefore, the Chronicler sought to show that the institutions and offices that had emerged under the leadership of the Zadokites by the end of the fifth century B.C.E. were not merely structures re-establishing customs and practices of the period immediately before the exile and then adjusted to political developments occurring under the new Persian hegemony, but were nothing less than the sacred institutions and offices that the anointed one of God, David, had created at God's command! The structures outlined in detail by this history accordingly were presented as descriptive of the community intended by God for God's people from the beginning and for all time. Proof that it was intended from the beginning was provided by the Chronicler, in the form of the genealogies appearing in the first nine chapters of the work, for they begin with Adam and they lead up to the true beginning of Israel, which in contrast to the Priestly Writing, was not the revelation of the Torah on Sinai, but the founding of the cult during the kingship of David. And the suggestion that this community was intended by God for all time was achieved by a notable downplaying of eschatology in the Chronicler's work. Hope resided not in realities yet to be revealed by a Messiah who would come in the future, but in careful observance and presentation of the cultic institutions revealed by God to David, handed down by the priests and kings of Judah, miraculously surviving the destruction of Jerusalem and the temple by being kept alive in the traditions of the true remnant of Israel, the exiles of Judah living in Babylon, and finding new life under the leadership of the Zadokite high priests once the true remnant had returned to Jerusalem.[7]

The Chronicler's History thus describes a community ideal that em-

---

7. P. R. Ackroyd writes, "It is as a subject people of this divinely guided empire that the Jewish community has to live" *I and II Chronicles, Ezra, Nehemiah* (London: Torch Bible Commentaries, 1973), p. 300. P. Welten emphasizes how ark and kingship were used by the Chronicler in developing a new theology for an age living without ark and king. They were applied not to cultivate a messianic hope, but to offer the basis for what was believed to be the correct understanding of cult and to offer an example of proper cultic praxis—"Lade-Tempel-Jerusalem: Zur Theologie der Chronikbücher," in *Textgemäss*, Festschrift E. Würthwein (Göttingen: Vandenhoeck and Ruprecht, 1979), pp. 169–183. In contrast, an eschatological/messianic dimension in Chronicles is stressed by R. Mosis, *Untersuchungen zur Theologie des chronistischen Geschichtswerkes* (Freiburg: Herder, 1973), pp. 147–163.

phasized continuity with temple structures of the past, and that proved powerfully influential in shaping the community of the Jews in the following centuries. The exile was not interpreted as a deep cesura or as an incisive turning-point between an old era and a new (as it had been interpreted by Second Isaiah), but as a brief interruption in an otherwise unbroken history of a sacred community and its cultic organization.

At the heart of the Chronicler's message was the warning that if future disaster was to be prevented, this community and its cultic organization would have to be preserved in their original purity. Guardians of this purity were the priests, with the high priest as undisputed head. This pre-eminence of authority had come to the high priest as a result of the pragmatic accommodation made by the Zadokite party to the political realities of the Persian period: although a foreign kingship had come to replace the kingship of the house of David, the Zadokite priestly house took on itself the exclusive responsibility of serving as guardian and bearer of the sacred traditions of the past.

At a time when rival definitions of the nature of Israelite community were being raised to challenge that of the Zadokites, the Chronicler followed the lead of Ezra and Nehemiah in defining community in terms of heredity. Thus Israel was in the first instance the remnant of Judah, which maintained the purity of the orthodox faith in exile. Once that remnant had returned and restored the temple cult, there was only one true place of worship—Jerusalem. Thus in the restoration accomplished by the Zadokites, the conditions of the Davidic period were restored, a period when there was similarly one united Israel centered around worship in Jerusalem.

On the basis of this clear definition of membership and leadership, it was possible for the Chronicler to express a conciliatory spirit vis-à-vis rival parties and Jews living outside of Judah. In the Chronicler's work, special care was apparently taken to accord the Levites a place of honor in the service of the temple, a notable fact when compared with the bitter polemic waged earlier by the Zadokite party against the Levites during the temple rebuilding and its aftermath.[8] To the Levites was assigned the important task of bearing the art (1 Chron. 15:15; 1 Chron. 5:4–5). And in the temple they were to serve as musicians (1 Chron. 15:16–22; 2 Chron. 5:12; 25:1–31) and as porters (1 Chron. 15:23 and 26:1–19), besides being responsible for many menial tasks.[9] At the same time, it must be recognized that the priestly structures inherited from the time of Josiah remained in force, with the Levites, in spite of their improved position, remaining minor clergy under the direction of the priests.

A tendency toward greater tolerance can be perceived also in the

8. See Ezekiel 44.

9. J. M. Myers, *I Chronicles*, AB 12 (Garden City, N.J.: Doubleday, 1965), p. LXIX.

Chronicler's attitude toward the Jews of the north. In 1 Chronicles 5:1–2, the Chronicler deviated from his sources in noting the privileged position of Joseph among the original tribes of Israel. And in connection with the Davidic monarchy, he pointed out that all the tribes of Israel played an important role in the key events of the kingdom (e.g. 1 Chron. 11:4; 13:1–5; 15:3).[10] Here too, however, the Chronicler's clear definition of the true Israel sets down the specific terms according to which Jews of the north could be readmitted into the true Israel—namely, through repentance and acknowledgment of the one true cult in Jerusalem with its priestly leadership (cf. 2 Chron. 11:13–17; 13:4–12; 15:9; and 30:1–11).

Finally, the conciliatory spirit of the Chronicler expressed itself also in the attention paid to the role of prophets in Israel's history. All groups could now find a common home under the overarching canopy of the Zadokite hierarchy. But once more the specific programmatic interests of the Chronicler domesticate the prophetic office into another agency of the temple cult, no longer critical of but subservient to the institutions of the kingdom. Jacob Myers has correctly observed this fact: "Closer examination of the oracles of the prophets recorded here reveals a somewhat different outlook or, rather, a different emphasis from those in Kings. Virtually all are lacking in specifically moral content and have to do almost entirely with oracular matters related to the cult or declaration of the principle of *quid pro quo*."[11]

In all three cases—treatment of Levites, attitude toward Jews of the north, and interpretation of prophetic activities—we do not witness a conscious distortion of historical sources, but rather the theological effort to gather all the important theological traditions of the past into a programmatic synthesis alone believed to be capable of reviving the Jewish community by reunifying it under legitimate leadership and reestablishing organizational structures resilient enough to withstand strife and outside challenge. Although the lofty heights of theological insight found in Jeremiah or Second Isaiah are lacking here, it must be remembered that the Chronicler's History stems from a community putting forth its best efforts in the struggle to balance the demands of the Persian sponsors with the needs of the people for a social and spiritual life true to its ancient heritage. Through acknowledgment of one holy city, one temple, one cult, and one priesthood, this people was to be drawn into the holy covenant and into the divine Torah, which alone were believed capable of assuring God's presence and its accompanying blessing and security. Within this delicate situation, the emphasis on exact performance of the holy rituals and strict observance of the Torah is completely understandable. It was the only means in the minds

---

10. Williamson, *Israel*, pp. 89–96.
11. Myers, *I Chronicles*, p. LXXVI.

of the Zadokite leadership capable of holding together a people, and safeguarding it from either assimilation to other religions or dilution by the infiltration of paganism. The harsh rules regarding relationships with foreigners found in the Chronicler's History are merely an extension of this basic norm and a particular expression of the underlying need it addresses (e.g., Ezra 4:3 and Neh. 13:1–3). The Chronicler and the official circles for which he speaks believed that for the sake of survival a very carefully defined circle had to be drawn around this community. Henceforth it was to be a holy people, in the sense of a people apart, a people defined by strict observance of the Torah and lead by priests whose lineage was proven (Ezra 2:59–63 and Neh. 7:61–65). One is able to appreciate the delicacies of this definition of community when one remembers that this exclusive view had to be held in balance with another fact dictated by the actual political realities of that time: Judah was also a cultic community living under Persian sponsorship, indebted to its emperors for its founding (Ezra 1:1–4) and dependent on its continued support (Ezra 7:11–18).

On the basis of the description just given, we now turn to evaluate the notion of community as it has evolved in the Chronicler's History, with an eye to determining how it contributes to the theological developments of the postexilic period. Once again it will be helpful to structure the evaluation on the basis of the triad constituting community in early Yahwism, namely, worship, righteousness, and compassion.

Worship, as portrayed in the Chronicler's History, may give the appearance of ritualized formality and hence may lead to the question of whether it gives expression to the community's acknowledgment of Yahweh's lordship with the depth and intimacy characteristic of early and prophetic Yahwism. In responding to this question, it must be remembered that forms of worship are vehicles, and as such may or may not be the carriers of deep worship experience. It is evident today that profound expressions of worship can occur as surely within a highly liturgical Anglican or Roman Catholic mass as within the freer forms of expression found in a Methodist or Baptist service. Therefore it is necessary to look beyond liturgical forms for further evidence of the Chronicler's concept of worship.

Such evidence is found both in breadth and in specific detail. In the broader picture, it is striking how eager the Chronicler seems to have been to portray Israel as responding to its historical experiences with worship and praise. In the entire span of history from the time of David on, he drew attention to the guiding hand of Yahweh preserving in Jerusalem and among the priests of the temple the Torah and the forms of worship that enabled the people to live within God's covenant and enjoy God's blessings. When threatened by hostile armies from other lands, the hand of God was also identified as Israel's sole source of security. In fact, in the archaic pattern of holy war, the warriors were prepared for battle by the Levites who blew the trumpets and led them in prayer. Thus worship was established as the basis on which Israel's wars were seen.

Even during the exile, this providential care continued, leading to the Lord's new act of mercy that inaugurated the Chronicler's own era, that of the second temple: ". . . the Lord stirred up the spirit of Cyrus the king of Persia so that he made a proclamation throughout his kingdom" (Ezra 1:1). Finally, in the same abiding care of Yahweh for his people the Chronicler recognized the source of the missions of Ezra and Nehemiah, which played such an important role in the subsequent reform of the community and which prepared the way for the program outlined by the Chronicler himself. For example, he interprets Artaxerxes's commissioning of Ezra in the form of a doxology:

Blessed by the Lord, the God of our fathers, who put a thing as this into the heart of the king, to beautify the house of the Lord which is in Jerusalem, and who extended to me his steadfast love before the king and his counselors, and before all the king's mighty officers. I took courage, for the hand of the Lord my God was upon me, and I gathered leading men from Israel to go up with me. (Ezra 7:27–28)

We thus find ample evidence that the Chronicler believed that Yahweh had not only guided the congregation of Israel over the centuries past, but continued to direct its life within the contemporary world ruled by Persians. And true to the pattern basic to early Yahwism, we find the Chronicler responding to God's initiative in worship and praise, both through the voice of the congregation and through editorial comment (e.g., Neh. 8:6–9:5).

As a specific example of the central role of worship in the Chronicler's notion of community, we can refer to the prayer of Ezra in Nehemiah 9:6–37. The pattern followed is that of classic Yahwism: recital of the great saving acts of Yahweh leading to praise. Thus this prayer can be compared with an early Yahwistic hymn such as Exodus 15, a prophetic recital such as Hosea 11, or later hymnic compositions such as Psalms 78, 105, 106, and 136. And the prayer of Ezra serves as an excellent example of how a classical form could become the vehicle of an expression of confession and worship filled with contemporary meaning. Against the background of the past relationship of Yahweh and people, characterized by God's faithfulness and righteousness and the people's repeated backsliding, Ezra addressed the present. It too was characterized by trial and affliction, but not due to any lack of divine grace. The present hardships were rather evidence of God's righteous judgment, aimed at evoking communal repentance:

Now therefore, our God, the great and almighty terrible God, who keepest covenant and steadfast love, let not all the hardship seem little to thee that has come upon us, upon our kings, our princes, our priests, our prophets, our fathers, and all thy people since the time of the kings of Assyria until this day. Yet thou hast been just in all that has come upon us, for thou hast dealt faithfully and we have acted wickedly. (Neh. 9:32–34)

Although a classical form served as the model for Ezra's prayer, it certainly does not fall into the category of lifeless ritual formalism. Its intimacy and passion are evident both in the elevated praise of its introductory address, "Thou art the Lord, and thou alone," and in its urgent concluding appeal, "we are in great distress." As a reflection of the Chronicler's theology, Ezra's prayer portrays Yahweh as the one true God who alone is worthy of worship and praise, a concept in harmony with the central quality of community in early Yahwism and prophecy.

We turn next to examine the Chronicler's portrait of community in relation to the second essential quality found at the heart of Yahwism since earliest times, namely, righteousness. It is clear that for the Chronicler David was the parade example of the righteous individual. By carefully abiding by the institutions and ordinances that David had introduced, Israel was to live in righteousness before its God (e.g., Neh. 12:45–46). Beyond such institutional and cultic regulations, however, the Chronicler did not give a vivid picture of the nature of the righteous life in everyday matters, nor did he explicitly draw a connection between the way of righteousness and its source in the saving acts of Yahweh. Whereas it was precisely that connection that characterized both the early collections of Torah and their explication in the prophets, the Chronicler tended to make more general reference to the Torah as the authoritative body of law that was to regulate the behavior of the community, especially in matters of the cult.

The tendency to view the Torah in rather abstract terms can be illustrated by reference to several episodes in the Chronicler's History. In Nehemiah 8 (a displaced section of the Ezra source), Ezra reads the Torah to a congregation of all the people in a great festivity culminating in the feast of booths. In this passage "the book of the Torah of Moses" (Neh. 8:1), or "the book of the law of God" (Neh. 8:18), or "the book of the Torah" (Neh. 8:3) or "the words of the Torah" (Neh. 8:9, 13) or simply "the Torah" (Neh. 8:2, 7, 14) is referred to as a known entity. As is characteristic for the Chronicler, the only specific content referred to in this book of the Torah is of a cultic nature (Neh. 8:14–15). A similar episode is mentioned in Nehemiah 9:3.

The Torah is also mentioned repeatedly in Ezra's prayer in Nehemiah 9:6–37, in a section reviewing the history of Israel as a history centering around the Torah given to Israel by God through Moses in which the well-being or the suffering of the people was directly tied to their relation to that sacred norm (Neh. 9:14, 26, 29, 34 [cf. 2 Chron. 33:8]). Once again, the passage does not give concrete expression to function of the Torah in the life of the community.

Finally, in the narrative in Nehemiah 10 describing the festival of covenant renewal, the Torah stands as the recognized authority, for the people "enter into a curse and an oath to walk in God's law (*tôrat hā'ĕl-ōhîm*) which was given by Moses the Servant of God" (Neh. 10:30 [Evv. 29] cf. 10:29 [Evv. 28]). Where specific content within that Torah is referred to, it relates to cultic ordinances (Neh. 10:34, 35 [Evv. 36, 37]). Thus we encounter here the pattern found throughout the Chronicler's History: the only aspects of the Torah that are specifically referred to are of a cultic nature (1 Chron. 16:40; 2 Chron. 14:3 [Evv. 4]; 23:18; 30:16; 31:3, 4, 11; 35:26; Ezra 3:2; Neh. 12:44; 13:1, 3).

Reference to these three episodes is not intended to suggest that when the Chronicler referred to Torah, he had in mind only cultic regulations. For example, when he portrayed the Levites going through all the cities of Judah teaching the Torah during Jehoshaphat's reign (2 Chron. 17:9), there is no reason to doubt that he understood that teaching to encompass all aspects of Torah, including the lofty ethical ideals of the Decalogue, the Holiness Code's command to "love your neighbor as yourself" (Lev. 19:18), and the *šĕma*'s focus on Yahweh's sole lordship (Deut. 6:4–9). In repeatedly holding up the Torah before the community as its standard, the Chronicler was holding up a truly lofty norm. As far as the Chronicler's own specific interests are concerned, however, there is no denying the fact that for him the cultic aspects of Torah command central stage. For example, when he observes that adversity came to Judah when Rehoboam "forsook the law of the Lord (*tôrat yhwh*), and all Israel with him" (2 Chron. 12:1), one can scarcely escape the conclusion that in the Chronicler's understanding Rehoboam's sin involved primarily matters concerning the cult.

Thus, with regard to righteousness as the second essential quality of Yahwistic community, we conclude that for the Chronicler righteousness had become closely associated with observance of the Torah. The quintessence of that observance, moreover, was reached in the proper conduct of the temple cult, as it had been instituted long ago by David under Yahweh's direction. As in Israel's past, blessing and security from internal and external threats would come only to a community faithful to this rich legacy. It would seem, therefore, that the social dimension of righteousness that came to expression in Nehemiah's reform was not subjected to further reflection in the final formulation in the Chronicler's History. Enjoying the central focus are concerns and insights of a priestly class viewing things from a somewhat different perspective than that of the pious governor Nehemiah. Whereas it is fortunate that the final version of that history included Nehemiah's Memoirs, it is quite evident that the center of focus had been shifted in the years between Nehemiah and the final edition of Chronicles.

As the third esssential quality of the classical Yahwistic notion of community, we recognized compassion, understood as the outreach of Yahweh, and then of the community faithfully following Yahweh's example, toward those hitherto exluded from the protection of the covenant. Certainly the laws included in the Torah safeguarding the rights of the poor and the vulnerable continued to receive attention in the Chronicler's History. Moreover, Yahweh was still understood as the God of love who offered an example for the people (Neh. 1:5). The question becomes more complex, however, in relation to the tendency toward isolationism running through the period of Ezra and Nehemiah and still visible in the final version of the Chronicler's History.

First, it is important to note that the horizons are somewhat broader in the Chronicler than in Ezra and Nehemiah, at least in the openness expressed toward the possibility of the return of the northern Jews to the community gathered around the Jerusalem temple. But within the larger history of the notion of community in the Bible, the general tendency toward a policy of exclusion advanced by Ezra and Nehemiah continues in the Chronicler's theology. The classic motif of Yahweh's mercy toward the stranger or the alien accordingly was eclipsed by the emphasis on separation from the peoples of the land as a necessary measure for the preservation of sanctity.

Whereas Second Isaiah's image of a servant commissioned to bring Yahweh's Torah and šālôm to the nations may have strained the resources of a Jewish community living under Persian domination, it did represent an important strand in classic Yahwism that this new tendency seriously threatened. It is true that the new historical situation had threatened the very existence of the people, and that visionary circles emphasizing Israel's role in a universal divine plan seemed to overlook the limitations imposed by historical realities. Nevertheless, one must pose this question in analyzing the isolationist tendency of Ezra, Nehemiah, and the Chronicler: Did not the concept of being a people called into covenant relationship with God not only for self but for all peoples of the world, preserve an essential quality of Israel's own unique spiritual identity?

Jacob Myers has suggested that a policy of relating to other nations by withdrawal leads to "a conception of the saved people, those who had returned from exile, joined by those who had remained in the land and who were ready to accept the returnee's direction and rule, dwelling in the chosen place of the Lord and maintaining their relationship with him in purity and in a kind of magnificent isolation from other peoples."[12] Myers then makes this comparison: "The wide horizons of the prophets were no longer evident."[13]

With regard to the role of compassionate outreach in the life of the commuity, and to some degree also in the understanding of righteousness and Torah, the Chronicler's History does not represent as significant a development as did the Book of the Covenant, Isaiah, Second Isaiah, or the Priestly Writing. We find in it tendencies toward a retreat

---

12. Myers, *I Chronicles*, p. LXXXIV.
13. Myers, *I Chronicles*, p. LXXXV.

into a carefully defined concept of community emphasizing the barriers protecting the holy people of Judah from the threats and dangers of contamination represented by the other peoples. These tendencies must be understood in terms of the political and social realities of the late fourth century. The loftier expectations of prophets such as Second Isaiah had been answered by repeated disappointments. The Persian empire seemed to be in firm control of the kingdoms of this earth. The rulers and leading families of Samaria seemed eager, in partnership with neighbors from Ammon and the Arabian Desert, to turn the weakness and uncertainty prevailing in Judah to their own advantage. The hour seemed to call for a clear, pragmatic program of self-preservation that came to grips with these realities. The answer was found not in the renewal of a daring eschatalogical vision focusing on Yahweh's cosmic drama and encompassing all time and nations. Rather it was found in reining in the expectations of the people by focusing their attention on what was in hand, a hierocratic structure centered in temple cult and a societal norm contained in the Torah of Moses, both recognized by the Persians as in harmony with imperial policy and self-interest. This modest expectation of the Chronicler is expressed with remarkable clarity in Ezra 9:8, in the prayer of Ezra:

> But now for a brief moment favor has been shown by the Lord our God to leave us a remnant, and to give us a secure hold within this holy place, that our God may brighten our eyes and grant us a little reviving in our bondage. For we are bondsmen; yet our God has not forsaken us in our bondage, but has extended to us his steadfast love before the kings of Persia, to grant us some reviving to set up the house of our God, to repair its ruins, and to give us protection in Judea and Jerusalem.   (Ezra 9:8–9)

This is not a vision for all times, but a specific program offering "a secure hold" and "a little reviving" for a community crossing very dangerous terrain.

Against this historical background, one can appreciate the contributions made by Ezra, Nehemiah, and the more complex entity, the Chronicler, to their time and at the same time subject their policies and principles to theological critique. For example, what seems to be an encroachment by the policy of hereditary purity on the primal quality of Yahwistic community—Yahweh's sole lordship acknowledged in worship—can be understood historically without being adopted as a theological principle binding for all ages. Certainly both earlier and later periods of biblical history offer more powerful examples of the faithful community responding to Yahweh's gracious divine acts in human acts of worship that acknowledge no norm for life aside from the one true God and the example God gives to those dedicated to lives of righteousness and compassion. Similarly, the Chronicler's emphasis on orthopraxis and on a priestly hierarchy need not be taken as a model for every religious community in such a way as to detract from responses that are new and fresh and coming from hearts filled to over-flowing with awe and wonder before the all-compassionate and righteous God who is present in every age to create, deliver, and sustain.

Also in relation to the qualities of righteousness and compassion, we can acknowledge that the exigencies of the time had led to a policy of isolation without uncritically accepting such a policy as normative for future communities living under other circumstances. The freshness characterizing the understanding of God's righteousness in early Israel, as that community sought to imitate the nature of the God it experienced in its daily life, must not be permitted to be lost in the face of later, more systematic efforts to define authority and to codify Torah. Although the tactical retreat into a more delimited concept of God's order of salvation can be understood within the context of the historical realities of the Persian period, the broader vision kept alive by dissident voices should also be drawn into a theological analysis of the period that tries to appreciate the rich diversity of Scripture. That vision preserved a motif that seems essential to the overall portrait of God's people: this people was called not only for its own salvation, but was called to play a role also in relation to the salvation of other peoples of the earth. With roots in the blessing to Abraham (Gen. 12:1–4), that motif developed the quality of compassion in the direction of an outreach that sought to draw the excluded and the oppressed into the orbit of God's šālôm, regardless of their racial background. As a servant people, Israel was not only to be preserved, but was to bring Yahweh's Torah and Yahweh's šālôm, to the ends of the earth. For this people, it was "too small a thing to raise up the tribes of Jacob" (Isa. 49:6). God's plan was much too comprehensive, and God's compassion too broad, to be thus limited. Within this prophetic vision, Torah retained a dynamic quality always related to God's ongoing relationship with God's creation.[14] Since we regard this vision to be a theologically appropriate development out of early Yahwism, we regard the Chronicler's program as a retreat necessitated by specific events, as a way-station to be regarded as transitional rather than definitive. Its emphasis on the pragmatic application of the qualities of Yahwistic community to the realities of this world was likely a necesssary correction to extremes within certain apocalyptic circles that could either have led to the extinction of the Yahwistic community, or to its development into a completely otherworldly cult akin to later gnostic communities. And its conciliatory program aimed toward reuniting estranged elements of the community within one cult perhaps forestalled the definitive division of the Jewish people along rigid party lines. Nevertheless, for the full richness and dynamism of the Yahwistic notion of community to continue its path forward to even fuller expressions of God's will for the human

---

14. Another beautiful example of this broad vision is Psalm 19 (cf. also Pss. 1 and 119).

family, the Chronicler's hierocratic pragmatism, though separated historically from the more universal visions of the apocalyptically minded dissidents, must be related by students of the Bible to the eschatological vision of prophetic faith. Only in this way can a confessional community exercise the self-criticism necessary to interpret the isolationism of Ezra, Nehemiah, and the Chronicler as an episode necessitated by historical exegencies rather than as a norm "chiseled" in stone and determinative for all future ages.

X

Witnesses to an Alternative Vision
(Joel, Ruth, and Jonah)

Historical Note: The reform efforts of Ezra and Nehemiah seem to have had the effect of ushering in a period in which the Judean community dwelt quite securely under the local leadership of its Zadokite priests and the more distant sovereignty of the Persian crown. This assumption must remain qualified by the fact that documentation for the last century of Persian rule (ending with Alexander's conquest in 332 B.C.E.) and the following century of Ptolemaic domination is very meager, with the Elephantine papyri helping little to shed light on the local situation in Judea. Several biblical books are best understood if placed in this period, however, books that seem to indicate that the Zadokite leadership and its carefully defined communal structure were not without critics. In the books of Joel, Ruth, and Jonah, we find evidence for the continued activity of circles dedicated to a broadly inclusive vision of the Yahwistic community that likely arose, at least in part, as a protest against what was deemed an unwarranted exclusivism and narrowness within the mainstream community.

The tendency to narrow the community's vision of God's future activity by scaling back the eschatological dimension of Yahwistic faith and by focusing exclusively on God's relationship to the "holy seed" of Judah did not go unchallenged. The reconstruction of the community that issued forth from the Zadokite program also had a significant effect on the editorial process that gave rise to the present shape of major parts of the Hebrew Bible. It is therefore not surprising that the theological stream fostering a broader and more eschatological vision is less conspicuously represented in the writings of this period than is the dominant stream with its notion of the hierocratic community as fulfillment of God's promises to David. Even if it were not represented at all, however, we could assume that it did not disappear entirely in the fourth and third centuries B.C.E., for the second century witnessed a reemergence of this stream in such strength as to suggest the resurfacing of an earlier tradition rather than the birth of a new one. But we are fortunate that the books of Joel, Ruth, and Jonah bear direct witness to two facets of such a stream in the otherwise dark period in question. Joel proclaims boldly an eschatological message in the direct style of the earlier prophets, while the other two books—Ruth implicitly, Jonah directly—portray God's righteous compassion as a dynamnic quality transcending national boundaries, and reaching out to embrace all peoples. Although evidence is lacking within these books that would allow precise dating, it does seem clear that they express a dissident movement within fourth- and third-century Judaism that did not weary of protesting against the tendency towards exclusiveness and isolationism perceived in Ezra, Nehemiah, and the Chronicler. Such light is valuable indeed. It is valuable historically as background to understanding the resilience with which Judaism in the Hellenistic era would carry on its mission of proselytizing among the Gentiles, a characteristic that in turn influenced the missionary programs of early Christianity. And it is valuable theologically as a reminder of the diversity found within the biblical traditions of every period, which we ignore at the cost of a more superficial understanding of the biblical notion of community.

A. JOEL

The Book of Joel reflects a fairly long history of development, throughout which the eschatological dimension of prophetic Yahwism was preserved and deepened. In its present form, the book presents a powerful protest against the claims of the Zadokite hierocracy in a manner reminiscent of Ezekiel 38–39.[1] Whereas the Zadokites responded to the historical crises of the postexilic period as challenges that could be met successfully through renewed commitment within the context of the existing sacral institutions, the Book of Joel interprets them as the final outbreak of evil leading to a fearsome battle in which only the Divine Warrior could prevail (1:15; 2:1–2, 11, 27). According to this eschatological view, what the people were witnessing were not events with which Judah's institutions and its leaders could cope, but the prelude to a final confrontation between God and all the evil forces of the world, in which the latter would be judged definitively.

Thus, while Ezra, Nehemiah, and the Chronicler represent an ideology emphasizing continuity with the past, and a claim to the absolute authority of existing institutional structures, the Book of Joel espouses the model of discontinuity we associate with the apocalyptic eschatology of postexilic dissident groups.[2] It obviously arises out of a move-

---

1. Cf. P. D. Hanson, *The Dawn of Apocalyptic*, 2d ed. (Philadelphia: Fortress Press, 1979), p. 234, n. 47.
2. Cf. O. Plöger, *Theocracy and Eschatology*, trans. S. Rudman (Richmond, Va.: John Knox, 1968), p. 103.

ment that did not place primary trust in the cultic apparatus of the Jerusalem temple, but looked instead to a radical reshaping of reality, in which Yahweh would initiate the destruction of the old, and the recreation of a new order:

And I will give portents in the heavens and on the earth, blood and fire and columns of smoke. The sun shall be turned to darkness, and the moon to blood, before the great and terrible day of the Lord comes. (Joel 3:3–4 [Evv. 2:30–31])

In Joel's vision, those who would be delivered by Yahweh in the dreadful day of battle were not designated as the Zadokite priests or the leaders of Judah and Benjamin, but by a term recalling Third Isaiah's designation of the faithful dissident, the "humble and contrite in spirit, [who] trembles at my word," and Malachi's related epithet, "those who fear Yahweh":

And it shall come to pass that all who call upon the name of the Lord shall be delivered; for in Mount Zion and in Jerusalem there shall be those who escape, as the Lord has said, and among the survivors shall be those whom the Lord calls. (Joel 3:5 [Evv. 2:32])

We thus meet here a spirit akin to that embodied in other protest writings already examined, an antiestablishment, eschatological spirit, one emphasizing the defiled and transitory nature of the institutions founded by Zerubbabel and Joshua and reimposed by Ezra and Nehemiah, one insisting moreover that Yahweh would soon act directly to reconstitute a people by pouring out the divine spirit "on all flesh." The broad, eschatological perspective of the group here challenging the authority of the Zadokite claims is expressed powerfully in the following passage:

And it shall come to pass afterward, that I will pour out my spirit on all flesh; your sons and your daughters shall prophesy, your old men shall dream dreams, and your young men shall see visions. Even upon the menservants and maidservants in whose days I will pour out my spirit. (Joel 3:1–2 [Evv. 2:28–29])

The egalitarian impulse characteristic of early Yahwism is still discernible in this passage, tied with the emphasis on the free movement of the spirit characteristic of Yahwism in its prophetic phase. It is thus not difficult to recognize the archaic sources to which this protest group appealed in its opposition to the less eschatological, more hierarchical polity of the Zadokite leadership.

B. RUTH

The Book of Ruth itself does not provide a historical "handle" for the reader seeking to peer behind its fictional premonarchical setting to its actual period of origin. But hints provided both by the presence of Aramaisms in the language and by some of its themes suggest a date in the early fourth century.

The book does not strike the reader as harshly polemical, for its tenor is idyllic, and its tone moderate. But this does not detract from the fact that the book gives elegant expression to a notion of community that takes radical exception to the one being enforced at the same time under the leadership of the Zadokites. When that difference is recognized, the book falls into position as another expression of an alternative vision of community. Before that difference is described, however, it is important to determine the tradition on which the book draws, and on which it bases its critique of the institutions prevailing in its own time.

The ultimate source of the book's community ideal is unmistakable, namely, the classical form of Yahwism that can be traced back through prophetic tradition to its ultimate source in the premonarchic cult of the League period. In fact, it is striking how clearly the central themes of classical Yahwism come to expression, appropriately placed in the fiction of the story within the time frame of the period of the Judges. As in the Book of the Covenant and other archaic and prophetic expressions of Yahwistic faith, Yahweh in the Book of Ruth is the protector of the widow and the foreigner, that is, of two of the three vulnerable classes singled out for special care in the religious community of early Israel. And when it is observed that Ruth and Naomi, through the hardships that had befallen them, also were forced to resort to gleaning for their sustenance, that is, to fall back on the provision established by their community to provide for the poor, it becomes clear that this idyllic story serves as a paradigm of the righteous passion that the genuine Yahwistic community was to extend to the three most vulnerable classes of humanity—the widow, the poor, and the alien. Also important to note is the central position that the Levirate marriage custom assumes in the story, for as observed in Chapter III, it functioned specifically in early Israel as a means of safeguarding the welfare of the widow and her children. It is truly remarkable how accurately the Book of Ruth recaptures the essential qualities of early Yahwism, even recreating for them the historical setting within which they were engendered.

Having recognized the source of the book's notion of community in the archaic institutions and customs of early Yahwism, we can now identify the important respect in which its notion of community differs from the one developed under the Zadokite priestly leadership. This can best be identified by noticing the most remarkable feature of the story: the person whose life served as the context within which the cardinal qualities of the Yahwistic community came to such paradigmatic expression was a *Moabite* woman, whose marriage to a Jew had brought her into the healing orbit of Yahweh's šālôm. The story unfolds by showing that this foreign woman, once having been drawn into the righteous community through marriage, could not be denied her right to remain a protected member of that community, so long as she desired so to remain. While this attitude toward the foreigner accords well with the social structures of early Yahwism, its intended function in its fourth-century setting must have been that of protest against the then ascendant Zadokite notion of the "holy seed"; that is to say, of a community within which blessing was restricted to the children of Benjamin and Judah (cf. Ezra 9:1–2), and in which those who were married to foreigners were commanded by law to put away their wives (Ezra 10:1–5; Neh. 12:23–27). How different is the ideal embodied by Boaz, who shows both compassion and a profound sense of justice in dealing with the Moabite woman Ruth. That ideal, in its sharp opposition to the law of obligatory divorce, is portrayed powerfully in the scene in which Ruth casts herself down before Boaz, and asks, "Why have I found favor in your eyes, that you should take notice of me, when I am a foreigner?" (Ruth 2:10) The reply given by Boaz formulates the early Yahwistic ideal beautifully: "The Lord recompense you for what you have done, and a full reward be given you by the Lord, the God of Israel, under whose wings you have come to take refuge!" (2:12)

There is disagreement among the scholars regarding the status of the genealogical note that the son born of the union between Boaz and Ruth was the great-grandfather of King David.[3] Whether original to the story or not, it fittingly amplifies the central theme of the book: none less than the glorious King David was a descendant of the kind of mixed marriage being condemned by the hierocratic leadership of Judah! For here was one offspring of the mixing of the "holy seed" with foreign blood who could not easily be condemned as an "abomination"!

C. JONAH

In the Book of Jonah, the alternative vision of Yahweh as a God whose compassion knows no limits, but reaches out to encompass all peoples, comes to expression even more emphatically and explicitly than in the Book of Ruth. While also written on a high level of literary sophistication, it uses satire and irony rather than idyllic romance to make its point. In two separate scenes, Yahweh is portrayed as a God whose compassion reaches beyond Israel to the nations. In the scene on the storm-tossed boat, we see a microcosm of the family of the nations, with each of the mariners praying to his own god. Yahweh, as the God who is the true Lord of nature, turns out to be the God who hears the

---

3. This problem is discussed by G. Gerlemen, *Ruth*, BK (Neukirchn-Vluyn: Neukirchener Verlag, 1965), pp. 7–10.

prayers of these pagans. The result is dramatic, and overall the scene recalls the universalism of Malachi 1:11: "Then the men feared the Lord exceedingly, and they offered a sacrifice to the Lord and made vows" (Jonah 1:16). Jonah thus learns that as a Jew, he does not have a monopoly on Yahweh. He earlier in the story had identified himself to his international hosts thus: "I am a Hebrew; and I fear the Lord" (1:9). But now the story goes on to explain that this mixed company of mariners also "feared the Lord." Jonah had prayed to Yahweh in his distress and was heard and delivered. But Yahweh also harkened to the prayers of these pagans, and saved them as well.

In the second scene, the point concerning Yahweh's universal compassion is made even more forcefully. Only after having witnessed his stubborn resistance broken under extraordinary circumstances by Yahweh did Jonah finally obey Yahweh's command by going to Nineveh to proclaim the impending judgment. And Jonah's fears were in fact corroborated: "The people of Nineveh believed God: they proclaimed a fast, and put on sackcloth, from the greatest of them to the least of them" (3:5). What is more, the King of Nineveh added his support to this overwhelming display of repentance, and explained his action with this remarkable reasoning: "Who knows, God may yet repent and turn from his fierce anger, so that we perish not?" (3:9). As H. W. Wolff has explained, the author of Jonah thereby made a very significant connection with Joel 2:12–14.[4] Joel had delivered Yahweh's word to *Israel*, a word that had described the very heart of God by revealing that the motivation even behind God's judgment was the compassionate desire to bring a wayward people to repentance and salvation.

Return to the Lord, your God, for he is gracious and merciful, slow to anger, and abounding in steadfast love, and repents of evil. Who knows whether he will not turn and repent, and leave a blessing behind him? (Joel 2:13–14)

Now in Jonah this prophetic probing is attributed to the Ninevite king, that is, one epitomizing all that is pagan and idolatrous. The result is a bold theological statement: Even as God cares for the inhabitants of Israel, and does not desire their destruction, so too God cares for the Ninevites, and seeks their repentance and deliverance from destruction. And since the Ninevites symbolized the Gentile nations in general, the story becomes a powerful confession in a divine compassion that is not limited to Israel, but embraces all the peoples of the earth.

But the story goes further, and in fact builds up to the most remarkable point of all, namely that the chief obstacle remaining in the way of this extension of Yahweh's salvation to the nations was Yahweh's own messenger, Jonah. Jonah manifests not commitment, but stubborn opposition to God's universal plan. He first tries to flee from the God

---

4. H. W. Wolff, *Jonah*, BK (Neukirchen-Vluyn: Neukirchener Verlag, 1977), p. 55.

commanding him to travel to Nineveh to preach. Once having been constrained to go there, and having witnessed the miraculous repentance of that evil city, he displays neither willingness nor capacity to emphathize with these foreigners who have come to accept his prophetic word. The irony is exquisite:

But it displeased Jonah exceedingly, and he was angry. And he prayed to the Lord and said, "I pray thee, Lord, is not this what I said when I was yet in my country? That is why I made haste to flee to Tarshish; for I knew that thou art a gracious God and merciful, slow to anger, and abounding in steadfast love, and repentest of evil. (Jonah 4:1–2)

This quotation of the classic expression of early Yahwistic faith in God's compassion (Exod. 34:6) makes the author's point powerfully.

Jonah is next portrayed as turning to his own selfish need to find creaturely comfort by withdrawing from the city and building himself a shelter. Yahweh lends a hand, "appointing" a plant for shade. One sees the story move toward its climax when Yahweh on the very next day makes a second "appointment," this time of a worm to destroy the plant. Jonah, suffering under the heat of the sun, wants no more of Yahweh's ways, and asks to die. Yahweh points out Jonah's total selfishness: so caught up is he in his own self-pity that he is unable to feel pity for one hundred and twenty thousand Ninevites (4:10–11)!

All in all, the Jonah narrative is most unusual, and profound in the message it delivers. Unfortunately that message is missed by most readers due to a misguided preoccupation with the question of the story's historicity. When understood as a theological tract addressing a pressing problem in the religious community of its time, it ceases to be a prophetic writing so "minor" in status as not to be taken seriously. Let us look at two of its contributions related to the subject of community.

First, consider the light this book sheds on the vexed problem of the so-called oracles against the nations; that is, the oracle type commonly arranged in collections by the final editors of the prophetic books and promising dreadful divine damnation of Israel's neighbors (cf. Isa. 13–23; 63:1–6; Jer. 46–51; Ezek. 27–32). Although some of the oracles against the nations are pre-exilic in origin (e.g. Amos 1–2), many of them stem from the postexilic period, which makes the message of Jonah in relation to the theological questions they raise all the more interesting. If one were to be restricted to the theological tradition represented by Ezra, Nehemiah, and the Chronicler in searching for the biblical framework within which to interpret these perplexing oracles, one would not get far beyond the conclusion that the exclusivism propounded by that tradition finds its logical extension in the condemnation of all that is foreign, and that the oracles against the nations are accordingly an appropriate vehicle for expressing Yahweh's hatred of all that is non-Judahite. The Book of Jonah points toward a vastly different conclusion. By offering a daring reinterpretation of Joel 2:12–14, according to which Yahweh's judgment is subservient to a divine plan not only in relation to Israel but to the foreign nations as well, the otherwise baffling harshness of the oracles against the nations becomes amenable to a new theological explanation. Yahweh's wrath is never to be construed as an end in itself, nor is it to be dedicated to nationalistic and self-aggrandistic goals. Even when directed against Israel's enemies, the judgment of Yahweh is dedicated to the restoration of an order of peace and justice predicated on true worship, and encompassing the entire human family. This angle of interpretation can be greatly expanded by other connections. For example, Jeremiah 18:7–8 gives expression to a similar belief:

If at any time I declare concerning a nation or a kingdom, that I will pluck up and break down and destroy it, and if that nation, concerning which I have spoken, turns from its evil, I will repent of the evil that I intended to do to it.

Moreover, on the basis of this interpretation it becomes possible to extend other passages beyond the compass of the Israelite community, in the manner of the Book of Jonah's reinterpretation of Joel 2:12–14. To cite one example, Ezekiel 33:11 (parallel in 11:32) takes on a new significance when subjected to such amplification: "Say to them, as I live, says the Lord God, I have no pleasure in the death of the wicked, but that the wicked turn from his way and live; turn back, turn back from your evil ways; for why will you die, O house of Israel?" When related to the interpretation of the oracles against the foreign nations, this passage from Ezekiel can suggest the following: because Yahweh feels this way about all humans, the prophets were sent with the shocking message of judgment of the unrepentant not only to Israel, but to all the nations. Through whatever mixture of human passions, these oracles were brought by their prophetic mediators to their listeners. Within the broader context of a biblical witness that includes the message of Jonah, those oracles must be interpreted as dedicated not to the destruction of the foreign nations, but to their repentance and salvation. Clearly, this interpretive insight has very broad implications for an adequate understanding of the meaning of community in the Bible, one that could serve as a basis for an entirely new approach to some of the most baffling passages of Scripture.

Within the various theological streams discernible in the postexilic period, Jonah is to be placed within the stream that drew on the universalism of the Servant Songs of Second Isaiah (e.g., Isa. 42:1–8 and 49:1–6), and that we have already discerned underlying Malachi 1:11 and Isaiah 56:1–8. The mission to the Gentiles defended by Paul and the other early Christian missionaries doubtlessly drew on this same stream: " . . . is God the God of the Jews only? Is he not the God of Gentiles also?" (Rom. 3:29). Yahweh, the one true God who, as Jonah expressed it, is "the God of heaven, who made the sea and the dry land"—that is to say, who is the sovereign Lord not only of history, but of the created order as well—is a loving God whose compassion extends to all humans, regardless of nationality. The Book of Jonah is unequivocal in locating this outreach in the identical source recognized by the earliest Yahwists as the basis of their own deliverance, namely, divine grace alone. Remarkably, the King of Nineveh joins the ranks of those appealing to God's boundless compassion: "Who knows, God may yet repent and turn from his fierce anger, so that we perish not?" (Jonah 3:9) As Israel's birth as a people was the result solely of God's prevenient grace, the alternative vision of Jonah was able to describe a further expansion of the orbit of salvation based on that same grace. From this it follows that if the community of faith in the postexilic period was to extend beyond the borders of Israel, it would do so by being faithful to the example of the earliest Yahwistic community; that is, as a gathering constituted by a communal response of gratitude culminating in worship and finding expression in a life of righteousness and compassion.

The Book of Jonah makes a second point having to do with the means by which knowledge of Yahweh was to reach the Ninevites, and all the other foreign peoples they symbolized. The answer is already implied in the formula of prophetic commission with which the story opens: "Now the word of the Lord came to Jonah the son of Amittai, saying, 'Arise, go to Nineveh. . . .'" True to the belief that had developed within prophetic Yahwism, the perfect expression of divine righteousness and compassion found in the Torah, though the only valid basis for šalôm throughout the family of nations, was nevertheless entrusted by God to a particular human agent, the people of Israel. The author of the Book of Jonah proves to be a worthy descendant of Second Isaiah in relation to this point. That it touches the very heart of the author's message is indicated by the fact that it is here that the polemical thrust of the story becomes most pronounced. The irony is exquisite: here we meet one who, like the prophets before him, is commissioned by God to proclaim God's word to a distant people (cf. Jer. 1:10). But far from carrying out his responsibility as agent of God's righteousness and compassion, Jonah becomes a vexing obstacle in the way of the outward movement of God's word to the nations. The message is clear, and it is programmatic in its intent: even as the Ninevites represent more than the inhabitants of one city by symbolizing all Gentile peoples, so too Jonah stands for more than one person. By being cast in a literary device long favored by the prophets (e.g., 2 Sam. 12:7 and Isa. 5:7), the key association would not have been missed by the hearers and readers of the story: Jonah was the Servant People, Israel, called and commissioned to "establish justice in the earth," to be "a covenant to the people, a light to the nations," "that [God's] salvation may reach to the end of the earth" (Isa. 42:4, 6; 49:6). But the Servant fails utterly in his vocation. Indeed, the openness of the pagan Ninevites to God's word of repentance in its contrast to the Servant's unfaithfulness and lack of compassion heaps shame on the agent called by God to be a partner in the divine plan of salvation. Here is a Servant who would rather die than to witness the successful fruits of his mission, so selfish and caught up in his own petty concerns is he!

When on the basis of linguistic and thematic evidence we place the provenance of Jonah in the late fifth or early fourth century B.C.E. (a view conforming to scholarly consensus), the location of the book within the theological streams of this period seems obvious: Jonah was written as a protest against the exclusivism and isolationism of the Ezra and Nehemiah reform movement. In a broad sense, it is thus a theological descendant of the Levitical-prophetic dissident movement that gave rise to the oracles of Isaiah 56–66. Its criticism of the Zadokite program also places it in close relation to the circles that produced Zechariah 11 and 12–14 as well as the Book of Malachi. Against the parochial tendencies of the Zadokite leadership of the time, it lifts up an alternative vision of Israel's universal misison, a vision not only renewing the universal message of Second Isaiah, but even betraying roots in archaic Yahwistic traditions (cf. Gen. 12:1–4; Exod. 34:6–7). Like the Book of Ruth, it registers a protest against a definition of community that, by focusing on the exclusivistic notion of "the holy seed," threatened the sole sovereignty of Yahweh as the only legitimate norm for defining the nature and vocation of God's people. The shocking judgment is made that by so doing, the Servant Community was opting for its own death. And the motivation for that choice was located in a myopic and selfish preoccupation with its own petty problems that blinded it to the bold, universal outreach of divine compassion. By redirecting attention back to the God of all creation and all humanity, the expansive dynamic inherent in Israel's early understanding of righteousness and compassion was recaptured. The reason for this is clear. Whenever the focus of the community rested solely on its God, its definition of the cardinal qualities of its communal life were extrapolated from the nature of that God, not from penultimate entities such as earthly rulers or genealogical lines. In such a situation, moreover, it is significant that the archaic picture of Yahweh as Deliverer of the lost and Protector of the weak was reasserted, for as this picture was the source of the vitality of early Yahwism, so too at this later period is persisted as a potential source for the revitalization of a community in danger of losing a sense of its vocation within an increasingly complex world.

D. THE THEOLOGICAL IMPORTANCE OF THE ALTERNATIVE VISION

Ezra and Nehemiah had addressed the need that was pressing itself on a community threatened on all sides by hostile neighbors and divided within by contending factions to reaffirm its unity and to give clear definition to its identity. This they achieved by turning the attention of the community to the institutions, beliefs, and customs that separated the people of Judah from the other peoples of the world. While fully understandable within the historical conditions of the period, this response nevertheless imperiled one of the most unique aspects to have developed up to that time within the Yahwistic notion of community. That aspect was its sense of being a member of the family of the nations not only for its own self-preservation, but as Yahweh's agent of righteousness, compassion, and blessing among all peoples of the earth. Joel contributed to the renewal of that vision by giving bold new expression to the eschatological dimensions of Yahweh's presence in the world, though in its focus on the negative side of divine activity it was a partial picture, in need of amplification. The other two books considered provide just such amplification. Ruth, in an idyllic way, reaffirmed the magnanimity of Yahwism vis-á-vis those of foreign birth who had been drawn into the Yahwistic community through marriage. And Jonah extended this affirmation by portraying Israel's prophetic mission of declaring God's word to all peoples, with the hope of bringing them to repentance and to deliverance from the wages of wickedness. This alternative vision finds expression in other passages, two of which are briefly discussed in concluding this section.

In Isaiah 19, a chapter that begins with the awful images of destruction typical of the oracles against the nations, one witnesses a conclusion that is most untypical of this genre. Rather than culminating with a picture of total destruction of the foreign enemy, Yahweh's final deliverance of Egypt is described in a manner reminiscent of Yahweh's earlier deliverance of Israel from its oppressors during the period of the Judges. And true to the pattern observed within the history of the early Yahwistic cult, the Egyptians respond to this deliverance by worshipping Yahweh:

. . . when they cry to the Lord because of oppressors he will send them a savior, and will defend and deliver them. And the Lord will make himself known to the Egyptians; and the Egyptians will know the Lord in that day and worship with sacrifice and burnt offering, and they will make vows to the Lord and perform them. And the Lord will smite Egypt, smiting and healing, and they will return to the Lord, and he will heed their supplications and heal them. (Isa. 19:20b–22)

Clearer expression could not have been given to the belief that the judgment of the nations, exactly like the judgment of Israel, was ultimately an expression of Yahweh's desire to open the human heart to divine deliverance and healing. The passage then goes on to envision the participation of the Assyrians in the worship of Yahweh. It concludes with an astonishing expansion of the Abrahamic blessing of Genesis 12:1–4:

In that day Israel will be the third with Egypt and Assyria, a blessing in the midst of the earth, whom the Lord of hosts has blessed, saying, "Blessed by Egypt my people, and Assyria the work of my hands, and Israel my heritage." (Isa. 19:24–25)

Since Isaiah 19, like the foreign nation oracles gathered together in Isaiah 13–23 generally, lacks historical allusions on which to date it, we must be content with an argument from the broader perspective of theological streams. Of the streams we have been able to identify, it would seem to stem from the same dissident group reacting against the Zadokite program in the fifth and fourth centuries, which came to expression in the books of Ruth and Jonah.

Finally, Psalm 145 is a beautiful formulation of the magnanimity of spirit this alternative vision sought to preserve and expand, though once again the difficulties in dating such a psalm must be acknowledged. Celebrated in this psalm is the God whose "greatness is unsearchable":

The Lord is gracious and merciful, slow to anger and abounding in steadfast love. The Lord is good to all, and his compassion is over all that he has made. (Ps. 145:8–9)

According to this psalm, the vocation of the faithful ones is at one with the works of Yahweh's whole creation, namely, "to make known to the sons of men his mighty deeds, and the glorious splendor of his kingdom," a kingdom that is everlasting. In the holy imagination of this psalm, the universal goodness of Yahweh reaches sublime expression:

The eyes of all look to thee, and thou givest them their food in due season. Thou openest thy hand, thou satisfiest the desire of every living thing. The Lord is just in all his ways, and kind in all his doings. The Lord is near to all who call upon him, to all who call upon him in truth. (Ps. 145:15–18)

It was in defense of this classical Yahwistic belief in God as the compassionate and righteous Lord of all peoples that the dissident group advanced its alternate vision. That the biblical legacy to later Jewish and Christian communities included the notions of Israel as a "light to the nations" (Isa. 49:6), of the temple as "a house of prayer for all peoples" (Isa. 56:7), of all the nations of the world contributing their children to the priesthood of Yahweh (Isa. 66:18–21), of offerings being made to Yahweh "from the rising of the sun to its setting" (Mal. 1:11), of a Moabite woman being adopted and protected by the Yahwistic community (Ruth), of a pagan king repenting and appealing to the mercy of Yahweh (Jonah 4:6–9), and of Assyria and Egypt joining Israel in becoming "a blessing in the midst of the earth" (Isa. 19:24), that these themes are a part of that rich and diverse inheritance is to the credit of that stream of tradition that is so downplayed by later editors and tradents that we must content ourselves with designating it as the group that kept alive "an alternative vision." Although eluding clear description as a social entity within the history of the postexilic period, however, its theological contribution to the religion of Isreal and the theology of the Bible will not be missed by sensitive readers. And this awakens the hope that its impact on the development of the biblical notion of community can be rediscovered, and appropriately applied to contemporary theological reflection.

XI

The People of the Torah: From Ezra to the Maccabean Revolt
(Judith and Ecclesiasticus)

We thank Thee who hast moved us to building, to finding,
   to forming at the ends of our fingers and beams of
   our eyes.
And when we have built an altar to the Invisible Light,
   we may set thereon the little lights for which our
   bodily vision is made.
And we thank Thee that darkness reminds us of light.
O Light Invisible, we give Thee thanks for Thy great
   glory![1]

Historical Note: In 332 B.C.E. the Judean Commonwealth passed over to Hellenistic rule as the result of the conquest of Alexander the Great. This introduced a period of intense Hellenization throughout the Near East, giving rise to pro- and anti-Hellenistic groups that competed for control of the nation and cult. During this period, the Zadokite priestly leadership of the temple and the new scribal class preserved many of the classical structures of Jewish community by adapting the Torah (the first five books of the Hebrew Bible) to the new setting without sacrificing its essential Jewish character to the Hellenistic spirit. The two centuries between Ezra and the Maccabean Revolt were thus very challenging ones to those of Jewish faith, ones in which distinctive forms of community and individual piety developed that would have profound impact on the major parties that arose in the Hellenistic and Roman periods. Unfortunately, however, the literary evidence for the period is very sparse, forcing us to generalize on the basis of meager sources (especially the Book of Judith) and to extrapolate backward from sources falling at the end of this period (especially Ecclesiasticus, or the Wisdom of Jesus the Son of Sirach).

---

1. T. S. Eliot, "Choruses from 'The Rock,' " in *The Complete Poems and Plays, 1909–1950* (New York: Harcourt, Brace, 1952), pp. 113–114.

A. THE ENCOUNTER WITH HELLENISM

The two centuries following the time of Ezra and Nehemiah witnessed the further development of diverse streams within Judaism toward the configuration of parties and movements familiar to us from the works of Philo and Josephus, and from early rabbinical and Christian writings. It was a period within which the Jewish faith and its cherished institutions came under the increasing pressure of Hellenization, in the form in which that world culture had been transmitted to the East by the missionary zeal of Alexander during his sweeping conquest of the Persian empire between the years 332 and 323 B.C.E.[2] Alexander's successors, the Diadochoi, continued this process of promoting the ideals of Greek culture. One of the chief questions facing subsequent Jewish communities was thus the question of the degree to which the traditional faith could legitimately be accommodated to foreign beliefs and customs. It is obvious that Yahwism, like every living religion, adopted themes and concepts from its environment at every stage of its history. The critical question was always whether the traditional faith was enriched or endangered in a given case. Although the process was more implicit than explicit, it seems that the Yahwistic faith survived its encounters with many different religions in part because its leaders were able to recognize when a particular foreign element posed a threat to the heart of that faith. The struggle to define the fine line between fruitful borrowing and threatening syncretism was unceasing. Although imagery originally associated with Baal is found in many of the Psalms, Elijah had combatted the Baal syncretism of Ahab and Jezebel in the ninth century B.C.E., recognizing it to be a deadly challenge to the central tenets of Yahwism. Eighth-century pilgrims worshipping at a sanctuary in the Negeb (Kuntillet 'Ajrud), however, apparently recognized Asherah as the consort of Yahweh, in keeping with the customs of their home sanctuary in Samaria.[3] But their practice was repudiated by the streams of tradition that shaped the received tradition. The Deuteronomonistic Historian accused Manasseh (686–642) of apostasy because he had erected altars to Baal and apparently permitted the worship of astral deities (1 Kings 21). Jeremiah, according to the report in Jeremiah 44, contended with fellow Jewish refugees in Egypt who

---

2. V. Tcherikover's treatment of this period remains a classic: *Hellenistic Civilization and the Jews*, trans. S. Applebaum (Philadelphia: Jewish Publication Society, 1961).

3. A colorful description of the Kuntillet 'Ajrud inscriptions is given by the archaeologist who discovered them in a Judean religious outpost in the Sinai desert, Ze'ev Meshel. "Did Yahweh have a Consort?" *BAR* 5 (1979), 24–35. For the texts, see Ze'ev Meshel, "Kuntillet 'Ajrud: A Religious Centre from the Time of the Judean Monarchy," Museum Catalogue 175 (Jerusalem: The Israel Museum). The most recent treatment is W. G. Dever, "Asherah, Consort of Yahweh? New Evidence from Kuntillet 'Ajrud," *BASOR* 255 (1984), 21–37.

were determined to return to a more "effective" deity than Yahweh, namely the Queen of Heaven, Astarte. But the prophetic critique did not always prevail, as illustrated by the Aramaic papyri of the fifth-century Jewish military colony at Elephantine on the Nile, where the gods Haram-bethel, 'Asam-bethel, 'Anath-bethel, and Anath-yahu are mentioned alongside Yahu (Yahweh),[4] though again such practices were apparently confined to circles on the fringe of Judaism.

In general it seems safe to conclude that neither in pre-Hellenistic times, nor in the period after Alexander, did forms of explicit syncretism become an abiding part of cult life within the mainstreams of Jewish religion. The syncretism of Ahab and Manasseh is remembered in biblical tradition only with derision, and the religious cults of Kuntillet 'Ajrud and Elephantine were short-lived. Similarly, during the Hellenistic period, the memory of protagonists of a genuine Hellenistic-Jewish syncretism such as the high priests Jason and Menelaus was preserved only for harshest condemnation. In fairness to such groups, we must remember that the judgments rendered came from the stream of tradition that eventually established itself as normative—that is, from the victors. During the periods of controversy themselves, no doubt the issues were much more complex than portrayed by later tradition. What later commentators judged to be pernicious syncretism and apostasy likely was deemed by the earlier protagonists of accommodation to be a progressive adaptation of the received tradition to new conditions; that is to say, a legitimate strategy for survival.

It is also important to realize that no new Jewish group escaped entirely the influence of the powerful Hellenistic movement. Hellenism represented the cultural values and artistic conventions of the wider world, and forced all Jewish groups to establish their identity via-à-vis those values and conventions. Below I describe the responses made by various groups to Hellenism, ranging from enthusiastic adoption to hostile rejection. But first, for the sake of completeness, one other community originating within postexilic Judaism should be mentioned: the community of the Samaritans.

B. THE SAMARITANS

It was the opinion of the Jews from the southern half of the land that their brethren to the north had been so completely intermingled with pagan elements as to obliterate their Jewishness, to the point of making them unworthy of participating in worship in the Jerusalem temple. Needless to say, this opinion was not shared by those who claimed to be survivors of the Assyrian conquest of 722, and who continued to worship at the cult located on Mount Gerizim. To the contrary, they

4. E. G. Kraeling, "Elephantine Papyri," *IDB* 2 (1962), 83–85.

claimed to be the only true descendants of Moses, a claim they backed
by rejecting all writings save the five Books of Moses as sacred scripture. Although many questions remain regarding the history of the
schism between the cultic community at Gerizim and the Jerusalem
temple community, the building of a temple a Shechem by the Samaritans—which probably occurred in the Hellenistic period—symbolized
their alienation from Jerusalem.[5] In their separate development, the
Samaritans developed a rigid and conservative position, both in relation to tradition and to the wider world. On the basis of their allegiance to the Torah (Genesis through Deuteronomy), to the exclusion
of the prophetic writings, the hagiographa, and every form of oral tradition, they developed a ritual legalism that resisted all change, whether of the sort generated by internal developments (such as prophecy or
Messianism) or external influences (such as Hellenism). Although a
remnant of the Samaritan community exists in the area surrounding its
ancient cult center to this day, its withdrawal from the kind of engagement with ongoing historical events that had characterized and ener-
gized Yahwism from the beginning and that persisted within the powerful Pharisaic party nullified every potential contribution it might have
made to religious communities beyond itself.

C. PRO-HELLENISTIC POSITIONS

After bracketing out the cults of Elephantine and Samaria from our
further study of the history of the biblical notion of community in the
four centuries before the Common Era, we are still left with a very
broad spectrum of movements and traditions. Indeed, they are of such
complexity as to require a far more extensive treatment than can be
given here. For our purposes, we must be satisfied with a broad
overview.

At one extreme were the groups and elements, both in Judea and
elsewhere, that adopted an emphatically pro-Hellenistic posture. The
Tobiad family serves as a good example of this tendency. Its history
traces back to the time of Nehemiah, when Eliashib, a high priest on
friendly terms with and connected to marriage to Sanballat the governor of Syria, provided a chamber in the temple for Tobiah during Nehemiah's absence from Jerusalem. When Nehemiah returned, he expelled Tobiah as one whose unsanctity (and, we can safely add, faulty
pedigree) made him unfit as a resident of the holy precinct (Neh. 13:
4–9).

This Tobiah in all likelihood was the ancestor of the powerful Tobiad family of the Hellenistic period. With its base of power east of the

---

5. See J. D. Purvis, *The Samaritan Pentateuch and the Origin of the Samaritan Sect*, HSM 2
(Cambridge, Mass.: Harvard University Press, 1968), and H. G. Kippenberg, *Garizim und
Synagoge* (Berlin: de Gruyter, 1971), pp. 33–93.

Jordan, it became the chief rival of the Zadokite temple priesthood of Jerusalem in the troubled times of the late third century B.C.E. The orientation of the Tobiads was thoroughly Hellenistic, and was clearly motivated by their widespread commercial interests.[6]

The interference of the Tobiads in Jerusalem politics increased during the priesthood of Onias II, who was forced to relinquish much of his power to Joseph, son of Tobias. From 240 until 218 B.C.E., Joseph was the chief political figure in Jerusalem. There is no doubt that his pro-Hellenistic posture, coupled with his high-handed abuse of his power, fanned the flames of revolution among many devout Jews.

Following the conquest of Judea by the Seleucids, the Tobiads moved closer to the center of the Jewish community, their primary goal being control of the office of the high priesthood. They exploited both the chaotic political climate and the open breach between the Zadokite high priest Onias III and his Hellenizing brother Jason by purchasing the high priestly office for Jason from Antiochus IV Epiphanes. The story of the subsequent happenings is well known, with the high priesthood becoming a pawn in the hands of rival parties, the temple treasure a source of booty, and the sacred Torah the beseiged bulwark of the pious against the threat of Hellenization. It seems likely that if the Hellenizing group had remained the dominant power in Judaism, the Jewish faith would have gone the way of the other local cults, obliterated and supplanted by the new world culture.

When it is recalled that the long struggle that culminated with the Maccabean revolt began, in a sense, with Nehemiah's stand against the "liberal" high priest Eliashib and his friend Tobiah, it is no longer possible to dismiss Nehemiah as a narrow legalist, whose blind distrust vitiated the attempts of people of goodwill to create an open community. Given the volative political circumstances of the whole period between Nehemiah and the Maccabees, the policy of the pro-Hellenistic party seemed to bring with it an assimilation that would have effaced what was unique within the biblical notion of community.

The combination of opportunism and zeal for Hellenization that characterized the Tobiad family had no more future within Judaism than the syncretistic position of the Elephantine colony. It simply had strayed too far from the true spirit of the ideals of biblical faith.

Later movements and individuals displaying an openness to the world culture of the time were judged by the community on the basis of their relation to the Torah. Accordingly, the Idumaeans Antipater and Herod were deeply despised as traitors to the faith, whereas Philo, who sought to translate the ideals of the Torah into the world view of his cultured neighbors in Alexandria, was admired by many of his compa-

---

6. Cf. J. H. Hayes and J. M. Miller, eds., *Israelite and Judean History* (Philadelphia: Westminster Press, 1977), pp. 572–575.

triots. Thus at the opposite end of the continuum from the Tobiads we see a whole group of writings, ranging in date from early Hellenistic to Roman times, and coming both from the Diaspora and from Judea, which are essentially characterized by fidelity to the Torah, but at the same time are open in varying degrees to Hellenistic forms of expression. In general, this group holds to positions that came to characterize the Pharisaic party, such as belief in the resurrection. As an example, we can cite the Wisdom of Solomon, a writing likely written in Egypt evincing a deep borrowing not only of literary conventions, but of philosophical concepts at home in Hellenism.[7] Reflected is a Jewish piety that, while upholding the Torah of Moses, sought to make that Jewish monument intelligible to sophisticated Hellenistic neighbors by emphasizing its ethical-universal aspects and paying little attention to ritual-particularistic dimensions. In this same spirit, the Jewish historian Artapanus, who was active in Egypt, could identify Moses with the Musaeus (the purported teacher of Orpheus), and with Hermes![8] The *Third Sibyl* illustrates well the fine line tread by Hellenistic Jews, for she blends devotion to Mosaic law with an appeal to natural law, and an insistence on the sole sovereignty of God with universalistic themes (lines 757–758).[9] Jewish piety combined with Hellenistic motifs also in the narrative works of Tobit and *Joseph and Aseneth*. Within this category also belongs the Book of *3 Maccabees*, within which loyalty to orthodox belief is defended in the face of persecution. We recognize in such writings a piety that is practical rather than utopian or extreme in relating Judaism to foreign powers and outside ideas.

D. TEMPLE AND TORAH, PRIESTS AND SCRIBES

While it is not possible to distinguish rigidly between those who sought to combine obedience to the Torah with a cautious openness to forms and concepts of the wider world from those who sought to defend their ancient traditions from the inroads of Hellenization, it seems that further refinements in defining the meaning of religious community occurred primarily among groups that placed the emphasis on preservation of the ancient faith from outside influences. This is true in part because such were the groups that survived and gave form to later Pharisaism and Christianity. But even among such groups we find a significant degree of diversity, though this did not clearly surface until the severe trials of the reign of Antiochus IV Epiphanes (175–163 B.C.E.). Before that crisis, it seems that the Zadokite leadership, at least in the homeland, had managed to maintain its control of the cult and

---

7. Cf. D. Winston, *Wisdom of Solomon*, AB 43 (Garden City, N.Y.: Doubleday, 1979).

8. M. Hengel, *Judaism and Hellenism*, vol. 1, trans. J. Bowden (Philadelphia: Fortress Press, 1974), p. 91.

9. J. Collins, *Between Athens and Jerusalem*, pp. 148–151.

community along lines consistent with the Priestly Writing and the fifth-century reform program of Ezra and Nehemiah, a program clearly presented in the Chronicler's History. Within this hierocracy, the Zadokite priests obviously exercised the dominant authority. But other groups had their assigned tasks as well. For example, the Levites served as temple attendants and singers, while the sages were able to continue their investigations of the vast realms of nature and human character, often in close contact with wisdom circles in other countries. Although some groups no doubt continued to feel excluded, and dreamed of a more ideal age to come, their apocalyptic visions seemed to have been repressed. Apocalyptic movements during the fifth, fourth, and third centuries were likely "underground" movements, comprising dissident and disenfranchised elements finding little with which to identify within the mainstream of the society, and therefore looking to an imminent intervention by God in which they would be vindicated and restored.[10]

At the center of the society, important developments were shaping the structures of community into a form that would become definitive for latter rabbinical Judaism. It was a period in which the Zadokite priests promulgated the sacrificial structures of the temple, and in which the Torah, in its canonical form consisting of the Five Books of Moses, came to be elevated to the sublime heights of an eternal order, the very basis on which creation itself was believed to be founded. In the Torah, God had pointed the way to the blessed life, complete in all things. This emphasis on the perfection and completeness of the Torah hastened further the eclipse of prophecy. The claim was later made that after Haggai, Zechariah, and Malachi the spirit of prophecy had departed from Israel.[11] Indeed, the prophetic personality fell suspect as endangering the stability of the community, a suspicion reinforced in the minds of many through their experience with the resurgent apocalypticism of the late Hellenistic and early Roman Period (later this wariness increased even further as the result of encounters with the prophetic emphasis of early Christianity).

It is likely that a practice prominent in later Pharisaic tradition also has roots in this period: the classical prophets of earlier times were

---

10. For a description of divergent groups within Judaism in the Hellenistic Period, see P. D. Hanson, "The Historical Setting of the Intertestamental Writings," *The Cambridge History of Judaism*, vol. 2, in press.

11. The view that the age of prophecy was past is found widely in the rabbinical writings: "When the 'latter prophets' Haggai, Zechariah, and Malachi died, the Holy Spirit departed from Israel" (*Sanhedrin* 11a; cf. *Baba Batra* 12b). Included among those things present in the era of the First Temple, but departed from the Second, is the Holy Spirit (*Song of Songs Rabbah* 8; cf. *Yoma* 21b; *Numbers Rabbah* 15, 10). The commentary on the words of Leviticus 27:34, "These are the commandments" reads: "Henceforth no prophet may make any innovation" (*Sabbat* 104a). The office of prophecy was thus regarded as a thing of the past, having ended with Malachi; the successors of the prophets were the *hkmym*, the "wise men," who came to be called Rabbis. Thus we read "A 'wise man' is greater than a prophet," (*Baba Batra* 12a; cf. *Jerusalem Berakot* 81 5:4).

themselves interpreted in such a way as to appear to be primarily expositors of the Torah. In general, it is clear that the creative edge of the community moved to the ongoing effort to apply the Torah to all facets of life in a rapidly changing world. In this new modality as a community patterning its life on Torah, and concerned with the faithful application of that norm to every detail of life, the new scribe class came to assume a position rivaling that of the priesthood over the course of the fourth and third centuries B.C.E. It is safe to say that, in everyday matters, the scribe exercised the greater influence over the life of the individual Jew. Increasingly, the role of the priesthood came to be associated with the ritual of the temple, though at certain times the high priest also exercised considerable influence in political affairs.

These important changes notwithstanding, the members of the priesthood continued to enjoy high esteem. After all, the eternal order symbolized by the Torah took form in this world precisely through the annual festivals, the observance of the Sabbath and the rite of circumcision, and the priests were the guardians of these observances. The Mishnah (completed ca. 200 C.E.) gives classic form to this view by picturing the blessed life as revolving around the temple, where the eternal order of heaven could reach out to the life of the people in their villages. Nevertheless, when it came to the day-to-day application of the Torah to the life of the villages of Judah or Egypt or Babylon, it was the scribe, and later the sage, who played the chief role. This change, perhaps more than any other, equipped Judaism for survival after the destruction of the temple in 70 C.E.

What was the nature of the idea of community that developed during the period between Ezra's reform and the crisis of the Maccabean period? Certainly an emphasis on continuity with the structures and beliefs of the past continued to characterize the Zadokite hierarchy. Indeed, the view arose that the Torah, in its every detail, traced back not only to Moses, but to the beginning of time. And the temple, with its orders of priests and sacrifices, was believed to stem from David's zeal for the Lord. Torah observance and temple worship thus became the principal vehicles of the ancient beliefs of Israel.

E. JUDITH

By way of example, we see in the Book of Judith, which originated perhaps in the late third century B.C.E. as an exhortation to faithfulness, an eloquent statement of the cardinal principles of traditional Yahwism. In spite of the arrogant claims of foreign potentates, there is one true God alone (6:2–4; 8:16–17; 14:18; 16:13). In a manner reminiscent of Second Isaiah, this God is described as the purposer who guides all history toward its intended goal (9:5–6). And this God is the righteous, compassionate One whose presence is with the oppressed and the weak:

For your power depends not upon numbers, nor your might upon men of strength. For you are God of the lowly, helper of the oppressed, upholder of the weak, protector of the forlorn, savior of those without help. (Jth. 9:11)

While some may take offense at the cunning and brutality of Judith's stratagem, and wonder where the magnanimity of Second Isaiah's attitude toward the nations had gone, we must interpret the Book of Judith within the context of the fundamental spiritual struggle of the Jewish community with Hellenism. And within that context, the book's confession in the sole lordship of God, and its emphasis on God's compassionate delivery of the oppressed, constitute a courageous statement in a threatening world. Judith herself is portrayed as a model of righteousness (8:4–6), devotion (8:8) and courage (9:11–17). Moreover, the book captures a central theme of Yahwism by picturing the response of the people to God's deliverance: "When they arrived at Jerusalem they worshipped God" (16:18).

F. ECCLESIASTICUS (THE WISDOM OF JESUS THE SON OF SIRACH)

Even more helpful as a witness to the Jewish community in the period just before the time of the Maccabees is Ecclesiasticus (or the Wisdom of Jesus the Son of Sirach). Once again, we find a community ideal emphasizing continuity with the institutions and beliefs of the past. In Sirach's overview of the past, the period of the exile and the return are ignored, as if those disruptive events had not occurred. In this respect, it is a historical portrait closely resembling that of the Chronicler. At the center of the Jewish community stands the Torah, which is God's plan for all life, embracing nature as well as the realm of human morality. The Torah is thus expanded to embrace the universal concerns normally associated with the wisdom schools. Chapter 24 draws out the identification explicitly. First, in a manner reminiscent of Proverbs 8 and 9, Wisdom describes herself as a member of God's heavenly assembly, spanning the heavens above and the depths below, and though created from eternity for eternity, nevertheless established by God in Zion to take up her dwelling with Jacob. Finally, the whole preceding catena of themes at home in the sapiental tradition is identified with the Torah:

> All this is the book of the covenant of the most High God,
>> the law which Moses commanded us
>> as an inheritance for the congregations of Jacob. (Ecclus. 24:23)

This wedding of wisdom with Torah emerges as a most natural one. We have seen how deeply concerned the Zadokite community was with stability within a fickle world. And it is well known that the agelong pursuit of wisdom was the pursuit of order, both in nature and in human relations. After Torah had come to be viewed as God's eternal plan for Israel, and by extension, for the world, it came to have much in common with wisdom. Hence the merging of the two in Sirach and in the late third-century community for which he serves as such an eloquent witness.[12]

According to Sirach, the God who revealed the Torah to Israel was a dependable, righteous God. Therefore the Jewish community could be assured of the order and harmony of the world, for all events and all individuals were under the retributive justice of God: "To the holy his ways are straight, just as they are obstacles to the wicked" (Ecclus. 39:24). "The blessing of the Lord is the reward of the godly, and quickly God causes his blessing to flourish" (11:22). Within this ordered world, prudence and caution are commended: "If you do a kindness, know to whom you do it, and you will be thanked for your good deeds" (12:1). "Give to the good man, but do not help the sinner" (12:7). The emphasis placed on a conservative sort of propriety is reminiscent of the courtly protocol at home in the earlier wisdom tradition:

> When a powerful man invites you,
>   be reserved;
> and he will invite you the more often.
>   Do not push forward, lest you be repulsed;
> and do not remain at a distance,
>   lest you be forgotten.   (Ecclus. 13:9–10)

The general impression one gets in reading Sirach is that it represents the legacy of an ancient tradition that had been tested and refined repeatedly, preserving for posterity only that which had proven to be supportive of life. The imprint of the era of Ezra and Nehemiah is unmistakable: security was to be found only within the community of fellow Jews, where a lofty ideal of fairness and compassion was to prevail. On the other hand, in relation to outsiders a deep-seated suspicion comes to expression, reminding the reader that Sirach spoke for a people struggling to maintain its identity in the face of powerful forces seeking its obliteration through assimilation. It is clear how in such a setting the Torah represented God's supreme gift to God's people. Through a life of obedience to the Torah alone could the snares of death on all sides be avoided and the life of blessing be preserved. It was in the effort to define that life of obedience that the tried and tested guidelines of the wisdom tradition proved to be a powerful ally.

Even as the Torah was the faithful guidepost for the blessed life, the Jerusalem temple occupied the position of vital life center for the Jew-

---

12. G. W. E. Nicklesburg, *Jewish Literature Between the Bible and the Mishnah* (Philadelphia: Fortress Press, 1981), pp. 59–62.

ish communities both in the homeland and abroad, with a couple of notable exceptions.[13] Typical of this period is the shift in emphasis in Sirach away from God's gift of the land to God's twin gifts of Torah and cult. This emphasis is seen in the attention paid to the various heroes of the past in chapters 44–50: Aaron receives three times as much space as Moses; Phinehas, space equal to Moses. And the obvious climax to this whole section comes in chapter 50, where Simon, the contemporary high priest (219–196 B.C.E.), is accorded the most lavish praise of all. Here then we see the figure who has inherited the splendor earlier accorded the Davidic king. In his presence, the community seems drawn into the blessing and glory that fulfills all God's promises. Within the temple and standing before its high priest, the people of God seems to have reached its final goal:

> How glorious was he when the
>   people gathered round him
>   as he came out of the inner sanctuary!
> Like the morning star among the clouds,
>   like the moon when it is full;
> like the sun shining upon the
>   temple of the Most High,
>   and like the rainbow gleaming
>   in glorious clouds.   (Ecclus. 50:5–7)

Although it is thus evident that strong lines of continuity connect Sirach to earlier tradition, it is equally clear that he was open also to the changes occurring within his religious community, such as the one mentioned earlier, the ascendency of the scribe to a position of influence rivaling that of the priest. Originally the scribes, as interpreters of Torah, were probably themselves of priestly descent. But in the second and first centuries B.C.E. the scribal office clearly evolved into a powerful autonomous force devoted to the ordering of all aspects of life—including those in the civil realm—in harmony with the Torah. Finally, by the period of the New Testament and the Mishnah, the heirs to the earlier scribal office, the sages (and rabbis), were, generally speaking, of the laity rather than of the priesthood.[14]

Whether or not Sirach was actually of Zadokite descent is a moot question. Regarding his relation to the scribal office the evidence is much clearer, for Sirach added considerable impetus to the ascendancy

---

13. For this period the known exceptions are twofold, the Tobiad temple at 'Araq el-Emir near Amman and the temple at Leontopolis in Egypt erected by Onias IV after the Jerusalem high priesthood had been purchased by the usurper Alcimus. We have already mentioned the earlier temples on Mount Gerizim and at Elephantine in Egypt.

14. In the later period, the term "scribe" (Greek grammatous) came to be applied to those whose activity actually was limited to the transmission of texts, in contrast to the earlier "scribes" who were interpreters of the Torah.

of the scribal class.[15] After describing the principal vocations of the Jewish community, and giving them their rightful due, he contrasts those occupying such vocations with the one whose worthiness is far greater:

> Yet they are not sought out for the council of the people,
>   nor do they attain eminence in the public assembly.
> They do not sit in the judge's seat,
>   nor do they understand the sentence of judgment. . . . (Ecclus. 38:33)

> On the other hand he who devotes himself
>   to the study of the law of the Most High
> will seek out the wisdom of all the ancients,
>   and will be concerned with prophecies. . . . (Ecclus. 39:1)

The description of the scribe that follows both betrays Sirach's own professional background and gives a picture of the scribe as the key figure of the Jewish community. Into the scribal portfolio were gathered functions earlier performed by the elders, the Levitical teachers, the prophets, and the sages. We witness here the emergence of a communal ideal within which the prophet receded into the background of the life of the community, and the priest increasingly became an official whose duties were concentrated on the cult, thereby leaving the interpretation of the Torah and day-to-day community teaching and leadership to the scribe. This emergent ideal in turn gave impetus to the development of the synagogue as a place of assembly for worship, study, and instruction apart from the temple. Finally, it is an ideal reflecting a community grown wary and even suspicious of the prophetic charisma, and dedicated to defining a more reliable method of determining God's will in relation to the frequently changing circumstances of life. What we witness here are the roots of the exegetical system of deducing God's will from Scripture, which would culminate in the Mishnah and the Talmud. Indeed, we see adumbrated at this stage the basic features of the Mishnah's picture of the community in the broad sense as revolving around the temple and the rites of the temple (which of course by the time of the Mishnah was strictly an ideal, the temple having long since been destroyed), but in its own village life living in faithfulness to the Torah under the guidance of its rabbis. To the extent that one can describe the world view underlying Sirach's communal ideals one can speak of a community at rest, a state made possible by the belief that the Torah given by God to the people was perfect and complete. Of course the assumption underlying this world view was that the community living in harmony with that Torah was thereby one that embodied God's will in its life and institutions.

---

15. D. Harrington, "The Wisdom of the Scribe According to Ben Sira," in G. Nickelsburg and J. Collins, eds., *Ideal Figures in Ancient Judaism*, Septuagint and Cognate Studies 12 (Chico, California: Scholars Press, 1980), pp. 181–188.

The implications of this ideal, which laid the groundwork for rabbinical Judaism, were profound, as regards both relations with the wider world and the concept this community came to adopt toward the future. Relations with gentiles were regulated on the basis of the concern to uphold purity. All contacts that rendered one impure were to be eschewed. The inevitable result was that strict separation had to be observed in the Jewish community's relation to outsiders. As regards the future, the emphasis on the perfection of the Torah left little room for eschatology. This was not a community waiting breathlessly for new acts of God, but devoted to patient application of that perfect gift given by God in the very beginning, the Torah, to all areas of life, and to meticulous protection of life from all forms of profanation. What we have characterized as a "realized eschatology" in Chronicles, Ezra, and Nehemiah is even more evident in Sirach's outlook. As the Chronicler took pains to locate the founding of all temple structures and offices in the reign of David and Solomon, Sirach looks to the even more distant past, indeed to the beginning of time, as the era of God's gift of the Torah. Nothing could give greater emphasis to the completeness and perfection of their communal ideal than this identification of the Torah's creation with the creation of the world.[16]

Although no doubt deemed parochial in the eyes of the more strident representatives of the Hellenizing party, the world of Sirach was characterized by a carefully refined internal structure that afforded its adherents a sense of order and security. Continuous on the one hand with the world of the Priestly Writing, the Chronicler, Ezra, and Nehemiah, it also was essentially the world bequeathed to Pharisaic Judaism, and codified in the Mishnah and the Talmud. Yet it is not possible to move directly from Sirach to the era of classical rabbinic Judaism, for there intervened between Sirach and the sages who gave form to the Mishnah a period of severe testing that would deeply affect the shape of Jewish religion.

Only a few decades after Sirach wrote his magisterial work, the world the Jews had hitherto managed to keep at arm's length began an ominous encroachment that soon struck at the very heart of the community centered around the temple and guided by the Torah of Moses. Between the years 175 and 163 B.C.E., the Syro-Hellenic King Antiochus IV Epiphanes set out to obliterate the Jewish community by banning its observance of the Torah, suspending temple sacrifice dedicated solely to the God of Israel, and seeking to assimilate the Jewish people to Hellenistic cultural and religious ideals. One result of this crisis was that the stable social and cosmic order portrayed by Sirach threatened to

---

16. Noting this emphasis in Sirach on purity and the eternal order of the Torah must not be carried so far as to deny the existence of contacts with the wider world of Hellenism (cf. 14:14, 16; 33:15; 38:1–8; 42:24–25) and an eschatological consciousness (cf. 48:24–25) within the community he represents.

come apart. Alternative communal ideals broke to the surface and began to compete for the allegiance of the people. Some drew on archaic ideals long repressed by the Zadokite leadership. Others sought to preserve lines of continuity with the more recent past. The results were of considerable significance for the further development of the biblical notion of community, for a process of differentiation occurred that led to distinct parties within Judaism. Alongside those who remained dedicated to a community centered around the temple cult and the concept of the eternal Torah as interpreted by the scribes, there arose others who, while also dedicated to lives of obedience to the Torah, interpreted the scriptural tradition with far greater dependence on prophetic and apocalyptic themes. On the basis of these themes, they called into question current temple practices, challenged the authority of the presiding priests, and announced decisive new divine acts of judgment and deliverance that would inaugurate a new age of enfranchisement and blessing for those excluded from roles of leadership by the presiding leaders. This period of intense religious ferment, extending through the second and first centuries B.C.E. and on into the Common Era, is of interest not only because of the fact that from it arose the classical parties of Judaism, the Pharisees, Sadducees, and Essenes, but also because it cultivated the eschatological perspective from which John the Baptist issued his urgent call to repentance, and from which the early disciples of Jesus interpreted their teacher's words and acts as signs of the long-awaited messianic kingdom.

Given the complexity of the period just assayed, and the paucity of sources shedding light on it, we need not be surprised to discover that theological evaluation in relation to this study of the development of the biblical notion of community is not a simple matter. What is more, this period is rarely studied from a theological point of view. Like the following two centuries, it tends to fall between the fields of Old and New Testament studies, and between the interests of Jewish and Christian scholars. Nevertheless, its influence on later developments should be clear in at least the following respects.

First, the development seen in Sirach of an understanding of Torah as not only the central guidepost for the Jewish community but as the eternal manifestation of the divine order of the universe had a profound effect on what would later emerge as Pharisaic Judaism. Strengthened by the identification of Wisdom with Torah, this understanding placed at the center of the life of many Jews a norm that was perfect and unchanging. On a fundamental level, this implied a static ideal of community, though in practice, the emerging exegetical methods of the new scribal class enabled the obedient community to bring new situations to this norm, and to experience its adaptability to every change. What could not change, however, was the norm itself, and hence every actual or even perceived threat to the supreme authority of the Torah, such as accommodation of its demands to the standards of another culture or religious cult, was resisted by the devout. This important development adumbrated the direction that would be taken by rabbinical Judaism; that is, the form of Judaism that emerged out of the various parties of the Hellenistic period as the wave of the future.

Second, it is obvious that this dedication to one supreme norm fostered a policy of separation from the Gentile world. Although every age had its exceptional figure who could address another culture in its own language without compromising the essence of the Jewish heritage, in general fidelity to Torah led to a distancing of self from the non-Jewish neighbor. When the geographical spread of the Diaspora is recalled, it is not surprising to note the steady increase of incidents of discrimination against Jewish settlements in the Hellenistic period.

Third, and closely related, is the development of a definition of Jewishness on the basis of strict obedience to the Torah and faithful observance of the temple rites and religious festivals. Since the Torah circumscribed cosmic order, whoever fell outside of its parameters lapsed into chaos. Since this was a deadly threat not only to the individual, but to the community thereby defiled by such an individual's presence, treatment of the offender was harsh.

These three points do not cover the entire spectrum of social and religious phenomena within the Jewish communities of the fourth and third centuries B.C.E., but rather ones whose importance would be particularly evident in the following centuries. I have noted in addition the persistence of alternative views, especially those dedicated to apocalyptic visions of radical reversal, on both cosmic and mundane levels. Of these I have more to say in the following chapter. Also present and influential throughout this period and on into the next two centuries was the wisdom, or sapiental tradition. Its influence on Sirach and his spiritual kinsfolk has been noted. But as a cultural stream permeating aspects of Jewish life during the Hellenistic period, it left its imprint on other groups as well, most especially on apocalyptic circles. The common tendency to treat Torah, Wisdom, and Apocalyptic as the property of discrete parties within Jewish religion of the Second Temple period therefore must be rejected on the basis of the writings of this period themselves. They indicate clearly that all three continued to be drawn on as the various movements and parties of the Hellenistic and Roman periods sought to relate their religious heritage to a rapidly changing world.

XII

Diverse Notions of Community in the Last Two Centuries B.C.E.
(Daniel, 1 Maccabees)

Historical Note: The struggle with Hellenization came to a head three decades after the control over Judea switched from the Ptolemies of Egypt to the Seleucids. In December 167 B.C.E., Antiochus IV Epiphanes desecrated the altar in the temple as the culminating blow against the elements within the Jewish populace that refused to yield to Hellenism. Righteous indignation and fury exploded in the revolt led by Mattathius and his sons, leading to the restoration of the first indigenous Jewish dynasty since 587 B.C.E. The ensuing Hasmonean period witnessed the emergence of several different religious parties, each with its own conception of religious community. This chapter describes the rise of the Sadducees, Pharisees, and Essenes in the period between Judas Maccabeus and Herod the Great with the help of the books of Daniel, 1 Maccabees, 1 Enoch, the sectarian writings of the Dead Sea community at Qumran, and Josephus's historical works, as well as various rabbinical writings. Since it remains the darkest of all biblical periods for most students of biblical theology, it will be necessary to devote considerable attention to the major events that impinged on and in important respects transformed the various Jewish communities. Only thus can an adequate foundation be established for a proper understanding of the subsequent rise of rabbinical Judaism and Christianity.

A. THE TRADITIONAL FAITH UNDER SIEGE

Although the third century B.C.E. must be characterized as a dark period with respect to the historical sources at our disposal, the fact that the Jewish communities reached a highly developed level of culture in places as distant from one another as the Nile and the Euphrates indicates how effectively the prayer, study, and instruction centered in the synagogues continued to nurture the lives of the Jewish people. It no doubt also reflects the relatively high level of tolerance with which they were allowed to observe their religious traditions by local civil authorities. The same generalization can be made about the Jews living in Judea, where the Ptolemies permitted them to pattern their lives on the Torah, so long as their religious observances did not lead to political insubordination. This is not to deny that there were periods of tension. For example, the struggles between the *diadochoi* (the generals of the sprawling empire left by Alexander) led to unrest in many of the areas settled by Jews. During such periods, the threat of Hellenism came in the form of a lure to compromise the stringent and exclusive demands of Jewish faith rather than as a systematic program to supplant that faith in the name of the gods of Olympus and the universal culture advanced under their standard.

A critical turn of events, however, transpired in 198 B.C.E. with the victory of Antiochus III ("the Great") over the Egyptian king Ptolemy VI Philometer at Paneion. As a result of that battle, the century-long domination of Egypt over Judah came to an end. The sweeping implications of that change were not immediately apparent. The leaders of Jerusalem in fact were divided in their political preferences, some favoring the older structures of Ptolemaic rule, others greeting the Seleucids as deliverers and guardians of the interests of the Jews. The divisions went so far as to split the powerful Tobiad family—whose members had managed to dominate Judaean politics at the end of the third and beginning of the second century—into pro-Ptolemaic and pro-Seleucid factions. The new overlord of Judea, who was not only a successful military leader but also an astute politician, took measures to win the support of the populace by granting them privileges beyond those they had possessed under the Ptolemies, including the right to internal autonomy under their Torah, certain tax exemptions and royal support for restoration of the temple.

This propitious beginning of the Seleucid rule over Judea soon proved to be deceptive, for already during the last years of Antiochus the Great's reign mounting hostilities with Rome led to a serious erosion of Seleucid power, and an accompanying strain on its economy. The able king was followed by a less able son, Seleucus IV Philopator (187–175 B.C.E.), who failed to ameliorate the mounting tensions between pro-Ptolemaic and pro-Seleucid parties in Jerusalem. Within the context of these tensions, the high priestly office had become the property of the one who could offer the highest bribe to the foreign ruler. But even this state of affairs was pale, compared to things to come.

Conditions in Judea rapidly declined during the reign of Antiochus IV Epiphanes. Granted, matters were already serious when he succeeded his murdered brother in 175, with his empire on the verge of bankruptcy, with Egypt eager to exploit his every mistake and with Rome in a position to determine his destiny. The Tobiads, for their part, recognized an opportunity to reassert their power, and made an attractive financial offer to the new emperor in return for his removing the legitimate high priest Onias III from office, and appointing in his stead Jason, who, though a brother of Onias, possessed the type of pro-Hellenistic proclivities that served well their commercial and political interests. The most strident pro-Hellenizing group within the Jewish community thus struck at the heart of the Jerusalem cult.

Antiochus was pleased to form a coalition with the resurgent Hellenizing party of Judea, the party dedicated to transforming Jerusalem from the holy center of Jewish faith into a Hellenistic *polis*, replete with a gymnasium and monuments to the Greek gods. Naturally, the new *polis*, bearing the name of "Antiochia," could no longer be constituted under the parochial Torah of the Jews or center its life around the traditions and rituals of its temple, but had to be assimilated to the cosmopolital polity of the other Hellenistic cities. Needless to say, the Hellenistic "reform" was perceived by many as a frontal attack on the substance of their religion and culture, and an attempt to undo the effects of the thousand-year history through which they had been formed into a people separate from the other peoples of the world. Their special relationship with the God of Abraham and Moses was threatened as they were invited to take their place among the pagan nations of the world.

Those holding fast to the Torah tradition as it had developed under Zadokite leadership from the time of Ezra down to the time of Sirach were subjected to another stinging insult when the high priestly office was again purchased, this time by an opportunist of non-Zadokite descent named Menelaus. The group identity of those wedding strict obedience to the Torah with the repudiation of all elements of Hellenism grew stronger. In one sense, they did not represent a new phenomenon, for their spiritual ancestors had protested against their civil and religious leaders in many instances during the period of the Second Temple. But the severity of the present crisis had the effect of galvanizing such elements into a new sense of solidarity and purpose. They viewed themselves as the remnant called by God to preserve the sacred traditions within a people characterized by growing laxity and apostasy. The same chaotic conditions engendering this remnant mentality also proved to be an inducement toward viewing the world increasingly in apocalyptic terms. Within this context there emerged within the Jewish community a broadly based movement of those designated simply as *ḥăsîdîm*; that is, "faithful ones." Although not a religious party in a strict sense, the *ḥăsîdîm* were to play an important role in the impending crisis. Beyond this, their concepts and beliefs were to have a lasting impact on the two parties that emerged out of their ranks, the Pharisees and the Essenes. Important aspects of the eschatological faith of early Christianity are also traceable to the *ḥăsîdîm*.

Ineluctably, the conflict between those faithful to a strict interpretation of the Torah and those devoted to the program of Hellenization escalated. Jason, the deposed high priest, fled from Jerusalem to Antioch, where he continued to use intrigue to regain his power. Among other deeds, he arranged the assassination of Onias III, the legitimate Zadokite high priest whom he and his supporters had forced from office. Antiochus, for his part, demonstrated the heartlessness of his approach to the problem when he executed three delegates sent by the Jerusalem Gerousia (the council of Jewish leaders) to negotiate a peace settlement. From this point on, international events added to the fatal escalation of tension. Antiochus's attention was directed in 170 B.C.E. toward an attempt to conquer Egypt, creating a vacuum in Jerusalem quickly filled by the outbreak of open conflict between the contending Jewish factions. In returning from Egypt the next year, Antiochus attacked Jerusalem, inflicting revenge on the populace. Then, with the cooperation of Menelaus, he sacked the temple, no doubt largely to replenish royal coffers depleted by the war.

Antiochus's next foray into Egypt, in the spring of 168 B.C.E., led to a dreadful setback and a blow to his pride, for the Romans intervened and forced him to break off the attack and to return to Antioch. Wounded pride and frustration contributed to the wanton acts that followed. Antiochus ordered his general Apollonius to attack Jerusalem, which he did on the sabbath, leading to a bloody massacre of the populace. The walls of the city were torn down, and a fortress called the Acra was established in the City of David for the occupying army. Direct Seleucid rule was thus established over the city. The Book of 1 Maccabees describes the action taken by Antiochus to obliterate the Jewish faith once and for all:

Then the king wrote to his whole kingdom that all should be one people, and that each should give up his customs. And the Gentiles accepted the command of the king. Many even from Israel gladly adopted his religion; they sacrificed to idols and profaned the sabbath. And the king sent letters by messengers to Jerusalem and the cities of Judah; he directed them to follow customs strange to the land, to forbid burnt offerings and sacrifices and drink offerings in the sanctuary, to profane sabbaths and feasts, to defile the sanctuary and the priests, to build altars and sacred precincts and shrines for idols, to sacrifice swine and unclean animals, and to leave their sons uncircumcised. (1 Macc. 1:41–48)

Antiochus's brutal measures culminated in an incredibly heinous act, which tradition remembered as "the abomination of desolation" (Dan. 11:31; 12:11): on the great altar of sacrifice in the temple, a pagan altar was erected, dedicated to Zeus Olympius. The revered Jerusalem temple had become a pagan shrine!

B. THE MACCABEAN REVOLT AND THE POSITION OF THE ḤĀSÎDÎM

The further development of parties and community structures during the Hellenistic period was deeply affected by the revolt that erupted among the Jews in response to the brutal and sacrilegious actions of

Antiochus IV Epiphanes.[1] The catalytic role played by Mattathias and his sons in that revolt and the ensuing dramatic series of victories over the Seleucids have become legendary, and need not be described in detail here. For present purposes, it is important to note that in the period immediately following the erection of the Zeus altar in the temple, the ranks of those rallying behind Judas Maccabeus and his brothers gave up their individual differences and fought as one body. An important role in this period was played by the ḥăsîdîm, the group already mentioned whose name bespeaks the unswering fidelity of its members to the Torah and their unflinching resistance to every outside influence threatening to obscure the uniqueness of the Jewish religious traditions. For in spite of their strict observance of the Torah, they became persuaded that the present state of holy war justified Mattathias's temporary suspension of the law of Sabbath, and they joined the ranks of his warriors. Their example likely had a profound effect on the masses. It is also noteworthy that the struggle temporarily erased the lines dividing those with apocalyptic propensities from those dedicated to the authoritative nature of the temple structures and the Zadokite priesthood and traditionally resistant to visions of apocalyptic reversal. The deadly threat posed by Antiochus for a time seemed to take on an apocalyptic appearance for all, leading to a fresh outpouring of the apocalyptic spirit that came to embrace a broad cross section of the populace.

Chapters 7–12 of the Book of Daniel arise from the circles of the ḥăsîdîm during the early period of the Maccabean revolt; that is, from the time before the subdivision of this group into the separate parties of the Pharisees and the Essenes. The wanton acts of Antiochus IV Epiphanes are interpreted by the writer of these chapters as the last onslaught of evil against God's elect people. And because the events being experienced were seen as reflecting events in heaven, and specifically the conflict between the angelic hosts of God and the forces of evil, hope for change was not vested in earthly leaders or programs, but in the outcome of a conflict being waged in heaven.[2] Antiochus was but the shadow of the evil hosts waging war on God's angels in heaven. And therefore Antiochus's brutal and sacrilegious acts were seen as a rebellion against God that would surely evoke divine judgment. In Daniel 7 and 8, the great empires of the earth are symbolized by fearsome beasts, culminating in the one, representing Antiochus, whose horn (i.e., power) assaults heaven itself:

It grew great, even to the host of heaven; and some of the host of the stars it cast down to the ground, and trampled upon them. It magnified itself, even up

---

1. For the history of the Maccabean and Hasmonean era, see P. Shäfer, "The Hellenistic and Maccabean Periods," in *Israelite and Judean History*, ed. J. H. Hayes and J. M. Miller (Philadelphia: Westminster, 1977), pp. 539–604.

2. See J. J. Collins, *The Apocalyptic Vision of the Book of Daniel* HSM16 (Missoula, Mont.: Scholars Press, 1977).

to the Prince of the host; and the continual burnt offering was taken away from him, and the place of his sanctuary was overthrown. And the host was given over to it together with the continual burnt offering through transgression, and truth was cast down to the ground, and the horn acted and prospered. (Dan. 8:10-12)

In the response adopted by the ḥăsîdîm of Daniel, we see how sharply this movement had come to distance itself from the military activism of the Maccabees (1 Macc. 7:12–18). Viewing the conflict as primarily a war in heaven, they saw it as their responsibility to wait patiently for the outcome of the war. Their cause was adequately represented by angels such as Gabriel and Michael, who were locked in fierce combat with the corresponding heavenly princes of Persia and Greece. As for the blasphemous adversary Antiochus, his fall was sure to come, but emphatically not by human resistance: "Without warning he shall destroy many; and he shall even rise up against the Prince of princes; but, by no human hand, he shall be broken (Dan. 8:25). With this assurance, the ḥăsîdîm were to be a community living in anticipation of what God would do to deliver and vindicate them. In this vision, the enigmatic "Son of Man" plays a key role, for after God—pictured as the Ancient of Days seated upon the throne of judgment—had broken the power of all adversaries, the Son of Man was presented to him, to whom "was given dominion and glory and kingdom, that all peoples, nations, and languages should serve him" (Dan. 7:14). Deliverance and vindication would finally come to the faithful as a result of that transfer of power to the Son of Man, for through him it would be passed on to the "saints of the Most High"—that is, the angels—and then to their people:

And the kingdom and the dominion and the greatness of the kingdoms under the whole heaven shall be given to the people of the saints of the Most High; their kingdom shall be an everlasting kingdom, and all dominions shall serve and obey them.   (Dan. 7:27)

The whole emphasis in this vision is on God's initiative. No credit is given to the contributions of the Maccabees, or for that matter to the efforts of any other military or priestly leader of Judea. The only allusion to the Maccabean campaign seems to call into question the great claims of its protagonists, an allusion made in connection with a description of the martyrdom of the pious ones: "When they fall, they shall receive a little help" (Dan. 11:34a). "A little help" and no more was given by the military effort of the Maccabees, for ultimately the Seleucid nightmare was part of a divine drama. Those who possessed wisdom therefore looked not to earthly leaders but to the heavenly realm for deliverance, a deliverance that led not to the acquisition of political power, but to everlasting life (Dan. 12:1–3).

The initial support given by the visionary members of the ḥăsîdîm to the Maccabean insurgents therefore was soon withdrawn, and the reason for their withdrawal is to be explained on the basis of their apocalyptic perspective. In the beginning of the Maccabean revolt, they may have felt that the conflict and resulting martyrdom of many of the faithful were signs of the imminent theophany of God, who would come to destroy all evil and inaugurate the perfect order of šālôm for which they yearned. But with the reconsecration of the temple and the restoration of the sacrificial rites, the religious objectives of the Maccabean campaign seemed to have been achieved. The continued fighting of the Maccabees seemed to betray their personal ambitions to establish an earthly reign in which they would serve both as kings and priests. Whereas the "faithful" at first believed that Judas and his brothers were motivated solely by their zeal for the Torah, their disappointment mounted as they saw that zeal compromised and accommodated to the pragmatics of an earthly state resembling not the righteous kingdom of God but the cities of the Greeks.[3]

The Book of 1 Maccabees gives ample evidence of the tension between traditional fidelity to the Torah and the new political pragmatism evolving among their leaders, a tension proving divisive within the Jewish community. The Maccabees proved in a political sense to be worthy heirs of the Zadokite leaders of the Persian period, for they willingly made compromises with the Romans or any other power when expedience required. The high praise heaped upon the Romans in 1 Maccabees 8 illustrates how sharply the policies of the Maccabees diverged from the spiritual ideals of the ḥăsîdîm as expressed in the Book of Daniel. 2 Maccabees contains a series of letters manifesting this same policy of accommodation. The importance of this position for the future of both Judaism and Christianity becomes evident when one realizes that it continues to persist in some forms of later Pharisaic Judaism and Christianity (cf. Rom. 13).

The tensions between the Maccabean leaders and the ḥăsîdîm were raised to the breaking point by the steady encroachment of the Maccabees on the high priestly office. In 152 B.C.E. Jonathan, who had succeeded his brother Judas as the leader of the Maccabean movement, assumed the title of high priest. This was interpreted by the ḥăsîdîm as a scathing attack on the sanctity of the sacerdotal office in the service of raw political power, for according to their traditions the Zadokite claim to the high priesthood had been established by God and hallowed by centuries of practice. The arrogations of the Hasmoneans (as the Maccabeans came to be known) reached a climactic point under the reign of the next of the sons of Mattathius, Simon. The Book of Maccabees records the inscription written by Simon's supporters in praise of their leader, which concludes thus:

3. See Tcherikover, *Hellenistic Civilization and the Jews*, trans. S. Applebaum (Philadelphia: Jewish Publication Society, 1961), p. 253, and John J. Collins, *Between Athens and Jerusalem* (New York: The Crossroad Publ. Co., 1983), p. 10.

And the Jews and their priests decided that Simon should be their leader and high priest for ever, until a trustworthy prophet should arise, and that he should be governor over them and that he should take charge of the sanctuary and appoint men over its tasks and over the country and the weapons and the strongholds, and that he should take charge of the sanctuary, and that he should be obeyed by all, and that all contracts in the country should be written in his name, and that he should be clothed in purple and wear gold. And none of the people or priests shall be permitted to nullify any of these decisions or to oppose what he says, or to convene an assembly in the country without his permission, or to be clothed in purple or put on a gold buckle. Whoever acts contrary to these decisions or nullifies any of them shall be liable to punishment. (1 Macc. 4:41–45)

A scenario familiar from earlier Jewish history thereby was repeating itself. Pragmatic leaders were claiming that their reign represented the fulfillment of divine will for the people. But among the people were those who held to a vision of God's purpose that the prevailing political and cultic structures contradicted. Their strict observance of the Torah seemed to make it increasingly difficult for them to live as integral parts of a state drawing deeply on the policies of the Romans, which policies were intolerant of exclusive devotion to the God of Israel. As had been the case in the time of Zerubbabel and again in the time of Ezra, visionary idealists kept their faith alive by yearning for the day when God would intervene directly to inaugurate the righteous kingdom, and by describing that day in apocalyptic visions. The rift between these Maccabees and their erstwhile supporters, the ḥăsîdîm, widened to the point of threatening the unity of the religious community. The community ideals espoused by the two sides had become so divergent as to render a common religious identity impossible.

C. THE EMERGENCE OF THE THREEFOLD DIVISION: SADDUCEES, PHARISEES, AND ESSENES

The threat to unity was not limited to the rift growing between the ḥăsîdîm and the Maccabees. During the reigns of Jonathan and Simon, a division also began to develop within the ranks of the ḥăsîdîm. On one side of that division were those fostering an apocalyptic vision of divine intervention, according to which all existing cultic and political structures would be removed by divine judgment, to be replaced by a new order characterized by the vindication of the faithful remnant and God's eternal reign of righteousness, peace, and prosperity. The Essene communities known to us from the writings of Josephus derive from this side of the Hasidean movement. Moreover, the archaeological finds at Qumran, including the library that has come to be known as the Dead Sea Scrolls, have given us a remarkably full picture of a group emerging from this apocalyptic wing of the ḥăsîdîm, a group, led by Zadokite priests recently expelled from the Jerusalem temple, that withdrew to the Judean wilderness in order to avoid what its members perceived to be the profanation of Jerusalem and the defilement of a cult controlled by an illegitimate priesthood.[4]

On the other side of that division, we find the emergence of the Pharisees, a powerful group standing in continuity with the tradition extending from Ezra to Sirach and preserving its devotion to the stringent demands of the Torah not through withdrawal from life within the Hasmonean state, but by delineating the path of fidelity as the life of holiness lived within the political structures of the world, in such a way as to ascribe to them only penultimate significance.

Guided by the interpretation of the Torah by their scribes, the Pharisees inherited and continued to develop the community ideal rooted in the notion of the eternal Torah. This ideal, as earlier observed, had evolved into its fundamental form by the time of Sirach. According to this ideal, the true order of life was the eternal order given by God in the Torah of Moses. It was an order unaffected by the flux of history.

Although wide diversity also existed within the Pharisaic movement, the Pharisees in general were apparently less impelled by eschatological expectation than were the Essenes. They were little troubled by the political actions of the Hasmoneans or, for that matter, of the Romans, so long as those actions did not interfere with their observance of the statutes and ordinances of the Torah, both in the temple and in their villages. This posture is reflected, for example, by the participation of some of their leaders in the Gerousia, or council of the elders, in the first decades of Hasmonean rule.

Before turning to a more detailed look at the Pharisees and the Essenes, mention needs to be made of the third party named by Josephus, the Sadducees.[5] The fact that the Pharisees played the dominant role in guiding Judaism into the classical form represented by the Mishnah often has eclipsed the significance of the Sadducees in the two centuries before the First Jewish Revolt against the Romans (66–70 C.E.). It must be called to mind, therefore, that from the time that the Hasmonean king John Hyrcanus I joined the party of the Sadducees until the devastation of the land by Vespasian and Titus, the Sadducees exerted the greatest influence within the Gerousia and various other Jewish councils. In other words, they were the aristocratic guardians of the social and economic structures of the land, and next to the king and high priest their influence was considerable.

When one considers the background of the Sadducees, it becomes

---

4. For a description of the historical-political background of the Dead Sea community, see F. M. Cross, *The Ancient Library of Qumran* rev. ed. (Garden City, N.Y.: Doubleday, 1961).

5. Josephus, *War* 2.8.14. Quotations from Josephus are from *Josephus: Complete Works*, 3d ed., trans. William Whiston (Grand Rapids, Mich.: Kregel, 1964).

apparent that the diversity that came to characterize the descendants of the Zadokite temple priests was even greater than that which evolved within the ranks of the ḥăsîdîm. On the one hand, the Hasmonean takeover of the temple priesthood led some of the Zadokites to lead a band of followers, including many ḥăsîdîm, to the Dead Sea, where they presided over the development of a full-blown apocalyptic community. On the other hand, another branch of the Zadokite priesthood eschewed such religious extremism in favor of a political position designed to protect their economic interests. Josephus's description of the high priests and men of power among the Jews describes their mentality well: "desirous of peace, because of the possessions they had."[6] By New Testament times, this branch, which we know as the Sadducees, had developed an ideology that was at once theologically conservative and politically pragmatic. This position was rooted in a view of oral interpretation that differed from that of the Pharisees. Although also fostering a tradition of oral interpretation, the Sadducees did not clothe it with an aura of scriptural authority in the manner of the Pharisees. Thus while the latter based their beliefs and practices on two "Torahs," one written, the other oral, and both purportedly originating on Mount Sinai, the Sadducees adhered to a strict reading of the written Torah as the sole authority in matters of belief. This led to the rejection of eschatological teaching such as the doctrine of the resurrection and all speculation relating to angels and demons. On the other hand, in relations with the political powers of the time, the Sadducees exhibited an almost unbridled capability to compromise and adapt. We are thus able to recognize the wealthy Saducean nobility of the Herodian period as heirs of the Zadokite priests of the Hellenistic era such as Jason and Alcimus. The Zadokites who constituted the elite priestly leadership of the apocalyptic community of Qumran must be understood as heirs to the strict piety of such priests as Simon the Great. Their piety was subsequently radicalized by their experience of the secularization of the new temple priests, the non-Zadokite Hasmoneans.

D. THE PHARISEES

It was the Pharisaic movement that emerged from the various Jewish groups of the Hellenistic and Roman periods as the bridge between biblical religion and the living Judaism of future ages. The reason for this is directly related to the inner dynamics of that movement, especially the balance it was able to maintain between fidelity to tradition and adaptability to changing conditions within the world. The importance the Pharisees attributed to oral tradition as the authoritative interpretation and application of Scripture and the trust they placed in

---

6. Josephus, *War* 2.16.7.

their master teachers enabled them to avoid both the socioreligious rigidity that led to the eclipse of the Samaritan cult and the theological orthodoxy of the Sadducean party that made the Sadducees ill equipped to win the support of anything but a very elite and conservative echelon of the Jewish community. At the same time, the Pharisees maintained a firm mooring in Scripture that equipped them with a historical foundation capable of surviving the tempestuous events of the Roman period, which swept away movements locked into a more futuristic-apocalyptic posture.

No mean part of the success of Pharisaism is attributable to its sages (later called *rabbis*) and the important role they came to assume within this movement.[7] They were the heirs to the stream of tradition stemming from the Priestly Writing, the reform of Ezra and Nehemiah, the Chronicler's History, and the community ideals and piety reflected in Sirach. By bringing together an exhaustive understanding of Scripture and an expansive knowledge of life through the application of a flexible hermeneutic, they made the Torah applicable to every situation and human experience that arose within the lives of their wide following. The Mishnah, the culminating accomplishment of their early masters, abounds in illustrations of the balance between fidelity to Scripture and adaptability. For example, the Priestly Writing's notion was accepted of the perfect order God granted God's people by revealing to Moses the rites and accouterments of the tabernacle. But the Levitical laws regulating temple worship were also applied to the Jewish home, where the family table became an extension of the temple altar.[8] The broadening tendency evident in this extension of temple laws was markedly strengthened by the merging of sapiental traditions and techniques with those found in the Torah. For the sapiental concern with ordering the diverse phenomena of the everyday world into one perfect unity became a powerful ally in the rabbis' efforts to draw all aspects of life into the order of reality revealed by God in the Torah. Especially in times as chaotic and threatening to Jewish existence as those of the late Hellenistic and early Roman periods, the effort to demonstrate that in spite of appearances all life fit into the pattern of meaning revealed in the Torah, became an urgent necessity.

In this effort to order all life, and to demonstrate how all experiences of life found their place in God's perfect order revealed in the Torah, the scribes initiated a process that culminated in more than the application of a corpus of sacred writings to a new setting. What emerged was nothing less than a whole new philosophy, which, while

---

7. For a thorough and lucid study of the sages, see E. E. Urbach, *The Sages: Their Concepts and Beliefs*, trans. J. Abrahams (Jerusalem: Magnes Press, 1975).

8. J. Neusner, *Judaism: The Evidence of the Mishnah* (Chicago: University of Chicago Press, 1981), p. 226. Cf. M. Smith, "Palestinian Judaism in the First Century," in M. David, ed., *Israel: Its Role in Civilization* (New York: Harper & Row, 1956).

rooted in the Torah, went far beyond the contents or the methods of the Torah. An illustration of this is given by Jacob Neusner, who first points out that the Mishnah stands in agreement with the conviction located at the heart of the Priestly Writing, and expressed in the creation story, that "creation comes to its climax at the perfect rest marked by completion and signifying perfection and sanctification." The world view of the Mishnah revolves around the conviction that it gives expression to an order that is perfect and complete, and thus dependable, notwithstanding all this world's contradicting evidence. Neusner then goes on to point also to the important difference between the Priestly Writing and the Mishnaic view: whereas the former bases its position on the myth of creation, the latter has adopted the "manner of the philosophers":

That is to say, the framers of the Mishnah speak of the physics of mixtures, conflicts of principles which must be sorted out, areas of doubt generated by confusion. The detritus of a world seeking order but suffering chaos now is reduced to the construction of intellect.[9]

By extrapolating backward from the time of the completion of the Mishnah to the period in which its underlying principles were being worked out, we are able to glimpse a movement that offered a clear alternative to that of the Sadducees. The Sadducees, benefiting both from the elite status accorded them by virtue of their priestly pedigree and from the added prestige coming through the enrollment of John Hyrcanus into their party, represented an aristocracy guarding their doctrine against all change, but pragmatically adapting their political position to current realities. The stricter members of the Pharisaic party, however, were more resistant to accommodation to political pressures in fidelity to the Torah, and thus they remind one of their spiritual ancestors, the ḥăsîdîm. They also refused to encapsulate religious observances within a realm held apart from everyday life in such a way as to allow the simultaneous rigid preservation of religious tradition and unfettered engagement with the world on its own terms, insisting that fidelity to the tradition had to be maintained even as that tradition was

---

9. Neusner, *Judaism*, p. 262. Recent reviews of Neusner's treatment of the Mishnaic period indicate that his monumental effort to make a mysterious and complex phenomenon comprehensible to nonspecialists must not be read uncritically (see S. J. D. Cohen, "Jacob Neusner, Mishnah, and Counter-Rabbinics: A Review Essay," *Conservative Judaism* 37 (1983), 48–63; Y. Elman, *Judaica Book News* 12 (1982), 17–25; H. Maccoby, "Jacob Neusner's Mishnah," *Midstream* 12 (1984). No doubt revision of some of the points in his reconstruction will be necessitated, for example, by closer attention to the Mishnah's connections with other rabbinical writings and to the coexistence of diverse viewpoints within the Mishnah, and certainly some points, like the degree to which the destruction of Jerusalem by the Romans influenced the world view of the authors of the Mishnah, must remain open, due to lack of direct evidence. In spite of many valid criticisms, however, we are indebted to Neusner for subjecting the rabbinical writings to the same kind of historical-critical study that has long been taken for granted by most scholars in their study of the scriptural writings. Like any other pioneering effort, Neusner's reconstruction must be viewed as a starting point and not as a finished product.

applied every aspect of life. The result was a twofold contrast with the posture of the Sadducees: (1) a dynamic understanding of tradition conducive to growth and change; (2) an insistence that no earthly power be allowed to inhibit the full application of the Torah to every aspect of life.

In reality, this stance meant that most Pharisees lived peaceably with both their own political leaders and their foreign masters so long as the political policies and practices of neither interfered with their observance of the mandates of the Torah. But when measures were taken by political authorities that crossed that critical line, Pharisees often proved stubborn unto death. This posture establishes such Pharisees not only as true heirs to the tradition of the ḥăsîdîm, but as godly individuals living true to their new designation, which etymologically derives from a Semitic word meaning "a person set apart."[10]

This dynamic understanding of tradition and the application of Torah to all aspects of life had a distinct influence on the communal forms that developed within the Pharisaic movement. During the earliest phase of their history—that is, in the early Hasmonean period—they apparently interacted quite freely with the Sadducees, no doubt in part out of the desire to bring the nation's political leaders into conformity with their interpretation of the Torah. The Gerousia of that time provided the forum within which king, high priest, Sadducees, and Pharisees struggled to promote their respective interests. During this period, the efforts of the Pharisees were met with mixed success, a fact not surprising when one takes into account that they demanded of others the same strictness of observance that they required of themselves. In the early Hasmonean period, their refusal to follow the radical otherworldly apocalypticism of their former co-religionists, the Essenes, and their continued support of the Hasmonean cause, resulted in relatively good relations with the governing authorities. Their opposition to the political pragmatism of the Sadducees, their criticism of the increasing secularization of the Hasmonean priest-kings, and their strict adherence to the Torah, however, led eventually to conflict with Hasmonean leaders who increasingly compromised Jewish religious tradition in favor of the ways of royalty in other lands. Already in the reign of John Hyrcanus I (135–104 B.C.E.) a bitter controversy broke out between Hyrcanus and a Pharisee named Eleazar.[11] When Alexander Jannaeus (103–76) took to the sword to bring the Pharisees into line with his political policies, the result was a massacre in which, Josephus reports, six hundred of them were slain. On the other hand, they found in Salome Alexandra (76–67) a leader sympathetic with many of their teaching who even took steps to upgrade their representation in the Gerousia, a development adumbrating their eventual rise to the status of the dominant party.[12]

---

10. Aramaic, pariš; Hebrew, paruš.
11. Ant. 13.10.5–6
12. Ant. 13.409

Throughout this history of changing fortunes vis-à-vis the Hasmonean leadership, however, the creative energy of many Pharisees seemed to be directed toward other than political or economic goals. Without denying different levels within Pharisaism, we can observe among those given to strict separation from the nonobservant (including those Pharisees who in their judgment were too lax!) the development of a lifestyle within which political structures played a strictly subordinate role to the structures of an order transcending all time and history. The true identity of such Pharisees was worked out not in the royal court, not in the marketplace, nor even in the Gerousia or later in the Sanhedrin, but within their synagogues and especially within their closed brotherhood (ḥăbûrâ), where they studied the Torah, listened as their sages worked out the system of exegesis that became the hallmark of Pharisaic Judaism, and above all, shared in the ritually pure table fellowship that was possible nowhere else. In the development of Pharisaism, later tradition (e.g., Pirke Abot) suggests that a highpoint was reached under the master teacher Hillel, who probably did much to shape the distinctive teachings that culminated in the Mishnah and the Talmud.

Thus by the beginning of the Common Era and the early years of the Christian movement, the essential qualities of the Pharisaic notion of community had likely evolved within certain leading circles, qualities based on the careful balance of respect for scriptural tradition and a daring hermeneutic. On this basis a remarkable edifice was built, allowing the vast and complex array of ritual laws to take on a new meaning and significance for the faithful Jew. The Pharisees in a real sense gave concrete expression to the utopian vision of the prophetic-Levitical community of the late sixth century B.C.E., which looked to the day when "your people shall all be righteous" and "you shall be called the priests of the Lord, men shall speak of you as the ministers of God" (Isa. 60:21 and 61:6). For they aspired to be the community fulfilling the condition and receiving the promise proclaimed by Moses at Mount Sinai:

Now therefore, if you will obey my voice and keep my covenant, you shall be my own possession among all peoples; for all the earth is mine, and you shall be to me a kingdom of priests and a holy nation.   (Exod. 19:5–6a)

The practical result of applying biblical laws, including those originally referring to priest and temple, to themselves was a life of dedication to the exact observance of sabbath laws and laws of purity. This dedication is reflected in the portrait of the Pharisees found in the Gospels, though the accusation that preoccupation with such observance led to the neglect of the ethical commandments must be viewed as an aspect of the intra-Jewish polemic of that time. Also lost in the New Testament portrait is the motivation behind this meticulous attention to the details of the ritual law. Pharisees felt obliged to live in a state of ritual purity out of a sense of being commanded by God through the

Torah to live a life separate from all defilement. What may appear to the modern reader to be an astonishingly high amount of attention was paid to the growing, preparation, and eating of food, for this involved an aspect of life particularly endangered by defilement. The perfect obedience to the Torah that was the goal of both the Pharisees and the Essenes presented more difficulties for the Pharisees because, unlike the Essenes, they lived their lives not in the isolation of a wilderness community but in the middle of the secular world. This fact enables us to understand the great emphasis they placed on avoiding every contact that could effect defilement, such as eating with "sinners"; that is, those not upholding their strict interpretation of the Torah. Since the sacred order defined by the Torah was the only order capable of sustaining life, it was critically important to maintain the state of holiness that allowed one to live within that order. The alternative was chaos, an alternative believed to be the inevitable outcome of disobedience. To the Pharisees, the destruction of the temple was tragic proof of this eternal statute.

This conviction explains the zeal with which the Pharisees applied the Levitical laws of ritual purity to all areas of life by elaborating, refining, subdividing, and reordering as new situations, new disputes, and new ambiguities called for clarification. It was thus not a fascination with trivialities and superficial legalities that provided the motivating force behind the laws of purity constituting a major portion of the rabbinical *hălākâ* culminating in the Mishnah. All such laws arose out of the basic conviction that unless the faithful maintained strict separation from all defilement, the fall back into chaos was inevitable. For as surely as Scripture had placed the priest entering God's presence while defiled by any sort of impurity under immediate divine condemnation, so too the Pharisee, living under the same laws of ritual purity, would not escape divine wrath if he intentionally neglected any of those laws. Maintaining holiness, and avoiding contact with the unholy, were thus complementary parts of maintaining cosmic harmony.

The emergence of this carefully refined and meticulously observed religious system as the dominant force within Judaism in the Common Era is due not only to its intrinsic vitality, but also to political circumstances. The Essenes, having chosen to flee from involvement in the political and social structures of their world to preserve, in unsullied form, their vision of the blessed world to come, lost every opportunity to influence a world now firmly under the control of the Romans. The Sadducees, in spite of their policy of cooperating with the reigning political powers of this world, fell on hard times as well. Already under Salome Alexandra, their influence began to be eclipsed by the Pharisees.[13] Then, during Herod's reign, they suffered bloody repression

---

13. *Ant.* 13.410–416.

under an Idumean king threatened by every representative of a legitimate priestly family. The Pharisees, as the lay leaders of the community, posed far less a threat to Herod, and it was during the Herodian period that they emerged as the undisputed leader of the Jewish
population. Although the split into two factions—the more progressive
Hillelites and the more conservative Shammaites—could have proven
damaging, they managed to confine differences to the level of lively in-
traparty debate, out of which the followers of Hillel emerged as the
stronger faction. Thus it was that following the shift of the center of
Pharisaic activity from Jerusalem to the academy (yĕšîbâ) at Jabneh in
the wake of the destruction of 70 C.E., the descendants of Hillel (with
the exception of Johanan ben Zakkai) apparently served as nĕsî'îm
(presidents) of the Sanhedrin, with fellow Pharisees representing the
majority of its members. Although from the time of Herod until the
destruction of the temple in 70 C.E. the Romans had stripped the Sanhedrin of genuine political power, it nevertheless provided the Pharisees with an important platform from which to seek to promulgate
their interpretation of the Torah as the official one for the Jewish community. And indeed, during this entire period, both the nation's leaders and the masses seemed increasingly to view the Pharisees as authorities in matters of religion.

Until finally disappearing as a force in the Jewish community after the
First Jewish Revolt, however, the Sadducees for their part continued to
contend with their rivals. For one thing, they refused to accept the decisions of the Sanhedrin, regarding its domination by largely Pharisaic lay
teachers as a violation of Scripture.[14] Guided by their literal reading of
Scripture, they of course would have found the rationalization devised
by the Pharisees completely unconvincing, according to which "if there
are none (that is, priests and Levites) in it, it is still valid."[15]

Even Josephus, in spite of his deep respect for Pharisaic teaching,
could not repress his own priestly background as he refused to recognize the Pharisees as permanent leaders of the Sanhedrin. He therefore
gives expression to a more perfect community ideal as an alternative to
the ascendant Pharisaic notion in the following passage:

Can there be a finer and more equitable policy, than one which sets God at the
head of the universe, which assigns the administration of the highest affairs to
the whole body of priests, and entrusts to the supreme high priest the direction
of the other priests?[16]

This position of Josephus, however, stands as a monument to a bygone era. The future of Judaism was securely in the hands of the Pharisees. For the dynamic hermeneutic of Pharisaism and the specific sys-

---

14. Cf. Deut. 17:9 with *Ant.* 13.10.6,297.

15. *Sifre Deuteronomy* 153. See Seth Mantel, *Studies in the History of the Sanhedrin*, Harvard
Semitic Series 17 (Cambridge, Mass.: Harvard University Press, 1965), p. 85.

16. *Contra Apionem* 2.21.185; cf. 2.22.188–189.

tem of practice cultivated by its strictest members enabled it to survive both the destruction of Jerusalem in 70 C.E. and the long history of domination by foreign powers that followed. Within the Torah, they discovered an eternal order that allowed them to treat with relative detachment the advent and passing of the world empires, and thus to eschew both the world accommodation of the Sadducees and the world escapism of the Essenes. While the community model of the hăbûrâ (closed fellowship) was separatist in nature, their daily lives were nevertheless lived out in close contact with nonobserving Jews (including Jewish Christians) and Gentiles (both Christian and non-Christian).

One example of the vitality inherent in Pharisaic tradition is the redefinition of ritual atonement that apparently arose in the aftermath of the destruction of the temple. While the Pharisees preserved traditions regulating temple sacrifice and the priestly orders in anticipation of the time when the temple would be rebuilt, they also began to cultivate a creative new understanding of atonement: "As long as the temple stood, the altar atoned for Israel. But now a man's table atones for him."[17] Although this formulation was written at a later time, the origin of the idea probably traces back to the pre-Mishnaic period, as does the story relating a conversation between Johanan ben Zakkai, the first master of Javneh after the gathering of the Pharisees to that center following the calamity of 70 C.E., and his disciple Joshua ben Hananiah, in which Johanan replies to Joshua's despairing cry over the ruined temple with this spiritualizing reinterpretation: "My son, be not grieved. We have another atonement as effective as this. And what is it? It is acts of loving-kindness, as it is said, *For I desire mercy and not sacrifice* (Hos. 6:6).[18] Jacob Neusner interprets this story as follows:

Earlier, Pharisaism had held that the temple should be everywhere, even in the home and hearth. Now Yohanan taught that sacrifice greater than the temple's must characterize the life of the community. If one were to do something for God in a time when the temple was no more, the offering must be the gift of selfless compassion. The holy altar must be the streets and market-places of the world, as formerly, the purity of the temple had to be observed in the streets and market-places of Jerusalem. The earlier history of the Pharisaic sect thus laid the groundwork for Yohanan ben Zakkai's response to Joshua ben Hananiah. It was a natural conclusion for one nurtured in a movement based upon the priesthood of all Israel.[19]

Although necessarily brief, this overview of the early history of Pharisaism gives a glimpse of how the community ideal bequeathed to the future by certain teachers within that movement emerged from its biblical roots as a progressive new stage of development. But it was not the only offshoot of the community of faith of the biblical period. Di-

---

17. *Babylonian Berakot* 55a.
18. *'Abot de Rabbi Nathan*, ch. 4.
19. Hayes and Miller, *History*, p. 672.

versity was a characteristic of that community during most periods, and its legacy was accordingly diverse. As already noted, groups placing a greater emphasis on divine acts that were yet to occur than on the perfection and completeness of the revelation given on Sinai, tended to develop their sense of identity apart from and often in opposition to the tradition stemming from Ezra and Nehemiah out of which the most famous rabbis emerged. This is not to deny that in many periods there were numbered among the Pharisees invididuals and groups espousing eschatological notions. Messianic hopes, as a part of their biblical heritage, were accepted by the rabbis from the beginning, and the role of oral tradition at least maintained some sense of openness to new eschatological interpretations of historical events. Especially during the peiod from the death of Herod the Great in 4 B.C.E. until the destruction of the temple in 70 C.E., the areas thickly settled by the Jews were characterized by serious unrest and much eschatological speculation. It was inevitable that events like the Passover slaughter of 40 C.E., in which Josephus reports that 20,000 Jews died, would lead many Pharisees to discern signs of the coming of the long-awaited Messiah who would establish the everlasting kingdom of peace and justice. And it must not be forgotten that the great Akiba himself heralded Bar Kochba as the Messiah who had come to deliver the Jews from the Romans in the tragic Second Jewish Revolt (132–135 C.E.). The tragic consequences of the political extremism advocated by certain apocalyptic circles, however, ultimately reinforced the position of leading Pharisees, who, in reflecting on the carnage left in the wake of the Zealots, and on the chaos spawned by the fanaticism of the Sicarii,[20] came to an important conclusion: they were to devote their lives not to the establishment of a kingdom of earthly power, but to the heavenly order in harmony to which they were called to live in defiance of every earthly allegiance. In addition, there was always present among the Pharisees a practical outlook that Neusner plausibly has described as the social setting of the Mishnah, an outlook strengthened by the two abortive Jewish revolts, in the wake of which the final formation of the Mishnah took place. It was the world of the householders, who were

people deeply tired of war and its dislocation, profoundly distrustful of messiahs and their dangerous promises. These are men of substance and means, however modest, aching for a stable and predictable world in which to tend their crops and herds, feed their families and workers, keep to the natural rhythms of the seasons and the lunar cycles, and, in sum, live out their lives within strong and secure boundaries, on earth and in heaven.[21]

---

20. The Sicarii were terrorists who created a climate of terror by mingling in the crowded streets especially during festivals and drawing out their daggers, which they carried hidden in their cloaks, to maim and to kill.

21. Neusner, *Judaism*, 255–256.

E. THE ESSENES

If the preceding description fits at least some of the Pharisees, it is far from descriptive of the third party named by Josephus, for the Essenes and related groups consisted of elements stubbornly unreconciled with existing social and political conditions. In fact, they seemed prepared to risk the peace and security of their present existence for the sake of an existence categorically different, purged of the trials and oppressions of this world, and free from the ambiguity caused by the coexistence of good and evil and the intermingling of the righteous and the wicked. Although the conditions underlying the alienation of such groups no doubt varied a great deal, disillusionment with political and religious structures seemed to have been a powerful force in creating a climate of apocalyptic expectation among broad segments of the Jewish population, especially in times of oppression and persecution.

Although standing in stark contrast to the outlook that finally prevailed within the Pharisaic movement, the notions of community found in these groups also betray deep roots in biblical tradition. Prominent in late prophecy is the theme that God's saving activity was not confined to the past, but was leading to a climactic denouement in the near future, specifically involving a great day of judgment on which all that was hostile to righteousness and opposed to "the elect" would be destroyed, making possible the inauguration of the everlasting kingdom of universal peace and justice. Although the dominance of the Zadokite party in the period between Ezra and Sirach led to the partial eclipse of groups cultivating this hope, anonymous writings such as Zechariah 12–14 that were added to prophetic books at a relatively late time indicate that apocalyptic-oriented circles continued to offer an alternative communal ideal to that being developed and refined under the auspices of Zadokites. During the fourth and third centuries, however, the prevailing political climate of Judea likely obliged such groups to limit their activity to secret gatherings of the like-minded.

The tumultuous events of the early second century B.C.E. brought the apocalyptic spirit into the open again. We have already seen how the ḥăsîdîm embraced an apocalyptic outlook during the persecutions inflicted by Antiochus IV Epiphanes. The influence and breadth of apocalyptic thinking during that period is evidenced by the significant number of writings embodying an apocalyptic outlook that have survived. Although Daniel alone among such writings was accepted into the Hebrew Bible, we find a whole "pentateuch" of apocalyptic writings, most of them from the late third and early second centuries B.C.E., collected in the so-called 1 Enoch (or Ethiopic Enoch). Joseph Milik has shown that the Enoch literature of this period was even more extensive than suggested by the final form of that book.[22] Also coming from apocalyptic circles of this period is the Book of Jubilees.[23]

A remarkably consistent outlook unifies these writings. They are characterized by a deeply pessimistic assessment of existing conditions. Their authors regarded the human race quite generally to have fallen under the spell of wickedness, and they gave mythic explanations for that sad state by explaining that the offspring of the fallen angels of Genesis 6 had gained control of the earth.[24] The earth was accordingly ripe for that which alone could cleanse it, a divine destruction comparable only to the flood of the time of Noah. Such a complete destruction finally would create conditions within which God could call into being a new order, perfect in all ways and holding for the elect unprecedented bliss:

And then all the righteous ones will escape; and become the living ones until they multiply and become tens of hundreds; and all the days of their youth and the years of their retirement they will complete in peace. And in those days the whole earth will be worked in righteousness, and all of her planted with trees, and will find blessing. And they shall plant pleasant trees upon her—vines. And he who plants a vine upon her will produce wine for plentitude. And every seed that is sown on her, one measure will yield a thousand (measures) and one measure of olives will yield ten measures of presses of oil. And you shall cleanse the earth from all injustice, and from all defilement, and from all oppression, and from all sin, and from all iniquity which is being done on earth; remove them from the earth. And all the children of the people will become righteous, and all nations shall worship and bless me; and they will all prostrate themselves to me. And the earth shall be cleansed from all pollution, and from all sin, and from all plague, and from all suffering; and it shall not happen again that I shall send (these) upon the earth from generation to generation and forever. And in those days I shall open the storerooms of blessing which are in the heavens, so that I shall send them down upon the earth, over the work and the toil of the children of man. And peace and truth shall become partners together in all the days of the world, and all the generations of the world.   (1 Enoch 10:17–11:2)[25]

The social setting of these writings is already suggested by the startling premise that underlies them, namely, that the entire apparatus of the temple cult was powerless to remove the defilement that was drawing the earth toward chaos. The dispute was clearly not over the existence of sin in the world. The temple cult was designed specifically to

---

22. See J. Milik, *The Books of Enoch* (Oxford, England: Clarendon Press, 1976).

23. See J. Vander Kam, *Textual and Historical Studies in the Book of Jubilees*, HSM 14 (Missoula, Mont.: Scholars Press, 1977).

24. See P. D. Hanson, "Rebellion in Heaven, Azazel and Euhemeristic Heroes in I Enoch 6–11," *JBL* 96 (1977), 195–233.

25. The citations from 1 Enoch are taken from J. Charlesworth, ed., *The Old Testament Pseudepigrapha*, trans. E. Isaac (Garden City, N.Y.: Doubleday, 1983).

deal with every type of sin, for according to its theology the delicate order that allowed the community to live in peace depended on the orderly removal of all sin and defilement; hence the elaborate sacrificial
system cultivated by the temple cult. The comprehensiveness of the
temple system comes to view especially in relation to the ritual of the
Day of Atonement: all sin that escaped the purifying effects of the normal sacrifices was removed once a year in this supreme sacrifice.

The dispute thus was not over the question of the existence of sin
and the deadly threat it posed. It rather stemmed from a flat denial
that the temple cult possessed an effective means for dealing with the
problem. Hence the radical alternative of the dissidents: only direct intervention by God, and the declaration of divine war on the evil powers
of heaven and earth, could purge the universe of evil and rescue it
from chaos. This message was not a new one. Its roots reach back to the
exilic period. What is new is that the visionaries who had cultivated the
apocalyptic message were now joined by former temple priests, more
specifically, Zadokite priests who found in the radical apocalyptic vision
of reversal a means of giving expression to the sense of hurt and alienation caused by their own fall from sacerdotal power. Excluded by the
Hasmoneans from their pre-eminent positions in the temple, some of
the most strict members of the Zadokite priesthood thus withdrew to
the wilderness, there to preside over an apocalyptic community that developed in detail an alternative notion of what it means to be the people of God. According to this view, the Zadokite succession was no
longer preserved in the era after Simon I, Onias II, and Alchimus within the Jerusalem temple, but in the Judean wilderness, whither the new
incumbent of the high priestly office, the Teacher of Righteousness,
had fled to build a new, undefiled "temple," consisting of the community of the elect, where God could be present until God returned to destroy the defiled temple and to replace it with a new one.

The resulting condemnation of the temple cult and its new priestly
leadership was total: its altar was polluted, its sacrifices unclean, its ritual
ineffectual in dealing with the deplorable conditions of the land and its
inhabitants. In fact, a view of the history of the temple developed that
was so bleak as to portray the entire sequence of events from the rebuilding of the temple under Zerubbabel and Joshua down to the present as
unmitigated disaster. The so-called Animal Apocalypse found in 1 Enoch 85–90 describes the ill-fated beginning of the Second Temple thus:

They again began to build as before; and they raised up that tower which is
called the high tower. But they started to place a table before the tower, with all
the food which is upon it being polluted and impure. Regarding all these matters, the eyes of the sheep became so dim-sighted that they could not see—and
likewise in respect to their shepherds—and they were delivered to their shepherds for an excessive destruction, so that the sheep were trampled upon and
eaten.   (1 Enoch 89:73–74)

With the temple defiled and the sacrifices "polluted and impure," the people were helpless before the hostile attack of foreign enemies (1 Enoch 89:75–90:5). The orientation of the "Animal Apocalypse" is similar to that of Daniel 7–12, likely betraying provenance within the circles of the *ḥăsîdîm*. The "lambs" of 90:6–7 who try to bring the "sheep" to their senses are probably the *ḥăsîdîm* making appeal to their lax brethren. But neither this, nor the Maccabean revolt, is able to change the disastrous course of history. As in Daniel, all such human efforts are at best "little help." Deliverance can come from one realm alone—heaven.

Within this vision, hope no longer resided within the institutional structures of the temple. Life in this world was no longer an ordered existence, regulated dependably by sacerdotal structures instituted by God through David and by a Torah coeval with the creation of the world. Due to defilement, the sacerdotal structures themselves had become problematic, and the prevailing interpretation of the Torah had the effect of blinding the people to its true meaning. Hope resided alone in an end-time vision, granted to the elect, of the destruction of all that existed, for all was fallen to defilement, including the temple. The only ones who had remained true to God's will were a group now located outside of the temple, who like helpless lambs, were afflicted and persecuted for righteousness's sake. Having given up hope within this world, they looked to heaven and awaited the time when God would come to draw them into the final conflict against all the hosts of wickedness:

I kept seeing till the Lord of the sheep came unto them and took in his hand the rod of his wrath and smote the earth; and all the beasts and all the birds of the heaven fell down from the midst of those sheep and were swallowed up in the earth, and it was covered upon them. Then I saw that a great sword was given to the sheep; and the sheep proceeded against all the beasts of the field in order to kill them; and all the beasts and birds of heaven fled from before their face. (1 Enoch 90:18–19)

According to this apocalyptic vision, the end-time battle was to be followed by a final judgment, in which God, seated upon the judgment throne, would cast into the fiery abyss first the rebellious stars (angels), then the shepherds (the unfaithful leaders of the community), and finally the blinded sheep (the apostates among the people). Only after the purification of the earth had thus been completed could the people of God be reconstituted around its worship center. But the defilement of the temple was so complete that it could not be cleansed. It had to be dismantled, piece by piece, removed to a distant land, and miraculously replaced by God with a new temple:

Then I stood still, looking at that ancient house being transformed: All the pillars and all the columns were pulled out; and the ornaments of that house were packed and taken out together with them and abandoned in a certain place in the South of the land. I went on seeing until the Lord of the sheep brought about a new house, greater and loftier than the first one, and set it up in the first location which had been covered up—all its pillars were new, the columns new; and the ornaments new as well as greater than those of the first (that is) the old (house) which was gone. All the sheep were within it. Then I saw all the sheep that had survived as well as all the animals upon the earth and the birds of heaven, falling down and worshiping those sheep, making petition to them and obeying them in every respect.   (1 Enoch 90:28–30)

Thus would the new era be born, and like the first creation, it would come by God's act alone. The sword was to be sealed up in the new temple, the distinction between Jew and Gentile was to be removed, enabling peace to abide forever (1 Enoch 90:30–39).

The social setting of the "Animal Apocalypse" seems clear: The former priestly class, the Zadokites, banished from their temple home and allied with visionary Hasideans suffering banishment for their own reasons, declare—in the name of the ancient seer Enoch—God's condemnation of the Hasmonean temple and its leadership. Having lost control of the situation, they look to the imminent intervention of God to vindicate them. God would judge their enemies, replace the defiled temple, and restore them to their rightful place of honor in the purified and glorified community.

The same view of history, no doubt reflecting the same social setting, is presented in another Enochan composition, the "Apocalypse of Weeks." The seventh week introduces the age beginning with the temple restoration under Zerubbabel and Jeshua, and is designated "an apostate generation," whose deeds are "many, and all of them criminal" (1 Enoch 93:9). But at the end of that period comes the turning point, when "there shall be elected the elect ones of righteousness from the eternal plant of righteousness, to whom shall be given sevenfold instruction concerning all his flock" (93:10). After thus designating themselves with terms that are also found in the Dead Sea Scrolls, the visionary dissidents go on to describe the end-time conflict to which they are commissioned. For in the eighth week they are given a sword, "in order that judgment shall be executed in righteousness on the oppressors and sinners shall be delivered into the hands of the righteous," following which the temple is rebuilt (91:12–13). In the ninth week, the great judgment takes place, and the world is purified. Finally, in the tenth week there occurs the "eternal judgment," followed by the passing away of the old heaven, the creation of the new heaven, and then endless bliss.

In the books of 1 Enoch and Jubilees, we find yet another clear indication of the radical nature of the protest leveled against the official cult by the opposition. It is the promulgation of a rival calendar. Recently much attention has been directed by students of religion and sociology to the importance of calendrical systems to the life of a cultic community. It is the calendar that keeps a people in harmony with the divine order of the universe. One of the most deadly threats to the well-being of a community is negelct of the holy observances called for by the sacred calendar. Equally deadly is the adoption of an erroneous calendar. In the Book of Daniel, one of the most heinous sins of the archvillain Antiochus IV Epiphanes was that he thought "to change the times and the law" (7:25); that is to say, the sacred calendar of the Jews and the holy Torah. Now, just a matter of two or three decades later, the banished Zadokites and their visionary followers scrutinize the upstart temple leadership, and accuse them of an equally heinous act, of regulating the cultic life of the people on the basis of a false calendar, thereby threatening to cast the whole universe into chaos (1 Enoch 82:5–6). The harmony of God's order thus slips away:

In respect to their days, the sinners and the winter are cut short. Their seed(s) shall lag behind in their lands and in their fertile fields, and in all their activities upon the earth. He will turn and appear in their time, and withhold rain; and the sky shall stand still at that time. Then the vegetable shall slacken and not grow in its season, and the fruit shall not be born in its (proper) season. The moon shall alter its order, and will not be seen according to its (normal) cycles. In those days it will appear in the sky and it shall arrive in the evening in the extreme ends of the great lunar path, in the west. And it shall shine (more brightly), exceeding the normal degree of light. Many of the chiefs of the stars shall make errors in respect to the orders given to them; they shall change their courses and functions and not appear during the seasons which have been prescribed for them.   (1 Enoch 80:2–7)

The entire third book of 1 Enoch (chapters 72–82) is devoted to a detailed description of a new calendar, one based on solar calculation. Revealed by an angel of the Lord, it covers "the rules concerning all the stars of heaven," "all their respective rules for every day, for every season, and for every year; the procession of each one according to the commandment, every month and every week" (1 Enoch 79:1–2). Here then was the astronomical basis for correcting the cosmic disorder inflicted on the land by an illegitimate and defiled priesthood. The third book of 1 Enoch, the so-called Book of the Heavenly Luminaries, can thus be seen as a companion piece of the "Animal Apocalypse" and the "Apocalypse of Weeks." It provides a detailed description of the cosmic setting of the true temple and the true Israel of the future.

Although the preceding discussion has given only a brief sampling of the radical critique of the temple and priesthood that arose in the midsecond century, it offers a vivid contrast to the position that prevailed within the Pharisaic party. The Pharisees, to be sure, also based their beliefs on the notion of an eternal, divine order, and this established their independence vis-à-vis the political powers of their day. But whereas the Pharisees adopted a lifestyle that permitted them to live in obedience to the Torah *within* the cultic and political structures of the Hasmonean kingdom, the apocalyptic circles of the time interpreted those structures as the deadly instruments of apostate leaders. It is easily understandable that their posture led to withdrawal, and to visions of divine judgment and vindication. Although beginning within the same movement of the *ḥăsîdîm*, the Pharisees and the Essenes thus developed in significantly different directions. The Pharisees tended to work out a *modus operandi* within a generally inhospitable world that allowed them to remain true to their faith by attributing no abiding significance to the political powers around them, whereas the Essenes broke at times with society and devoted themselves to preparation for a final, deadly battle with the dark powers of this world and their heavenly counterparts.

F. THE APOCALYPTIC COMMUNITY OF THE DEAD SEA SCROLLS

We now turn to the most vivid and complete example of an apocalyptic community from this period, the community of Qumran, as documented by the Dead Sea scrolls. The basis for assuming that the residents of that wilderness habitation were Essenes rests on a comparison of the description given of the Essenes by Philo, Josephus, and Pliny the Elder, with the picture emerging from the Qumran scrolls themselves. Geza Vermes summarizes the evidence found in the ancient historians thus:

Thus Essenes and Qumran desert societies both favoured the common ownership of property, both refused to participate in Temple worship, both had purificatory baths, both partook of a sacred meal blessed by a priest. Both furthermore were opposed to taking vows apart from the vow of entry, and both appear to have been interested in healing (in the Scrolls it figures at the head of the spiritual blessings). As for celibacy, although it is not positively referred to in the Qumran Community rule, its probability in the monastic brotherhood has been shown to be great.[26]

Beyond this positive correlation between ancient descriptions of the Essenes and the scrolls themselves, the many lines connecting the sectarian writings of Qumran with the books of Enoch and Jubilees, such as the solar calendar, the apocalyptic outlook, the rejection of the Jerusalem temple cult, the vision of a temple of the future that would supplant the existing temple, and even self-designations such as "the plant of righteousness," strongly suggest that the community of Qumran was a part of a rather broad apocalyptic movement. Corroborating this conclusion is the fact that 1 Enoch, Jubilees, and the Genesis Apocryphon were all found among the scrolls of the Qumran library.

In treating the early history of the *ḥăsîdîm*, and the development out

---

26. G. Vermes, *Perspective* (Philadelphia: Fortress Press, 1977).

of that movement of the apocalyptic-oriented Essenes, we have thus uncovered the roots of the Qumran community. We are dealing with
those elements within the Jewish population that took every act of compromise with the leaders of this world as betrayal of the Torah. As the
position of the Hasmoneans became established, they willingly accommodated sacred traditions to the political exigencies of the time, and
silenced religious opposition by combining the prerogatives of the high
priesthood with their regal authority. The Essenes interpreted these
developments as signs that the dark powers of the universe had taken
control of their own nation. The increasing alienation that characterized their relationship to their own leaders reinforced their apocalyptic
proclivities, nurturing a self-consciousness of being the righteous remnant of God within a nation and world fallen irretrievably to evil.

One added factor completes our accounting for the origins of the
Qumran community, namely, the influx into the Hasidean circles in the
mid-second century B.C.E. of a considerable number of Zadokite priests,
now themselves acquainted with alienation as the result of their being
forced from the temple priesthood by the Hasmonean usurpation. For
the training and background of the Zadokites had equipped them with
the leadership skills and sense of authority necessary to forge the dissidents into a well-organized apocalyptic community, founded on obedience to the Torah and yet self-consciously distinct from the temple
community. Through their presence, the apocalyptic orientation of the
ḥăsîdîm was imprinted with the priestly mentality of Zadokite purists,
resulting in the unique blend of strict legalism with an apocalyptic
world view that is the hallmark of the Dead Sea community. That ar-
chaeology has recently uncovered such rich evidence for a community
representing the culmination of a socioreligious movement otherwise
known only through scattered literary references is very fortunate, for
it enables us to give a rather complete description of the concrete setting of an apocalyptic community. Here we see the biblical texts they
read, copied, and interpreted, the particular sectarian writings with
which they formulated their own structures of community and doctrine, the vision they held of the new temple God would build to supplant the existing one, and the physical layout of their public buildings.
Qumran thus offers indisputable proof that in the apocalyptic writings
of the time, we are not merely dealing with the fantasies of highly
imaginative seers, but with an eschatological program on which large
groups of people staked their entire lives and fortunes.

The Dead Sea scrolls do not give unequivocal evidence for the precise date of the break of this group from the temple cult of Jerusalem.
In general terms, it is clear that the break came as a result of the Zadokites being forced from their priestly offices by the Hasmoneans. The
chief clue to the specific catalyst is in the form of references in the
scrolls to a bitter conflict between the community's founder, the Teach-

er of Righteousness, and the "wicked priest" of the Jerusalem temple, who exhibited great cruelty in oppressing the Teacher, even to the extent of coming to the Qumran settlement and harassing its inhabitants during their celebration of the Day of Atonement (1 QpHab xi). The intriguing question of course is, "Who was the 'wicked priest'?" Jonathan was the first Hasmonean to lay claim to the title of high priest, in 152 B.C.E., and is thus the first possible candidate. The more likely candidate, however, is his brother Simon (143–134), who after succeeding Jonathan, adopted such a high style of rule and made such extravagant claims as to bitterly insult and offend traditionalists like the Zadokites and the separatist ḥăsîdîm, who not only were being asked to accept the Hasmonean usurpation of the high priesthood, but to tolerate the pompous propaganda evident in the bronze inscription quoted in chapter 14 of 1 Maccabees. Accordingly, it seems probable that the definitive break leading to the flight to the wilderness occurred during Simon's reign.[27]

Thus there had occurred the culminating event in a long series of experiences proving to the Zadokites and their Hasidean followers that their position in the present temple community had been lost definitively. In their assessment of earthly realities, they concluded that the temple had been desecrated, the covenant broken, and the land polluted. True to their apocalyptic proclivities, they did not formulate their opposition in the form of a program of cultic and social reform, but rather in the form of a vision of impending divine intervention. No human was capable of purifying the old temple, of drawing the apostates back to obedience to the Torah, of cleansing the land. The collapse of the present order was too advanced. Only God could rescue humans from the doom they had brought on themselves. The Essenes of Qumran portrayed that divine act in vivid colors as an eschatological battle in which they alone would be drawn into an angelic host to perform a final act of judgment on the hosts of darkness and their human followers. The community of Qumran lived in anticipation of the final battle and the glorious new creation that would follow. And as years passed without the arrival of God and the angelic hosts, its anticipation was translated into a rigid system of communal institutions and structures.

As a people regarding themselves as the sole remnant remaining faithful to God, the Qumran community members placed great stress on obedience to the Torah in every detail. But there was a further facet to their concept of authority that had a great influence on the development of their notion of community, namely, the vital role played in the formation of their thinking by the Teacher of Righteousness. The rigidly exclusive doctrine of authority that developed at Qumran is also in-

---

27. On the dating of the origin of the Qumran community, see F. M. Cross, *Ancient Library*.

timately related to this community's apocalyptic outlook. Its members viewed themselves as a righteous remnant standing on a threshold between two ages. The old age was one hopelessly fallen to evil, the enemies being both the foreign enemies of God, especially the Kittim (the Romans), and the leaders of their own nation, the Hasmoneans. God had preserved them as witnesses to the truth in this fallen age and as human agents assisting the angels in the inauguration of the new age, when its time had finally come. They alone knew the secrets of the age's coming, secrets contained in Scripture, but opened up only to the one to whom God had given the key of interpretation. That key had been given to the Teacher of Righteousness, "[in whose heart] God had set [understanding] that he might interpret all the words of His servants the prophets, through whom He foretold all that would happen to His people and [His land]" (1 QpHab ii, 8–10).[28] Here was a claim which arose directly out of apocalyptic enthusiasm: No longer was the spirit of prophecy silent! Nor was knowledge of God's will any longer limited to those trained in scribal methods of interpretation. The time toward which all Scripture pointed had arrived, and with it, one whom God had granted the gift of interpretation in a measure exceeding even that of the earlier prophets (1 QpHab vi:1–2). Without denying the flexibility inherent in the exegesis of the Pharisees, whose scribes were able to apply Scripture to every new situation through the use of a dynamic hermeneutic, we nonetheless recognize in the *pēšer* method of interpretation used by the Teacher of Righteousness a far loftier claim to inspiration. By way of the *pēšer* method, a commentary method in which the verses of a prophetic book are quoted and then interpreted so as to unlock their hidden, contemporary meaning, the message of biblical prophecy was brought to focus on the Teacher and his followers as the exclusive human instruments of God's eternal plan.

What was the nature of that plan according to the thinking of the Teacher and his followers? In keeping with the apocalyptic dualism of the Essenes, it was a plan anticipating radical discontinuity with the realities of the present. This is manifested vividly by the titles they applied to their community: the present leaders of the nation and the majority of the people had broken the covenant, but God was now establishing this commnity as his "New Covenant." The assessment of past history in the scrolls is as bleak as the ones we have seen in the "Animal Apocalypse" and the "Apocalypse of Weeks," viewing the Israel of the Jerusalem temple as an apostate Israel, ripe for destruction as God prepared to create the "true Israel." The inhabitants of Jerusalem had become corrupt and defiled, but here in the wilderness God had gathered together the "Men of Holiness." The temple in Jerusalem had become

---

28. Translations from the Dead Sea Scrolls are from G. Vermes, *The Dead Sea Scrolls in English* (Baltimore: Penguin Books, 1962), unless noted otherwise.

desecrated by its unfaithful priests, but now in this unlikely place God was creating a "New Temple." The inhabitants of the earth had so fallen under the power of the Prince of Darkness as to be designated the "Sons of Darkness," but now God had drawn into his heavenly hosts a human community prepared to fight in the final battle against all agents of wickedness, in heaven and on earth, a community called the "Sons of Light." By looking at each of these titles in turn, we can get a rather complete understanding of the notion of community that prevailed at Qumran.

That the community at Qumran chose to designate itself the "New Covenant" is very significant. As seen in a previous chapter, it was the term used by Jeremiah (or his disciples) to designate the people of the coming age, whose perfect obedience would be the result of the Torah being written on their hearts. This covenant was contrasted with another, that formerly made with Israel's ancestors, which they broke. A fundamental similarity in anthropology connects the Qumran group with Jeremiah, deeply pessimistic in attitude, holding out little hope of any alternative to divine wrath short of God's calling into being a *new* people, characterized by a more intimate embodiment of the Torah than its ancestors.

In the thinking of this apocalyptic community, its members constituted that new people of God. God had commissioned the Teacher of Righteousness to gather them from the nation that had wantonly abandoned the Mosaic covenant, and to lead them to a wilderness sanctuary. There they organized themselves in imitation of the tribes in the wilderness period; there they received the definitive interpretation of God's will from their new Moses, the Teacher of Righteousness; there they vowed to follow the Torah with perfect obedience; there they entered into an intimate covenant with God; there, in short, they became the "Men of the New Covenant." This term carries with it a meaning that is both radical and exclusive. It is radical in stressing that the old era had ended, and that the final age had begun. It is exclusive in claiming that all but this remnant had been cut off from the covenant with God and were consigned to divine wrath on the day of judgment. In their community alone was the salvation of Israel preserved: "They shall separate from the habitation of ungodly men and shall go into the wilderness to prepare the way of Him: as it is written, *Prepare in the wilderness the way of . . . make straight in the desert a path for our God*" (1 QS vii, 13). For all those falling outside the sanctity of their community they were to cultivate "an everlasting hatred in a spirit of secrecy" (1 QS ix, 21). This too was a part of their preparation, for in the day of judgment to follow they were to witness God's judgment on the apostate majority within Israel—with special harshness reserved for the priests (1 QpHab ii, 10 to vi, 12; ix, 3 to x, 1–5)—and on the nations (1 QpHab xii, 10 to xiii, 4). This exclusiveness of course is tied to the community's concept of authority: They bound themselves by oath to perfect obedience to the Torah of Moses and the teachings of the prophets, but with the added stipulation, "in accordance with all that has been revealed of it to the sons of Zadok" (1 QS v, 9). Since authority was thus centralized in one person (and his successors), none of the flexibility in the interpretation of the law that characterized the debates between the various rabbinical schools is found at Qumran. This rigidity is not unrelated to the fact that the designation "New Covenent" was not adopted by Pharisaic Judaism. The rabbis, in sharp contrast to the Covenanters of Qumran, viewed it as their responsibility to interpret the Torah of Moses to an age benefiting neither from a fresh outpouring of prophecy nor from the presence of the Messiah.

The wilderness community claimed that the majority of the nation, by forsaking the covenant, had abdicated their claim to the title "Israel," or at best, they were the "unfaithful Israel." The inheritors of the ancient title were of course those constituting the "remnant" of the faithful. Hence, they designated themselves the "True Israel." This term they defined in a way signaling a shift in the concept of election. One did not belong to the "True Israel" by virtue of belonging to the ʿam yisrāʾēl, the "People of Israel," but by a personal divine call to break with the old Israel to take up membership in the ʿēdâ, or "congregation," of the elect. Involved, moreover, was a long and arduous process of initiation and examination, at various stages, that determined how high one advanced within the hierarchy of the community. The emphasis placed on the necessity of personal choice and on the vow to obedience taken by each initiate shows distinctly how far the emphasis had moved from the people as a corporate body to the individual. But having once been drawn together by the foreknowledge of God, they now reconstituted the original people of God, lead by the "priests of Zadok" with the laity divided into the twelve tribes of Israel, and then into camps of one thousands, one hundreds, fifties, and tens, in meticulous imitation of the organization of the wilderness community of Moses's time!

The members of the Qumran community also called themselves the "Men of Holiness," and their community they called the "House of Holiness." Naturally, this involved the adoption of a term central both to biblical tradition and the traditions of all the Jewish parties of that time. But here too a new connotation evolved, with vows to a life of perfect obedience being accompanied by the reinterpretation of many biblical laws so as to heighten their demands. This new legalistic severity is also seen in the policy relating to transgression: any full member of the Council, that is, the inner assembly of the community, who broke any law of the Torah, whether willfully or through neglect, was immediately excommunicated. Finally, the Qumran community distinguished itself from other groups, at least among the members of the Council, by practicing celibacy and eschewing private ownership of property.

I have already noted the Qumran community's total condemnation of the Jerusalem temple. This condemnation raised for a community of priests a serious question: with the defiled state of that temple leaving the divine presence without an earthly home, Israel's most essential connection with the source of all blessing had been broken. What could be done to recreate a hospitable setting for God's presence? The answer they gave to this question demonstrates the creativeness of their apocalyptic thinking. In the interim period within which they were living, between the old age of wrath represented by the old temple and the new age of blessing in which God himself would create a new temple, they, through their lives of perfect obedience and ritual purity, would provide for God an earthly temple. They *were* the "New Temple." Although calling to mind the spiritualization of the concept of the temple that occurred within the early church, it is distinct in that the messianic kingdom was not understood to be temple-less. Here their thinking is thoroughly priestly. The messianic age would indeed have a temple, located on Mount Zion, in which they, the Zadokites, as the sole legitimate priesthood, would once again preside in holy splendor. The situation in the wilderness was strictly liminal, but nevertheless important as a preparatory stage in the transition to the new age.

In the interim period, how did the community function as the "New Temple"? Great emphasis was placed on the life of perfect holiness as the proper worship of God. But beyond this the priestly orientation of this comunity comes to expression in the careful attention that was paid to the Mosaic ritual laws. In this area, the precise calculations based on the solar calendar figure prominently, so that each festival would fall on the precise day intended by God and determined by the "Great light of heaven," the sun. Whether these priests, deprived of their temple, and trying to live as an interim temple in the wilderness, also engaged in sacrifice is a moot question. Bones found at Qumran had been advanced as evidence by some scholars to argue that the Zadokites had rationalized that until a pure temple had been rebuilt in Jerusalem, they were obliged to uphold the laws of sacrifice in their wilderness "temple." Others conclude that this is unlikely, and that the bones did not belong to sacrificial animals. Whatever was the case as regards sacrifice, it is clear that life revolved at Qumran around worship, both in the sense of obedience to the Torah in daily life and in a carefully regulated schedule of ritual acts.

One of the most interesting aspects of their ritual life was the daily common meal.[29] Although involving one of life's most basic activities, it was clothed in an aura of sanctity.[30] In imitation of the rites of the temple priests, the participants first prepared themselves through the

---

29. Cf. G. Vermes, *Perspective*, p. 94.

30. Josephus, in his description of the cultic meal of the Essenes, depicts its aura of sanctity thus: "After purification, they assemble in a special room which none of the uninitiated is permitted to enter; pure now themselves, they repair to the refectory, as to some sacred shrine" (*War* 2.8.5).

ritual bath, by which act they assured that all would be entering the meal in a proper state of ritual holiness. Beyond cultic cleansing, the bath also assumed the sacramental function of mediating God's forgiveness (1 QS iii, 3–6). Then the meal itself was structured with regard to seating and order in a manner identical to the directions for the messianic meal.[31] Here was obviously a time and space in the life of Qumran when the community experienced its membership in the heavenly congregation, a foretaste described thus in one of the sect's hymns:

> Thou hast cleansed a perverse spirit of great sin
>> that it may stand with the host of the Holy ones,
> and that it may enter into community
>> with the congregation of the Sons of Heaven.   (1 QH iii, 21–22)

The leaders of the Qumran community were very creative in finding terms of self-description, as indicated by the heaping up of such terms in this section of the community's rule:

> It shall be an Everlasting Plantation, a House of Holiness for Israel, an Assembly of Supreme Holiness for Aaron. They shall be witnesses to the truth at the Judgment, and shall be the elect of Goodwill who shall atone for the Land and pay to the wicked their reward. It shall be that tried wall, that *precious corner-stone*, whose foundations shall neither rock nor sway in their place [Isa. 28:16]. It shall be a Most Holy Dwelling for Aaron, with everlasting knowledge of the Covenant of Justice, and shall offer up sweet fragrance. It shall be a House of Perfection and Truth in Israel that they may establish a Covenant according to the everlasting precepts. And they shall be an agreeable offering, atoning for the Land and determining the judgment of wickedness, and there shall be no more iniquity.   (1 QS viii, 4–9)

Although each of the terms in this description is interesting in itself, I shall comment on only one more designation, one that has close connections with the previously discussed "New Temple." For in imitation of the congregation of ancient Israel in the wilderness, a state of purity was to be maintained not only in preparation for sacred worship, but also for sacred war. As those living in a perpetual state of ritual purity in preparation for Holy War, they referred to themselves as the "Sons of Light." Because in the war to come they would be fighting beside God's holy angels, preservation of a state of perfect holiness was absolutely necessary. Accordingly, they believed that they stood in the long succession of the chosen heroes of God, and indeed they saw themselves as the culmination of that succession, for God had called them

---

31. Comparison of the description of the daily common meal found in 1 QS vi, 1–6 with the messianic banquet described in 1 QS ii, 17–22 indicates that the Qumran community believed the two to be the same in all essential features. This equation of their daily meal with the messianic banquet is brought out explicitly at the end of the 1 QSa fragment: "And they shall follow this prescription whenever the meal is arranged, when as many as ten meet together" (D. Barthelemy and J. T. Milik, eds., *Discoveries in the Judean Desert*, vol. 1: Qumran Cave I (Oxford, England: Clarendon Press, 1955), p. 111. For the above translation and further discussion of the Qumran meal, see F. M. Cross, *Christian Century* 72 (1955), 969.

out of a world of darkness to join the heavenly host in the final battle that would usher in the messianic kingdom. Nowhere does this apocalyptic dualism and the severe legalism of the Qumran community come to clearer expression than in their manual of war, entitled "The Sons of Darkness against the Sons of Light." Here we see that their meticulous attention to every detail of the Torah, their practice of celibacy, and their life of severe personal discipline were inextricably tied to their self-image as warriors preparing for the end-time battle.

Taken together, these terms give a rather complete picture of the community ideal that developed at Qumran. It is an ideal determined by a combination of severe legalism with an apocalyptic world view. Having turned its back on this world as fallen beyond redemption, it is quite natural that this community located its true home in heaven, and defined its membership with a rigidity excluding all others. It is also understandable that such a lofty self-concept would bring with it a deeply felt need to attain a state of holy perfection befitting those who mingled with angels:

> All them that follow Thy counsel
> hast Thou brought into [com]munion with Thee,
> and hast given them common estate
> with the Angels of Thy Presence.
> They are Thy courtiers,
> sharing the high estate
> of [all the heavenly beings].   (1 QH vi, 12–14)[32]

Through the ranking of the community according to priestly and lay status as well as levels of perfection, through the ritual baths and the sacred meals, through perfectionist attitudes toward Torah obedience and the observance of the sacred rituals—in all these ways, a manner of life was practiced that was believed to adumbrate the messianic kingdom. At the same time, all these "heavenly" practices did not remove the harsh realities of the menace of the Jerusalem priests, the threat of the Romans, and the indifference to their message of judgment on the part of the majority of the Jewish people. Hence, these aspects of "realized eschatology" existed side by side with a more futuristic dimension, seen especially in their meticulous plans for the final war against the hosts of darkness.

G. IMPLICATIONS OF SECOND AND FIRST CENTURY B.C.E. DEVELOPMENTS FOR LATER COMMUNITIES OF FAITH

This chapter began with an account of the ebbing of a movement that threatened the Jewish people with a force comparable to that of

---

32. Translation by T. Gaster, *The Dead Sea Scriptures*, 3d ed. (Garden City, N.Y.: Doubleday/Anchor Books, 1976), p. 168.

the Philistines, the Assyrians, or the Babylonians of earlier periods. This was the mighty movement of Hellenization, which had found enthusiastic supporters within the nation, most notably among the Tobiads but in some cases also within the wing of the Zadokite priesthood out of which arose the Sadducean party. The Hellenizing movement itself was unable to capture the soul of the Jewish people, a soul that had nurtured a vision of what it meant to be a people of God into a form too precious and clear to abandon in favor of the world culture sweeping over the other nations. This assessment is not to deny, however, that the spirit of Hellas made its contributions to Jewish thought, albeit a rather indirect one. For the encounter with Hellenism forced the Jews to think through many of their teachings in a new light, and not infrequently, the resulting reformulations reflect many of the concepts and themes of the rival.

A second contribution of Hellenism is even more important for this study. This contribution was the effect its challenge had on inducing the various streams of tradition within Judaism to clarify their positions, this time vis-à-vis a very formidable opponent. The result was that the second century B.C.E. witnessed the birth of important rival parties, each seeking to preserve what it believed to be the essential qualities of the Jewish heritage within the new environment. As already noted, the parties defining their identity solely on the basis of their pro-Hellenistic posture made little lasting contribution to the development of community notions within Judaism. We turn now, therefore, to evaluate the groups that adopted a course opposed to the encroachments of the mighty Hellenic world culture, for among them the Jewish heritage continued to supply a sense of the uniqueness of their way of life.

The Hasmoneans rose to power as warriors filled with God's spirit and dedicated to the eradication of every vestige of the cult of Zeus Olympius and the anti-Jewish customs connected with it. As success followed success, they began to model their objectives after the glorious kingdom of David and Solomon. It is therefore not surprising to notice some of the snares that threatened to dilute the Yahwistic qualities of the latter re-emerging to plague the Hasmoneans. There is no reason to doubt that zeal for the Torah and commitment, much in the style of the early judges of Israel, motivated Mattathias and Judas Maccabeus, and that it was out of recognition of and in response to these qualities that the ḥăsîdîm rallied to their support in the early stages of the Maccabean Revolt. But when we come to the reigns of the full priest-kings of the Hasmonean Kingdom, such as John Hyrcanus I and Alexander Jannaeus, we encounter rulers after the example of the typical Hellenistic potentate. What accounts for this change?

At the outset, and out of fairness, we must acknowledge one undeniable accomplishment of the Hasmoneans: without their military successes and organizational accomplishments, the Jewish people might have disappeared as a separate religious and cultural entity. Once this has been said, however, we must account for the fact that in their dealings with the Romans as in their treatment of the religious parties in their own land, they seemed to be guided by a policy of self-interest indistinguishable from the tyrant kings of other lands. With few exceptions, the Hasmoneans, from the time of Simon I on, acted in a manner ill fitting to guardians of the classical qualities of Yahwism. One searches in vain for evidence that their ultimate allegiance was to the divine Deliverer and Protector of the vulnerable, the impoverished and the oppressed. And consequently, the norm informing their policy decisions seemed to be self-generated, rather than inferred from the classical image of God as righteous, compassionate deliverer. The result was a very partisan definition of righteousness, and a severely limited notion of compassion. But little more could be expected of a royal and priestly house that maintained its control by ruthlessly repressing all opposition, defined the strength of the Jewish people according to the canons of worldly power, and willingly compromised traditional values and practices on behalf of a worldly pragmatism.

It is no accident that the traditional supporters of the Hasmoneans, except during the reign of Salome Alexandra, were the Sadducees, for like the Hasmoneans, they seemed to be guided by economic and political objectives more sensitive to world markets and powers than to traditional religious values. Through the agency of the Hasmoneans and the Sadducees, the religious tradition was therefore handed down as a torso, convenient as a sign of religious piety and placing no obstacles in the way of the opportunities presented by alliances with the Romans or any other power.

The Hasmoneans and the Sadducees prided themselves on noble family histories. But to the eyes of their more pious contemporaries and to the eyes of critical historians, they presented themselves as the victims of their own self-serving objectives. Neither figures significantly in the ongoing history of the notion of community in Israel, for they both failed to live beyond the deaths of the earthly structures with which they had become entangled.

Was any group within this period capable of preserving and expanding on the dynamic Yahwistic notion of community that had managed to survive so many other threats and crises? Clearly, such a group could be constituted only by those who above all clung to the cardinal principle of biblical faith, namely, worship of no God besides the God of Abraham, Isaac, and Jacob, the God who delivered Hebrew slaves from their house of bondage and thereby set forth an example of righteous compassion for the called people to follow. The focus comes to rest on the Essenes and the Pharisees, the two groups stemming from the Hasidean movement, a movement representing from its inception repudiation of all those worldly entanglements that lured the hearts of the people toward gods other than Yahweh.

For both the Essenes and the Pharisees, the basis for the repudiation of such entanglements was found in the life of unswerving obedience to the Torah. Righteousness, as the God-given norm that guides the obedient one in every decision and action, thus was preserved with force in both parties. And in both, worship was upheld as the activity constituting the heart of true community, as is clearly illustrated by both the Community Rule of Qumran and the writing into which was later gathered the formative thoughts of the early Pharisaic masters, the Mishnah.

Nevertheless, when contrasting the writings of the Pharisees with the writings that are the most complete example of Essene thought, the Dead Sea Scrolls of Qumran, one is struck by the vast differences in tone separating the two. The contrast seems to contradict the wide-ranging theological similarities alluded to in the previous paragraph. The rabbinical writings show a basically world-tolerating spirit, moderate in its style of relating to earthly structures and powers. In the Qumran writings, one finds a harsh vindictiveness, a hatred of the world, and a fanatic dedication to a vision of the world's destruction. What accounts for the difference?

The single most decisive factor seems to be the definition of authority found in the two parties. In the case of Qumran, there is one authority, the Teacher of Righteousness, whose gift of interpretation outstrips that of the prophets (1 QpHab vi,2–3). To him alone God granted the key that unlocks the hidden meaning of Scripture! The Teacher of Righteousness, as we have seen, organized his community after being overcome and banished by his opponents, the new Jerusalem priests of the Hasmonean line. All Scripture comes to be interpreted through the lens of that conflict. God's activity is narrowed down to God's plan to defeat the "Wicked Priest" and his apostate people. God's election is limited to the Teacher and his small circle of followers. All creation and all history is fit into the rigid, dualistic apocalyptic vision of this victimized priest. Worship, though central to his community's life, becomes a part of the preparation for the final war in which God is expected to join with the small wilderness community in destroying all other humans, Jews and Gentiles alike. Righteousness, though again picking up on a central theme of the classic Yahwistic notion of community, becomes a quality possessed singularly by those initiated into the Qumran congregation, leading to an exclusivism unprecedented in Jewish cult history. Similarly, compassion is narrowed down by the exclusive sectarianism of Qumran. God's mercy is not forgotten; indeed, in relation to the members of the community itself, God's mercy reaches out at the time of deepest need, to deliver.[33] But

---

33. For example, see 1 QS xi, 11–12.

in relation to those outside the community of the elect, compassion, defined by early Yahwism as the embrace of the oppressed, the weak, and the impoverished after the example of the Deliverer God, flees before a new concept, that of "perfect hatred," a distinguishing mark of these "men of holiness."

In the earlier discussion of the conflicts that tore into the fabric of the Jewish community in the postexilic period, I observed the effects of the resulting disharmony of spirit on that community's attitude toward the other nations: bitter hatred of fellow Jews produced an inner chaos that grew to engulf the whole world, resulting in the most vitriolic oracles of judgment against the nations found in Hebrew Scripture. The Qumran writings seem to be the product of the same bitterness of soul. This is not to place sole blame on the desert exiles. But it does illustrate how delicate a balance is represented by the triad of worship, righteousness, and compassion that characterizes the classical Yahwistic notion of community. Where the experience of intracommunal šālôm enables the community of faith to discern the creative, redemptive activity of God in all parts of the earth, its vision of restoration expands until it embraces all nations. As a negative counterpart, Qumran serves as a shocking illustration of the effects of intracommunal conflict, bearing the bitter fruits of deep pessimism, strict determinism, and a rigid, authoritarian, communal structure. Life is ordered not in service of God's world and God's people, but in preparation for a battle devoted to the destruction both of the world and of its inhabitants, a destruction seen as the only means of inaugurating the blessed era.

In contrasting this narrow and vindictive definition of the people of God at Qumran with the thought of the stricter representatives of the Pharisees, there is no denying that an attitude of exclusivism plays a role in the writings of the latter as well. This attitude is inextricably related to their undivided acknowledgement of the Torah as the perfect and complete revelation of God's will for God's people. Only by living in obedience to that divine order could the Jew hope to enjoy the blessings of a rich and harmonious life. Since obedience to the laws of purity necessitated separation from all that defiled, the strict Pharisees were careful to avoid contact with all that was ritually unclean, such as certain foods, people with specific diseases, or quite generally, sinners; that is, those not living in obedience to the Torah. For the same reason they felt obliged to remove, as a threat to the community, any member who was guilty of transgressing the Torah.

Having recognized this, however, it becomes important to specify just how this notion of exclusivism functioned in contrast to what we observed in the Qumran writings. Again, the concept of authority as it relates to the interpretation of Scripture provides the key. In Pharisaism, interpretation involved a process far more dialectical and subtle than the rigid, authoritarian dogmatism of the Qumran pêšer method.

While the Torah was the perfect expression of God's will, its application to the changing circumstances of life was worked out through a lively hermeneutical process, in which divergent opinions frequently emerged. The resulting problems of interpretation were not resolved by appeal to a single human authority, but by recording the debates themselves and allowing them to guide further debate in subsequent generations. This process reflects important underlying attitudes.

First, it is clear that the ongoing historical experience of the community was viewed as more than a passage out of a dying world into the heavenly realm. Life's experiences were valued as a source of insight into the Torah, and hence provided narrative material for illustrating the meaning of specific statutes and commandments. This attitude, while distinct from the worldly pragmatism of the Hasmoneans and the Sadducees, stands also in marked contrast to the rigid apocalyptic schema through which the Teacher of Righteousness and his followers viewed historical events and related Scripture to these events.

Second, the Pharisees' attitude toward other creatures betrays nothing of the Qumranian cosmic death-wish. True, the household of faith was to be protected conscientiously from the profane world through meticulous observance of the ritual laws. Yet this did not produce the deep-seated pessimism, rigid predestinationism or severe hatred of the world found in the Qumran writings. The Jews removed from fellowship (*niddûi*) for reasons of deviating from halakic decisions, could repent and be received back into full participation in the community. That is to say, the action was disciplinary and educational, not eschatological and deterministic in the manner of Qumran, where the corresponding punishment was designated "exclusion from the pure meal of the Congregation," that is, from the daily common meal eaten as anticipation of, and in a proleptic sense, as participation in the messianic banquet (1 QS vi, 25). The fact that membership in the Pharisaic party was not interpreted as an eschatological category stemming from a rigid apocalyptic dualism and predestinationism also meant that the lines between Pharisees and other Jews, and even between Pharisees and non-Jews, was not as unyielding as at Qumran. Nonmembers could join the party, if they accepted the interpretation of the Torah, and converts from among the Gentiles were not uncommon.

In contrasting Pharisees and Qumranians, it is readily apparent that the concrete effects resulting from such disparity in attitudes toward the world, toward nonmembers, and toward authority were immense. On the one hand, we find a desert community structuring all aspects of its communal life, from eating to study to worship, in anticipation of an imminent battle in which it, in the company of God and the angelic hosts, would destroy all flesh in preparation for its own life of endless bliss. On the other hand, we find a community developing a style of life within gatherings of the faithful scattered among the cities and villages of the Roman empire. It was a life style of holiness through obedience to the Torah dedicated to preserving a witness to God's perfect order in a world dominated by wickedness and apostasy, a world they regarded as not likely to end soon.

The subsequent histories of these two communities were as different as their attitudes toward the world around them. In the case of Qumran, history had an abrupt ending, but not the one anticipated by its members. At first events ran true to the mythic scenario: the Kittim (Romans) attacked, and the holy warriors, after hiding their secret writings in caves, no doubt went out to meet them, equipped with the assurance that God and the heavenly hosts would join them in the mighty slaughter. But from that point something went wrong. The divine intervention did not occur, and those living lives of preparation for war were swept off the pages of history by war, leaving for posterity a pitiable story of misspent zeal, of violence sown and violence reaped.

In the case of the Pharisees, history went on and on, quite as expected. And the *modus vivendi* worked out by the leading early sages equipped them well for living through future ages by combining fidelity to the Torah with a willingness to learn from the ongoing lessons of history, and by providing sanctity for the strictly observant among them within the table fellowship of the ḥăbûrâ, an important refuge for those obliged to conduct their day-to-day affairs amid the profane realities of this world.

When we evaluate rabbinic Judaism in relation to the long history of the Yahwistic notion of community, we accordingly come to results vastly different from those emerging from our examination of the Qumran writings. We see a notion centering on worship of the one true God, the God of Abraham, Isaac, and Jacob, deriving its example from the God who delivered Hebrew slaves from their bondage, and ordering life through a lively, ongoing process of interpreting the Torah. The vitality with which this community was able to face the future is illustrated by the response of its leaders to the very catastrophe that wiped the Qumran community from the face of the earth. To the destruction of the temple in 70 C.E., they reacted neither in capitulation nor in suicidal resistance. Their focus on the eternal Torah and its perfect order, which they incorporated into their communities of worship, study, and fellowship, enabled them to live on as members of that order even without the temple. In fact, the vitality of which we speak is manifested by more than accepting the catastrophe, for as we have seen, it apparently became the occasion for a bold new definition of temple, altar, priest, and sacrifice. In the new era, home and hearth were to be the temple, the dinner table the altar, the householder the priest, and the act of loving-kindness the atoning sacrifice. This community was thus capable of summarizing the heart of the law in the commandments to love God and fellow humans, and to derive from that heart the example of a life of righteousness and compassion. There can be no question that Pharisaic Judaism both inherited and refined essential qualities of the classical Yahwistic notion of community.

That certain dimensions and facets that had developed in the long history of growth of the biblical notion of community, however, were not fully incorporated in the communal ideals of the Pharisees will come as no surprise to anyone aware of the rich diversity characteristic of biblical expressions of community, not to mention to the one appreciative of the complexity of the theological task of defining what it means to be "the people of God." Our study of the period from Ezra down to Hillel has shown that the Pharisaic movement represents the culmination of a particular stream of tradition, one placing great emphasis on God's gift of the eternal Torah as the most significant distinguishing mark of the Jewish people. But there were other traditional themes that received less attention among the Pharisees, especially those drawn from prophecy and developed during the postexilic period within circles fostering a more eschatological perspective than the one cultivated by Ezra, Sirach, and the Pharisees. Arising from such circles as a part of their eschatological outlook was commonly a critique of the ideology of their more established fellow Jews. To their perception, the cultic institutions and social structures for which their opponents were claiming a perfection originating in divine revelation were flawed with human error and even ritual defilement. As for divine disclosure of God's perfect order, it was their claim that God's decisive intervention to establish a religious order lay not in the past, but in the future, and that they were the privileged recipients of a vision of that denouement. Rather than deriving a pattern of life and institutional structures solely from a model era of the distant past (such as the Mosaic or Davidic eras), such circles patterned their communal structures largely on the basis of their vision of the perfect kingdom that was to come. Hence communal forms and cultic rites, while not uninfluenced by tradition, were more anticipatory in nature than imitative. And relations to current religious leaders and existing cultic institutions were usually characterized by a harsh critique based on the vision of God's decisive future act.

This contrast, as we have drawn it, has been oversimplified for heuristic purposes. In reality, most Jewish circles of that time embodied aspects of both the imitative and the anticipatory. For example, many Pharisees did entertain messianic ideas, and the Qumranians did imitate what they took to be the communal structures and practices of the Mosaic period. But this does not deny the importance of recognizing the relative weight generally ascribed to these aspects in the different parties. It seems quite clear that most Pharisees tended to eschew apocalyptic speculation in favor of living in harmony with the eternal Torah given by God to Israel on Sinai, whereas the adherents of the

Qumran commune ordered their relations with nonmembers, ate their meals, and planned their military strategies, all on the basis of their end-time visions.

This contrast between Essenes and Pharisees (a contrast that becomes even more pronounced when the Sadducees are included in the comparison) gives expression to the recurrent polarization between visionary and pragmatic dimensions of religious experience we have recognized during earlier periods as well (e.g., reflected in the prophetic "reform" emphasis via-à-vis the emphasis of the kings on "form"). And once again, true to the social coordinates typical of this type of polarization, the Essenes, with their focus on a vision of end-time reversal, were constituted by elements alienated from existing institutions and conventions, whereas the Sadducees represented the party with the greatest investment in existing social, political, and economic structures. As for the Pharisees, while dedicated to a spiritual order co-opted by no earthly system, they had worked out a style of living true to the order that at the same time encouraged toleration of the existing earthly powers.

This sketch of the diverse ways in which these three parties within Judaism sought to translate the biblical heritage into the realities of the Pax Romana is essential as background to any attempt to take the next step, namely, that of studying how the biblical notion of community was further developed within the early Christian movement. What is too often ignored is that all such attempts that overlook the roots of early Christianity in the Jewish tradition are doomed to failure.

Since Jewish tradition presented itself to the early followers of Jesus not as a unified tradition, but as one characterized by widely divergent interpretations, it offered not only rich resources for those seeking to understand the meaning of Jesus' life and teaching, but profound questions as well. Was Jesus' message to be interpreted as a summons out of this world into an otherworldly apocalyptic vision, in the manner of the Essenes? Was it to be regarded as an exposition of Torah in the tradition of the scribes of the Pharisees, thus calling for obedience within a community living in, and yet carefully holding itself separate from the "sinners" of this world? Was it to be translated into a political program designed to confront Rome with the power of the Davidic kingdom, now represented by the messianic figure Jesus? Or did Jesus' message point in some other direction, not yet explored by the existing groups within the Jewish community? Although the first half of the first century C.E. was a time of relative political stability within the Roman empire in general, the problem of defining what it meant to be a people of God continued to be a very difficult one for a people claiming a special place in God's plan for the world and yet living under the powerful hand of the Romans. Under the surface of apparent calm, therefore, was to be found a deep yearning for a Messiah who would throw off the

Roman yoke and restore the freedom and dignity of the Jewish people. But in relation to this yearning, there were as well deep divisions as to when and how this redemption would come, and considerable confusion regarding the religious, social, and political posture called for in such an ambiguous situation. Basically, therefore, it was a period of profound social and spiritual crisis, adumbrating the tragic events of the next eighty years.

We have come now to an important juncture in this study of the notion of community as it developed over the course of biblical history. From this point on, further development occurred along two distinct trajectories. On the one hand, the Pharisees—with the "moderate" Hillelites gaining ascendancy over the "stricter" Shammaites—emerged by the time of the convening of the academy at Jabneh under the leadership of Johanan ben Zakkai as the normative party within Judaism. Within the following century, the great rabbis of the Pharisees would codify their interpretation of the Torah, culminating in the Mishnah. During this same period of time, Christianity would develop from its beginnings as a Jewish sect devoted to the teachings of Messiah Jesus into a predominantly Gentile movement with congregations scattered throughout the Mediterranean lands. Although it would be of great profit to follow both trajectories into this formative period, I focus in the remainder of this study on the birth of Christianity, making reference to the Pharisees and Essenes where necessary for purposes of contrast and clarification. But as I thus continue with this specific objective, I shall keep clearly in mind the questions and options, mentioned earlier, that were posed by the Sadducees, Pharisees, Essenes, and Zealots. These questions point to unresolved issues with which the youngest of the Jewish sects would be obliged to struggle as it sought to interpret, in light of its Hebrew Scriptures, the event it perceived to represent God's newest saving act on behalf of humans, and from that interpretation, to determine the notion of community that was to guide its corporate life.

XIII

Community in the Teaching of Jesus
(Matthew, Mark, and Luke)

Then came, at a predetermined moment, a moment
  in time and of time,
A moment not out of time, but in time, in what
  we call history: transecting, bisecting
  the world of time, a moment in time but
  not like a moment of time,
A moment in time but time was made through
  that moment: for without the meaning
  there is no time, and that moment of time
  gave the meaning.[1]

Historical Note: Jesus of Nazareth carried on his ministry in
the third decade of the Common Era, that is, during the
reign of Tiberius (14–37 C.E.) and the procuratorship of Pontius Pilatus (26–36 C.E.). Although this was a time of international stability under the hegemony of the Romans, locally
there was considerable unrest and division within the Jewish
populace. Activists such as the Zealots were engaged in strata-
gems aimed at fomenting revolution against the Romans.
The Sadducees were committed to maintaining good relations with the Romans as a means of protecting their own
economic, political, and theological interests. The eschatological themes intertwined in Pharisaic teaching drew some
of the Pharisees into messianic speculations and even into
messianic movements at times. In general, however, the
Pharisees were primarily concerned to preserve their right to
pursue a life of fidelity to the Torah, which they did within
the cities and villages of the land. In contrast, the Essenes cultivated their eschatological visions in places apart from the
main centers of population. Within the context of these diverse streams of tradition, Jesus went about teaching a message with many themes in common with both the Pharisees
and Essenes, and yet in important respects distinct. The problem of identifying even the general lines of that teaching

---

1. From T. S. Eliot, "Choruses from 'The Rock,'" *The Complete Poems and Plays, 1909–
1950* (New York: Harcourt, Brace, 1952), p. 109.

within writings produced considerably later is a most difficult one. Nevertheless, a study dedicated to shedding light on the lines of continuity extending from the Hebrew Bible and early Judaism on into Christianity cannot bypass the question of the impact Jesus had on the way the early Christians reflected on the nature of true community. Although Jesus himself did not establish the early church, there is no denying that his life and teaching had a decisive impact on the thinking of those who gradually began to define the character of a Jewish community centered around the confession that Jesus of Nazareth was the Christ—that is, the Messiah sent by God to redeem the world. We turn now to the attempt to uncover in the gospels of Matthew, Mark, and Luke the major themes bearing on community that, with a reasonable degree of confidence, can be traced to Jesus.

A. CONTINUITY AND CHANGE

Two major religious communities stem from the history we have traced thus far in our study. Modern Judaism is the child of Pharisaism, its canon of authoritative writings being the Hebrew Bible, the Mishnah, the Palestinian and Babylonian Talmuds, and the rabbinical biblical commentaries (Midrashim). Modern Christianity is the child of the movement arising from the life and teachings of Jesus of Nazareth. It is heir to a tradition that added to Hebrew Scripture the writings arising in the early years of the church, which eventually were canonized as the New Testament. One of the most fascinating challenges facing Jews and Christians in our own day is the clarification of the relationship between these two religious communities. What values, beliefs, and visions do they share? At what points do they differ? How can they best cooperate in working for peace and justice in our world? How can they move beyond the misunderstandings of the past to a new era of mutual respect and appreciation?

The bulk of this book has dealt primarily with the vast range of values, beliefs, and visions shared by both. But attention to divisions, especially the party divisions that developed during the Hellenistic and Roman periods, also has clarified some of the distinct teachings and practices that divide those of Jewish and Christian faith. Of course, such historical study also sheds light on divisions that continue to exist within the Jewish community, and differences that often divide one Christian group from another. Often too, it clarifies why individual Jews or Christians not infrequently find their convictions leading to a stronger sense of affinity with members of the other confession than with some members of their own.

Further light on this complex and fascinating set of questions derives from the study of the origins of the Christian community in the first two centuries of the Common Era. Although what we call the Christian Church developed in the period after the death of Jesus, the character of that community was so deeply imprinted by the life and teachings of the Galilean as to commend as a starting point a careful evaluation of what can be ascertained concerning Jesus' own notion of community.

According to the Gospel of Mark, Jesus' first public words were "The time is fulfilled, and the kingdom of God is at hand; repent, and believe in the gospel" (Mark 1:14). Modern biblical scholarship has established that this statement indeed captures the central theme in the preaching of Jesus. When the religious situation in Judah in the Roman period is recalled, it seems clear that such an announcement would have addressed the concerns of many in his Jewish audience. First of all, it was a theme with deep roots in their tradition, with prophets such as Isaiah and Ezekiel envisioning the day when Israel, delivered from the threats of all hostile neighbors, would live securely under God's reign. Especially among apocalyptic circles, like the one gathered on the shores of the Dead Sea at Qumran, this vision functioned at the center of life. But beyond such circles, this vision also stirred the hearts of men and women of all parties. Secondly, the humiliation of living under the subjugation of the Romans heightened the appeal of the promise that God would come to re-establish his reign over the Jewish people.

But to say that a broad cross section of the Jewish population would have been concerned with the contradiction between the promises found in their sacred writings and the circumstances within which they lived their lives is not to say that all agreed on how God's reign and their own freedom could come to fulfillment. The fact that Jesus did not lead his followers into conflict with the Roman occupation indicates that his views regarding the kingdom of God differed sharply from that of the Zealots. And although distinct lines of connection can be drawn between Jesus' teachings and those of the Qumranians, sharp differences are immediately apparent. One need only compare the Qumranian vision of the heavenly battle against all flesh that would usher in God's reign with Jesus' teaching that the kingdom was already present in the world where the sick were healed and those suffering from demon possession were released. Finally, in relation to the Pharisees, it is likely that the eschatological theme was far more fully developed and was treated with a greater sense of urgency by Jesus than by most Pharisees, though not necessarily all.

The eschatological vision coming to expression in Jesus' preaching illustrates the nature of the relationship between early Christianity and its parent community. The vision of the kingdom of God incorporates familiar themes of the past, but also develops them in new ways. In other words, it was a relationship characterized by both continuity and change. In this respect, it is harmonious with the pattern seen in all the paradigmatic events of the Bible. From the time of the exodus on, we have seen that the new was interpreted in light of the confessional heritage. Thus at every stage in the history of the biblical understanding of community, the emerging understanding arose as an intricate interweaving of the old and the new. Before turning to an examination of the life and teachings of Jesus himself, let us consider further this phenomenon of continuity and change as it is found in early Christianity, since it represents such a fundamental theological problem throughout the period of the early church.

Matthew, in what may well be a self-portrait, pictures the true interpreter of this dynamic process in this saying of Jesus "Therefore every scribe who has been trained for the kingdom of heaven is like a householder who brings out of his treasure what is new and what is old" (13:52). The advent of the Messiah was viewed by the disciples of Jesus as an astonishing new act of God, and they responded with an enthusiasm born of a fervent sense of God's nearness. Yet the nature of Jesus and the significance of his message and life were worked out by constant reference to ancient Scripture, as the fullness of quotations from Hebrew Scripture (in its Greek version) in the New Testament indicates. Although viewed as a fresh chapter in God's saving approach to humans, it was one growing organically out of the long antecedent history recorded in the Torah and the Prophets.

Similarly with reference to the Hellenistic-Roman world within which early Christianity took shape, recognition of the deep biblical roots of the Jesus movement does not deny the contributions of that new world, with its broad horizons, rich philosophical traditions, and deep esthetic and religious sensitivities. It is simply to recognize that we are dealing with a notion of community that took shape in continuity with a deeply grounded Jewish confessional heritage, within which new borrowings from the various world cultures always involved assimilation to a dynamic, theocentric view of reality with a carefully defined sense of its own center and ultimate loyalty.

That Jesus and the earliest disciples viewed the events they were experiencing as developing in an unbroken continuity out of their Jewish religious history can be illustrated in many different ways. First, themes that formed the heart of Jesus' teaching, such as the twin commandment to love God and neighbor as well as the petitions of the Lord's Prayer, flow out of his ancestral faith and are paralleled by traditional Jewish prayers and sayings attributed to rabbis from the same period.[2] Second, Jesus understood it to be his calling to proclaim the kingdom to the Jews (Matt. 15:24; 9:35–38), a mission that was continued by the twelve apostles (Matt. 10:5–23), whose very number recalled the twelve tribes of Israel.[3] This was very much in keeping with the expectation

2. Compare, for example, the traditional Jewish prayers *Amidah* and *Kaddish*.
3. See also Galatians 2:7–10 and the Book of Acts.

widely held within Judaism that the Messiah would gather together the Jews who were dispersed throughout many lands,[4] and may have been one of the "signs" taken by some as indicating that he was the Messiah. Third, even Paul, the "apostle to the Gentiles," devoted much attention to his collection for the "remnant, chosen by grace"(Rom. 11:5), the congregation in Jerusalem (Gal. 2:10; 1 Cor. 16:1–4; 2 Cor. 8:1–9:15; Rom. 9:4; 15:24). And when Paul defended his mission to the Gentiles, he did not do so as the advocate of a new religion, but by proclaiming that through faith in God's redemptive act in Jesus converts from the Gentiles became "Abraham's offspring" (Gal. 3:20). Fourth, the Book of Acts reports how the disciples visited the temple in Jerusalem (2:46; 3:1, 11), a report joined by later tradition portraying James as one who continued to be a supporter of the temple cultus. Fifth, Matthew, who begins his account of Jesus' life with a genealogy depicting Jesus as son of Abraham and son of David, and thus heir to the two unconditional promises of Hebrew Scripture, goes on to portray the early history of Jesus as a recapitulation of the exodus and settlement events, and then presents him as the new Moses delivering God's new Torah on the mountain.

This list of examples of continuity between the old and the new could be expanded, but the preceding suffices to indicate that Jesus and the early disciples interpreted the events of their time as guided by the same divine purpose revealed throughout Scripture. In light of this analysis, we must realize that the wide diversity of traditions and interpretations in the Bible, the fragmentation into different parties that characterized the history of Israel, and even the eventual separation into two religious communities do not belie this unity of purpose, but rather stand as constant reminders of the partiality and fallibility of the responding human community. One of the most exciting challenges of biblical theology is to discern beneath such disparity and diversity their common grounding in the one true God, whose purpose throughout time is one.

From this challenge, it follows that a special attitude will characterize the Christian tracing his or her spiritual roots back to the faith of Israel, an attitude of deep gratitude and profound rejoicing over the riches entrusted by God to God's first people (Rom 9:4–5). And that attitude is not confined to an antiquarian interest, but characterizes our relationship to religious Jews today, who continue to serve as witnesses to God's choice of a special people "as a light to the nations, that my salvation may reach to the end of the earth" (Isa. 49:6). This attitude prepares us, moreover, to understand the position of the New Testament writers, who do not deny that Israel had been elected to live in a unique

---

4. For example, in *Song of Songs Rabbah* 2:7 we find this comment: "For what reason is the Messiah to come? To gather the scattered of Israel."

relationship with God, but who build on that election in announcing that through Jesus, the Jew from Nazareth, that unique relationship had been made available by a gracious God to all people, regardless of race or background. Of course, as in the case of earlier divine initiatives experienced by previous biblical communities, Christians believe new depths of understanding into the meaning of being a people of God were opened up through the Christ event. That is why, as we trace the development of the biblical notion of community on into the New Testament, we will do well to follow the style of the Matthean "scribe who has been trained for the kingdom of heaven," the one who like a householder "brings out of his treasure what is new and what is old" (Matt. 13:52).

The nature of the confluence of old and new occurring at this juncture in history is implied by the words of Jesus placed by Mark as the introduction to his ministry: "The time is fulfilled." Paul incorporates the same theme in his letter to the Galatians, "But when the time had fully come [KJV: But when the fulness of time was come], God sent forth his Son, born of woman, born under the law, to redeem those who were under the law, so that we might receive adoption as sons" (Gal. 4:4). Obviously the concept the "fulfillment" or "fulness" of time bears directly on the phenomenon of the confluence of old and new in early Christianity. What does it mean? Wherein lay the special significance of this particular time?

Paul's letters aid us in answering this question, and indeed, they suggest both positive and negative dimensions to the concept. In a positive sense, Paul was aware of the history of redemptive acts that had prepared the remnant of the faithful to hear and respond to God's new word. God's promises to the patriarchs, God's deliverance of Hebrew slaves from Egypt, God's giving of the Torah on Sinai, God's guidance through the wilderness, and much more are recalled by Paul in his letters. But Paul also points to a negative dimension to the concept. He argues that the holy law had been perverted by sinful humans to ends never divinely intended (Rom. 7:7–12). Indeed, Paul gives expression to an anthropology reminiscent of Jeremiah 17:9 when he cries out, "Wretched man that I am! Who will deliver me from this body of death?" (Rom. 7:24). All in all, one could say that from the Pauline perspective, the redemptive history beginning with promises to Israel's ancestors and guided by God's gracious providence had been disrupted by a history of sin and perversion of what God had given. The "fulness of time" was thus a time caught between God's promise and human sin.

For a religiously sensitive Jew such as Paul, this clash between God's faithfulness to ancient promises and the faithless response of humans placed the human race before a life-or-death decision. In this connection, he differed with many of his former co-religionists among the Pharisees on an important point, namely, in his assessment of the possibility of experiencing reconciliation with God within the framework of their interpretation of the Torah. For Paul, the religious significance of the moment lay not in the sense of purity accompanying careful obedience of the law, but in a sense of brokenness arising out of the contradiction between the law's holiness and the human perversion of the law's divine intent. And it was the human experience of brokenness that was seized by God as the opportunity for addressing the human family in a new way. For Paul, the gospel message was that in Christ God had responded to humans in their brokenness, and the result was a new community of the faithful based not on human resourcefulness, but on "the righteousness of God through faith in Jesus Christ for all who believe" (Rom. 3:21).

In a deep theological sense, the openness to God's new initiative that characterized the early disciples was not a new phenomenon, but arose as a rediscovery of the primal moment found in all the paradigms of Yahwistic faith, as experienced, for example, by Hebrew slaves in Egypt, Jewish exiles in Babylon, and Torah-faithful ḥăsîdîm in the face of persecution inflicted both by the Seleucids and their own leaders. What all these groups shared was that awesome moment of discovering that human resources are ultimately useless as regards deliverance and salvation. From the eschatological perspective that Paul shared with prophets such as Isaiah and Jeremiah, this moment was of highest religious significance when held together with a memory of God's promises, for human brokenness was to divine wisdom the opportunity for a new initiative to break through sinful pride to the human heart. For the repentant, this fact represented an invitation to turn to the gracious God as the only hope for deliverance. Since to this moment of human brokenness, Paul believed that God had replied with his son Jesus, he was able to conclude that this particular confluence of divine promise and human sin constituted the "fulness of time," the climactic point in the history of God's relationship with humans, a moment of unprecedented grace recalling God's creation of the first Adam. Through Jesus, God was inviting humans to the fulfillment of Israel's long history of promise.

There is thus a distinctly archaizing or primal quality in Paul's interpretation of the Christ event. In contrast, the Pharisees are portrayed in the New Testament as guardians of an established and carefully defined religious system. Although shaped by early polemic into something of a caricature, the New Testament reflects the actual position of the Pharisees as a party committed to preserving the received Mosaic tradition. In his argument for a sense of identity based on God's new initiative in Christ, Paul repeatedly goes behind the authorities enlisted by the Pharisees; for example, behind Moses to Abraham, and behind the law to the promise. Paul's archaizing, of course, was actually designed to prove that something radically new had occurred, a new age had dawned, the age of the new Adam. What becomes clear in this process of drawing on the archaic to establish the radically new is this: the early Christian writers distanced themselves from the tradition reaching back to Sirach, Ezra, and Nehemiah, the tradition based on a concept of the Torah as an eternal order given by God to Israel in conformity to which the life of holiness was to be found. They believed that their perception of God's presence was more closely akin to their most ancient forebears such as Abraham and the descendants of Jacob in Egypt. That is to say, they believed that in Jesus, God had re-entered history to deliver a lost people from their bondage.

Accompanying that new initiative was a new outburst of prophetic activity. This is characteristic of a movement construing its role less in terms of received traditions than in terms of responding to what was perceived as a fresh divine initiative. The situation was typical of the early charismatic stage of a religious movement in its tendency to foster the development of new confessional formulas and even new communal structures. It is thus not surprising that in some respects the confessional and communal patterns emerging from early Christianity find close analogies in early Yahwism.

It does not follow from this that developments within Judaism in the period between Ezra and Hillel are irrelevant for a proper understanding of earliest Christianity. Although interpreting the events of their time as manifesting God's saving entry into history in a manner recalling the time of the patriarchs or the exodus, the followers of Jesus used traditions and concepts that were in large part the legacy of postexilic Judaism. In this study, therefore, it is important to keep clearly in mind the particular setting of the early Jesus movement—namely, a religious community divided in its perception of how fulfillment would occur, a division represented by the separate paths being followed by the Sadducees, Pharisees, and Essenes. Too frequently Christianity is viewed either as a timeless phenomenon unrelated to its socioreligious environment, or as the culmination of a prophetic tradition last represented by Second Isaiah, and somehow "springing over" 550 years of Jewish history.[5] In either case major aspects of early Christianity are misunderstood, aspects that address precisely the world of beliefs, hopes, and fears coming to expression in the teachings of the Sadducees, Pharisees, and Essenes. Indeed, only by grasping the tensions characterizing the interrelationships between those three parties can one understand the fundamental tensions addressed by and lying at the heart of the Jewish messianic movement within which distinctively Christian reflections on the nature of community began to develop.

---

5. See J. Blenkinsopp's accurate description of this common approach to the study of the Old Testament in "Tanakh and the New Testament: A Christian Perspective," L. Boadt, H. Croner, and L. Klenicki, eds., *Biblical Studies: Meeting Ground of Jews and Christians* (New York: Paulist Press, 1980), pp. 96-119.

It will be important to keep in mind that the Jewish community at that time was one torn by the tension between an ancient vision of a kingdom of šālôm and the contradictory realities of a world dominated by a powerful pagan empire. Over much of the Second Temple period, the leaders of the Jewish community tended to cope with the repeated disappointments and dashed hopes by accommodating that ancient vision to the existing realities. The purest expression of this tendency in Jesus' time remained the Sadducean party, as it continued to hold a very conservative view of Scripture that allowed its members in the political and economic spheres to carry on their affairs unencumbered by religious or moral restraints. The eschatological elements of Jewish tradition speaking of an end of the present order and the advent of the messianic kingdom were repudiated by the Sadducees on the basis of their limited canon and conservative hermeneutic. Similarly, though cultivating an oral tradition of their own, they refused to ascribe to it the degree of authoritativeness that led the Pharisees to speak of two Torahs, with the result that they were not nearly as radical as the Pharisees in applying the norms of the Torah to all areas of life.

At the opposite extreme, it is evident that the Essenes continued to emphasize the radical disjunction between a world fallen to sin and the world intended by God, a disjunction they resolved by centering their faith on a future divine intervention in which this world would be destroyed in preparation for the New Creation. Community life for the Essenes thus was otherworldly in orientation. In eschewing every connection with a world doomed to annihilation, refuge was found in a "monastic" existence far apart from city and village life. In their refusal to accommodate their vision to worldly realities, the Essenes were able to maintain the universal scope of the restoration vision of late prophecy and early apocalyptic, but in a rigidly vindictive form focusing on the destruction of all flesh, with the resulting loss of the theme of God's salvation extending to all nations.

Radical political activists such as the Zealots and the *sicarii* shared with the Essenes the sense of disjuncture between this world and the world to come, but differed with them in their attitude toward the imperative that the end-time vision placed on the faithful here and now. While the Essenes tended to await the arrival of the messiah and the heavenly hosts, the radical activist groups sought through their contemporary actions to defeat the Romans and their allies. Especially at times of political unrest, this radical position also found supporters among the Pharisees.

In general, however, the mainstream of the Pharisaic party continued to live true to its middle way. In substance, its teachings were much closer to those of the Essenes than to those of the Sadducees. The order to which the Pharisees committed their life energies was not of this world, and their prayers gave expression to eschatological hopes for the manifestation of God's righteous reign before all peoples. But they differed from the Essenes in two respects: (1) as regards the implications they drew from the disjuncture between God's order and the order of this world for the form of their communal life, and (2) as regards the degree to which eschatology determined the mode of their daily existence. By expecting of this world's powers no more than that the Pharisees be allowed to live true to their interpretation of the Torah, and by fulfilling their need for fellowship within their ḥăbûrôt, the Pharisees were able to live their lives in the cities and villages rather than in wilderness communes. And as the result of the tendency to downplay the eschatological themes of prophetic tradition, the apocalyptic enthusiasm that so deeply imprinted the teachings and lifestyle of the Essenes was less evident among the Pharisees, with notable exceptions such as Akiba and his disciples during the Bar Kochba period.

The Sadducees, Essenes, Zealots, and Pharisees are thus not mere supporting actors in the drama of early Christianity. They embody in differing degrees important aspects of the tradition that would also provide the lens through which the early disciples would seek to understand the happenings transpiring around them. And the tensions characterizing the interrelations between those parties would continue to affect the lives of the followers of Jesus.

In the ensuing process of community formation in early Christianity, the option of the Sadducees played little part. We already have seen that it was an alternative with little future in Judaism itself. It simply had strayed too far from the classical ancestral faith.

Far more central to the development of the early Christian notion of community were the traditions and customs of the Essenes and the Pharisees. Like the Pharisees, Jesus and his followers refused to resolve the tension between God's order and the order of this world by a retreat into monastic communes. They lived and carried on their teaching mission in the cities and villages of Galilee and Judah. But they differed with the Pharisees insofar as this lifestyle was not maintained through downplaying the eschatological aspects of prophetic and apocalyptic tradition. Indeed, the themes of the great day of judgment and the coming of God's universal reign, themes that formed the heart of Jesus' message and the early kerygma that build on it, call to mind similar themes in the literature of Qumran and in such writings as Daniel and 1 Enoch.

Given this high eschatology, how did the disciples of Jesus maintain their connections with the social and political structures of their world? The answer is tied to the particular form of eschatology that developed within primitive Christianity. Key to this form were the twin confessions that the Messiah was not being awaited as in the case of Qumran, but had arrived, and that the long-awaited Kingdom had already begun to unfold in the very midst of this world. According to this eschatology, the resurrection of the Messiah Jesus from the dead was the most vivid sign of the Kingdom's presence. Whereas the Essenes lived in *anticipation* of that point in time, the disciples of Jesus confessed that they were *experiencing* it. The battle with the forces of chaos was not a future event, but one already in progress. More than that, the tide of battle had already turned, with Jesus' resurrection viewed as a sign that the forces of chaos were in retreat. This difference is seen even in the case of the Gospel of John, the gospel in many respects closest to the sectarian writings of Qumran: The battle between the sons of light and the sons of darkness is not consigned to the future, but is described as a present event in which light is already triumphant over darkness, and in which humans, far from being locked into the rigid predestinationism of Qumran, are called to act out their God-given freedom in rallying behind the victor, Jesus Christ.

Although sharing important elements of biblical faith with both the Essenes and the Pharisees, the specific character of the eschatological faith of early Christianity was distinct in the manner in which it addressed the fundamental issues and tensions of its religious environment. And this distinctness was reflected in the type of community that arose among those confessing the arrival of the messiah and the messianic kingdom. In the place of the withdrawal and esotericism that accompanied the eschatology of Qumran, Jesus and the disciples proclaimed their message openly in city, village, and countryside, and invited all to welcome the Kingdom, and to live in harmony with this new reality. This openness of style, found already in Jesus' preaching, found its natural extension in the world mission of the second and third generations of disciples.

All in all, while continuous with many of the traditional themes found also in the other Jewish groups, the Christian messianic movement, especially due to its belief that the Messiah and the Kingdom of God had already arrived, had a strong transforming effect on those traditional themes. A style of expressing the faith in the everyday lives of its members emerged that was distinct from that of either the Pharisees or the Essenes. For example, the inbreaking of the messianic kingdom was taken to imply that the message of salvation preserved by Israel was now to reach out to all peoples and all nations, which led to a redefinition of membership in the community of faith with stress on repentance rather than on closed fellowship emphasizing ancestry and safeguarded by laws of purity. This universal theme also led to a very different attitude toward the nonmember, whether Jew or Gentile. Whereas the Qumranians cultivated an attitude of "perfect hatred" vis-á-vis the outsider, Jesus admonished his followers to love their enemies. Whereas the Pharisees limited table fellowship to fellow members, Jesus ate with publicans and sinners. The overall effect of the eschatological dimension within the Jesus movement was thus a more thoroughgoing transformation of tradition than found in the teachings of either the Pharisees or the Essenes.

We might cite two further examples of this transformation, noting how it related to the major religious parties of that time. First, we have seen that the Essenes and the Pharisees both subjected tradition relating to the temple to reinterpretation, the former already in the two centuries before the Common Era, the latter after the destruction of 70 C.E. For the Essenes, the existing temple, defiled and under the control of an illegitimate priesthood, would be destroyed in the final assize. But essentially, the traditional theology of the temple remained unaltered, for they expected God to provide in the future a new temple, one in which they would officiate in splendor. Within Pharisaic circles, there arose new teachings regarding the form the sacrifice could take in an age deprived of a temple, but here too we witness an adjustment to new circumstances rather than a fundamental change in doctrine. In contrast to both, the spiritualization of attitudes toward the temple found in the New Testament goes further, and does involve a fundamental theological change. In the Gospel of John, Jesus says to the Samaritan, "Woman, believe me, the hour is coming when neither on this mountain nor in Jerusalem will you worship the Father. . . . For the hour is coming, and now is, when the true worshippers will worship the Father in spirit and truth, for such the Father seeks to worship him" (4:22, 24). A corresponding transformation forms the basis of the Book of Hebrews.

The second example relates to attitudes toward the Torah. In their transformation of the tradition, the Essenes actually heightened the legalism involved in obedience to the Torah. For their part, the leading teachers of the Pharisees continued a tradition of meticulously explicating the implications of the Torah for all aspects of life, especially in those gray areas where ambiguity existed. Although a high degree of diversity existed in early Christian circles, an attitude toward the Torah prevailed that radically changed the function of Torah in the lives of the faithful.

As we turn, therefore, to an examination of the origins and early development of the communal structures in the New Testament, we must tread carefully between the extremes of either accentuating the uniqueness of early Christianity to the point of overlooking important connections with its ancestral heritage, or emphasizing continuity to the point of obscuring important innovations. For example, the argument that the roots of Christianity lie in Old Testament prophecy, with the intervening five and a half centuries offering nothing of significance, greatly obscures many essential features of early Chrisitanity. Its refutation, however, must not blur a basic distinction: the nature of the response arising among Jesus' disciples to the events they were experiencing does differ in important respects from the response of either the Pharisees or the Essenes to the events of their time. In fact, their response resembles in important respects the pattern of response we described at the birth stage of Yahwism among those recalling their deliverance from Egyptian bondage. We have already observed that the background of the early Yahwistic response to God's saving initiatives was tied to a sense of brokenness and an awareness of the futility of all human plans for escape. Those for whom earthly realities offered no means of escape found their salvation in Yahweh. The response of praise and worship thus arose from the depths of their being. And from that primal experience of worship the development of structures of community (including the rules of life called Torah) were inferred, under the conviction that in the salvatory event God was present and God's nature was revealed. From that presence and nature, the community sought to extrapolate its forms of community and style of life in the world.

It is clear that the first disciples came to believe that in Jesus, God was acting in a new, decisive way. However, even as the early Hebrews did not interpret their experience of deliverance *tabula rasa*, but rather through the lens of their confessional heritage, so too the early disciples drew on their long, rich Jewish heritage in explicating the meaning of this new event. From that heritage, they derived the categories of "Messiah," "Kingdom of Heaven," "righteousness of God," and "nation of priests." But these rich concepts, symbols, and categories were transformed on the basis of their new encounter with God's righteousness and compassion, now manifested in the life of Jesus. Their response was thus at once traditional and primal, much in the manner of Second Isaiah who could first admonish his hearers to "remember the former things of old" (Isa. 46:9), and then encourage them to face the future with a daring openness: "Remember not the former things, nor consider the things of old. Behold, I am doing a new thing" (Isa. 43:18–19a). The former side of this dialectic again found expression in the early church's confession that God is faithful to God's universal purpose: ". . . till heaven and earth pass away, not an iota, not a dot, will pass from the law until all is accomplished" (Matt. 5:16). The other side of the dialectic was also preserved, namely, that the surprising newness of God's creativity can never be exhaustively captured in human formulations: "You have heard that it was said to men of old . . . , but I say to you" (Matt. 5:21–22). As we turn therefore to trace the New Testament stage in the growth of the biblical notion of community, we must keep in mind this dialectic, for it functions within the early history of Christianity as it had in all previous stages of biblical history. Which is only to say the origin of the church must be understood both as a continuation of what preceded and as a new beginning.

B. JESUS' ANNOUNCEMENT OF THE KINGDOM AND A CALL TO DISCIPLESHIP AS THE PRIMAL EVENTS IN THE BIRTH OF THE CHURCH

Alongside many lines of continuity with received tradition, early Christianity included forms of belief and practice that cannot be explained as simply derivative of earlier forms. Although Jesus did not establish a new organization in any strict sense, the fact that a close analysis of the new elements in earliest Christianity points back inevitably to his life and teaching underscores the unique role he must assume in any reconstruction of the early church. In spite of the fact that the attempt to recover the "historical Jesus" has been beset by major difficulties, and has proven that the sources do not provide the basis for a biography in the modern sense of the word, nevertheless a theological study of the origin of the church that passes over the Jesus of history leaves a bewildering gap in our understanding. Although opinions vary broadly regarding the question of how much can be recovered of Jesus' teachings, I believe it is possible to move behind subsequent redactional levels to give an accurate portrayal of the major themes of Jesus' ministry, including his notion of community.

The Synoptic Gospels, though each in its own style and with its own structural and thematic features, are united in presenting Jesus and his mission within a very distinct frame of interpretation. Jesus is the Messiah, announced long ago by the prophets, who has come to inaugurate the reign of God, the Kingdom of righteousness and peace long awaited by the faithful of Israel. The quotations they use from prophetic and early apocalyptic biblical texts offer an important clue to the stream of tradition within which the early followers of Jesus stood. It was a distinctly eschatological tradition, one commonly borne by devout Jews from undistinguished backgrounds, whose piety had led them to be critical of the pragmatism practiced by their political and religious leaders and to look to the ancient prophetic promises of the messianic deliverer who would come to re-establish a righteous people of God within which levels of status would be overcome and the humble and the poor would be fully reintegrated into the life of the community.

Since the Gospels in their present form are the product of careful theological reflection, Chapter XIV relies on them as sources for describing the notion of community that was emerging within the early church as its members sought to infer, from all that they knew of Jesus' life, death, and resurrection, a picture of who they were as a people of God. First, however, we engage in the difficult task of seeking to shed light on the major themes of Jesus' own teaching on the subject of the life of God's people, a task involving the attempt to peer behind the final redacted form of the Gospels.[6] Although this cannot be done with anything approaching scientific accuracy, the results do point to the roots of many of the early church's ideas in Jesus' preaching. Of course, they also help us to see where the church introduced significant changes, especially in the Pauline and post-Pauline periods.[7]

The Gospels are unanimous in their portrait of John the Baptist as one preceding Jesus and preparing for the latter's public ministry. It is clearly a historically based tradition, and offers a valuable connection with the religious background just described. For in his ascetic style of life and through his message of judgment and repentance, John bears the marks of an Essene, with one qualification. He is an Essene differing from the members of the Qumran commune in that he has moved out of holy isolation to proclaim his apocalyptic message to all who will hear. The reason for this move seems clear: John has come to the conclusion that the Kingdom of God is at hand.

This connection with the religious movements of the time is significant. It corroborates what was suggested earlier. The Christian messianic movement arises within a stream of tradition reaching back to classical prophecy, a stream mediated by eschatological and apocalyptic circles during the Second Temple period. Within this stream, focus was centered over the centuries on the prophetic promise of the universal Kingdom of righteousness and peace intended by God for God's people, a promise obstructed according to this view by unfaithful leaders and apostate people. Through much adversity, hope was maintained in the form of a vision of radical reversal in which God would definitively eliminate the obstacles that had blocked the fulfillment of divine promise. The generation of visionaries to which John belonged read the signs of their time as indicating that the decisive reversal was imminent. John, after hearing about Jesus, seems to have taken the next step. The reversal had already begun. God's judgment on all sinners was about to occur. One escape alone could be offered to a threatened world: repentance! Therefore John went about preaching repentance, and teaching the way of the Kingdom (Luke 3:7–14).

A distinct line of continuity connects the ministry of John the Baptist

6. Important works relating to the problem of Jesus' teaching written since the ground-breaking research of M. Dibelius and R. Bultmann include G. Bornkamm, *Jesus of Nazareth* (New York: Harper & Row, 1960); N. Perrin, *Rediscovering the Teaching of Jesus* (London: SCM, 1967); H. Koester, "The Historical Jesus: Some Comments and Thoughts on Norman Perrin's *Rediscovering the Teachings of Jesus*," in Hans Dieter Betz, ed., *Christology as a Modern Pilgrimage: A Discussion with Norman Perrin* (Missoula, Mont.: Scholars Press, 1974), pp. 123–136; H. Koester, *Introduction to the New Testament*, vol. 2: *History and Literature of Early Christianity* (Philadelphia: Fortress Press, 1982), pp. 73–86; G. N. Stanton, *Jesus of Nazareth in N.T. Preaching*, STSMS 27 (London: Cambridge University Press, 1974).

7. For a clear description of the core of parables and sayings that can be ascribed to Jesus with a reasonable degree of assurance, see James Breech, *The Silence of Jesus: The Authentic Voice of the Historical Man* (Philadelphia: Fortress Press, 1983), pp. 1–20.

with that of Jesus. This is suggested already by the synoptic tradition that Jesus was baptized by John. Moreover, from the words that make the strongest claim to authenticity, such as the parables, it is clear that Jesus assessed the human situation essentially from the same eschatological perspective, and preached accordingly: "The time is fulfilled, and the kingdom of God is at hand; repent, and believe in the gospel" (Mark 1:15). God's long-awaited decisive action in addressing evil was about to occur, making way for the Kingdom of God. Humans could prepare by repenting of their rebellion against God, and, in showing true remorse for their waywardness, by accepting God's exclusive claim on their lives. Although the evidence we have for the preaching of the Baptist is very limited, it seems clear that Jesus' message, in contrast to John's emphasis on judgment, had a more positive orientation: to believe in the gospel was to be assured that even now God was the compassionate Deliverer, not willing the death of the sinner, but the sinner's salvation.[8]

At the heart of Jesus' message was thus the announcement of God's new initiative, God's drawing near to establish the Kingdom. No single theme is more central to Jesus' message than this one, and without a clear and full understanding of its connotations we miss the profound meaning of that message. Jesus' choice of the term "Kingdom of God" was obviously related to the eschatological tradition from which he viewed the world, and it is from that tradition, viewed in connection with Jesus' own words, that we can derive the clearest understanding of its meaning. With the prophets, Jesus believed that God had made known to Israel God's will, as expressed in the commandments and elaborated by the prophetic speeches. And with Isaiah and Jeremiah and Ezekiel, Jesus looked to the day when God would break the bonds of sin that enslaved humans, freeing them truly to be God's people. According to Jesus, that day was to be a day of healing not only for humans, but for all creation, for according to the eschatological tradition from which he spoke, the ravages of human sin had left their mark on the entire created order. So far advanced was the decay that Jesus believed with John and others that the world was actually dominated by the archangel of evil, namely Satan, and that God's reign could be established only be the final defeat of Satan and Satan's hosts. For those interested in signs of such a cosmic struggle between the forces of evil and good, the world of that time afforded ample evidence, as the writings of the Qumran community indicate. In a word acknowledged by biblical scholars as authentic, Jesus describes his own time as locked in that eschatological struggle: "From the days of John the Baptist until

---

8. For a perceptive description of the relationship between the messages of John the Baptist and Jesus, see Breech, *Jesus*, pp.28-31, 37, although it seems that Breech goes too far in de-emphasizing the eschatological dimension in Jesus' teaching in favor of a world view that he describes in rather modern-sounding existentialist terms.

now the kingdom of Heaven has suffered violence, and men of violence take it by force" (Matt. 11:12). In the Baptist's suffering and death (Matt. 14:1–12), and now in the persecutions Jesus and his followers would endure for the sake of the Kingdom, the final battle was being fought.

The distinctness of the eschatology of Jesus and his followers is related to the belief that that battle had already entered its final phase, and that the tide had turned against the forces of chaos. The teachings of Jesus accordingly were presented as instructions for life in the Kingdom that God was now raising up around and within them. And the miracles were nothing less than the mending of the created order, as sickness, infirmity, demonic possesion, and death were driven back in defeat. God's reign of peace and justice was unfolding in their very midst. It is this aspect of his teaching more than any other that sets Jesus apart from the apocalyptic leaders of his time:

Being asked by the Pharisees when the kingdom of God was coming, he answered them, "the kingdom of God is not coming with signs to be observed; nor will they say, 'Lo, here it is!' or 'There!' for behold, the kingdom of God is in the midst of you." (Luke 17:20–21)

1. JESUS TEACHES THE WAY OF THE KINGDOM

Jesus was an effective teacher. This was evident to friends and foes alike. He was especially skilled at drawing images from the rural and village surroundings familiar to him. Beyond this, he had a thorough knowledge of his own religious traditions, in both their scriptural and oral forms. This enabled him to draw effectively on those traditions in answering those who asked what they must do to be saved, in replying to those asking for signs. He referred to Abraham, to Moses, to David, to Elijah, to Zechariah and Jonah. Jesus was very much a teacher in the Jewish tradition.

More specifically, he was a teacher deeply impressed with the eschatological faith of the prophets, a fact that must be kept in mind if we are to understand the notion of community that informs his sayings and actions. When he entered into public ministry, he did so as one feeling called by God to address the people of Israel at a critical juncture in their history. What he believed he was called to proclaim was the final opportunity being offered to the people by God for repentance before the day of judgment: "The time is fulfilled, and the kingdom of God is at hand; repent, and believe in the gospel" (Mark 1:14). This verse offers a poignant summary of that proclamation, for the sayings and parables of Jesus, in a language at once simple, colorful and powerful, revolve around the greatest of life's mysteries, the growth of God's Kingdom among humans. Let us describe several of the main points in Jesus' teachings.

First, Jesus called above all for undivided devotion to God, in which life became integrated around its rightful center by removing all idols and distractions and freeing the faithful to focus on the one ultimate, life-giving Reality in worship. He thus began with the heart of classical Yahwism, as it earlier had come to expression in the first commandment, the šĕmaᶜ, and Isaiah's call to trust in God. To those tempted to turn for security to their wealth, he told the stories of the foolish rich farmer, and the rich man and Lazarus. "You cannot serve God and Mammon," he insisted. And when his disciples observed that they had given up everything to follow him, he gave the assurance:

Truly, I say to you, there is no one who has left house or brothers or sisters or mother or father or children or lands, for my sake and for the gospel, who will not receive a hundredfold now in this time, houses and brothers and sisters and mothers and children and lands, with persecutions, and in the age to come eternal life. (Mark 10:29–30)

Jesus gave unforgettable expression to the claim the Kingdom of God places on the true follower in the images of the pearl of great price and the treasure in the field. And when he saw how difficult it was for the otherwise righteous young ruler to take the last step to discipleship by breaking loose from the bondage of his wealth, he grieved. Like the Deuteronomist and the rabbis before him, he insisted that two ways lay before every mortal, the way of life and the way of death. With the added urgency born of his sense of the nearness of the Kingdom, and with a unique sense of authority (Mark 1:22), he promised life to those who renounced the entanglements of this world and who followed the way of the Kingdom he, Jesus, was called by God to announce.

Such renunciation can of course lead to a rigid asceticism, if, as in the case of Qumran, it is motivated by a slavish legalism. But Jesus located its motivation elsewhere, in a love for God and God's Kingdom that led to a discarding of all else as simply not worth preserving. Out of love and anticipation, the disciples were to give up all else and follow their Master. They were to renounce the temptation to lay up treasures on earth not out of fear of punishment, but because of the far superior value of the treasures in heaven. And out of the assurance that they were precious to God, they could break with a false sense of security based on earthly possessions: "Seek first his kingdom and his righteousness, and all these things (that is, earthly needs) shall be yours as well" (Matt. 6:33). On the basis of joyous participation in the Kingdom, the disciples were to live fully in the present and without anxiety for the future (Matt.6:25–33).

The same sense of priorities vis-á-vis the Kingdom allowed them to face danger and opposition without fear, for they were not alone, but accompanied by God's Spirit (Matt. 10:19). And God's care was not a distant and impersonal providence, but an intimate love like that of a parent (Matt. 18:1–14; 19:13–15). These words of assurance were an important concomitant to his call for undivided devotion to God, for the relentlessness with which he preached such singleness of devotion drew increasing opposition. And as in the case of the prophets during the First Temple period, such opposition came from the highest echelons of the community, for this message was consistent, whether his hearers were priests, Pharisees, Sadducees, or Roman officials: the most noble of deeds, be they acts of prayer, tithing, charity, or temple services, were useless when motivated by anything other than devotion to God. Satan himself was obliged to hear this fundamental lesson: "You shall worship the Lord your God, and him only shall you serve" (Matt. 4:10).

Second, Jesus redefined community membership in a new, inclusive way. When seen within its original first-century setting, this theme, addressing the age-old question—"Who belongs to the people of God?"—must be regarded as one of the most revolutionary in Jesus' teaching. We must recall how important this question was during the Roman period. In the minds of this war-weary nation, nothing less was at stake than their identity as a people. It is this question that drove the Essenes to their wilderness refuge, where they erected around them the stout barrier of isolation. The Pharisees chose the more progressive option of striving to live true, within the villages and cities of that alien world, to the eternal order that gave them their sense of identity, the Torah. But for some of them this meant maintaining a very strict separation from "sinners"; that is, all who did not observe their interpretation of the Torah. All meaningful contact, such as table fellowship, was restricted to the undefiled. In considering Jesus' teaching about fellowship, one must remember that the ḥăbûrâ Pharisees upheld a system that was the product of centuries of careful reflection and refinement, a system ultimately derived in their view from God's supreme gift to Israel on Sinai, the Torah. From the interpretation of Torah deriving from their sages, they learned how to remain ritually pure through avoiding all contact with unclean vessels, foods, and persons. Only by maintaining this ritual purity could they expect God's blessing to abide with them, thereby upholding their people in peace and blessing.[9]

The parables and sayings of Jesus seemed to turn this delicate order on its head! For example, in offering an example of the good neighbor, Jesus rejected the priest and the Levite in favor of the one who symbolized the unclean and inferior—the Samaritan. The epithet "Good Samaritan" would have struck most observant Jews of Jesus' time as a contradiction in terms. Again, in describing the order he was commending, he told the story of the unjust steward (Luke 16:1–7), which

---

9. C. J. Neusner, "The Fellowship (Haburah) in the Second Jewish Commonwealth," *HTR* 53 (1960), 125–142; see also J. Bowker, *Jesus and the Pharisees* (Cambridge, England: Cambridge University Press, 1973).

ran in the face of common standards of honesty and decency. And in summoning others to follow him, he had the audacity to declare, "Leave the dead to bury their own dead," in a society that regarded being left without proper burial as the greatest of all disgraces. Such stories must have struck many listeners as a shocking outrage against the holy order by which they carefully regulated their lives.

Contemporary scholarship has confirmed that such parables and stories were intended to provoke the most fundamental questions regarding existing religious and social presuppositions. As J. D. Crossan has written in commenting on the Parable of the Good Samaritan:

The literal point confronted the hearers with the necessity of saying the impossible and having their world turned upside down and radically questioned in its presuppositions. The metaphorical point is that *just so* does the Kingdom of God break abruptly into human consciousness and demand the overturn of prior values, closed options, set judgments, and established conclusions.[10]

Stories and sayings such as those just mentioned are not of the type used by those conceiving of their role primarily in terms of preserving an existing order. They obviously are intended to call into question existing presuppositions. But on what basis, and to what end? The correct answer to these questions will be completely missed if it is not found in relation to Jesus' conception of the Kingdom as the reality entering life that had the effect of changing all things, of ending an old era and thrusting humanity into a new order. Jesus and many of his contemporaries among the Pharisees thus disagreed because of a different interpretation of the events around them. The Pharisees experienced those events as essentially in continuity with events of the past, which meant that faithfulness involved upholding the tradition. Jesus' view was more radically eschatological. In those events he saw evidence of God's breaking into this world in a fresh, new way. As in the case of the Hebrew slaves in Egypt or the Jewish exiles in Babylon, this level of expectation subjected tradition to a new scrutiny in light of contemporary events. However, for those not prepared to accept Jesus' claim that God's Kingdom had entered this world, thereby placing an ultimate claim on the faithful and reordering all life in light of a reality challenging and even superseding present structures, the natural inclination was to reject such a view and the teachings growing out of them as representing a frightening threat to communal and social stability.

The implications of Jesus' eschatological message of the Kingdom for the composition of religious community must have been particularly troubling for many devout Pharisees. Much of the polemic between Jesus and the Pharisees as described in the Gospels hinges on this question, and doubtlessly has roots in the life of Jesus. Whereas the strict

---

10. J. D. Crossan, *In Parables: The Challenge of the Historical Jesus* (New York: Harper & Row, 1973), p.65.

members of the Pharisaic party maintained their identity as God's people in a predominantly pagan world by preserving purity within their closed fellowships, Jesus went about inviting into his fellowship "tax collectors and sinners"—that is, people who, whether due to their occupation or to choice of lifestyle, did not conform to traditional dietary laws and who from the Pharisaic perspective were thus a source of defilement. It seems inevitable that the Pharisees would have asked, "Does this not jeopardize the entire concept of religious community by obliterating all distinctions between holy and profane?"[11]

At no point does it become more important to see clearly the bearing of Jesus' eschatological perspective on an issue than in relation to this question of community definition. We can clarify the essential point by reference to the following passage:

Then the disciples of John came to him, saying, "Why do we and the Pharisees fast, but your disciples do not fast?" And Jesus said to them, "Can the wedding guests mourn as long as the bridegroom is with them?" (Matt. 9:14–15)

In light of the eschatological reality of the Kingdom, all traditions and customs pale before the new reality. And it is this new reality that evokes the fitting response. It was precisely Jesus' urgent sense of the Kingdom's coming that led to his redefinition of community membership. The invitation list was not determined by existing party rolls or lists of individual achievements. One criterion alone applied: Repentance of one's sin, and acceptance of God's grace. The banquet list thus read as follows: "You poor, for yours is the kingdom of God," "you that hunger now, for you shall be satisfied," "you that weep now, for you shall laugh," along with the "merciful," the "pure in heart," the "peacemakers," and "those who are persecuted for righteousness' sake" (Luke 6:20–22; Matt. 5:3–12). This membership list, in other words, consists of those whose identity rests solely on God's gracious initiative. They are the ones drawn out of brokenness and bondage of various kinds and given salvation as a pure gift of God. It is a people resembling those described in the Song of Hannah or Mary's Magnificat, people viewing themselves not in self-possessing terms, but in terms of self-denial and surrender to the only One able to save. To such belong the Kingdom of God, for they are the people called, the people

---

11. The polemic between Jesus and the Pharisees with whom he debated must not be interpreted as evidence that the issue of the relation of Jews to Gentiles was seen in post-biblical Judaism in purely negative terms. For example, Rabbi Jeremiah (380–430 B.C.E.) gave this interpretation of 2 Samuel 7:19 ("This is the law of man, O Lord God"): "The text does not read, This is the law of priests, Levites, lay Israelites, but, This is the law of man. Open the gates and let them enter . . . not priests, Levites, lay Israelites that are mentioned, but the righteous nation keeping faith. This is the gate of the Lord . . . it is not priests, Levites, lay Israelites that are mentioned, but the righteous, who shall enter it. Exult . . . , not priests, Levites, lay Israelites, but the righteous in the Lord . . . So that even a heathen who carries out the Torah is as the High Priest"—as translated by R. Levy, *Deutero-Isaiah* (London: Oxford University Press, 1925), p.64.

emptied of self, open to grace, and filled to serve as servants of the Kingdom. To whom would such a definition of community appeal? Predictably not to those already satisfied and secure in their own exclusive communities. Although all except the highest classes were represented among the followers of Jesus, the observation is probably correct that Jesus' summons was heeded especially by those not securely integrated into the existing social structures of the time.[12] As we shall see below when we describe Jesus' life as the manifestation of the Kingdom, he seemed to gather about him what against the prevailing religious standards of the time could only have appeared as a very "mixed company." But this is very much to be expected of one who announced that he had come "not to call the righteous, but sinners" (Matt. 9:12).

Once more, the parables furnish us with a very good illustration of Jesus' teaching. In this case we recall the story of the man who "gave a great banquet, and invited many," only to be disappointed at their excuses and refusal to accept the invitation. At which point he said in anger to his servant, "Go out quickly to the streets and lanes of the city, and bring in the poor and maimed and blind and lame." When the servant explained that room remained, the householder commanded further, "Go out to the highways and hedges, and compel people to come in, that my house may be filled. For I tell you, none of those men who were invited shall taste my banquet" (Luke 14:21–24).

This was obviously a very unusual concept of fellowship, incomprehensible within the standard presuppositions of the society. But what perspective explains such a notion? Consider the form of invitation commended by Jesus to his disciples:

When you give a dinner or a banquet, do not invite your friends or your brothers or your kinsmen or rich neighbors, lest they also invite you in return, and you be repaid. But when you give a feast, invite the poor, the maimed, the lame, the blind, and you will be blessed, because they cannot repay you. You will be repaid at the resurrection of the just.   (Luke 14:12–14)

What is clear is that an eschatological perspective underlies this invitation, for this is not an invitation to a religious gathering in the customary sense of the word, such as that of one of the Pharisaic ḥăbûrôt. Rather, it is an invitation to the eschatological banquet, with the guest list derived from the announcements of the Jubilee year in ancient Israel. As we shall see later, the invitation was extended by Jesus wherever he went, and a large company accepted. The banquet at which they found themselves was heavenly, in a sense, but also very much a part of this world, for true to Jesus' teaching, the Kingdom of God was experienced in their very midst.

All this indicates that Jesus did not destroy the notion of community

---

12. W. Meeks, *The First Urban Christians: The Social World of the Apostle Paul* (New Haven, Conn.: Yale University Press, 1983), pp.51–73.

by obliterating all distinctions, but rather redefined community by removing it from normal social conventions, and placing it directly within the eschatological context of divine initiative and human response. In so doing, he recaptured the primal pattern of ancient Yahwism. The archaizing tendency within early Christianity referred to in the first section of this chapter thus has roots in Jesus' own teachings, and as observed there, the concomitant of that archaizing was the introduction of something very new, relative to the customs of the time. The degree to which Jesus removed questions of membership from human control is illustrated by his refusal to be troubled over the question of whether an act of compassion was performed by a member of his specific group or not. In Mark, we read of his criticism of the narrow sectarian attitude of his disciples:

John said to him, "teacher, we saw a man casting demons out in your name, and we forbade him, because he was not following us." But Jesus said, "Do not forbid him, for no one who does a mighty work in my name will be able soon after to speak evil of me. For he that is not against us is for us." (Luke 9:38–40)

Notions of membership and group identity were not to be tied up with organizational concerns or party labels, even as they were to be free of concerns for numbers or strength as judged by worldly standards. Their identity was to be derived solely from their relation to the living God, and their purpose solely from their having been called to be representatives of God's Kingdom. The righteousness of that Kingdom was to be embodied by the disciples not as a recruiting device, but that others "may see your good works and give glory to your Father who is in heaven" (Matt. 5:16). For such a people of God, in the world not for themselves but for the reconciliation of all humans with God and for the mending of the entire fallen creation, Jesus had poignant images. All of them pointed to the new sense of fellowship, in which the disciples were freed from worldly concerns with proprietorship and control to live in the new eschatological reality: The Kingdom was present like leaven in the dough, quietly bringing about the good for the whole loaf. It was like the mustard seed, tiny, but containing a surprising potential. The disciples were to be the salt of the earth not there to transform everything else into salt, but there for the health of all. They were to be a lamp held high, present in the world for God's glory.

Third, Jesus redefined the function of the Torah by relating obedience to an intimate sense of God's presence. In considering this third theme in Jesus' teaching, it is first important to remember that Jesus treasured the commandments as a trustworthy guide to God's will. When the rich young man came to him asking what he must do to inherit eternal life, Jesus began his instruction with the commandment of the Decalogue. To the scribe who answered wisely regarding the greatest of all the commandments, he replied, "You are not far from the

Kingdom of God" (Mark 12:34). To the lawyer who answered similarly, he said, "You have answered right; do this, and you will live" (Luke 10:28).

Although the details of these stories have evolved in the oral tradition behind the Gospels, the quotations of Jesus are likely historical. In them we see this pattern: Jesus points to obedience to the commandments as an important indication of one's spiritual health. But obedience is never construed strictly as a formal matter, but is always understood within the context of the individual's relation to the God who is a living presence in life. Thus Jesus sought to clarify the heart of the Torah, and to point to the mysterious realm of intentionality as the key to true obedience; where God's intention was clearly identified behind a particular law, and where the human response to that intention was the desire to obey the loving God and to love the fellow human, the righteousness intended by the Law-giver was fulfilled.

One must be careful not to oversimplify this matter by offering a caricature of the Pharisee and then arguing that Jesus' position was diametrically the opposite. To do so is to miss the much more subtle, though important difference. The position of the Pharisees must be understood against the background of the tradition we traced back to Sirach and even Ezra. We have seen that according to Sirach, God's eternal order, known as ḥokmâ ("wisdom"), was with God from the beginning, and will be forever: "From eternity, in the beginning, he created me, and for eternity I shall not cease to exist" (24:9). This eternal wisdom, moreover, is identical with the Torah: "All this is the book of the covenant of the Most High God, the law which Moses commanded us as an inheritance for the congregations of Jacob" (24:23). Out of this background Torah had become for the great Pharisaic sages of Jesus' time the cardinal principle in a carefully defined religious system. It portrayed the eternal, divine order that alone upheld life, on its personal, communal, and cosmic levels. This being the case, obedience to every detail of the Torah was the unquestioned requirement for the righteous person. And hence the life of the Pharisee was dedicated to the fulfillment of all aspects of the Torah, without exception.

We can perhaps observe that Jesus' view of Torah was less systematic and philosophical and more historical. For Jesus, God's will obviously came to expression in Torah, but always within a specific historical context. Interpretation of the Torah thus involved for him attention both to the original setting within which a particular law had been given and to the present setting to which it was being applied. This historical approach opened up the possibility of grasping the divine intention behind the law, which in his view was the aspect applicable to the life of the believer. Let us turn to an example.

In a debate over the validity of traditional divorce law, the Gospels portray the Pharisees as presenting their argument on the basis of Mosaic law, which from everything we know about the hermeneutic of the Pharisees is essentially an accurate portrait: "Moses allowed a man to write a certificate of divorce, and to put her away." According to their exegesis, this established divorce as a provision within an eternal order. Then Jesus is portrayed as interpreting that divorce law within a different framework, namely, an historical-theological one: "For your hardness of heart he wrote you this commandment." This opens up the possibility of testing whether this Scripture provides the answer: "But from the beginning of creation, 'God made them male and female.' 'For this reason a man shall leave his father and mother and be joined to his wife, and the two shall become one.' So they are no longer two but one. What therefore God has joined together, let not man put asunder" (Mark 10:5–9; cf. Matt. 19:3–9). Within a hermeneutic that understands the Mosaic law to be a divine word to a specific setting, a search for clues to the deeper intention underlying the law is called for. This Jesus locates in the Genesis story, which is offered as a more profound insight into God's will regarding marriage and divorce, and hence as an authority more weighty than the specific Mosaic law, whose validity was limited to a specific setting.

How then is the Torah to be interpreted and applied to life? Does it not lose its validity entirely, raising the specter of moral chaos. The answer is best answered by reference to another specific text. We have noted that Jesus' discussion concerning eternal life with the rich young man began with the question of obeying the commandments (Mark 10:17–31; cf. Matt. 19:16–30; Luke 18:18–30). "Teacher, all these I have observed from my youth," the young man was able to reply. Then Jesus focused specifically on the individual ("Jesus looking upon him loved him"), apparently concerned to identify the state of his relation to God. And he identified an obstacle, the lad's love of his possessions. It is that obstacle he felt constrained to address. What is obvious in this is that true faith is a matter of one's ultimate loyalty. Morality, obedience, and righteousness are lacking if they do not arise from true devotion to God. Why? A clue comes in this same story. The young man ran up to Jesus and addressed him with "Good Teacher . . ." To which Jesus replied, "Why do you call me good? No one is good but God alone." This reply indicates why conformity to the law itself cannot constitute true righteousness. No human is righteous, except as that human is declared righteous by God through forgiveness. Now this begins to sound Pauline, but it is already the principle that lies at the heart of Jesus' teaching concerning obedience and the Torah. Apart from grace and forgiveness, true obedience, and hence righteousness, is not possible. On the basis of this conviction, Jesus directed the attention of his disciples to the disposition of the heart.

It is against this background that we can understand the so-called antitheses found in the Sermon on the Mount (Matt. 5:21–48). Although the precise formulation of these antitheses probably bears the imprint of Matthean redaction, the underlying hermeneutic seems to preserve the approach taken by Jesus to the question of the Torah's validity. In each case, the command is radicalized not in the spirit of the Qumranians—that is, by intensifying its formal requirements—but by locating its intent in the will of the individual. The result is to establish the sinfulness of every human, the same result that allowed the Jesus portrayed in the Johannine narrative to command with confidence, "Let him who is without sin among you be the first to throw a stone at her" (John 8:7). However, it must not be overlooked that the antitheses conclude with this injunction: "You, therefore, must be perfect, as your heavenly Father is perfect," or as Luke records this conclusion, in what is perhaps its original form, "Be merciful, even as your Father is merciful" (Matt. 5:48; Luke 6:36).

This juxtaposition of a definition of righteousness that establishes the sinfulness of every human and the command to be merciful as God is merciful could give the appearance of a insidious guilt trap, were it not for the relational interpretation Jesus gave to the Torah. For the intended result of this shocking juxtaposition is to drive the sinner to give up claims of personal goodness, confessing indeed that "no one is good but God alone," and then rejoicing in the goodness and mercy of the God who forgives sinners. Through confession of sin and acceptance of forgiveness as a gift of pure grace, the relationship between God and human is restored, within which obedience as the inclination of the heart toward God is fulfilled.

Thus it is that the present relationship with the living God is the context within which discernment of God's will occurs, and moral decisions are made. As seen in Jesus' words to the rich young man, the scribe and the lawyer, the commandments are a valuable witness to God's will within that living relationship. But it is important to note the nature of their witness: not as abstract requirements, but as expressions of the bond between divine will and the response of the grateful, forgiven mortal.

Within this relational setting, the heart of the Torah comes to clear expression. Jesus was not innovating when he described that heart as follows: "You shall love the Lord your God with all your heart, and with all your soul, and with all your strength, and with all your mind; and your neighbor as yourself" (Luke 10:27; cf. Matt. 22:37–38; Mark 12:29–31). The rabbis of his time had come up with the same formulation. And this is not surprising. As our entire study has shown, both early Yahwistic and prophetic tradition maintained that the heart of righteousness lies in undivided devotion to God, from which stems love for the neighbor and a clear understanding of one's responsibility for the neighbor at her or his point of particular need. But what might seem to be a restatement of the obvious nevertheless proved to be extremely controversial, for Jesus' age was not different from the age of the prophets in having among its political and religious authorities individuals disposed to allowing penultimate loyalties and selfishness to encroach on the ultimate loyalty expressed in love of God and neighbor. In his own surrender to God's will, Jesus freely exposed all areas of life to the holy presence of God, and from that holy center he declared what God demanded. This hermeneutic exposed every idol that obstructed a true relationship to God, even the idol of the self-righteousness that sought to hide an unloving heart behind a display of piety intended to humiliate "sinners."

By establishing this inextricable tie between love of God and love of neighbor, Jesus was revivifying the early Yahwistic pattern of divine initiative and human response. For within the primary relationship to God, the responding human community's understanding of righteousness and compassion was inferred from the example of God's righteousness and compassion. This pattern is seen in the last of the antitheses, which is also in a substantive sense climactic:

You have heard that it was said, "You shall love your neighbor and hate your enemy." But I say to you, Love your enemies and pray for those who persecute you, so you may be sons of your Father who is in heaven; for he makes his sun rise on the evil and the good, and sends rain on the just and on the unjust. (Matt. 5:43–45)

The pattern here is the same as that found in the Yahwistic laws of the Book of the Covenant: The standard for behavior within the community of faith is ultimately God's antecedent gracious behavior toward humans. Therefore, "Be merciful, even as your Father is merciful" is the dynamic basis of true obedience. Since knowledge of that basis can be found only in a living relationship with God, the Torah can be rightly understood and applied to life only within the life of devotion to the living God. In that process, earlier formulations of Torah, while taken seriously as records of God's will in the past history of the people, are not clothed with an aura of immutability. Nor is Torah in its received form simply preserved as a timeless monument, but is renewed through reformulation as the inferential process of perceiving God's will in God's ongoing saving activity continues.

This manner of relational interpretation rests on an important presupposition having to do with the eschatological significance Jesus attributed to the events of his time: Jesus believed that God was present and that God's Kingdom was unfolding in his world, and that an intimate relationship with God was therefore possible. The more formal approach to the Torah that developed within Pharisaism was tied to the growing sense that God was far removed from everyday life, that God's Spirit had been silent in Israel since the days of Haggai, Zechariah, and Malachi, and that God was represented through the mediation of the

Torah. While the subject of the "absent God" and the "removal of the Presence" is a subject too large to enter into here, we should note that the tendency to interpret the Torah as an eternal order was tied to this development. Of course, the Pharisees did not believe that this post-prophetic state was final. Their eschatology anticipated the time when God's spirit would again address the people, an anticipation tied to their messianic reflection.

The high level of eschatological and then messianic enthusiasm of the early Jesus movement indicates that the followers of the Nazarene teacher saw signs that that hope was being fulfilled. The second chapter of Acts shows how early Christians saw their experience with the Spirit as a fulfillment of Joel's prophecy (Joel 2:28–32). The signs of the Spirit proved to them that they stood at a decisive turning point in God's history with God's people. This charismatic and eschatological perspective probably traces back to an early stage in the Jesus movement.

Already in Jesus' teaching a renewed sense of the spirit of prophecy is in evidence, and it provided the vantage point from which the Torah could be reinterpreted in the manner we have described. Here too then a sense of the nearness of God's Kingdom explains an important difference between Jesus and the Pharisees: deeply impressed with the signs of God's presence in the events around him, Jesus developed an interpretation of the Torah with a level of authoritativeness equal to that ascribed by the scribes to Moses (and by extension, to their own Mosaic exposition). The process of interpretation thus was more than reapplication, or adaptation to new situations; it was derivation of a new, deeper sense of God's will from life lived in God's presence now. Thus it was that Jesus was perceived to teach "as one who had authority, and not as their scribes" (Matt. 7:28–29). For he related both tradition and contemporary experience to the heart of the Torah, the one true God present and redemptively active in the world now, a reality he could proclaim on the basis of intimate personal communion with One he addressed as his Heavenly Father. And from that relational context, he was able to give fresh expression to God's will to those who were accompanying him into God's reign of righteousness and peace. In so doing, we feel that Jesus recaptured the dynamic understanding of Torah found in early Yahwism, which explains the affinities between his process of interpretation and that underlying the Book of the Covenant, as noted earlier. For he related obedience directly to fellowship with God within the context of a life centered on God alone, and deriving its direction from God's righteous, compassionate example as seen both in Scripture and in events of the present. To this process of interpretation, Jesus added the following guideline: the believer could be assured that the inclination of the heart was properly centered if obedience was motivated singularly by the desire to glorify God: "let your light so shine before men, that they may see your good works and give glory to your Father who is in heaven" (Matt. 5:16).

Fourth, we find a related theme: Jesus' teaching that the Kingdom of God was a *present* reality. The new eschatological order of life that he announced, and that led to a redefinition of community membership and of Torah, was a reality *already* present in the lives of those responding to his call. The reordering of life's priorities that it caused called into question old ways of life, and introduced a new style of living. Therefore it is not accurate to speak of the reality of the Kingdom as simply the object of a future expectation. It was experienced in the presence of Jesus as a present reality.

Jesus' parables and sayings were intended to shock his hearers out of the kind of complacency that accepts the unjust social structures and unmerciful personal habits of the present as normal. His teaching placed before them an alternative way of life that called into question their present existence. One of the remarkable themes of his teaching was thus its emphasis on the contemporaneity of God's reign.

In using the symbol of the Kingdom, Jesus was drawing on an apocalyptic tradition that could have fostered a distinctly futuristic outlook in the minds of his hearers.[13] He seems intentionally to have offered a corrective to that popular notion, as indicated by his reply to the Pharisees: "The kingdom of God is not coming with signs to be observed; nor will they say, 'Lo, here it is!' or 'There!' for behold, the kingdom of God is in the midst of you" (Luke 17:20–21). Another synoptic tradition likewise speaks out against the popular preoccupation with signs: "Why does this generation seek a sign? Truly, I say to you, no sign shall be given to this generation" (Mark 8:12; cf. Matt. 16:1–4; 12:38–9; Luke 11:29).

For Jesus, the Kingdom was not to be the object of apocalyptic speculation. Given the nearness of its arrival, such speculation was idle, and, if anything, a distraction from the Kingdom's claims on the individual. As many of his parables indicate, it called for watchfulness, repentance, and a radical reordering of life's priorities. Although futuristic and cosmic speculation became an early part of the gospel tradition (likely in the wake of the Roman War of 70 C.E.; cf. Mark 13), Jesus seemed to describe God's reign as a time of the restoration of God's people to wholeness and a time of the healing of creation. In other words, his was a notion continuous with the Servant Songs (cf. Isa. 42:1–8 and 61:1–4). Luke, therefore, was either drawing on an accurate historical tradition, or supplying a very pertinent interpretation of Jesus' career, when he depicted Jesus' reading the Servant passage of Isaiah 61 in the synagogue at Nazareth at the beginning of his career:

The Spirit of the Lord is upon me, because he has anointed me to preach good news to the poor. He has sent me to proclaim release to the captives and reco-

---

13. See, for example, Daniel 7–8 and *Assumption of Moses* 10.

vering of sight to the blind, to set at liberty those who are oppressed, to proclaim the acceptable year of the Lord. (Luke 4:18–19)

As we shall see shortly, Jesus recognized the signs of that restoration and healing as occurring wherever he taught and ministered. And these he saw as proof that the Kingdom was at hand. In his teaching, there is no indication of the sharp distinction that grew later between a sense of the Kingdom being a present phenomenon and an understanding of it as an event of the future. Perhaps no passage captures Jesus' own sense of the contemporary reality of the Kingdom as powerfully as Matthew 25:31–46, which contains the added feature of being placed in the form of a Son of Man passage—that is to say, the form that developed into the most popular carrier of Christian apocalyptic eschatology. Here, however, on the day of the Son of Man's great judgment, the spotlight comes to rest not on lofty cosmic phenomena and their earthly reflections, but on very recognizable happenings out of the everyday and the mundane. The end-time setting of the drama recedes into the background as the substance of the Kingdom is recognized as present in the life of those obedient to God's invitation to the Kingdom in their everyday lives: the Kingdom is in essence the concrete act of justice and mercy, the cup of water to the thirsty, the visit to the imprisoned, the garment for the naked. Where such acts are performed from a grateful and loving heart, God reigns!

Fifth, it is fitting that what is perhaps the most sublime expression of Jesus' teaching was given in the form of a prayer, that is, in the quintessential form of response to the one true God. Like his other teachings, it directs the attention of his disciples to God's Kingdom, so as to establish it at the center of their lives. It arises from the heart of his own Jewish faith, as can readily be recognized when compared with the following two passages from the *Amidah* and the *Kaddish*, respectively: "Our father . . . who are gracious and dost abundantly forgive . . . " "Sanctified be his great Name in the world which he has created. May he establish his Kingdom . . . even speedily and at a near time."

Jesus teaches his disciples to address God with the title "Father," which conveys his sense of God's nearness and involvement, like unto that of a parent. It is the same sense conveyed by the following saying: ". . . what man of you, if his son asks him for bread, will give him a stone? . . . If you then, who are evil, know how to give good gifts to your children, how much more will your Father who is in heaven give good things to those who ask him!" (Matt. 7:9, 11). And then he begins by praying for the time when all creation will acknowledge and give glory to God.

We have already seen how the coming of God's Kingdom was at the center of Jesus' concern, and here we see that it is to form the center of the prayer life of his disciples: "Thy kingdom come," that is, the new order in which all creation, restored and healed, will be embraced by

God's *šālôm*. As in the thought of the early Yahwistic community, that order would prevail where God's creatures lived out of gratitude to their Creator in obedience to God's will: "Thy will be done." As we have seen, Jesus devoted much of his teaching to an explication of God's will, rooting it in the day-to-day relationship of the faithful with God, and identifying its motivation in the desire to glorify God. Of course, the supreme example of such devotion was Jesus' own life: "Father, if thou are willing, remove this cup from me; nevertheless not my will, but thine, be done" (Luke 22:42).

"Give us this day our daily bread." This petition ties into one indivisible unity the bread needed for daily sustenance, and the future bread God will give (literally, the Greek reads, "our bread for the next day"). Since we have seen how Jesus' teaching the way of the Kingdom repeatedly stressed the contemporaneity of the Kingdom in the lives of the disciples, it is not surprising to find this double entendre here, as it is found also in the eucharistic meal, the bread eaten now in anticipation of the messianic banquet with Lord. There is simply no conflict here between the bread needed on earth to sustain life, the bread that according to divine justice is the right of everyone, and the bread of heaven!

Forgiveness is the subject of the next petition, and here the quality of mutuality is stressed. Without God's forgiveness, we are lost, but as Jesus stressed in the parable of the unforgiving servant (Matt. 18:23–35), it is a mockery of God to receive forgiveness and then to be unforgiving of others. Here again we see the pattern that characterized the community of faith since early Yahwistic times, the pattern of initiating divine act and the faithful response in *imitatio dei*. The Kingdom is present where forgiveness is freely received and freely given, and where human calculations and balance sheets are discarded in favor of the open generosity shown by God to all creatures, which is the hallmark of the Kingdom of God (Matt. 18:21–22).

The fact that the Kingdom stands at the threshold, while an occasion for rejoicing, is also a time for watchfulness and prayer, for it means that Satan and his allies, driven against the wall, are more fierce and beguiling then ever before (Matt. 11:12). Jesus does not appeal to the disciples' sense of heroism, as if in the style of Greek tragedy, but urges them to turn to God in prayer, in full awareness of the willingness of the spirit and the weakness of the flesh, a human condition ever haunting disciples disposed to fall asleep at the moment of their Master's greatest need, arguing over who would be first in the Kingdom, following up their bravado with cowardly denial, and doubting their way to faltering faith. It is the realism of Jesus' anthropology that allowed such a motley band to survive, a realism leading to a renunciation of human triumphalism and an appeal to a divine escape: "And if those days had not been shortened, no human being would be saved; but for the elect those days will be shortened" (Matt. 24:22).

In the parable of the wise and foolish maidens, Jesus gave vivid expression to the need for watchfulness (Matt. 25:1–13; cf. 24:42–44 and 12:35–40). The temptation story gives a glimpse into Jesus' own struggle with temptation and the "Evil One." And here in this prayer he teaches his followers to appeal to God for help in the time of temptation and encounter with the powers of evil, a theme developed beautifully in Jesus' prayer in John 17. Wherever the Kingdom was present, Satan would be there in force, tempting the disciples of the Kingdom to give up the power of patient, suffering love for the power of worldly dominion. We shall presently see how Jesus' own passion became the most unforgettable lesson in the way of the Kingdom, which, as the way of the cross, made suffering and glory indivisible parts of one faithful response to God.

2. JESUS' LIFE: THE MANIFESTATION OF THE KINGDOM

Indivisibly related to Jesus' teaching the way of the Kingdom was his manifesting the way of the Kingdom in his own life. In his miracles, in his forgiveness of sins, in his style of reaching out to and drawing into his fellowship all manner of people, his disciples recognized the advent of God's reign. Even as he explained the way of the Kingdom in parables and sayings so too in his own day-to-day living he was utterly given to God's will. Even as he taught his disciples to pray, "Our Father who art in heaven, hallowed be thy name, thy Kingdom come, thy will be done," God was being glorified, the Kingdom was coming, and God's will was being fulfilled in the events occurring in his own life.

This recognition led the followers of Jesus to confess that in Jesus God was present, drawing a lost human family back to fellowship with God, and healing a broken creation. The signs of that redemptive, healing process were seen wherever Jesus went, a theme running through all four Gospels, in statements such as the following:

And he went about all Galilee, teaching in their synagogues and preaching the gospel of the kingdom and healing every disease and every infirmity among the people. So his fame spread throughout all Syria, and they brought him all the sick, those afflicted with various diseases and pains, demoniacs, epileptics, and paralytics, and he healed them. (Matt. 4:23–24)

We have noted how in his teachings Jesus had turned the attention of his disciples away from apocalyptic speculation and directed it instead toward the impact of God's reign on their present lives and the world in which they lived. He had taught his disciples that were one fed the hungry, healed the sick and drove out the demons of the possessed, the Kingdom was present. In his own life, wherever Jesus encountered the hungry, the sick, and the possessed, he fed, he healed, and he delivered. For those raised with the hope of the day when God would again come to them to free the imprisoned, heal the lame, restore sight to the blind, and inaugurate God's eternal reign of peace, the reports of Jesus's acts raised a critical theological question: "Was Jesus the long-awaited one sent by God for this purpose?" It was the question conveyed by John the Baptist to Jesus, according to a narrative in "Q" (the source drawn on by Matthew and Luke): "Are you he who is to come, or shall we look for another?" (Matt. 11:3 and Luke 7:20). Jesus' answer invites the questioner to compare the traditional prophetic descriptions of God's day of healing (i.e., the long-awaited Jubilee year) with the events then occurring, and to draw his own conclusion: "Go and tell John what you have seen and heard: the blind receive their sight, the lame walk, lepers are cleansed, and the deaf hear, the dead are raised up, the poor have good news preached to them. And blessed is he who takes no offense at me" (Luke 7:22–23).

The question raised by this response of course was not one that any Jew, longing for the messianic age, could take lightly. And it was complicated both by a history of disappointment with messianic pretenders and by the fact that the world of that time displayed no lack of miracle workers and magicians claiming to have come from God. The Gospels of Matthew and Mark portray Jesus himself issuing a warning to his followers regarding imposters:

And then if anyone says to you, "Look, here is the Christ!" or "Look, there he is!" do not believe it. False Christs and false prophets will arise and show signs and wonders, to lead astray, if possible, the elect. Lo, I have told you beforehand.   (Mark 13:21–23; cf. Matt. 24:23–25)

The critical issue that arose in relation to this teacher and miracle worker was the one expressed in Jesus' reply to John the Baptist: ". . . blessed is he who takes no offence at me." It was inevitable that the religious leaders of the Pharisees and the Essenes—that is, of the two parties whose beliefs included messianic expectations—would subject this teacher and prophet to very close scrutiny before making a judgment. This was especially true of the Pharisees, given the increasingly influential role they were playing in the life of the Jewish community during the Roman period. Moreover, it is natural that the criterion they used was their interpretation of the Torah, for it was unthinkable to them that the Messiah could live in any manner other than in perfect obedience to God's eternal will.

Against that criterion, what did they see? One who broke sabbath, did not observe the laws of purity, mixed with known sinners, and challenged their interpretation of the Torah of Moses. They drew the conclusion that alone seemed possible within their frame of interpretation. Jesus was one who lived outside of the perfect order ordained by God and given by God to Israel as an eternal ordinance. And by convincing others to live in disregard of this order, he represented a serious threat to their sacred heritage, and indeed, to the order of the world. For one thing, they knew how delicate was the balance they maintained with the Roman occupation of their land that enabled them to live true to their ancestral faith. Moreover, they were aware of the chaos that threatened to engulf any land that conducted its life in disregard of God's laws. On the basis of this criterion, they judged Jesus to be an impostor and a serious threat. The acts that some were taking as signs of Jesus having been sent by God accordingly appeared to the Pharisees in a different light (in this portrait, the Gospels are likely accurate): his pronouncement of the forgiveness of sins was an act of blasphemy (Mark 2:7), and his healing was not by the power of God, but by "Beelzebul, the prince of demons" (Matt. 12:24; Luke 11:15; cf. Mark 3:22)—that is to say, the evil power under whose dominion most of the world of their time suffered.

Of course, the threat Jesus posed was not confined to the realm of religion. The many activities housed within the temple serve to remind us of the impossibility of drawing rigid distinctions between the realms of religion, politics, and economics in that period. The account of his driving the merchants and moneychangers from the temple dramatizes the threat posed by his sole allegiance to the demands of God's Kingdom to the religious, political, and economic system of which the temple was a part. Jesus did not show the respect demanded by the temple officials. From the perspective of his absolute loyalty, only one activity was justified within the temple, namely, worship of the one true God. Similarly, he did not subscribe to the whole system of sacrifices and oaths associated with the temple (Matt. 5:23–24; 33–37; 23:15–22). The official response to his position seems to have taken the form of an accusation that he was involved in a design to destroy the temple (Mark 14:58).

There can be little doubt that the division within the Jewish community caused by Jesus was closely related to a clash between eschatological expectations and interpretations. The answer given by those pondering this question was influenced largely by two factors, the specific eschatological tradition from which they viewed the issue, and the degree to which their personal encounter with Jesus engendered either trust or doubt. As for the latter factor, Jesus' influence was profound in the lives of those who had left behind their former lives to become his disciples, and was also a major factor for many who had been healed by him, or had been accepted into his fellowship. Of course, the response of those with whom Jesus differed sharply on important matters of interpretation was very negative. As for the matter of the eschatological traditions of the respondents, a great diversity was characteristic of that period. Many held firmly to popular Davidic messianism, which had a distinctly nationalistic-political flavor, and taught that the Messiah would come as a victorious warrior who would defeat the Romans and re-establish the glorious Davidic kingdom. Indeed, Herod's death seemed to create a vacuum in the land that was particularly conducive to messianic movements, and claimants to the messianic title were not lacking; for example, Judas in Galilee, Simon in Peraea, and Athronges in Judea (*Ant.* 1.10.5–7; Acts 6:33–39). Those viewing Jesus' life from the perspective of the popular Davidic hope saw scant evidence that he was the "son of David," though aspects of the Davidic tradition later did come to be applied to Jesus in parts of the Synoptic Gospels, such as Matthew's genealogy of Jesus and the story of the triumphal entry into Jerusalem.

Alongside the Davidic tradition, other restoration traditions also existed. One harked back to the Servant of Yahweh described in Isaiah 42, 49, 50, and 53, and on that basis taught that God would redeem a fallen people through the vicarious suffering of an obedient servant. Another, developing among apocalyptic circles, described the Son of Man, who would come down from heaven to defeat the powers of evil that held creation in bondage and to establish God's universal Kingdom.

It is not possible with any degree of precision to determine the contents of Jesus' own eschatological beliefs. It seems that he avoided applying the term "Messiah" to himself, the reason perhaps being his desire to eschew association with the popular nationalistic-political tradition. This may account for the saying recorded in all three Synoptic Gospels in which Jesus quotes Psalm 110 in refuting the tradition that the Messiah is the son of David (Matt. 22:41–46; Mark 12:35–37a; Luke 20:41–44). As for the term "Son of Man," scholars are divided over the question of whether Jesus used it either to refer to a future figure or to himself. It seems likely that both the title "Son of Man" and the title "Messiah" were first applied to Jesus by the disciples in the post-Easter period as they used every resource offered by their tradition to explain the significance of this unique person.[14]

As for Jesus himself, it would seem that he was guided by a deep sense of the nearness of God's reign, coupled by the desire to live utterly true to the way of the Kingdom. We have seen how closely his conception of the way of the Kingdom was related to the vision of restoration and healing found in the Servant Songs of Second Isaiah. This connection makes it plausible to suggest that as Jesus perceived that his faithfulness to the Kingdom was leading to suffering and even to the likelihood of an untimely death, the image of the Suffering Servant became a key to his own self-understanding. The Synoptic Gospels record at three points how Jesus reflected on his upcoming passion, death, and resurrection (Mark 8:27–33; 9:30–32; 10:32–34; and parallels). While this reflects the redactional structure of the gospel writers, it may draw on utterances of Jesus prompted by his reflection on the growing animosity and hostility of his adversaries, which reflection led to an awareness of the inevitability of his suffering and dying for the sake of God's Kingdom.

---

14. H. Koester, *Introduction*, Vol. 2, 88–89.

The attempt to clarify Jesus' own self-understanding is of course most difficult. But the suggestion that the tradition of the Suffering Servant guided his thinking rather than the nationalistic-political Davidic tradition adds a significant degree of clarity to many aspects of his life as pictured in the Gospels. It means that Jesus anticipated God's drawing near to restore a broken and fallen creation, and God's drawing those who were faithful to God's plan of healing and justice into participation in the Kingdom, which would break through all obstacles to establish universal peace. This eschatological perspective explains more adequately than any other factor his posture vis-á-vis the religious traditions and practices of the time and the manner of his relating to marginalized elements of the society. To this we may add one further source of influence.

Within certain apocalyptic circles, such as those represented by Daniel and the Book of Enoch, there had developed an eschatological tradition with a distinctly universalistic tendency. At various periods, this tradition gave rise to criticism of the more particularistic attitudes characteristic of the religious leadership associated with the Jerusalem temple. Within that tradition, a greater emphasis was placed on the mighty acts of God transcending all human boundaries than on the appeal to party affiliation or human ancestry.

This type of universal vision fostered within apocalyptic circles during the Second Temple period seems also to have influenced Jesus' eschatological outlook. This is not to say that his perspective was apocalyptic. Indeed, his affinities with prophetic eschatology are more pronounced than his connections with the apocalyptic movements of that time, as seen in his persistent relating of the Kingdom to present realities. Moreover, the vision of God's activity was already universal in scope in the great prophets of the classical period, such as Isaiah and Jeremiah, a vision that may be described as one of the most important legacies of pre-exilic prophecy, with Second Isaiah playing a key role in handing that legacy on to later, especially apocalyptic, circles. At any rate, it seems to have been that universal vision, coupled with the Servant of Yahweh tradition, that lies at the heart of Jesus' own perception of the world and his mission of announcing the Kingdom. In light of the coming Kingdom, and the consequent ingathering of the nations to worship Yahweh, Jesus seemed to have had no compunctions about eating and drinking with "tax collectors and sinners." To those who appealed to laws of purity in criticism of such behavior, Jesus replied, "Those who are well have no need of a physician, but those who are sick. Go and learn what this means, 'I desire mercy, and not sacrifice.' For I came not to call the righteous, but sinners" (Matt. 9:12; Mark 2:17; Luke 5:31). The fact that the eschatological Kingdom was at hand mandated not the drawing of a tight enclosure around the righteous, but an invitation to all to repent and receive the Good News of God's redemption of creation.

That this definition of community and fellowship differed sharply with that which emerged as the dominant view among the Pharisees is obvious in light both of the New Testament narratives and of our knowledge of the Pharisaic movement. It is perfectly understandable that a Pharisee, dedicating his whole life to maintaining strict separation from impurity so as to safeguard the state of holiness within which alone God could be present, would be dismayed and appalled at the sight of a prophet who allowed a woman of questionable reputation to kiss his feet, wash them with her tears, dry them with her hair, anoint them with ointment, and who then commended her for her faith, sending her away with the assurance that her sins were forgiven (Luke 7:36–50). While such an action makes no sense within a notion of community predicated on the preservation of a state of ritual purity by a chosen few in an otherwise defiled world, it is fully consonant with the belief that even now God was active in the world creating a new universal community to which all peoples were invited and through which all creation would be mended and restored to its intended wholeness. For it was of the very nature of the new eschatological community that it was to be composed not only of those with an established reputation of holiness, but of all those repenting of their sinfulness and accepting the new fellowship as a gift of a gracious God.

This eschatological criterion of community membership was by nature unrestrained by the types of group controls typical of most associations of that time, both religious and social. Membership was open to whomever accepted the invitation extended by Jesus and the disciples. The result was that human distinctions of race, gender, and social status disappeared. Although the apostle Paul formulated this principle theologically, it is already present in narrative form in the stories about the grateful Samaritan leper (Luke 17:11–19) and the centurion's servant (Matt. 8:5–13; Luke 7:1–10; cf. also the Johannine narrative about the Samaritan woman in John 4:7–26).

What is more, this eschatological understanding of community and the open quality it engendered permeates Jesus' entire life. We have already seen how it figured prominently in his teaching; for example, in the parables of the rejoicing over the one lost sheep, the prodigal son, and the marriage feast. But it is seen even more vividly in the reports about his own life experiences. To begin with, the composition of the group he gathered around himself defies explanation if one does not recognize the acceptance of the invitation to the Kingdom of God as the sole operating criterion of membership. We see no trace of the standard criteria functioning in contemporary groups, such as common class and shared interests in the Roman clubs, common vocation in the commercial guilds, and a common interpretation and observance of the Torah in the ḥăbûrôt of the Pharisees. Only the eschatological criterion can explain the presence of the tax collector (Matt. 10:3) alongside the zealot (Luke 6:15), or the spirit of openness extended to a soldier of the Roman army (Matt. 8:5–14), or the graciousness accorded a woman of questionable reputation (Luke 8:36–50). Beyond this, if the group's cohesiveness were explained on the basis of a political ideology, it would be impossible to reconcile the Kingdom's demand for ultimate loyalty with permission to pay taxes to the occupation government of the Romans. The eschatological criterion for membership of course is what fostered the reinterpretation of the Torah, and we could even say, of ethics in general. With human barriers thus removed, it became possible to love the enemy even as it became impossible to define another as categorically distinct from oneself so as to give one the right to cast the first stone. When viewed from the perspective of God's Kingdom and God's righteousness, the commonly drawn distinction between those who were holy and those who were sinners disappeared. From this it followed that the sole requirement for membership was repentance of one's own sinfulness and acceptance of God's grace.[15]

The divisions caused by Jesus' invitation thus did not fall along conventional lines. Standard distinctions between sinner and pure, holy and defiled, even Israelite and non-Israelite no longer retained their traditional validity. What were outsiders or "the children of darkness" to the Pharisees and the Essenes were to the Jesus movement "the lost sheep of the house of Israel." While the religiously elite in large part took offence at Jesus' summons, the simple folk (the 'am hā'āreṣ, and even foreigners like the Samaritan woman and the centurion from Caesarea) responded in trust. The former applied tests of credibility carefully refined over the course of a long scholarly tradition and rejected Jesus, saying, "Behold, a glutton and a drunkard, a friend of tax collectors and sinners!" (Matt. 11:19; Luke 7:34); the latter experienced healing and acceptance, and believed (e.g., Matt. 15:31). In one of the narratives exemplifying the openness of the Jesus movement and the far-reaching effect it had on conventional divisions, namely, the story of the healing of the centurion's servant, Jesus responds to the example of the faith of the "outsider" with this comment: "Truly, I say to you, not even in Israel have I found such faith. I tell you, many will come from east and west and sit at table with Abraham, Isaac, and Jacob in the kingdom of heaven, while the sons of the kingdom will be thrown into the outer darkness" (Matt. 8:10–13).

The radical departure from conventional divisions even affected the most basic social unit, the family:

Do you think that I have come to give peace on earth? No, I tell you, but rather division; for henceforth in one house there will be five divided, three against two and two against three; they will be divided, father against son and son

---

15. G. Theissen, *The First Followers of Jesus: A Sociological Analysis of the Earliest Christianity*, trans. J. Bowden (London: SCM, 1978), p. 64.

against father, mother against daughter and daughter against her mother, mother-in-law against her daughter-in-law and daughter-in-law against her mother-in-law. (Luke 12:51–53; cf. Matt. 10:34;–36; Luke 11:27–28; Mark 10:28–31; Luke 14:26)

Then his mother and his brothers came to him, but they could not reach him for the crowd. And he was told, "Your mother and your brothers are standing outside, desiring to see you." But he said to them, "My mother and my brothers are those who hear the word of God and do it." (Luke 8:19–21; Matt. 12:46–50; Mark 3:31–35).

We thus see how the eschatological faith of Jesus and his acknowledgment of the sole criterion of the coming reign of God led to a restructuring of life on all levels, personal, social, political, and economic. Out of the urgent sense of the advent of the Kingdom, human behavior in relation to various laws and customs was redefined. Hence the criticisms raised by Jesus' gathering food and healing on the sabbath (Matt. 12:1–14; Luke 13:10–17), and by his eating without observing the laws of ritual purification (Matt. 15:1–20; Luke 11:37–41). That it was Jesus' eschatological understanding of the Kingdom that led to his taking issue with both Essenes and Pharisees concerning the traditional religious observances is stated clearly in Matthew 9;14–15: "Then the disciples of John came to him, saying, 'Why do we and the Pharisees fast, but your disciples do not fast?' And Jesus said to them, 'Can the wedding guests mourn as long as the bridegroom is with them? The days will come, when the bridegroom is taken away from them, and then they will fast'" (Matt. 9:14–15).

From the perspective of Jesus' eschatological vision, humanity stood before its most decisive moment. The reality it faced defined its existence in the most ultimate sense. That reality was the Kingdom of God. All other considerations were suspended in the light of this one. This was the pearl of great price. It was the treasure in the field. It was the invitation to the wedding banquet. Decisions were henceforth to be made solely in the light of the Kingdom. Those who delayed in order to purchase a house, or to bury the dead, would be left clinging to that which perishes. Repeatedly we see that Jesus was guided by this vision of the new thing that God was doing on behalf of a lost humanity and a fallen creation.

Of course the commentary on life, the interpretation of Scripture, and the critique of current practices that arose from this singleness of focus on the Kingdom sounded rash, and even blasphemous, to those operating from a world view predicated on normalcy and caution. But it is significant to note that in answering to the charges of blasphemy and apostasy, Jesus did not defend himself on the basis of his own credentials, but asked that his words and actions be judged strictly on the basis of their relation to the reality of the Kingdom:

Every kingdom divided against itself is laid waste, and no city or house divided against itself will stand; and if Satan casts out Satan, he is divided against himself; how then will his kingdom stand? And if I cast out demons by Beelzebub, by whom do your sons cast them out? Therefore they shall be your judges. But if it is by the Spirit of God that I cast out demons, then the kingdom of God has come upon you. (Matt. 22:25–28; cf. Mark 3:23–26 and Luke 11:17–20).

This passage indicates that Jesus did not base his authority on personal claims, but understood all that he proclaimed and did in relational terms, that is, in relation to his dedication to divine purpose. The power and authority visible to others were derived solely from his total dedication to God's purpose. Those who followed him were thus not his personal retainers, but servants of the God who called them to bear witness to the Kingdom. Jesus' miracles did therefore pose a question, but one that referred beyond himself. Those witnessing these things were obliged to ask whether what they saw was evidence of God's Spirit active in their world, or evidence of the demonic. It was of the very nature of this question that it set "son against father, daughter against mother." For it asked whether people believed that in this Jesus God was inaugurating the Kingdom of *šālôm*. There is every reason to believe that this question arose directly from Jesus' own life, for the Gospel writers and the sources they draw on are unanimous in portraying the life of one given utterly to the new saving act of God unfolding around and within him.

3. JESUS DIES FOR THE KINGDOM

As suggested earlier, the experiences of Jesus' short career had likely fostered a growing sense that his single-minded devotion to a Reality that called into question so much that the worldly-minded cherished, would lead to opposition and death. Early in the formation of Gospel tradition, a passion narrative evolved (its earliest form is seen in Mark) that portrayed Jesus, even as he approached death, clinging to God's will and devoted to the Kingdom's claim on his life. This portrait is consistent with the pattern of Jesus' entire life, and undoubtedly captures the spirit of one who was prepared to die for those he loved. The eschatological traditions with which Jesus had grown up had prepared him to face fierce opposition as evidence of Satan's war against God's reign. It had also instilled in him full confidence in God's ultimate victory. His eschewal of every method of violence and force clearly shows that he had rejected the bellicose vision of divine intervention cultivated by apocalyptic communities such as Qumran, confident instead that God's reign would come through quiet, patient obedience and a willingness to suffer for the redemption God intended for the human family. This is very much in the spirit of the Suffering Servant tradition (Isa. 42:1–8; 49:1–7; 50:4–9; 52:14–53:12; cf. Zech. 12:10–14). It is no accident that the Gospel writers drew heavily on that tradition in interpreting the events of Jesus' last days.

We saw in an earlier chapter how the Suffering Servant tradition grew out of the brokenness and despair of the Babylonian peiod as a bold alternative to the national-political vision of restoration associated with the royal house of David. One of the important roots of that tradition reaches back to Jeremiah, the much abused prophet who identified intimately with the sufferings of his people, bore their abuse in his own body, reflected on their incorrigibility, and kept hope alive only by refusing to abandon his vision of God's new initiative, what he called "a new covenant." Out of this background of prophetic suffering, there grew within the thought of Second Isaiah the picture of the faithful one who would patiently accept the punishment of his wayward people, and lay his life down as a sin offering for their redemption. That this picture was preserved within visionary circles in subsequent generations is suggested by the reference in Zechariah 12:10–14 to "the one whom they have pierced."

That Jesus accepted the task of the Suffering Servant by being faithful to God's will even when it was clear that it was leading to the executioner's cross became a central theme in the kerygma of the early Christians.[16] For it drew together for them the deepest lessons of their people's entire history. As the prophets had declared, they were an incorrigible people, lost like sheep without a shepherd. They had failed to obey God, and were suffering from their apostasy. Most tragic of all, nothing within their existing institutions seemed to offer them a means to be released from their spiritual bondage. Therefore they had joined those who, like John the Baptist, awaited God's bold new initiative in bringing them to their senses through repentance. Naturally, visionary brothers and sisters before them had had their hopes raised by a would-be messiah, only to be disappointed, as the one who should have delivered them from their bondage seemed disposed only to look after his own personal interests. But now that history of bitter disappointment was ended, for their Master, Jesus, far from attending to his own interests, had been totally given to the will of God, and had drawn them and all who heeded his call closer to the orbit of the Kingdom's healing power.

There is no doubt that the execution of their Master by the Romans cast them into a serious crisis. In pondering on that seemingly tragic end, however, they were able to make an important connection with their prophetic heritage that explained this happening as well: here was the true Messiah, the Suffering Servant, dying a cruel death *for them.* The will of God, which was so clearly the motivating force behind his entire life, was now seen upholding him in death as well. God was pres-

---

16. Contrast this interpretation of the relation between the bibilical tradition of the Suffering Servant and the life of Jesus with that of M.D. Hooker, who regards the influence of Second Isaiah on Jesus (and the early church) in a broader sense: "Jesus, therefore, the true representative of Israel, may well have seen in Deutero-Isaiah's oracles the description of Israel's sufferings, of which his own were a part" (*Jesus and the Servant* [London: SPCK, 1959], p. 162).

ent in this faithful Servant, redeeming a lost people, reclaiming them as his possession by drawing them into the long-awaited Kingdom of peace and justice. But how could they know that this was in fact from God, and not just an instance of the death of a courageous martyr?

For the early Christians, this question was answered by Jesus' resurrection: by raising Jesus from the dead, God had announced to the world that the enemy that had presided over their bondage, death, had been overcome. The last obstacle in the way of the Kingdom had been removed. The invitation could now go out to all peoples.

All Jesus' teachings, all his miracles, all his acts of compassion found their deepest meaning in the sight of this righteous, faithful Servant of God dying on the cross for his people, and in the subsequent experience that death had no power over him, that he was the "first fruits" of the Kingdom of šālôm. It is no accident that those teachings, miracle stories and narratives began to grow into interpretive biographies only after this experience, for Jesus' death and resurrection gave to his early followers the key that opened up to them the meaning of their sacred Scripture, of Jesus' teachings and acts, and of human existence as a whole.

4. THE RENEWAL OF THE TRIADIC NOTION OF COMMUNITY

In Jesus' response to what he interpreted as God's new initiative of ushering in the Kingdom, we can recognize the reaffirmation of the classical triadic communal pattern tracing back to early Yahwism.

It is first of all clear that Jesus was so devoted to his heavenly Father that his whole life was an act of undivided *worship*. The childhood story surely grasps an essential truth in identifying his rightful home as "my Father's house" (Luke 2:49). His whole life must have appeared to his followers as one of unbroken fellowship with God, a quality captured by the prayers attributed to Jesus, but permeating all other aspects of his life as well. The effect of this devotion was that his teachings and miracles directed the attention of those around him not to himself ("See that you say nothing to any one . . . " Matt. 8:4, *inter alia*), but to God ("And great crowds came to him, bringing with them the lame, the maimed, the blind, the dumb, and many others, and they put them at his feet, and he healed them, so that the throng wondered, when they saw the dumb speaking, the maimed whole, the lame walking and the blind seeing; and they glorified the God of Israel" Matt. 16:30–31).

Secondly, God's *righteousness*—as the order of justice according to which every person is equally entitled to the protection of the community and no person is exempted from responsibility for others, especially the weak and the vulnerable—lies at the very heart of Jesus' life. For that reason Matthew captures the essential point when he places "righteousness" in parallelism with "kingdom" in Jesus' statement on life's ultimate priority: "But seek first his kingdom and his righteousness, and all these things shall be yours as well" (Matt. 6:33; cf. Luke 12:31). For Jesus, the Kingdom was the reign of God's universal justice, within which there was room neither for special privilege nor its ghastly counterpart of hunger and oppression. God was just, and the people of God was to be the human agent of God's justice in the world. A special quality was to characterize its relationships, one that, by embodying God's righteousness, redefined current norms: "If any one would be first, he must be last of all and servant of all" (Mark 9:35). It was a quality that could not be gotten by imitation of the leaders of the earth: "You know that those who are supposed to rule over the Gentiles lord it over them, and their great men exercise authority over them. But it shall not be so among you; but whoever would be great among you must be your servant, and whoever would be first among you must be slave of all" (Mark 10:24–44).

If the powerful of the earth did not offer a model for the citizens of the Kingdom, who did? Jesus responded to that question in a surprising way: ". . . whoever does not receive the kingdom of God like a child shall not enter it" (Mark 10:15; cf. Luke 18:17)—that is, with an open heart, without reservations, hesitations, calculations, and doubt. To this example, the gospel tradents added a most pertinent addition: "For the Son of man also came not to be served but to serve, and to give his life as a ransom for many" (Mark 10:45).

Finally, the third cardinal quality in the classical biblical notion of community comes to its most emphatic statement in the entire Bible in the life of Jesus. Indeed, the meaning of *compassion* is both broadened and deepened, broadened within the context of his eschatological vision, deepened through his own passion.

As observed already, early Yahwism had an audaciously expansive dimension to compassion, rooted in the encounter with a God who did the unusual and surprising thing by taking up the cause of the outcasts of the earth. In embodying this divine quality, the early Yahwistic community showed a degree of concern for the alien, the widow, the orphan, and the poor that was unique in antiquity. We also have observed how this quality was constantly endangered by the tendency for the earlier openness to be lost due to the concern of many to protect their interests by an appeal to special privileges. Jesus gave powerful expression to the prophetic theme that since God's mercy was unlimited, the people of God was to be a community openly showing compassion to all in need. Even as we had earlier observed the manner in which the example of Yahweh's compassion counteracted the natural tendency for righteousness to become a basis for excluding those who failed to measure up to its demands, so too we observe Jesus taking issue with a definition of Torah that made a strict division between those on the inside and those on the outside of the community of faith. The Kingdom of God knew no such boundaries, but issued an urgent invitation to all to enter into fellowship with God through repentance and faith. Believing that he was called to extend that invitation, Jesus looked beyond all human norms of righteousness, which is to say, he was guided by the divine example of righteous compassion:

When he saw the crowds, he had compassion for them, for they were harassed and helpless, like sheep without a shepherd. Then he said to his disciples, "The harvest is plentiful, but the laborers are few; pray therefore the Lord of the harvest to send out laborers into his harvest." (Matt. 9:36–37; cf. Mark 6:34 and Luke 10:2)

The compassion Jesus felt for the throngs of people with their diverse needs runs as a leitmotif throughout the Gospels (e.g., Matt. 14:14; 15:4–32; 20:34; Mark 1:41). And in keeping with the spirit of early Yahwism, his heart was especially open to those rejected by others. Because of his deep compassion for the lost, the invitation of the Kingdom went forth into the "highways and byways." As a result, those who by human standards were denied the benefits of the community were drawn into the true community of šālôm, including the blind, the deaf, the dumb, those suffering from demon possession, lepers, and the lame. It is not surprising to see the classical pattern of worship, righteousness and compassion of the early Yahwistic period recapitulated within the circle of those following Jesus, for like the 'apiru coming out of their Egyptian bondage, one thing united the followers of Jesus, their common experience of having been in bondage and now experiencing the freedom and open fellowship only God can give.

Finding the Yahwistic triad of worship, righteousness, and compassion once again in the gospel narrative corroborates the suggestion that it constitutes the heart of the biblical notion of community. Throughout the history of community spanned by the Bible, a remarkably consistent pattern recurs at those points where the community experiences God's presence intimately and intensely, a pattern in which the primal response of worship is followed by the desire to embody the qualities recognized in God's redemptive initiative on behalf of humans, the qualities of a righteousness that looks out for the rights of all people and a compassion that draws into the protection of the community of šālôm those excluded by human standards. Jesus, through his teaching, infused that communal notion with new life, and beyond that, gave to his followers its most memorable example with his own life. With prophetic zeal, he opposed human attempts to distort the biblical notion through deletion or addition. Matthew captures this prophetic zeal in one of his "woes against the scribes and Pharisees:"

Woe to you, scribes and Pharisees, hypocrites! for you tithe mint and dill and cumin, and have neglected the weightier matters of the law, justice and mercy and faith; these you ought to have done, without neglecting the others. (Matt. 23:23)

At issue here was not the Torah, but how the Torah was being interpreted. The Torah was not to be construed as a long list of demands, but as a faithful guide to life in fellowship with God and other humans, a guide with a very distinctive heart. Tithes of mint and dill and cumin were not located at that heart. The classical triad of justice and mercy and faith *were!* To be sensitive to these "weightier matters" meant to live from the center of the covenant relationship rather than on its periphery. That center was clear to Jesus because of his profound sense of God's presence, and the nearness of the Kingdom. By living in daily fellowship with God and by devoting himself utterly to God's Kingdom, Jesus was able to rediscover the essence of community in worship, righteousness, and compassion. And he gave expresssion to that essence in the form of the twin commandents that stand as the central pillars of the classical biblical faith:

You shall love the Lord your God with all your heart, and with all your soul, and with all your strength, and with all your mind; and your neighbor as yourself. (Luke 10:27; cf. Matt. 22:37–39 and Mark 12:29–31)

This center did not remove from the life of the faithful all the other contents of the Torah. It ordered them by receiving them daily from God within the context of a life lived for the Kingdom.

XIV

The Birth of the Church as Response to God's New Initiative

(Matthew, John, James, 1 and 2 Timothy, and Luke—Acts)

> Then it seemed as if men must proceed from
>   light to light, in the light of the Word,
> Through the Passion and Sacrifice saved in spite
>   of their negative being;
> Bestial as always before, carnal, self-seeking as
>   always before, selfish and purblind as ever before,
> Yet always struggling, always reaffirming, always
>   resuming their march on the way that was lit
>   by the light;
> Often halting, loitering, straying, delaying, returning,
>   yet following no other way.[1]

Historical Note: The church developed as a community separated from the Jewish synagogue in the several decades after Jesus' death (30 C.E.). Originally constituted as a Jewish congregation in Jerusalem, it began to spread into non-Jewish areas through the efforts of missionaries such as Paul. In 49 C.E. an important council meeting in Jerusalem decided in favor of Paul and his supporters, that Gentile converts not be required to undergo circumcision or to observe Jewish dietary laws. The following decades witnessed the spread of Christianity widely through the Roman empire. Out of this period arose the writings I shall use in tracing the development of the notion of the church as the community of those acknowledging Jesus as God's Messiah and Redeemer, including the Pauline and Deutero-Pauline letters, Mark, Matthew, the Book of Revelation, John, James, the Didache, 1 Clement, the Pastoral Epistles and Luke-Acts.

---

1. From T. S. Eliot, "Choruses from 'The Rock,' " in *The Complete Poems and Plays, 1909–1950* (New York: Harcourt, Brace, 1952), p. 108.

Jesus did not organize an institution. Rather, he conformed his life completely to his vision of the order that be believed alone could create true community among humans and true harmony throughout creation. In the vocabulary of his religious tradition, he called that order the "Kingdom of God." And with the conviction that that order, long awaited by the faithful among his people, was now entering into this world, he dedicated himself to extending to all who would hear an invitation to become a part of God's people—that is, the company of those acknowledging God's reign as the central reality of their lives.

The first followers of Jesus consisted of those who responded positively to that invitation. In Jesus they recognized the Spirit of God at work, and they placed their trust in him as the one who could lead them into the covenant with God and the loving fellowship with other humans that characterized life within the Kingdom of God. From their Master they learned that heeding his call entailed placing the Kingdom of God as the first priority in their lives, and ordering all else on that basis. Concretely, it meant leaving their vocations, their families, their property, and their communities, finding a new community in the wandering company of those following Jesus, and becoming part of his mission of announcing the Kingdom of God.

The pattern of community formulation that we see here bears close resemblance to the one we recognized in the emergence of the early Yahwistic community out of the exodus experience. In that early period, the Hebrews who found themselves gathered in worship around the Deliverer God Yahweh were united solely by the common experience of having been called forth from bondage to freedom by a gracious God. Community in that early period arose as a response to God's gracious initiative, a response expressed in worship and in a life patterned on the divine qualities manifested in that initiative, the qualities of righteousness and compassion. The Yahwistic community was on its most primal and basic level "the people called."

The experience of having been called into community by the gracious initiative of God is fundamental to the entire subsequent history of the notion of community in the Hebrew Bible. The *qāhāl yhwh* or *qāhāl yisrā'ēl* (the congregation of Yahweh or Israel) was the assembly of those who could gather together because of what God previously had done. The Greek word, used first by Luke, that came to designate the Christian church (*ekklesia*), with its root meaning of "those called forth," makes explicit the nature of the people of God as a *called* people. Its identity was not self-generated, it was not supplied by the dominant society, it was not the invention of a wise founder. Rather, it was derived solely from the experience of having been delivered and gathered together by a gracious God. The community of faith throughout the biblical period was the company of those responding in worship and gratitude to the God who calls humans into fellowship.

The fact that the same primal pattern is found at the beginning of both early Yahwism and the church is indicative of the bond between those two communities. Furthermore, the reliance of the first disciples on their Hebrew Scripture to grasp the meaning of Jesus' life and teaching strengthened that bond, for it was based on the confession that the God of Abraham, Isaac, and Jacob, and of Sarah, Miriam, and Ruth, was also the God of Jesus of Nazareth, and that through the entire history from Abraham to Jesus God had been graciously active on behalf of God's people. The strong position that the church took against Marcion's claim that the God of the Old Testament was not the same as the Father of Jesus Christ assured that that bond would remain strong in the subsequent history of the church, for it led to the reaffirmation of the unity of God's salvific work in the catholic creeds.

The entire history of God's salvific work, however, was also characterized by a dynamic, forward-moving thrust. It is a basic tenet of biblical faith that until God's purpose had been reached of the entire creation being united through worship in righteousness and peace, God would be experienced as the "jealous God," relentless in seeking to win back the hearts of a wayward people. Therefore unity of purpose did not preclude God's doing "a new thing." Yahwistic tradition had long spoken of God's "new things": revealing a new name, commissioning a new servant, establishing a new covenant, and creating a new heart. And for this reason, biblical history is in a real sense a history of endings and new beginnings. Therefore, the unity of the biblical confession in the God who remains faithful to one purpose is not contradicted by the birth of the Christian community. For that birth arises within the broad span of the history of God's initiatives as the response to the new thing that a group of believers perceived God to be doing on behalf of humans.

Chapter XIII noted the sense of urgency and devotion with which Jesus responded to the new initiative of God to which he felt called. It was the event toward which all prior history had pointed, toward which all hearts longed, and as the Apostle Paul would add, toward which creation itself was groaning in travail. It was the event of the coming of God's Kingdom. Although, as noted earlier, Jesus did not organize an institution, in a profound sense the roots of the church are to be found in the response of Jesus and the first generation of disciples to this new divine initiative. As had been true in earlier periods of biblical history, this new response, though certainly growing in part out of earlier confessions, would introduce new insights into God's will that in time would have to be related back to the antecedent confessions. Much of the theological activity of the first three generations of the church was devoted to this question of the relation between the old and the new, as seen in the debates between Jewish-Christians and those who like Stephen and Paul were carrying the gospel beyond Judah. In studying this period, it is important to remember once again that unity and diversity are not mutually exclusive qualities. For as the first three generations of the Christian movement sought to work out a faithful response both to their ancient religious heritage and to the new initiative of God they were experiencing, the deep unity called for by the God of holiness and mystery was one capable of preserving the rich diversity that was a part of God's long history with the covenant community.

A. THE FIRST GENERATION

The formation of community in earliest Israel began within a band of former slaves in the form of a response to the Deliverer God who had saved them. The primal phase of that response was worship, finding expression in praise and in a commitment to devote themselves to no God but Yahweh. Salvation was thus interpreted as a call to fellowship with God. From this primal response grew the qualities and structures of community necessary to preserve the new freedom and to hand it on to future generations.

The first disiciples came to recognize in the wandering prophet and exorcist Jesus the hand of God actively at work in their world to deliver the lost from their bondage to sickness, demon possession, greed, and self-righteousness. They responded by worshipping God, and heeding Jesus' call to follow him. The call to follow an itinerant teacher was common in the ancient world since the time of Socrates. The nature of the circles of disciples varied, however. In some cases, the purpose was the promulgation of the master's philosophy. In others, a secret knowledge (gnōsis) was the attraction. Some groups were dedicated to learning their leaders' methods of healing. Yet others followed a master to a monastic retreat to await the end of the world. While some of these qualities were present in the circle of disciples that gathered around Jesus, none of them describes the essential quality of that fellowship. That quality can be grasped only by calling to mind the central theme running through Jesus' own life; namely, dedication to God at a time when God was believed to be inaugurating the Kingdom of righteousness and peace, a dedication that mandated extending the invitation of the Kingdom to all people. If in calling the disciples to follow him, Jesus had focused that call on himself rather than on God and God's Kingdom, we should be encountering a very different phenomenon, fraught with dangers of self-aggrandizement and exploitation. The disciples were able to place their complete trust in Jesus because they believed that this holy man was not drawing them into a human program, for his call always pointed beyond himself to God. Jesus' life was transparent to God's reign. They were able for this reason to trust him completely, and to follow him in the confidence that to follow Jesus was to abide in the presence of God.

In calling the disciples to follow him, Jesus called them to imitate the dedication to God and God's Kingdom that characterized his own life. Jesus gathered them around him to teach them the way of the Kingdom through his parables, sayings, and miracles. In that circle they experienced the Kingdom, and that experience became for them their commission: "Whenever you enter a town and they receive you, eat what is set before you; heal the sick in it and say to them, 'The Kingdom of God has come near to you' " (Luke 10:8–9). This eschatological emphasis reminds one of the apocalyptic orientation of the covenanters of Qumran. But beyond this similarity a huge gulf opens, for the disciples of Jesus did not hear their Master summoning them to a retreat from society where they might preserve their purity until God had destroyed the rest of the world. They heard the command to *enter* the world, to save it through the word of repentance and the invitation to accept God's reign.

At the center of the communal life of the disciples, we can recognize above all the unique type of eschatological confession that characterized the teachings of Jesus. They believed that they stood at life's most important crossroads. The Kingdom was at hand; yet a vast world filled with lost and confused people lay before them (Luke 10:2). This created a new situation that old precedents did little to clarify. Old customs and conventions suddenly became passé. What once was deemed prudent was now foolish. While there was once a time to purchase fields, attend funerals, and go about the motions of daily professions, the message of the Kingdom established a new situation and a new priority. Abandoning all, they were to follow the one who had abandoned all for the sake of God's Kingdom. And in this devotion, they were to learn the way of the Kingdom in preparation for the day when their Master would no longer be with them.

They proved to be an average group of students. They had their high moments, and their low ones, for they kept wavering between the customs of this world and the way of the Kingdom. So they squabbled over who was greatest, until their Master reminded them that the Kingdom belonged to servants. They brushed aside children until their Master took the children into his arms and explained that unless one received God's reign like a child one could not enter it. They doubted and they betrayed. But through it all Jesus taught them that even as the cause was not their own but God's, the power to perform their duty did not come from them but from God. In the time of persecution, "do not be anxious how you are to speak or what you are to say . . . for it is not you who speak, but the Spirit of your Father speaking through you" (Matt. 10:19–20). In facing hostility, they were to recall from their Master's life that God's power is of a different order than the power of this world. While the leaders of this world resorted to weapons of violence, and though those weapons would at times be turned against them, they were to remember the superior power of faith and love, the power that came to victory by choosing to suffer rather than to inflict suffering. As a constant reminder of the Reality for which they lived, and the Power from which they received their strength, Jesus bequeathed to his disciples his prayer of the Kingdom.

In association with the one whose sense of identity and mission was derived from complete devotion to God and God's purpose, the disciples learned that such devotion was the cardinal quality of the way of the Kingdom to which they were called. Thus if we are to trace the roots of the church to the fellowship of the earliest disciples, we find that it was called into being specifically to carry on the mission of its Master by living a life in imitation of its Master, with the full assurance that in so doing it was sustained by a loving heavenly Parent. This sense of continuity between the life and mission of Jesus and that of the disciples is captured by a passage in Matthew following the list of the twelve:

These twelve Jesus sent out, charging them, "Go nowhere among the Gentiles, and enter no town of the Samaritans, but go rather to the lost sheep of the house of Israel. And preach as you go, saying, 'The kingdom of heaven is at hand.' Heal the sick, raise the dead, cleanse lepers, cast out demons. You received without paying, give without pay." (Matt. 10:5–8)

The message was to be the same; the remuneration was to be the same; even in regard to the focus on "the house of Israel," the disciples continued in the mission of Jesus. Of course, as Jesus' own activity took him beyond Judah to Galilee and beyond the house of Israel to Samaria, the disciples would find the openness and compassion of Jesus' own example compelling them to move ever outward. But they began with the central focus of their Master, and never abandoned a sense of responsibility to preach to the "lost sheep" of their own household.

To understand the notion of community that existed within the first circle of Jesus' followers, therefore, we must recognize a particular consciousness that they received through their intimate fellowship with their Master. They learned to view all things from the perspective of God's reign, enabling them to sort out what was valid from what was indifferent or useless, and to determine what bound them and what did not. In light of the announcement that the Kingdom was at hand, life took on a totally new look. This consciousness of God's reign is conveyed nicely in the following story:

Then the disciples of John came to him, saying, "Why do we and the Pharisees fast, but your disciples do not fast?" And Jesus said to them, "Can the wedding guests mourn as long as the bridegroom is with them? The days will come, when the bridegroom is taken away from them, and then they will fast." (Matt. 9:14–15)

To the one desirous, either then or now, of understanding this group of disciples, the central requirement is the recognition of the new reality to which it was dedicated, and from which it derived its sense of identity and purpose. Their conduct could not be understood apart from the alternative order by which they came to regulate their lives. Measured against the political order of the Romans, they fell under suspicion of sedition. Measured against the religious order of some Pharisees, the disciple was, like the Master, "a glutton and drunkard, a friend of tax collectors and sinners" (Matt. 11:10). Only the one aware of their consciousness of God's order of reality could recognize that their conduct in relation to earthly rulers and their behavior in relation to the ritual practices of their time did not stem from sedition or disrespect, but reflected their desire to conform their lives to their vision of the "higher righteousness" of the Kingdom that was coming.

At this point it may be helpful to remind ourselves of how this consciousness compared with that of the Pharisees. To begin with, that which the two groups held in common is considerable, especially the dedication to a higher order of reality to which the faithful felt committed to remain true in spite of the pressures of the orders of this world. In both cases, moreover, that higher order was known through God's gracious acts and words on Israel's behalf as revealed in Scripture. On the other hand, the controversies reflected on all levels of the New Testament give expression to a major difference in orientation, and that difference is best understood in relation to the role that eschatology played in the two groups. Although some Pharisees did identify with the apocalyptic activism of the Zealots, for the most part the Pharisees during the time of the first generation of Jesus' disciples likely held to a very mild, restrained form of eschatology. Their primary focus rested on God's ancient gift of the eternal Torah, which, perfect and complete, called for interpretation and application to new situations but not alteration. When allowed by the ruling civil authorities to live true to the Torah, they felt secure in the order of life God intended for them, and were little inclined toward visions of reversal and change. In contrast, the disciples of Jesus found themselves in a world in which all was becoming new in the path of the advent of God's reign. How could they be expected to fast when the marriage feast had already begun?

And so the disciples went forth in imitation of their Master's devotion to God and out of an urgent sense of the nearness of the Kingdom to which they were to invite all that would listen to their word of repentance and forgiveness. And it is likely that they interpreted both their successes and the bitter opposition they faced as signs of the final battle between the angels of the Kingdom and Satan. This is the sense of the following passage that Luke includes in his report on the mission of the seventy:

The seventy returned with joy, saying, "Lord, even the demons are subject to us in your name!" And he said to them, "I saw Satan fall like lightning from heaven." (Luke 10:17–18)

As those understanding their mission as an extension of that of their Master, the first disciples no doubt shared Jesus' sense of the nearness of God's reign, which in turn determined their style of mission. They were not sent out to organize communities and reform political structures, but to bring in the lost into the Kingdom through repentance before the day of judgment.

The events leading up to and culminating in the death of their Master must have cast the circle of Jesus' disciples into a state of serious self-questioning and doubt. The stories of Judas's betrayal, Peter's denial and Thomas's doubting are not the types of legends invented to glorify founding fathers; they reflect the crisis caused by the crucifixion within the circle of disciples closest to Jesus. Although the death of their Master must have heightened their sense of responsibility to carry on where he had left off, the horrible fate suffered by Jesus at the hands of the Romans must have had a paralyzing effect. If there was any source of hope at that dark moment, it must have come from recalling Jesus' teaching about the power of God's reign in relation to the powers of this world. Victory was assured not by meeting worldly power with power in kind, but by trusting in the alternative power of God.

The experience of Jesus' resurrection confirmed in the lives of the disciples the reality and trustworthiness of that alternative power of which their Master had spoken when he instructed them to turn the other cheek, to walk the second mile, and to love the enemy. If Jesus had been brought to defeat by this world's powers, that instruction would have been thrown into serious question. His victory over death, however, they interpreted as a dramatic manifestation of the Kingdom's power. Jesus, a righteous servant at one with the will of the Heavenly Father, could not be bound by death. God's raising him from the dead had broken the power of evil, and thereby removed the last obstacle of the Kingdom. Jesus was the "first fruits" of God's reign.

Above all, this meant that in their continued mission of proclaiming the Kingdom, they were not alone. Their Master was with them. Thus in the post-Easter period, the focus of the disciples came increasingly to rest on Jesus as the Christ, as the Messiah of the Kingdom. As the Torah represented God's presence to the Pharisees,[2] Christ came to represent God's presence to these disciples: "For where two or three are gathered in my name, there am I in the midst of them" (Matt. 18:20). Devotion to God, dedication to the Kingdom, commitment to Christ and care for the "sheep" became indivisible aspects of one way of life within the christological notion of community that began to develop. When the Son of Man was portrayed as presiding in the Last Judgment and declaring to the faithful, "As you did it to one of the least of these my brethren, you did it to me," there is no question that those hearing

2. See 'Abot 3:2.

the story identified the speaker with the risen Christ. He was the one who, after obediently pointing beyond himself to God, was now united with God, and yet present through his Spirit with the faithful as they continued the Kingdom's mission of compassion and justice.

In the ongoing activity of the first generation of disciples, the tenor of the mission was the one set by Jesus during his life. It centered on proclamation of the coming of God's reign, and it carried out the works of healing, comforting, and preaching repentance as the signs of the Kingdom. In all this, the openness of Jesus to the outcasts, the lame, and the possessed continued to provide the example for the disciples (Mark 3:14–15; Luke 14:21). No doubt this openness continued to elicit opposition both among the Romans, who interpreted the disciples' allegiance to the Kingdom of God as a sign of sedition, and among fellow Jews, who took offense at their laxity in relation to their interpretaion of the Torah of Moses. But all such opposition, even in violent form, continued to be seen as a sign of the final resistance of Satan to God's reign. And the stories of the Book of Acts probably capture the posture of the disciples as they faced martyrdom: unwavering confession in the Christ and confidence in the ultimate victory of Christ over the powers of evil. Their eschatological faith thus led them to regard themselves as participants in the final battle, but participants who, unlike the Zealots or the Qumranians, did not engage to curse and to maim, but to bless and to restore and to heal in the name of the Kingdom.

By the time we approach the end of the first generation of the Christian movement, we can recognize the emergence of certain aspects of communal life that adumbrate things to come. To be sure, among the Jewish Christians in Jerusalem structures were minimal, in large part showing continuity with traditional Jewish customs and practices. We read in Acts that the disciples in this period continued to participate in the temple cult, they practiced circumcision, and they observed dietary laws. During this time, the twelve apostles came to be respected as preserving a living link with the Lord. The number 12, associated with the twelve tribes of Israel, was probably upheld as a symbol of the new, eschatological Israel. As the community grew, and as the conversion of Gentiles increased the burdens of leadership, deacons were appointed to assist the apostles. but we are still witnessing the point midway between charisma and institution, for the literature stemming from this period betrays no great interest in establishing formal structures. Rather, the most important bonding element throughout the first generation was the experience of the abiding presence of the risen Lord. As indicated earlier, the experience of Christ's presence functioned in a manner similar to the Torah among the Pharisees.[3] In their regular

---

3. Compare 'Abot 3:2 with Matt. 18:20.

worship and daily common meals, it was Christ's presence that constituted them as God's people: "This is my body which is for you. Do this
in remembrance of me" (1 Cor. 11:24). In their acts of mercy, it was the
perceived presence of Christ in their world that constrained them:
" . . . as you did it to the least of these my brethren you did it to me"
(Matt. 25:40).

During this period, the words of Jesus and traditions concerning his
life were collected and interpreted from a messianic perspective. Another important development that stems from the Jerusalem congregation has to do with the manner in which the risen Christ's presence was
perceived, namely, as the Holy Spirit. The tradition drawn on by Luke in
the second chapter of Acts portrays the coming of the Spirit as an eschatological even that broke all linguistic and geographical barriers and
demonstrated powerfully the universality of the Kingdom to which the
disciples had been called by Christ and to which they were now to bear
witness in the world. It also gives us a glimpse of the nature of the early
apostolic kerygma, according to which Jesus was the key to God's plan of
salvation for the world. Although crucified, he had been raised by God,
and now united with the Father he had poured out the Holy Spirit to
guide and comfort the community of the faithful (Acts 2:14–36).

Chapter XIII observed that the disciples gathered around Jesus were
those who responded to his call. The doctrine of the Holy Spirit provided the means by which this notion of being the people called by God
through Christ could be preserved. This notion is seen in the community's initiatory rite, in which individuals and members of households
were baptized "into Christ" (Rom. 6:3a). This and the longer baptismal
formulas[4] that Paul drew on and that played such an important part in
the development of the confessions of the early church, indicate vividly
how the most important cohesive factor among the Christian congregations was their sense of living in the presence of the risen Lord. It was
Christ's presence that called them into being, preserved them, and
gave them their sense of identity and purpose.

The importance of the Holy Spirit in the life of the early Christian
community can scarcely be overemphasized. Sociologists have long observed how the charisma of new movements tends to be replaced rapidly by the rigidity of organizational structures.[5] This tendency can be
observed in the Essene community of Qumran. Shortly after the death
of the Teacher of Righteousness, a rigidly legalistic organizational
structure evolved that stifled further development or adaptation to
changing circumstances. The authoritarian style of the Teacher of
Righteousness no doubt accounts in large part for this fact. In contrast,
we have seen that Jesus' teaching emphasized the freedom characteriz-

---

4. E.g. Galatians 3:27–28.
5. See M. Weber, *The Theory of Economic Organization*, trans. A. M. Henderson and T.
Parsons (New York: Oxford University Press, 1947), pp. 363–369.

ing the life of the one who lived in communion with God. The doctrine of the Holy Spirit preserved the sense of the living Lord's presence, and served as a counterforce to the natural tendency for the young community to develop legalistic attitudes functioning to preserve the forms and structures of the past. In other words, belief in the Holy Spirit as the presence of the risen Lord in the community kept alive the dynamic inferential process at the heart of early Yahwism and prophetic faith according to which the quality of life of the community was clarified and renewed by each generation through the ongoing encounter with the living God in life's experiences.

Christ's presence accordingly was experienced in what came to be called the gifts of the Spirit, including preaching, healing, and speaking in tongues. The experience of the Spirit accounts as well for another development, one that would become the chief characteristic of the second generation of the church, namely, the outward movement of the Christian proclamation into the entire known world. For though centered in Jerusalem, and observant of the Jewish festivals and customs, the testimony of the early Jewish Christians had led to the conversion of Gentiles from among the Hellenistic elements of the Jerusalem populace; the Holy Spirit seemed blind to distinctions of race and gender! This led to the next step in the development of the Christian notion of community as members of the Jerusalem congregation carried the gospel to Samaria, Damascus, and even as far as Antioch, a movement that was a logical extension of the openness that characterized Jesus' own ministry, including his contacts with people of Galilee and Samaria. Matthew 28:19–20 stands as a monument of this important development: "Go therefore and make disciples of all nations, baptizing them in the name of the Father and the Son and the Holy Spirit, teaching them to observe all that I have commanded you; and lo, I am with you always, to the close of the age."

We can summarize our portrait of the first generation of the church therefore by recognizing the centrality of the experience of the abiding presence of the risen Christ. In their common life, this experience gave rise to the forms of community that began to emerge, especially the initiatory rite in which the convert was baptized "into Christ," and the common meal in which wine was drunk and bread was eaten in memory of Christ and in anticipation of the messianic banquet with him in the Kingdom. To the experience of the Holy Spirit as Christ's presence, we can also trace the custom of sharing goods in common, speaking in tongues, and continuing Jesus' acts of exorcism and healing. Finally, it was the experience of the disappearance of all human barriers in the presence of the risen Christ that gave impetus to the Gentile mission. Thus it was that the Pentecost experience took its place among the other paradigmatic experiences of the early Christian movement. Indeed, it grew intimately out of the earlier experiences of the disciples, especially their receiving instruction in the way of the Kingdom by Jesus, and their witnessing the manifestation of God's reign in his life, death, and resurrection. Pentecost showed them that the one who had drawn them into the Kingdom would continue to abide with them as they brought the invitation to the Kingdom to others. The Holy Spirit thus would be their source of confidence and power as they moved into the future to proclaim and to embody the righteousness and compassion that had its source in the one true God, for the Holy Spirit was God's Spirit, even as Jesus was God's Christ.

B. THE PAULINE CHURCH: A COMMUNITY WITHOUT DISTINCTIONS

Two characteristics stand out when we look back on the first generation of the church: first, the way in which it continued to live in communion with the risen Lord through the experience of the Holy Spirit, and second, how diverse its membership was becoming by the end of that period. These two characteristics set the stage for the second generation, whose leaders would continue to seek to place all life under the rule of the Spirit, but whose diverse membership would increasingly create problems and tensions calling for another sort of rule, namely, that regulated by organizational structure.

The problem of diversity was raised especially by the conversion of Gentiles, which as noted already had occurred among the first generation of disciples in Jerusalem. Here was a classic conflict between continuity and change. The Jewish Christians confessed that in Jesus Christ, their Messiah, they had experienced God's new saving initiative. But beyond this basic confession differences in emphasis arose. Some emphasized that Jesus was the *Jewish* Messiah, who had come to restore the *Jewish* people, and accordingly they continued to practice circumcision and observe the dietary laws of their tradition. Moreover, they expected converts to do the same. Others stressed the *newness* of God's initiative in Christ, as manifested by the influx of *Gentiles* into the community of faith and the solidarity experienced in the Spirit, and concluded that circumcision and food laws were not binding on non-Jewish converts.

The latter point of view ultimately prevailed, and the chief reason for this outcome was the organizational skill, theological acumen, and deep devotion of the apostle Paul. The struggle between the many different groups, including the observant Jerusalem Christians and various missionary groups, some of them with pronounced gnostic leanings, was often bitter and surely very complex. Here we can focus only on the position that after the Apostolic Council in Jerusalem in 49 C.E. asserted itself over the others, that stemming from the teachings of Paul and centered especially in Antioch.

Paul, who had received a first-class training within the Pharisaic tradition under the master teacher Gamaliel, was converted through a visionary encounter with the risen Christ, by whom he believed he had been called to become a missionary to the Gentiles. More than any other figure, it was Paul who took up the mandate implicit in Jesus' dealings with outsiders such as the Samaritans and Romans, in the words of his parable of the marriage feast ("Go therefore to the thoroughfares, and invite to the marriage feast as many as you find" [Matt. 22:9]), and in his response to the faith of the Centurion ("Truly I say to you, not even in Israel have I found such faith. I tell you, many will come from east and west and sit at table with Abraham, Isaac, and Jacob in the kingdom of heaven, while the sons of the kingdom will be thrown into the outer darkness" [Matt. 8:10b–12a]).

It is important to recognize the basis of this dramatic turn in the life of one trained as a Pharisee, for it has bearing on Paul's entire message. Stated simply, the basis was Paul's eschatological belief that Jesus the Messiah had inaugurated the new age of reconciliation. The conclusion Paul had drawn was thus deeply rooted in his Jewish faith, and indeed, his repeated recourse to Scripture and to the events of biblical history indicate clearly that he saw Christ as the fulfillment of divine promises given to the ancestors of the faith. But alongside this stress on continuity Paul placed great emphasis on the radical newness of God's act in Christ.

A classical formulation of the contrast between the old era and the new is found in Galatians 3:23–29. In his Letter to the Galatians, Paul sought to establish that the crucifixion of the Messiah was the eschatological event that erased all distinctions between Jews and Gentiles, for it inaugurated the age of freedom under God's grace transcending every human effort to erect restrictive barriers.[6] Specifically in 3:23–29 Paul addresses the question of membership and eligibility, and states emphatically that all distinctions had been erased, for salvation comes through faith, signified by "baptism into Christ." He goes on to point out, however, that this is not an upstart religion, but rather the fulfillment of the classic faith revealed in Scripture. For those who are Christ's are thereby "Abraham's offspring," the heirs to the ancient promise.

The kinship between Paul's eschatological perspective and that found at the heart of Jesus' proclamation of the Kingdom is obvious. We have seen that Jesus' attitude toward the sabbath and toward fasting and eating with sinners was tied to his belief that a new era had dawned. Paul argued strenuously against those who would subject the Gentile converts to the law of circumcision precisely because that

---

6. See W. A. Meeks, *The First Urban Christians: The Social World of the Apostle Paul* (New Haven, Conn.: Yale University Press, 1983), pp.180–183.

would amount to a repudiation of the good news that the new age had come. It would be tantamount to "turning the clock backward" in God's history of salvation. In the New Age, life "under the law" was abolished in favor of the new order established by God through Christ. In 1 Corinthians 9:21, Paul even uses the term "the law of Christ" to refer to the new order of freedom, in which the believer obeys the will of God incarnate in Christ and revealed by the Holy Spirit as a grateful response to God's antecedent grace (cf. Rom. 8:1–4). We can recognize in this a reform impulse as well: obedience is related back to the primal moment of faith, its response to the God experienced as present and active in the world on behalf of the lost. Paul's emphasis on justification by faith is thus closely akin to the early Yahwistic community's stress on God's gracious initiative in saving those lacking both human resources and any special claim on God's grace as the foundation of authentic human community.

Paul does not deny that "the advantage" of the Jew is "much in every way" (Rom. 3:1–4). He readily expresses his indebtedness to his tradition (cf. Rom. 9:4–5). But the point he makes is an eschatological one: God's plan has reached the stage where redemption has been extended to all peoples:

But now the righteousness of God has been manifested apart from law, although the law and the prophets bear witness to it, the righteousness of God through faith in Jesus Christ for all who believe. For there is no distinction; since all have sinned and fall short of the glory of God, they are justified by his grace as a gift, through the redemption which is in Christ Jesus, whom God put forward as an expiation by his blood, to be received by faith. (Rom. 3:21–25a)

It was Paul's specific eschatological perspective that led him to take issue with his former co-religionists, the Pharisees. According to their eschatology, the messianic age had not yet arrived, and understandably they structured their lives on a different basis than that developed by Paul. The age in which they lived was one continuous with that of Moses, and the order by which they regulated their lives was the Mosaic Torah. As a minority group dedicated to maintaining ritual purity in a defiled world that seemed unlikely soon to pass away, they felt it their sacred duty to maintain strict separation from all that defiled, such as ordinary food and utensils, and sinners. This was a communal ideal with roots reaching all the way back to Haggai (cf. Hag. 2:11–14), and coming to expression especially in Ezra's strict separation of the Judahites from their foreign wives aimed at restoring the purity of the "holy seed" (Ezra 9–10). In contrast to this cautious posture resulting from centuries of experience as a righteous remnant in the midst of a defiled world, the eschatological faith of Paul fostered a daring enthusiasm. Like Jesus, he believed that the day of reversal had arrived, and that the new era had dawned in which all nations would be invited to become members of God's people. The result was a reversal of the relation between the holy and the profane. No longer was the holy threatened, under seige, or on the defensive. The reign of evil had been broken, and the unholy was in retreat. This is seen by contrasting Ezra's policy against mixed marriages with Paul's position. Ezra felt constrained to enforce separation, because the unclean, as the more potent or "infectious" state, threatened the ritually clean, a position maintained by strict Pharisees and necessitating their separation from those who did not observe their interpretation of the Torah. Paul's eschatological faith led to a reversal of this relationship. Holiness had taken the offensive in the age-long struggle. This he illustrated with the problem of mixed marriages:

For the unbelieving husband is consecrated through his wife, and the unbelieving wife is consecrated through her husband. Otherwise, your children would be unclean, but as it is, they are holy. (1 Cor. 7:14)

This new state of relationships between the holy and the profane led to a very different posture vis-á-vis the world. Paul could state, " 'All things are lawful for me,' but not all things are helpful. 'All things are lawful for me,' but I will not be enslaved by anything' " (1 Cor. 6:12). The conduct of the Christian is accordingly regulated not by written laws, but by the new fact of his or her redemption. More specifically, conduct arose from the righteousness of God, which was given as a gift to the believer through faith in what God had done in Christ. Therefore Paul could root his conduct directly in the presence of the risen Christ in his life: "For the love of Christ controls us, because we are convinced that one has died for all; therefore all have died" (2 Cor. 5:14). We thus see that for Paul, the "turning of the tide" in the long struggle between righteousness and evil had occurred with the resurrection, for in Christ's victory over death God's victory over the chaos of defilement and sin had occurred.

Paul's defense of his Gentile mission is likewise squarely based on his eschatological perspective. He does not argue that circumcision or the law is at fault: "We know that the law is spiritual" (Rom. 7:14), he insists. But he refuses to regard the traditional formulation of the law as eternal, or as a binding authority limiting God's freedom. He looks historically behind the law to God's promise to Abraham, who "believed in God, and it was reckoned to him as righteousness" (Rom. 4:3; cf. Gen. 15:6). His view of the purpose of the law is likewise thoroughly historical: "It was added because of transgression, till the offspring should come to whom the promise had been made" (Gal. 3:19). To this he adds a second equally historical explanation: through the law "scripture consigned all things to sin, that what was promised to faith in Jesus Christ might be given to those who believe" (Gal. 3:22). A variation on this explanation follows immediately, "The law was our custodian until

Christ came" (Gal. 3:24), watching over God's people till they had reached maturity, so to speak. The point behind these various interpretations of the role and the function of the law was historical and eschatological. The point was at hand in God's plan when God was now reaching out beyond Israel, and in this extension of salvation to all peoples the law was no longer to define limits or set boundaries: "For neither circumcision counts for anything, nor uncircumcision, but a new creation" (Gal. 6:15). To prove this point, Paul points out that Jesus, by being crucified, had fallen under the curse of the law, thereby redeeming mortals "from the curse of the law" (cf. Gal. 3:13 with Deut. 21:23). And he goes on to insist that this eschatological act was at the same time the fulfillment of God's original plan, "that in Christ Jesus the blessing of Abraham might come upon the Gentiles, that we might receive the promise of the Spirit through faith" (Gal. 3:14). It is thus a thoroughly eschatological confession when Paul can claim that all those baptized into Christ are Abraham's offspring, whether Jew or Greek, slave or free, male or female (Gal. 3:27–29). The event had occurred that brought to fulfillment an important aspect of Israel's history. The blessing of Abraham had come to embrace all peoples, the light borne by the servant Israel had been given to all nations, God's salvation had reached the end of the earth. All things had become new under this new order of salvation. To emphasize the fulfillment of that history of promise, Paul refers to those who belong to Christ as "children of God through faith" (Gal. 3:26), and "the Israel of God" (Gal. 6:16).

In the eschatological concept of the "new creation"—that is, the order of reality with which God brings to fulfillment the divine plan for creation by breaking down all human distinctions that had led to the exclusion of certain groups and individuals—we find the heart of Paul's notion of community. Here the radical egalitarianism of early Yahwism, the expansive vision of the prophets, and the uninhibited compassion of Jesus find a worthy successor. And here later generations have found an expression of the dynamic creativity of the biblical notion of community that has continued to challenge the people of God to become what God has intended them to be. For Paul, the principle that guided the life of the community of the faithful was the principle of the Spirit of Christ that constituted the body of those who were equal before God at the same time as they remained divergent in the gifts they had to offer. According to Paul, the essential division of responsibilities in the church was not between those exercising roles of authority and those following their direction, or between those ministering and those passively being ministered unto. Instead, it was between all members each of whom was drawn into God's service by receiving a particular charisma—that is, a particular type of ministry within the whole body. This understanding of the division of the diverse forms of ministry among all members of the congregation is described as follows by Ernst Käsemann:

For Paul, to have a charisma means to participate for that very reason in life, in grace, in the Spirit, because a charisma is the specific part which the individual has in the lordship and glory of Christ; and this specific part which the individual has in the lord shows itself in a specific service and a specific vocation. For there is no divine gift which does not bring with it a task, there is no grace which does not move to action. Service is not merely the consequence but the outward form and the realization of grace.[7]

This attitude allowed Paul to be very open, even casual with regard to forms of community leadership. Only in the Letter to the Phillipians does he even mention bishops and deacons (Phil. 1:1). He seemed to be confident that the community open to the spirit would not lack cohesiveness.

Unfortunately, the challenge to be a community guided by the Spirit and fundamentally egalitarian in structure has rarely been heeded, leading to recurrent attempts to establish certain groups, whether defined by gender, race, or social status, as privileged and in possession of superior authority in the community of faith. In certain instances, Paul and Paul's immediate followers and interpreters themselves succumbed to this temptation. In this connection, the question whether it is Paul himself or later interpreters of Paul who admonish women to be silent in the meetings of the church (which question remains much debated) is a secondary matter (1 Cor. 14:33b–36). What is far more important to understand is that the *heart* of Paul's vision of God's people is not found in such a pronouncement, a point reinforced by Paul's full inclusion of women as co-workers elsewhere.[8] It is only fair to distinguish between Paul's vision of the new community, and some of his own reactions to specific situations. For he was much aware that the church was still weighted heavily by the old era. Indeed, he turned to his vexing fact repeatedly.

What was to be said of the undeniable indications visible on all sides that all had *not* come to fulfillment, Paul was led to ask. Members of the community of faith were still afflicted by sickness, and the struggle with sin went on. Something had to be added to the description of "Jesus Christ, who gave himself for our sins, in order to rescue us from the present evil age, according to the will of our God and Father" (Gal. 1:3–4). For Paul was vehemently opposed to the Corinthian enthusiasts of the church who argued that they had already passed from the cor-

---

7. E. Käsemann, *Essays on New Testament Themes* (Philadelphia: Fortress Press, 1982), p. 65.

8. E.g. Philippians 4:2–3; even 1 Corinthians 11:5 takes it for granted that women pray and prophesy in church. For a discussion of the problem of the role of women in the Pauline Church, see R. Scroggs, *Paul for a New Day* (Philadelphia: Fortress Press, 1977).

ruptible to the incorruptible. Paul therefore stresses the paradox of "already" versus "not yet." The present manifests "first fruits," but the believer waits for the glory that is to come.[9]

Indeed, this waiting is cosmic in scope:

We know that the whole creation has been groaning in travail together until now; and not only the creation, but we ourselves, who have the first fruits of the Spirit, groan inwardly as we wait for the adoption as sons, the redemption of our bodies. (Rom. 8:22–23)

Since the decisive eschatological event had occurred, Paul could speak of the New Creation and the New Age. But his eschatological perspective did not blindly overlook the persistent signs of evil's presence in the world. He rejoices over the Thessalonians who "wait for his Son from heaven, whom he raised from the dead, Jesus who delivers us from the wrath to come" (1 Thess. 1:10). And he replies to the despairing grief of those who have lost loved ones before Christ's return with the assurance that they are not lost, but will be the first to rise to the Lord in the resurrection (1 Thess. 4:13–18). And then he goes on to issue a warning against apocalyptic speculation with a clear word of instruction in 5:1–11. Their eschatological faith is not to direct their attention away from their participation in life, but to equip them "to encourage one another and build one another up" (v. 11). "Since we belong to the day, let us be sober, and put on the breastplate of faith and love, and for a helmet the hope of salvation" (v. 8). The victory Christ had won was to be a part of their experience now, but not in a self-indulgent abdication of their participation in the community. For as the Body of Christ they were passing through the way of testing leading to the parousia, when God's reign would be universally revealed. In contrast to a form of enthusiastic apocalyticism or gnosticism leading to a denial of social and ethical responsibility, we find Paul's eschatological faith expressing itself in a moral rigor reminiscent of Jesus' coupling the teaching of the Kingdom with moral watchfulness and sobriety. The person of faith remains a pilgrim in this world, who looks yet "to the things that are unseen" (2 Cor. 4:18). And since that pilgrim shares with fellow believers an important role in God's plan for the redemption of creation, Paul's eschatological paradox lies at the heart of his understanding of the community of faith.

This eschatological paradox comes to expression in Paul's metaphor of the church as "the body of Christ." He wholeheartedly accepts the confession of the earliest church that in becoming a Christian one is baptized "into Christ." Paul elaborates on this understanding by pointing out that through this baptism the believer dies to sin, is raised to

---

9. Concerning the eschatological dimension of Paul's concept of salvation, see V. P. Furnish, *Theology and Ethics in Paul* (Nashville, Tenn.: Abingdon Press, 1968), pp. 122–126.

"newness of life" as one forgiven and redeemed, and looks with confidence to the resurrection:

Do you not know that all of us who have been baptized into Christ Jesus were baptized into his death? We were buried therefore with him by baptism into death, so that as Christ was raised from the dead by the glory of the Father, we too might walk in newness of life. For if we have been united with him in a death like his, we shall certainly be united with him in a resurrection like his. (Rom. 6:3–5)

Paul's understanding of baptism and justification alone allows us to grasp what he means when he describes the community of faith as "the body of Christ." It is neither a Stoic community living in indifference to the world, nor a gnostic community claiming that it has already passed beyond earthly life into the heavenly realm. The force of sin, evil, and Satan still manifest in the world is too real to deny. But Paul recognizes that Christ had ushered in the new reality of God's righteousness. Through baptism and forgiveness, the believer is transferred from the fallen world into that new reality present in this world where Christ is confessed. The community of faith accordingly is characterized by "loyal participation in the body of Christ, in which the power of God is at work and to which final vindication is promised."[10] Thus we see how Paul preserves the paradox, and places the believer between the decisive victory that was Christ's resurrection and the final fulfillment, which will be the resurrection of all believers.

As an eschatological community, the church is to be a unique body in the world. It is characterized by a unique source of origin, a unique perspective, and a unique mission:

For the love of Christ controls us, because we are convinced that one has died for all; therefore all have died. And he died for all, that those who live might live no longer for themselves but for him who for their sake died and was raised. From now on, therefore, we regard no one from a human point of view; even though we once regarded Christ from a human point of view, we regard him thus no longer. Therefore, if any one is in Christ, he is a new creation; the old has passed away, behold, the new has come. All this is from God, who through Christ reconciled us to himself and gave us the ministry of reconciliation; that is, God was in Christ reconciling the world to himself, not counting their trespasses against them, and entrusting to us the message of reconciliation. So we are ambassadors for Christ, God making his appeal through us. We beseech you on behalf of Christ, be reconciled to God. For our sake he made him to be sin who knew no sin, so that in him we might become the righteousness of God. (2 Cor. 5:14–21)

When Paul describes the origin of the church, he remains true to the primal pattern of early Yahwism. Its source is strictly and solely in an antecedent act of divine grace: " . . . we are convinced that one has

10. Meeks, *Urban Christians*, p. 189.

died for all . . ." For our sake he made him to be sin who knew no sin, so that in him we might become the righteousness of God." In the fullness of time, at the point where the brokenness of creation was fully in evidence, God acted in a dramatic new way to break down the barrier of sin that humans had constructed between themselves and their only source of life. What was impossible for humans to accomplish God accomplished for them through the devotion and sacrifice of his son: "All this is from God, who through Christ reconciled us to himself." The community of faith is thus the body of those who have responded in worship and praise to God's gracious initiative in Christ.

The result of this response is a new creation. The old order of sin and evil and chaos has "passed away." The believer is no longer enslaved to the bonds of death, to self-centeredness and greed: "that those who live might live no longer for themselves but for him who for their sake died and was raised." Life for Christ, which means life for those Christ loved, is life in the new age of God's righteousness. The one thus reborn is "a new creation," experiencing that "the old has passed away, behold the new has come."

According to Paul, reconciliation and new birth create within the people of faith a radically new way of looking on life. Formerly, they, like the rest of the world, saw things from "a human point of view." They saw corruption, decay, and the dominion of evil in the world. They despaired, and reacted by grabbing what they could get for themselves as a source of security in a dying world. But with the new creation comes a new perspective, seeing the world and the neighbor from the viewpoint of the new age, which began with Christ's resurrection. The power of evil and death no longer has control over the community of faith. In hope, faith, and love, the community lives within the sphere of God's reign in Christ.

Many forms of salvation, of course, are ultimately self-indulgent, as the "saved" adopt an attitude of privileged chosenness implying freedom from all responsibility for the perishing masses.[11] Paul cannot draw this conclusion from the example of the Savior "who, though he was in the form of God, did not count equally with God a thing to be grasped, but emptied himself, taking the form of a servant, being born in the likeness of men" (Phil. 2:6–7). Pointing to this example, Paul declares, "Have this mind among yourselves." The implication is very clear: the community of faith is to be present in the world for the sake of the world's reconciliation with God, even as Christ was in the world for the world's salvation. The gift is to be passed on, for God's love is not diminished, but comes to fullness as it is shared: "All this is from God, who through Christ reconciled us to himself and gave us the min-

---

11. Cf. Scroggs, *Paul*, pp. 49–50, concerning the tension between equality and elitism. He observes, "The worst sin of all is to create an elitism out of precisely that act that eliminates any possibility of elitism" (p. 50).

istry of reconciliation; that is, God was in Christ reconciling the world to himself, not counting their trespasses against them, and entrusting to us the message of reconciliation." As Christ devoted his life to extending the invitation of God to all mortals, the Body of Christ was to be in the world as "ambassadors for Christ," through whom God extends that invitation: "Be reconciled to God."

The theological basis for community as clarified by Paul is of fundamental importance. If it is not grasped, the church loses its uniqueness by losing its source and perspective and mission. It is extremely easy for the church to view itself as a voluntary agency, following high ethical norms, and dedicated to worthy goals. But Paul's vision of the church's origin is fundamentally different. True human community is created only where the community between God and humans is restored. The key is reconciliation. And reconciliation between human and human is possible only where preceded by reconciliation between humans and God. For Paul, the entire area of ethics is approached from this fundamentally theological understanding of life in community.[12] This is reflected, for example, in the structure of the Letter to the Romans, where the ethical section beginning with chapter 12 is based firmly on the preceding eleven chapters of theological reflection. Another implication of this theological framework is that ethics is not construed in individualistic terms, say, as the means of attaining personal perfection, but is understood as an aspect of responding to the antecedent love of God. Ethical behavior is thus Christ-like behavior, always focusing on the building up of the whole body of Christ, always motivated by concern for the weaker brother or sister.[13]

Because Paul stood firmly against the gnostics' seductive beckoning to abdicate responsibility for the world, his theological foundation for community led to a deeper grounding for social and personal ethics than that found in voluntary organizations. For no voluntary organization is able to put forward as profound a source of dedication to the well-being of all humans as this: "For the love of Christ controls us." It should be clear that the pattern of community building here is again true to the early Yahwistic example, where the group responding to God's antecedent act of grace in worship and praise proceeded to draw its principles of righteousness and compassion from the example of the Deliverer God. To be the body of Christ meant for Paul not only to be the benefactors of Christ's sacrifice, but to embody *in* the world, *for the sake of* the world, the mind of Christ. And that meant a very special way of being human:

So if there is any encouragement in Christ, any incentive of love, any participation in the Spirit, any affection and sympathy, complete my joy by being of the

---

12. See Furnish, *Theology and Ethics*, pp. 208–226, for a clear exposition of the indivisible union between the gospel and ethics in Paul.

13. D. Bonhoeffer, *The Cost of Discipleship*, trans. R. H. Fuller (New York: Macmillan, 1957), pp. 187–189.

same mind, having the same love, being in full accord and of one mind. Do nothing from selfishness or conceit, but in humility count others better than yourselves. Let each of you look not only to his own interests, but also to the interests of others. Have this mind among yourselves, which you have in Christ Jesus, who though he was in the form of God, did not count equality with God a thing to be grasped, but emptied himself, taking the form of a servant. (Phil. 2:1–7)

A connection with the tradition of Second Isaiah's Suffering Servant seems likely here. We recognized in the Servant an alternative to the customary way in which the ancient world construed leadership. Instead of a dazzling king, imposing order by force, we saw the one offering an example of patient suffering for the sake of the lost, and a willingness to die to atone for the sins of others. This alternative power of love was the one that Jesus embodied in contending with the powers of evil, as he repudiated Satan's invitation to come to victory by pitting violence against violence. Clearly, Paul continues this tradition, and models his notion of community after it. He holds up before the eyes of his congregation the crucifixion-resurrection paradox, and encourages them in their affliction. They are thus following in the way of their Lord, and having suffered with him, will also be victorious with him (Rom. 5:1–11; 2 Cor. 1:3–7; 4:14). Notice how the inferential process moving from divine example to norms for human behavior found in early Yahwism is followed by Paul:

We who are strong ought to bear with the failings of the weak, and not to please ourselves; let each of us please his neighbor for his good, to edify him. For Christ did not please himself; but, as it is written, "The reproaches of those who reproached thee fell on me." (Rom. 15:1–3)

Welcome one another, therefore, as Christ has welcomed you, for the glory of God. For I tell you that Christ became a servant to the circumcised to show God's truthfulness, in order to confirm the promises given to the patriarchs, and in order that the Gentiles might glorify God for his mercy. (Rom. 15:7–9)

Paul appeals to the same source of motivation in urging participation in his collection for the poor in Jerusalem:

For you know the grace of our Lord Jesus Christ, that though he was rich, yet for your sake he became poor, so that by his poverty you might become rich. (2 Cor. 8:9)

The patience and perseverance that characterized Paul's activities on behalf of the Jerusalem congregation attest to the depth of his own conviction that the unity of the church was secured precisely in showing acts of mercy and mutual support. We know that important theological differences existed between Paul and the pillars of the Jerusalem church. But even these did not deter him from following Christ's example of compassion as the most powerful of all bonding agents in the community of faith.

This inferential pattern continued on in the Pauline tradition, as illustrated by the following:

Put on then, as God's chosen ones, holy and beloved, compassion, kindness, lowliness, meekness, and patience, forbearing one another and, if one has a complaint against another, forgiving each other; as the Lord has forgiven you, so you also must forgive. And above all these put on love, which binds everything together in perfect harmony. And let the peace of Christ rule in your hearts. (Col. 3:12–15a)

Let all bitterness and wrath and anger and clamor and slander be put away from you, with all malice, and be kind to one another, tenderhearted, forgiving one another, and God in Christ forgave you. (Eph. 4:31–32)

Therefore be imitators of God, as beloved children. And walk in love, as Christ loved us and gave himself up for us, a fragrant offering and sacrifice to God. (Eph. 5:1–2)

As a body dedicated to the ministry of reconciliation and to the goal of a creation drawn out of decay into the sphere of God's healing power, the church was able to assess realistically the hazards of this world, and yet confess with confidence, "neither death, nor life, nor angels, nor principalities, nor things present, nor things to come, nor powers, nor height, nor depth, nor anything else in all creation, will be able to separate us from the love of God in Christ Jesus our Lord." (Rom. 8:38–39)

Paul was able to be equally realistic about the diversity that characterizes human community, for the unity that he envisioned was dynamic enough to integrate the many different gifts of individual members into the whole. Thus the body was not threatened by the individuality of its members, nor was the individuality of the members threatened by the corporateness of the body: "Now you are the body of Christ and individually members of it" (1 Cor. 12:27). The reality of Christ's Spirit in its midst was enough to integrate the diversity of gifts (1 Cor. 12:4–11) and offices (1 Cor. 12:28–31a) into one harmonious agent, for all were derived from the same divine source, even as all members were baptized into the same Lord: "For just as the body is one and has many members, and all the members of the body, though many, are one body, so it is with Christ. For by one Spirit we were all baptized into one body—Jews or Greeks, slaves or free—and all were made to drink of one Spirit" (1 Cor. 12:12–13).

It is not incidental, of course, that Paul's discourse on the higher unity culminates in 1 Cor. 13 with his description of "a still more excellent way," without which one has nothing. For Paul captures the essence of the Christian gospel with a sublime celebration of love:

Love is patient and kind; love is not jealous or boastful; it is not arrogant or rude. Love does not insist on its own way; it is not irritable or resentful; it does not rejoice at wrong, but rejoices in the right. Love bears all things, believes all things, hopes all things, endures all things. (vv. 4–7)

Love, as a quality known through the example of Christ, and embodied as a gift of the ever-present Spirit, served for Paul as the norm for all situations in life. Especially where customary norms proved inadequate, the "law of love" was a reliable guide.[14] It alone could preserve the freedom the believer had been granted by a God who saved sinners "apart from the works of the law," and at the same time safeguard against the misuse of that freedom for self-gain at the cost of the well-being of others.

One final issue remains to be considered in relation to which Paul combines his customary realism with his eschatological perspective. Although Paul believed that the Messiah had come in the person of Jesus, the historical fact remained that most Jews of his time had not accepted this messianic claim. Had God abandoned his plan for the salvation of Israel? Had the ancient promise that they would become a blessing to all the families of the earth been abandoned?

Paul approaches the question of the future of his "kinsmen by race" from the same eschatological perspective informing all his theological discussions. He begins his discussion in Romans 9–11 with a celebration of Israel's rich religious heritage, to which the church remained deeply indebted, a heritage culminating, "according to the flesh" with "the Christ" (Rom. 9:4–5). He then goes on to draw the careful distinction between two different ways of understanding who are the descendants of Abraham—namely, as "children of the flesh" and "children of the promise"—and points out that the latter belong to Israel, for "the children of the promise are reckoned as descendants" (Rom. 9:9). This assures that salvation will be understood as resulting from the free grace of God, both among Jews and Gentiles.

After pointing out that the rejection of God's new initiative by the majority of Israel was tied to God's free, gracious move to draw the Gentiles into the plan of salvation, he clarifies the relation of the Gentile church to historical Israel with the aid of the metaphor of the olive tree. He insists that God's new outreach in Christ to the Gentiles was not separate from, but a part of his long prior relationship with Israel: "Remember, it is not you that support the root, but the root that supports you" (11:9). Indeed, forgetting this relation of dependence would bring with it the threat of a fatal fall to pride (11:20–22). From this contemporary problem, Paul turns his attention to the future, and sees the time beyond the Gentile mission when God would return to his first people, "so all Israel will be saved," "for the gifts and the call of God are irrevocable" (11:26, 29). It is clear how important for Paul is the belief that the separation occasioned by Israel's rejection of the mes-

---

14. Paul's application of the "higher law" of love to a situation eluding customary legal solutions is illustrated by the problem of food offered to idols discussed in 1 Corinthians 8.

siahship of Christ was not a final state. He took the long history of salvation and the promises made to Israel's ancestors too seriously to accept any other vision than the eschatological vision of God's final salvation of the Gentiles and of "all Isreal," "that he may have mercy upon all" (11:32b). It is this vision that moves Paul to a shout of praise:

> O the depth of the riches and wisdom
> and knowledge of God! How unsearchable
> are his judgments and how inscrutable
> his ways!
> "For who has known the mind of the Lord,
> or who has been his counselor?"
> "Or who has given a gift to him
> that he might be repaid?"
> For from him and through him and
> to him are all things. To him be glory
> forever. Amen.   (Rom. 11:33–36)

C. THE CHURCH AFTER THE FIRST JEWISH REVOLT (THE THIRD GENERATION)

The major theological challenge facing the Christian congregations of Paul's time was that of relating the new Gentile mission to the Jewish heritage of Christianity. Paul struck the balance that allowed the church to emerge from that challenge strengthened as he insisted on the freedom of the Gentile Christians from circumcision and the dietary laws and at the same time demonstrated his respect and concern for the "mother church" by seeing to the collection of the contribution for "the poor" of Jerusalem.

As the delay of the parousia became more obvious, another problem emerged and became the primary challenge of the post–70 C.E. period. As Paul had already experienced within the churches of Corinth and Philippi, many Christians were growing impatient in the face of the continued postponement of the Second Coming, and began to claim that already in this life they had passed from the corruptible to the incorruptible. Gnostics played a large part in this development as they claimed that for the true believer this world retained no reality. And their hand was strengthened by their appeal to the writings of Paul to support that claim. Those following in the Pauline tradition who stressed the Pauline theme of ethical and social responsibility thus found themselves drawn into bitter controversy with gnostic teachers preaching a gospel of otherworldly knowledge and salvation that turned the backs of its followers on moral engagement with the issues of this world.

Because the gnosticizing enthusiasts drew on themes central to Pauline and even earlier teachings, especially those relating to the presence

of the Revealer in the form of the Spirit, the lines of battle were difficult to demarcate. Let us sample some writings of the period from 70
to 130 C.E. to see how this controversy, along with other factors being
pressed on the church by the outside world, such as the growing separation from Judaism and periodic persecution by the Romans, affected
the development of the notion of community. We shall see in this sampling especially the tendency, among Christians who were not only
aware that the eschaton had not arrived as expected but believed that
the world was likely to be their home for a long time to come, to stress
church order as the reply to otherworldly enthusiasm, and true doctrine as the fitting response to what was coming to be defined as heresy.
It will be clear that this period carries us a significant step in the direction of early Catholicism.

One of the most important groups of writings for this period is also
the most difficult to use, because of the difficulty in dating its various
levels of redaction. These are the New Testament Gospels, containing
as they do materials stemming from the historical Jesus, collections of
stories and sayings from the first generation of disciples, and then subsequent redactional levels down to the final editions. The sayings
source commonly referred to as "Q" (for German *Quelle*, "source")
shows how the words attributed to Jesus already at an early stage were
edited from a specifically eschatological perspective, probably to function in the teaching activity of the early church both in relation to potential converts who were to be made aware of the need to repent and
in relation to members of the Christian community who were to be instructed to remain prepared for the Lord's return. In Q, Jesus is accordingly identified with the Son of Man, and awaited as the one who
was to come after a period of tribulation (Luke 17:22–37; Matt. 24:26–
27, 37–39). And the Lord's Supper is presented as the solemn meal
celebrated in anticipation of the banquet to be eaten with the Lord "in
the Kingdom of God."

Shortly after the destruction of the temple the effort to gather the
words of Jesus was carried a step further by the author of the Gospel of
Mark. On the basis of and with focus on a passion narrative, this author
"fleshes out" the early confessions contained in baptismal and eucharistic formulas by presenting a biography of Jesus. In this manner a new
genre was born, one particularly treasured within a community seeking
to live as had its apostles in the presence of its Lord. In the form of the
gospel narrative, they were able to visualize that presence, and to identify with the passion of Christ as they themselves suffered for their
confession.

The later Gospels were patterned after Mark. Written circa 85 C.E.,
Matthew was written as a catechism for the church, being structured
on the basis of five major discourses (the "Sermon on the Mount" in
chap. 5–7, the discourse on the apostolic mission in chap. 10, the dis-

course on the nature of the Kingdom in chap. 13, the discourse on church discipline in chap. 18, and the discourse on false leaders in chap. 23).[15] The claim to authority advanced by Matthew is more explicit than that found in Mark. Jesus is presented as the one who in the events of his life gave the definitive revelation of God's will, and who was the fulfiller of the Jewish Scriptures. This view of Jesus' role as Revealer comes to expression in the so-called formula quotations; for example, "All this took place to fulfill what the Lord has spoken by the prophet . . . " (1:22).[16]

The background of the Gospel of Matthew is clearly that of the growing separation of the Christian church from Judaism as the former moved toward the status of a distinct religion. It is to be remembered that in the wake of the destruction of the temple in 70 C.E. the Pharisees moved their center of activity from Jerusalem to the academy founded in Jabneh, thereby initiating a period of intense study and reorganization resulting in the forms of Judaism that remain normative to the present day. On its side, the Christian church was defining its relationship both to this reconstituted Judaism of the rabbis and to the heritage common to both, the Jewish Scriptures. This it did by making the claim that it, and not the synagogue, was the legitimate heir to the biblical promises. The Gospel of Matthew reflects this polemical position. In fact, the opening volley comes in the first verse of the Gospel of Matthew with the heading to the genealogy of Jesus: "the son of David, the son of Abraham." The latter term appeals to the covenant promise standing at the very beginning of Israel's history, thus out-archaizing the standard appeal of the Jewish leaders of the time to the authority of Moses. Moreover, Jesus is presented as the authoritative interpreter of the Torah, as opposed to the "false teachings" of the "scribes and the Pharisees." This is seen especially in the Sermon on the Mount (e.g., "Think not that I have come to abolish the law and the prophets; I have come not to abolish them but to fulfill them," followed by the "antitheses" [5:17–48]). As chapter 23 indicates, the polemic against the "scribes and Pharisees" was very sharp, though one must keep in mind that the controversy was one *between* Jewish parties, for the nature of the polemic undergoes a radical change when falsely reapplied—as has so often been the case in the history of Christian interpretation—as words of *Gentiles* directed against Jews.

The post–70 C.E. situation is reflected also in the additions that Matthew makes to the parable of the wicked tenants (21:33–46), which he has taken over from the Gospel of Mark (Mark 12:1–12). In verses 41 and 43, we recognize an allusion to the destruction of the temple,

---

15. Koester, *Introduction to the New Testament*, Vol. 2, History and Literature of Early Christianity (Philadelphia: Fortress Press, 1982), p. 173.

16. On the use of the formula quotation in Matthew, see K. Stendahl, *The School of St. Matthew and Its Use of the Old Testament* (Philadelphia: Fortress Press, 1961), pp. 97–127.

which is interpreted as God's judgment on the official leaders of Judah: " 'He will put those wretches to a miserable death, and let out the vineyard to other tenants who will give him the fruits in their seasons. . . ' Therefore I tell you, the kingdom of God will be taken away from you and given to a nation producing the fruits of it."

That a new people of God was being called into being through the life of Jesus, Matthew demonstrated by the unique way in which he presented the life of Jesus, beginning with his early years. It is especially interesting to note how his account of Jesus' infancy recapitulates the events that gave birth to God's first people. It begins with Joseph the dreamer, who having experienced the terrible jealousy and wrath of a godless king, flees to Egypt, and later returns after that king's death (cf. Matt. 2:19–21 with Exod. 4:19). The future savior of the people, named Jesus (in Hebrew, named Joshua), thus escaped premature death, enabling him to embark (like Moses's successor of the same name) on the task of saving his people and establishing a new home for them. But as remarkable as the similarities to the ancient story are the differences. For while Joshua's conquest was by force and bloody conflict, the only blood shed by Jesus was his own. Jesus as Messiah was thus a kind of king hitherto unheard of in the world, though adumbrated by the Suffering Servant. Matthew uses the synoptic story of the temptation of Jesus to demonstrate that his Kingdom was not like the kingdoms of this world, and that his power offered a sharp alternative to the power of this earth's rulers.

After introducing how the Kingdom of God entered the world as a fulfillment of biblical history, Matthew proceeds to the main body of his gospel, structuring it around the five discourses, mentioned earlier, that offer instructions in the life of the Kingdom. The first of those discourses, the Sermon on the Mount, pictures Jesus as a second Moses delivering God's will to the people from the mountain. Here is the Torah of the new people of God, fulfilling the old by peering more deeply into the righteousness God intends for the people of the Kingdom. With this Torah, Christians are to live the Kingdom of God now, in their everyday lives. The other four discourses similarly draw traditional materials together into Matthew's unique catechism for the church.

Like Mark, therefore, the Gospel of Matthew helped to present the living Lord to a community centering its life on his example and basing its hope on his victory over death. The Son of Man, though not yet returned, was not far removed from the community of the faithful, but present in its very midst in the eucharist (26:20–29), in its members' acts of compassion on behalf of those in need (25:31–46), and in its going forth to all nations in his name and under his commision (28:18–20). Moreover, it is now a community conscious of no longer being under the authority of the Jewish leaders or belonging to "their synagogues" (Matt. 10:17), and striving to prove itself rather than its rivals to be the true inheritor of the biblical promises.

The decade from 80 to 90 C.E. thrust the young church into a serious crisis. It had confessed before the world that its God was the ruler of all nations, and that tne resurrection of its Messiah had marked the beginning of a new age. One of its foremost leaders, the apostle Paul, had admonished Christians to obey governing authorities, "for there is no authority except from God" (Rom. 13:1). But now a Roman emperor named Domitian had come to the throne (81–86 C.E.) who claimed to be divine. The gnostics of that time could merely accept that claim as evidence of the fallenness of the world. Christians who claimed that God was active in history according to divine purposes faced a serious challenge.

John of Patmos drew on prophetic, apocalyptic, and mythic motifs to declare that despite appearances, the sovereign God was very much in control of history. What Christians were experiencing was the last, ill-fated onslaught of evil, but the universal reign of Christ was unshaken. On the basis of this conviction, Christians facing or already experiencing persecution could be confident of ultimate salvation. Indeed, since the victory was secured, and secured by a power superior to the weapons of this world's rulers, resorting to such weapons was wrong. Christians were instead to commune with the victorious King through worship and praise (this is the meaning of the hymns appearing throughout the Book of Revelation), and wait with patient confidence for their final vindication. It seems likely that the Book of Revelation was presented to the worshipping community to be read aloud in its communal gatherings as an encouragement to persevere in its faith. What remained were the final trials, but in their worship they could already experience proleptically the final victory.

The Book of Revelation shows us how apocalyptic forms and images were transformed in the early church. It is characterized neither by the pseudonymity nor the claim to esoteric knowledge found in most apocalyptic works. Rather, it is presented as an open message to the congregations to guide them through a difficult period. And although much of the language is mythic, it describes a battle and a victory carried out not in the heavens, but on earth, for the event that secured the victory on which hope was to be based was the death and resurrection of the Lamb, Jesus Christ. It is true that the members of the Christian community are presented as observers and not as combatants, but this argues not for an otherworldly apocaltypicism, but for the particular nonviolent political posture adopted by first-century Christians in periods of persecution. This portrait is also in harmony with their conviction that the conflict was one that had already been resolved, a conflict between God and all forces of evil. The Roman emperor was therefore

not to be feared, being merely an embodiment of one of the penultimate realities placing demands on Christians but possessing no genuine
power before the Ultimate. Although the dimension of myth in such a
view of reality is not to be denied, it functioned in the life of the community of faith not as a means of escaping moral involvement with the
issues of this world, but as a means of *empowerment* for such involvement. For living proleptically, through word and sacrament, in the reality of the Ultimate had the effect of declaring the unreality of the
penultimate. The latter thus lost its power over the faithful community, as they lived in the assurance of God's victory over evil, which gave
them the courage to eschew every form of accommodation with the
emperor cult (in contrast, for example, to the Nicolaitans mentioned in
2:6 and 15).

The Book of Revelations not only reflects a period of persecution,
but also—and in this respect it resembles the Gospel of Matthew—a
period of growing separation from Judaism. Jewish Scripture is drawn
on to demonstrate that the Christian church now occupies in the world
the role once played by Israel, for Christ "has freed us from our sins by
his blood and made us a kingdom, priests to his God and Father" (1:5–
6), thereby fulfilling the important promises of Exodus 19:6 and Isaiah
61:6: ". . . for thou wast slain and by thy blood didst ransom [people]
for God from every tribe and tongue and people and nation, and has
made them a kingdom and priests to our God, and they shall reign on
earth" (5:9–10). The universalism of this passage is in keeping with the
theology of the apostle Paul, though Paul's careful attention to the
abiding significance of the Jewish people is missing, reflecting the
growing gap between the two communities.

From roughly the same period comes the Letter to the Hebrews.
Though standing within the Pauline theological tradition, like the
Book of Revelation it betrays both a more hostile disposition on the
part of the Romans and further alienation of church from synagogue.
Drawing on an allegorical method of interpretation reminiscent of
Philo, the heavenly realm is portrayed as the prototype with this world
as its shadow. In this world, Christians are a pilgrim people focusing on
the land of rest, which is the final sabbath rest with God. Against the
contrast of the rebellious and apostate Israel of old, this new people of
God is admonished to remain firm in its faith so as to reach its goal
(Heb. 4:1–13). Even as the author looks on unbelieving Israel as a van-
ishing people, he views the institutions of the old covenant as superseded by the life of the church under its high priest Jesus. Thus the
nuanced treatment of the relationship between the church and Israel
found in Paul has yielded to what Daniel Harrington has called a "re-
placement" theology in the Letter to the Hebrews.[17]

---

17. D. J. Harrington, S.J., *God's People in Christ: New Testament Perspectives on the Church
and Judaism*, OBT 1 (Philadelphia: Fortress Press, 1980), pp. 13–14 and 85–89.

Other writings from within the Pauline tradition move in somewhat different directions. The author of the Letter to the Colossians polemicizes against those who would attempt to reimpose Jewish ritual law on the church. And in Ephesians we find a daring description of the church as the body of Christ, which is universal, even cosmic in scope. Paul's theme of the overcoming of the distinction between Jews and Gentiles is amplified, but in the reformulation of the notion of the body of Christ, the gnostic terminology applied blurs the theological distinctions that had remained very clear in Paul. One result of this theological blurring seems to have been the displacement of the polemic with gnosticism away from the theological arena into the realm of ethics. Out of this grows the attempt to probe the truth of the Christian claim on the basis of its superior ethical posture in comparison with that of the gnostic communities.[18]

Consideration of the growing influence of gnosticism brings us to the Gospel of John. Also written circa 90 C.E., one of its chief concerns seems to be the portrayal of the presence of the risen Lord through long discourses bearing distinct affinities with some of the gnostic discourses found in the Nag Hammadi library.[19] The eschatology found in Mark and Matthew is accordingly spiritualized, with the Second Coming accounted for in terms of the gift of the Spirit (14:15–17; 16:7–15). The same emphasis on the immediate experience of the Lord is seen in John's treatment of baptism and the eucharist (3:1–15 and 6:25–51). Nevertheless, a huge gap separates this Gospel from a genuinely gnostic writing such as the Gospel of Thomas: John remains true to the earlier gospel tradition by portraying Jesus as the revealer of heavenly truth, who actually became human, suffering and even dying like other mortals. The victory over evil is won within the stuff of human existence. In keeping with this historical emphasis, the disciples are summoned not to an otherworldly paradise, but, in the manner of Jesus, are sent "into the world" (17:18). Ultimately, therefore, what on the surface gives the appearance of a gnosticizing writing is on a fundamental level directed against a gnostic reinterpretation of the Christian gospels.[20]

Alongside the effort to define itself over against gnostic reinterpretations of the gospel, the community giving rise to the Gospel of John was one also determined to establish its identity vis-á-vis the synagogue. By the end of the first century, the division had been sharply defined, which in concrete terms meant that Jewish Christians had been expelled from the synagogue (cf. the term *aposynagogos* in 9:22; 12:42;

---

18. Koester, *Introduction*, vol. 2, p. 271.

19. The Nag Hammadi texts are conveniently available in J. M. Robinson, ed., *The Nag Hammadi Library in English* (New York: Harper & Row, 1977).

20. On the relation of the Gospel of John to gnostic writings, see Koester, *Introduction*, vol. 2, pp. 185–193.

16:2). In John 9:28, the Jews are quoted as reviling the man whom Jesus had restored to sight with the words, "You are his disciple, but we are disciples of Moses." Not only does this reflect the sense of division, but indicates that the experience of separation has left the realm of historical polemic and become an abstract assumption, for here, as generally, the author of John refers not specifically to particular groups or individuals in the style of the Synoptic Gospels (e.g., "scribes," "Pharisees," "high priest"), but to "the Jews." Reflected is a Gentile Christian attitude according to which the Jews, because of their disobedience and rejection of God's son, have been supplanted by a new chosen people (8:31–47).[21]

In the discussion thus far, we can see that one major impetus for the direction of development taken by Christian theology within the powerful Pauline tradition was polemic with groups identifying closely with earlier Jewish tradition. In the mid-first century, the polemic was directed against the Jerusalem Christians of Jerusalem who sought to preserve circumcision and dietary laws as binding on all Christians. After 70 C.E. considerable energy was directed against the Pharisees. These two controversies raise the question of whether the church's connection with its ancient Jewish heritage was not seriously threatened by these efforts to define Christianity as opposed to Jewish traditions, especially within the new Hellenistic-Roman environment within which the vast majority of Christians found themselves.

The question is a complex and important one. In addressing it, two observations must be kept in mind from earlier chapters. First, pre-Christian and pre-Rabbinical Jewish tradition does not constitute a monolithic heritage. Pharisaism, which as the ascendant party within Judaism was the one in relation to which the early Christian church had to define itself, developed especially out of one strand of Judaism discernible in the last two centuries of the previous era—the one tracing back through the teachings of the sages to Sirach and Ezra. This strand, basing its identity chiefly on the Torah of Moses, also incorporated certain eschatological and sapiental traditions. Early Christianity, while also drawing deeply on Jewish halakic traditions (as seen both in Jesus' teachings and in the parenesis of the second and third generations of the church), inherited from visionary streams within Judaism a highly developed form of eschatology. This form drew especially upon the biblical prophets, though it was also influenced by later apocalypticism. Thus the separation that developed between the two communities was not a phenomenon with a history confined to the first centuries of the Common Era, but had roots reaching back to the diversity that characterized Judaism during the Persian and Hellenistic periods. This is not to overlook the effects of the more recent polemics, for as the

---

21. See Harrington, *God's People*, pp. 101–105.

two groups grew further apart, the very fact that the one emphasized one side of the common heritage increased the tendency of the other to focus more exclusively on its traditional position. Therefore, the rabbis continued to appeal primarily to the Torah of Moses, with their own oral traditions defined as also deriving from Sinai. The leaders of the Christian church continued to stress the prophets. This was hardly a situation encouraging rapprochement, especially since both (unlike Paul) seemed convinced that only one line of descent (their own) could be legitimate. It is important that this phenomenon of polarization be understood today, at a time when many Jews and Christians desire to move beyond polemic to mutual respect and beyond enmity to an understanding of the potential contribution of the other and a deeper appreciation of the breadth and richness of our common heritage. Historical study shedding light on the origins of separation can render valuable service in demonstrating the complementarity of many traditions long divided by religious controversy.

Second, it is also important to remember that an awareness of the dynamic nature of the Torah in the life of the community of faith was not lost in early Christianity. The threat of such loss was real, as illustrated by the antinominianism of some gnostic and Marcionite groups. But as we have seen, neither Jesus, nor Paul, nor Matthew set the gospel of the Kingdom in opposition to the stringent righteousness of the godly life. Moreover, a powerful impetus soon arose within the church for a reappropriation of much of that threatened Jewish heritage. That impetus was the growing need for church order within a community that had grown difficult to regulate both because of the development of different theological movements, and due to the great distances separating the individual congregations. We shall now turn to important witnesses to this reappropriation.

The founder of the branch within early Christianity that held firmly to earlier Jewish customs and practices was James, the leader of the primitive Jerusalem congregation and brother of Jesus. The biblical Letter of James, though probably not written by him, gives us a good indication of the piety of the Jewish Christians of that early period as it became translated into the language of the Greek-speaking world ("the twelve tribes of the Dispersion," v. 1:1). It is a piety based squarely on a traditional Jewish sense of the way of righteousness. The piety of the poor (the 'ebyônîm of the Psalms) is commended (1:9–11; 2:5), whereas the unjust ways of the rich come under harsh condemnation (2:6–7; 5:1–6). The root of sin is located in the desire of the impure heart, which ultimately leads to death (1:13–15). The author exhorts the faithful to be obedient to the whole law (2:8–13), and to beware of being hearers and not doers (1:22–25). There is no need here to give a full list of the virtues urged by the author, for it is thoroughly traditional. What is noteworthy, however, is the severe criticism that the author exercises against a gnosticizing form of Pauline theology that emphasizes faith to the neglect of good works (2:18–26), and a related appeal to a boastful and selfish form of wisdom that undermines the peace of the community (3:13–18). This writing thus makes a passionate appeal for faithfulness to the classical virtues of biblical tradition as the community awaits the coming of the Lord, virtues reaching all the way back to the triadic notion of community found in earliest Yahwism: "Religion that is pure and undefiled before God and the Father is this: to visit orphans and widows in their affliction, and to keep oneself unstained from the world" (1:27).

Two writings from the end of the first century draw deeply on this same classical biblical parenesis, the *Didache* (or *Teaching of the Twelve Apostles*) and *1 Clement*. In both cases, the reason for this appeal to traditional Jewish law is clear: the need for church order has directed the attention of practical-minded church leaders to the richest thesaurus of moral wisdom available to them, Jewish Scripture.

The *Didache*, which is the oldest preserved church order, embodies a Christian version of the traditional Jewish doctrine of the Two Ways. The doctrine of the Two Ways, which can be traced all the way back to Deuteronomic parenesis, became the most popular form in which the faithful were trained in the way of perfect obedience to the Torah. In the *Didache*, it is fused with the teachings of Jesus, and presented as a catechism not only for the elite, but for all members of the community. The forms of communal life are regulated by orders for baptism, fasting, prayer, and the eucharist (chapters 7–15).

Hand in hand with this regulation of church order is the development of a defined order of leadership: the duties of apostles, prophets, and teachers are defined, and limits are placed on the function of more charismatic mendicant types (10:7–15:4). Visible throughout this writing are thus signs of what Max Weber called the "routinizaton of charisma."[22] Although a short apocalypse concludes the work (chapter 13), the tone throughout reflects a community expecting to be living in this world for a long time to come, and regulating its life so as to minimize the ferment of enthusiasts and to unify factions under the umbrella of the apostolic church.

This same conciliatory tone and obvious desire to minimize the divisive effects of different groups appaling to their favorite apostolic authorities is also found in a writing contemporary with the *Didache*, *1 Clement*. What gave rise to this letter was a report reaching Rome of unrest in the Corinthian church. It seems that enthusiasts, claiming special spiritual gifts (38:2) and gnosis (48:5), were challenging the established leadership of that church. Clement, a leader of the Roman church, follows the precedent set by Paul of offering advice to a distant

---

22. M. Weber, *Theory*, p. 364.

congregation by letter, a practice, already widely adopted at that time, which reflects the consciousness of the various congregations as belonging to one wider church. The fact that it is in this case the Roman church that offers its advice adumbrates the later claim to papal primacy.

One of the most noteworthy characteristics of the letter is the preponderance of parenetic material drawn from Jewish Scripture, both in the form of ethical teaching and examples of virtue taken from the lives of biblical figures. As in the case of the *Didache*, the author's dependence on the doctrine of the Two Ways is again obvious. This is seen especially in the catalogues of virtues and vices and general rules of the community found in chapters 1–17. To the materials drawn from Jewish Scripture, he adds sayings of Jesus as well as teachings derived from pagan (especially Stoic) sources (for example, he adduces the myth of the Phoenix as proof of the resurrection, in chap. 25).

When compared with the Pauline letters, after which it is modeled, *1 Clement* illustrates a line of development from a Pauline theology and notion of the church toward the ecclesiology that would prevail under the leadership of Rome. First, Paul's theological emphasis on justification by faith has been overshadowed by an emphasis on morality and good order. This is seen by contrasting Paul's appeal to Abraham as the champion of faith with Clement's appeal to the same hero as an example of obedience, hospitality, righteousness, and humility (10:1, 7; 17:1; 31:2). It is seen again by contrasting Paul's treatment of the problem of gnostic antinominianism by use of the theological concept of "dying to sin" with Clement's recourse to natural theology (chap. 33; cf. a similar argument for church unity made by reference to the harmony of nature in chap. 20).

Another aspect of this letter's stress on church order is its special instructions regarding the offices of the church. The presbyter-bishops who preside over the affairs of the church and direct its liturgical life trace back to the appointment of the apostles (chap. 42). Moreover, the apostles, in their foreknowledge of the latter situation of the church, laid down the rules for orderly succession of the presbyter-bishops. Interference in this "apostolic succession" was not a trivial matter, but had direct bearing on salvation itself (chap. 44).[23]

We thus see in *1 Clement* clear evidence of the unfolding of a Catholic notion of the church through the harmonization of Pauline and Petrine streams of tradition under one authoritative church order centered in Rome. Although the letter recognizes a multiplicity of presbyter-bishops with no explicit claim of the Roman leader as enjoying primacy, the later claim to papal authority is foreshadowed in this

23. Cf. C. C. Richardson, "Introduction" to Clement's First Letter, in *Early Christian Fathers*, Library of Christian Classics 1 (Philadelphia: Westminster Press, 1953), pp. 37–39.

strong admonition for church unity and hierarchical order issued by the Roman church.

The Pastoral Epistles, written circa 120 C.E., will be the last example we shall give of the tendency away from the eschatological perspective of the earliest Christian movement toward a concept of the church as an established institution within the Roman society. Although Philemon is a letter addressed to an individual, 1 and 2 Timothy and Titus are actually addressed to the leadership of the church in a general sense, and fall into the category of church orders. For example, 1 Timothy sets down rules regulating the appointment and expected behavior of bishops (3:1;–7), deacon (3:8–13), and presbyters (5:17–22), in addition to general ethical admonitions and warnings with the traditional catalogues of virtues and vices (4:1–5; 6:3–16), and specific rules applying to widows (5:3–16), slaves (6:1–2) and the rich (6:17–19).

Although written in Paul's name, the letter expresses a very different spirit from the genuine letters of Paul. Motivation for the special way in which the Christian is to live in the world is not rooted in the eschatological sense of the passing away of this world before one far more glorious, but in presenting to the world an example of decency and submission both to civil authority and to the established leadership of the church. The life prescribed for the Christian is thus that after which any good Roman citizen could model his or her life. Part of this pattern of integrity is "to be submissive to rulers and authorities" (Titus 3:1), and to pray "for kings and all who are in high positions, that we may lead a quiet and peaceable life, godly and respectful in every way" (1 Tim. 2:2). Another side of the same pattern is to contribute to the preservation of sound doctrine by repudiating false teachers and being attentive and obedient to the properly appointed teachers of the church.

While recognizing that the unique motivation for life found in Paul's eschatological perspective is muted in the Pastoral Epistles, with the result that the Christian life commended begins to look like civil respectfulness and submission to orthodox doctrine, we should not ignore the opposite extreme against which this position is being worked out. The church is being threatened, according to the author, by false teachers who seek to deceive the members of the Christian community through "myths and genealogies which promote speculations rather than divine training" (1 Tim. 1:4) and "godless and silly myths" (4:7). Perhaps being referred to are Jewish-gnostic teachers (Titus 1:6–7) who are confusing the people with a manner of life contradicting the established Christian virtues ("godless chatter and contradictions of what is falsely called knowledge [gnōsis]," 1 Tim. 6:20). As Helmut Koester has pointed out, an important aspect of Pauline ethics is at stake:

The Pastoral Epistles resurrect this element of Paul's ethics [e.g., the legitimacy of rational moral decisions after prudent consideration of the alternatives] in their fight against the gnostics, who had made Paul their chief witness of a sectarian morality that had no concern for the moral norms of the society, because the "world" of which that society was a part had no rightful claim to be taken seriously.[24]

The Pastoral Epistles are thus not only interesting as witnesses to an important stage in the development of the church. They also pose theological questions that still confront every community of faith once its members find themselves an accepted part of a larger social universe: "How is the unique way of life born of the ardent eschatological faith of Jesus and Paul to be balanced against the demands placed by state and society on its citizens? Does one divide one's life into two spheres, for example, applying a more explicitly Christian ethic to one's private life and a more rational ethic to one's affairs in the realms of politics and economics? Alternatively, does one insist on unifying life on the basis of one Christian ethic, either by striking a compromise between two ideals, or by adopting the posture of an alien in a strange land?" We return to such questions in the next chapter, for they arise inevitably out of the issues raised by a biblical notion of community.

This survey of representative writings from the period between 70 and 130 C.E. concludes with a composition falling at the end of this timespan, the history comprising the books of Luke and Acts. *1 Clement* and the Pastoral Epistles are valuable background to our consideration of this work, for it was written by one who shared the concern found in those works of presenting Christianity as a very positive contributor to the well-being of the world of which it was now a part. Whereas those works presented primarily the moral teachings and formal structures of the church, Luke-Acts was written to present the story of Christianity, tracing its roots back to ancient promises in the Jewish Scriptures (Acts 3:24), locating its origin in the miraculous circumstances surrounding Jesus' birth (Luke 1:26–38), and tracing it from its early stage in Jerusalem all the way to the capital of the Roman empire (Luke 24:44–49 and Acts 28:30–31). It is thus an apologia conceived on a grand scale, and aimed at convincing Gentile readers that the conquest of Christianity was not a political threat to the Roman empire, but instead offered healing and stability and salvation to the whole world, according to the plan of the God who directs history from its very beginning to its very end.

That the birth of the Christian community was a miraculous gift of God representing a different order of power than that occupied by Roman emperors and generals is stated emphatically by the birth narrative in Luke. Jesus was not born in the circumstances of the kings of this world. In fact, as the human matrix of his birth, God chose Mary, a young, poor maiden, and as the delivery room, a stable. The unbroken connection between this creative act of God and God's creation of ancient Israel is shown by Mary's taking up the song of another Jewess

24. Koester, *Introduction*, Vol. 2, p. 303.

who eleven centuries earlier had captured in sublime poetry the redemptive act of the Deliverer God Yahweh:

> He has shown strength with his arm,
> he has scattered the proud in the imagination
>   of their hearts,
> he has put down the mighty from their thrones,
> and exalted those of low degree;
> he has filled the hungry with good things,
> and the rich he has sent empty away. (Luke 1:51–53)

The account of the king born of humble circumstances to minister to the lowly and the poor is continued in the description of the first to receive the good news, namely, shepherds—that is, marginal elements of society whose very vocation imposed on them the stigma of being unable to live true to Jewish sabbath law. Yet it is this one of lowly birth, who is announced to shepherds as they watch their flocks, whom the angel Gabriel celebrates as the "Son of the Most High," whose kingdom would be forever (1:32–35).

Luke follows the pattern established by gospel tradition of introducing Jesus' public ministry with John the Baptist's call to repentance, a theme he then picks up after John's arrest with Jesus' explanation: "I must preach the good news of the kingdom of God to the other cities also; for I was sent for this purpose" (4:43). This then according to Luke was the starting point of the gospel, whose movement out into the Gentile world he wished to document.

"For I was sent for this purpose." After the temptation story—another narrative unit taken from the gospel tradition that pointed to the spiritual nature of Jesus' kingship—Luke offers a powerful lesson in the nature of the purpose to which Jesus had been sent by God. Jesus was in his home synagogue for the sabbath worship, and there read from the sixty-first chapter of Isaiah:

> The Spirit of the Lord is upon me,
> because he has anointed me to preach
>   good news to the poor.
> He has sent me to proclaim release to the captives
> and recovering of sight to the blind,
> to set at liberty those who are oppressed,
> to proclaim the acceptable year of the Lord.   (Luke 4:18–19)

He closed his reading with the words, "Today this scripture has been fulfilled in your hearing" (4:21). This passage presents the mission of Jesus in very specific terms, for in it Jesus identifies with the Servant of Yahweh's task of restoring at torn creation and a broken human family to wholeness.[25] The humble king Jesus is thus the alternative to the

---

25. Cf. Isaiah 61:1–3.

kings of this world who impose their will on their subjects by force. Through proclaiming the good news of divine forgiveness, through healing the sick, releasing those in bondage and freeing the oppressed Jesus would inaugurate the Kingdom that would finally restore peace and justice on earth. The reign of šālôm envisaged by early Israel and kept alive by the prophets in the concept of the Jubilee ("the acceptable year of the Lord") had begun with the ministry of Jesus.

This introduction offers an important key for the next stage of Luke's history, that covering the life of Jesus. For Jesus' teachings and miracles are interpreted as the signs of the inbreaking of the Kingdom of God. In this manner, Luke's presentation of the traditional gospel material makes a very strong statement. Jesus' Kingdom is not an earthly kingdom, and thus comes as no threat to the political rule of the Romans. But this does not mean that it is unrelated to everyday life. To the contrary, it brings into the world the redemptive power of God that has the effect of changing the quality of life in a fundamental way by healing all that is broken and restoring all that has fallen. The gospel of the Kingdom is thus presented as the good news of peace on earth offered to all peoples and nations.

In keeping with the gospel tradition, Luke goes on to tell of the opposition of this world to that good news by relating his version of the passion of Jesus. But since the Kingdom was God's gift, the opposition was overcome, and Jesus was raised from the dead. According to Luke, after Jesus had explained that all this was in fulfillment of Scripture, he went on to describe the next stage of the salvation drama: "Thus it is written, that the Christ should suffer and on the third day rise from the dead, and that repentance and forgiveness of sins should be preached in his name to all nations, beginning from Jerusalem" (24:46–47).

The Book of Acts takes up the narrative from this point, beginning in Jerusalem and then following the spread of the gospel to the nations. In this second half of Luke's narrative, Pentecost was interpreted as God's act of empowering the followers of Christ to move beyond Jerusalem to the Gentile world, and breaking down all barriers separating human communities from one another. From that point on the Spirit of the risen Christ would accompany the missionaries as they ventured forth to proclaim the good news of what God had done for all peoples. Luke pictures as the heroes of that next stage Peter and Paul, indicating the same harmonization of traditions found in *1 Clement*. In all their plans and activities, the various congregations are portrayed as working together in oneness of spirit (e.g., 2:36 and 4:32). By combining various traditions, some of them historical, many legendary, Luke continues his account until the goal is reached, and Paul, the hero combining unyielding fidelity to God with perfect civil responsibility ("Neither against the law of the Jews, nor against the temple, nor against Caesar have I offended at all"—Acts 25:8), takes up his residence in

Rome, "preaching the kingdom of God and teaching about the Lord Jesus Christ quite openly and unhindered" (28:31).

The Lukan history of early Christianity offers us an appropriate place to end this study of the development of the biblical notion of community, for it reflects a community that has worked out a clear definition of its origins, its nature, and its purpose in the world. Taken together with the other writings examined from the fifty or sixty years after the destruction of the temple in 70 C.E., it gives us a picture of a church that has worked out a *modus vivendi* in a world dominated by a powerful pagan empire. The intense eschatology of the primitive church has given way to a more pragmatic posture.

Apostolic doctrines and structures of authority have begun to evolve that serve the purpose of eradicating heresy and fostering unity within the widely scattered young churches. The break with Judaism is complete, and the dominance of the Gentile elements within the Christian congregations has begun to replace the Jewish character of Christianity with a distinct Greek flavor. Although periods of persecution would from time to time renew something of the sense of eschatological urgency characteristic of earliest Christianity, we have in the main moved into the world of early Catholicism and an era in which the church emerged as an increasingly powerful institution defining its place among other institutions in the world and predicating its decisions on the assumption that human history would go on for a long time to come. In other words, we have already made the move into the world experienced by most people today, and the world within which the church or the synagogue seeks to define itself as an institution among other institutions. The problems we saw facing the third generation of the church thus have become our legacy: first, how is the eschatological perspective that was at the heart of Jesus' life and teaching and that was so central to the primitive church to be treated by a church attending to matters of defining doctrine and maintaining structures as aspects of self-preservation and worldly respectability? Second, are life in the spirit and church order compatible or mutually exclusive elements? Third, what is the relationship between the Kingdom of God and the kingdoms of this world? What is the nature of the Christian vocation in this complicated situation? Fourth, does the separation of church and synagogue and the development of a church that is overwhelmingly Gentile imply a complete breakdown of mutually enriching intercourse between the two, or even a subsequent history of distrust and hostility? Here again we encounter questions to which we return in the next chapter.

XV

The Biblical Notion of Community: Contemporary Implications

The community of faith in the Bible is the people *called*. It is the people *called* forth from diverse sorts of bondage to freedom, *called* to a sense of identity founded on a common bond with the God of righteousness and compassion, and *called* to the twin vocations of worship and participation in the creative, redemptive purpose that unifies all history and is directed to the restoration of the whole creation within a universal order of šālôm.

Perhaps the single most important source of renewal for contemporary communities of faith lies in the rediscovery of their identity as "the people called." That is, they are one branch of the movement that continues to derive its sense of being and purpose from the vision of God's unceasing dedication to the healing of creation and the reconciliation of the entire human family among its diverse members and with its God.

In an age when the future is thrown into jeopardy by a widespread loss of any profound sense of roots or tradition and the consequent loss of a sense of direction and purpose, it is extremely important for churches and synagogues to remind their members that their communities are not a new or accidental product of recent social or historical developments. They are rather the descendants of a four-thousand-year history of God's seeking to form with humans an abiding and blessed relationship. To be sure, many divisions characterize the branches constituting the extension of that history into our own day. The negative effects of those divisions, however, diminish as God's people today find their identity in a gratitude and devotion to God that is singular and wholehearted, and comes to expression in a dedication to a vocation of healing and reconciliation that transcends all differences because it is directed by the *God* who transcends all differences, the God who has promised to gather together a human community both for its own blessing and for the extension of that blessing to all peoples.

If our common ancestry in the biblical community of faith can be re-discovered, a powerful spirit of renewal can enter the communities of faith to which we belong. We have been divided by the petty strife emanating from efforts to discredit the communal structures and teachings of others, which dissipates so much of the energy of contemporary religious bodies and which usually is based on a totally routinized and static sense of identity. This strife can be replaced by a far more dynamic and positive sense of purpose in response to the call to be full participants in the advocacy of mercy and justice in all areas and facets of life.

We miss the spirit of the biblical message, therefore, if we seek to extrapolate from our study one ecclesiastical form as the supposedly definitive one for all places and all time. Not only do we find in Scripture ample examples of monarchical, oligarchical, and democratic structures that can be used to defend episcopal, presbyterian, and congregational forms,[1] but more importantly, throughout biblical history such structures seemed to be more the accidents than the substance of the mission of the community of faith. Although much can be learned from the different polities reflected in the Bible, the essential issue is located on a deeper level. For whenever and wherever God's people has been faithful to its calling, it has allowed its communal structures to emerge from its central mission of embodying the qualities of God's righteousness and compassion in all aspects of its life. That is to say, the specific forms giving structure and order to the common life of the faithful have been inferred from their experience of God's gracious initiative and have arisen as an aspect of the response deemed appropriate and fitting for those acknowledging the gift character of their life together. For example, in ancient Israel this acknowledgment led to a covenant community centered around festivals of worship and *tôrâ*, and to such concepts as the Jubilee Year and the inalienable right of each family to its inheritance. In early rabbinic Judaism, it led to the redefinition of the atoning sacrifice as the act of loving-kindness. In the early church, the sense of living in the presence of Christ led to a disregard of distinctions between Jew and Greek, slave and free, male and female, to the idea of a universal church and even to the practice of sharing all goods in common.

The contemporary community of faith that seeks to live true to the biblical model will similarly be a community adapting its institutional structures to its central confessions and missions. In other words, as the God in response to whom we are called into fellowship is living and active, so too the structures of our communities will be maintained or changed on the basis of the desire to respond faithfully to God's redemptive presence in our world within the specific and often changing conditions of our time.

---

1. See B. Reicke, "Die Verfassung der Urgemeinde im Lichte judischer Dokumente," *ThZ* (1954), 95–113.

Since our God is experienced as a God patiently dedicated to the redemption of all creation, it should not be surprising that the forms of community emerging from our response to God in many respects will resemble those of our spiritual ancestors. But always the source of such similarities is the initiating activity of God, and not any authoritativeness intrinsic to the forms of a bygone age. For this reason, we have been able to discern a fundamental pattern underlying the community-building of God's people in every age, the pattern of divine initiative and human response, which constitutes the heart of the biblical concept of covenant. This pattern comes to expression in the recurrent biblical formulation of covenant: "I shall be your God, and you shall be my people."

Because of the dynamic, relational nature of the notion of community in the Bible, this attempt to capture its essential characteristics and point to some of its implications for contemporary communities of faith must be presented in a way that preserves that essential dynamism. And that is best done by beginning with a brief summary of those essential characteristics as they developed over the centuries of biblical history.

A. A SUMMARY OF THE BIBLICAL LEGACY

The biblical notion of community was born out of the experience of having been delivered from slavery to freedom. This humble origin imprinted the communal consciousness of Israel in a way that profoundly affected its thought for all time. For one thing, it created a sense of unity based not on the accomplishments of individual leaders, but on the gracious initiative of God who raised up those who had no status, no freedom, and no influence over their own destiny to be a people called to a life of blessing for themselves and others. The theological and social consequences of this starting point were far-reaching. In it are to be found the seeds of the ethical monotheism that developed in Israel and became such a clear distinguishing mark between its faith and that of the other ancient cults. Moreover, the conviction that all members of the community shared a common origin in the despair and self-degradation of slavery, from which they had been raised to hope and freedom by grace alone, led to the cultivation of several distinctive communal qualities.

The early Yahwistic community was committed to the *equality* of its members, and indeed we can recognize a persistent egalitarian impulse influencing the laws and institutions of early Israel. Both in terms of the benefits enjoyed by the members of the community and the responsibilities they bore toward others, the emphasis placed on equality and inclusiveness stands out within the ancient world. This observation is neither to deny that early Israel's vision was parochial in comparison with modern conceptions of global community nor that there were powerful counterforces opposed to the Yahwistic ideals, as we have seen reflected in the Book of Judges. These facts notwithstanding, the social and ethical legacy of early Yahwism is one of the most remarkable in history. And the ultimate source of the ideals that formed the heart of that legacy is clearly identified in the earliest traditions of the Bible, namely, the God Yahweh. The veritable touchstone of Israel's sense of identity was the Deliverer God, from whom it traced the gift character of its life. Thus from the example of Yahweh Israel inferred other qualities that characterized it as a people. As Yahweh was a righteous God acting to establish and preserve the rights of every individual, however lowly or oppressed, Israel, in order to be true to its own birthright, was to be a *righteous* people present in the world on behalf of all those finding themselves in similar circumstances. The example of the God who reached out to those who had no special claims on God's attention also functioned in the biblical community to counteract the natural human predisposition to claim special privileges for the "in-group" and to dismiss outsiders as undeserving of concern. As God had acted to deliver precisely those who had been excluded from the privileges of the Egyptian social system, so too Israel was to act on behalf of the vulnerable and dispossessed around it, giving rise to the quality of *compassion* as another cardinal characteristic of her notion of community.

Born within the foundational experience of deliverance from bondage was a corresponding world view that contrasted sharply with that which prevailed in antiquity. Whereas the heavenly realm functioned within the dominant societies of that time to rationalize and stabilize the *status quo*, the fact that Hebrew community was born out of a decisive break with the "eternal" social order of the pharaohs directed attention to the God who interacted with the human family within the stuff of history so as to replace oppressive structures with forms conducive to the well-being of all creatures. The God Yahweh, "who brought you out of the land of Egypt, out of the house of bondage," was the center of attention in the cult, which established *the happenings of this world* as an essential aspect of the religious and moral life. Within such happenings Yahweh was encountered, and there the quality of Israel's response to its God was inextricably tied to the quality of Israel's response to the humans caught up within those happenings.

Not only did this establish ethical responsibility as a thoroughly religious concern, but it lent to the concept of God a *relational and dynamic quality*, for God related to humans within a *covenant* of promise and commitment. That concept was not defined for all time in the endless cycle of nature, or in the eternal drama of the theogonic and cosmogonic myths. God was not the manifestation of a specific aspect of the natural order. God was rather the one who reached out to humans to establish a relationship, and in that reaching out called Israel to be the agent through which the blessing of that relationship could finally reach all the peoples of the earth. This unique understanding of the nature of the divine-human relationship explains the dynamic character of the biblical vision of divine purpose. And that vision in turn can be seen as the key to the vitality of the Yahwistic community that enabled it to grow amid the challenges, threats, and changes of the surrounding world.

The legacy of the earliest period of biblical community is thus great, both because of the fresh new way in which it redefined the fundamental concepts of life and because of the particular contributions it made to the history of institutions and social structures. Subsequent generations would continue to build on its fundamental idea of life as based on the pattern of divine initiative and human response. Moreover, the experience of being related to the God who continued to oppose injustice and to defend the oppressed fostered within Yahwism an openness to self-criticism that prepared the way for the prophetic movement. All the counterforces we contend with daily in our own private and public lives were present in Israel to stifle the sense of humaneness and equality emanating from the example of the righteous and compassionate God Yahweh. Nevertheless, a triadic notion of community had been born that was powerful because of the power inherent in its interrelated component parts—that is, in its finding identity and unity in worship of the saving God Yahweh, and in its imitation of that God in the life of righteousness and compassion dedicated to the final goal of drawing all humans into the *šālôm* intended by God for all creation.

As novel and powerful as was the early Yahwistic notion of community it could not carry within it the guarantee that the *šālôm* to which it was dedicated would in fact be preserved within future generations. Indeed, it could not proffer such a guarantee precisely because of the intrinsically relational nature of its concept of community. *Šālôm* was the concomitant of a faithful, wholehearted response to God. It arose where the community acknowledged its source in divine grace, and responded in worship, and in righteous compassion. This relational quality of the Yahwistic notion of community is both its most sublime, and its most disquieting aspect. No generation had the privilege of resting on the reputation of its ancestors. The heart of any living relationship lies in its commitment to daily renewal. And in the case of a historical entity like Israel, that renewal had to occur within the particular circumstances of a rapidly changing world. In the final years of the tribal confederacy, the rather loose communal structures first developed among the clans began to prove inadequate in relation to new developments both within the community and beyond. The phrase that concludes the Book of Judges is an accurate summary of the conditions reflected by the preceding stories in that book: "Everyone did what seemed right in his own eyes." Whatever value earlier generations may have attached to clan autonomy, a community dedicated on a fundamental level to šālôm had to face the rude fact that the twin specters of anarchy and foreign invasion posed a deadly threat to its very existence as a people.

We have seen the resulting tension between two responses that arose within Israel to the threats of anarchy and military defeat, the move toward *kingship* in the absolute form dominant in the ancient Near East, and attempts to introduce a limited form of monarchy that would remain true to the fundamental values of early Yahwism. Out of the former arose an exalted image of the role of the king in the cult, which became a significant threat to the sole sovereignty of Yahweh—that is to say, to the keystone of the triadic notion of community. Out of the latter was born the office of prophecy as Yahwism's institutionally commensurate response to kingship.

It was within *prophecy* that the notion was kept alive that the divine presence could not be completely routinized and institutionalized. The examples of Ahab's four hundred compliant prophets and the obsequious priest of Jeroboam II, Amaziah, amply illustrate that the influence of absolute notions of monarchy persisted in Israel. The prophetic movement could have functioned as a compliant part of such a system if the prophets had been willing to confine their vision to a heavenly realm removed from the realm of politics and economics, directing their devotees to an otherworldly concept of salvation. In this manner a compact of peace could have been maintained between prophets, priests, and kings, for such a religious position could have contributed to a populace kept docile and content in their spiritualized concept of religion. Aside from the cult prophets, however, Israel's prophets refused to divorce their vision of the šālôm God intended for all people from the institutions and the structures of society, and hence they kept alive the early Yahwistic ideal of a covenant community acknowledging *one* Sovereign and defending the equality of *all* individuals.

Conflict between kings and prophets was inevitable, with priests often, though not always, aligning themselves with the kings. Involved were two very divergent views of community, the one egalitarian, the other hierarchical and authoritarian, the one dedicated to a continuous process of reform of existing structures on behalf of the disadvantaged, the other placing a higher value on security and stability. Any study that characterizes kingship as utterly alien to Yahwism and prophecy as alone representative of biblical faith, however, is theologically naive. For it was within the lively encounters between kings and prophets that the Yahwistic notion of community was tested and refined in many important respects. The nature of that testing varied with each age, but overall we can recognize certain developments that had a far-reaching effect on the biblical notion of community.

First, we recognize that the challenge thrust on prophecy (as the heir to the earlier Yahwistic values and beliefs) to represent the traditional faith before rulers and citizens often devoted to antithetical allegiances had an important result. It became the occasion for the development within Yahwism of a rigorous *political realism*. The triadic notion of community that formed the foundation of the identity of early Israel was preserved, but it was tempered into a vastly more powerful force by the necessity of defining and defending its vision within an often hostile environment. Specifically, it established more clearly than before the autonomy of the people of God. The community of faith was neither beholden to nor bound by earthly institutions or ideologies. Since the royal cult, with its symbol of the temple as the chapel of the king, influenced many to view Yahweh as a patron deity tied to the self-interests of king and nation, the prophets incurred much opposition as they insisted that Yahweh was the sovereign God unfettered by the self-interests of the national cult, who judged Israel, its kings, and all its people on the basis of a standard of justice that could be co-opted by no political or religious authority. In this way Yahwism was transformed from a rather parochial tribal cult into a vital force preserving an egalitarian sense of righteousness and compassion and a radical allegiance to no authority but Yahweh within a pluralistic environment.

The period of the monarchy was not just a time of a developing pluralism within Israel, but a time of a growing international consciousness. The great empires of Egypt and Mesopotamia began to wax in strength and to encroach on Israel, a phenomenon that continued throughout the history of the divided monarchy and the remaining history of Judah. This led to a second significant development within the Yahwistic notion of community: its vision expanded in the direction of a universal perspective of God's purpose and the community of faith's role within that purpose. This meant that Yahweh came to be recognized as Sovereign over all nations whose standard of justice and deep compassion extended beyond Israel to all peoples. It also meant that other nations could be the instruments of Yahweh's judgment on the apostasy of Israel. This development was to have far-reaching effects on biblical faith, especially as it moved toward the time of the Diaspora of the Jews and the accompanying phenomenon of increased Gentile conversions.

A third development was the cultivation of a far more profound understanding of Yahweh's role within the realm of nature. This was due in no small part to the hymnic celebration of creation within the temple cult. Closely related was the unfolding of an indigenous wisdom tradition, which related the God of Israel to such problems as the harmony existing between different aspects of reality, the presence in the world of evil, and how evil could be explained in relation to belief in God's goodness and power.

A fourth development was that of an understanding of the community of faith as a *remnant* within the larger nation. Once again we find a phenomenon born of necessity within an inhospitable environment, one however that equipped Yahwism with a critical self-consciousness well suited for meeting the challenges of even more difficult times ahead. The development of the remnant idea occurred as a part of the struggle of the prophetic movement to preserve the integrity of the covenant community within an increasingly secular and pluralistic society. Within such a setting, how was the people of God to be identified? In resisting the nationalization of the cult attempted by some of the kings, prophets such as Isaiah and Jeremiah insisted that the nation as a whole could not be designated as the people of God, save in an eschatological sense. Instead God's election of a people was believed to be carried by the remnant that remained faithful to the covenant in the midst of a largely apostate nation. Within the faithful remnant, the righteousness and compassion and true worship that were the unmistakable marks of the people of God could be preserved, until such time that the nation repented and God's sovereignty was universally acknowledged.

A fifth development arising within prophetic Yahwism was also to have a profound effect on future generations, the development of *messianic and other types of eschatological thinking*. In this case the abetting factors involved were complex, and the outcome manifests the high level of flexibility of which Yahwistic faith was capable. This study has recognized in 1 Samuel 12:19–25 a poignant formulation of prophetic realism, indicating how the prophetic movement, while accepting the alterations in political structures imposed by changing historical and social forces, nevertheless insisted on the preservation in Israel of the fundamental Yahwistic principles of sole worship, righteousness, and compassion. The greatest enigma posed by the monarchical period was the figure of the king. How did the king fit into God's plan for God's people? While the prophets were deeply critical of many of the practices of their kings, their position was not one of condemnation of kingship *per se*. They were willing to accept the limited form of kingship called "the Samuel compromise," provided the kings conformed to and led their people in the example of obedience to the ancestral faith. Occasional instances of sincere devotion on the part of the king no doubt deeply moved people, including the prophets. Kings such as David, Jehoshaphat, Hezekiah, and Josiah accordingly exercised considerable influence over the hearts of their subjects. Fervent Yahwists in such instances looked with hope on their king, and asked whether the time had arrived when God's anointed one would faithfully fulfill God's mandate by leading Israel back to the example of divine righteousness and compassion, thereby inaugurating the era of šālôm for which their hearts yearned. Isaiah was the prophet who gave the most sublime expression to this yearning (Isa. 9 and 11).

This yearning for the faithful king and for the reign of justice and peace was battered repeatedly, however, both by the failure of the few "righteous" kings to persevere in their divine mandate and especially by the indifference or even hostility of the majority of Israel's kings toward the ancestral faith. Repeatedly, devotion to Yahweh was subsumed by these kings under personal ambitions. Repeatedly, faithful Yahwists were disappointed by the failure of their kings to set an example of godly piety. The resulting history of disappointment gave rise to messianism. Although kings repeatedly failed to lead the nation back to undivided devotion to the heavenly King, God had not abandoned the ancient promise of gathering a righteous people as a blessing to themselves and to all nations and as a source of glory to God. In the later years of the monarchy, the yearning for the fulfillment of this promise focused increasingly on the future, and with the destruction of Jerusalem and the temple by the Babylonians in 587, it broke out into eschatological forms of expression that persisted within certain circles through the next six centuries and on into the Common Era.

There was considerable variety in the eschatological visions that developed in the aftermath of the Babylonian destruction. Some continued to focus on the hope of restoration under a Davidic messiah. Others seemed to look to Yahweh's unmediated intervention on behalf of a faithful remnant. What united these various eschatological visions, however, was a bleak assessment of the human situation that had developed within prophetic circles during the course of the monarchy. Especially toward the end of this period, prophets such as Ezekiel and Jeremiah looked back on the history of their nation and came to the shocking conclusion that Israel was a people bent on destruction, motivated by a totally corrupt heart. The promise of blessing was maintained only by directing the focus of prophetic proclamation increasingly toward God's radical new initiative of the future, and this within a more threatening and all-encompassing understanding of the consequences of sin and rebellion than had characterized earlier Yahwism. The disintegration of the community of righteous compassion had set in motion a calamity that threatened the entire created order.

Within the world view of the royal cult, it was the task of the nation's kings and priests to maintain the sacral and civil structures that were essential to šālôm. Jeremiah and Ezekiel, however, observed that the kings and priests of their time were purveyors not of order but of chaos (Jer. 4:23–26; 22:13–19; Ezek. 9–11). While clinging to the hope that the final outcome of God's struggle for the human heart would be one of a righteous, obedient nation, their deeply pessimistic anthropology and historiography led them to conclude that nothing less than a new divine initiative was required, a new creation, a new heart, a new covenant (Jer. 31:31–34; Ezek. 36:22–32).

A deep pessimism regarding the unaided human situation and a yearning for God's new initiative were the common element underlying the various eschatological visions that began to develop after 587, and that persisted throughout the entire Second Temple period. It is important to note that although the eschatological perspective had a pronounced effect on the way in which visionaries conceived that God would finally bring into being the faithful, righteous community, and on the way they judged existing leaders, institutions and social structures, a strong connection with the religious heritage was nevertheless maintained. For the classical triadic notion of community as the gathering of those giving expression to their devotion to God through worship and following the divine example of righteous compassion was preserved and indeed continued to be refined within the context of the new eschatological perspective. The remnant of the faithful came to be seen as God's chosen agent called to give witness to true community within a chaotic world, and to keep alive the hope of the restoration of creation until the time of fulfillment finally came. At times the harsh treatment received by eschatological circles from their adversaries had the effect of abetting an otherworldly orientation that seemed to cut faith off from serious involvement in the realities of this world. But in general that orientation was a strategic move preserving the identity of the remnant groups until such time when conditions permitted them to re-enter the larger society with programs of reform embodying the classical ideals of Yahwism.

The eschatological vision of Second Isaiah in particular had unique features worthy of specific mention in this summary, since they later came to exercise considerable influence on the eschatological thought of Christianity. According to this anonymous prophet of the exile, Yahweh intended to reconstitute the broken and scattered people, but not through the expected agency of a Davidic messiah. Indeed, the political side of the restoration would be accomplished by a "messiah" of a pagan nation, Cyrus the Persian. On the other hand, the inner transformation of the people from unrighteousness to fidelity was to come through the faithful mediation of Yahweh's Servant, one who would patiently and quietly bear witness to God's alternative order of justice and peace, and through suffering and death would finally win the hearts of God's people, and the nations, to Yahweh. Although the immediate impact of the Servant image on the religion of Israel was limited, it introduced into the tradition a valuable means for struggling with suffering and the experience of God's absence. For the experience of Job frequently was repeated in the life of the Jewish community: the righteous often do suffer more sorely than the wicked. But through the suffering of the Servant, the prophet and those following in the tradition of Second Isaiah came to recognize that such adversity bespoke neither God's distance nor God's indifference, for the Servant was not the victim of a distant God, but the faithful representative of the compassionate God ever seeking new ways to redeem the lost. Unlike Israel's kings, with their predisposition to draw attention and even adoration toward themselves, the servant directed attention solely to Yahweh. And through this self-transcending orientation, a way out of the destructive chain of sin and death that had held Israel in bondage for so long was envisioned. Here in the Servant, God's people would come to recognize the "sin offering" that was God's means of atonement for the lost. That the exilic period was a period of profound theological reflection on the problems of sin and alienation is indicated as well by the theological interpretation given by the Priestly Writing to the Day of Atonement: in providing the blood of the sacrificial victim, God made possible the atonement of the people (Lev. 17:11).

While recognizing variations in the way eschatological circles viewed the future, I do not want to overlook the fact that in a very basic matter they were in fundamental agreement: the reconstitution of God's people in faithfulness and peace would occur when God's sovereignty was acknowledged by all, and all were united in worship of the one true God and in imitation of God's righteousness and compassion. In those forms of the future hope in which a Davidic figure played a part, the Davidide was to be totally dedicated to God's will. In other forms, the Son of Man functioned similarly. In fact, right on into the period of early Christianity and rabbinic Judaism, this classic criterion for the messianic age persisted: God's reign would be inaugurated when God's sovereignty was acknowledged, and God's will was obeyed by all.[2] Neither Hellenistic Judaism, nor Pharisaism, nor early Christianity can be understood without recognizing the formative influence of this eschatological dimension of the notion of community in the later biblical and postbiblical periods.

The centuries following the return from exile were characterized by deep searching for a form of community that was both faithful to the ancestral heritage and appropriate for the radically changed situation of living under Persian dominion. In that searching disagreements arose over the question of what in fact represented the correct interpretation of the ancestral heritage. Some stressed the role of the Zadokite priestly leadership, especially after the last Davidide, Zerubbabel, fell into eclipse. Others held to a vision of restoration giving more attention to marginalized segments of the community, including disenfranchised Levites and members of prophetic circles. Defining the nature of the people of God became entwined in what was largely a political struggle between contending groups for control over the present shape and future orientation of the Jewish community.

The group that prevailed was the priestly party that since the time of

<hr>

2. Cf. *Jerusalem Ta'anit*, and C. Thoma, *A Christian Theology of Judaism* (New York: Paulist Press, 1980), pp. 166–167.

Josiah had enjoyed pre-eminence in the cultic realm, and had found its influence greatly enhanced during the exile, namely the Zadokites. We have seen the emergence of a hierocratic ideal of community under their aegis, with an emphasis on continuity with the temple structures of the past and a policy of cooperation with the Persian authorities. We can understand how from their point of view community restoration was unthinkable without the restoration of the temple cult, for within it were conducted the rites provided by God to serve as the channels through which order and prosperity could re-enter the land. It is equally understandable that groups rejecting their claims to authority and refusing to cooperate with their restoration efforts would have been repudiated as an obstacle to God's plan for Israel. Thus accompanying their zealous efforts to rebuild a community centered around their Zadokite-dominated temple cult was the inability to understand the concerns of dissident groups who sought to regain a recognized place in the temple and covenant community by appealing to what was at once a more archaic and a more eschatological view of the restoration. Efforts to maintain order increasingly took the form of excluding those who held to the broadly inclusive vision of restoration delineated by Second Isaiah, and of defining the Zadokite temple order as definitive, established in the golden age of David and Solomon, and intended for all time. Under Zadokite leadership, we thus witnessed a twofold tendency toward a more narrow definition of community membership and a less eschatological notion of God's ultimate plan for Israel.

Intracommunity polemic thus had the effect of separating off into a collateral stream the nascent universalism and rather lofty eschatology of Second Isaiah. Sensitive theological evaluation of the postexilic situation must recover the significance of these visionary themes in the history of the biblical notion of community without losing sight at the same time of the abiding significance of the Zadokite restoration program. To the latter must be attributed the not insignificant fact that faith in Yahweh survived the Persian period as an historical confession. More than that, it refined a form of community that was able to preserve the essential principles of Yahwism in a form adapted to the new situation of life under a foreign power. Central to this development was the elevation of Torah to a place of pre-eminence as the distinguishing mark of Jewish community. Not to be forgotten were also more practical matters aimed at safeguarding Judaism from assimilation into the religions and customs of neighboring peoples, matters such as reforming economic order, rebuilding fortifications, and enforcing divorce from foreign-born wives.

At the same time the lasting contribution of eschatological circles to a vision of God's broad outreach to redeem all nations and restore the entire creation must not be ignored. The way in which both tendencies, the more pragmatic tendency of the Zadokite leadership, and the more visionary tendency of the dissidents, can be given their due is by a dialectical evaluation of the divergent streams of the postexilic period. Such an approach looks beyond the historical and intracommunal determinants that abetted such separation to a situation in which stability and inclusiveness, viable communal structures, and a vision of the perfect order of šālôm intended by God for all creation, work hand in hand in creating and recreating, forming and reforming God's people as a blessing both to themselves and to all peoples.

The study of the history of the community of faith during the Second Temple period is a fascinating exercise in such a dialectical approach. For it seems that tension between contending religious groups and separation into divergent streams of tradition are two of the most characteristic marks of that period. Of course, it is an exercise evoking much sadness and some bewilderment as well. It is sad to recognize how torturous intracommunal struggle at times led to the projection of disharmony onto the broader world and universe in portraits of God's vengeful judgment on the nations and in apocalyptic visions of cosmic calamity. And it is bewildering to witness the emergence of separate streams of tradition that seem to move inexorably toward the split of the parent faith into separate Jewish and Christian communities, with the ensuing history of their often hostile interrelationship down to modern times.

Yet the strongest impression arising from the study of the Second Temple period is a positive one. In this period of emerging traditions, we find valuable clues to the nature of the connection between the faith communities to which we belong and those of biblical times. We have seen, for example, how a monumental formulation of what it meant to be God's people arose in the stream of tradition extending from Ezra and ben Sirach to Hillel and the Mishnah, thereby providing the foundation for rabbinical Judaism. The deep Torah piety and eschatology of the Hasideans contributed both to the Maccabean Revolt against the inroads of Hellenism and later to separation from the reconstituted monarchy of the Hasmoneans and to an eschatological reformulation of the faith of Israel. These observations in turn contribute to our understanding of the complex ancestry of early Christianity, including the teachings of Jesus.

Specifically as regards the origins of Christianity, the study of the Second Temple period offers a basis for a more adequate understanding of both the essential nature of the early Christian notion of community and of its relation to the contemporaneous Pharisaic and Essene movements. The connections between the teachings of Jesus and those of the Pharisees were both many and profound. At the same time, the eschatological perspective that obviously made such a deep imprint on all Jesus' teachings and actions can be understood best in light of the antecedent history of eschatological and apocalyptic thought spanning the long history from Second Isaiah down to the Roman period.

The central themes as well as the style of Jesus' teaching indicate that he was imbued with the same classic notion of community that the Pharisees sought to preserve. Those holding to this notion recognized that in contrast to the order of government imposed on the Jews by the Romans, God had provided the faithful with an alternative order of life according to which the reign of God was acknowledged over all that is, and within which the faithful sought to embody God's righteousness and compassion as depicted by the Torah and the prophets. The intra-Jewish controversies between Jesus and other Jewish teachers and between early Jewish Christians and the Pharisees, controversies no different in nature from those found both in the earlier biblical period and in the later debates between the rabbinical schools, must not detract from the vast areas of agreement between Jesus and the Pharisees. At the center of both lay the vivid sense of God's presence with those who lived in harmony with God's will. The points at which Jesus differed with some of the Pharisees of his time probably stemmed in part from differences in the way traditional eschatological themes were applied to historical events. In this connection, comparison of his teachings with what we know of the Essenes is instructive, though his insistence on giving expression to his eschatological vision within rather than apart from the social structures of his time suggests that even here his closest affinities were probably with eschatologically oriented circles within Pharisaism rather than with the separatist Essene communities.

However one decides that historical question, the essential theological point remains clear: Jesus' eschatological perspective, and specifically his sense of the imminent inbreaking of God's reign of justice and peace, provided the context within which received traditions and contemporary experiences alike were interpreted. The Torah was accordingly understood as a guide to God's will amid events interpreted as God's final initiative to end the reign of Satan and to establish the eschatological reign of righteousness and šālôm. Within that setting, the Torah was not abolished, but was applied to the situation toward which it was believed to have been ultimately directed, the situation in which God's presence in the world acting to save the lost determined how any given commandment was to be applied so as to bring out its intended meaning. For example, at the point at which the healing of creation toward which the history of God's people was directed was occurring, sabbath law was not to inhibit that salvatory process. The very notion of sabbath arose out of God's willing health and wholeness for all creatures: "Ought not this woman, a daughter of Abraham whom Satan bound for eighteen years, be loosed from this bond on the sabbath day?" (Luke 12:16; cf. Exod. 20:8–11; Deut. 5:12–15; Mark 2:23–27). God, the giver of the Torah, had again drawn near to God's people, and the faithful were to permit nothing, not even earlier formulations of the Torah, to stand in the way of their responding with full hearts:

"Can the wedding guests fast while the bridegroom is with them?" (Mark 2:19; cf. Matt. 9:15; Luke 5:34).

Jesus' eschatological interpretaion of the events he was witnessing was accompanied by a belief that the Torah was not a haphazard collection of commandments, but had a distinct heart that accurately reflected the will of God:

> The first is this, "Hear, O Israel: The Lord our God, the Lord is one; and you shall love the Lord your God with all your heart, and with all your soul, and with all your mind, and with all your strength." The second is this, "You shall love your neighbor as yourself." (Mark 12:29–31; cf. Deut. 6:4–5 and Lev. 19:18)

A vivid sense of God's nearness together with a recognition of the summation of the Torah in the love of God and neighbor provided a living context within which to interpret the meaning of all of the Torah and the prophets.

Nowhere is Jesus' eschatological perspective and understanding of the love commandment expressed more clearly than in relation to the question of the nature of the community willed by God. Dedication to preserving God's will from defilement in a fallen world had led some of the Pharisees to separate themselves strictly from "sinners"; that is, from all those who did not observe the Torah in the manner prescribed by Pharisaic interpretation. The sincerity and devotion motivating them to seek refuge in their ḥăbûrôt need not be doubted. Their history was filled with stories of the tragic consequences of mixing with foreigners and sinners. In a world in which God's order was under siege on all sides by the powers of this world and the powers of Satan, they believed that their ancestral faith could be preserved only by carefully avoiding every contact that would defile that which God had separated out as a witness to holiness.

Jesus also viewed the world as caught up in the struggle between God and Satan, the faithful and apostates. But while most Pharisees seemed to expect no imminent, dramatic change in world realities, and remained dedicated to preserving their witness until God eventually acted to establish universal reign, Jesus understood his life as being drawn into events that marked a dramatic turning point: the long-awaited reign of God had come. In that light he interpreted the healings and exorcisms that he was performing: "If it is by the Spirit of God that I cast out demons, then the kingdom of God has come upon you" (Matt. 12:28; cf. Luke 11:20).

It was this sense of the turn of the ages that perhaps more than any other single factor explains Jesus' disagreement with many Pharisees of his time regarding community membership. It was an essential part of that turning point that God was extending a final, urgent invitation to all who remained outside of the Kingdom. This was not a time to safeguard the remnant of the faithful from contact with sinners, but for the faithful to accept God's call to become participants in the Kingdom's coming. This involved going out precisely to sinners with a call to repentance proclaimed urgently in light of the imminent judgment of the world (Matt. 9:12; Mark 2:17; Luke 5:31–32). It involved becoming agents of the divine healing that was a sign of the end-time. It involved taking risks and enduring hardships for the sake of the only reality that was eternal. It meant being receptive to God's Spirit and thereby being empowered with the words and deeds of the Kingdom. Since the sole criterion for membership in the blessed community was repentance and acceptance of God's reign, traditional divisions between the pure and sinners were rejected by Jesus. He saw God's Kingdom as breaking all human barriers and coming to expression in the invitation to all people to accept their oneness under God's universal reign. By associating with publicans and sinners, he gave expression to his understanding of the events of his time. That this appeared to some as evidence that he was a glutton and a drunkard was similarly the outgrowth of their carefully defined interpretation of reality.

As Christians and Jews today seek to establish their relationship on a more adequate historical foundation than has characterized the past, it is important that all of us recognize the integrity of *both* ancestral religious movements, and to understand that differences arose largely through the differing degrees of emphasis being placed on certain themes—all of which, however, developed out of the common biblical heritage. It is also important to recognize that both sides were dedicated to the same ultimate reality, God's universal reign of justice and peace. Moreover, it must never be forgotten that the belief that God's anointed one (i.e., the Messiah) would be God's agent inaugurating that Kingdom both has deep roots in Hebrew Scriptures and continued to be the object of hope and prayer in postbiblical Judaism. Especially when one considers the delicate dialectic between "realized" and "futuristic" eschatology that has developed as a part of the church's interpretation of Jesus Christ, it becomes obvious how openly and fruitfully Jews and Christians can discuss their different understandings of God's reign and the Messiah with one another. Both look at history as the arena of God's purpose. History is not closed, but open to that purpose. Together, Jews and Christians long for God's final victory over all that diminishes and threatens life in a world in which evil is all too evident. And together they seek a fuller understanding of the vocation of communities of faith dedicated to hastening the day when the blessing that the true God alone can bring will be known to everyone. What a great impoverishment is suffered by both communities when they deny themselves the enrichment in understanding that can come from drinking deeply from each other's chalice! But for that enrichment to occur, old stereotypes must be replaced by more accurate knowledge of one another. Christians, for example, must realize that Jews are not unmessianic, but remain true to their eschatological beliefs by waiting for and praying for the Messiah, and by bearing witness to that hope by remaining faithful to their traditions. Christians, moreover, should give expression to their openness to God's grace by continuing to rediscover lost aspects of biblical faith from the people with whom God first entered into covenant relationship, the people to whom they owe their membership in the community of those responding to God. To do so is to follow the lead of the Apostle Paul, who not only recalled Israel's rich spiritual legacy (Rom. 9:4–5) but also looked forward to the new chapter of God's dealing with Israel (Rom. 12:25–27), and to the final fulfillment of creation when God would be all in all (1 Cor. 15:28). In like manner, countless themes both in the Bible and in the rabbinical writings, like the Noachic covenant and the Abrahamic blessing, provide a firm basis on which Jews can base their discussion with Christians.

Or does the figure of Jesus finally represent an insuperable obstacle in the way of Jewish-Christian dialogue? When Christians look back to Scripture in search of their spiritual ancestry and the roots of their communal consciousness, there is no denying the fact that Jesus occupies a special, central position. Properly understood, however, this does not obscure but rather illuminates the deep roots of the church in the faith of Israel and its indebtedness to the Torah and the Prophets, for Jesus provides the church with its strongest link with God's first covenant people. As a Jewish rabbi and prophet drawing on the ancestral faith within which he had been raised, and living with a sense of divine calling and an intimate awareness of God's nearness instilled in him by that same faith, Jesus sought not to break with his Jewish tradition, but to reform and to amplify that tradition, much in the spirit of the dynamic, forward-moving nature characteristic of biblical faith from its earliest stages. And the early church confessed that Jesus both reaffirmed the central tenets of early and prophetic Yahwism and impelled them toward a new stage of development. His role in this regard can be fruitfully compared to the role of the great rabbis who helped mold the traditions culminating in the Mishnah and Talmud.

Thus, while Jesus did not organize the church in any formal sense, he laid down the foundation on which the church would grow, in a manner analogous to the role of Hillel in the history of rabbinical Judaism. For in calling together disciples, in teaching them the way of the Kingdom of God and giving them an unforgettable example of the life lived in conformity to God's will, Jesus drew some of his fellow Jews into the challenge that formed the heart of his own life, the challenge to accept God's reign as the only ultimate reality in life, and to dedicate life fully to drawing others into the orbit of the Kingdom's healing power. These followers came to attribute to Jesus a key role in the inauguration of God's reign, confessing that through him God had entered history personally to grapple with the demonic forces that bound humanity. In him they saw a renewal of God's order of righteousness and compassion, and the beginning of the restoration of creation to health through miracles of forgiveness, feeding, healing, and kindness. In him they became acquainted with a power unlike the destructive powers of this world, a creative power expressing itself in patient, suffering love. All of this seemed to come together in his death and resurrection as an announcement of God's final victory on behalf of humanity over sin and sin's consequences of hopelessness and death.

We have come to recognize the disciples, therefore, as a group continuing the mission of announcing the good news of God's reign. Not that all evidence of the old order of sin had disappeared. Indeed, those who set out to proclaim the gospel of redemption had to deal with their own weaknesses and doubts and with the hostility of many to whom they preached. But they believed that the decisive battle had been won. And they celebrated God's reign as a present reality by being baptized "into Christ" and commemorating their Lord's passion in the meal eaten in anticipation of the eschatological banquet. One can readily see the continuation of the sense of eschatological urgency that characterized Jesus' life, therefore, at the center of the early Jerusalem church, a sense fostered by its experience of Jesus' resurrection and the abiding presence of the risen Lord in the form of the Spirit.

This eschatological and charismatic perspective further cultivated the inclusive attitude toward community that was such a pronounced characteristic of Jesus' life. Actually the issue that soon was to lead to controversy within the church, the terms under which Gentiles could be admitted into fellowship, was not a major one within Jesus' Judean and Galilean environment. Nevertheless, his consistent opposition to the divisions creating separations between those around him—such as the separation between observant and sinners, between Jews and Samaritans, between patriots and the occupational forces—had created an environment conducive to the conversion of non-Jews. This was interpreted as a further sign that the fulfillment of God's plan for creation was at hand. The fledgling movement saw in its witness to God's act in Jesus Christ the renewal of Israel's vocation of being agents in bringing God's salvation to all peoples. Having experienced the "first fruits" of the Kingdom, the young church felt called to participate in that Kingdom's coming in fullness. It was to be prepared to encounter the same suffering and abuse experienced by its Lord, confident that its solidarity with Christ guaranteed that nothing could separate it from God and from life with God (Rom. 8:35–39).

The eschatological sense of witnessing and being called to participate in the fulfillment of God's reign over all creation was a key element in the next stage of development of the notion of community as it moved in a direction distinct from that of Pharisaic Judaism. In this stage, the Apostle Paul played a decisive role in defining Christianity as a universal faith. Working within an eschatological understanding of his time as transitional between the Old Age of wrath and the New Age of reconciliation, Paul contributed to the development of a Christian understanding of community by relating it to the primal pattern of divine initiative and human response. The church accordingly was not viewed primarily as a guardian of received tradition, but as a body growing in response to God's new initiative in Christ, and within the context of that response interpreting the contemporary meaning of that tradition.

Since for Paul Christ's resurrection and the abiding presence of Christ's Spirit within the community of faith formed the center of God's new initiative, he defined the church as the body of Christ, called by grace to carry on the mission of reconciliation it had already experienced (2 Cor. 6:16–21). Applying an eschatological hermeneutic in which Christ was the key to the meaning of Scripture, Paul concluded that Torah and the prophets were not timeless expressions of divine will, but witnesses to God's involvement in the life of God's people pointing to the fulfillment he believed was at hand, the dismantling of every barrier separating humanity from God and humans from one another, and the redemption of creation culminating in God's universal reign. In this interpretation, he did not dispute the importance of God's promise to Israel. Indeed, in Romans 11 he bases his hope for Israel's salvation squarely on God's faithfulness to that promise. But he shifts the emphasis away from physical to spiritual descent, and focuses on faith in Christ as the One sent by God to accomplish what even the holy Law was unable to accomplish, namely, reconciliation of humans to God: ". . . in Jesus Christ you are all sons of God through faith" (Gal. 3:26). Aware of the terrible separation from God caused by sin in a manner reminiscent of Jeremiah and Ezekiel (e.g., Rom. 7:13–25), Paul believed that God had taken a bold new initiative to break the impasse by "sending his own Son in the likeness of sinful flesh and for sin" (Rom. 8:3). Although a radically new initiative, Paul believed that this act was in fidelity to the ancient promise made to Abraham, whom he sees as a paradigm of faith: "And if you are Christ's then you are Abraham's offspring, heirs according to promise" (Gal. 3:29). The church, as the body of those accepting God's gift of salvation through Christ, was thus rooted in the earliest stages of Israel's history with God at the same time as it was constituted as a people of God by this new divine initiative. Through this initiative, the ancient promise was extended to all peoples, in fulfillment of both the Abrahamic promise of Genesis 12 and the Servant Songs of Isaiah 42 and 49. This extension of the biblical community to the nations was made possible in no small part by Paul's proclamation that baptism into Christ was sufficient to make one a member of God's people, in spite of the insistence of some that circumcision and observance of the dietary laws were binding on all converts. Paul's position concerning community membership was of course tied to his eschatological perspective. In Christ, God's plan of salvation had been extended to all peoples; in him had been manifested "the righteousness of God through faith in Jesus Christ for all who believe" (Rom. 3:22). "For as many of you were baptized into Christ have put on Christ. There is neither Jew nor Greek, there is neither slave nor free, there is neither male nor female; for you are all one in Christ Jesus" (Gal. 3:27–28).

On the one hand, Paul's notion of the church builds on Jesus' dedication to the reign of God that overcame all distinctions and drew all those responding in faith into the healing power of the Kingdom, and on the experiences of the Jewish church. On the other hand, the setting within which the Pauline churches carried on the proclamation of God's reign was sufficiently different from the earlier Jerusalem setting to necessitate significant changes and new emphases. It is inevitable that strains between different groups arose, such as the one between the Jerusalem congregation under the leadership of James and the missionary group that began to work out of Antioch. When we look back on such early controversies within the church, we should resist the temptation of accepting uncritically the options that emerged victorious, while ignoring others. It would seem to be a fair extension of Paul's own injunciton regarding the freedom of the believer in Christ, for example, to acknowledge the legitimacy of the choice of some Christians, whether in antiquity or today, to give expression to their close relation to Judaism by observing dietary laws, so long as such a practice is not then held up as binding on all other Christians.

Already during Paul's lifetime, as in subsequent years, another serious problem arose in the form of a gnostic interpretation of the gospel. Jesus, in keeping with his Jewish tradition, expressed deep concern with the well-being of all people within the structures of their everyday life. The inbreaking of God's reign did not lead him to withdraw from life, but to engage fully in the acts of teaching and healing that manifested God's active involvement in mending a broken creation. Opposition and abuse were not avoided, but regarded as signs of the continued resistance of Satan. Accordingly, Jesus looked to the future for the fulfillment of God's redemptive plan. Paul similarly taught that the Christian, while confident that the decisive battle against evil had been won by Christ, nevertheless continued to live in hope of creation's final redemption. Gnostic teachers, however, including some claiming Pauline authority, proclaimed a gospel of immediate escape from this world into the sphere of the incorruptible. And for centuries they threatened to break Christianity off from its ancient biblical heritage by declaring that this world was not the creation of the true God, but a lesser order undeserving of the believer's attention.

Paul and those standing in the Pauline tradition were able to limit the inroads of gnosticism in part by developing church structures and disciplines capable of preserving the historical confessions of the young church. We have seen in the gospels and epistles confessional formulations that summarized the central teachings of the church, and provided a norm for distinguishing between true teaching and heresy. We have also noticed in the Pastoral Epistles and in writings like the *Didache* and *1 Clement* that the further elaboration of such formulations were accompanied by the development of offices of authority. These developments, while necessitated by genuine problems, introduced a new strain, that between the model of allowing communal structures to arise as a response to a vivid sense of God's presence and a more rigid sense of an authoritative structure dedicated to preserving true doctrine and an orderly communal discipline.

The results were particularly pronounced and far-reaching in the area of community structure. What we witness is the development of a church moving away from the notion of leadership provided by the Holy Spirit through the granting of *charismata* to each individual and toward the notion of offices arranged hierarchically and invested with the authority to impose proper discipline and true doctrine on all members of the churches. Already in *1 Clement*, this authoritative structure has even begun to acknowledge one bishop, the bishop of Rome, as endowed with a special status. By the time of Tertullian, efforts to restore a more charismatic notion of community structure were repudiated. The episcopal structure had become identified with orthopraxy. Not only did this introduce a sharp distinction and then an ever widening gap between clergy and laity, but also excluded certain groups, notably women, from positions of leadership in the church.[3] While this routinization of community structure was occurring within the mainstream church, certain groups that had been renounced as heretical, notably gnostic groups, were continuing to practice a more open community polity closer in spirit to the early Pauline congregations. The biblical era thus came to a close with many important issues relating to the theological notion of community unresolved, inviting much further reflection and struggle by future generations of the faithful.

B. RECAPTURING A VISION: FAITH COMMUNITIES TODAY

One of the clearest implications of this study for efforts to relate the Bible to contemporary issues is that the Bible is not a "reference manual" supplying direct answers to modern problems. Indeed, if the central message of the Bible were the claim to provide answers to the di-

---

3. Cf. E. Schüssler Fiorenza, *In Memory of Her: A Feminist Theological Reconstruction of Christian Origins* (New York: Crossroad Publishing Company, 1984), pp. 285–342.

verse problems faced by believers of all ages in the concrete settings of their lives, biblical faith would be a very archaic and fragile phenomenon. The conditions within which the faithful live change as empires come and go, customs are transformed, and the relationship of communities of faith to governing authorities changes. For example, Christians living in the United States and asking how to translate their faith into responsible political action must take into account the fact that their country is politically independent, exercises considerable economic and often even military influence over other countries, possesses a huge nuclear arsenal, and is related to the other major military world power in a manner often characterized by tension and confrontational tactics. The political tactics urged by Isaiah on the king of a tiny Judean nation threatened by far superior foreign empires, or the political tactics enunciated by the Apostle Paul to a community living under the domination of the might of Rome obviously are not simply transferable to this new setting. But Isaiah's underlying principal argument that a people's security can be established on no foundation save ultimate trust in God accompanied by dedication to justice and peace, and Paul's stress on reconciliation with God followed by the ministry of reconciliation as the hallmark of those dedicated to God's order of righteousness, retain their validity as profoundly today as in ancient Israel or in the Roman era. We must therefore tutor ourselves in the quality of theological discernment that enables us to grasp the dynamic vision of divine purpose that lies at the heart of the biblical witness and still can enlighten the vision of communities of faith today.

This study has illustrated that the biblical notion of community, and the vision of an order of righteous compassion and peace that that community was to embody, experienced rebirth and renewal in the concrete situations faced by each new generation of believers. As I have sketched elsewhere,[4] the essential ontology of biblical faith (and its descendant faiths) is historical in the sense of developing over the ages in a dialectical relationship with new experiences. Unlike mythopoeic systems with their visions of the primordial acts of the gods that established timeless structures and values, biblical faith looks to the God who invites a responding community to recognize the presence of God in the events it encounters, and to infer from that presence what is the just and loving way to live. This thoroughly relational aspect of the biblical and Judeo-Christian ontology explains both the enduring quality of Jewish and Christian faith and the error implicit in construing the Bible as a manual of timeless answers to specific personal, political, or social problems.

This distinction is an important but frequently misunderstood one. The fear is often expressed that it leads to an erosion of biblical author-

---

4. In Hanson, *Dynamic Transcendence* (Philadelphia: Fortress Press, 1978).

ity and a subsequent normlessness for communities of faith. It is not enough to reply that the approach that expects to find specific answers to contemporary problems by applying biblical proof-texts both over-looks the huge gap between the biblical settings of such texts and the contemporary situations to which they are applied and encounters con-flicting answers even within the biblical writings. While true in itself, it is necessary to go beyond negative judgments to a clear description of the true nature of biblical authority, which in my judgment means a de-scription of the abiding validity of the biblical notion of community and its vision of God's plan for the world. Although this descriptive-constructive task is of such magnitude as to demand resources far ex-ceeding those available to me, the main purpose of this study would be missed if it did not contribute to this important task of clarifying the identity and purpose of contemporary faith communities. Accordingly I now shall draw on the study of the growth of the notion of communi-ty in the Bible in addressing three typical problems that impose them-selves on communities that continue to look to the Bible for guidance. This exercise is simply illustrative in nature, for examples could be mul-tiplied, and those chosen could each be subjected to book-length treat-ment. But this section indicates how the concrete witness given by the biblical paradigms of faith to its vision of divine purpose is not lost but renewed and extended as the contemporary community of faith grasps, or better still, is grasped by those paradigms and their underlying vi-sion and is inspired to embody them in its own life. This exercise is then followed with an attempt to offer a summary formulation of the biblical notion of community and of the vision of divine purpose as they can take shape in the life of a community of faith today.

Guiding the selection of specific problems with which to illustrate how a proper understanding of the biblical notion of community and the vision it embodies might function today has not been the desire to isolate those that are necessarily of greatest theological or social conse-quence. Rather, my choice has grown out of a sense that the three problems discussed relate specifically to the question lying at the heart of this study—namely, how can a community that seeks both to live true to its confessional heritage and to live as a responsible part of to-day's world define and constitute itself? Accordingly, we shall consider the questions of community structure, relation to civil authorities, and Jewish-Christian relations.

1. COMMUNITY STRUCTURE

Historical studies leave no doubt that the causes abetting divisions between spiritual descendants of the communities of faith in the Bible, and not infrequently giving rise to bitter struggle and persecution, have included the determination of certain groups and their leaders to preserve inherited structures with little reference to the more dynamic apsects of the classical religious heritage. For example, such "power politics" is clearly discernible in the treatment of the Montanists in the late second and third centuries C.E. Zeal for specific structures frequently distracted Roman Catholics and those seeking to reform the church from the essential underlying theological issues at stake in their controversies. And it is patently clear that fragmentation among the reformers themselves occurred in no small part due to questions of communal structure and style that often were argued without due regard to the deeper dynamics of the Christian heritage. The contemporary ecumenical discussions occurring between various Christian bodies today (e.g., Catholics and Lutherans, Lutherans and Episcopalians, Episcopalians and Methodists) underscore a problem that has haunted the Christian churches for centuries. Such discussions, now removed from the heated political battles of earlier times, have repeatedly pointed to far greater agreement on important doctrinal issues than had earlier been apparent (cf. the recent Catholic-Lutheran statement on the doctrine of justification).

The study of the biblical roots of contemporary communities of faith places specific ecclesial structures and polities in proper historical and theological perspective as subservient to and derivative of something more ultimate and dynamic than particular institutional forms. That ultimate form is God's ongoing gathering together of a people to carry on God's purpose of restoring a broken world and bringing it to its intended wholeness. This is not to deny for a moment the important role that institutional structures play in preserving and administering the traditions and means of grace that renew God's call and sustain the people in the vocation to which they have been drawn. But it emphatically places such structures in a subservient role to a drama directed by God, and establishes a clear criterion by which those structures must continually be evaluated and reformed, namely, the degree to which they draw the community into the creative, redemptive purposes of God.

Since the God described by biblical faith is experienced as a Reality present in the concrete happenings of this world and dedicated to the redemption of all creation, it is only natural that the responding community must be one alive to organizational and tactical changes necessitated by changing conditions. For example, the forms within which an East African culture can experience God's call and God's means of grace will be different from those which have evolved within a Western European culture, and the specific nature of those forms can be discovered only by those experiencing God's presence in that particular setting. The dynamic notion of community to which the Bible bears witness has been a faithful guide to people precisely in such settings, for the Bible is filled with examples of new communities being born out of the experience of God's presence, and offers a wide range of possible forms and structures that can be used in constituting the people of

God. In Egypt a group of slaves encountered God as their Deliverer, and in responding to that divine initiative they were constituted as a people in a way largely unique in the ancient world. In Galilee and Judea, a band of women and men responded to Jesus' announcement that God's Kingdom was drawing near to them, and in responding they were gathered into a community once again in ways unique within its social setting. And in between, many different groups discovered and rediscovered their identity as a people called by God's initiative to a life of blessing for themselves and others. In our own day, those discovering community in response to God's grace for the first time, as well as those rediscovering community within structures that had grown stale, will recognize that faithfulness is determined not by conformity to a particular polity or institutional structure, but by conformity to the redemptive purposes of God. That this conformity requires of older, established religious bodies both a relinquishment of control and a willingness to allow other groups to take risks as they seek to find the particular structures and styles of discipleship that allow them to give faithful expression to their vision cannot be doubted. Such relinquishment and risk taking is possible, however, only if definitions of community predicated on notions of human accomplishment are relinquished in favor of a definition growing out of a vision of a universal redemptive process that is of God's making and in relation to which responding communities adopt such institutional forms as are in harmony with their dedication to embody God's will in the world. By clearly keeping its attention focused on the order of reality that transcends every human institution, and defining its own identity strictly in terms of participation in that order, communities of faith can avoid the common confusion between the human and the divine: "[The Church] announces the Kingdom, but is not the Kingdom itself."[5]

Once patterning its life after this dynamic, biblical model, a community of faith will not react to challenges to its particular institutional structures as threats to be repulsed, but very possibly as signs of the Spirit prodding it to new life and a more fitting response to God's presence. This is why the common neglect of the doctrine of the Holy Spirit is a worrisome sign, perhaps even an indication of the retreat away from the challenges and surprises inevitably occurring where a people is open to God's presence into the false security of human institutions. Such institutions by outward appearances may seem to be hallowed, and indeed may have their origins in the faithful response of earlier generations to divine initiative. But if perpetuated as ends in themselves and cut off from ongoing scrutiny and reform, they may become obstacles rather than instruments of God's order, and agents of human rather than divine purpose. When a spiritual and eschatological per-

---

5. D. Harrington, *God's People in Christ: New Testament Perspectives on the Church and Judaism* (Philadelphia: Fortress Press, 1980), p. 27.

spective is supplanted by the dedication to traditional forms, the goal of self-preservation threatens the goal of participating in a universal redemptive process transcending every institutional form. The stakes in human structures increase, and the willingness to take risks for God's order of righteous compassion decreases. As suggested by the metaphor "salt of the earth," God's people can carry out their important task of bearing witness to God's alternative order only if they refuse to blend into habitations that have grown comfortable through a refusal to question old values and assumptions. To be "salt of the earth," a people must persist in radically reorienting life away from every idol toward the one true God.

The early disciples experienced in Jesus the call to a radical denunciation of every penultimate loyalty in response to the only loyalty worthy of laying claim to one's life. And succeeding generations of the church saw the continuation of that call in the presence of the Holy Spirit, which kept alive both the sense of being redeemed from death solely through God's atoning act in Christ, and the sense of being called to a divine purpose in life. The early church offers a good example of how earlier forms of community were tested on the basis of the experience of God's presence, with the result that many traditional Jewish forms were retained or adapted, even as new forms evolved in relation to new situations. One need only consider the role of the twelve, the eschatological meal, the simultaneous respect of and freedom from the Torah, sabbath observance, differing positions in relation to dietary laws and, in support of these various practices and beliefs, the application of traditional Jewish methods and principles of scriptural exegesis, to see the lively manner in which the early church both retained the old and adopted the new. Paul of course tied these various practices, as well as miracles of healing and speaking in tongues, to the Holy Spirit by identifying them as *charismata*; that is, gifts of the Spirit. If one contrasts the viridity of this early stage of the church with the organizational structures that prevailed at Qumran, the central importance of the doctrine of the Holy Spirit becomes apparent. In the absence of such a teaching, we witness at Qumran an archaizing, biblicizing rigidity leading, after the death of its founder, not to new growth under the guidance of the Spirit, but to life strictly regulated by a legalistic, rigid institutional structure. We need only remember that similar tendencies toward legalism and rigidity at times arose within the church as it moved toward a routinization of its charisma in the service of a more tightly controlled hierarchical concept of organization as a final argument in support of what should be an important lesson for communities of faith today: if they are to remain a life-giving presence contributing to justice and peace, it is essential that they preserve a lively sense of God's Spirit. That sense alone seems to preserve the primal experience at the heart of both early Yahwism and the early church, the experience of God's gracious initiative as that which alone calls, constitutes and defines the mission of a genuine community of faith.

If communities of faith today are both to preserve the freedom to adapt communal structures to changing situations and to preserve the classical themes and doctrines that enable it to address with prophetic clarity and courage the critical issues of this world, they must be dedicated to the ongoing process of clarifying the central vision of divine purpose that is their sole legitimate source of identity and purpose. When a community lives with an intimate sense of the presence of the God by whom it is called and sustained, it is able to keep both confessions and communal structures in harmony with its ultimate devotion, for both are inferred from its experience of the living God. On the other hand, wherever the vision of God's ongoing activity on behalf of the whole human family and the entire created order is lost, the dynamic process of inferring confessions and structures from divine example is lost, with the inevitable result that mundane examples move to center stage and abet the desire to preserve received forms as definitive. A community of faith is able to confess that no human formulations or institutional structures are eternally valid and at the same time maintain a healthy communal stability if it lives from the belief that its life is created ever anew as an aspect of God's ongoing creative, redemptive activity, of which it is a modest part. The true community of faith is thus a pilgrim people, seeing its forms and structures as provisional within a world being transformed from brokenness to wholeness, and trusting that ultimately its own transformation is being guided by a God whose promises are trustworthy and whose purposes are dedicated to the redemption of all creation.

2. RELATION TO CIVIL AUTHORITIES

The problem of the relation between communities of faith and the prevailing civil authorities is age-old. It was the problem faced by Micaiah ben Imlah when requested by the king's messengers to give an oracle favorable to King Ahab. It was the one that Amos confronted when ordered by Amaziah to desist from criticizing King Jeroboam II and to depart from the Bethel sanctuary (Amos 7:10–17). It was the problem that weighed heavily on the Jews of Jerusalem and Alexandria during the Hellenistic period. It was a life and death issue for Christians during the reigns of the Roman emperors Nero and Domitian. In the post-Constantinian era, it took on a new form, and underlay serious tensions between popes and emperors for centuries. Nor has the problem diminished in our own era, an era living with the terrible memories of a German church divided over this very issue and witnessing the horrible consequences of that division, the persecution of Jews and Christians in many lands due to their insistence on following the mandate of their beliefs.

Through all these ages, appeal has been made to Scripture in support of diverse positions on the issue of the relation of the community of faith to civil authorities. The government of South Africa has enlisted the efforts of sympathetic theologians to spell out a rationale in support of the policy of apartheid. The Roman Catholic Church has recently increased its criticism of liberation theologians in Latin American countries such as Peru and Brazil in part because of their defiance of civil authorities. In the United States, both Jewish and Christian communities find themselves divided over what has come to be called "civil religion," that is, the close alliance between civil and religious interests and authority.[6] A massive gathering of the National Association of Evangelicals and the National Religious Broadcasters was able to enlist both white and black religious leaders, both Christian and Jewish clergy to lift up triumphal litanies hailing the new militant conservative religious coalition and to extol the moral and religious virtues of the Reagan administration.[7] The Reverend Jerry Falwell has even issued an edition of the Bible emphasizing U.S. patriotism by embossing the liberty bell on the cover and binding with the pages of Scripture the pages of the presidents and a text of the U.S. Constitution.

In support of a close tie between faith and patriotism, appeal commonly has been made to the logion ascribed by all three of the Synoptic Gospels to Jesus, "Render to Caesar the things that are Caesar's, and to God the things that are God's" (Matt. 22:15–22; Mark 12:13–17; Luke 20:20–26). Of course, this logion is open to diverse interpretations, depending on what one understands to belong respectively to Caesar and to God. Less ambiguous seems to be Romans 13:1–7, which begins with the sentence, "Let every person be subject to the governing authorities," and then goes on to point out that all such authorities "have been instituted by God," and that the one in authority is "God's servant for your good."

Chapter XIV observed a growing concern among church leaders of the post-Pauline period with civil respectability, as reflected in the so-called Pastoral and Catholic Letters. 1 Peter said, "Be subject for the Lord's sake to every human institution, whether it be to the emperor as supreme, or to governors as sent by him to punish those who do wrong and to praise those who do right" (1 Pet. 2:13). As a proof text for obedience to civil authorities, this too seems to offer strong support.

One approach to this problem would involve lining up biblical texts that reflect a different attitude toward the governing authorities, such as those already mentioned from the time of Ahab and Jeroboam II, or

---

6. See R. N. Bellah, *The Broken Covenant: American Civil Religion in Time of Trial* (New York: Seabury Press, 1975); and P. D. Hanson, "The Role of Scripture in Times of Crisis," *Word and World* 1 (1981), 116–127.

7. Reported by Marjorie Hyer, *L.A. Times–Washington Post* News Service, January 31, 1981.

passages from the Book of Revelation, and then trying to argue which attitude is most authentically "biblical." But this approach is faulty on a fundamental methodological level. Attention to this level reveals that the problem of the relation to civil authority parallels the problem of community structure. The Bible, properly understood, does not set forth timeless policy on either matter. The diverse positions found in different writings of the Bible indicate that different solutions arose depending on the nature of the particular situation. Does this mean that a contemporary community of faith can expect to find no help in the biblical writings. No, but it does direct attention to a deeper level, namely, to the level of the dynamic notion of community that develops within Scripture and the vision of divine purpose that defines the faith community's vocation in the world. On this level, the central message of the Bible is clear, namely, that the community of faith can be devoted ultimately only to one authority, the one true God, and hence the order to which it is committed is the order of reality ordained by God. The relation of the community of faith to other orders, such as those of emperors and magistrates, must be determined by this ultimate devotion. Any other posture would lead to idolatry.

Accordingly, the specific positions adopted by Amos, Isaiah, Jesus, Paul, or the author of 1 Peter are to be seen as examples of how the principle of God's ultimate authority was applied to concrete situations by different biblical communities. Simply to adopt one or the other of these concrete applications is to miss the point that, for example, Paul is speaking to a very specific situation, namely, one in which Christians live in a relatively peaceful but often delicate relationship to Roman authorities. This situation in turn is quite different from that of Micaiah ben Imlah, an Israelite prophet addressing his own king, or from that of John of Patmos, a seer addressing Christians suffering persecution under the Romans. Needless to say, the situations under which believers live in various parts of the world today are equally diverse. Specific concrete applications may be very helpful in aiding the faithful in one situation or another to see how the principle of sole allegiance to God's order may be translated into a responsible posture within a particular setting. But what unites believers of all nations and ages is the duty so to embody its vision of God's creative, redemptive purpose on behalf of all creation as to find itself taking a stand in relation to civil authorities in harmony with that universal purpose. Entailed is not a mindless imposition of a simple solution on complex situations. The biblical vision as it had developed over centuries of history is itself complex, embodying dimensions that often can best be described in terms of polarities like form and reform, or pragmatic action and eschatological hope. In this duty, the criticism and support of the community of faith in its broadest scope is utterly essential if temptations to yield to idolatrous parochial, nationalistic, or personal definitions of divine purpose are to be resisted.[8] In addition, a thorough knowledge of the struggles of previous generations of the faithful adds examples to the paradigms of the Bible in equipping believers for the difficult task of relating to their civil authorities.

3. JEWISH-CHRISTIAN RELATIONS

Throughout the history of Christianity, the manner in which Christians have related to Jews has been one of the most important indicators of their own spiritual health. Residing within the relation of Christians to Jews is something essential to the identity of the former, perhaps to both. Christians have often failed to understand their indebtedness to Judaism and the contribution Jews continue to make to a proper understanding of what it means to be a person of biblical faith. The resulting loss has been tragic, and has fostered the kind of sickness of soul that turns against the very people sent by God as a blessing to all people. When tempted by this sort of ingratitude, I find it helpful to substitute for the common anti-Jewish interpretation of the Parable of the Wicked Tenants (Mark 12:1–12) a reading that stresses that God came to Gentiles as a Jew, and *continues* to come to us through the witness of Jews who live true to their ancestral faith and their messianic hope. The common tendency to belittle the faith of the Jew has nothing to do with the freedom to which God calls God's people, a freedom from all need to establish our own goodness by diminishing the goodness of others.[9] It has been one of the central themes of this study that within the Bible the identity of God's people is not established by human acts or pronouncements, but by the unmerited initiative of God, and by the response of humans to that initiative that gathers them into a community devoted to sharing God's grace and glorifying the Sovereign One. At points in this study where we found evidence of divisions between different groups, it was not possible to draw a simple distinction between the one side's truth and the other side's error. Indeed, the message of dissidents was commonly found to point to important aspects of the tradition that had been lost by the mainstream. Unfortunately polemic with its resulting polarization usually exacerbates the narrowing of a group's grasp of its spiritual heritage.

Sadly, polemic and misunderstanding have stood in the way of a full appreciation of the close spiritual kinship that should unite Christians and Jews. Renewing a sense of that kinship does not entail denying or

---

8. Cf. Hanson, *Transcendance*, pp. 84–85.

9. This same acknowledgment of the divine origin of the call to peoplehood should create an openness for a gracious engagement with non-Judeo-Christian religions as well, predicated on a respect for the specialness and beauty of their religious traditions, and an eagerness to learn. Since communities of faith owe their existence to God's initiative, any sense of arrogant proprietorship is unseemly. The issue is not to determine who has been called and who excluded, but to rejoice in God's gracious calling and gathering that surpasses the understanding of any human individual or community.

ignoring differences. Indeed, if Jesus as the central figure of Christian faith is understood in proper historical relation to Judaism, he is restored to his proper place between the two religious communities, namely, as the *primary link that connects them*. If we recognize the central message of Jesus in the announcement of God's reign—that is, the order of *šālôm* toward which Jewish Scripture points and around which the faith and hopes of Jews of Jesus' time revolved—we will see how intimately the origins of the Christian faith are tied to the history of the Jewish people.[10] Jesus also becomes a link rather than a barrier when we recognize that he described the Kingdom of God in stories and sayings resembling those of other rabbis of his time, and that his prayers resembled theirs.[11] As for his emphasis on the openness of the fellowship of faith to all peoples, we must recognize that he was announcing a stage in God's redemptive activity that did not nullify Israel's special calling, but that extended the blessing handed down by the teachers and prophets of Israel to the Gentiles. As the parallelism of Simeon's blessing in Matthew's 2:32 so beautifully states, God's new initiative in Jesus was simultaneously "a light for revelation to the Gentiles, and for glory to the people Israel." As discussed at greater length in the Appendix to this book, Paul develops a similar notion by advancing a model for understanding the relationship between Jews and Christians in terms of parallel traditions growing out of God's redemptive acitivity, which traditions, while yet distinct, would one day be drawn together into the oneness of God.

We perhaps can best understand the differences dividing Jews and Christians by noting two different views regarding the point at which the world is situated in God's movement of reality from promise to fulfillment. Christians confess that the Messiah has come, whereas Jews still await the Messiah's coming. Although a difference not to be ignored, it must be understood as a difference in the interpretation of a commonly held belief in God's promise to draw near to finish what has been begun in the lives of God's people. The messianic order, after all, is a term we use to point to the mystery of God's reign, the state wherein God's will is acknowledged and obeyed by all and for the blessing of all. In other words, it is God's presence and the universal human acceptance of that presence that are being expressed by this metaphor. To

---

10. D. Flusser, (in the Foreword to C. Thoma, *A Christian Theology of Judaism*, p. 17) has written, "It would, indeed, be a great Christian event, were many people to recognize that Jesus' faithfulness to his Jewish people, his burning compassion for Jewish suffering, and his Jewish hope in Christians belong to the *imitatio Christi*."

11. D. Flusser, (in the Foreword to C. Thoma, *A Christian Theology of Judaism*, p. 16) has observed, "By his thinking and his message, Jesus proved himself a true son of his people and a representative of its faith and hopes. It would be absurd and somehow malicious to construe an essential antagonism where none existed. . . . Consequently, faith in Christ cannot be in earnest unless that form of Jewish faith which stamped Jesus becomes a part of Christian faith and morality."

recognize that in Jesus the messianic reign has begun is to confess that in Jesus' life God was intimately available to those gathered around him. Throughout the history of the Jewish people, there have been times when God's presence has been intimately felt as well. As for Christians, they look to the time when God's presence will be yet more fully manifested in the world, a hope traditionally represented by the concept of the Second Coming. In both forms of messianism, therefore, we see believers giving expression both to their experience of God's presence and to their hope of a final fulfillment. Both have experienced what God's nearness is like in the events of their sacred history, but that experience has not been so complete as to exclude the yearning for unbroken communion. For the histories of both include times when God has seemed to be distant, even absent. A longing for the fulfillment of God's reign is thus an essential aspect of the messianism of Christians as well as of Jews, a longing, that is, for the time when the brokenness so evident around us will be ended and God's righteous compassion will embrace and be embraced by all.

In the meantime, as Jews and Christians continue to look forward to the fulfillent of their hopes as a future event, it is important that they see clearly that the unique perspective of each of these ancient traditions plays a major role in the interpretation of both biblical and later traditions, not to mention contemporary events. It is, for example, a part of my legacy as a Christian that in studying the biblical notion of community that I should stress eschatological themes, both in the Hebrew Bible and in the New Testament. It is likely that a corresponding study by a Jewish biblical scholar would emphasize more than has this study the significance of the land, and the eternal validity of traditional practices of Judaism. This contrast is stated clearly by Moshe Goshen-Gottstein: ". . . historic mainstream Judaism can have no place for 'biblical theology' in the sense of an exegetical insight that would change practice."[12] The reason for this axiom, which obviously influences the conclusions derived from the study of Scripture, is found in the particular theological perspective from which Goshen-Gottstein works, according to which the rabbis had fixed the interpretation of Scripture into the rules of observance, rules that were henceforth binding on the faithful. This is not to suggest that Goshen-Gottstein's position is representative of all Jewish scholarship.[13] Rather, it serves as an example

12. M. H. Goshen-Gottstein, "Tanakh Theology: Religion in the Old Testament and the Place of Jewish Biblical Theology," in *Ancient Israelite Religion: Studies in Honor of Frank Moore Cross*, (P. D. Miller, Jr., P. D. Hanson, and S. D. McBride, Jr., eds., Philadelphia: Fortress Press, in press), note 41. In this same article, note 50, Goshen-Gottstein has also observed: ". . . it is through becoming aware of contrasting biases that combined Christian and Jewish biblical scholarship can progress."

13. J. J. Petuchowski, for example, has pointed to the innovativeness that often has characterized the development of Jewish law: ". . . there are also occasions when, instead of its usual meticulous reasoning on the basis of precedent and analogy, Jewish law has, in fact, performed what might be called 'quantum jumps' "—"The Everwidening Holiness Franchise: Quantum Jumps as Jewish Tradition," *Moment* (May, 1985), pp. 60–62.

of the important role of our particular religious traditions in our theological reflection and study.

In the final analysis, however, even the most distinct differences are not a barrier to understanding and appreciation between Jews and Christians. Since such a long history, and such important longings and beliefs unite Jews and Christians, and above all, since it is God who calls and redeems and judges us all, we should freely and graciously recognize in our differences the opportunity to share our unique perspectives with the hope of enriching our partial visions. This free flow of fellowship will in turn release the prayers and loving desires for God's redemption of all creation, which have been blocked by our distrust of each other. Truly, the faith of both communities unites us in praying for the final sabbath when all God's people will be united in holiness, rest, peace, and joy (Babylonian Talmud, *Shab* 118a–b), when "God will be all in all" (1 Cor. 15:28) [NEB].

C. THE ABIDING VALIDITY OF A BIBLICAL NOTION OF COMMUNITY

What enables the Bible to continue to offer guidance to people who today seek to find patterns of living in communities that offer a healing alternative to so much that seems destructive of life in the world around us? We have suggested that the answer is to be found in a unique vision of the entire creation as an intricate organism created by God for the benefit of all creatures, and as a home within which humans experience life's highest purpose in giving praise to the Creator.

This vision maintains its credibility first of all because it takes into account the dark sides of life that modern people experience, such as mass starvation alongside overindulgence, repressive governments creating explosive situations in countries in all parts of the world, and confrontation among the superpowers that holds before the consciousness of all nations the dread prospect of the extinction of life on planet Earth. These dark sides are interpreted within the vision fostered by biblical faith as the effects of a broken covenant. At the heart of the created order, God has placed a human family guided by moral commandments and charged with the maintenance of justice and peace. If these responsibilities are repudiated, a process of disintegration is initiated whose end result is cataclysm. Although the curses pronounced by the prophets on a disobedient covenant community may have had an archaic ring in the ears of more optimistic ages, they describe all too poignantly the experience of an age whose rape of nature and abdication of mutual respect and moral responsibility have led to specters of destruction inconceivable to earlier generations.

The biblical vision remains arresting for many thoughtful people today primarily, though, because of its clear description of the nature of the hope that lies beyond shattered human dreams and ominous threats of catastrophe. It is not a facile hope (indeed it is unlikely that any form of facile hope could commend itself to thoughtful people today, given the magnitude and complexity of the problems we moderns face). Rather, it is a hope maintained in the face of a history marked by much tragedy, stemming from the persistence of humans to disregard what is good and just, and permitted by a God who refuses to deny humans the freedom that is an essential part of their nature. The source of this hope is found in a Reality that has proven to be equally persistent throughout that history, namely God, whose presence in the midst of human tragedy is the dominant theme of the biblical confessions. It is the nature of this hope, therefore, that it directs the attention of the faithful back to the stories of God's presence and God's entering human bondage as Deliverer, beginning with the primal moment of Israel's history as a people, the deliverance from bondage that culminated in a call to become a covenant people.

The biblical vision of community can thus point beyond tragedy and threats of destruction because it both explains the true nature of the human dilemma and describes the only means of escape: Humans are in a precarious situation, and threaten to bring the delicate created order to a dreadful end, because they are in bondage to diverse forms of slavery. And their escape can come only through the gracious act of a God who seeks to deliver, to heal, to restore, and to reconcile the human family, members with members, and all with their God.

The biblical vision seeks application today not by luring moderns, grown weary of the struggle for justice, into a peace of mind achieved by escape from social involvement. It enters our world precisely at the juncture of human disobedience and divine will to save. This means that those who accept the challenge of this vision accept a vocation of struggle. For the battle between righteousness and injustice that characterizes the entire biblical history continues today. But neither does this vision simply direct world-weary humans back to the battle to continue muddling through endless skirmishes. It transforms the nature of the battle by revealing the presence of God in the middle of the fray, standing on the side of the poor, the oppressed, the sick, and the forgotten of the earth, and supporting those working for peace and justice. This is the same God whom the biblical accounts identified in the decisive events of the past, the God present with the human family from the beginning in an untiring effort to break the bondage that held its victims in sickness, hunger, sin, and despair. This is the same God, moreover, who has promised the faithful that the tide has turned, and that God's reign is even now reaching out to heal and restore a broken creation.

Although this vision does not sweep believers into a mythical paradisiacal realm, it does transform the appearance of a world torn between good and evil by identifying the Deliverer God at its center, and by calling the faithful to accept as their vocations participation in God's act of restoring the broken world. In this call to a vocation at the center of life, the community of faith discovers its origins. True to the history of the community of faith of all ages, its birth thus is marked by the passage from its own bondage to freedom, and by the relativization and desacralization of all penultimate loyalties based on confession of God as life's sole Sovereign.

Let us now look at two dimensions of a genuine community of faith, namely, as life-sustaining fellowship, and as agent of healing in the world.

1. LIFE-SUSTAINING FELLOWSHIP

It would be inaccurate to characterize the members of a true community of faith as solitary heroes of righteousness in the world. In fact, the faithful in the Bible are not portrayed as invincible individualists capable of single-handedly vanquishing the foe. Moses, Jeremiah, and Jesus are portrayed as humans with genuine needs for comfort, encouragement, and support. In creating community, God has graciously provided for a deep human need. The biblical notion of being in the world begins with supportive community, where the faithful can gather to celebrate all that is good and worthy in life as a gift of divine grace, and can commemorate the central events of their common spiritual history together, like the event of deliverance from slavery in the Jewish passover, or the events of rebirth and atonement in Christian baptism and the eucharist.

This fellowship in the faith becomes the context for growth into full personhood. So many patterns of being human encourage, whether consciously or unconsciously, the aggrandizement of self over others that leads to alienation of humans from other humans and even from nature. In the community of faith, personal identity is grounded in a Reality that transcends every individual, creating a basis for equality and freedom and the redress of wrongs committed. In Christian community, this equality and freedom is expressed in the access every individual has to God through the mediation of Christ. This mediation constitutes the people as a priesthood of believers, within which no privileged classes are recognized, but only redeemed sinners all standing equally under God's judgment and grace. A deep solidarity is created in such a community as forgiven sinners confess to each other the deliverance they have experienced from their paritcular kinds of bondage, and their passage to the wholeness of life intended by God for all.

The fact that the Bible is filled with the stories of specific individuals indicates that while identity is not self-generated, but received by all from the Sovereign One, the covenant relationship does not obliterate individual personhood, but restores it to its full potential. Dietrich Bonhoeffer thus describes the dialectical relation between oneness in fellowship and individual personhood within the Christian faith: "[Christians] are compelled to decide, and that decision can only be made by themselves. It is no choice of their own that makes them individuals: it is Christ who makes them individuals by calling them."[14]

The need for communal fellowship is sharpened when one calls to mind the nature of the world within which we live. Being witnesses to an order of reality that challenges many existing values often leads to difficult choices, even to sacrifice and suffering. Disciples in an often inhospitable environment need the support of others who share their vision, and who derive sustenance from their relationship to God, as experienced especially in common worship and prayer. This grounding in God and in God's righteous order give the faithful strength to stand united in their testimony that what multitudes call real is ultimately illusory, and that what to many seems illusory is the "pearl of great price."

In many ways, and in all types of life experiences, the individual believer is thus sustained within a community whose trutworthiness is not the product of human virtue, but of the mutual respect and caring that arises out of the common acknowledgment of God's sole sovereignty. And as the lives of the faithful throughout the ages have shown, this support within the community of faith is accompanied by the support of another community, what the Letter to the Hebrews calls "the great cloud of witnesses," or what is commonly referred to as the "communion of saints." The example of ancestors in the faith continues to be a source of great strength to individual believers, as they find that in their trials and decisions they are not alone, but mysteriously accompanied by those who have already passed through similar situations and prevailed. The comfort experienced by the hospital patient in reading the Psalms, the encouragement experienced by the base community leader in reading the exodus story, or the hope experienced by the imprisoned victim of civil injustice in reading the gospel passion narrative are thus communal experiences, as the community of faith defies the limits of both time and space to unite all who acknowledge the sole sovereignty of the one true God, and who work together to free all who suffer under the self-proclaimed sovereignties of penultimate powers.

Within the community of faith living in the consciousness of possessing no intrinsic merit, but of being sustained solely by divine grace, individuals are able to abandon efforts to demonstrate superior virtues and strength in relation to others in favor of genuine sharing. Problems are not hidden, but discussed honestly with an openness encouraging the honest sharing of others. Such honest sharing, which is so essential for the building of understanding and trust, is fostered within the com-

---

14. D. Bonhoeffer, *The Cost of Discipleship*, trans. R. H. Fuller (New York: Macmillan, 1957), p. 78.

munity whose vivid sense of God's presence enables it to renounce the common temptation to derive a sense of smug satisfaction over the lesser fortunes of others or to respond to the misfortunes of others with condescending paternalism. The community of faith that lives true to its calling is thus a place fostering the process of restoration and healing that lies at the heart of the biblical vision of the inbreaking of God's order. Such a community, united with all other true faith communities, can be seen as a part of the reconstitution of a healthy nucleus that in turn becomes a source of healing for the entire created order. Here we recall the biblical image of the "city set on a hill" as a vivid metaphor for the role that the healthy community of faith assumes in the world. For as its individual members experience forgiveness, reconciliation, and healing, they become a part of the process by which God seeks to renew the entire creation. In the very process of being restored, they are drawn into true community as those called to become agents of restoration. This leads us to the second dimension of the community of faith, its role as an agent of healing in the world.

2. AGENT OF HEALING

Although not itself God's order (Luther was right in describing the members of the church with the term *simul justus et peccator!*), the true community of faith, by experiencing in its own life the creative redemptive presence of God, holds before the world an alternative vision, the vision of the whole human family reconciled and living together in peace. Although imperfectly, it gives witness by its word and by its actions to the orbit of *šālôm* toward which God seeks to draw all people. We have found it helpful to visualize that orbit of *šālôm* as constituted where God is worshipped as sole Sovereign, and where the righteousness and compassion experienced in God's own creative and redemptive acts are embodied in the lives of those responding in gratitude. The people of God is thus a community that, in finding its own needs satisfied by the abundant grace of God, is freed to be present in the world for others in need. It is of the very nature of the community of faith, therefore, that its purpose is not exhausted in its providing for the needs of its members, but extends outward to a self-transcending calling to be present wherever there is loneliness, sickness, hunger, or injustice. The indivisibility of these two aspects of a faith community's life is pictured vividly by the image used by Paul of the body of Christ. Christ's body is first broken on the cross as a part of God's reaching out to the lost. Believers receive the grace of Christ's body in the eucharist, and having been thereby healed and strengthened, are gathered together as Christ's "body" in the world; that is, as the mediating presence through which God's grace is extended to all people. This image excludes every self-indulgent definition of the community of faith, and boldly sets forth the mode of such a community's life as incarnational, present in the world for the sake of the people of the world. Before turning to examples of this incarnational mode, recall the triadic notion of community that equips an otherwise typically human organization to be a mediation of divine grace, an agent of healing.

The faith community that is guided by an integrative vision ultimately finds its identity in relation to the creative, redemptive Center of all life, the God it has come to know through its scriptural-confessional heritage. It is this Center that integrates what is otherwise fragmented, unites what is otherwise divided, and gives harmony to what otherwise is discordant. In a world smarting under the heavy blows of dictators and sect leaders who enslave their followers under the cloak of absolute authority, the nature of the life deriving from acknowledgment of the sole Sovereignty of God must be clarified.

For many understandable reasons, countless people today are deeply suspicious of any kind of authority, and the notion of an ultimate divine authority strikes some as repulsive. If God were another power seeking to deprive humans of their freedom, this fear would be justified. But it is the bold claim of Scripture that freedom is found only by those who submit to the one Reality able to grant true freedom by actually delivering humans from the bonds that enslave. From this perspective, those who find God threatening appear to be those so bound by their own penultimate loyalties, so identified with and enamored of their own idols, as to regard loss of such loyalties and idols as a loss of freedom. Typically, such loyalties and idols, far from granting freedom, function to rationalize special privileges and private sins. And economic power and wealth, though common, are not the only forms such idolatry assumes. One's political or social movement, one's ideology, religion, or philosophy, may be deemed so far superior to that of other people as to secure one's own privileged status in the order of things. The fact remains that whatever idol one clings to, the twofold result is the victimization of others who suffer from the disharmony and injustice that accompanies idolatry and the enslavement of self.

It is because of the virulence and virility of such idols in our world that the severe message of Scripture must be reiterated in the name of authentic freedom and true community: freedom from the countless penultimate loyalties that enslave and oppress can be found and preserved solely through submission to the one Reality in relation to whom devotion entails not enslavement but deliverance. Only when a community bases its life together on worship of this one Reality is there hope that some of its members will not diminish the wholeness of other members through appeals to special privilege. Or more realistically, since every community experiences such abuse, we rather should state that only within the community where the presence of the one Sovereign is still experienced is there a recourse for those wronged by the idolatry and self-centeredness of others.

In ancient Israel, the centrality of the first commandment was not merely the result of conflict with other cults. It gave expression to the deep awareness that the heart not united with the one Reality that delivers inevitably became ensnared in the traps of deadly alternatives.

That central confession abides as the cornerstone of true community. When life is reduced to its most basic level, the life and death question revolves around true and false worship. To that basic biblical lesson, there is nothing to add:

See, I have set before you this day life and good, death and evil. If you obey the commandments of the Lord your God which I command you this day, by loving the Lord your God, by walking in his ways, and by keeping his commandments and his statutes and his ordinances, then you shall live and multiply, and the Lord your God will bless you in the land which you are entering to take possession of it. But if your heart turns away, and you will not hear, but are drawn away to worship other gods and serve them, I declare to you this day, that you shall perish. (Deut. 30:15–18a)

With regard to this basic principle of community, our tradition has been a history of reformulation and elaboration, including, for example, Augustine's famous depiction of God as the heart's only place of true rest,[15] and Kierkegaard's description of true devotion as "the purity of heart . . . to will one thing."[16]

Modern psychologists and theologians both have pointed out that true community is impossible without a grounding in a common source of empowerment and healing. Paul Tillich, among recent theologians, was the most vivid in describing the malaise experienced by people whose lives are controlled by "ultimate concerns" other than the "Ground of Being."[17] Fragmentation is a severe malady afflicting both individuals and societies today, as life is trivialized and debased in the absence of the one Reality capable of uniting without repressing and enslaving. What basis of harmony can be found in a society that becomes a marketplace for idols such as insatiable materialism, the endless search for self-indulgent thrills, sadistic bigotry as a means of puffing up empty egos, triumphalistic and chauvinistic nationalism, exploitative sexism, and shameless selfishness? A faith community can be a place of hope not by being immune to the attraction of such idols, but by being a place exposed to the Reality capable of freeing humans from such forces of death and despair, and being a place where sisters and brothers can confess their apostasy, and be as unashamed of repentance as they are assured of forgiveness and healing.

The community of faith is thus in the first instance a place of *worship*.

---

15. *Confessions* I.1.

16. S. Kierkegaard, *Purity of Heart Is to Will One Thing* (New York: Harper & Brothers, 1938).

17. P. Tillich, *Systematic Theology*, vol. 1 (Chicago: University of Chicago Press, 1951), pp. 11–15, 155–157.

In worship, unity and healing recurs in remembering that community was born of a divine act of deliverance and in experiencing that community is renewed by that same gracious act. In ancient Israel, awareness of the central grounding of community in divine grace was preserved by means of a sacred calendar that placed memory of the prevenient gracious acts of God at the very heart of life. Once a year deliverance from slavery was remembered at Passover and the Feast of the Unleavened Bread; once a year thanks was given for the land and its harvest at the Feast of Weeks; once a year God's protection in the wilderness was commemorated in the Feast of Booths; and once a year the solemn fast of the Day of Atonement was observed. The rhythm of the order God had established for the people of the covenant was also celebrated weekly, commemorating God's creation of the world and Israel's release from bondage in Egypt, and reminding the people that they were a holy possession of their God. This rhythm in turn radiated outward in time to be marked by the observance in the seventh year of God's gift of the land, and in the fiftieth year of God's gift of freedom. This calendar lent a harmony to life both by reminding Israel of the history of God's covenant relationship and by placing the community within the broader context of God's care for the entire created order.

Although the sacral calendar has fallen into neglect in many religious communities today, there is no question that much is lost when a people no longer symbolizes its communal life and the holy events of its past as parts of the much more encompassing order over which God reigns.

To a world instinctively suspicious of invitations to submit to an absolute authority as a condition for freedom or prosperity, biblical faith therefore insists that an authentically fulfilled life can be discovered only within the fellowship of those submitting to the one Authority who does not divest one of freedom, but grants one genuine freedom, the kind of freedom that can occur only where all people are equally valued and cared for. For this reason, the doctrine of God is more than a cherished relic of the past. It is the indispensable key to a community of caring, equality, and justice. "There is no life that is not in community, and no community not lived in praise of God."[18] James Luther Adams recently has drawn attention to a powerful symbol for this transcendant reference point of community:

I am thinking about Albrecht Durer's 1507 picture of The Praying Hands. The praying hands point to the source of being and meaning beyond all creatures. As Boswell's Johnson would say, these hands express more than wonder; they express awe before the divine majesty. Or as Augustine would remind us, they warn us against giving to any creature the love that belongs alone to the

---

18. T. S. Eliot, "Choruses from 'The Rock,'" in *The Complete Poems and Plays, 1909–1950* (New York: Harcourt, Brace, 1952), p. 101.

Creator, whether that creature be a liturgical formula, an institution or a document. Each of these creatures may point to the ultimate ground, but none exhaust it or define its bounds. It cannot be spatialized. Vocation is then from a formative and transformative power that is sovereign and is the enemy of idolatry whether it be religious, ecclesiastical, cultural or secular.[19]

Only when its unity is rooted in its sense of devotion to the one true Sovereign can a community of faith transcend the webs of pettiness, parochialism, and self-interest that so rapidly belittle and destroy human fellowship. For only when a person's primary relationship, in the ultimate sense of the term, is to God can the inordinate and unhealthy neediness and insecurity that blights our relationships with others be replaced by a genuine sharing predicated on a sense of wholeness dependent on no human, be it self or another, but on God's grace. A community of faith that takes seriously the central theme of its heritage will therefore hold up before the world, by means of paradigms and symbols both old and new, the sole sovereignty of God as the only proven safeguard against the myriad penultimate loyalties that promise abundance and deliver death. To choose life is thus to submit to the only one who as Creator of all life is graciously willing and able to sustain the life and freedom of all. To choose life is to let go of all that holds the heart back from embracing that which alone possesses intrinsic worth, to relinquish all forms of bondage, and to find fulfillment in belonging to the order of life over which God reigns.

United in worship and reconciled with its God, the community of faith is restored to the health and wholeness that enables it to be a nucleus of health for the broader human community around it. Its own blessing and health is not a gift intended for it alone, but willed by God for all. And it is indeed in worship that the truth of God's absolute Sovereignty brings into focus a vision of God's reign of peace and justice over all creation. This vision is the faith community's invitation to give expression to its devotion through a life of service in the world. And its experience of having its needs fulfilled by God in worship empowers it to speak out courageously against all that tears the fabric of the human family, and to ally itself with all peacemakers and agents of caring in the world.

The advocacy of peace and justice is not a simple challenge. Issues are complex, and the consequences of decisions often very serious. How is a community of faith to be guided in its vocation of opposing the idols of nationalism, greed, elitism, militarism, and materialism and of speaking out on behalf of the oppressed, the hungry, the sick, and the poor. We recognize in the paradigms of the Bible two qualities that developed out of the experience of God's presence in the world: the standard of righteousness and the way of compassion. United in wor-

19. J. L. Adams, "The Vocation of Ministry," Lowell Lecture, Harvard Divinity School, June 5, 1985.

ship, these two qualities defined the orbit of *šālôm* within which God's healing power was both experienced and made available in the world. In describing the community of faith as agent of healing, it is necessary now to recall these two qualities as they developed within the historic communities of biblical times.

It is a central and persistent theme of Scripture that God's people is to be *a righteous people*. The source of its righteousness is also clearly stated: "You shall be holy; for I the Lord your God am holy" (Lev. 19:3). "You therefore must be perfect, as your heavenly Father is perfect" (Matt. 5:48). The community of faith has as its standard none other than the example of God's impartial justice. And faithfulness to that standard is not a matter of ethical decision alone, but is a fundamental aspect of faithfulness to God. That is to say, working for social justice, opposing discrimination in its many forms, giving sacrificially to battle world hunger, and seeking to change social and political structures that favor the powerful at the expense of the weak are expressions of the individual's and the community's devotion to God. A religious system that merely justifies a life of self-indulgence is accordingly a blatant form of idolatry.

The concreteness with which the biblical understanding of righteousness comes to expression in Scripture is noteworthy. Although based on the community's perception of God's activity, it unfolds in everyday matters, as we have seen in the Book of the Covenant, in the Gospels and in the letters of the early Christian church. For it is in such matters that God's order becomes visible. The slave, the impoverished widow, the drought-stricken land, and the devastated city are not only human tragedies; they testify to the violation of God's order of *šālôm*, and call on all who have experienced God's reconciliation to be messengers of that reconciliation and ministers of healing and restoration. Underlying the faith community's every activity on behalf of peace and justice is God's activity to heal the broken creation. To be God's people is therefore by definition to be a people dedicated to righteousness in all areas and spheres of life. At the heart of its calling is concern for the just treatment of all people, the equitable distribution of the earth's resources and fruits among all the families of the earth, and the translation of its belief in God's sovereignty over all people into social and political policies predicated on the principle of equality.

That the problems facing the world today are threatening and complex is undeniable. The response called for by the faithful community must accordingly be worked out in a careful and well-informed way. What blocks the cause of peace and justice in the world, however, is not primarily lack of knowledge, but lack of commitment. The divine mandate in relation to world hunger, domestic poverty, racial tension, inequal opportunity in education and the job market is usually very clear.

Even an issue as frightening as the threat of nuclear war calls for very specific actions on the part of communities of faith when treated not in the abstract, but with attention to specific problem areas. For the nuclear threat has grown to such magnitude primarily due to age-old problems such as inequal distribution of the earth's produce, distrust based on misunderstanding, nationalistic self-aggrandizement, and ideologies of special privileges.

We have noted time and again that the advocacy of justice on the part of the communities of faith in the Bible was not guided by a rigid prescription. No immutable rule guided the faithful in early Israel in their treatment of the alien or the widow. Isaiah did not appeal to a manual of Yahwistic diplomacy in advising Ahab during the Syro-Ephraimite crisis. And the early church in Jerusalem had no handbook of biblical sociology to follow in dealing with the problem of poverty. What they all had, however, was a living sense of God's involvement in all life in harmony with a plan of peace, equality, and justice. A contemporary community of faith can remain true to its heritage, accordingly, not necessarily by adopting early Israel's system of the *naḥălâ* or the early Jerusalem church's communist pattern of community, but by grasping the vision of righteousness that motivated such developments and then working out commensurate ones within the conditions of today's world. If that vision is grasped, there is no denying the fact that the response will be specific and emphatic; and it will often represent a radical departure from existing structures. But that can occur only if the ingredients of what constituted a faithful response in the biblical period recur today, namely, thorough knowledge of the confessional heritage; passionate engagement with the issues of this world, motivated by seeing them as the arena of God's creative, redemptive activity; acknowledgment of God's sovereignty celebrated in worship; and commitment to participating in God's creative, redemptive plan for the world. The dynamism that characterizes this relation to the events of the world has been demonstrated throughout this study. The study has also given sufficient examples of the unfaithful response to serve as warning against laxness in the matter of the community's responsibility for righteousness. What strikes one with particular clarity is the inextricable relation between a deep commitment to God and a deep commitment to social justice. Being related to the living God renders most conventional ways of dealing with injustice unsatisfactory, for they are largely determined by myopic self-interest. Being an agent of healing requires of the community of faith a clear discernment of God's presence in the world, and an unswerving commitment to the transformation of personal habits, family patterns, and social and political structures until they conform to the standard of righteousness manifested by God's creative, redemptive activity on behalf of all creatures.

The thoroughly social nature of biblical faith is stressed throughout the history we have studied. Moreover, this social nature characterized not only the biblical community's response to its own time, but its vision of the future as well. God's future reign was not construed in terms of a blissful union of the elect with God that removed them from the world of humanity, but as a reign of justice and peace that repaired all wounds and restored righteousness as the standard among humans.[20] This vision of a redeemed world is found in all types of biblical writings, from law codes (Lev. 25) to promises of eschatological salvation (Isa. 61:1–3 and Luke 4:18–28). And that vision took on a new importance as the result of Jesus' announcement that God's reign was imminent, indeed "among you." An urgent sense of the nearness, and thus of the reality of God's reign still is an important reminder to the faithful that the unjust structures of this world are not to be tolerated as inevitable. Rather, to the extent that the community of faith allows itself to be drawn into the reality of God's alternative order of righteousness, it becomes an example of the future that God intends for all creation. Believers should therefore pray daily that the Jubilee vision of a redeemed and healed creation might captivate the imagination of every community of faith leading to a deeper commitment to global harmony, justice, and peace throughout the world!

In considering the biblical notion of righteousness, we thus must conclude that an asocial private piety is simply unbiblical. Where God's people is present in the world, it is present on behalf of the God of righteousness, and thus on behalf of those who suffer from discrimination, poverty, and injustice. It is a people that no longer distingushes between its personal needs and the needs of others. Ministering to the least esteemed or most despised human is thus a concrete act of attending to its own most urgent personal concern.

This description of righteousness already implies the third quality of the triad, since righteousness and compassion are indivisible. Indeed, our separation of these two qualities is merely a heuristic exercise, intended to give a fuller picture of the kind of response that is called forth in a people dedicated to the righteous, compassionate God. While righteousness describes the holy standard by which the community of faith is to guide and test its conduct, *compassion* describes the way of life that seeks to imitate the mercy of the God who delivers and sustains those in need not because of any worthiness of their own, but rather because it is simply of the divine nature to love and care for all creatures. Compassion therefore describes the empathy that the faithful feel for those who are excluded from the normal protections offered

---

20. J. Moltmann has written, "For Christianity's hope is not directed towards 'another' world, but towards the world as it is changed in the Kingdom of God." *The Church in the Power of the Spirit: A Contribution to Messianic Ecclesiology*, trans. M. Kohl (New York: Harper & Row, 1977), p. 164.

by a society to the ingroup. It describes their openness to fellowship with all people, regardless of race or social class. It draws on the example of the God who, in the events of biblical history, was recognized as reaching out especially to the most vulnerable and weak to free them from their bondage and to restore them and empower them to live a full and productive life. Compassion is rare in a society filled with fear and distrust, and within which many people feel that another's well-being decreases their own chances of success. The community patterning its life after the example of the God whom it acknowledges as the source of its every need should not be plagued by such anxiety. It is able to give because it has already received abundantly from God. The community of faith imitates the example of the benevolent, compassionate God when it demonstrates that there is enough for all on this earth if people live simply and generously. Clearly, this entails for those living in unhealthful luxury (and that means most of us!) a radical reorientation of lifestyle. But the deep satisfaction that comes when one's life is brought into harmony with the way of life that allows everyone on this planet to lead a decent life abundantly repays all sacrifice. This is especially so when it becomes clear that the simple, generous life alone can reunite the members of the human family who are presently so sharply divided between the "have's" and the "have not's." For the very overabundance that is the bondage of the rich is what is needed to remove the bonds of hunger that debilitate the poor of the earth. As a people believing in the rights of all peoples, the community of faith today must speak out against every structure, institution, and habit that abets the injustice of unequal distribution of the earth's goods, and work courageously for fundamental changes both in national priorities and in personal lifestyles. Another clear message of our biblical heritage is that if the covenant people do not do their part to restore the righteous and compassionate order placed before the human race by a loving God, the result will be judgment. "And if [they cry] out to me, I will hear, for I am compassionate" (Exod. 22:27b). From this perspective the tragedies of our own historical period are seen to result not from pure chance or divine caprice, but, within a world under the righteous judgment of God, as the inevitable consequence of human repudiation of the order of šālôm that alone can assure peace and harmony in the world. If catastrophe falls, it will be for the same tragic reason envisioned by the seer of Isaiah 24:

> The earth mourns and withers,
>   the world languishes and withers;
>   the heavens languish together with the earth.
> The earth lies polluted
>   under its inhabitants;
> for they have transgressed the laws,
>   violated the statutes,

> broken the everlasting covenant.
> Therefore a curse devours the earth,
> and its inhabitants suffer for their guilt;
> therefore the inhabitants of the earth are scorched,
> and few men are left. (Isa. 24:4–6)

Within a world threatened as never before with the specters of mass starvation and apocalyptic devastation, the major theme a community of faith receives from Scripture is nevertheless one of hope. God has called a people to be God's possession as a part of a process of restoration and healing. A people defined by worship, righteousness, and compassion, in living true to its divinely ordained attribute, experiences in its common life the reconstitution of *šālôm*, that is, the order of life intended by God for the human family. Although any given community of *šālôm* gathered in response to God's call embodies that order but imperfectly, it, along with all such responding communities, becomes, so to speak, a laboratory of the Kingdom, sort of an experiment being carried out by God on behalf of the whole creation. I recall Krister Stendahl once referring to the one responding to God's call as a "guinea pig of the Kingdom." The image is a poignant one, for where these "guinea pigs" gather together in worship, and are guided by their symbols and paradigms along a path defined by righteousness and compassion, novel things happen. Individual lives are changed as diverse forms of bondage, from substance abuse to selfish materialism, are broken by a God who continues to deliver slaves and to gather them into community both for their own blessing and for the well-being of others. And whole communities are changed too, as God's Spirit addresses them, whether through their own leaders or outside figures and events, leading to a clarified vision and a renewed zeal for God's blessed order.

The hope that upholds a true community of faith today is not based on an optimistic view toward human possibilities. It is not blind to the ominous signs around it, such as decaying cities, advancing drought, epidemic alcohol and drug abuse among youth, and an insane arms race. Its hope derives from a vision handed down by its confessional heritage, which describes a new world that has begun to infiltrate the old, like healing into a sick body. The qualities of that new world are the very qualities the community of faith has been called on to embody in its life, qualities inferred from the history of God's activities on behalf of the human family. This implies that in a sense, though again imperfectly, the community of faith is a front line for that new world. It is to be a faithful servant, not glorying in itself, but in the One it serves. It is not to display an otherworldly scorn for the world, or a sanctity that eschews contact, but is to incarnate the qualities of God's order right in the midst of everyday life. This radical incarnational style of living was emphasized by the Apostle Paul through the application of a very daring metaphor: the church is the body of Christ on earth!

Because it embodies the message of God's redemptive activity and models itself after God's righteousness and compassion, the otherwise outrageous claim can be made that, within this rather average group of humans who are only fledglings in the life of compassion and justice, a new order is dawning. This claim is open, of course, to awful abuse if it is separated from its underlying principle: a human community that otherwise participates in the typical sins and imperfections of humanity can participate in the dawning of God's reign only if it locates the center of its being not in its own self-interest, but in the self-transcending purposes of God. This transcendant center is also its only hope for breaking the narrow parochialism so typical of religious bodies. Ultimately, neither its doctrines nor its practices can claim to define, in any exhaustive manner, the reign of God to which it is devoted, and thus it must be open to all agents of the Kingdom, whether they happen to be insiders or outsiders.

Talk of visions of the future, to be sure, evokes a mood of caution in many people, for visions may be nothing but illusions. A community that seeks to imitate the style of the God encountered in Word and world, however, will cling only to the vision of a restored creation that seeks embodiment in the everyday lives of the faithful. Ultimately, therefore, the followers of this vision will be known for the quality of their lives, for their love, honesty, sense of justice, and selfless caring.

In the final analysis, therefore, a book devoted to the study of such a community cannot conclude with a prescription, but must be content to refer back to the description that has unfolded in the preceding chapters, and to extend to people of goodwill an invitation to recognize in the writings of Scripture a testimony to God's presence among humans and to God's unceasing efforts to gather together a community of faith and to draw it into the process of creation's healing. We are speaking here of a body that is not of human making, and thus not under human control. The initiative that has drawn together and sustained a people of faith through the generations is God's. The "people called" is the gathering of those who have experienced deliverance from bondage, healing from brokenness, birth from spiritual death, reconciliation with God and fellow humans, and have seen in these passages signs of God's inbreaking reign. Owing all to God, beholden to no human authority, they are free to respond to God's gracious initiative by being in the world of the sake of others. In the sorrows and weaknesses of others, they see evidence of the Kingdom seeking to enter the world, and they are present as God's hands to assist in the birth. And where new birth occurs, they rejoice over signs of God's order of šālôm. They rejoice over the small woman walking between the dying outcasts of Calcutta binding wounds and cooling feverish brows. They rejoice over the small company of Arabs and Jews who travel the land speaking of reconciliation and peace. They rejoice over the poor Peruvian villager who bakes her loaves and distributes half of them to her even poorer neighbors. They rejoice over the corporation executive who switches off her phone to pray and reflect before making a business decision involving complicated moral issues. They rejoice over the village priest in an embattled section of Central America who, though threatened and harassed, nevertheless serves his peasant parishioners the bread of life and courageously stands up for their dignity and human rights. Combined with the witness of Scripture and the history of the saints and martyrs, such modern miracles are received by faith communities as signs of the order that is entering the world, opposed, to be sure, by determined coalitions, yet powerful in a mysterious manner known not to the ungodly but to the peacemakers and the pure in heart.

The community of faith is thus a gathering of those responding to God's saving grace by devoting themselves to God's plan for the restoration of all creation. Even as the members of the faith community give thanks to God for the new life they have received, so too they look to God's Spirit for guidance in living true to their commitment to God's order of šālôm. They are thus characterized by an openness to the Spirit's leading, and live in expectation of continued transformation and growth in their beliefs, their communal structures and their relations to others. From the small and personal to the large and international, their thinking is characterized by the new perspective that permits them to look on the world not with the eyes of fallen humanity, but with the eyes of those restored to wholeness by a loving God.[21]

In personal relationships, those who are devoted to God's reign are mediators of a godly love, a caring that allows them to be truly present with the other, bearing gifts that are not their own, but God's, abundant gifts freely received and freely passed on to others, gifts of bread and gifts of the glad tidings of forgiveness and rebirth. Their homes become a microcosm of the harmony that thrives where God is worshipped, and where God's righteousness and compassion become the heart's foremost desire. Their friendships are genuine, honest, and committed to mutual growth and fulfillment.

In their life in community, they are able to overcome partisan conflicts through a shared consciousness of a devotion to one Sovereign and a commitment to a cause that transcends the self-interests of any

---

21. It is important to remember that on all levels of its involvement with life the community of faith equips its members not with exact tactics and solutions, but with a perspective derived from the vision of God's order, of a reign of universal peace, equality and justice. This is in keeping with the function of Torah in both the Yahwistic and the early Christian communities. As an example, one can take the community ideal represented by the Gospel of Matthew, which T.W. Ogletree describes thus: "Rather than functioning chiefly to describe the moral requisites of social order, [the law's] primary impulse is to portray the wholeness of existence to which disciples are summoned." *The Use of the Bible in Christian Ethics* (Philadelphia: Fortress Press, 1983), p. 128.

individual. Among them dissident voices are not silenced, but heard in the effort to discern God's will more clearly. Authority is not held up as a human possession, but acknowledged as God's prerogative intended to empower all humans with direction and purpose. In prayer and reflection, the guidance of the Spirit is sought, and the welfare of God's whole family is held up as the faith community's sacred vocation in the world.

In the political arena, the community of faith represents a prophetic perspective that opposes every form of idolatry and rationalization of greed and special privilege, and proclaims the alternative order of universal justice, equality, and peace. This stance involves risktaking, and sometimes danger. For when the principles of righteousness and compassion are applied to international policy, economics, and human relations, complex and controversial issues emerge. Some would argue that communities of faith have no business addressing problems undreamed of in biblical times, and should confine themselves to baptizing children, marrying young adults, burying the dead, and preaching repentance and salvation. Problems involving genetic engineering, nuclear policy, and global hunger are claimed to be the sole concerns of experts in government and business. But if the community of faith is the people called to draw all areas of life into the orbit of God's order of šālôm, such an attitude is unacceptable. It must be active in encouraging experts in such complicated areas to form policy not solely on the basis of expedience, national self-interest and defense, but also with an eye to the effect of decisions in these areas on life in the broadest sense. In all such discussions, the faith community exercises its responsibility by representing its unique perspective from which all problems are seen in relation to the one Reality that alone can bring lasting peace and prosperity. Even in a most pragmatic sense, this perspective is valuable as a means of distinguishing between ultimate and penultimate loyalties, ends and means, limited and universal goods.

The impact of a community of faith on political and social issues is not limited to its collective activities, however, but depends as well on the witness of its individual members in their special areas and fields. In challenging its members to give expression to their faith in their jobs, a faith community acknowledges that power should not be ignored, but transformed into a force of justice and peace in the world. Too much power resides in Congress, in Exxon, IBM, or Kennecott for a faith community to be disinterested in their impact on human life around the world. If the dangerous drift of our world toward catastrophe is to be arrested, people of vision and courage must represent the perspective of righteous compassion in Congress, on the boards of international companies, in our universities and in every other sphere of our common life. World starvation, disintegration of family life, and war are far too formidable an obstacle to the order of šālôm to allow a community of faith to fail in its task of challenging those with influence and power to put indispensable resources behind missions of reconciliation, peace, justice, and healing. It is not merely a romantic dream, but a sobering fact that if all those who belonged to faith communities were guided by the perspective of God's alternative order of universal justice and peace, we would witness a world in which far fewer martyrs were imprisoned for conscience, far fewer babies starving before feeling the flush of life, far fewer aged freezing to death in unheated homes, far fewer middle aged destroying themselves with overwork and excess stress, calories, and alcohol.

Finally, in the realm of ecological concerns, a community drawing on the Bible for its sense of vocation also is charged with an urgent mandate. For the rich theology of creation that is part of its scriptural legacy urges that God's righteousness and loving concern be extended to embrace the entire cosmos in prayers for healing and actions directed toward ending the heartless exploitation of nature that scornfully disregards the well-being of humans both living and yet to be born and the very integrity of a beautiful, fragile, and endangered planet.

On all these levels, then, the community of faith is called on to be an agent of healing in the world. Although religious bodies sometimes resemble pathetic relics of the past searching current trends for a cause, the people of God is to be the bearer of a redemptive vision that can have a powerfully transforming effect on all levels and areas of life. For when it addresses issues, as address it must, it speaks on behalf of its understanding of what God intends for all creation, an understanding that has developed over a very long history of experiences and testing. Granted, its decisions and acts are hammered out amid lively discussion among members who are no less fallible than those around them, members who often disagree among themselves and must struggle to subsume personal biases and interests under their passion for God's reign of justice. But while one must never confuse a faith community that serves God's reign with that reign itself, the community that draws on its heritage of symbols and paradigms and applies them humbly and diligently to the problems of our world is a beacon of hope. And especially when such a community has a sufficiently mature vision of God's reign to allow it to cooperate with all other agents of reconciliation and healing in the world, its impact for justice and peace should not be underestimated. For how rare are organizations that define themselves as present in the world for the world, and stand subservient to no authority but the authority of the Sovereign of all? Needless to say, communities of faith all too frequently become indistinguishable from clubs and organizations whose sole purpose is self-service, and whose vision is no larger than the collective interests of the ingroup. But wherever a group gathers in response to God's creative and redemptive presence and commits itself to God's purpose, there arises a true community of faith, a people called by God, which is capable of transcending self-interests in serving a world sorely in need of loving servants and courageous peacemakers.

Above all, therefore, "the people called" is a people belonging to God. This sense of being God's possession constitutes its identity, its vocation, and its vision. Its charter is God's covenantal promise, "I shall be your God, and you shall be my people." Although God's people has undergone much change over the centuries that we have studied, the type of community we describe is still indelibly marked by the experience of God's first people, called forth from Egyptian slavery to be a nation of priests consecrated to God's purpose.

Reality seen from the perspective of belonging to God is not simple, static, or timeless. In fact, it is as dynamic and forward-moving as God is actively present in the events of the world and the cosmos. Life accordingly presents itself to the faithful as a summons to participate in God's purpose of redeeming all who remain in bondage, and of restoring a creation long ravaged by sin to a state in which righteous and peace prevail. Although this notion of vocation can be perverted into a utopian dream inviting escape rather than engaged, humane living, it serves the faithful community living in the example of its Sovereign as a clear guide to a life of self-transcending purpose that issues forth in patient, generous advocacy of the case of the poor and the oppressed and in loving care for God's creation. Far from diverting attention and energy away from life toward dreams of otherworldly escape, the sense of belonging to God releases a free flow of vitality for life by assuring the faithful that their lives are secure in the providence of a gracious God who has redeemed them and abides with them, thus enabling them to give freely without anxiety over success, merit or destiny. Out of this alternative community, this new creation called forth by God, there arises a dedication to justice and peace, free from conditions or restraints. For the people called is a people viewing life from a new perspective, the perspective of God's order of šālôm. As such it is a blessed community not only as recipient of divine blessing, but as mediator of God's šālôm to the world. For having experienced God's šālôm within its own life, which releases it from every form of bondage and fear, the community of faith becomes a nucleus of blessing from which reconciliation and healing radiates outward into the rest of the world.

Many are the images that have arisen out of the yearning of the faithful community for the time when God's blessed order would be fulfilled and when God's sovereignty would be recognized by all. As the people called moves through life as a pilgrim people, glimpsing a vision of that fulfillment, but seeing it opposed by powerful forces and embodied only imperfectly in its own life, it is upheld by such images, images of the creation of new heavens and a new earth, of the marriage of justice and peace, of the swallowing up of death and sorrow forever, of the great wedding banquet. We therefore end our study of "the people called" with a vision that gathers several of those images into one beautiful picture, for it continues to be offered to weary pilgrims as refreshment for their souls and sustenance for their spirits as they continue to grow in the community of faith that is one of God's most precious gifts to humanity:

Then I saw a new heaven and a new earth; for the first heaven and the first earth had passed away, and the sea was no more. And I saw the holy city, new Jerusalem, coming down out of heaven from God, prepared as a bride adorned for her husband; and I heard a loud voice from the throne saying, "Behold the dwelling of God is with [humans]. [God] will dwell with them, and they shall be [God's] people, and God will be with them; [God] will wipe away every tear from their eyes, and death shall be no more, neither shall there be mourning nor crying nor pain any more, for the former things have passed away. (Rev. 21:1–4)

APPENDIX

Underlying Presuppositions and Method

A. WORLD CRISIS AND THE RESPONSIBILITY OF COMMUNITIES OF FAITH

Anyone with a moderate knowledge of world history can cite many examples of contributions made by religious communities to the cause of peace and justice. But such a person can go on to cite examples of the opposite phenomenon as well, for much suffering and oppression has been prepetrated with appeal to sacred scripture and religious authority. Any community of faith that chooses to address social and political problems today must accept the responsibility to think carefully through the presuppositions it draws on in applying its sacred traditions to contemporary realities, and to explain them in an articulate manner to other groups and individuals.

One claim presented in this book is that contemporary religious communities tracing descent from the Bible are heirs to a vision both open enough to chart a path into an expanding universe and reliable enough to oppose irresponsible policies and blind passions, which in recent decades have been moving civilization toward the abyss. The reader, therefore, deserves an explanation of the presuppositional and methodological basis on which this claim is made. If a satisfactory explanation is given, there seems to be a good chance that this study will be taken seriously, for few thoughtful people would deny that in a world threatened with the specters of mass starvation, economic collapse, and nuclear holocaust, the need for a trustworthy guide into the future is urgently needed.

But we are immediately beset with a serious problem. In a world more consciously aware than ever before of pluralism and of the wide spectrum of beliefs and values found even within a particular society, one could easily come to doubt whether any faith community could articulate clearly its religious vision by answering questions relating to its identity and purpose, its ultimate allegiance and its understanding of authority. For example, in the face of widely divergent Christian movements, all claiming to represent the true church, but each with its own interpretation of the gospel and the gospel's relation to the current world, what defines a group as faithful to the Christian faith? Some (myself included) would argue that a parochial version of Christianity that promises divine grace apart from confession and repentance, and that promulgates the notion of a particular nation as enjoying a privileged place in God's favor, is a betrayal of the biblical tradition that is at the heart of the Christian heritage, a tradition that develops a universal mission of divine justice and peace. Since this argument obviously appeals to a specific understanding of that heritage, and to a particular perspective and set of presuppositions, to what authority can it appeal? It is to this question of authority, and to the related questions of presuppositions and theological understanding that I offer the following methodological reflections.

B. A SCRIPTURAL BASIS THAT INCLUDES THE HEBREW BIBLE

Although the problem addressed presses equally on all Scripture based religious traditions, and although the particularly close relationship between Judaism and Christianity is a central focus throughout this book, we must here focus specifically on that problem as it relates to Christianity. The reason for this focus is that it is complicated by the historical fact that the Christian church inherited the sacred writings of a religious community that had already passed through a long antecedent history, adding to them other writings that were specifically Christian in origin. Given this curious situation, what weight is accorded the "Old" Testament in relation to the "New"?

Light can be shed on this question by reference to recent treatments of the church by two pre-eminent Tübingen theologians, the Catholic Hans Küng and the Protestant Jürgen Moltmann.[1] In both treatments, the authority of Scripture is emphasized, though as is fitting, the later confessions of the chruch and insights derived from contemporary experience are drawn on freely as well.

While agreeing wholeheartedly with Küng and Moltmann that Scripture is the essential starting point for an adequate contemporary understanding of the church's nature and mission, and learning much from their deep insight into biblical faith, I feel that the full potential of Scripture's contribution to that understanding has not been exhausted in their studies. The reason lies in the tendency to focus on the New Testament to the neglect of Hebrew Scripture. Naturally, few Christians would dispute that without God's decisive new act in Christ, and in the outpouring of the Spirit in the primitive church, the church re-

---

1. Hans Küng, *The Church*, trans. Ray and Rosaleen Ockenden (New York: Sheed and Ward, 1967); Jürgen Moltmann, *The Church in the Power of the Spirit: A Contribution to Messianic Ecclesiology*, trans. M. Kohl (New York: Harper & Row, 1977).

mains a riddle. Moreover, the specific emphasis of Moltmann on the crucified One and of Küng on the resurrection are both germane and helpful, and serve to complement one another in delineating the central event in the church's historical development. Nevertheless, the emergence of the church from the experiences of the crucifixion and resurrection of Christ represents the culmination of a dynamic process limited not to the period from Jesus' birth to Paul's letters and the testimony of the Gospel writers. Its history reaches from patriarchal promises and the deliverance of Hebrew slaves out of Egypt to the founding of a covenant community, then on through struggles between kings and prophets and priests and apocalyptic seers until God's new initiative occurred in what the Letter to the Ephesians called "the fulness of time" (1:10).

The slight qualification I raise in relation to the studies of Küng and Moltmann does not constitute a serious criticism of these two scholars. Their assessment of the theological significance of the faith of Israel up to the present time is very positive. Blame rests primarily on the field of biblical scholarship that has failed to produce the type of background studies on which we have every reason to believe theologians like Küng and Moltmann would have gladly drawn had such studies existed. This observation provides the challenge to which the present work responds.

This challenge has both positive and negative sides. On the negative side, we face a history of inexcusable neglect of the Hebrew Bible in formulations of the nature of the church. Küng and Moltmann actually are not poignant examples of that neglect, for in comparison with other scholarly works they have made considerable progress in the direction of finally acknowledging the debt of Christianity to the people of God's first covenant. More typical is Rudolph Bultmann's "Marcionite" presupposition concerning the "miscarriage" of the Old Testament hope, a bleakly negative view of Jewish faith that lends to Christianity a decidedly gnostic cast, obscuring the universality of the church's nature and calling, and threatening to weaken the rootedness of the gospel in social realities by narrowing salvation along individualistic lines. For example, Paul's treatment of the theme of "justification by faith" has become the occasion for a narrow, introspective individualism or privativistic pietism when uprooted from the rich historical and broad social context of righteousness and salvation in Hebrew Scripture. Similarly, attempts to interpret the interrelationship between law and gospel falter when focus on *nomos* in the New Testament obscures the dynamic meaning of *tôrâ* in the Hebrew Bible. The best possible Christian response to this challenge would be for us to acknowledge that we are neither true to our own heritage nor fair to religious Jews if we do not allow our understanding of the church to be rooted in the fullness of the biblical testimony to what it means to be a people of God.

The positive side of the challenge is by far the more significant. In a time of deep human need, when voices are badly needed that suggest an alternative to the natural and political crises that loom so large before us, the committed community of faith has a rich heritage from which to draw in inviting humans into a community that both cares tenderly for its own and extends to all those around it the best that it has to offer, a spirit of compassion and justice that transcends all parochial concerns by being grounded in the love of the God who loves all with impartiality. Convinced that the Hebrew Bible is an integral part of that rich heritage, I have defined my task as that of explicating the contribution that a biblical theology based on both Testaments makes to an understanding of a vital and life-giving community of faith. For not only do the books of the Hebrew Bible provide background history and teaching without which the New Testament cannot be adequately understood; more importantly, they also unfold a dynamic view of God as universal creator and redeemer, and corresponding to that view, a notion of the community of faith as unfolding in response to and as participant in the creative, redemptive acts of God on behalf of all creation. I undertake this task with the conviction that the community of faith that bases its identity on a broad, dynamic understanding of its confessional heritage can indeed offer the world an alternative to the numerous hollow promises and wrong-headed programs that raise hopes even as they hasten catastrophe. This it can do as God's agent for justice and peace in the world, an agency incorporating a carefully reflected ontology, a specific perspective from which the world is viewed, and a clear concept of authority on the basis of which decisions are made. But unless it is realized that this ontology, this perspective and this concept of authority can be properly understood only when seen in their dynamic process of emergence from the *entire* drama of Scripture, the community of faith's vitality is threatened, as is that of any organism when cut off from its source. Only by understanding itself as the extension of the *biblical* community of faith, which was called into existence by God and which derived life and direction solely from communion with God, can the *contemporary* community of faith fulfill its divine calling. Apart from this source, it is fully as capable of diminishing and destroying life as any other human agency—perhaps even more capable, because of the fear evoked in the hearts of many anxious humans by the invocation of the divine.

C. THE METHOD USED IN THIS STUDY

Given this essential need to define itself on the basis of a proper grasp of Scripture, no religious community with roots in the biblical writings can avoid the problem of method. Only if we can explain how Scripture can offer the basis for an understanding of a contemporary community of faith that is both faithful to Scripture's intrinsic nature and at the same time comprehensible to modern minds can we hope to go on to develop and then commend a definition of religious community that can claim to be more than a product of subjective presumptiveness. While the full development of such a definition lies beyond the scope of this study, the basic questions concerning method in biblical study cannot be avoided, given their impact on theological conclusions.

1. PRESUPPOSITIONS

Undeniably, subjectivity and presumptiveness lurk in every form of theological discourse. And so they must be acknowledged and addressed as unavoidable aspects of the methodological problem. It is sheer folly to imagine that one can apply a presuppositionless method. In fact, there is no such method, but only methods, whether out of self-deception or attempts to deceive others, that make such a claim. While presuppositions are unavoidable, clarity in understanding the nature of one's presuppositions is of critical significance in any study. Therefore they must be brought out of the area of unquestioned dogma or unconscious belief, and exposed to the light of criticism. Such critique the community of faith owes not only to its own members, but to the society of which it is a part. For apart from the influence that presuppositions have on doctrines or ontological principles, their determinative role in directing the activity of faith communities in the world has far-reaching consequences. The position such communities take on the basis of those presuppositions affects the lives of countless individuals, influences the quality of life of many societies, and at times can even have an effect on the course of world history. When tempted to leave presuppositions unscrutinized on the level of unconscious values or blind prejudices, one need merely reflect—to cite one example—on the divergent presuppositions that gave rise to two vastly different definitions of the church in the Third Reich in Germany. No one can deny the consequences on all levels of life of that particular conflict over definitions. Therefore, constant restudy of the nature and vocation of a given community of faith, including all underlying presuppositions, is a responsibility it must accept simply by virtue of its existence as a social institution. When one adds to this a major theological consideration, the answerability of such a community to God, this responsibility of self-critique takes on an even more awesome significance.

Out of responsibility to both spheres mentioned, the social and the theological, the evaluation of presuppositions should take into consideration the degree to which they are conducive to the fullness of life that God intends for all. There should be no conflict between social and theological responsibility in a community deriving its identity from the historical faith of the Bible. Indeed, both aspects converge in the critical examination of presuppositions when the fulfillment of life is found to lie in communion with God.

An important feature of the presuppositions—or to use the term current in interpretation theory (the discipline called *hermeneutics*), the "prior understandings" (*Vorverständnisse*)—that guide biblical interpretation is that they should be harmonious with the central message of Scripture itself. Since determination of that message is the goal of biblical theology—that is, the purpose to which the presuppositions are dedicated, it is obvious that the process of interpretation that first uses presuppositions to arrive at conclusions, and then uses those conclusions to revise and refine its presuppositions, is a circular process. And this is totally in keeping with both our casual experience with texts, and with the most sophisticated insights of hermeneutical reflection. We enter the intepretive task equipped with presuppositions that influence the questions we ask and the form that answers derived from the text take, but in this very contact with the text, our presuppositions, both consciously and unconsciously, are influenced and changed.

What then are the presuppositions that underlie this study of the biblical roots of our understanding of faith communities? I describe four such presuppositions in the spirit of openness just suggested; that is, with the belief that they are true to the spirit of Scripture, and yet amenable to criticism and correction:

a. Since the world's beginning, God has been active in fidelity to a creative, redemptive purpose, and will remain active until this world has completed its divinely ordained intention.

b. Since the dawn of human consciousness, God's purpose has included fellowship with the human family, fellowship arising out of confession of God's sovereignty and expressing itself in gratitude and praise. Such confession has in turn motivated the desire within the responding community to pattern its life on what it grasps to be the nature of the divine Sovereign.

c. The sacred writings of many peoples reflect this pattern of fellowship and response. Among them, the writings of the Bible assume a unique role for Jews and Christians, for they are believed to have arisen as confessional responses from a people experiencing God's fellowship within a covenantal relationship that bears significance for all peoples, a significance that is a part of God's plan for creation. These responses accordingly, in their organic connection with God's initiating activity and in their long history of interpretation and development within ancestral communities of faith (a history itself guided by God's Spirit), when interpreted historically, critically and with theological sensitivity constitute a trustworthy witness to the order God intends as the basis for human society. This presupposition does not deny that the confessional responses constituting the Bible are genuine human responses, and thus couched in the biases and limitations of the historic cultures that gave rise to and transmitted them. Their trustworthiness resides, however, in the transcendant dynamic discernible as the unbroken strand running throughout Scripture, which dynamic provides the basis for rigorous critique of the culturally determined vehicles within which the biblical message finds its human expression. It is perhaps the most demanding task of biblical theology to give clear expression to this transcendant dynamic, and to free it as a principle of critique in relation both to biblical traditions and to more recent concepts and values.[2]

d. Within God's purpose for creation, a specific vocation as human partner and historical agent is accorded the individual and the community responding in faith to God's creative, redemptive activity. A lively sense of this vocation, experienced as divine call and guided by a vision of God's purpose for creation, was the constitutive element of the people of God in Israel and of the community of faithful responding in faith to Jesus' ministry of the Kingdom. This sense of vocation remains the source of identity and purpose of many religious communities down to the present.

2. THE PROCESS OF INTERPRETATION AND THE IMPORTANCE OF THE FAITH COMMUNITY AS CONTEXT

From the presuppositions underlying interpretive method, we turn now to the process of interpretation itself. Here modern hermeneutical theory has done a great service in delivering us from a sterile set of interpretive techniques and directing attention toward the much more profound problem of understanding. As we seek to understand the Word by which we are addressed in Scripture, and as we open ourselves to the influence of the God active in the history of Israel and in our world, we need more than a scientific technique, however important philological, historical, and philosophical tools are in the larger task of understanding. If we seek to understand the biblical Word originating as a response to divine initiative, and if we seek to open ourselves to discernment of the presence of the divine Creator and Redeemer both in biblical times and in our own world, there is only one context within which we can hope to receive the necessary perspective and empowerment that makes such theological understanding and discernment possible. That context is the gathering of those who continue to live life in communion with God. The knowledge communicated by the Bible is knowledge intertwined with God's activity of creating, redeeming, and sustaining life. That knowledge can be properly understood only by those whose lives are drawn into the orbit of God's ongoing creative, redemptive and sustaining activity. It is clear that the community of faith we are studying in the Bible arose on the most fundamental level

---

2. Concerning the nature of this task, see P. D. Hanson, *Dynamic Transcendance* (Philadelphia: Fortress Press, 1978), pp. 46–94.

out of its experience of God's presence. The nature of that community, and its relation to our own communities of faith, can be understood only if we live in the presence of the One whose creative, healing presence bridges all intervening ages, thereby making the inner reality of that community the source of our identity as well.

Essential to an adequate method of interpretation, therefore, is its location wtihin a community of faith that finds its unity in worship of the one true God. Interpretation of Scripture, and the effort to understand its entire confessional heritage, is an aspect of a faith community's living in the presence of God for the sake of the world. As in all aspects of its interpretive task, therefore, its effort to define itself as a faith community is broadly communal and ongoing. All those drawn into a community of faith are full partners in the task of self-definition by which it clarifies to itself, to other religious communities and to the wider world the nature of its God-given vocation. Theological scholarship aggravates the dangers of deception and self-service if it is carried on in academic isolation. For the criterion of fidelity to the one true God becomes a reality within a community that submits all its endeavors, including its scholarly and reflective ones, to worship of God alone, and to service of all God's creatures. A community of faith can preserve the safeguards every scholarly endeavor needs by relating scholarship to the total life context, and by subjecting all methods, theories, and conclusions to a lively critique deriving from a membership inclusive of both sexes, all races, classes, and regions. Within this context of worship, self-transcending service and inner critique, presuppositions, methods, and results all will be held open to an addressing Word that no one group is allowed to domesticate or claim for its personal purposes.

Although diversity characterizes both the received confessional heritage and its contemporary expressions, contemporary communities of faith can begin to rediscover what unites them as they grow more conscious of the primal experience they share, communion with the life-giving center of life, God. There the myriad facets of life cease to resemble a meaningless chaos, and fall into the pattern of a world becoming whole again within a divinely initiated and directed redemptive process. There the confessional witness of the past unites with contemporary events, and together they are guided toward the unfolding of God's purpose by the Spirit of God experienced in worship. Even as the myriad facets of life find their pattern of meaning at this center, so do the diversity of peoples acknowledging one Sovereign over life. Here diversity begins to manifest a deeper unity in which all humans become parts of one family, sharing a common vocation and destiny, albeit with different ways of celebrating and understanding that vocation and destiny.

That vocation and destiny itself derives from the process of being drawn toward God in worship, for in the worship life of a community a vision is fostered of the universal order of peace and justice in relation to which diverse peoples become a people of God. That order is intended to embrace all of creation, for according to this vision it is God's will that all be drawn into the divine order of justice wedded with peace planned from the beginning. To be drawn into a community united in worship, therefore, is to be drawn toward the center of life. This centering in turn places one in solidarity with the whole human family, which is seen from the perspective of faith as deriving from the same heavenly Parent.

In discussing the method used in defining a community of faith on the basis of its confessional, and especially its biblical heritage, context is therefore of crucial importance. Knowledge and self-understanding are not sought for their own sakes, but as one aspect of participation in the process to which all human structures and activities are subservient, the unfolding of God's order of universal justice and peace. In devotion to this self-transcending purpose, and in a givenness to the world that has its source in first having received life from God as a gift of grace, a community of faith draws deeply on its scriptural heritage in an act of self-definition that is an aspect of its becoming the universal fellowship God intended from the beginning for all people. For example, the Christian church defines its nature as church as it *becomes* church, and it becomes church as it gives up all personal claims and allows itself to be drawn, through communion with God in worship and through commitment to universal justice and peace in the world, into a reality vastly greater than itself.

3. A HERMENEUTIC OF ENGAGEMENT

Since the interpretive method described ties study with worship, and reflection with action in the world, I call it a "hermeneutic of engagement."[3] I turn now to describe this process of interpretation more closely as it relates to the problem of defining the nature and mission of a contemporary faith community.

a. The Nature of This Method of Interpretation

A hermeneutic of engagement is an appropriate tool for relating a community to its confessional heritage, inasmuch as it is modeled after the interpretive process through which the community of faith in the Bible discerned the presence of God in its world and defined itself in relation to that presence. In the Bible, the confessional heritage, in the course of recitation and re-enactment in worship, provided the perspective from which the community could relate the new events of its time to the plan of God. From the resulting process of transmission and

---

3. Ibid., pp. 76–90.

interpretation was derived a view of God as Creator, Redeemeer, and Sustainer involved in the concrete realities of life, a God resisting reduction into set formulas or concepts, a God ever addressing new areas of life so as to eradicate all that diminishes and destroys life and to foster all that contributes to the reign of peace and justice.

This view of God in turn gave rise to a correspondingly dynamic view of the community of faith. The circle of believers called into being by God was a responding community, using the confessional heritage of its past to live forth confessionally into a future as participants in God's creative and redemptive drama.

A method of interpretation appropriate for this kind of scriptural heritage is one that fosters a similar living forth from the confessional heritage in response to an ever-active God. Freezing the symbols of faith or definitions of community into static categories is as inappropriate now as it was in biblical times, if my presupposition regarding the dynamic nature of God and God's purpose is true. In other words, I feel that the Bible itself calls for the kind of engaged interpretation described here. And in particular, the materials of the Hebrew Bible by their very nature urge on us this kind of approach! Its legends, confessions, hymns, narratives, and laws are all responses to a God experienced within the struggles of life, struggles accordingly interpreted as manifestations of God's efforts to release humans from bondage to all that diminishes life, and to free them for the life of shared blessing in communion with God and in human fellowship.

In order to understand the message of Scripture to communities of faith today, we therefore must be daring enough to try to glimpse the restless, dynamic heart of Scripture, and be willing to be drawn into that heart; that is, into communion with the God who was so vividly experienced by that ancient people that their response was a testimony that still addresses us as divine Word today. We miss the essential nature of Scripture if we go to it in search of institutional structures in a surface sense of the word. In the history of the Bible, structures were drawn inferentially from the confessions, or were destroyed and replaced as an aspect of a confessional response to the God addressing humans in prophetic word and historical event. In the community patterning itself on this biblical model, structures are justified only as they serve the creative, redemptive purpose of the living God. And in our day communal forms and structures can properly emerge, be transformed, or be supplanted, only as communities of faith are conscious of living in the praise and service of the God present and active in every age and place.

This study therefore is not ecclesiological in the normal sense of that word. It will rather be a theological portrayal of the history of God's people in the Bible, and on the basis of that portrayal a description of the qualities characterizing the biblical community of faith. This portrayal and description are then presented to contemporary religious communities as an invitation to learn from the style of God's people in the biblical era how a community of faith might constitute itself in our own day; that is, an invitation to engage itself, under the guidance of the Spirit of God, in the dynamic interrelationship of Scripture and contemporary realities.

b. Two-Dimensional Exegesis: Word and World

A hermeneutic of engagement does not entail exegesis of texts from the perspective of scholarly detachment. Involved instead is a two-dimensional exegesis that keeps alive the dynamic ontology of biblical times. Within biblical communities of faith, God's activity in the world was discerned in the interaction between confessional heritage and new events. And Word and world continue to interrelate in the life of religious communities today. Utmost care must be given to both sides of this two-dimensional exegesis. As much harm can be done by applying an inadequately understood Word to a well-understood world as in applying a well-understood Word to an inadequately understood world. In an increasingly complex society, biblical interpretation can be carried out faithfully only as an aspect of the community of faith's mission of justice and mercy engaging the committed from all countries, races, socioeconomic backgrounds, and professions in a common task. Seeking a Scripture-based understanding of the ontology, perspective, and authority of the community of faith is clearly a corporate task of all God's people. As a reality in the world born of God's initiating activity witnessed in Scripture, such a community receives its directions and inspiration by continual immersion in the Word. That immersion conditions its presence in the world as a presence for the world, and as such it participates in the unfolding of the order God intends for all creation. Through this participation, in turn, it is opened anew to the address and the challenge of the Word, and thereby prepared for the next stage of God's activity in redeeming the world. Moreover, its immersion in the world as an instrument of God's love safeguards its theological exercises from becoming mere abstractions, and its hermeneutic circle from becoming self-indulgent.

c. Levels of Discernment: Paradigms and a Vision of Divine Purpose

In its engagement with Scripture, the faith community recognizes two levels of meaning: (1) paradigms and (2) a vision of divine purpose.

(1) PARADIGMS

It is a central biblical confession that God is present in all reality, as its Creator and Purposer. But in the Bible the nature of God's purpose comes to expression so vividly in certain events that they become paradigms for the community of faith. As such they are treasured by the tradition through retelling, reinterpretation, and in special cases such as the Passover *sêder* or the Lord's Supper, through re-enactment that takes on sacramental significance. Through these paradigms, in the concreteness and particularity of the historical event, a community learns what it means to be a people responsive to God in the real stuff of life. Here it experiences the mystery of encountering the eternal God in the ordinary and the unexpected. Here earthen vessels are recognized as carriers of transcendent meaning, a recognition that translates from the concrete paradigms of Scripture to the concrete occurrences of our everyday life. It is a recognition dawning in the consciousness of small children as they hear the Passover narrative or the parables of Jesus, a recognition occurring each time the family of faith recites the *kiddush* or gathers around the Lord's Supper, a recognition that moves into daily life experiences as the vexation of yet another social crisis or yet another outstretched hand is transformed into the blessed discernment of the atoning act of loving-kindness or of "the least of these my sisters or brothers . . . unto *me*!"

(2) VISION OF DIVINE PURPOSE

The paradigms of faith, as described, perhaps may be pictured as windows through which the community of faith is given the opportunity to glimpse the divine presence at the root of all reality. They are vivid reminders that earthly phenomena are not ends in themselves, but when properly understood are vessels or agents of a transcendent purpose. When focus is raised in turn from the individual paradigm to the whole sequence of paradigms preserved by biblical tradition, it becomes apparent that they are not isolated episodes, but links in an unbroken chain. Motifs—like the deliverance of oppressed people, the disenthronement of the insolent proud and the healing of the broken—are recurrent, suggesting that essential connections bind the individual paradigms into a larger unity.

Recognition of this larger unity prompted communities of faith in the biblical era to use earlier paradigms as a key to interpreting the theological meaning of the events of their world and the experiences of their people. The exiles in Babylon, for example, compared themselves and their hope to the people of the exodus, even as the later Essenes of Qumran derived a sense of direction from the generation of Babylonian exiles. Hosea likened the experiences of his age to the wilderness generation, and the apostle Paul compared baptism in his time to the crossing of the sea by the people of Moses. This typological method reflects the belief that the individual paradigms are episodes in one universal drama of salvation. Second Isaiah was the first to give explicit theological formulation to this view: the God encountered in the concrete events of history is a God faithful to a long-range—indeed, an eternal—plan of salvation for the whole creation. In the biblical writings in general, the recurrence of patterns of meaning in the paradigms is viewed as evidence for the trustworthiness of God, and the faithfulness of God to the promises of the covenant. The paradigms, taken as a whole, thus provide the basis for a vision of reality as directed by a gracious divine Purposer.

Any contemporary community that bases its identity on a sense of being called to participate in God's universal purpose will seek to envision as clearly as possible the transcendent dynamic that gave rise to biblical confessions and that is still perceptible to the eyes of faith as that which beckons all reality toward peace and justice. Without clarification of its vision, it cannot be confident that its response is in harmony with God's will. It is for this reason that the community of faith, seeking to evaluate the significance of Scripture for its self-understanding, will include, alongside its depiction of the paradigms of faith, a second level of biblical interpretation: a description of its vision of the all-embracing, creative, redemptive drama that unfolds in the Bible.

This is of course an awesome challenge, requiring both intimate knowledge of that drama and a high degree of creative imagination in giving expression to it. No one form of description will be completely satisfactory or definitive. Nevertheless, the community of faith that accepts the responsibility of honestly giving account of itself both for the sake of its own members and of other segments of the society must be committed to a clear formulation of its central vision. In some cases this formulation will take the shape of a root metaphor, which for a given group captures its perception of the God revealed in Scripture and experienced in life. Such metaphors can be found today in the writings of groups experiencing the presence of God in their own liberation struggles.

For its part, the field of biblical theology can contribute another type of formulation of this vision, namely a description of the purposeful movement that it discerns unfolding through the writings of Scripture and that it regards as an essential source of our knowledge of God's will and of the perspective from which we can understand the events of this world and the role of the community of faith in relation to those events. The fresh new metaphors of liberation movements and the more conceptual descriptions arising from biblical scholarship should be allowed to enrich one another as complementary aspects of one united effort. In this ongoing process, it is the responsibility of biblical theology to resist all attempts to reduce the vision to narrow, self-serving formulations. This is one reason among many why the interdenominational character of biblical scholarship should be fostered. Unfortunately, in pursuit of the central meaning of Scripture, and no doubt in response to the partial perspectives of the specific theological traditions of which they are a part, biblical theologians have often contributed to parochialism and oversimplification. For example, Gerhard von

Rad selected as normative for his biblical theology the history of salvation tradition, to the virtual neglect of other important streams within the Hebrew Bible. Such oversimplification threatens the biblical principle that God's presence cannot be captured in the univalent formulation or the immutable image. Believers can hope to communicate to posterity a faithful vision of that presence only by preserving its rich confessional diversity as a witness to its encounter with God in the whole range of life settings and experiences.

As one struggles with the question of how to foster a vision of God's ongoing universal purpose without losing a sense of the rich diversity that resists verbal idolatry, it seems necessary to visualize the transcendant dynamic of Scripture as one that unfolds precisely within the tensions and polarities represented by divergent biblical traditions. One must be able to appreciate how the lofty visions of seers and the pragmatic policies of priests both contribute to our vision of divine purpose. One must be able to recognize the contribution that kingship made to social form and stability, and at the same time see that life under kings was quickly debased when left unscrutinized by prophets with their vision of a heavenly order of reality and their dedication to the reform of every structure that grants privilege to some and excludes others. One must even be able to visualize the importance of the tension between the cosmic dimension of reality portrayed by mythical, sapiental, and hymnic traditions in the Bible and the teleological dimension described by the history of salvation tradition.[4]

Obviously the picture of the community of faith emerging from this dynamic and often tension-filled vision of divine purpose is dynamic and often tension-filled as well. What comes into view in this study therefore is something very different from a timeless blueprint for contemporary faith communities. It is rather a verbal portrait of an emerging community, one constantly growing in response to divine initiative. What will be held before the contemporary community of faith therefore is the model of a community with a vision of God's presence in the events of its world, and with the courage to allow itself to be drawn toward that presence as a servant of the broken, the oppressed, and the despised.

But why locate the significance of the Bible for the contemporary community of faith in this model and the vision of divine purpose to which it is related rather than in a simpler structural model; for example, the polity of the pastoral epistles? The answer is rooted in the presuppositions underlying this study that were described earlier, and can be stated thus: the transcendent dynamic discernible in Scripture in response to which a community becomes a people of God does not stop abruptly at the end of the biblical era. If the biblical vision of a God

---

4. See further, P. D. Hanson, *The Diversity of Scripture* (Philadelphia: Fortress Press, 1982), pp. 14–82.

acting true to a plan of universal peace and justice is trustworthy, that activity does not end with the last event recorded in the Bible, for up to the final stages of the formation of Scripture the fulfillment of God's plan is still awaited in the future. According to this model, a contemporary community of faith is thus not primarily an archive where members can study records about ancient happenings, or an institution committed to perpetuating structures of a bygone age, but rather a community called by God to participate in an *ongoing* drama. This necessitates the same interpretive process that was an essential characteristic of most communities of biblical times, namely, one drawing from the paradigms of its confessional heritage and from its vision of divine purpose a perspective from which to understand the religious and moral issues raised by contemporary realities, and then responding in keeping with this understanding in confession and action. The magnitude of this challenge must not be minimized; identifying where God is present (for example, on what side of a conflict) is perhaps the most risky of all human enterprises, and description of contemporary events in terms of their relation to a universal plan of justice is not something a community dares to engage in lightly, especially when one calls to mind the mixed record of communities that have been guided by transcendent visions in the past. If a contemporary faith community is to make sense out of a complex world by bearing witness to a unifying vision and at the same time is to avoid the snares of triumphalism and self-aggrandizement, it must take seriously the biblical motif of the servant people, a people responding with fear and trembling to God's initiatives and mindful of its solidarity with the entire human family. From this perspective, the diversity that characterizes biblical traditions is interpreted not merely as an indication of divisiveness within the religious communities of biblical times. On a deeper level, it can be seen to reflect deference vis-á-vis the mystery of divine presence, a tentativeness that did not deem inappropriate the coexistence of responses that on the surface appear self-contradictory—for example, the fulfillment was now (realized eschatology) and not yet (futuristic eschatology); God's reign would come down from heaven (spatial metaphor), or it would come at the end of time (temporal metaphor). On the model of the biblical community, contemporary faith communities can hear openly the often diverse testimonies of their own seers and prophets, whose differing angles of vision contribute to the modesty befitting those living in the presence of God, and to the self-criticism that is an essential component of any genuinely humane community. Here the existentialist perspective can enrich the eschatological; the black liberation position can contribute to the feminist; the Marxist critique can be taken seriously by more traditional religious groups. Although this model guarantees debate and tension, it is totally in keeping with the spirit of a community that derives its sense of direction from a very long confessional history and its sense of vocation from the desire to participate in the unfolding of an order of peace and justice intended by God for *all* people, and subject to the parochial claims of *none*.

The description of its vision of divine purpose is therefore an aspect of the hermeneutical task that demands a high degree of graciousness and judiciousness. The record of divine activity in Scripture is not reducible to a simple formula. And as overall patterns of meaning emerge from the paradigms, we must not be tempted into making a community's task of relating the overall trajectory of its heritage to contemporary events easier by eliminating fundamental polarities. On the other hand, it would only invite despair if biblical theology were to commend to the communities it served an unordered set of dichotomies that seemed to imply blatant contradictions. On this level, the challenge is to describe the vision of divine purpose running through our confessional heritage in a manner true to the mystery of divine presence and the complexity of mundane reality, and at the same time to delineate the dynamic Reality active through all time and space in the creation and preservation of a righteous habitation—that is, an order wedding justice and peace. Only by fostering such a nuanced description of its transcendent vision combined with vivid descriptions of the fundamental paradigms can biblical theology discharge its responsibility of offering the community of faith a reliable point of reference for defining its proper relation to the overarching reality within which every mundane reality finds its rightful place.

Although useful in the theological task of grasping the contemporary meaning of Scripture, technical terms such as "paradigm" and "vision of divine purpose" must not obscure the inextricable relationship of biblical research to the worship life of actual communities of faith and their life of engagement in the everyday world. Nor can they be allowed to obscure the communal nature of the mission of the church in both aspects of its engagement—that is, in relating Word and world. There is no denying that Scripture embraces a richness and diversity of testimony to God's activity that challenges the most discerning and well trained of minds. But it is equally clear that the schoolchild or the illiterate adult is able to grasp and be grasped by the central paradigms of faith in Scripture. This complexity and simplicity corresponds to the world we live in. The questions of how a community living forth into the world from its confessional heritage is to respond to the peaceful use of nuclear energy, to various forms of abortion legislation, and to different monetary theories are difficult to the extreme. Yet, because of their impact on human well-being, they represent a direct challenge to believers possessing specialized training and wisdom in the fields in question. Yet who can deny the simplicity and purity of love's mandate in the vast majority of our experiences as human beings?

This polarity of the simple and the complex is another aspect of the rich diversity that characterizes the life of faith, and here too unity is found as the polarity itself is drawn into the unity of the divine mystery in worship and devotion. This means that a religious community that locates its unity in communion with God will not be tempted into premature dissolution of the polarities of Scripture or the polarities of this world. How often have not a religious group's "simple" answers been the by-product of its own insecurity, its need to display to the world a superficial (and dishonest) unity because of its failure to ground true unity in worship of and devotion to the one living God! A community grounded in the God of mystery whose presence faithfully guides all worlds to their final goal is a community capable of treating every opinion honestly and fairly with a freedom rooted in communion with the ultimate Reality, in whom all polarities find their final rest.

Once believers accept their role within such a hermeneutic of engagement, and witness their diversity gathered up in the unity of worship, both competitiveness and envy will give way to a partnership in which God alone is exalted. When understanding is obscured by the scholar's stammering attempts to describe God's presence through technical formulations, the fresh metaphor born of the struggles of the poor against the oppressor will refocus the community's vision. When the preacher's exposition fails to correlate the ancient Word with a suffering world, the tender courage of the peacemakers in the congregation may keep alive the testimony of Scripture. It is within the vast choir of witnesses to God's presence in our world that the message is proclaimed that a people is God's people not when it copies a past polity or perpetuates its own image, but when, guided by its scriptural and confessional heritage, it glimpses God's presence in the world, and responds faithfully to that presence in confession, worship, and action. For that glimpse and that response have constituted the true community of faith through all ages. They form the heart of its transcendent vision.

d. A Hermeneutic of Engagement and the Problem of Biblical Authority

For some people, the suggestion of openness to God's new initiative in contemporary social and political events threatens the authority of Scripture. Undoubtedly a static view of authority, a view of the Bible as a collection of immutable laws and infallible truths, poses less problems for leaders of some religious groups. But such a static view and the alliances between religious bodies and repressive political powers that it commonly engenders pose too blatant a contradiction of the biblical view of reality to enjoy the support of biblical theology. From a biblical perspective, world events are viewed as the arena of an ongoing salvation drama, and communities adopting this perspective must be open to the God who is engaged in their world to "raise up the poor from the dust." This openness to the presence of the living God implies for a community of faith the need for constant renewal and reform.

The authoritative guide to the communal life dedicated to renewal and reform of self and world is not a static organizational structure, but the living example of a merciful God that moves the responsive community to adopt the role of servant within a suffering world. Although the process of working out an authentic communal form and style is inextricably tied to engagement with the concrete realities of this world, it does not exclude but draws on disciplined study as well. Indeed, it is through careful study of the paradigms of the confessional heritage that a community of faith is able to recapture and even sacramentally relive the events in which its spiritual ancestors patterned their lives after the example of the Deliverer God. And through the effort to capture the central meaning of its scriptural heritage with the aid of the master image, the root metaphor, or the imaginative description of its vision of divine purpose moving through space and time, it begins to glimpse the creative, redemptive stream that flows steadily through the heart of all reality, unifying all life as it draws all reality toward its final fulfillment.

A community of faith submits to its proper authority to the extent that it allows itself to be drawn into that redemptive stream, giving up all penultimate values for the one eternal value, the universal order being created by the Redeemer God. Submission to such an authority is not a simple matter, but one replete with struggle, testing, and difficult decisions. But while resisting eternal tests of verification, it is an authority that proves itself to be self-authenticating within the servant community that takes the side of the weak and the oppressed as its divine calling. The dynamic manner in which this inner authority functions is exemplified in the history covered in this book, for its nature is most readily learned from the individuals and groups of the past that lived intimately with the divine presence.

We turn to our scriptural heritage, therefore, as an essential dimension of our response to God in an ongoing, living relationship. We draw on the patterns of transcendent meaning that emerge in Scripture as a guide to our own effort to make sense of an often baffling world. It is not with a merely antiquarian interest that we look to the people of God in the Bible. They are our spiritual ancestors, and their encounters with God were instrumental in the formation of a concept of life that has been bequeathed to us as the foundation on which we can construct an authentic life of faith and humaneness. As people responding to the creative, redemptive God today, we represent an extension of the biblical community of faith. Their ontology, as responding agents in God's purposeful activity, is our ontology. Their notion of community is the source of our own efforts to renew life as God intends it within a human family embodying righteousness and compassion. Without a clear understanding of the biblical community's role as participant in the unfolding of God's order of universal peace and justice out of chaos and sin, we shall fail to define adequately our own identity to ourselves or to our world.

It is therefore salutory that we look to the Bible for orientation, for it is in effect our spiritual autobiography as people drawn to the living God. By tracing the life of the biblical community of faith—its birth, its growth amid crisis and struggle, its fragmentation and near demise, its rebirth and further pilgrimage—in this way we clarify who we are, where we have come from, where we are going, and above all, to whom we belong. In recognizing the disparity between our ancestral community's vision of divine purpose and its parital response, a disparity that led to fragmentation and confusion of identity, we are led to a posture that repudiates the temptation to idealize and defend our past. It leads instead to repentance of the unresponsiveness of our spiritual forebears and of ourselves. It creates a deep desire to be reconciled with those from whom we are cut off due to misunderstandings and conflicts growing out of our confusing our own "tribalism" with God's universal reign. Where communities of faith allow themselves to be guided by such a biblical realism, there is hope for the overcoming of the temptation to employ Scripture to justify perversities such as the arrogant presumption of some to have earned special privileges within the human family and to have escaped from the harsh realities of this world into blissful otherworldly delights. The result can be a sense of discernment distinguishing clearly between God's steadfast love that is the central theme of Scripture and the persistent hardness of a human family preferring its idols to life in the presence of the true God. This sense of discernment will establish for biblical theology the unco-optable function of subjecting all structures and beliefs to critique in submission to the sole authority of the living God, and in full acknowledgement that every human response, even those found in the Bible, participate in and perpetuate elements of a partial and often idolatrous vision. Within Scripture, faith encounters the basis for a thorough-going critique that alone can purge religious communities of their idols, and re-establish communities of faith as servant communities dedicated to the earthly vocation of mercy and justice as a part of the perennial stream that has borne faithful servants of all ages, upholding them in their struggles for God's reign, and enabling them to repudiate all who seek to substitute human desires for God's will, even when such include some of the most powerful political and religious leaders of the world.

D. WHY A HISTORICAL STUDY IS ESSENTIAL TO UNDERSTANDING THE NATURE OF CONTEMPORARY COMMUNITIES OF FAITH

If we were seeking to construct a definition of community on the basis of a universal notion of the human psyche, we might appeal to the twin basic human needs for ego expression and dependency, somewhat in the manner of Ludwig Feuerbach. Or if we sought a sociological basis for understanding religious organizations, we might begin with Friedrich Schleiermacher's definition: "The Christian Church takes shape through the coming together of regenerate individuals to form a system of mutual interaction and cooperation."[5] Or in the effort to supply a universally recognizable definition of religious community on the basis of a philosophical-theological and comparative-religion premises, we might follow a recent suggestion of Gordon Kaufmann and base the definition of community on the category of humaneness."[6] Without denying the value of such attempts in clarifying aspects of the notion of religious community in a pluralistic world, we must be aware of the fact that within the Judeo-Christian tradition the notion of community has emerged not through reflection on abstract psychological, sociological or philosophical principles, but as an historical development understood in relational-covenantal terms. For example, the universal scope of the biblical notion of community emerged through stages from a narrow clan henotheism through a national cult to a prophetically based and eschatologically oriented universalism. From the outset it must be acknowledged that this historical development is not an ineluctable evolutionary process. Not infrequently we find the retreat into earlier forms. And commonly divergent tendencies compete with one another within the community. The complexity of the development does not deny, however, that it is historical, through and through.

The value of the historical approach to defining community found in our biblical heritage is considerable, even when viewed in relation to the above mentioned methods, for it stands as a reminder that all understanding is historically conditioned. For example, Feuerbach's and Schleiermacher's definitions of human psychological and social structures inevitably reflected their early and middle nineteenth-century German milieu, even as Kaufmann's understanding of "humaneness" is more easily grasped by an American Mennonite theologian than, say, by a Brazilian Catholic peasant or a Black South African Methodist minister, which is simply to illustrate that the effort to identify universals itself is an aspect of historical process. Once this is acknowledged, much can be gained from studies of community using psychological, sociological, and philosophical methodologies. In a religious tradition, however, within which the notion of community has emerged historically, redefinition will be carried on primarily through a study of its heritage, with other methodologies being used to assure self-criticism, to safeguard against faulty reasoning, and to foster an attitude of openness to traditions subscribing to different notions of community and world.

Added to these rational considerations is another that contributes a theological dimension to a community's effort to define itself through

5. F. Schleiermacher, *The Christian Faith*, eds. H. R. Mackintosh and J. S. Steward (Edinburgh: T. & T. Clark, 1928), p. 532, para. 115.

6. G. D. Kaufmann, *The Theological Imagination: Constructing the Concept of God* (Philadelphia: Westminster Press, 1981), pp. 172–206.

a critically informed study of its confessional heritage. This is the belief that the development of the notion of the community of faith in the Bible is not only the record of a human process, but on a deeper level can be interpreted as the human response to a divinely initiated relationship within which God has been fashioning a people called to participate in the unfolding of a divine plan for creation. This belief finds expression in a confession that runs throughout the Bible: out of the families of the earth God chose one people as the instrument of his purposes, "that by your descendants all nations of the earth shall bless themselves" (Gen. 26:4); "to be a people for his own possession" (Deut. 7:6); "and I will be their God, and they shall be my people. Then the nations will know that I the Lord sanctify Israel, when my sanctuary is in the midst of them forevermore" (Ezek. 37:27b–28); "as a light to the nations, that my salvation may reach to the end of the earth" (Isa. 49:6). Naturally, this claim was open to misuse; for example, claims of superiority or smug self-confidence. Correct understanding of the nature of this election, that is, as an election based not on merit and dedicated not to self-glorification, but based on a call to a self-transcending task and dedicated solely to God's purpose and God's glory, maintained a touchstone for persistent criticism of all human efforts to exploit election for personal or national gain. We see this criticism running through biblical prophecy, as illustrated by this word of Amos:

> "Are you not like the Ethiopians to me,
>   O people of Israel?" says the Lord.
> "Did I not bring up Israel from the Land of Egypt,
>   and the Philistines from Caphtor and the Syrians from Kir?" . . . .
> All the sinners of my people shall die by the sword,
>   who say, "Evil shall not overtake or meet us." (Amos 9:7, 10)

It also accompanied Israel's development of its understanding of election and Torah: ". . . not because you were more in number than any other people that the Lord set his love upon you and chose you, for you were the fewest of all peoples" (Deut. 7:7; cf. Deut 32:21). It was on the basis of this understanding of God's election of a servant people that the New Testament church worked out its understanding of community. Unlike the mystery cults, the early Christian community based its identity not on mystical communion with an otherworldly Savior figure, but on a mission in continuity with the ministry of Jesus of Nazareth, whom they acknowledged as the long-awaited Messiah of the Jewish people. This was a mission based on the call to repentance, and a return to the righteousness of God that was to be the mark of God's people. Those who carried out this ministry with a living sense of the presence of the resurrected Christ Paul could call "the Israel of God" (Gal. 6:16;), thus emphasizing the continuity of God's earlier people with this new gathering of disciples "in Christ."

E. THE HISTORICAL RELATIONSHIP BETWEEN THE COMMUNITIES OF THE TWO TESTAMENTS

Paul treats the relationship between the people of the first covenant and the new "Israel of God" most extensively in Romans 9–11. There he anguishes over the unwillingness of the "kinsmen by race" to accept the gospel, and goes on to describe their special history: "They are Israelites, and to them belong the sonship, the glory, the covenants, the giving of the law, the worship and the promises; to them belong the patriarchs, and of their race, according to the flesh, is the Christ." This splendid heritage evokes a doxology: "God who is over all be blessed for ever. Amen" (9:4–5). Against this background, Paul puzzles through the phenomenon of the rejection of the Christ by the majority of his kinsfolk, and the election of the Gentiles: "But it is not as though the word of God had failed. For to all who are descended from Israel belong to Israel, and not all are children of Abraham because they are his decendants" (9:6–7a). This Paul illustrates by pointing to Jacob and Esau, and the fact that the promise was not handed down by natural inheritance or by human merit ("though they were not yet born and had done nothing either good or bad"), but "in order that God's purpose of election might continue" (9:11). He then draws on an ancient liturgical formula (Exod. 33:19) to identify the source of God's election: "I will have mercy on whom I have mercy, and I will have compassion on whom I have compassion" (9:15). And thus it is that Paul explains the new Israel of God, "even us whom he has called, not from the Jews only but also from the Gentiles" (9:24). In this new chapter of God's relationship with the human family, in which righteousness is based on faith, the people of God is a people in which "there is no distinction between Jew and Greek" (10:10). As indicated by Paul's frequent quotation of prophetic texts to support his argument, this conception of the people of God breaking with a strict ethnic definition is rooted deeply in Hebrew prophecy, a conception mediated in the post exilic period within apocalyptic circles.

At the same time as Paul makes his case for this spiritual understanding of the Israel of God, he also hastens to observe that the new people of God is threatened by the same temptation on which the first Israel stumbled, pride of election. Therefore he goes on to teach a lesson that speaks urgently to every Christian individual and congregation, not only in Paul's day, but in every age down to our own, a lesson in what I earlier called "biblical realism:" God, in an act that was at once judgment and mercy, broke off some of the branches of the original Israel, in which place the Gentiles ("a wild olive shoot") were grafted on. The warning to the newly grafted people is clear: "Do not boast over the branches" (11:18a). Rather, the Gentiles were to acknowledge the direction of dependency, that is, the true nature of the indebtedness (recalling the heritage enumerated in 9:4–5):

"If you boast, remember it is not you that support the root, but the root that supports you. You will say, "Branches were broken off so that I might be grafted in." That is true. They were broken off because of their unbelief, but you stand fast only through faith. So do not become proud, but stand in awe. For if God did not spare the natural branches, neither will he spare you. Note then the kindness and the severity of God: severity toward those who have fallen, but God's kindness to you, provided you continue in his kindness; otherwise you too will be cut off.   (Rom. 11:18–22)

Boasting is excluded, ultimately (as Paul insists) because justification comes by faith alone, and "it is the root that supports you," and excluded historically because of the distinction between the "natural branches" (Israel), and those "cut off from what is by nature a wild olive tree and grafted, contrary to nature, into a cultivated and live tree" (the Gentiles).

The overall witness of Scripture, therefore, as well as this specific elucidation of salvation history by Paul, gives us the order that must be followed if we are to understand the community of faith within the only context that reveals its essential being, the context of God's creative and redemptive activity from creation to the coming of God's reign. The order is sketched by Paul in Romans 9:4–5, and traces the history of the Israelites, to whom "belong the sonship, the glory, the covenants, the giving of the law, the worship . . . the promises, and the patriarchs." Only by reliving the history of God's intimate relationship with God's first people can communities of faith today avoid the trap of blind arrogance and instead grow into a realistic and mature understanding of what it means to be "God's people," "the children of the promise." And only by reliving this rich history are Christians prepared to enter the next chapter mentioned by Paul, "and of their race, according to the flesh, is the Christ."

The reason why this *praeparatio* in the history of God's first people is essential to understanding the Christ and the community of Christ's followers is clear. In the birth of a people of God in Christ, God's anointing Jesus as the Messiah was not a solitary happening, but one within a long history of salvation. Jesus is not a gnostic savior, a disembodied spirit emanating from the *pleroma* to draw forth divine sparks entrapped in this aeon within prisons of flesh. Jesus, who was anointed God's Messiah to go to the lost of the tribes of Israel, is the carpenter's son from Nazareth; that is, of a particular people according to the flesh. That people is the Jewish people. The Christian kerygma goes on to profess that to that people, and then to all the nations of the earth for which the Jews were called to be a blessing, Jesus came as the Messiah; that is, the anointed King long awaited out of the House of David who would deliver the people from their dark prison. Christians today

are as indebted as were those in Paul's Roman audience to their ancestors in the faith, God's first people the Jews, for the perspective that
alone can protect us from the arrogance that evokes God's wrath. That
perspective alone can safeguard us in our calling to be a servant people
of God, the perspective of God's universal purpose revealed first to
Israel and then spreading from this servant people to the ends of the
earth.

Paul, moreover, goes on in Romans 11 to explain that we are indebted to God's first people for our essential orientation not only by virtue
of our origins in Israel's past, but also in view of Israel's future role in
God's purpose: "Now if their trespass means riches for the world, and
if their failure means riches for the Gentiles, how much more will their
full inclusion mean!" (11:12). God's history with God's first people has
by no means come to an end. For the present, "those who do not persist in their unbelief, will be grafted in, for God has the power to graft
them in again. For if you have been cut from what is by nature a wild
olive tree, and grafted, contrary to nature, into a cultivated olive tree,
how much more will these natural branches be grafted back into their
own olive tree" (11:24). But Paul goes even further in penetrating the
mystery of God's relation to the Jewish people: "Lest you be wise in
your own conceits, I want you to understand this mystery, brethren: a
hardening has come upon part of Israel, until the full number of the
Gentiles come in, and so all Israel will be saved" (11:25). On what basis
can Paul make this confession? The trustworthiness of God's promises:
"For the gifts and the call of God are irrevocable" (11:29).

In relation to the past in which the nature of our calling as God's
people was born and developed, and in relation to the future toward
which our participation in the unfolding of God's purpose impels us,
we are dependent for our sense of orientation on God's relationship
with the people through whom the nations of the world will bless themselves, the Jews. I personally do not derive from the overall trajectory
of Scripture or from Paul's penetrating interpretation of that trajectory a millenialistic historiography such as that expressed by Jürgen
Motlmann in *The Church in the Power of the Spirit*. It seems rather that
Paul uses a teleological framework to portray the unique role of the
Jews in God's purpose for God's creation, and while that purpose certainly has an historical dimension, this is accompanied by an existential
dimension as well. In this respect, Paul's vision of God's relation to the
Jews is analogous to the view of God's reign that grows out of the Gospels: Christians celebrate the advent of God's reign in Jesus' life and
preaching and its victory in his resurrection, awaiting its culmination in
the return of the Son of Man, and at the same time engage in its present inbreaking as their vocation in the world. In a similarly multiva-
lenced manner, Christians should celebrate the peoplehood of God's

first Israel in the foundational events recorded in the Hebrew Bible, and look forward to God's new "covenant with them when I take away their sins" (11:27). But at the same time, we live with the present ramifications of God's purposes with God's first people: "For the gifts and the call of God are irrevocable."

Our relation to the Jews thus implies both present communion and future hope. This is a view sympathetic to that of Moltmann, with the exception that it is critical of a millennialism that lacks solid support either in Romans 9–11 or more broadly in Scripture as a whole.

We must acknowledge with deep sadness that, taken as a whole, the history of Christendom's relation to God's first (and God's future!) people was summarized accurately by Paul, "wise in your own conceits." All too frequently Christians have laid claim to being God's people with an arrogance reminiscent of that which called forth God's wrath on ancient Israel in the time of the prophets. Too often Christians have sought to insulate themselves against God's judgment on sectarian pride by narrowing the vision of the peoplehood of God so as to identify it exclusively as a Christian possession. What more vivid proof of this could be given than the long history of wrongs committed by Christians against Jews, beginning in the early centuries of the church, continuing through medieval and reformation times, and culminating in the greatest human atrocity of modern history, the Nazi holocaust. Within the church, this shameful record calls for a repentance leading to a more accurate understanding of the Jewish-Christian relationship: "natural branches" related to branches "cut off from what is by nature a wild olive tree, and grafted, contrary to nature, into a cultivated olive tree." For clarity on this historical relationship will keep Christians mindful of the dependency implicit in this relationship: "Remember, it is not you that support the root, but the root that supports you." Acknowledgment of their historical dependence on God's first people in turn prepares Christians to acknowledge their ultimate dependence on God.

Much is to be gained by finally healing this important relationship and placing it firmly upon a true historical foundation. If Christians learn to reaffirm their covenant with God by reaffirming the eternal validity of God's covenant and promises with Israel, they will recapture a clear vision of their place as a covenant people in God's universal plan for Israel and the whole human family.

From the perspective of this vision alone can Christians hope to develop an authentic relationship with Judaism, a relationship opened up by repentance of past sin and by devotion to God's reign of righteousness first revealed to the Jews. Without claiming to know the mind of God by specifying timetables for God's future with the Jews or precise formats for contemporary rapprochement between Jewish and Christian communities, Jews and Christians together can take an important step forward by living with faith and quiet trust based on the testimony of their common biblical heritage to God's fidelity to God's plan for the human family. That is to say, because that plan is one, and is inclusive of all God's people, Jews and Christians can work together, pray together, and celebrate together in the confidence that all those doing justice and loving-kindness, and walking humbly with their God are on a pilgrimage leading toward the reign of peace that one day will unite all the faithful under God's righteous sovereignty.

F. SCRIPTURE: THE FOUNDATIONAL CHAPTERS IN A FAITH COMMUNITY'S AUTOBIOGRAPHY

This study of the community of faith in the Bible thus is not an exercise in disinterested historical construction of an ancient cult. It is rather to be viewed as an important aspect of learning what it means to be a community of faith today. All those who find themselves called into such a community are present in the world as an extension of an unbroken community of God's people extending over the ages through the confessional response of believers to what they discerned as the presence of God in their worship and in the events around them. In our time as well, the authentic community within which life's meaning is discovered continues to grow through the gathering of those responding to God's call to fellowship and being drawn by God's Spirit into participation in the ongoing creative, redemptive stream that continues to be present for the redemption and healing of individuals, nations, and the whole creation.

As Karl Barth observed in the preface to his epoch-making Romans commentary, we go to Scripture not as aliens but as spiritual descendants.[7] We are open to the testimony of our ancestors in the faith as to how we can more fully live in the presence of God, for we are a community deriving our identity and vocation from the same divine Presence who constituted them as a people of God. For this reason, we find that the kind of history presented by the Bible is well suited for our purposes. It is obviously not a history designed in the first instance for reconstruction of the *bruta facta* of antiquity. From the time of its birth as a people, Israel *interpreted* its history, and then transmitted that history in oral and written tradition as an expression of life in fellowship with God and in response to God's call, God's promises, and God's commandments. In other words, the history we receive from the Bible is the history of a community of faith.

The interpretation of history as the expression of a divine-human relationship runs throughout Scripture. Israel's birth as a people in the exodus was interpreted as a call to fellowship with Yahweh, its incorpo-

---

7. K. Barth, *The Epistle to the Romans*, trans. E. C. Hoskyns (London: Oxford University Press, 1933), p. 1.

ration as a people of the Covenant was traced to God's revelation of divine will on Sinai, its discovery of a land to live in was regarded as the fulfillment of promises made long before to the patriarchs and so on. This history, though interpreted in the relational terms of a covenant between God and Israel, nonetheless was not utopian, but remarkably realistic. More often than not, events interpreted as evidence of God's initiating grace were seen to elicit within the people not obedience of trust, but rebelliousness and hardness of heart. Therefore the group keeping alive this history of interpretaion was often a slender minority in Israel. But persistently that minority interpreted even the resulting tragedies and catastrophes within the framework of the relationship between God and responding people; even wantonness and a turning to other gods was interpreted as a response to God, albeit a negative one. It was within the history of this covenant relationship that each new generation was summoned to respond as a community of faith; that is, as a people defining itself primarily in relation to its participation in God's purpose for the world.

As communities of faith today draw on this heritage for their own sense of identity, they draw on a vividly comprehensible history, for faithfulness and hard-heartedness are the alternatives they also face as they seek to bear witness to compassion and justice in the world. And from the community of faith in Scripture they learn a fundamental lesson of life: in the day-to-day vocation of relating to the challenges and needs of the world, they are either retreating from or being drawn more intimately toward the heart of all reality, the God whose presence in the world defines decisions and actions as either faithful or perfidious.

We see, therefore, that the confessional quality of biblical history makes it a source ideally suited for the contemporary community of faith in its search for an understanding of its life as a people of God and of world events as manifestations of God's ongoing creative and redemptive acts.[8] But this confessional quality also raises an important question: is the history in relation to which God responds in the Bible merely a construct of faith, an inner or spiritual history bearing little or no relation to the *bruta facta* of the real world? If so, the relevance of this source as a pattern for a faith community's response to contemporary events is called into question, for these events *are* concrete, *are* historically real. Although a particular school of existential interpretation has emphasized the spiritual nature of the biblical traditions at the

8. M. H. Goshen-Gottstein, in reflecting on the character of Jewish biblical theology, has written, ". . . the truth of the Tanakh theologian is not that of the historian, for the theologian looks for truths embedded in the depths of the text—not for truth on the surface of events." "Tanakh Theology: Religion of the Old Testament and the Place of Jewish Biblical Theology," *Ancient Israelite Religion: Essays in Honor of Frank Moore Cross*, in P. D. Miller, Jr., P. D. Hanson, and S. D. McBride, Jr., eds. (Philadelphia: Fortress Press, in press), p. 59.

cost of their grounding in concrete happenings of history,[9] a balanced approach will not overlook one of the unique characteristics of the confessional traditions of the Bible, namely, their firm grounding in the actual happenings of history. The existentialistic overemphasis on the subjective was, to be sure, encouraged by a naive historiography that defined historical tradition in narrow, positivistic terms, and then went to ancient sources, biblical and extrabiblical, literary and artifactual, to prove or disprove the biblical account. Once a more adequate historiography is adopted, however, it becomes clear that from the exodus period onward (and to a certain extent even from patriarchal times in the Middle Bronze and Late Bronze Ages), the historical traditions of the Bible betray roots in the actual events of the ancient world. It was in the concrete realities and happenings of this world that Israel encountered and responded to its God.

The ontology of events that enables us to deal in a balanced way with the "objective" and "subjective" dimensions of Israel's historical traditions has been described in detail elsewhere.[10] It is sufficient here to note that Israel's and the early church's interpretation of history serves as a model of precisely the kind of interpretation called for in communities of faith today. It will be an interpretation taking into full account the actual happenings of the real world, viewing them from the perspective of the confessional heritage in an effort to understand their meaning in relation to divine purpose. On the basis of such an interpretive process, the community of faith today can respond to contemporary events as an agent in the world dedicated not to the partial plans for humanity of different nations or interest groups, but to the universal plan for peace wedded with justice intended by the God of all nations and peoples.

In tracing the development of the notion of the community of faith in the Bible, we use all available tools and sources of data so as to reconstruct the unfolding of this phenomenon as accurately and as comprehensibly as possible. What comes into view is an ongoing chain of the community of faith's responses to historical events interpreted as episodes in one divine drama. The situation varies among these responses regarding the degree of accuracy with which reconstruction can be accomplished. And it is clear that the overall reconstruction of the emergence of the community of faith in the Bible that we sketch will be subject to constant revision. Nevertheless, we believe that one of the lessons gained from this study will be this: if we open our eyes to the community of faith that took shape in biblical times, the way in which we look on the communities of faith of which we are a part will be radically transformed.

---

9. See F. Hesse, "The Evaluation and the Authority of O.T. Texts," in *Essays on Old Testament Hermeneutics*, C. Westermann, ed., J. L. Mays, trans. (Richmond: John Knox Press, 1963), pp. 285–313.

10. See P. D. Hanson, *Dynamic Transcendence*, and P. D. Hanson, *Diversity of Scripture*.

A Select List of Related Books

CHAPTERS I–III

Albright, W. F., *From Stone Age to Christianity.* New York: Doubleday, 1957.
———. *Yahweh and the Gods of Canaan.* New York: Doubleday, 1968.
Alt, A. *Essays on Old Testament History and Religion.* New York: Doubleday, 1968.
Anderson, B. W. *Creation Versus Chaos.* New York: Association Press, 1967.
———. *Understanding the Old Testament.* Englewood Cliffs, N.J.: Prentice-Hall, 1975.
Baltzer, K. *The Covenant Formulary in Old Testament, Jewish and Early Christian Writings.* Philadelphia: Fortress Press, 1971.
Cross, F. M. *Canaanite Myth and Hebrew Epic.* Cambridge, Mass.: Harvard University Press, 1972.
de Vaux, R. *Ancient Israel: Its Life and Institutions.* New York: McGraw-Hill, 1961.
Eichrodt, W. *Theology of the Old Testament.* 2 vols. Philadelphia: Westminster, 1961 (vol. I), 1967 (vol. II).
Frankfort, H. *Before Philosophy.* London: Penguin, 1949.
Freedman, D. N., and Graff, D. F. *Palestine in Transition: The Emergence of Ancient Israel.* Scheffield: Almond Press, 1983.
Gottwald, N. *The Tribes of Yahweh.* Maryknoll, N.Y.: Orbis Books, 1979.
Hanson, P. D. "The Theological Significance of Contradiction in the Book of the Covenant." In G. W. Coats and B. O. Long, eds., *Canon and Authority.* Philadelphia: Fortress Press, 1977.
———. "The Decalogue Within the Covenant Community." *Lutheran Theological Seminary Bulletin* 61 (1981): 14–36.
———. *Dynamic Transcendence.* Philadelphia: Fortress Press, 1978.
———. "War and Peace in the Hebrew Bible." *Int* 38 (1984): 341–362.
Harrelson, W. *The Ten Commandments and Human Rights.* Philadelphia: Fortress Press, 1980.
Hayes, J., and Miller, M., eds. *Israelite and Judaean History.* Philadelphia: Westminster, 1977.
Herrmann, S. *A History of Israel in Old Testament Times.* Philadelphia: Fortress Press, 1981.
Hillers, D. R. *Covenant: The History of a Biblical Idea.* Baltimore: Johns Hopkins University Press, 1970.
Kraus, H. J. *The People of God in the Old Testament.* New York and London: Association Press, 1958.
———. *Worship in Israel.* Richmond: John Knox Press, 1965.
McCarthy, D. H. *The Old Testament Covenant.* Richmond: John Knox Press, 1972.
Mendenhall, G. E. "Ancient Oriental and Biblical Law." *BA* 17 (1954a): 26–46.

————. "Covenant Forms in Israelite Tradition." *BA* 17 (1954b): 50–76.

Noth, M. *The History of Israel.* New York: Harper and Brothers, 1960.

————. *The Laws of the Pentateuch and Other Essays.* Philadelphia: Fortress Press, 1967.

————. *A History of Pentateuchal Traditions.* Englewood Cliffs, N.J.: Prentice-Hall, 1972.

Orlinksy, H. *Ancient Israel.* Ithaca, N.Y.: Cornell University Press, 1960.

Ringgren, H. *Israelite Religion.* Philadelphia: Fortress Press, 1966.

Rowley, H. H. *Worship in Ancient Israel.* London: SPCK, 1967.

Stamm, J., and Andrew, M. E. *The Ten Commandments in Recent Research.* Naperville, Ill.: Allenson, 1967.

von Rad, G. *Old Testament Theology.* 2 vols. New York: Harper & Row, 1962 (vol. I), 1965 (vol. II).

————. *The Problem of the Pentateuch and Other Essays.* New York: McGraw-Hill, 1966.

Waltzer, Michael. *Exodus and Revolution.* New York: Basic Books, 1984.

Weippert, M. *The Settlement of the Israelite Tribes in Palestine.* London: SCM, 1972.

Wright, G. E. *God Who Acts.* Naperville, Ill.: Allenson, 1952.

CHAPTERS IV–VI

Alt, A. "The Formation of the Israelite State in Palestine." In *Essays in Old Testament History and Religion*, trans. by R. A. Wilson. New York: Doubleday, 1968.

Birch, B. C. *The Rise of the Israelite Monarchy: The Growth and Development of I Samuel 7–15.* SBLDS 27. Missoula, Mont.: Scholars Press, 1976.

Blenkinsopp, J. *A History of Prophecy in Israel from Settlement in the Land to the Hellenistic Period.* Philadelphia: Westminster Press, 1983.

Bright, J. *Jeremiah.* AB 21. New York: Doubleday, 1965.

Brueggemann, W. *The Prophetic Imagination.* Philadelphia: Fortress Press, 1978.

————. *Genesis.* Interpretation. Atlanta: John Knox Press, 1982.

Bryce, G. E. *A Legacy of Wisdom.* Lewisburg, Pa.: Bucknell University Press, 1979.

Clements, R. E. *God and Temple.* Philadelphia: Fortress Press, 1965.

————. *God's Chosen People: A Theological Interpretation of the Book of Deuteronomy.* London: SCM, 1968.

————. *Prophecy and Tradition.* Atlanta: John Knox Press, 1975.

Clifford, R. *The Cosmic Mountain in Canaan and the Old Testament.* HSM 4. Cambridge, Mass.: Harvard University Press, 1972.

Crenshaw, J. L. *Old Testament Wisdom. An Introduction.* Atlanta: John Knox Press, 1981.

Halpern, B. *The Constitution of the Monarchy.* HSM 25. Chico, Calif.: Scholars Press, 1981.

Hanson, P. D. *The Diversity of Scripture.* OBT 11. Philadelphia: Fortress Press, 1982.

Ishida, Tomoo. *The Royal Dynasties in Ancient Israel. A Study on the Formation and Development of Royal-Dynastic Ideology.* BZAW 142. Berlin: de Gruyter, 1977.

Kaiser, O. *Isaiah 13–39*. OTL. Philadelphia: Westminster Press, 1974.

———. *Isaiah 1–12*. OTL. 2nd ed. Philadelphia: Westminster Press, 1983.

Levenson, J. *Sinai and Zion: An Entry into the Jewish Bible*. Minneapolis: Winston Press, 1985.

Malamat, A. "Organs of Statecraft in the Israelite Monarchy." *BA* 28 (1965): 34–65.

Mays, J. L. *Amos, A Commentary*. OTL. London: SCM, 1969a.

———. *Hosea, A Commentary*. OTL. London: SCM, 1969b.

McCarter, P. K. *I Samuel*. AB 8. New York: Doubleday, 1980.

Mettinger, T. N. D. *Solomonic State Officials: A Study of the Civil Government Officials of the Israelite Monarchy*. ConBOT 5. Lund, Sweden: Gleerup, 1971.

———. *King and Messiah: The Civil and Sacramental Legitimization of Israelite Kings*. Lund, Sweden: Gleerup, 1971.

Miller, P. D., Jr. *The Divine Warrior in Early Israel*. HSM 5. Cambridge, Mass.: Harvard University Press, 1973.

———. *Genesis 1–11: Studies in Structure and Theme*. JSOTSuppl 8. Sheffield, England: JSOT Press, 1978.

Mowinckel, S. *He That Cometh*. New York: Abingdon Press, 1956a.

———. *The Psalms in Israel's Worship*. New York: Abingdon Press, 1956b.

Murphy, R. E. *Wisdom Literature: Job, Proverbs, Ruth, Canticles, Ecclesiastes, and Esther*. FOTL 13. Grand Rapids, Mich.: Eerdmans, 1981.

Nicholson, E. W. *Deuteronomy and Tradition*. Oxford, England: Blackwell, 1967.

Noth, M. "God, King and Nation in the Old Testament." In *The Laws of the Pentateuch and Other Studies*. trans. D. R. Ap-Thomas. London: Oliver and Boyd, 1966.

Roberts, J. J. M. "The Davidic Origin of the Zion Tradition." *JBL* 92 (1973): 329–44.

Tadmor, H. "Traditional Institutions and the Monarchy: Social and Political Tensions in the Time of David and Solomon." In T. Ishida, ed., *Studies in the Period of David and Solomon and Other Essays*. Tokyo: Yamakawa-Shuppansha, 1982.

von Rad, G. *Deuteronomy*. OTL. Philadelphia: Westminster Press, 1956.

Weinfeld, M. *Deuteronomy and the Deuteronomic School*. Oxford, England: At the Clarendon Press, 1972.

Welch, A. C. *Prophet and Priest in Old Israel*. New York: Macmillan, 1953.

Whilelam, K. W. *The Just King: Monarchical Judicial Authority in Ancient Israel*. JSOTSuppl 12. Sheffield, England: JSOT Press, 1979.

Wilson, R. R. *Prophecy and Society in Ancient Israel*. Philadelphia: Fortress Press, 1980.

Wolff, H. W. *Hosea*. Hermeneia. Philadelphia: Fortress Press, 1974.

———. *Joel and Amos*. Hermeneia. Philadelphia: Fortress Press, 1977.

CHAPTERS VII–X

Ackroyd, P. R. *Exile and Restoration*. Philadelphia: Westminster Press, 1968.

Bickermann, Elias. *From Ezra to the Last of the Maccabees: Foundations of Post-biblical Judaism*. New York: Schocken Books, 1962.

Cross, F. M. "A Reconstruction of the Judaean Restoration." *JBL* 94 (1975): 4–18.

Freedman, D. N. "The Chronicler's Purpose." *CBQ* 23 (1961): 436–42.

Greenberg, M. *Ezekiel 1–20.* AB 22. New York: Doubleday, 1983.

Hanson, P. D. *The Dawn of Apocalyptic: The Historical and Sociological Roots of Jewish Apocalyptic Eschatology.* Philadelphia: Fortress Press, 1979.

———. "Israelite Religion in the Early Post-Exilic Period." In P. D. Miller, Jr., P. D. Hanson, and S. D. McBride, Jr., eds., *Ancient Israelite Religion: Essays in Honor of Frank Moore Cross.* Philadelphia: Fortress Press, 1986.

Japhet, S. "Sheshbazzar and Zerubbabel—Against the Background of the Historical and Religious Tendencies of Ezra-Nehemiah." *ZAW* 94 (1982): 66–98.

Kaufmann, Y. *The Babylonian Captivity and Deutero-Isaiah.* New York: Union of American Hebrew Congregations, 1970.

Klein, R. W. *Israel in Exile. A Theological Interpretation.* OBT 6. Philadelphia: Fortress Press, 1979.

Koch, K. "Ezra and the Origins of Judaism." *JSS* 19 (1974): 173–97.

Levenson, J. D. *The Theology of the Program of Restoration of Ezekiel 40–48.* HSM 10. Missoula, Mont.: Scholars Press, 1976.

McEvenue, S. E. "The Political Structure in Judah from Cyrus to Nehemiah." *CBQ* 44 (1981): 353–64.

McKenzie, J. L. *Second Isaiah.* AB 20. New York: Doubleday, 1968.

Meyers, J. *I Chronicles.* AB 12. New York: Doubleday, 1965a.

———. *II Chronicles.* AB 13. New York: Doubleday, 1965b.

———. *Ezra and Nehemiah.* AB 14. New York: Doubleday, 1965c.

Mowinckel, S. *He That Cometh.* Nashville: Abingdon Press, 1955.

Petersen, D. L. *Late Israelite Prophecy: Studies in Deutero-Prophetic Literature and in Chronicles.* SBLMS 23. Missoula, Mont.: Scholars Press, 1977.

Plöger, O. *Theocracy and Eschatology.* Richmond, Va.: John Knox Press, 1968.

Smith, M. *Palestinian Parties and Politics That Shaped the Old Testament.* New York: Columbia University Press, 1971.

Steck, O. H. "Theological Streams of Tradition." In *Tradition and Theology in the Old Testament.* Philadelphia: Fortress Press, 1977.

Westermann, C. *Second Isaiah.* OTL. Philadelphia: Westminster Press, 1969.

Williamson, H. G. M. *Israel in the Books of Chronicles.* Cambridge, England: Cambridge University Press, 1977.

Whybray, R. N. *The Second Isaiah.* Sheffield, England: JSOT Press, 1983.

Zimmerli, W. *Ezekiel 1.* Hermeneia. Philadelphia: Fortress Press, 1979.

———. *Ezekiel 2.* Hermeneia. Philadelphia: Fortress Press, 1983.

CHAPTERS XI–XII

Collins, J. J. *The Apocalyptic Vision of the Book of Daniel.* HSM 16. Missoula, Mont.: Scholars Press, 1977.

———. *Between Athens and Jerusalem. Jewish Identity in the Hellenistic Diaspora.* New York: Crossroad, 1983.

Cross, F. M. *The Ancient Library of Qumran.* New York: Doubleday, 1961.

Hanson, P. D. "Rebellion in Heaven, Azazel and Euhemeristic Heroes in I Enoch 6–11." *JBL* 96 (1977): 195–233.

———. "Apocalyptic Literature." In D. A. Knight and G. M. Tucker, eds., *The Hebrew Bible and Its Modern Interpreters.* Philadelphia: Fortress Press, 1985.

Hartman, L. F., and DiLella, A. A. *Daniel.* AB 23. New York: Doubleday, 1978.

Hengel, M. *Judaism and Hellenism. Studies in Their Encounter in Palestine During the Early Hellenistic Period.* 2 vols. Philadelphia: Fortress Press, 1974.

Koch, K. *The Rediscovery of Apocalyptic.* SBT 22. London: SCM, 1972.

Lacocque, A. *The Book of Daniel.* Atlanta: John Knox Press, 1979.

Milik, J. *The Books of Enoch.* Oxford, England: At the Clarendon Press, 1976.

Montgomery, J. A. *The Book of Daniel.* ICC. Edinburgh: T. and T. Clark, 1927.

Neusner, J. *Judaism: The Evidence of the Mishnah.* Chicago: University of Chicago Press, 1981.

Nickelsburg, G. W. E. *Jewish Literature Between the Bible and the Mishnah.* Philadelphia: Fortress Press, 1981.

Purvis, J. D. *The Samaritan Pentateuch and the Origin of the Samaritan Sect.* HSM 2. Cambridge, Mass.: Harvard University Press, 1968.

Russell, D. S. *The Method and Message of Jewish Apocalyptic.* OTL. Philadelphia: Westminster Press, 1964.

Schäfer, P. "The Hellenistic and Maccabaean Periods." In J. H. Hayes and J. Miller, eds., *Israelite and Jewish History.* Philadelphia: Westminster Press, 1977.

Tcherikover, V. *Hellenistic Civilization and the Jews.* New York: Jewish Publication Society of America, 1961.

Towner, W. S. *Daniel.* Interpretation. Atlanta: John Knox Press, 1984.

Urbach, E. E. *The Sages: Their Concepts and Beliefs.* Jerusalem: Magnes Press, 1975.

Vermes, G. *The Dead Sea Scrolls: Qumran in Perspective.* Philadelphia: Fortress Press, 1977.

CHAPTERS XIII–XIV

Bornkamm, G. *Jesus of Nazareth.* New York: Harper & Row, 1960.

Bowker, J. *Jesus and the Pharisees.* Cambridge, England: Cambridge University Press, 1973.

Breech, J. *The Silence of Jesus: The Authentic Voice of the Historical Man.* Philadelphia: Fortress Press, 1983.

Crossan, J. D. *In Parables: The Challenge of the Historical Jesus.* New York: Harper & Row, 1973.

Fiorenza, E. Schussler. *In Memory of Her: A Feminist Theological Reconstruction of Christian Origins.* New York: Crossroad, 1984.

Furnish, V. P. *Theology and Ethics in Paul.* Nashville: Abingdon Press, 1968.

Gager, J. G. *Kingdom and Community: The Social World of Early Christianity.* Englewood Cliffs, N.J.: Prentice-Hall, 1975.

Harrington, D. J. *God's People in Christ: New Testament Perspectives on the Church and Judaism.* OBT 1. Philadelphia: Fortress Press, 1980.

Käsemann, E. "Ministry and Community in the New Testament." In *Essays on New Testament Themes,* trans. by W. J. Montague. Philadelphia: Fortress Press, 1982.

Koester, H. *Introduction to the New Testament.* 2 vols. Philadelphia: Fortress Press, 1982.

Meeks, W. *The First Urban Christians: The Social World of the Apostle Paul.* New Haven, Conn.: Yale University Press, 1983.

Perrin, N. *Rediscovering the Teachings of Jesus.* London: SCM, 1967.

Richardson, P. *Israel in the Apostolic Church.* SNTSM 10. New York: Cambridge University Press, 1970.

Robinson, J. M., and Koester, H. *Trajectories Through Early Christianity.* Philadelphia: Fortress Press, 1971.

Scroggs, R. *Paul for a New Day.* Philadelphia: Fortress Press, 1977.

Stendahl, K. *The School of St. Matthew and Its Use of the Old Testament.* Philadelphia: Fortress Press, 1968.

Theissen, G. *The First Followers of Jesus: A Sociological Analysis of the Earliest Christianity.* London: SCM, 1978.

CHAPTER XV

Birch, B. C., and Rasmussen, L. L. *Bible and Ethics in the Christian Life.* Minneapolis: Augsburg, 1976.

Goshen-Gottstein, M. H. "Tanakh Theology: Religion of the Old Testament and the Place of Jewish Biblical Theology." In P. D. Miller, Jr., P. D. Hanson, and S. D. McBride, Jr., eds., *Ancient Israelite Religion: Essays in Honor of Frank Moore Cross.* Philadelphia: Fortress Press, in press.

Gutiérrez, G. C. Inda and J. Eagleson, eds., *A Theology of Liberation: History, Politics and Salvation.* Maryknoll, N.Y.: Orbis Books, 1973.

Hanson, P. D. "The Role of Scripture in Times of Crisis." *Word and World* 1 (1981): 116–27.

———. "The Identity and Purpose of the Church." *Theology Today* 42 (1985): 342–52.

Küng, H. *The Church.* New York: Sheed & Ward, 1967.

Moltmann, J. *The Church in the Power of the Spirit: A Contribution to Messianic Ecclesiology.* New York: Harper & Row, 1977.

Ogletree, T. W. *The Use of the Bible in Christian Ethics.* Philadelphia: Westminster Press, 1983.

Segundo, J. L. *The Community Called Church.* Trans. J. Drury. Maryknoll, N.Y.: Orbis Books, 1973.

———. *Liberation of Theology.* Trans. J. Drury. Maryknoll, N.Y.: Orbis Books, 1976.

Sider, R. J. *Rich Christians in an Age of Hunger.* London: Hodder and Stoughton, 1977.

Thoma, C. *A Christian Theology of Judaism.* New York: Paulist Press, 1980.

General Index

Aaron, 226–27, 231f, 335
ʿabdê hammêlek, 115
Abiathar, 102, 105
Abner, 101
Abraham, 16f, 450
Acra, 343
Acts, Book of, 465f
ʾādām, 130f
Adonijah, 105
Adultery, 61
Ahab, 65, 141–47
Ahaz, 187–90
Ahijah, 133f, 137–38
Akiba, 357
Alexander Jannaeus, 352
Alexander the Great, 326
Alien, 46, 83
Altar, 356
Amarna, 38n
Amaziah, 150
Amenemopet, 209
Amidah, 411
Amos, 48–58, 150–51
Anathoth, 198
Androcentric bias, 165n
Animal Apocalypse, 360–62
Anthropology, 206
Antiochus III, 341
Antiochus IV Epiphanes, 329f, 337, 340, 341–44, 363
Anti-Semitism, 86, 543
Apocalypse of Weeks, 362
Apocalypticism, 268–77, 344, 346–57: Christian, 455f; second century BCE, 360: at Qumran, 364–72
Apostasy, 193, 198f, 218f
Apostle Paul, 79
Apostles, 461
Apostolic succession, 461
ʾAraq el-Amir, 335n
Aristocracy, 115f
Ark, 33, 102, 175, 179
Artapanus, 330
Artaxerxes I, 294–98
Asa, 179–80
ʾāšām, 247, 249
Asherah, 326
Assyria, 160
Astarte, 327

Atonement, 226–30, 246–49, 356, 360
Augustine, 58
Authority, 375–77, 421, 487; biblical, 488f, 520, 535–37; divine, 504

Baal, 110, 141–47, 150, 165
Baal religion, 35f
Babylon, 225
Babylonians, 216
Banquet, 273, 371n, 402, 412
Baptism, 436–39, 444f, 457, 485f
Bar Kochba, 357
Baruch, 203
Bathsheba, 103, 105
Benjamin, 36
Bethel, 137–38, 151, 156
Biblical theology, xiii
Birth narrative of Jesus, 463f
Bishops, 443, 462, 487
Blessing, 229
Blood, 40, 228–29
Blood guilt, 227f
Bondage, 27, 56, 115, 119, 228, 235, 397, 422, 425, 430, 500, 511
Brokenness, 24, 219, 236f, 388
Bureaucracy, 106

Calendar, 362f, 370, 506
Called people, 428
Canaanite religion, 88, 129, 140–42, 167
Case laws, 44f, 51, 71
Change, 4, 76–77
Chaos, 109, 113, 118, 128, 161–62, 190, 199, 226, 230, 254, 258, 267, 273, 276, 354, 359, 363, 475
Charismata, 492
Children, 431
Chosen people, 458
Christ, body of, 444f, 447, 449, 457, 485, 503
Christology, 434–36
Chronicler's History, 199f, 263, 265, 300–11
Church, 429, 466, 483, 527; order, 452, 462, 466, 487
Church-state relations, 493–96
Circumcision, 435, 438f
City-states, 16
Civil authority, 462, 465f, 493–96

Civil religion, 494
Code of Hammurabi, 47, 112
Colossians, Letter to the, 457
Common meal, 370f, 371n, 437
Communal structures, 42, 44
Community: as agent of divine healing,
    503–18; as context for biblical
    interpretation, 537; origin of, 21–29; as
    participating in redemptive activity,
    513f, 533; as a possession of God, 517;
    qualities of, 1f, 5, 28, 70–78;
    terminology, 6–9
Compassion, 5, 27, 30, 45, 47, 49, 52,
    72–76, 80, 84, 91, 119, 146, 156–57,
    166, 174, 183, 193, 211, 223, 239, 241,
    247, 259, 295–97, 307f, 316f, 320,
    375f, 408, 424f, 470–71, 507f, 510
Confederacy, 30
Confessional heritage, 4, 394
Continuity, 76; and change, 208, 230f,
    283–94, 438
Cosmic mountain, 28, 108f
Covenant, 3n, 10, 11f, 17, 27, 33, 39–41,
    43, 70, 76, 103, 152–53, 155, 158, 163f,
    165–67, 169, 171, 180, 195, 198f,
    206–07, 220, 229, 240, 271, 278f, 295,
    470f, 472, 501; Abrahamic, 225; book
    of the, 33, 42–52, 55, 154; broken, 499;
    conditional, 170, 179–81, 185, 204f;
    Davidic, 101–04, 107–09; with death,
    185f, 188; with Levi, 282f; Noatic, 225;
    unconditional, 109, 119, 122f;
    Yahwistic, 103f
Creation, 60, 127–32, 225, 473, 486f,
    499, 516
Cross, 422f
Crucifixion, 434, 439
Cult, 42, 154f, 222, 227, 234, 307
Cult festivals, 107
Cyrus, 215, 233, 235f

Dan, 137f
Daniel, 344
dāt, 293
David, 101–04, 264, 269, 301, 316
Deacons, 443, 462
Dead Sea Scrolls, 347, 364–72, 375
Death, 246–47; of Jesus, 421–23, 434
Deborah, Song of, 37
Decalogue, 11, 53–63, 161, 171, 404
Democratization, 257, 274
Despair, 253
Deuteronomistic History, 31, 34, 199f
Deuteronomy, Book of, 167–76
Devotion, 69–70
Dialectic, 76, 80, 89, 193; visionary-
    pragmatic, 250f, 253, 256, 347, 380,
    478f
Didache, 460
Dietary laws, 435

Discipleship, 430–33
Discrimination, 53, 174
Dissidents, 269–77, 288–90, 313, 321,
    365, 478
Diversity, 313, 356f, 380, 499, 526, 531f,
    533f; of talents, 449; theological, xiii, 4,
    6f
Divine: assembly, 234f; council, 265;
    curse, 262; grace, 439; mountain, 181;
    name, 176; order, 226; purpose, 4, 5,
    19, 29, 162, 421; wrath, 319
Divorce, 405
Doctrine, 452; of the Two Ways, 460–61
Domitian, 455
Doubt, 212
Dynamism, 75
Dynasty, 120, 122f

Early Catholicism, 466
Earth's resources, 508
Ecclesiastes, 213
Ecclesiasticus, 333–39
Ecclesiology, 461, 468
ʿedâ, 7, 24, 138f, 369
Edict of Cyrus, 255
Egyptian religion, 112
ekklesia, 7, 24, 428
Election, 109, 181, 275, 539
Elephantine, 327, 335n
Eliashib, 328f
Elijah, 141–45
Elisha, 142
Elohist Document, 17n
Empowerment, 26, 67, 456
Enemies, 392
I Enoch, 358
Enūma eliš, 130
Equality, 23, 174, 469, 472, 501, 509
ʿēreb, 2, 299
Eschatology, 3, 126f, 191–93, 231f, 258,
    268, 283, 301, 313f, 337f, 379f, 433,
    466, 474–77, 480f, 482; early Christian,
    395f, 401, 409, 415f, 417–21, 431;
    among Essenes, 358; in Jesus' teaching,
    384f, 391f; in Paul, 440–42; among
    Pharisees, 357
Essenes, 338, 342, 347–48, 352, 354,
    358–65, 374–82, 390; eschatology
    among, 358
Ethical responsibility, 444
Ethics, 462f; in Paul, 447f, 457, 462f, 470
Eucharist, 454, 457
Evil, 276
Exclusivism, 375–76
Exile, 224–29
Exodus, 2, 10f, 12, 19, 19n, 42
Exploitation, 48
Ezekiel, 216–24
Ezra, 291–93, 305, 309

Faith, 78, 206, 439–42, 485; social nature of, 510
Faithfulness, 29, 189
Fellowship, 501–03
Fertility, 110–11, 142
Festivals, 51, 51n
Flood, 272, 359
Foreign: nations, 319; policy, 106, 161, 187
Foreigners, 289, 298, 304, 315f, 317
Forgiveness, 185, 412
Freedom, 2, 56, 66, 116, 173, 212, 425, 436f, 440, 450, 469, 501, 504, 506
Fulness of time, 387f

Gabriel, 345
Gender, 53; bias, 165n
Genealogies, 16
Gentiles, 337, 437–39, 466, 484; Gentile mission, 437f, 450, 451
gēr, 46
Gerizim, 327f, 335n
Gerousia, 343, 348, 352
Gilgal, 31, 33, 37–39, 91, 91n
Gilgamesh, 130n
Gnosticism, 451f, 457, 486f
God: as center of a community's devotion, 455, 493, 504–07; as deliverer, 2, 12, 20f, 21, 25, 43, 47, 321, 397, 470, 500f; as initiator of community, 2–5, 24, 40, 50, 69, 447, 469, 513; as judge, 184; as participating in redemptive activity, 513f; as purposer, 332; as redeemer, 27; as sole sovereign, 124–25, 145, 158, 161, 171, 186, 188, 190, 207, 235, 242, 258, 399, 472f, 477, 504–07; as sustainer, 28; as warrior, 21, 37, 258, 267f, 270–73, 283, 313, 344f, 360
Gomer, 164–65
Grace, 2, 11f, 24, 43, 56, 80, 172, 175, 236f, 244, 250, 320, 402, 407, 440, 445, 471, 502f

ḥābûrâ, 353, 356, 378, 400
Haggai, 257, 261–63
hakkōhēn, 232
hălākā, 354
Hannah, Song of, 65–69, 74
Harmony, 3n
hăsîdîm, 343–49, 352, 358, 361, 364–66
Hasmoneans, 346, 365f, 367, 373–74
Heavenly Luminaries, Book of the, 363
Hebrew Bible, 520–22
Hebrews, Letter to, 456
Hellenism, 340f, 342, 373
Hellenization, 325–27, 329f
Heredity, 298–300
Heresy, 452, 487
Hermeneutics, 487–89, 524, 524–37; existentialist, 545f

Herod, 354f
ḥêsed, 27, 28, 43
Hezekiah, 197, 201–02
High priest, 265, 277, 335; Jesus as, 456
High priesthood, 329
Hillel, 353, 355
History, 12n, 230, 544f; as context of biblical faith, 538; as religiously significant, 470
ḥokmâ, 405
Holiness, 26, 40, 43, 173, 217f, 228, 256f, 261, 354, 369–71, 378
Holy Spirit, 436–38, 491f; see also Spirit of Christ
Holy war, 142, 234; see also God, as warrior
Hope, 499f
ḥopšî, 52, 52n
Hosea, 158–67, 198
ḥps, 246f
Human response, 3, 469
Hymn, 26–28, 37, 67
Hyrcanus I, John, 352

Idolatry, 57–59, 124, 138, 158, 504–05
ʿimmanûʾēl, 189
Inclusiveness, 40, 400, 403f, 417–20, 424f, 442f, 469, 481f, 486, 526
Indictment, 161
Individual, 208–11, 214, 222f; personhood, 501f
Institutions, 23, 491f
Interest, 49
Isaiah, 181–94
Isaiah Apocalypse, 271–73
Ishbaal, 101
Israel, 38; savlation of, 450f

Jabneh, 355, 453
Jacob, 165f
James, Letter of, 41f, 459
Jason, 329, 342f
Jehoiakim, 203
Jehoshaphat, 142
Jehu, 147, 165
Jeremiah, 198–209, 368, 422
Jeroboam, 133f, 136–39
Jeroboam II, 148f, 159
Jerusalem, 102, 109f
Jerusalem Council, 427, 438
Jesus of Nazareth, 338, 382–87, 480–82; in Christian faith, 483; eschatological teachings of, 384; the historical, 395f; as link between Judaism and Christianity, 497f
Jethro, 20
Jewish roots of Christian faith, 541f
Jewish-Christian relations, 383, 386, 458f, 466, 482f, 496–99, 540
Jezebel, 140f, 144

Jezreel, 165
Joash, 180
Job, Book of, 212
Joel, Book of, 313f
Johanan ben Zakkai, 356, 381
John, Gospel of, 457
John of Patmos, 455
John the Baptist, 338, 396f, 464
Jonah, 317; Book of, 316–21
Jonathan, 346, 366
Jordan, 31
Joseph, 303
Joseph and Aseneth, 330
Josephus, 347–49, 348n, 352, 355, 357, 370n
Joshua, 261–63, 265; Book of, 31–34
Joshua ben Hanahiah, 356
Josiah, 200–07, 216
Jubilee, 240, 255, 403, 464f, 465, 510
Jubilees, Book of, 359
Judah, 81–84
Judaism, 86, 453; separation of Christians from, 456f, 479
Judas Maccabeus, 344
Judgment, 162f, 195–96, 199, 219, 279, 368
Judith, 333
Judith, Book of, 332f
Justice, 23, 41, 47f, 52, 78, 114, 117, 153, 172–73, 187, 193, 204, 242f, 411–12, 423f, 426, 500, 507–09
Justification, 79, 247, 445; by faith, 440, 521

kābôd, 218, 221–22, 225, 261f
Kaddish, 411
kappōret, 229
kērem, 144
King, 474; as reformer, 197f
Kingdom of God, 384, 397–413, 417–20, 431–33, 454, 465f, 512f
Kings and prophets, 98f, 103, 105, 123f, 472
Kingship, 30, 36, 97; absolute, 93f, 102, 104, 133, 143; limited, 90–92, 97f, 101, 104, 126, 133f, 139, 142, 150, 170, 175f, 203, 472, 474; northern, 159f; theological dimension, 116–27
Kuntillet 'Ajrud, 326f, 326n

Land, 28, 31, 64f, 145, 175, 221, 225, 227f, 506
Law, 11n, 82, 441f, 457, 459f
Law and gospel, 57, 79f, 85, 521
League, 11, 11n, 15f, 30, 35 133f
Leontopolis, 335n
Levi, 283
Levirate marriage, 84, 315
Levites, 169, 221, 226–27, 231f, 233, 253, 256, 260, 281f, 288–89, 302, 477

Liberation, 26n, 119
Limited kingship, 90–92, 97f, 109
Liturgy, 40
Lord's prayer, 411–13
Love, 172–74, 233, 407f, 426, 447, 449–50, 450n, 481
Luke, 463–65

Maccabean revolt, 344
Maccabees, 345f
2 Maccabees, 346
3 Maccabees, 330
Magnificat, 402
Malachi, Book of, 266f, 277–87
mal'ākî, 278
Marcion, 429
Marduk, 112
Mari, 16, 64n
Mark, Gospel of, 452
Marriage, 61, 406
māšîah, 235
Mattathias, 340, 344f
Matthew, Gospel of, 452–55
mêlek, 92
Memory, 88
Menelaus, 342–43
Mercy, 78, 411, 426
Merneptah, 38
Mesopotamia, 44
Messiah, 235f, 385f, 391f, 395, 416, 422, 497f; Jesus as, 438f, 450, 497f
Messianic banquet, 437
Messianism, 126f, 192, 263, 415f, 474f, 482f; among Pharisees, 357; at Qumran, 370
Metaphors, 531
Method in biblical research, 7, 12n, 522–37
Micah, 194–97
Micaiah, 142
Michael, 345
Miracles, 413f, 421
Miriam, 30; Song of, 74
Militarization, 116
Mishnah, 336f, 350f, 351n, 354, 357, 381
mišpāt, 243
mišpātîm, 71
Mixed marriages, 294f, 298, 316, 441
Moses, 12, 29, 31, 170, 335
Murder, 61
Mushite priesthood, 105
Mystery, 533f
Myth, 16, 108f, 130, 182f, 222, 272f, 359; conflict, 109f, 455f

Nabaoth, 65, 143–45
Nag Hammadi, 457
nāgîd, 92
nahălâ, 63–65, 104, 144, 149, 195, 240, 294, 509

Nathan, 103
Nations, 258, 267f, 290, 308, 313, 318f, 417
Natural theology, 461
Nature, 118, 127, 129, 132, 167, 473
Neco, 202
Nehemiah, 291–93, 294–98, 309, 329
Nehemiah Memoirs, 292
nepeš, 46
New Covenant, 367f, 369
New Creation, 221, 442, 444, 446, 475
New Testament Gospels, 452
niddûi, 377
Nineveh, 317f
Ninevites, 320f
Noah, 359
nomos, 11n, 78
Northern Kingdom, 302
Nuclear war, 509

Obedience, 161, 173, 206–08, 376, 378, 404f, 409
Omri, 140
Onias II, 329
Onias III, 329, 342f
Onias IV, 335n
Ontology, 488, 529
Openness, 25, 388, 435
Oppressed, 23f, 25, 28, 41, 45, 47, 68, 150
Oppression, 24
Oral tradition, 349f
Order, 109, 112–14, 119, 128, 230, 273
Orphan, 46f, 84
Outsiders, 337, 392f, 400, 439

Papal authority, 461
Parables, 398f, 401
Paradigms, biblical, 8, 529f
Parents, 61
Passion narrative, 421
Passover, 21, 31, 56, 200f
Pastoral Epistles, 462f
Paul, 438, 465, 485
Peace, 3n, 183, 465, 507–09
Pentateuch, 11n
Pentecost, 437f, 465
Persecution, 455
Persians, 255f, 265f, 272f, 292f
pešer, 367
Peter, 465
Pharisees, 82, 338, 342, 348–58, 363f, 375–82, 384, 388, 390f, 400f, 402n, 405, 414f, 433, 440, 453, 458, 479; eschatology among, 357; messianism among, 357
Phinehas, 335
Phoenician religion, 106, 111f, 140
Pluralism, 519f
Polarities, 74–75, 495, 532

Polemic, 233; Jewish-Christian, 458f
Political criticism, 94
Pontius Pilate, 382
Poor, 41, 48, 64, 83, 153, 211, 315
Poverty, 49
Power, 67, 434
Pragmatism, 255–56, 260f, 346, 374
Praise, 28, 67
Prayer, 411
Presbyter-bishops, 461
Presbyters, 462
Presuppositions, 523–25
Pride, 186, 193, 236
Priesthood, 159, 227, 370
Priests, 231f, 332, 376, 472
Priestly writing, 17n, 44, 44n, 130, 224–33, 224n, 261
Privilege, 22, 25, 66, 106, 119, 150, 443
Process, 2f, 23f
Prophecy, 125–26, 136f, 141–47, 151f, 163f, 331f, 331n, 409, 472–73; birth of, 96–100; function of, 99f
Prophet, 97, 303, 336
Prophetic critique, 126
Prophets and kings, 137
Psalms, 117
Ptolemies, 341
Public policy, 515f
Purity, 217f, 221, 226f, 229, 231, 337, 353f, 370f, 376, 402, 414, 440
Purpose, divine, 26, 236, 249f, 301, 527, 530–35

Q source, 452
qāhāl, 7, 24
Qoheleth, 213
Queen of Heaven, 216, 327
Qumran, 348f, 364–72, 377f; messianism at, 370

Rabbi Jeremiah, 402n
Rabbinical Judaism, 337f
Rabbis, 350
Ramesses II, 10, 12
Ransom, 227f
Realism, 126, 189, 276, 473f; historical, 99
Recital, 26
Reconciliation, 227–29, 246–49, 388, 446f, 485
Reform, 76, 179, 199
Rehoboam, 133f
Relinquishment, 25, 491
Remembering, 172
Remnant, 126, 169, 192, 196, 342, 365, 367–69, 474
Repentance, 165f, 199, 233, 392, 396, 398, 402, 419
Responsibility, 47, 276
Restoration, 240, 255, 257, 261

Resurrection, 423, 441, 445f, 485
Retribution, 210, 212f
Revelation, Book of, 455f
Revision, 76, 81
rib, 152f
Righteousness, 5, 27, 30, 63, 71f, 74–76,
    80, 84, 91, 117, 144, 156f, 161, 166,
    173f, 183, 193, 210f, 222f, 233f, 238f,
    255, 259, 295, 306f, 406–08, 423f, 424,
    459f, 470f, 507f
Rights of the individual, 93
Ritual, 40
Romans, 355, 367, 382, 384, 455f, 463;
    Epistle to the, 447
Rome, 460f
Royal ideology, 89, 92f, 102f, 104,
    108–09, 117, 128, 138
Royal theology, 181f, 192f, 201, 241
Ruth, Book of, 314–16

Sabbath, 60, 225, 344, 414, 480
Sacrifices, 39f, 227f, 246f, 370
Sadducees, 338, 348f, 351f, 354f, 374,
    382
šālôm, 3, 5, 61, 125, 157, 162, 165–66,
    175, 185, 220, 222, 240, 243, 254f, 258,
    267, 269, 275, 277, 411f, 425, 465, 471,
    480, 503, 508, 512, 517
Salome Alexandra, 352
Salvation, 162f, 191f, 235, 240f, 439
Samaria, 140, 291, 309
Samaritans, 327f
Samson, 36
Samuel, 91, 97
Sanballat, 294, 328
Sanctuary, 225, 226f
Sanhedrin, 355
Satan, 397
Saul, 89–92, 100
Scribes, 209, 332, 335f, 335n, 338
Second exodus, 237, 240
Second Isaiah, 233–50, 476
Second Jewish Revolt, 357
Security, 119, 188
ṣĕdāqâ, 71, 83
ṣĕdeq, 71
Seleucids, 341
Self-criticism, 471
šĕmā^c, 69
ṣĕmaḥ, 262
Separation, 339, 353, 368f, 376, 400
Sermon on the Mount, 406, 452–54, 453f
Servant, 446; songs, 240–47, 410f, 416; of
    Yahweh, 233, 274, 416f, 464f, 476f
Shammai, 355
Shechem, 36
Sheshbazzar, 261, 263
Shiloh, 134, 204f
Sicarii, 357, 357n
Simon, 335, 346, 366

Sin, 226–30, 233, 248, 359f, 397;
    offering, 246f, 249f
Sinai, 225
Sirach, 333–39
Slave, 52, 66–67, 69
Slavery, 14f, 22f, 48, 53, 115f, 469, 500
Social: anthropology, 38; ethics, 79;
    justice, 508; sciences, 7, 15;
    stratification, 115f, 149; structures,
    112–27, 250f, 472
Society: Egyptian, 13–15; tribal, 16, 36f;
    village-pastoral, 19
sôd, 24
Solidarity, 501
Solomon, 104–07, 122f
Son of Man, 345, 411, 416
šôpēṭ, 34, 90, 97
Sovereignty, 26n
Spirit of Christ, 434–36
Steadfast love, 27
Stranger, 46
Structures: of community, 468, 489–93;
    institutional, 528
Suffering, 213, 257, 416, 421f; Servant,
    257, 421f, 448; vicarious, 244–49, 422f
Synagogue, 336, 353, 457f, 466

Talmud, 336f
Tamar, 81–85
Taxation, 116
Teacher of Righteousness, 360, 365–68,
    375
Temple, 106, 108f, 110f, 120f, 122, 181,
    204, 221, 226, 231, 256n, 257f,
    261–64, 269, 302, 334f, 359f, 360f,
    363, 367, 370, 393, 415, 435, 478;
    destruction of, 356
Temptation, 413
Tension, intra-community, 253, 257–59,
    261, 266f, 275, 347, 376, 438, 479
Theft, 62
Third Sibyl, 330
Tiberius, 382
Tiglath-pileser III, 188, 190, 192
I Timothy, 462
Tobiads, 328f, 330, 341f
Tobiah, 294, 329
tôrâ, 11, 11n, 30, 33, 42, 53, 57, 78–81,
    83–85, 153, 169f, 171, 199, 207, 231f,
    243, 286–87
Torah, 293, 297, 297n, 303f, 306f, 309,
    331–39, 342, 348–54, 356, 361, 365f,
    376–79, 389, 393, 404f, 407–09, 426,
    433, 478, 480
tôrat mōšeh, 293
Traditions, 351f; ancestral, 10, 13–20;
    apocalyptic, 410; biblical, 467; conquest,
    31f, 35; Davidic, 192f, 208, 220, 415f;
    diveristy of, 269; exodus, 11–13, 20–28,
    31; exodus-wilderness, 164; general,

Traditions *(continued)*
13n; Hebrew Bible in the New
Testament, 385f, 454; League, 103;
Yahwistic, 133f, 152f, 161, 181, 198,
201, 315
Tribal confederacy, 11n
Trust, 161, 181, 186–88, 190f, 193, 212,
502f
Trustworthiness, 76
Typology, 530f

Ugaritic: Baal cycle, 114; epics, 15; texts,
63, 109
Universalism, 151, 242f, 258, 286, 289,
317, 319f, 322, 417f, 456, 473
Uriah, 103

Vision, 5, 9, 218, 250, 254–56, 258, 263,
276, 283, 360, 467, 530–35; of God's
order, 514n
Visionaries, 261
Vocation, 5, 467, 501, 517; of the
community of faith, 503f, 507–18, 525

War, 97; eschatological, 366, 371f, 378,
392, 455f
Widow, 46f, 83f, 315
Wilderness, 27, 168f, 206, 225f, 237, 360

Wisdom, 112, 208–14, 333, 338f, 405,
473; of Solomon, 330
Women, 443, 443n, 487
World hunger, 508f
World religions, 496n
Worship, 5, 24–26, 28, 30, 39, 41, 43, 50f,
53, 58, 69f, 73–75, 77, 80, 107–12,
120–23, 146, 154–58, 161, 171, 175,
182f, 193, 212f, 222, 237f, 295, 304f,
375, 399, 423, 471, 504–06, 526f, 535

Yahweh, 20, 56, 73, 89, 125, 171
Yahwist, 129f
Yahwistic: Document, 17n; laws, 44f;
tradition, 133
ydᶜ, 46
yir'ê yhwh, 283f

Zadok, 102
Zadokites, 221, 233, 253, 255–68, 277,
279–83, 287, 301f, 347f, 349, 360, 363,
365f, 477f
Zealots, 357, 382, 384, 390
Zechariah, 257, 261–63
zéraᶜ haqqōdeš, 298
Zerrubbabel, 261–66
Zion, 108f, 110, 181, 183, 186, 191

Scripture Index

HEBREW BIBLE

Genesis **1–11**, 129–31; **1:28**, 225; **2:7b**, 17, 130; **3:1–7, 14–19**, 131; **4:1–16, 7–24**, 131; **6:1–4**, 131; **9:8–17**, 225; **9:20–27**, 131; **12:50**, 15; 15, 16; **15:6**, 17; **17:1–27**, 225; **18**, 17; **22:18**, 17; **26:4**, 539; **28**, 17; **38**, 81; **38:25–26**, 83

Exodus **1–3**, 17; **1:11**, 13n; **1:15**, 21; **1:17**, 18; **2:10, 11–15**, 18; **2:11**, 14; **2:23b–25**, 17; **3:15**, 17; **6:2–9**, 18; **15**, 11, 20f, 26, 33; **15:1**, 26; **15:11–13**, 27; **19:1–8**, 285; **19:3–8**, 39; **19:5–6a**, 353; **19:6**, 40; **20:2**, 11; **20:21**, 11, 12; **20:21–23:19**, 42–52; **20:22–26**, 50; **21–23**, 33, 42–52, 55; **21:1–11**, 44, 53; **21:12–14, 18–19**, 44; **21:12, 16–17**, 55; **21:28–30**, 227; **22:21–24**, 85; **22:23**, 62; **23:1–8**, 50; **23:9**, 46; **23:14–19**, 51; **23:19**, 11f, 44, 51; **24:1–2, 9–11**, 41; **24:3–8**, 33, 39; **24:9–11**, 229; **29:10–21**, 228; **29:42b–46**, 225; **29:45**, 229; **34**, 55; **34:6–7**, 74; **34:6–8**, 68f; **34:8**, 69; **40:34–38**, 225f

Leviticus **1:1–17**, 232; **8:5–22**, 228; **16:14, 26**, 229; **17:11**, 229; **19:1, 3–4**, 228; **19:35f**, 71; **19:18**, 233; **25:35–46**, 53

Numbers **6:23–27**, 280n; **14:21**, 231; **26:52–56**, 64; **27**, 64; **36:6**, 65

Deuteronomy **1:1a**, 169; **4:44–45**, 170; **5:1–3**, 169; **5:6–21**, 171; **5:12–18**, 53; **5:22**, 54, 171; **5:33**, 169; **6:4–9**, 171, 175; **6:14**, 53; **6:20–21, 23–25**, 172; **7:6**, 172, 539; **7:7**, 539; **7:7–8**, 172; **7:7b, 9a**, 174; **7:9–11**, 173; **7:11**, 174; **7:25**, 363; **8:11–20**, 172; **12:5**, 170; **15:12–15**, 174; **17:14–20**, 170, 200; **17:19b–20**, 170; **21:1–9**, 227; **23:1–6**, 287f; **27–28**, 58; **31:9–13**, 200; **32:8–9**, 40, 68

Joshua **3:1–5:1**, 31, 33, 39; **13–19**, 33; **24**, 33

Judges, 34–38; **1**, 35; **2:1–5**, 34; **3:31**, 36; **5:4–5, 13**, 35, 37f; **6:1–8:32**, 35; **6:7–10**, 34; **6:13, 32**, 36; **7:1**, 36; **8:22–23**, 36, 91; **8:24–27, 29**, 36; **9:1**, 36; **10:6–16**, 34; **17–18**, 36; **19–21**, 36; **35**, 36

1 Samuel **2:1–10a**, 67; **4–6**, 89; **8**, 93; **8:9**, 100; **9–10:16, 11, 14**, 89; **10:27b–11:15**, 89; **11:15**, 90; **12**, 98; **16:14–2 Sam 5**, 101; **22:2**, 101; **23:1–13**, 101; **24–26**, 101

2 Samuel **2:4**, 101; **5:3**, 101; **6**, 89; **7:13–14**, 103, 120; **8**, 124; **8:10–18**, 146; **9–20**, 89; **11–12**, 103; **23:1–7**, 102; **23:3–4**, 103; **23:5**, 101; **24**, 104

1 Kings **1**, 133; **1–2**, 89, 105; **3:16–27**, 114; **4:2–6**, 106; **4:29–34**, 112; **5:12**, 106; **9–10**, 147; **9:25**, 107; **10:1–10**, 112; **11**, 123; **11:17**, 180; **11:28**, 133; **11:33**, 38, 138; **12:4, 14, 18**, 133; **12:16**, 115, 134; **12:25–33**, 137; **13**, 138; **14:7–11**, 138; **15:11–13**, 179; **15:14b**, 180; **16:3**, 140; **16:7–8**, 188; **18:2, 3b–4**, 141; **18:39**, 42; **19:15–18**, 142; **21**, 62, 143–45; **22**, 142; **22:41–46**, 180; **23:29**, 202

2 Kings **4:1**, 149; **9:25–26**, 143; **11:17**, 180; **18:4–6**, 197; **18:5**, 201; **22:11–20**, 200; **23:2, 3**, 200; **23:13, 22, 25**, 201

Isaiah **1:10–20, 16–17**, 185; **1:21–23**, 183; **1:26**, 182; **3:4, 13–15**, 184; **3:16–26**, 186; **5:1–12, 20**, 184; **5:15–16**, 186; **6:6b–13**, 189; **7:1–9:6**, 187; **7:9b**, 188; **7:10–9:6**, 189–91; **8:5–10, 11–15**, 190; **8:11–15**, 190; **8:21–22**, 191; **9:1–2, 6b, 7**, 192; **9:6**, 208n; **9:7b**, 193; **10:1–4**, 184; **10:5–15**, 187; **11:3–5**, 183; **14:24**, 187; **17:1–4**, 182; **19**, 322; **19:24–25**, 323; **22:8b–11**, 186; **24:1–20**, 271; **24:4–6f**, 511; **24:5**, 277; **24:14–16a**, 272; **24–27**, 271–73; **25:6–8**, 273; **28:16–17, 21b**, 186; **29:1–8**, 191; **30:15–17**, 188; **31:1**, 187; **40:1–11**, 233; **40:1–3, 5, 21–23**, 235; **40:8**, 26; **40:10–11**, 239f; **41:17–19**, 236; **42:1–4**, 242; **42:2–3, 5–9**, 243; **42:10–13**, 238; **42:13–16**, 237; **42:21–25**, 234; **43:49**, 239; **44:28a**, 235; **45:3**, 236; **46:22**, 242; **47:6a**, 234; **49:1–6**, 242; **49:6**, 243, 275; **49:7–12**, 240; **49:13**, 238; **49:15**, 239; **50:4–9**, 244; **51:4**, 243; **51:12, 13**, 244; **51:17–20**, 234; **52:12–14, 15a**, 244; **52:15b**, 245; **53:1–6**, 245; **53:8–10**, 246; **53:11b**, 247; **54:5–8**, 239; **55:1**, 236; **56:1–8**, 287–89; **56:7**, 289; **57:13b**, 257; **59:9, 14**, 257; **59:18**, 258; **60:20**, 257; **60–62**, 238; **61:1–3**, 464; **61:1–4**, 255, 410f; **61:6**, 255; **63:1–6**, 258; **63:16, 18–19**, 257; **65:1–7**, 257; **65:5**, 268; **65:5b–7**, 280; **65:13–15**, 275; **66**, 264; **66:1–2**, 260, 285; **66:1–4**, 257; **66:5, 15–16**, 258; **66:18–21**, 289; **66:22–23**, 290

Jeremiah 2:13, 199; 2:23–24, 206; 3:21–
23, 199; 4:23–26, 199; 7:1–15, 204;
9:23–24, 205; 11:3–5, 11, 205; 17:9,
206; 18:7–8, 319; 22:13–17, 203f; 23:5,
6b, 208; 31:31–34, 206, 207n; 32:36–41,
207, 207n; 44:15–19, 216
Ezekiel 1:28b, 218; 3:16–21, 223; 8:6, 10,
218; 11:22–25, 221; 16:1–14, 223; 18:5–
9, 19–28, 31–32, 223; 20, 217; 20:23–
26, 228; 22:15, 12–31, 218; 33:1–20,
223; 33:10–11, 21, 219; 33:11, 319; 34,
269; 34:23–24, 262; 36:22–23, 28, 217;
36:26–28, 220; 37, 269; 37:9–10, 219;
37:12–14, 27–28, 220; 37:27–28, 220;
38–39, 269f; 38:11, 270; 40–48, 221,
256, 261; 40:44–47, 221; 43:6–9, 18–19,
221; 43:18–27, 228; 44, 232, 260, 268;
45:1–5, 7–10, 221; 47:1–12, 222; 47:26,
65; 48:35, 269
Hosea 1:4–5, 147–48; 2:1–13, 165; 2:14–
15, 19–20, 23, 165; 2:16, 166; 4:1–3,
161f; 4:4b–6, 7–10, 159; 4:12–13a, 158;
5:6–22, 171; 5:14b, 163; 6:1–3, 5–6,
163; 7:3–4a, 5–7, 160; 8:1, 4b–5, 160;
8:4a, 159; 8:11–13a, 14, 161; 9:8, 163,
165; 10:12, 167; 11:2, 158; 11:4, 5–7, 8–
9, 164; 12:4, 6, 166; 12:13, 163, 170;
12:15, 170; 13:4–6, 158; 14:3, 167
Joel 1:15, 313; 1:16, 317; 2:1–2, 11, 27,
313; 2:12–14, 317, 319; 2:28–32, 409;
3:1–5, 314; 3:5, 9, 317
Amos 1–2, 151; 2:6–12, 154f; 3:2, 152;
3:7–8, 151; 3:15, 153; 4:4–5, 156; 5:2,
157; 5:4b–5a, 156; 5:10–13, 154; 5:15,
168; 5:18, 158, 272; 5:19, 272; 5:21–24,
156; 6:8, 157; 7:10–17, 150; 7:12–15,
151; 9:7–10, 539; 9:11–15, 157
Jonah 3:9, 320; 4:1–2, 10–11, 318
Micah 1:5b, 6, 195; 2:2, 195; 3:1–3, 5, 9–
12, 195; 5:1–4, 196; 6:3–5, 196; 6:6a, 8,
197; 6:8, 77; 6:11, 195; 7:5–6, 195; 7:7,
18–20, 196
Zephaniah 1:12b, 216
Haggai 1:8, 260, 264; 1:9, 262; 2:5b–9,
262
Zechariah 1:16–17, 262; 2:8–9, 270; 4:14,
263; 6:9–14, 265; 8:9–13, 16–17, 262;
10–14, 273; 10:2–3a, 279; 14:20–21,
231; 14:21, 273
Malachi 1:1, 278; 1:10, 13a, 280; 1:11,
286, 289; 1:16–2:9, 280n; 1:17, 279; 2:3,
280; 2:10, 279; 3:1–4, 7, 16–21, 283;
3:5, 281; 3:14–15, 279; 3:16–18, 285;
3:16, 18, 20–21, 286
Psalms 2, 108; 15:1–5, 113; 24, 113; 24:3–
5, 7–8, 114; 48:7–9, 93; 48, 109; 50,
117; 65:9–13, 118; 68, 110; 68:5–6, 49;
72:1–2, 117; 72:1–4, 113; 73:26, 213;
82, 68; 84:1–2, 120; 89:25, 35–36, 109;
89:25, 128; 95:2–5, 111; 104, 110;
104:1–6, 9, 118; 110, 107; 110:2–3, 117;

115:9–13, 284; 122:1–5, 111; 132, 101–
02; 135:19–20, 284; 144:10, 89; 145,
323; 147:10–11, 284f
Job 8:3–7, 212; 12:3–6, 212; 19:21–22,
212f; 19:24–26, 213; 22:29–30, 212;
23:1–17, 212; 42:5–6, 213
Proverbs 1:1–7, 209; 2:6–22, 210; 8, 210;
10:10–12, 211; 11:11, 211; 14:21, 211;
14:31, 210; 21:3, 13, 211; 22:17, 209;
22:22–32, 211; 24:22, 209; 25:1, 209;
25:21, 211; 31:9, 210
Ruth 2:10, 12, 316
Ecclesiastes 2:24–26, 213; 3:16–22, 214;
8:11–16, 214
Daniel 7–12, 344; 7:14, 27, 345; 8:10–12,
344; 8:25, 345; 11:34a, 345; 12:1–3, 345
Ezra 1:1, 305; 1:1–4, 304; 2:59–63, 304;
7:1–5, 292f; 7:11–18, 304; 7:12–26, 293;
7:27–28, 305; 9:1–2, 289; 9:8–9, 309
Nehemiah 5:11, 294; 7:61–65, 304; 8:2–3,
53; 8, 306; 9:6–37, 305–06; 9:32–34,
305; 9:38–10:39, 295; 10, 306f; 12:27–
43, 295; 13:3, 295; 13:4–9, 328
1 Chronicles 5:1–2, 303; 9:29, 105n;
15:12–15f, 179–80; 15:15, 16–22, 302;
19:6–7, 180; 28:2, 264; 29–31, 197

NEW TESTAMENT

Matthew 1:1, 453; 1:3, 81; 2:19–21, 454;
2:32, 497; 4:10, 400; 4:23–24, 413, 415;
5:3–12, 402; 5:16, 394, 404, 409; 5:17–
18, 78; 5:17–48, 453; 5:21–22, 394;
5:21–48, 406; 5:23–24, 415; 5:43–45,
408; 5:48, 407; 6:25–33, 399; 7:28–29,
409; 8:4, 423; 8:5–13, 418; 8:10–13,
419; 8:10b–12a, 439; 9:12, 403, 417;
9:14–15, 402, 420, 432; 9:36–37, 425;
10:5–8, 432; 10:5–23, 385; 10:19, 399;
10:19–20, 431; 11:3, 414; 11:10, 433;
11:12, 397f; 11:19, 419; 12:1–14, 46–50,
420; 12:24, 415; 13:52, 385, 387; 14:1–
12, 398; 15:1–20, 420; 15:24, 385;
15:31, 419; 16:30–31, 423; 18:20, 434,
435n; 18:21–35, 412; 21:36–46, 453f;
22:25–28, 420f; 23:23, 77, 425; 24:22,
412; 25:31–46, 411; 25:40, 436; 28:19–
20, 437
Mark 1:14, 398; 1:15, 297; 1:22, 399; 2:17,
417; 3:14–15, 435; 3:31–35, 420; 8:12,
410; 8:27–33, 416; 9:30–32, 416; 9:35,
424; 10:15, 24–45, 424; 10:5–9, 17–31,
406; 10:29–30, 399; 10:32–34, 416;
12:1–12, 496; 12:34, 404f; 13:21–23,
414; 14:58, 415
Luke 1:26–38, 463; 1:32–35, 51–53, 464;
1:46–55, 81; 2:36, 465; 2:49, 423; 3:7–
14, 396; 4:18–19, 410f, 464; 4:21, 464;
4:32, 468; 5:31, 417; 6:20–22, 402; 6:36,
407; 7:1–10, 418; 7:20, 22–23, 414;
7:34, 419; 8:19–21, 420; 9:38–40, 404;

Luke *(continued)*
  10:2, 8–9, 431; **10:17–18**, 433n; **10:27**,
  407, 426; **12:51–53**, 420; **14:12–14, 21–
  24**, 403; **14:21**, 435; **16:1–7**, 400; **17:11–
  19**, 418; **17:20–21**, 398, 410; **22:42**, 412;
  24:44–49, 463; **24:46–47**, 465; **28:31**,
  466
John **3:1–15**, 457; **4:7–26**, 418; **4:22, 24**,
  393; **6:25–51**, 457; **8:3–6a**, 82; **8:7**, 407;
  8:31–47, 458; **9:22**, 457; **9:28**, 458;
  12:42, 457; **14:15–17**, 457; **16:2**, 458;
  16:7–15, 457; **17:18**, 457
Acts **2:14–36**, 436; **3:24**, 463; **28:30–31**,
  463
Romans **3:1–4**, 440; **3:21**, 388; **3:21–25a**,
  440; **3:29**, 319; **3:31**, 79; **4:3**, 441; **6:3a**,
  436; **7:7–12, 24**, 387; **7:14**, 442; **8:1–4**,
  440; **8:22–23**, 444; **8:38–39**, 449; **9:4–5**,
  386; **9–11**, 450, 540; **10:14**, 78; **11:5**,
  386; **11:9, 20–22, 26, 29**, 450; **11:33–36**,
  451; **13:9–10**, 83; **15:1–3, 7–9**, 448
1 Corinthians **6:12**, 441; **7:14**, 441; **8**,
  450n; **9:21**, 440; **11:15**, 443n; **11:24**,
  436; **12:4–13, 27–31a**, 449; **13**, 449;
  14:33b–36, 443
2 Corinthians **4:18**, 444; **5:14**, 441; **5:14–
  21**, 445; **6:2**, 249; **8:9**, 448
Galatians **1:3–4**, 443; **3:13–14, 24, 27–29**,
  442; **3:19, 22**, 441; **3:23–29**, 439; **4:4**,
  387; **6:15, 16**, 442
Ephesians **5:1–2**, 449
Philippians **1:1**, 443; **2:1–7**, 447; **2:6–7**,
  446f; **4:2–3**, 443n
Colossians **3:12–15a**, 449
1 Thessalonians **1:10**, 444; **4:13–18**, 444;
  5:1–11, 444
1 Timothy **1:4**, 462; **2:2**, 462; **3:1–7, 8–13**,
  462; **4:1–5, 7**, 462; **5:17–22**, 462; **6:20**,
  462
Titus **1:6–7**, 462; **3:1**, 462

Hebrews **4:1–13**, 456
James **1:1, 9–11, 13–15, 22–25**, 459; **1:27**,
  460; **2:6–13**, 459; **2:15–17**, 41; **2:18–26**,
  460; **3:13–18**, 460; **5:1–6**, 459
Revelation **1:5–6**, 456; **5:9–10**, 456; **21:1–
  4**, 518

APOCRYPHA, PSEUDEPIGRAPHA
AND EARLY PATRISTIC BOOKS

1 Clement, 460f
Ecclesiasticus **11:22**, 334; **12:1, 7**, 334;
  13:9–10, 334; **24:9**, 405; **24:23**, 333,
  405; **39:1**, 336; **39:24**, 334; **44–50**, 335;
  50–57, 335
1 Enoch **10:17–11:2**, 359; **72–82**, 363;
  79:1–2, 363; **80:2–7**, 363; **85–90**, 360;
  89:73–74, 360; **90:30–39**, 362; **90:18–
  19, 28–30**, 361–62; **91:12–13**, 362;
  93:10, 362
Judith **6:2–4**, 332; **8:16–17**, 332; **9:5–6**,
  332; **9:11**, 333; **14:18**, 332; **16:13**, 332;
  16:18, 333
1 Maccabees **1:41–48**, 343; **4:41–45**, 347

RABBINIC TEXTS

'*Abot* **3:2**, 434n, 435n
'*Abot de Rabbi Nathan* **ch.4**, 356n
Baba Batra **12a and 12b**, 331n
Babylonian Berakot **55a**, 356n
Babylonian Talmud Sabbat **118a–b**, 499
Jerusalem Berakot **81 5:4**, 331n
Numbers Rabbah **15, 10**, 331n
Sabbat **104a**, 331n
Sanhedrin **119**, 331n
Sifre Deuteronomy **153**, 355
Song of Songs Rabbah **8**, 331n; **2.7**, 386n
Yoma **21b**, 331n

Index of Authors

Ackroyd, P. R., 301n
Adams, J. L., 506f
Albright, W. F., 52n
Alt, A., 91n, 170n
Anderson, B. W., 10n
Augustine, 505
Avigad, N., 266

Baltzer, K., 143n
Barth, K., 544
Bell, D., 544
Bellah, R. N., 494n
Betz, H. D., 396n
Birch, B. C., 98n
Blankensopp, J., 389n
Bonhoeffer, D., 213, 447n, 501f
Bornkamm, G., 396n
Bowker, J., 400n
Breech, J., 396n, 397n
Bright, J., 12n
Bultmann, R., 396, 521

Calvin, John, 54n, 58
Campbell, E. F., 38n
Chaney, M., 38n
Charlesworth, J., 359n
Chaucer, 158f
Clark, N. M., 15n
Clements, R. E., 170f
Cohen, S. J. D., 351n
Collins, J. J., 330n, 344n, 346n
Cone, J. K., 23n
Coogan, M., 129n, 212n
Cross, F. M., 15n, 31n, 92n, 100, 120n,
    137, 232n, 263n, 348n, 366n, 371n
Crossan, J. D., 401, 401n
Crusemann, F., 247

Dever, W. G., 15n, 326n
Dibelius, M., 396n
Dodd, C. H., 82n
Dumbrell, N. J., 16n

Eichrodt, W., xiii
Eissfeldt, O., 170n
Eliot, T. S., 177n, 215, 253n, 325n, 382n,
    427n, 506n
Elliger, K., 232, 232n
Ellul, J., 30n
Elmann, Y., 351n

Fensham, F. C., 45
Feuerbach, L., 537
Finkelstein, J. J., 15n
Fishbane, M., 280n
Flusser, D., 497n
Freedman, D. N., 38n, 263n
Furnish, V. P., 444, 447n

Gaster, T., 372n
Gerlemen, G., 316n
Gese, H., 53, 228n
Goshen-Gottstein, M. H., 498, 498n, 545n
Gottwald, N., 38n
Graf, D. F., 38n
Gutierrez, G., 23n

Haag, E., 246n
Halpern, B., 98n
Hanson, P. D., 3n, 12n, 19n, 21n, 44n,
    54n, 108n, 118n, 232n, 254n, 260n,
    263n, 271n, 313n, 331n, 359n, 494n,
    525n, 532n
Harrington, D., 336n, 456, 458n, 491n
Hayes, J. H., 329n, 356n
Hengel, M., 330n
Hesse, F., 546
Hiebert, T., 20n
Hooker, M. D., 422n

Jacobsen, T., 22n
Janowski, B., 225n
Janzen, J. G., 212n

Käsemann, E., 443, 443n
Kaufmann, G., 538
Kierkegaard, S., 59, 505n
Klein, R. W., 231n
Koch, K., 226n, 292n
Koester, H., 396n, 416n, 453n, 462f, 463n
Kraeling, E. G., 327n
Kramer, S. N., 212n
Kraus, H. J., 31n
Küng, H., 520f

Levenson, J., 256n
Levy, R., 402
Lohfink, N., 231n
Luther, Martin, 54n, 58, 60n, 62, 78-79,
    127, 127n

Maccoby, H., 351n
Malamat, A., 64n
Mantel, S., 355n
Martin, J. D., 232n
Mays, J. L., 166
McCarter, P. K., 91n, 98n
Meeks, W. A., 403n, 439n, 443n
Mendenhall, G., 38n
Meshel, Z., 326n
Mettinger, T. N. D., 98n, 241n
Milik, J., 358, 359n
Millar, W. P., 271n
Miller, J. M., 12n, 329n, 356n
Moltmann, J., 510n, 520f, 542f
Mosis, R., 301n
Murphy, R. E., 209
Myers, J., 265n, 302n, 303, 308

Neal, M. A., 25
Neusner, J., 350n, 351, 351n, 357, 400n
Nicholson, E. W., 170n
Nicklesburg, G. W. E., 334n
North, C. R., 241n
Noth, M., 10n, 12n, 15n

Ogletree, T. W., 514n
Orlinsky, H. M., 242n
Otto, R., 43

Pederson, J., 21n
Perrin, N., 396n
Petuchowski, J. J., 498n
Pfeiffer, R. S., 212n
Plöger, O., 313n
Pope, M., 212
Purvis, J. D., 328n

von Rad, G., xiii, 21n, 57, 88n, 227n,
    242n, 531-32
Reicke, B., 468n
Richardson, C. C., 461n
Robinson, H. W., 228
Rosenbaum, J., 197n
Rowley, H. H., 228

Schleiermacher, F., 537f
Schüssler-Fiorenza, E., 487
Scroggs, R., 443n, 446n
Shäfer, P., 344n
Smith, M., 350n
Smith, N. H., 242n
Soggin, J. A., 31n
Speiser, E., 130
Spenser, E., 130
Stanton, G. N., 396n
Stendahl, K., 80, 453n
Sterk, O. H., 143n

Talmon, S., 293n
Tcherikover, V., 326n, 346n
Thiessen, G., 419n
Thoma, C., 477n
Thompson, R. T., 247n
Thompson, T. L., 15n
Tillich, P., 58, 95, 505, 505n

Urbach, E. E., 350n

Vanderkam, J., 359n
de Vaux, R., 51
Vermes, G., 364, 367n

Waltzer, M., 8n
Weber, M., 436n, 460
Weippert, H., 207
Weiser, A., 91n
Welch, A. C., 117
Welten, P., 143n, 263n, 301n
Westermann, C., 240n
White, L., Jr., 132n
Willi, T., 263n
Williamson, H. G. M., 294n, 296n
Wilson, A., 242n
Wilson, J. A., 209, 212n
Wilson, R. R., 16n
Winston, D., 330n
Wolff, H. W., 159n, 317, 317n

Zimmerli, W., 59, 232n